Years of Renewal

European History 1470

Edited by John

Contributors Catherine Brice,
David
Caroline

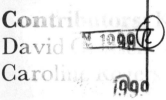

Hodder & Stoughton

A MEMBER OF THE HODDER HEADLINE GROUP

British Library Cataloguing in Publication Data

European history, 1450–1600.—(Years of renewal).
  I. Lotherington, John   II. Brice, K.
  III. Series
  940.2

  ISBN 0 7131 7743 8

First published 1988
Impression number 12 11 10 9
Year 1999 1998 1997 1996 1995

Typeset by Rowland Phototypesetting Limited
Printed in Great Britain for Hodder & Stoughton Educational, a division of Hodder Headline Plc, 338 Euston Road, London NW1 3BH by Clays Ltd, St Ives plc

Contents

List of Maps

List of Diagrams

Acknowledgements

The maps for this book were drawn by the expert and patient Alison Ryder. The authors would like to express their gratitude to her, to Robert Hanks, Carol Lockwood, Clare O'Brien, Stephen Rogers and Doris Storey for their help in typing the manuscript and to Richard Tarrant for his help in proof reading.

We are also much indebted to Nicholas Davidson and Bob Wolfson for encouragement and advice and to Phebe Kynaston and Holly Gothard for their editorial guidance.

Finally, our thanks must go to all those Sixth Form students who have helped, whether they knew it or not, in the preparation of this book.

Preface: How to Use This Book

1. General

The A-level student, it has been claimed, has ever more to do and no more time to do it in. Booklists grow longer as more specialist knowledge is required. In addition to writing essays derived from secondary sources, documents have to be examined and evaluated. The purpose of this book is to help you, the student, to tackle all this more efficiently.

While this is a standard textbook in that the basic narrative is given and most chapters match traditional A-level topics, it is also a guide to recent approaches in research and a workbook containing documents and exercises. As well as providing information, it is designed to help you to acquire an awareness and a method so that you can put the limited time you have for further researches to the best use.

2. Documents

Interspersed in the text are documents and questions relating to them. These are not just illustrations or separate exercises but an important part of the narrative. They fill a gap in the text—by answering the questions on the documents you will in effect be writing that part of the text for yourself. It is important to note down the facts and quotations you draw from these documents to ensure your notes are complete.

3. Bibliographies

At the end of each chapter there is a short bibliography, one of general use for the whole period being found at the end of Chapter 1. The books chosen are those most suitable for A-level students, rather than the more daunting specialist works, and they should be readily available in libraries or paperback editions.

A problem with any reading list is that it becomes almost instantly out of date. One way to keep up with the latest views is to read a journal regularly, with an eye on the reviews section. *History Today* would be a good choice being cheap, readable and well-illustrated as well as attracting contributions from leading historians. For the more adventurous, *Past and Present* has a record of publishing articles with stimulating new approaches.

4. Discussion Points

The points for discussion emphasise the various themes outlined in the chapter preceding them. They are intended to test understanding and to stimulate debate in class. Written answers would also be useful and, if taken in order, would form a summary of the chapter.

5. Essay Questions

It is unlikely that you will write more than one or two essays on any given topic—but the A-level examiner could well ask something completely different. The essay questions listed at the end of each chapter give a range of questions so that, by giving some thought as to how to answer them, you can be better prepared and can open up new lines of thought. It is a good idea to read through the essay questions before you work on the chapter to help you to pick out what is most important in the text.

6. Exercises

There are a variety of exercises following each chapter to help in developing your ideas and in organising the material. Two types of exercise recur frequently—structured essay writing and documentary exercises.

The essay writing exercises will help you to develop the skills necessary to avoid just 'telling the story' and to construct a clear and convincing argument instead.

The documentary exercises go further than the use of documents in the text. Several sources will be used and, as well as comprehension and the detection of bias, comparisons will be made and conclusions compiled to give an overall picture. This should give at least a taste of the creativity and the problems of the practising historian.

I Introduction—Renaissance Europe

1. The Countries of Renaissance Europe—The West

If you look at the adjoining map you will be most familiar with the boundaries you see in the West. **England**, although its relationship with the other parts of the British Isles was to change considerably in the ensuing centuries, had established its own boundaries in Saxon times. The major change of the fifteenth century had been that the Plantagenet kings of England had finally lost their possessions in France. Only Calais was salvaged at the end of the Hundred Years' War during the disastrous reign of Henry VI (1422–61).

A revived **France** looms much larger in Early Modern history. It had the greatest area, the biggest population and the richest agriculture of any country in Europe. But such resources in themselves do not make power; the resources must be tapped by a centralised government. Once the threat of the English Plantagenets had been overcome, the French kings attempted this by resuming a campaign which had begun centuries earlier against the independence of the outlying provinces of France. Louis XI (1461–83), known as the universal spider, was well-equipped with the necessary political skills. He took Anjou to the south west, Provence touching the Mediterranean coast, Burgundy to the east and Artois and Picardy in the north. It was only left for Louis' son Charles VIII (1483–98) to acquire Brittany through marriage to its Duchess, Anne, after some forcible political wooing in 1491.

It seems almost as if there was a masterplan for the French nation to be turned into a 'nation state', a unified state extending to its 'natural frontiers' such as the Atlantic or the Pyrenees. But the ambitions of the French kings were never so clear or consistent. Louis XI had extended the area of his sovereignty but there was still much to divide France. He did not unify the country's system of law, with Roman law still predominating in the south and customary law in the north. Customs barriers divided France economically and were to do so until the French Revolution of 1789. The French equivalent of Parliament was the Estates-General, but it met so irregularly that it did nothing to unite the interests of the country. Even Charles VIII, who had filled in the last gap in France's Atlantic border by taking Brittany, was quite happy to hand

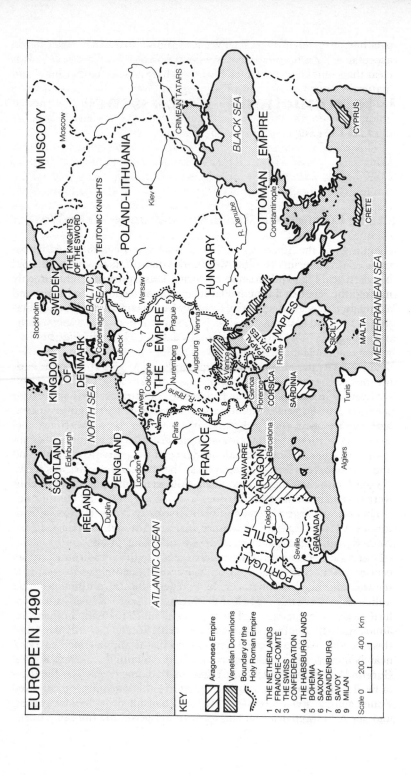

EUROPE IN 1490

KEY

(diagonal hatch)	Aragonese Empire
(dense diagonal hatch)	Venetian Dominions
(dotted boundary)	Boundary of the Holy Roman Empire

1 THE NETHERLANDS
2 FRANCHE-COMTÉ
3 THE SWISS CONFEDERATION
4 THE HABSBURG LANDS
5 BOHEMIA
6 SAXONY
7 BRANDENBURG
8 SAVOY
9 MILAN

Scale 0   200   400   Km

MUSCOVY
Moscow

SWEDEN
Stockholm

THE KNIGHTS OF THE SWORD
TEUTONIC KNIGHTS

POLAND-LITHUANIA
Warsaw
Kiev

CRIMEAN TATARS

BLACK SEA

OTTOMAN EMPIRE
Constantinople

CYPRUS
CRETE

MEDITERRANEAN SEA

BALTIC SEA

KINGDOM OF DENMARK
Copenhagen
Lübeck

NORTH SEA

SCOTLAND
Edinburgh

IRELAND
Dublin

ENGLAND
London

ATLANTIC OCEAN

FRANCE
Paris

Antwerp
Cologne
R. Rhine
Nuremberg
Augsburg
THE EMPIRE
Prague
Vienna
HUNGARY
R. Danube

Venice
PAPAL STATES
Genoa
Florence
Rome
NAPLES
CORSICA
SARDINIA
SICILY
MALTA
Tunis
Algiers

NAVARRE
ARAGON
Barcelona
CASTILE
Toledo
Seville
PORTUGAL
GRANADA

over hard-won territory on the Pyrenees frontier to Spain in order to win acceptance for a hare-brained invasion of Naples *(see Chapter III)*. It is clear that some concepts which historians use, such as 'nation state' and 'natural frontier', must not be allowed to obscure the slow-changing realities and political waywardness of the period. And if there was a guiding concept for the rulers of the time, it must have been that of the dynasty—keeping politics in the family, as it were.

This certainly seems to have been the case with regard to **Spain**. When King John of Aragon needed help against his rebellious subjects in 1469, he married off his son Ferdinand to Isabella, the heiress to the throne of neighbouring Castile. When, by 1479, both had inherited their respective kingdoms, the shape of modern Spain was established *(see Chapter II)*. It was rounded off in 1492 when the two monarchs finally conquered Granada, the Moorish territory to the south. This was the completion of the 'Reconquista', the reconquest of Spain by the Christians driving out the Islamic Moors who had originally invaded from North Africa. It had taken seven centuries. Unsurprisingly, it had deeply marked the Spanish national character with a religious confidence and aggression. It was men of the Reconquista tradition, the 'Conquistadores', who would venture across the Atlantic to convert and exploit the pagans of the New World. It was the fiercely Catholic Spanish who would be the most immune to Protestantism and the readiest to strike against it. With such a unifying tradition, it might seem almost inevitable that Spain should have been united.

Given the chances of politics, 'inevitable' can be a misleading word for the historian. **Portugal**, another kingdom formed by the Reconquista, had more in common with Castile given the great rivers which connect the two countries; and the King of Portugal did make a military bid for Castile on Isabella's accession in 1474. It was the victory of Ferdinand and Isabella in battle, not geography or tradition, which made the union of their crowns safe for the time being. And in most respects their realms were to remain distinct entities.

Dynastic arrangement was to tie Spain to the **Netherlands**, a territory which today includes Belgium as well as the modern kingdom of the Netherlands. The Netherlands had never been a united, independent country, and never was to be except for a few years in the nineteenth century. In the later Middle Ages, almost the whole territory belonged to the Duke of Burgundy but technically he ruled over each province under a different title as the Count of Flanders, the Duke of Brabant and so forth, and his territories, extending further south towards Switzerland, almost formed a middle kingdom between France and Germany. But this is a 'might-have-been' as Duke Charles the Bold was killed in battle near Nancy in 1477 and his duchy all but collapsed. The province of Burgundy itself, from which the Duke took his title, reverted to the King of France. The territory that was left, the Netherlands in the north and Franche-Comté to the east of France, passed to Mary of Burgundy and then, through her marriage to the Emperor Maximilian, to the

Habsburgs, the leading dynasty of Germany. Their son, the Archduke Philip, then made the connection with Spain by marrying a Spanish princess, the Infanta Joanna. Such were the intricacies of dynastic links, of very little interest to the average Fleming or Brabanter or Dutchman of the Netherlands, except if more taxes were one of the results. Then cries would go up in the defence of ancient liberties. There was no unity or sense of national interest to over-ride the particular interests of each province and the towns within it.

Such particularism might be seen as essentially medieval but in other ways the Netherlands was one of the most advanced areas of Europe. It straddled the delta of the Rhine and was therefore the crossroads for the trade of north-western Europe. This bred great wealth and there were more towns and larger urban populations than anywhere else but Italy. Antwerp was the chief city, a centre of financial institutions and industrial innovation. Netherlanders were pioneers in the arts and technology. They were socially advanced in that the feudal nobility in most parts had to share power with the burghers, the leading magistrates and merchants of the towns. It was not that feudalism in general, the structure of aristocratic control of the land, was declining; it had never made much of a mark in this river-patterned land where merchants could sail their barges but where barons could rarely afford the drainage for a feudal estate. This was the background to events later in the sixteenth century (*see Chapter XIV*) when a breakaway section of the Netherlands in the north, equipped with great mercantile fleets, was to become the first commercial world power.

For all the restraints, there was much dynamism in the West. The Netherlands, whatever its changing political circumstances, was significant for its economic and social development. The kings of France and of Spain, although limited by the divisions within their nations, had established themselves strongly enough by the end of the fifteenth century to think of competing with each other. In the first instance that was to be in the Italian Wars (*see Chapter III*).

2. The Countries of Renaissance Europe—The Centre

Italy was at the heart of European affairs. Christendom looked to Rome as the location of the shrine of St Peter, to which travelled hundreds of thousands of pilgrims and Rome was the home of the popes, whose bureaucracy and international taxation system made the city a worldly as well as a spiritual centre. Europeans as Crusaders had valued Italy strategically. It was the gateway to the Mediterranean and the Holy Land to the east. The Crusades had long since ended but their imprint, and that of Italy's importance, remained on the European mind and the European economy. The fleets of Venice and Genoa had carried the troops to the Holy Land and had supplied them. Their voyages had become the major trade routes across the Mediterranean, enduring even though the Holy Land had finally been lost in the thirteenth century, and so Europe looked to Italy for its trade in oriental luxuries. The profits from that trade were ploughed into other enterprises, such as international banking. There had been an economic recession in the fifteenth century but Italians found things other than trading enterprises to put their capital into—there was no shortage of money to further that explosion of learning and artistic creativity which made up the Italian Renaissance *(see Chapter V)*. The religious, economic and cultural primacy of Italy held the attention of Europe, inspiring resentment as well as admiration.

These feelings were compounded by the Italians' development and confident use of the new craft of diplomacy *(see page 17)*. The problem was that diplomacy, in arriving at a precarious balance of power after the Peace of Lodi of 1454, had just succeeded in disguising the political instability of the peninsula. Italy was divided into a profusion of small states, many no bigger than a small city and its immediate surroundings. But amongst those city-states there were five of greater size and power.

Only one of the five states had a stable system of government, Venice, which was a republic ruled by its leading aristocratic families and which possessed a trading empire stretching across the eastern Mediterranean. Milan was the least stable state, having been taken over by the families of mercenaries, first the Visconti and then the Sforza, whom it had once employed. Florence was subject to family feuding but, for the greater part of the fifteenth century, it was dominated by the Medici family who held no official position but ruled through money and influence. The problem was that, when Lorenzo de Medici, known as 'The Magnificent', died in 1492, he was to have no effective successors. The Papal States straddled central Italy and were technically ruled over by the popes. However, the popes had lived in Avignon for much of the fourteenth century and their return to Rome in 1376 had been followed by the chaos of the 40 year Great Schism, a split in the Church when there were two, and sometimes three, rival popes. The cities of the Papal States had fallen into the hands of local tyrants who ruled nominally as papal vicars. The popes were to spend much of the later fifteenth and early sixteenth centuries as warriors as well as priests, winning back their lost territories. To the south of the Papal States lay Naples, a poor feudal kingdom threatened by the rival dynastic claims of Aragon and France. Within the kingdom itself the barons ganged up in factions, and played out their family feuds and engaged in banditry.

Italy was made up of an unstable group of states expanding and pressing against one another. There were no such pressures to the north, where the Alps prevented political space being so rapidly filled up. There was the Duchy of **Savoy**, for instance. Apart from one or two commercial centres it was a collection of valley communities only loosely controlled by its Duke. His main role was to play off the nearby great powers of France and Spain who competed well into the seventeenth century to control the military routes across the mountains.

Switzerland too was in the game of selling its military potential, its main export being mercenaries renowned for their toughness and discipline. They fought with pikes and their steady marching proved more than a match for the dramatic, 'each man for himself' charges of feudal cavalry *(see page 16)*. It was the Swiss who had caused the dismemberment of the old Duchy of Burgundy in 1477, when Charles the Bold had gone too boldly into battle believing that his mounted knights would have no difficulty in disposing of a mass of Swiss peasants on foot. The Swiss had developed this military capacity and their political organisation in defending themselves against their former rulers, the Habsburgs of Austria. The small valley and city republics of the region, known as cantons, had joined in a confederation. In reality, it was no more than a loose alliance and prone to civil wars, but it proved durable and flexible enough to keep the greater powers of Europe at bay through to the present.

Switzerland was technically part of the **Holy Roman Empire** until 1648, but in practice was fully independent; the same was true of northern Italy. In many respects the princes and free cities of the heartland of the Empire north of the Alps acted as though they were fully independent as well. This sprawling territory, covering all of Germany and more, had never been centralised at all. There was an Emperor but no Imperial army and no Imperial taxes except in the most dire of emergencies. The Emperor himself could not claim powers through right of inheritance; he was elected to the position by the seven leading princes of the Empire known as the Electors. These included the Elector Palatine, the Electors of Saxony and Brandenburg, the Archbishop Electors of Mainz, Trier and Cologne, and the King of Bohemia. Decisions, supposedly binding on the whole Empire, could be made by the Diet, the Imperial parliament, which was attended by princes and the delegates of the free Imperial cities. But powerful rulers, such as the Elector of Saxony or an ecclesiastical prince like the Archbishop Elector of Cologne, ruling over part of the Church as well as part of the territory of the Empire, might take little notice of an Imperial law if it did not suit them. They knew that there was little chance of such a law being enforced, especially as the emperors had for centuries diverted much of their resources in futile attempts to control Italy. Most princes seemed set on developing their own independent, sovereign authority. It almost seems as though the Holy Roman Empire had a grand name but counted for nothing.

This would be wholly true if day-to-day politics were all that mattered but the Holy Roman Empire embodied an ideal which obstinately survived all the cynicism and institutional weakness. There were attempts at Imperial reform to reinforce justice and end private war within the Empire. In 1495 an Imperial Supreme Court, the *Reichskammergericht*, was established and this was followed up by an Imperial Governing Council, the *Reichsregiment*, in 1500. Unfortunately there was a conflict between the desire for greater Imperial unity and the fear of increasing the power of the Emperor so the reforms failed. The Imperial ideal, though, could outlive any such failure.

It was the Habsburg dynasty which controlled the largest territories in the Empire from their main base in Austria. This impressed the Electors sufficiently to elect a Habsburg as Emperor at each election from 1440 until the abolition of the Empire in 1806. In 1519, when Maximilian's son became Emperor as Charles V *(see Chapter VIII)*, he had at his disposal the inherited territories of Burgundy, Spain and part of Italy as well as his German lands. This was an excellent basis for a revival of the Imperial ideal. But the more power that Charles had, the more fear and enmity he inspired from all sides. He failed to crush the Lutheran Reformation in Germany and so the Holy Roman Empire was further divided. Both the survival of the old Imperial ideal of unity and its failure to be realised were to be bequeathed to modern Germany.

3. The Countries of Renaissance Europe—The North and East

The countries to the north and east were remote at this time from the mainstream of European history. This was a result of a much lower population density. Even at the end of our period in 1600, a population density of 44 per square kilometre in Italy or 34 in France compares with 14 in Poland and just 1.5 in Sweden and its neighbours. Given the slowness of communications—villages could be several days' journey from one another—there was little chance for advanced economic or political organisation. Indeed, this peripheral region of Europe was in what might be described as a prehistoric stage. Many of the forests, mountains and river systems were only just being explored and colonised by small groups moving amidst the vast but silent drift of population from Germany towards Siberia. There were islands of Christianity from which missionaries throughout the Middle Ages had moved out to combat paganism, backed up by the Crusading orders of the **Knights of the Cross** and the **Teutonic Knights** who were the only effective political authority in their regions. It is against this background that the achievements of some traders and rulers seem all the more remarkable.

The lands around the Baltic were colonial in the economic sense as well as in terms of the movement of populations. They could provide the raw materials which the more developed economies of the south needed. These included timber, the other materials needed for shipbuilding (naval stores) and grain. The trade had been developed by the merchant rulers of the cities on the Baltic shore of Germany and Poland. They had banded together in what was known as the Hanseatic League to avoid cut-throat competition and to strengthen their bargaining hand with the countries which bought their goods. A strict code of conduct was imposed. Funerals took place at night so as not to waste business time and sex was forbidden on a tour of duty abroad—although secret staircases in merchants' houses suggest that their energies were dissipated after all. For all its regulations, the Hanseatic League was subject to market forces. In the fifteenth century the returns on sales of grain fell and the Hanse merchants could ill afford the increasingly expensive cloth and other industrial goods from the south. The sixteenth century was to see a steady invasion of Dutch and English ships into the Baltic; the Hanseatic League, being unable to resist such aggressive well-financed competition, declined and the Baltic region became more and more an economic colony.

This was particularly the fate of the largest country which bordered on the Baltic, **Poland-Lithuania**, with its reserves of timber and grain. The constitution of that kingdom was much like that of the Holy Roman Empire—the king was elected and any attempt at centralised power could be defeated in the Sejm, the Polish parliament. And with the king often preoccupied with the far-off borders with Muscovy and the Ottoman Empire, Polish nobles were in effect answerable only to themselves.

The ruler with the greatest authority around the waters of the Baltic was the King of **Denmark** who, since the Union of Kalmar in 1397, had ruled Norway and **Sweden** as well. However, the Swedes in practice handled their own affairs. Christian II of Denmark caused this to become a formal separation by his tactless response to a rebellion in 1520—he had himself crowned hereditary king of Sweden and then celebrated by killing 80 of the Swedish nobility and bishops. By 1523, Christian found himself uncrowned, being deposed in Denmark by his uncle and being replaced in Sweden by the founder of a new dynasty, Gustavus Vasa. The new King of Sweden built up his authority steadily, culminating at the Diet of Västerås in 1544. There, the Crown was declared hereditary in the Vasa family. The Lutheran Reformation of the Church in Sweden was made fully official which also confirmed the takeover of Church lands by king and nobles. A national army was formed to be based on conscripting a proportion of the men of every village. Through such measures, Gustavus Vasa and his successors could exploit the thinly spread resources of their kingdom to the full.

The Grand Dukes of **Muscovy** also made the best of thinly spread resources. Russia had been carved up in the thirteenth century by the Tatar hordes invading from the east. Their leaders, the Khans, exacted tribute—protection money—from Russian cities and principalities but in 1480 Ivan III of Muscovy refused to pay and got away with it. The Tatars were in decline and they left a power vacuum which Ivan was eager to fill. He continued the 'gathering of Russia' which his predecessors had begun, taking Novgorod, Tver and other territories. And his imperial pretensions expanded beyond his conquests. He claimed to be the heir of the Byzantine empire of Constantinople, lost to the Turks in 1453, and so assumed the title of Tsar, meaning Caesar. He certainly acted in an imperial way, assuming more absolute power over his subjects than any other European ruler. Muscovy would have been a highly centralised state if its administration, over-stretched and corrupt, had matched its political thought. Only through brute force were the difficulties of communicating power over such vast areas occasionally overcome. It was trade, not brute force, which was appropriate for opening up communications with the West at this time, but that was not to happen until the middle of the sixteenth century *(see Chapter XVI)*. Muscovy was known about before then but it was viewed as remote and barbarous. While it shared a continent geographically with countries such as France or Italy, Muscovy was not yet European in any political or economic sense.

Its remoteness from the rest of Europe was also religious. Muscovy was the bastion of Orthodox Christians who had become separated from the Latin Christianity of Rome in the eleventh century. They jealously guarded the purity of the forms of their services—their liturgy—and so gave a distinct character to the culture of much of eastern Europe. That culture was very resilient. In the Balkans, it was to endure five centuries of rule by the Ottoman Turks.

By the end of the fifteenth century it looked as though the Sultans of **the Ottoman Empire** might redraw the map of Europe, Mohammed II (1451–81) having moved in on the remnants of the Byzantine Empire and leaving Ottoman forces poised to advance towards central Europe from what is now Greece and Bulgaria *(see Chapter X)*. To make up those forces, the Sultan could draw on subject populations from south east Europe through most of the Middle East. He had no need to fear rebellious noblemen as leading Turks did not have a secure base in inherited land, only holding estates in return for service to their ruler. The Grand Vizier, the head of government, was technically a slave. Selim I, 'the Grim', (1512–20) emphasised this by executing eight of them. With such a concentration of power in his hands, the Sultan could tap resources as he chose. Islam gave an added impetus to Ottoman conquests in the name of Jihad, or holy war.

It was not just neighbouring south east Europe which was under threat from such a well-organised and determined power. Their navy gave the Ottomans striking power across the eastern Mediterranean as far as Italy. They controlled an enclave there, Otranto (1480–81). Their power was to be carried into the western Mediterranean by supporting the Barbary pirates who worked from North African bases, preying on Christian shipping and raiding the coasts of Spain and Italy. But the Ottomans' most solid advances were in the Balkans. They did face powerful resistance—for instance, there was the freedom fighter (or terrorist from the Turkish point of view) in the mountains of what is now Rumania, named Vlad Dracul. He rallied his countrymen and terrified his enemy by building up a reputation for extreme cruelty. One woodcut shows him eating a meal while gazing contendly on the Turks impaled on stakes around him. (His bloodthirsty tactics won him fame as a national hero in his home country and he passed into legend as the original for Count Dracula.) The Turks were held up by the likes of Vlad the Impaler, but not stopped. They were to threaten south eastern Europe for two centuries. Their last siege of Vienna was as late as 1683.

In the late fifteenth century it was not the Habsburgs who were expected to be the major bulwark against the Turks but the kings of **Hungary**. Some success in this was achieved by King Matthias Corvinus (1458–90). He was a great soldier and consolidated what he had won with careful administration and attention to justice. But the Turks could always rely on Christians to fight amongst themselves and Matthias was no different. He was diverted first into Bohemia where he tried to have himself made king in 1469 and then into wars against the Habsburgs. And then on his death in 1490, all his work collapsed. Hungary's monarchy, like Poland's, was elective and this gave the nobility a chance to weaken the monarchy after it had threatened their liberties. The members of the Jagiellon family who were elected to rule in Hungary from 1490 could not keep control. For instance, it was the Church, not the king, which gathered tens of thousands of peasants together in 1514 to crusade against the Turks. Lacking proper leadership, the peasants attacked their closer enemies, the noble landlords, and were in turn slaughtered by them. When the Ottomans destroyed the kingdom of Hungary at the battle of Mohacs in 1526, they did not immediately realise what they had done, assuming that the pitiful enemy could not be a national army.

Bohemia was similar in its weakness to Hungary, being an elective monarchy and also ruled by the ineffective Jagiellon family. It had been divided by religious wars as well which followed the death of Jan Hus, a Bohemian Church reformer. He had been condemned as a heretic by the General Council of the Church at Constance and was burnt at the stake in 1415. His followers, the Hussites, fought for a generation to maintain his cause, fired not just by religion but by national resentment at the domination of the Bohemian Church by Germans. By 1436 they won their right to worship in their own way but tensions continued throughout the century with the Roman Church authorities. Making these divisions worse were the wars of succession over who should win the election to be king, wars in which Poles, Hungarians and Austrians got involved. This just made way for the German domination the Hussites had fought against. After the death of the last Jagiellon king in 1526, the Crown of Bohemia passed to the Habsburgs and was to be held by them, apart from one brief interlude, until that family's empire finally disintegrated in 1918 and Bohemia emerged in Czechoslovakia.

The map of late fifteenth century Europe shows us a wide variety of disputes and developments. During the sixteenth century the map would in some ways be simplified. Nearly all the issues of international importance would depend upon the policies and capacities of the Habsburgs, their dynasty coming to dominate Europe through diplomacy and marriage alliances. The map of Europe was to be renewed as Habsburg Europe.

According to tradition, Renaissance Europe also saw renewal as the

Early Modern world. Our map, in the west at least, was coming to resemble more closely the Europe we know today.

But we must beware of imposing our view of things onto the past. There may have been some signs of modern nation states emerging but a look at France and Spain shows that those signs are few and often ambiguous. And the people of the late fifteenth century would not have thought in terms of a political map of Europe at all. They thought in religious terms; their map was of Christendom. Its centre might not be seen in Europe at all but in Jerusalem which, from the eleventh to the thirteenth centuries, the Crusaders had won and finally lost to the forces of Islam. Apart from religion, Europe was seen in terms of trade. The markings on their map would not be mainly of national boundaries and capital cities like ours; it would concentrate on trade routes and commercial cities, its coastlines would be indicated by the names of the many ports strung along them.

4. Society

Just as the people of Renaissance Europe did not see boundaries on a map in the same way as we do today, so their conception of social boundaries was very different. For them the family, particularly in southern Europe, might mean not the nuclear family of parents and children but the extended family of several generations, cousins and servants. The place of women within the family and within society in general was changing in the sixteenth century *(see page 174)*. As widows controlling estates and as members of guilds, they had had considerable economic influence but they were increasingly subordinated within a patriarchal society—despite those eminent examples of powerful women such as Elizabeth I.

The people of Renaissance Europe did not think in terms of classes but of social 'orders' determined by rank and function rather than economic status. In theory there were three orders—those who fought (the nobility), those who prayed (the monks and the priests) and those who worked (the townsmen and the peasants). In practice it was more complicated, with much variation in relationships between and within each order.

The nobility were distinguished by symbols such as coats of arms and liveries (uniforms) for their servants. They were noted not for production but consumption—conspicuous consumption of luxuries which indicated their rank. They enjoyed a wide range of privileges, an important one being exemption from direct taxation in most countries on the (increasingly spurious) grounds that they served as feudal warriors. Hereditary rank automatically endowed them with status but real power depended on their control of the land. They had seigneurial rights over the peasantry which meant that they not only acted as landlords but had independent powers as judges. Where a nobleman controlled large

11

estates he could often act as a prince in his own right, paying homage to his king but in practice virtually ignoring him. The nobility, however, were not all magnates (great aristocrats). Alongside *les grands* in France or the *grandees* of Spain, there were also the poor noblemen whose rank remained but whose fortunes had declined so that they pushed a plough and were indistinguishable from the peasants apart from the gloves they wore and the sword they hung above the fireplace to symbolise their noble heritage. At a lesser extreme were the gentry, not so powerful landowners as the magnates but of great importance in that any nobleman with political aspirations relied on support from amongst them. The ambitious nobleman supplied his supporters with favours or bribes—it was patronage which fuelled rank with power.

Churchmen could be the social equals of the nobility. Indeed, there had been a claim in the Middle Ages that the lowliest priest, by virtue of his spiritual vocation, was superior to the greatest nobleman. In practice, it was the bishops and abbots who did wield power because they were often as great landowners and seigneurs as the leading noblemen *(see page 20)*. Although it was common for a bishop to be a younger son of a noble family, the Church was still the main career open to talent. With an education and a command of the language of the Church, Latin, an ambitious clergyman could go far within the Church or in government service. This was social mobility but it was limited, especially as the clergy were not permitted (legitimately) to father families to whom they could pass their honours and lands. Also, like the poor nobility, many of the poorer priests were indistinguishable from the peasants they served.

The peasants were the workers on the land *(see page 27 for their role in the economy)*. During the Middle Ages they had mostly been serfs, not quite slaves, as they were permitted their own plots of land, but bound to work on their lords' estates and pay feudal dues such as heriot, a death duty. By the fifteenth century, as a result of the post-Black Death labour shortage when peasants could demand a better deal, serfdom had largely died out in western Europe. However, this did not mean that the lot of the peasants permanently improved. In eastern Europe there was to be a 'second serfdom' established during the Early Modern period by nobility eager to make profits out of the expanding grain trade. Even in Western Europe, by 1500 the population was starting to increase again and there was a growing shortage of land. Some peasants profited from economic changes, with inflation outstripping customary rents, and they became well-to-do farmers—yeomen in England, 'laboureurs' in France —but many were reduced to being landless labourers, dependent on the chances of employment to avoid starvation. Occasionally the more articulate peasants would protest or even rebel *(see page 145)* but, for the most part, the peasants laboured silently and were exploited, regarded by their superiors as being little better than brutes.

Townsmen did not fit easily into the scheme of three social orders. Some were poor wage-labourers but the burghers who governed the towns often had a lifestyle akin to that of the nobility, living off the rents on land they had bought or the interest on government bonds. Indeed, the aim of many wealthy merchants was to commit 'class treachery', as it has been called, and acquire titles of nobility through purchase or office. Between the extremes of wage-labourer and powerful office-holder or merchant, there were many gradations of social status. So much depended on which craft guild or religious confraternity the townsman belonged to—the group counted for far more than the individual *(see page 28 on the economic basis of urban society)*.

In several areas, cities had been largely independent and the most dynamic force in historical developments during the Middle Ages. During the Early Modern period they were to be gradually brought under control by the princes of Europe. They were to come into their own again with the onset of the Industrial Revolution and large-scale urbanisation. Before then, the nobility remained the most important element in society, as princes were continually forced to recognise in their attempts to secure or extend royal government.

5. Government by Princes

There were independent cities and small republics in the Early Modern period but government was largely in the hands of princes (the term used to describe all those with sovereign powers and not just the sons of kings). They were once seen as the creators of 'New Monarchies', exercising centralised authority through administrators who were lawyers or gentry and not dependent on the nobility. Although such administrators were used—for instance, lawyers with the names of *letrados* in Spain or *maîtres* in France—their use was not new, stretching back in France, Spain and England into the Middle Ages. And the co-operation of the nobility was still crucial to effective government.

There was no simple chain of command, however. For all his prestige, a prince's authority was just part of a system of interlocking rights and obligations. He had to respect his subjects' liberties—not yet universal liberty but instead the numerous individual privileges of all the corporations, the towns, the provinces, the Church and, of course, the nobility which made up the realm. A major obstacle to royal authority was provincial privilege where the province was remote from the centre of government and sometimes unassimilated in terms of language, custom or trade. Very often, the main loyalty was to the province rather than to the realm—this is known as particularism. Many of the political problems of the Early Modern period resulted from the prince attempting to impose his will on a province and being fiercely resisted. The alternative to what was often futile confrontation with particularism was to win the support of the local nobility.

A prince had various ways of securing the co-operation of his nobility and the realm in general. He was usually on the move, bringing his direct personal influence to bear on as many of his vassals as possible. (As a consequence of this constant movement capital cities had not yet fully developed and the prince took many government officials with him as he travelled. Mules carried the government records and if there were too many they might just be dumped wherever the royal court happened to be.) The prince's authority was supported by his status as God's anointed deputy and myths were cultivated which indicated the sacred powers of monarchy—the 'King's touch', for instance, whereby it was claimed that the kings of France and England could cure scrofula, a skin disease. He was at the centre of great rituals, such as ceremonial crown wearings, which enhanced his prestige. If he was an effective commander in battle he won the allegiance of that warrior caste, the nobility, with their strong sense of man-to-man loyalty.

Prestige, however, was not always effective in bending the nobility to the prince's will. The truly successful prince had the ability to assess and serve the self-interest of the most important noblemen and to gather together active supporters from amongst his subjects of standing. It was patronage which oiled the wheels of the government machine. The prince was the 'fount of honour' and had at his disposal prestigious and profitable offices as well as pensions and lands. Whenever there were not enough offices to go around, the solution seemed to be to create new posts in order to give them away. When a prince was insufficiently generous or gave benefits only to less important royal favourites, then opposition to the point of rebellion could result.

The demands of patronage led to the expansion of bureaucracy in Early Modern Europe. In its most crude form, called venality, offices were not just given away but sold. The prince would gain often desperately needed ready cash and the buyer of the office could then enjoy the status and the perks that went with it—a judge might pocket the fines he imposed, for instance. Such a bureaucracy was scarcely that of a centralised 'New Monarchy' and it was a long way from a professional civil service, given that office-holders tended to regard their offices as personal property. But it has to be said that the creation of offices itself represented a new royal interference at various levels of society. And one of the features of Early Modern politics was the attempt by princes to use further patronage or royal agents to control the administrations they had created.

For the prince to achieve anything he nearly always needed money. He might be putting up royal buildings or paying the dowry involved in a marriage alliance or engaging in that most expensive princely pastime, war. According to custom, he had to live off the revenue from his own estates like any great noblemen, except in cases of limited feudal dues and emergencies. (Royal finance was still a personal matter for the prince; what counted was what he had at his disposal in his treasure chests.) Taxation was regarded as extraordinary, even though the majority of princes during the Early Modern period had an ordinary, regular need for it. There were alternatives—borrowing heavily from a great banking family like the Fuggers, or even pawning the Crown jewels—but taxation was generally necessary.

In many realms, taxation could only be granted by the equivalent of Parliament, usually called the Estates but known as the Cortes in Spain and the Diet in Germany. They were not elected in our sense but they usually brought together the nobility with representatives of the towns and country districts and sometimes clergy. The king of France, as we have seen, could collect some taxation on his own authority and bypass the Estates General but up to half of France's provinces had Provincial Estates with which he had to bargain. The nature of any bargain between prince and Estates depended on the issue of 'redress before supply'; if the Estates could secure the principle that their grievances must be redressed (i.e. notice taken of their interests) *before* they granted supply of taxation then they would have the upper hand over the prince. If the prince managed to establish the principle of 'supply before redress' (i.e. he got his money before he had to listen to complaints) then he obviously had an advantage. However, even where the prince had to take notice of the Estates this was not necessarily detrimental to his authority. With careful management he could persuade the Estates to support him and that could help to secure acceptance for royal policies in the country as a whole.

Notions of patronage and careful management take us away from too schematic a view of Early Modern politics. Some historians have seen a movement in the period towards absolutism, royal authority freed from any restraints. Admittedly there were lawyers and humanists who welcomed such a development in theory, the political philosopher Jean Bodin in late sixteenth century France, for instance. And there were institutional developments in the form of reformed treasuries, administrative councils or the despatch to provinces of royal agents; but they were as likely to disappear as to be created and they had not replaced the medieval institutions of government by the end of the sixteenth century at least. Monarchs still had to grapple with the complexities of those rights and obligations which they and their subjects shared.

There were developments, though, which disturbed those ordinary procedures of politics. The Reformation was to bring the Church more closely under princely control but, at the same time, the controversies involved were to create civil disturbance which it was one of the two main duties of the prince to prevent *(see Chapters XIV and XV on the subject of religious civil war)*. The other main duty of the prince was to go to war in defence of his realm and his rights. It was usually the latter which provoked conflict. Warfare was to grow in scale and expense during the Early Modern period and the gathering of men and money for it was to strain loyalties and the machinery of government to the utmost.

15

6. Warfare

Medieval warfare is characterised, or perhaps caricatured, by the picture of a great charge of chivalric knights. Every man would fight for himself, concerned about his own honour and the potential ransom for any enemy he managed to capture. While there were more organised tactics than this on some medieval battlefields, there was a general lack of discipline and too great a reliance on the social rank of the combatants. That is why the Swiss were able to inflict such dreadful slaughter on the chivalry of Burgundy at Nancy in 1477 *(see page 6)*. The Swiss were common mountain men but they had learnt to fight with pikes in close ranks. They had learnt discipline.

Some armies copied the Swiss and fought with pikes but there were variable responses to this dominance by the infantry. The chivalry of the Middle Ages gradually became the Early Modern cavalry, able to charge in a disciplined group with the aim of bursting through the infantry formations, rather than just being skewered by them. The other new development on the battlefield was the use of firearms.

Artillery, in the form of cannon trains, were of doubtful use on the battlefield. The cannon were slow, unpredictable in their accuracy and inclined to blow up and kill the artillerymen rather than the enemy. Artillery were to be used in the more settled conditions of siege warfare but it was the primitive gun held to the shoulder, the arquebus, shortly to develop into the musket, which was to be most devastating on the battlefield. At first, more or less random firing by the gunners, known as arquebusiers, was used to harrass the enemy before the pikemen went in to do the main job. Then, during the Italian Wars *(see Chapter III)*, the well-trained Spanish infantry went over to the use of the pike like the Swiss, except with the variation that arquebusiers were promoted to a vital defensive role. The pikemen were still responsible for the main thrust in an attack but the arquebusiers aimed to prevent enemy cavalry or infantry getting close enough in their assaults to break up the pikemen's formation. These formations of pikemen and arquebusiers were the *tercios* of the Spanish army which were to dominate the battlefields of Europe for most of the sixteenth century. The chivalry despised this use of the arquebus rather than the sword and seemed to regard it as cheating. The flower of the French chivalry, Chevalier Bayard, executed any arquebusiers he captured—until he himself was felled by a bullet.

Dominance was less obvious concerning siege warfare. Cannon had been battering down the proud walls of medieval fortresses since the early fifteenth century. The solution for defenders was to build lower walls. The *trace italienne* was developed—low, broad walls protected by extensive earthworks with bastions jutting out, diamond-shaped projections of masonry making it very difficult to approach the main wall. All this meant that sieges tended to be long and very expensive.

Artillery also had some effect on naval warfare. The aim in battles at sea had long been to grapple with the enemy, board his vessels and fight what was almost a land battle at sea. This form of warfare was slow to change in the Mediterranean. The great Battle of Lepanto in 1571 saw 100 000 men join battle in the traditional way. However, in the Atlantic, the sixteenth century saw more and more ships being fitted out with cannon and the broadside became a possibility. All the same, at sea there were other factors which could intervene before the artillery became of any use. Too many cannon on board could make a ship topheavy and sink it. And the Spanish Armada was defeated not by broadsides but by fireships and the weather.

The development of gunpowder technology was important but in battles the tactical response and the deployment of infantry seemed even more important. These changes taken together, the beginnings of the so-called Military Reformation, may also have had a significant social and political effect. The nobility, if they were to continue to be successful in war, had to become rather more like professional soldiers than uncontrollable feudal warriors. As to cannon specifically, J R Hale has stressed that big guns were not a royal monopoly—aristocrats and fortified towns often owned them—but it is still the case that the expense of full artillery trains was so great that only princes, and the greater princes at that, exploiting national resources, could regularly afford them. The gap between princes and nobility was growing greater.

Princes also tried to bring to an end private wars amongst the nobility, although the limited success of that policy could be seen in the great religious civil wars of the late sixteenth century. However, at the same time they encouraged another brand of independent soldiering. Given that princes could rarely raise enough native troops for their purposes, they hired mercenaries. Mercenary captains in Italy, the *condottieri*, had long been showing how much profit could be derived from war. There was ambition aplenty but not always aggression to be seen on the field of battle, as the first aim of the mercenary was to preserve himself and his forces. Swiss mercenaries and some of the German *landsknechtes* may have been made of sterner stuff but all mercenaries were parasites. Princes had to pay dearly for them, increasing their difficulties with their Estates and overtaxed subjects.

If a prince wished to pursue an energetic foreign policy there was one way of avoiding the costs of war or making wars more cost effective. That was through careful use of diplomacy. A diplomatic system was just starting to develop in the fifteenth century and it is known as Renaissance diplomacy.

7. Renaissance Diplomacy

'An ambassador is an honest man sent to lie abroad for the good of his country'. These words of Sir Henry Wotton, English ambassador in Venice in the early 1600s, give us a caricature of what diplomacy had become by the end of our period. It would not have been seen that way in the late Middle Ages. Ambassadors did not lie, in the sense of stay, abroad. They travelled, often in great pomp, but only to deliver messages—perhaps a marriage proposal or a threat of war—quickly returning home without having negotiated or got to know their host country. They would not joke about lying, in the sense of misleading, as that would be to break the code of chivalry which governed diplomatic practice. And they might not represent a prince or country as it was quite normal for great noblemen and cities to despatch ambassadors on their own account. It was Renaissance diplomacy, developed by the advanced states of Italy in the fifteenth century, which was to transform all this into a system resembling our own.

The instability of Italy made its politicians more creative. Few rulers could claim to rule because they had a right to do so (remember the Sforza of Milan or the Medici of Florence) and few had dependable allies or borders unthreatened by expanding neighbours. They relied on cunning as an alternative to expensive military strength and that called for diplomats who could argue with brilliance and haggle with tenacity, knowing all the strengths and weaknesses of their potential enemies or allies. To perfect that knowledge, it was necessary for the ambassador to live in the country of the potential enemy or ally. The use of resident ambassadors with powers to negotiate may seem obvious to us but it was an innovation in the Early Modern period.

It was not without precedent. There had long been permanent representatives of international banks such as that of the Medici, and they could act as informal ambassadors. But it was not until the 1450s that Italian rulers regularly used resident ambassadors. They were forced to do this by the turnabouts in alliances which were becoming more and more frequent. There was a rush to send residents to Rome to find out what was going on and, better still, to anticipate what was about to happen. The Vatican was then, and was to be well into the twentieth century, one of the best international listening posts. Then most of the Italian states exchanged ambassadors after the Peace of Lodi in 1454, a defensive alliance with invitations to all Italian states to join and with provision for consultations to maintain the peace. This does not reflect the medieval ideal of Christian unity. Each ambassador was eyeing his fellows suspiciously, expecting treachery at any time. For these diplomats in Italy, more than anywhere else in Europe, the sovereign secular state was of the highest value and its security, rather than any promises which had been made or even the fate of Christendom, was of supreme importance. As Garrett Mattingly put it in his pioneering work on Renaissance diplomacy, 'the state, by the law of its being, could think only of itself'.

The states of Italy did not, however, compete with each other chaotically. Renaissance diplomacy showed itself to be creative, with the emergence of a balance of power for the first time in Italy after the Peace of Lodi in 1454. The various rulers and diplomats recognised that it was in their own interests to join together to restrict any one state which appeared to be getting too powerful and therefore a threat to everybody else. This balance of power did not survive the French invasion of 1494 but there was by this time a most willing student who was to carry some aspects of Renaissance diplomacy into the rest of Europe—Ferdinand of Aragon.

Despite an absence of orderly records (in 1508 not one copy of an important Spanish treaty with England could be found) and a marked reluctance to pay the necessary costs, Ferdinand sent skilled and loyal resident ambassadors to the royal courts and leading cities of Europe. And he inspired the secular objectives of the state to be given the highest value. Fonseca, one of his diplomats and a bishop, said of breaching a treaty oath, 'I place this object of His Highness higher than the safety of my immortal soul'.

Ferdinand used diplomacy to try and encircle France with a series of Spanish alliances with her neighbours, but no balance of power emerged. The great states of western Europe were too secure and too unwieldy—only one state had to change sides to wreck completely any chance of a balance. And Renaissance Europe became Reformation Europe. Religion by the mid-sixteenth century had once again become the dominant theme in international affairs and was to remain so for a century. Power and profit could be placed in a balance but the claim that God was on your side overturned the scales altogether.

8. The Church

For most of us today, the state regulates the way we live our lives. For people at the end of the Middle Ages, the Church shared that dominant role. The parish priest had a more direct effect on an ordinary person's life than any government official. The beliefs that mattered most were not those of a political ideology but the teachings of the Church. And in 1500, apart from some surviving pockets of heresy and the Orthodox Church in the easternmost part of Europe, the Church meant the Church of Rome.

(a) Structure
The pope as Head of the Church was the supreme legislator and judge, issuing instructions called papal bulls. But power over this greatest of European institutions could not be completely concentrated in one man. Cardinals were appointed by the pope but they were not merely servants; they had increasing influence in the Curia, the papal civil service in Rome, and they were the ones to gather in conclave to elect a new pope as soon as the old one had died.

With regard to other important ecclesiastical appointments, princes demanded influence and the popes were regularly forced into compromises with them. Church and state could never be disentangled. Bishops were, after all, amongst the most powerful landowners in any kingdom and no prince could allow an entirely free choice of who they should be. The sensitivity of this issue had been seen in the Middle Ages when disagreements over the appointments of bishops had led to a series of wars between popes and emperors known as the Investiture Contest.

While a bishop had powers over the ordinary parish priests, the so-called secular clergy, he had no direct power over monks, the regular clergy. They were organised in various monastic orders which were international and subject only to the Pope. The larger monastic houses were ruled over by abbots who might control extensive estates and be as powerful—and as independent—as any bishop or lord. There were also the friars, mainly the orders of the Franciscans and Dominicans. They had started to settle down in one place like monks although some kept to their original task as wandering preachers, thereby much annoying the secular clergy who saw them as competitors and trespassers in their parishes. And the Dominicans had taken on a special role as inquisitors, rooting out heresy; that could lead as much to quarrels over jurisdiction, who could judge whom, as to the preservation of the Faith.

Ordinary laymen had no say in running the Church but they did form their own religious clubs called confraternities. Some cities had several dozen of them and John Bossy estimates that at least 10 percent of all adults from the thirteenth century onwards were members of one or more. Members would worship together, feast together and support each other in sickness or provide for burial. Some confraternities had special duties such as those which organised the procession on the Feast of Corpus Christi and put on the Mystery Plays, dramatised stories from the Bible. These confraternities posed no threat to the Church but there could be anxiety that they were independent of clerical control.

The Church was organised as a hierarchy but there was no simple chain of command. Bishops, abbots, chapters (the governing bodies of cathedrals) and confraternities all had a clear sense of their privileges and the independence which went with them. That much restricted the power of the pope to interfere in the day-to-day working of the Church. And if the pope were to think of himself as a monarch there was always the memory of the Conciliarists who, in the early fifteenth century in the aftermath of the Great Schism *(see page 5)*, had argued that General Councils rather than popes should have supreme authority in the Church.

(b) The condition of the Church

When surveying the late medieval Church, historians have often high-lighted its abuses, the ways in which it had been diverted from its spiritual mission by the corruption of the world. There was simony, the raising of cash through the sale of posts in the Church hierarchy. Pope Leo X raised half a million ducats by selling 2000 Church offices. Not surprisingly, this led to pluralism, the holding of several offices, and to absenteeism when a clergyman acquired offices solely for their income rather than because he was going to perform any of their duties. The absence of some clergy from their posts, though, was not necessarily their own choice. They might have been called away on government service or found it necessary to spend some time at a university. And Cardinal Jean of Lorraine could hardly have been blamed for failing to perform his duties as Coadjutor of Metz, given that his family had got him appointed in 1501 at the age of three. Apportionment of blame aside, the Church was being exploited by many of its officials rather than being served by them.

There had been attempts to keep the Church separate from the world through the rule of celibacy. Priests without wives, it was hoped, would be that much more dedicated to the Church and, as a distinct caste, would stand apart from worldly society and could bequeath no Church property to descendants. Many priests, perhaps most, kept their vows of celibacy but priests were as much prey as anyone to the lusts of the flesh and there was no effective discipline to keep them to their vows if they chose to wander. A cardinal or bishop might have his courtesan, as a high-class prostitute was known, an ordinary priest his concubine, a wife in all but name. Where a bishop got to know about a priest and his concubine, the routine was to exact a fine rather than to split them up. It seemed to be that, in some respects, the rules of the Church were there to be broken so that money could be made.

This was borne out by the activities of Church courts. Religious matters and many we would regard as secular, such as the regulation of wills, came within the jurisdiction of Church courts. Although they may have offered justice more often than many Protestant historians have allowed, they could be put to corrupt uses. As one papal official is quoted as saying, 'The Lord desireth not the death of a sinner but rather that he should pay and live.' It is certainly the case that these ecclesiastical courts looked after their own. Any criminal who could claim 'benefit of clergy', and simple literacy was regarded as pretty good evidence, would be tried before a Church court and guaranteed a light penalty, even for so serious a crime as murder. Such abuses bred resentment amongst many of the laity, that mass of people without benefit of clergy.

Church taxation provoked laymen more than anything else. The tithe, 10 percent of all produce, had to be paid over to support the Church and there were other taxes as well, such as Peter's Pence, a tax on hearths paid to the pope. Demands were voiced in Estates (Parliaments) throughout Europe that the jurisdiction and the financial exploitation by the Church should be cut. But this did not lead inevitably to that rebellion against the Church which became the Reformation.

The Church seemed secure in that it was on the whole serving the needs of the world. Its very abuses made it valued. Powerful families could add Church offices to their other acquisitions. Convents might be scandalously lax but that was because they were so useful as dumping grounds for the excess daughters of well-to-do families. Relics of saints, which pilgrims travelled to see and to touch, and to pay for the privilege, were often frauds. The venerated forearm of Saint Andrew might just be a pig's bone; sceptical travellers noted enough nails from the Cross to make a forest of crosses and enough of the Virgin's milk to launch ships. But, where the fraud was successful, the people were content with what the Church provided. Indulgences, which were sold by the Church as though they were passports from the torments of purgatory directly into the bliss of Paradise, had become crude money-raising devices but that was possible because there was so much ready demand for them.

Most abuses were not new. Some gave rise to objection and there were movements for reform. But many abuses were generally accepted as part of the natural order of things. They fitted the Church into the way of the world and they could be accommodated to the religious beliefs of the time. It was only when those beliefs changed in the Reformation that abuses were seen by more than an élite of reformers as destructive of the Church. And certainly the Church's concentration on worldly affairs was to prevent a rapid spiritual response to Luther's challenge.

(c) Religious rituals and beliefs

Social and religious boundaries were often the same. The community was generally a parish. Apart from perhaps a manor house, the church was the most substantial building in the village and more than likely to be the most permanent structure, being built of stone. Outside the church would be the graveyard where the dead, the ancestors of the parish, could lie still gathered in community. In processions around the church and within it there took place the ceremonies which marked the stages of the individual's life and gave the community its identity.

The Church's religious calendar was paralleled by the seasons, all important in an agrarian society, and so the community's spiritual and material lives could reinforce each other. Easter, the celebration of life coming forth from death, could take on extra meaning being also the time to celebrate the renewal of fertility in Spring. Christmas, the celebration of birth amidst darkness, is near to the winter solstice and still carries with it many of the traditions associated with ancient Roman ceremonies and the pagan festival of Yule. Saints' feast days marked other stages in the agricultural cycle and, where appropriate, the saint's image could be carried in procession to bring blessings and fertility to the fields.

Saints, increasing in number at the end of the Middle Ages, both official and locally invented, could be prayed to as individuals concerned with particular aspects of life. Before you commenced a journey, St Christopher could be called upon for his protection, for instance. Sometimes the statue of a saint came to be thought of as having magical powers but, if it had been prayed to and had failed to deliver the goods, it might be mutilated or tossed in a river. A more orthodox approach to saints was to seek their services in interceding with Christ to forgive sins. Cults grew up around those saints thought to be most effective and the most widespread cult was that of the Virgin Mary. It seemed in some cases as though she was being worshipped almost as a mother goddess.

Saints and the services of the Church in general were in greatest demand when calamity threatened. When the plague was nearby, St Roch, the saint thought to guard against it, would receive more votive offerings (gifts dedicated to the saint in return for help). In fear of hail which might destroy the crops, special prayers would be said to ward off the evil spirits which stirred up such tempests. And when a storm began, the church bells would be rung in an attempt to quell it—a practice which Protestant reformers, try as they might, never managed to stamp out.

There is much in the above religious practices which seems more pagan than Christian. Jean Delumeau sees the people of medieval Europe as being, in effect, pagan while paying lip service to official Christianity. (His views will be considered in more detail in relation to the Counter-Reformation.) John Bossy has argued differently, suggesting that there was an authentic Christianity which treated spiritual and social needs as one. This can be seen most clearly in the seven sacraments, the most important ceremonies of the Church.

The seven sacraments were seen as the special channels of Christ's grace, His power of redemption for mankind. There was ordination, the service when a man is set apart as a priest for the service of Christ. There were the four sacraments which introduced the individual to the Church soon after birth (baptism), brought him or her into full adult membership (confirmation), sanctified union with a fellow Christian (marriage) and prepared for the passage into the after-life (the last rites known as Extreme Unction). The religious function of these four sacraments merged with a social function. Baptism introduced the new individual to the community and enabled social bonds to be made with people of different families who acted as godparents. Confirmation varied in age but it often marked the onset of puberty and the adult responsibilities which go with it. Marriage could actually be contracted outside church simply by the oath of the two concerned in front of witnesses but, more and more, the blessing of the priest was taken to be an essential addition to the sacrament. Only a ceremony in church was properly public and could unite two families as well as two individuals. The anointing with oil at the last rites mirrored the use of water at baptism, separating the individual from the living community just as baptism had brought him into it.

Ever since Adam and Eve's original disobedience to God, people had been doomed to inherit original sin as part of their humanity. And the penalty for sin was eternal torment. All the sacraments were intended to qualify the effects of sin. The sacrament of penance dealt with the individual's specific sins. The individual would confess his faults to the priest, undertake a suitable penalty and then receive absolution, i.e. release from the consequence of his sin. Penance served any number of social purposes as specific sins needed to be controlled lest they disrupted the community. Pride, say, was one man trying to set himself above his fellows; lechery might destroy a family. But Sin itself could not be eradicated through man's individual efforts. The penalty for Sin could only be paid by Christ's sacrifice on the Cross and it was the Eucharist which celebrated His sacrifice.

The Eucharist was a sacrament and a miracle. The priest at the altar would consecrate bread and wine and they would then become the Body and Blood of Christ, His sacrifice on the Cross thus being brought into the physical experience of the priest and, unless it was a private Mass, the congregation. There was the problem that the bread and wine continued to look like bread and wine but doubters could be told of the miracle at Orvieto when the consecrated bread supposedly bled, and men of learning could grapple with the doctrine of transubstantiation. Academic philosophers of the time differentiated between the appearance of something (its 'accidents') and its essential physical being (its 'substance'). Given that, it made sense that the 'accidents' of the bread and wine could remain the same while their 'substance' could be transubstantiated into the Body and the Blood. For the ordinary parishioner, however, what mattered was the occurrence of the miracle and not its technicalities.

The consecrated wine was reserved to the priest in his more-than-human role and attendance at the Eucharist to receive the Body in the form of consecrated bread might take place for some parishioners only once a year at Easter, but that emphasised the special holiness of the ceremony. The community was brought together to be relieved of its sin. And a vital part of the ceremony was the Peace, usually symbolised by a kiss. It was the purging of the community from anxiety and conflict, the restoration of charity. Charity meant much more than our giving to good causes. It meant that which gives life to a community and the Eucharist was an essential part of it. This social importance of the Eucharist explains, paradoxically, why men would fight to the death over differing interpretations of it once the Reformation had begun.

9. Thought and the Printing Press

The Church dominated intellectual pursuits in the Middle Ages. Intellectuals were churchmen and, although other subjects such as law and medicine were studied, the 'Queen of the Sciences' was theology. There had, however, been influences from outside the Christian tradition, principally Aristotle, one of the greatest philosophers of classical Greece, whose ideas became known in western Europe by the thirteenth century through the mediation of Arab scholars. Aristotelianism was at the heart of medieval philosophy, which was known as scholasticism.

The philosopher who did most to reconcile Christianity with Aristotelianism was St Thomas Aquinas (c1225–74). For him, the pursuit of knowledge, including knowledge of God, was the search for 'universals', the essences underlying the diversity of the natural world. To understand a 'universal', the philosopher had to see through the 'accidents' (surface appearance) of something to the real 'substance' beneath *(see page 24)*. The scholastic philosophers who shared Aquinas' point of view were known as 'realists'.

Despite the dominance of the Church and its accepted Aristotelianism there was no lack of dispute. The 'realists' were opposed by the 'nominalists', who argued that the supposed essences were just the names we give to things. However, knowledge was slow to spread through books laboriously copied out by scribes and slow to change. Whatever the disputes conducted in the Middle Ages, they were still framed within Aristotelian logic and there was a tendency to debate the minutest details of acknowledged authorities rather than to think afresh.

It was not until the Early Modern period that there were serious challenges to Aristotelianism. The men of the Renaissance attacked it on aesthetic and ethical grounds—they asserted that the logic-chopping of the scholastics was barbaric in style and entirely useless in pursuit of the good life. The men of the Reformation, starting with Martin Luther, attacked scholastic thinking as the basis for the theological errors of the medieval Church. But it was the development of printing which, more than anything else, helped to break the monopoly over thought of Aristotelianism and the medieval Church.

In 1454 or thereabouts in the German city of Mainz, Johann Gutenberg produced what became known as the Gutenberg Bible. It looked like other bibles of the period with the same style of lettering and painstakingly hand-painted illuminations. The difference was that it was the first to have been printed with movable type—there were three hundred Gutenberg Bibles rather than just one copied out by scribes. Gutenberg tried to keep his invention of printing to himself in order to sell his books in the same market and at the same price as handwritten volumes. That was why hand-painted illuminations were added. But one of the most revolutionary developments in European history could not be kept secret for long.

In 1483 a Florentine scholar had to pay three times as much for the preparation of his text by a printer as he would have paid to a scribe. The printer, though, was to provide not one copy but over a thousand. Access to knowledge was increased immensely. Those of the literate élite who had always read books could now obtain more; those with money, but not enough to pay scribes, could now afford to buy books.

Historians who play down printing's importance point out that, while it helped to spread knowledge, the books being printed were entirely traditional, at least until the early 1500s. The new technique did not seem to be giving rise to new ideas. Elizabeth Eisenstein has challenged this view with her account of scholars being confronted for the first time through the variety of printed texts with the anomalies and contradictions of the traditional academic authorities of the Middle Ages. For Eisenstein, printing is a crucial element in the intellectual ferment of the Early Modern period whether in culture, religion or science.

The Renaissance and the Reformation will be examined later *(see Chapters V and VI)* but some points can be made about them jointly with regard to printing. There had been 'renaissances' of classical ideas in the earlier Middle Ages just as there had been attempted 'reformations' by those whom the Church labelled as heretics. But such efforts, whether in culture or religion, had been localised and temporary. Printing certainly had a part to play in making the Renaissance and the Reformation international and permanent in their effects in contrast to their medieval forerunners.

The business of science was also driven forward. Copernicus (1473–1543) suggested that the earth orbits the sun. This contradicted the Ptolemaic model of the universe upheld by the Church, which held that the sun orbits the earth. Copernicus could contradict this most fundamental assumption about the universe not because of 'modern' scientific observation but because he was able to cite the discrepancies in calculations presented to him in printed texts. Tycho Brahe (1546–1601), another great astronomer, was to concentrate much more on direct observation of the stars but he also employed up to 50 printers in order to publish the accumulated data. It must be noted that this did not guarantee immediate advance for science. The printing presses rolled off far more works by alchemists and other pseudo-scientists. And the presses also made it easier for the authorities, mainly the Church, to declare what was orthodox in opposition to new ideas such as those of the astronomers. But another feature of printing is that it makes knowledge much more difficult to control. Censorship was attempted by governments and the Church but there were always printers somewhere in Europe who could ignore it and guarantee that the new ideas, such as in science, stayed in circulation.

This ambiguity in the effects of printing can be seen in affairs of state as well as of the mind. A prince could now have a decree printed, guaranteeing that all copies would be identical and so enabling him to demand much more precise obedience. On the other hand, the publication of definite texts of laws gave the subject a defence against an arbitrary government trying to claim the law was on its side when it was not.

Beyond the relationship of prince and subject, the development of nations was affected by printing owing to national languages, the vernaculars, becoming standardised. Such standardisation was encouraged through what printers chose to publish because they wanted as broad a market as possible, neither restricted to the dialect of one region nor the exclusive intellectual world of Latin. However, the effect was more than commercial. Loyalties to a region had been expressed through dialects, loyalties amongst churchmen or scholars through Latin. Now the possibility of national loyalty was much increased as people became used to thinking in a national language.

Printing does not 'explain' the Early Modern period but, as Eisenstein notes, it greatly affected the pattern of continuity and change. Francis Bacon thought that printing, gunpowder and the compass were the three inventions which had 'changed the appearance and state of the whole world', *(see page 16 on warfare and Chapter IV on maritime exploration)*. He might also have noted that the armourer needed printed treatises on weapons in order to make good use of gunpowder and the navigator needed reliable printed maps as much as he needed the compass. The invention of printing assuredly had multiple effects.

10. The Economy

It is important to know something about the material basis of life in the sixteenth century but there are difficulties in discussing 'the economy' of Early Modern Europe in general terms. It is a technical and controversial subject and, while some massive studies have been made, the evidence is scattered and incomplete. It is also the case that the European economy scarcely existed for many of the Continent's inhabitants who were far away from the main trade routes and who were farming little above subsistence level; that is, aiming to grow just enough to live on and to pay their share of supporting lords and priests. There was often precious little of a surplus for trading purposes. For them it was the local economy which mattered, focused on a town unlikely to be further than 15 miles away.

The fate of most people was to plough the fields in the lowlands, growing rye, barley, oats or wheat, or to be shepherds or herdsmen in the upland areas. Change came slowly in the routine of their lives. That does not mean everything was uniformly the same. The Dutch took advantage of nearby urban markets to develop intensive dairy farming by the end of the Middle Ages. In northern Italy the value of maize, imported from America in the sixteenth century, was recognised and a maize cake called 'polenta' is still one of the staple foods of that region today. But despite regional innovations, traditional crops and methods dominated and yields could be dangerously low—for instance, only five grains of wheat grew for every one sown, and that was if all went well.

The people of Europe around 1500 lived constantly under the threat of disasters such as famine or epidemic disease. Such calamities could destroy much with great rapidity but that did not necessarily force on the rate of change. Where the economic basis was sound, a commmunity would return to the normal routine of life within a few years. Where the local economic basis was not sound, villagers were likely to migrate, taking their traditional skills with them rather than changing their farming techniques. The many sites of deserted villages are evidence of this.

Towns might be thought of as centres of change and certainly they contained a greater variety of livelihoods, but they need to be viewed very differently from towns today. Naples' bloated population touched 200 000 by 1500 but a respectably sized central European city might number only 2000 inhabitants—scarcely more than a village in our view. But such cities or towns defined themselves physically by their city walls and legally by the charters which had established their corporations and guilds, the bodies which controlled local government and industry. The guilds were associations of those engaged in a particular trade, laying down regulations for the price, size and quality of their products and generally discouraging disruptive change as much as possible. And they protected their trade from being flooded by rural labourers.

For people around 1500 there was a clear distinction between town and country. For us, if we were to walk around such a town, that distinction might seem less clear. We would see no factories but small workshops which we would be tempted to define as cottage industries. We might see the carpenter or cooper or cloth-worker farming part time on a plot of land inside the city walls—countryside within the city. Our main impression would be of the small scale of the urban economy and how closely it was integrated with the traditional needs of an agrarian economy.

While we need to be aware of the enormous difference in scale and in the rate of innovation between the modern economy and that of sixteenth century Europe, it would be a mistake to think of the latter as simply being undeveloped. There had always been some international trade and since the eleventh century it had been growing as merchants, especially from Italy, took goods from the Mediterranean and the East into northern Europe. This north–south European trade axis rested on the fairs of Champagne which reached a prime importance in the thirteenth century. By 1500, seaborne trade from Portugal and Spain and barges plying the Rhine had become ever more important; Antwerp had become the city where the commerce of the south met northern Europe.

Along with the trade routes, high finance was developing. At the fairs of Champagne merchants had exchanged goods and money directly. By 1500 at Antwerp they were using bills of exchange, through which, for example, a Florentine merchant could pay for goods in Antwerp by drawing on funds owed to him in that city rather than having physically to take the money there from Florence. The bill of exchange is the ancestor of the modern cheque. Other business techniques were being innovated by this time, double-entry book-keeping being of particular importance. More rational accounting enabled the merchant to establish whether he was actually making a profit.

Despite such innovations, there were some brakes on commercial development. It was not so easy to raise a loan given that the Church saw lending money at interest as a sin, called usury. It used to be thought that the Protestants were the first to ignore this restriction but Catholics had already seen ways of lessening its effect. In 1515 Johannes von Eck, a

Catholic spokesman who was to be a leading opponent of the Protestants, argued that it was not sinful to charge up to five percent interest
a year on a loan as that just covered the risk, the potential loss to the
lender. Eck was arguing on behalf of the Fuggers, an Augsburg banking
family who practised capitalism on an international scale.

In the later Middle Ages an increasing number of banking families
had grown up exploiting the new financial techniques and providing the
finance for trading expeditions and for princes whose warlike ambitions
outstripped their income. Some of these families attained considerable
power—the Medici, for instance, were to be the rulers of Florence—but
it was the Fuggers who had the most diverse interests. They traded in
spices, wool and silk throughout Europe. They were the biggest of
mine-owners with interests in silver in the Tyrol and copper in Hungary.
They 'farmed', that is, leased the right to collect the revenue from the
huge estates of Spain's three Military Orders of crusading knights. And
they had won such concessions from the Habsburgs, the rising dynasty of
Europe, whose finances they virtually ran until the middle of the
sixteenth century. Even then, before concerted attempts by governments
to direct the overall economy, the requirements of politicians had a great
impact on the shape of the economy.

Governments sometimes directed trade through monopolies. For
instance, the kings of Castile had granted the city of Burgos a monopoly
in the marketing of wool which was to be the foundation of its prosperity.
Such monopolies were used by governments to reward the favoured with
privileges or to bring trade under closer control so that it could be more
easily taxed. There was no sign yet of consistent national trading
policies. Customs duties had to be paid when travelling within a country,
not just on its borders; for example, between Paris and Rouen a
merchant would have to pay 15 tolls. But princes, with an eye to the
amassing of bullion they could share, did sign treaties which encouraged
trade or passed laws, known in England as Navigation Acts, to confine
trade to their own subjects' shipping. All this amounts to a fair amount of
'state intervention' but it was mostly a matter of regulation and not the
large-scale financial intervention which modern governments have
regarded as normal until recently.

The government's impact on the economy was not confined to
intentional intervention, however. When short of ready cash a prince
might debase the coinage, replacing some of the silver content with
copper. That could lead to a sharp burst of inflation, ruining some or
making fortunes for more astute speculators. But the most regular
spin-off of government policy came from the amount that was spent on
war. The men of an army needed food, clothing and other supplies. By
1500 more faith and more cash were being placed in artillery which
created an armaments industry, metal foundries becoming amongst the
biggest of industrial operations at the time. Armies were certainly agents
of destruction but they could also act as stimulants to economic activity.

There was one state which had developed its economy far more fully than any other by 1500. That was the city-state of Venice which controlled an extensive maritime empire stretching down the Adriatic and through to the easternmost part of the Mediterranean, the Levant. Venice had become the main gateway for those goods such as silks and spices which were so highly prized in northern Europe. This was not just due to its secure position as an island city protected by its lagoon; even more important was an aristocracy who shared none of the feudal nobility's distaste for trade. The Venetian nobleman was brought up as part of an extended family which operated as a group of business associates; he might go to sea as a trader in his earlier years and later on manage affairs at home or take part in the government which was controlled by the aristocracy. In government, he might help to regulate the marine insurance on offer at the Rialto, a vital business service, or to manage the *galere de mercato*, the 'nationalised' shipping which was leased out to individual merchants. The ships themselves could be built in the state-run Arsenal which employed up to 4000 men and operated something very close to the production line system—Henry Ford's innovation, which influenced twentieth century industry so much, was not entirely new. It seems as though Venice had developed many of the forms of capitalism, even state capitalism.

Economic historians disagree about when capitalism originated—claims range from the thirteenth century through to the eighteenth century. A consensus view on this is unlikely as so much depends on the definition of the concept of capitalism. We can, however, be certain that industrial capitalism as we know it today scarcely existed in the Early Modern period. There were some examples—the Venetian Arsenal for instance, or the Fugger's mines where there was heavy investment and a large, wage-paid workforce—but most industry was still craftwork with limited investment in those small workshops governed by conservative guilds.

If we were to track down many capitalists around 1500, we would find them engaged in commerce, as the great profits were to be made in the transfer of goods and not in their production. But, although those profits enabled some merchants to live like aristocrats, there were limits to the development of commercial capitalism in the later Middle Ages. It was partly because most merchants were likely to value the leisure of aristocrats when they could afford it, in contrast to the Venetian aristocrats who valued work as merchants; it has been estimated that a merchant family which grew in wealth through three generations would then become *rentiers*, living off rents or government bonds. The Medici, a great example of capitalistic success, depended not so much on their bank as on what they could siphon off from the government by the middle of the fifteenth century. There was a spirit of enterprise but it was not that strong or regarded as being especially good.

Although merchants had moved towards capitalism's 'rational control of resources' through, for instance, book-keeping, and were finding ways around the usury laws, they did not organise themselves into the modern company. Firms of merchants were often of the same family which, like family businesses today, can founder when the talent runs out. There were 'compagnies', but these were more like clubs and, although they did foster economic co-operation, the merchants did not share the investments and profits, the risks and the tasks, as in a modern company.

Merchants' attitudes and organisation perhaps just reflected the main restriction to the development of capitalism in Europe around 1500, namely a slow-changing, narrow agrarian base. As the sixteenth century progressed there were two new developments which made this less of a determining factor—the opening of sea routes to the Indian and Pacific Oceans and general, nearly continuous inflation.

While the creative error of Christopher Columbus in finding the New World in 1492 may be seen as more momentous in the long term, the culmination of the Portuguese search for a sea route to India in Vasco da Gama's voyage there in 1497 was to have far more immediate economic impact *(see Chapter IV)*. New sources of supply were opened up for the spice trade, costs were brought down and the monopoly hold of Mediterranean merchants on the eastern trade was broken. Trading posts were set up along the coasts of Africa, India and into the East Indies. The Portuguese tried to keep these new trade routes to themselves but later on in the sixteenth century they were to be invaded by the Dutch and by the English. Those two nationalities of north western Europe were to seize the new opportunities, developing a more expansive, aggressive commercial capitalism than had been known before. A world economy was emerging and the expansion of Europe had begun.

The economy within Europe had been sluggish for most of the fifteenth century but from 1470, for the next hundred years or so, it was to grow. Along with that growth came inflation, the great Price Rise of the sixteenth century. In explanation of it, Earl J Hamilton writing in the 1930s pointed to the influx of bullion from the New World which meant an increased amount of money in Europe chasing the same amount of goods, thus allowing for prices to rise. However, the Hamilton thesis, although still represented as standard in some textbooks, has been attacked quite regularly by a succeeding generation of scholars on the grounds of its theoretical inadequacies and the lack of evidence. The arrival of the bullion (even when that mined in Europe is included) does not correlate in time or place with the greater part of the inflation. In place of Hamilton's, there are many competing theories. Although no consensus view has emerged, it is recognised that an increase in the volume of commercial transactions and a growth in the European population after its late medieval downswing could have contributed to a pressure on prices through a greater demand for goods. Certainly the population growth correlates much more closely with the Price Rise than does the influx of bullion.

The inflation averaged about two percent a year. That may not seem much to modern eyes but it made a relentless impact over a century on

Sixteenth Century Rulers

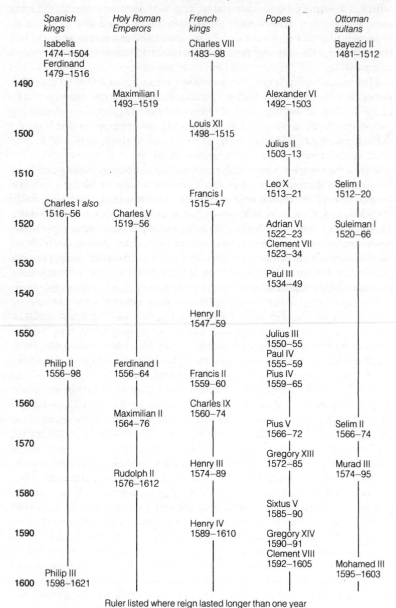

	Spanish kings	Holy Roman Emperors	French kings	Popes	Ottoman sultans
	Isabella 1474–1504 Ferdinand 1479–1516		Charles VIII 1483–98		Bayezid II 1481–1512
1490		Maximilian I 1493–1519		Alexander VI 1492–1503	
1500			Louis XII 1498–1515	Julius II 1503–13	
1510	Charles I *also* 1516–56	Charles V 1519–56	Francis I 1515–47	Leo X 1513–21	Selim I 1512–20
1520				Adrian VI 1522–23 Clement VII 1523–34	Suleiman I 1520–66
1530				Paul III 1534–49	
1540					
1550			Henry II 1547–59	Julius III 1550–55 Paul IV 1555–59 Pius IV 1559–65	
	Philip II 1556–98	Ferdinand I 1556–64	Francis II 1559–60		
1560		Maximilian II 1564–76	Charles IX 1560–74		
1570				Pius V 1566–72 Gregory XIII 1572–85	Selim II 1566–74 Murad III 1574–95
		Rudolph II 1576–1612	Henry III 1574–89		
1580				Sixtus V 1585–90	
1590			Henry IV 1589–1610	Gregory XIV 1590–91 Clement VIII 1592–1605	
1600	Philip III 1598–1621				Mohamed III 1595–1603

Ruler listed where reign lasted longer than one year

the more primitive economy of sixteenth century Europe. It helped to stimulate industrial growth as wages lagged behind prices and so profits were greater and more money was available for investment. By 1560, 'real' wages (that is, in terms of purchasing power) were down between 20 percent and 50 percent from the last half of the fifteenth century. It is an irony that, for the economy in general, the Price Rise was a part of its health and development while for countless numbers of individuals it meant poverty or destitution.

11. Bibliography

J R Hale *Renaissance Europe* (Fontana, 1971). E F Rice *The Foundations of Early Modern Europe* (Weidenfeld & Nicolson, 1971). H Kamen *European Society 1500–1700* (Hutchinson, 1984). P Zagorin *Rebels and Rulers 1500–1660 Vol 1* (CUP, 1982). M Howard *War in European History* (OUP, 1976). G Mattingly *Renaissance Diplomacy* (Jonathan Cape, 1955). J Bossy *Christianity in the West 1400–1700* (OUP, 1985). E Eisenstein *The Printing Revolution in Early Modern Europe* (CUP, 1983). F Braudel *Civilisation and Capitalism* (Fontana, 1985) in 3 volumes, but well worth browsing in. *The New Cambridge Modern History Vol 1* (CUP, 1957).

II Ferdinand and Isabella

1. Introduction

In October 1469 Isabella, the eighteen-year-old half-sister of the King of Castile, married Ferdinand, the seventeen-year-old son of the King of Aragon. It was an arranged marriage and the two were an ill-assorted pair. Isabella was a serious-minded, devout and unattractive woman whereas Ferdinand was warlike, ruthless and lecherous and drew reluctant praise from contemporaries as a master of plot and subterfuge. The Italian writer Machiavelli summed him up superbly by saying he 'kept his subjects' minds uncertain and astonished and left no time for men to settle down and act against him.' Superficially dissimilar, the pair were to work together in relative harmony until Isabella's death in 1504.

Undoubtedly the most politically effective marital partnership of this, or perhaps any other, period, they faced huge problems at the start of their married life. It was by no means sure that Isabella would take the throne of Castile and in the event it was necessary for Ferdinand and Isabella to defeat internal opponents and foreign invasion to enforce her claim after the death of her half-brother in 1474. Ferdinand became King of Aragon in 1479. They then had to govern the very different kingdoms of Aragon and Castile, taking into account the traditional hostility between their subjects. However, their royal marriage had established a dynastic union which was, apart from some periods of crisis, to hold the realms of Spain together permanently.

The historical importance of Ferdinand and Isabella was once seen in their unification of Spain. This is now disputed. Those historians who stressed unification were often looking for the origins of nation states prematurely and exaggerated the degree to which Ferdinand and Isabella created a centralised 'New Monarchy'. Historians working today, such as Elliott, Lynch and Kamen, recognise that there were important developments under Ferdinand and Isabella, but they also stress just how much the realms of Spain remained separate entities. As Elliott reminds us, when we refer to Spain under Ferdinand and Isabella and their successors, we often mean Castile, its largest, wealthiest and most easily governable realm. The monarchs had little need or incentive to integrate their disparate territories.

Another issue to be considered is the extent to which the monarchs were innovatory in dealing with the problems they faced in the government of Spain. In many respects they used medieval methods in a revived, energetic way, rather than creating a 'New Monarchy'. The need for such revived and energetic government can be shown by a consideration of the condition of Aragon and Castile at the time of their marriage.

2. Spain in 1469

At the time of the marriage of Ferdinand and Isabella, Iberia was divided into five main political entities—Castile, Aragon, Portugal, Navarre and Granada.

The kingdom of Castile sprawled across most of central Spain, being by far the largest state in the peninsula. It was four times greater in area than the Spanish territories of Aragon and, with about five million people, accounted for 70–80 percent of the population of Iberia. During the early Middle Ages much of southern Castile had been occupied by invading Moors from North Africa. The long struggle to regain this lost territory (known as the 'Reconquest') did much to determine the nature of Castilian society. The warrior nobility, or *hidalgo* class, had taken the lead in the Reconquest and their values of military prowess and conquest became the dominant ones in Castile. The most important aristocratic families carved out massive domains which gave them considerable political and economic power in relation to the Crown. Below the nobility in the social scale, there was almost no middle class in rural Castile and only a small one in the towns of the kingdom. The mass of the population was made up of poor, often landless, peasants who had little prospect of escaping a life of grinding poverty but who were to provide the armies of Spain with a constant flow of hardy recruits. Economically, Castile depended heavily on the revenue from wool exports provided by the huge flocks which grazed on the grasslands of the Castilian interior.

In the mid-fifteenth century the most notable feature of the political scene in Castile was the weakness of the Crown. King Henry IV, who came to the throne in 1454, was a sovereign who lacked personal authority and the institutions to impose his will on the country. It was strongly rumoured that Henry was unable to produce an heir (he was nicknamed 'the Impotent') and when a daughter was born to him and his queen it was believed by many that the baby was the product of the liaison between the Queen and one of the King's noble favourites, Beltràn de la Cueva. The young Princess Joanna became widely known as 'la Beltraneja' and her right to succeed to the throne was disputed by many nobles who looked to Henry's half-sister, Isabella, as the rightful heir. Henry had proved totally unable to control his warlike nobility, anarchy reigned in many parts of the kingdom and a contested succession seemed the best recipe for continued instability. Castile did,

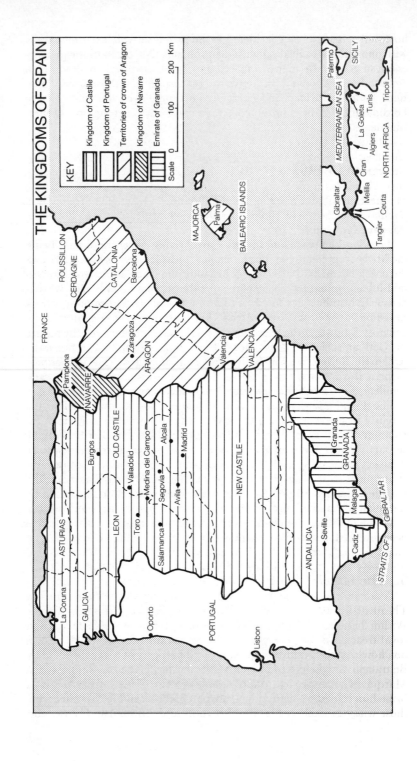

THE KINGDOMS OF SPAIN

KEY

Kingdom of Castile
Kingdom of Portugal
Territories of crown of Aragon
Kingdom of Navarre
Emirate of Granada

Scale

0   100   200 Km

FRANCE

ROUSSILLON
CERDAGNE

CATALONIA
Barcelona

Zaragoza
ARAGON

Pamplona
NAVARRE

Valencia
VALENCIA

MAJORCA
Palma

BALEARIC ISLANDS

La Coruna
GALICIA

ASTURIAS

LEON

Burgos
OLD CASTILE

Valladolid
Toro
Medina del Campo
Salamanca
Segovia
Avila

Alcala
Madrid

NEW CASTILE

Oporto

PORTUGAL

Lisbon

ANDALUCIA
Seville

Cadiz

Granada
GRANADA

Malaga

STRAITS OF GIBRALTAR

MEDITERRANEAN SEA

Palermo
SICILY

Tripoli

Tunis
La Goleta

Algiers
Oran
Melilla
NORTH AFRICA

Gibraltar
Tangier   Ceuta

however, possess one great political advantage: it was a unitary state with one language, one system of taxation, one Cortes (Parliament) and one system of law.

Turning to Aragon, there too political disorder had been prevalent. King John II at least possessed a clear male heir in the person of Ferdinand but he was faced by civil war in the period 1462–72. Unlike Castile, Aragon was split into a number of states—Aragon itself, Catalonia and Valencia. Each of these jealously guarded its own Cortes, language, laws and privileges *(fueros)*. The power of the Aragonese Crown was thus restricted by particularism (assertion of local independence) in a manner that the Castilian monarchy was not. In the Mediterranean the Crown of Aragon also ruled Sardinia and Sicily. The population of Aragon in Spain was about one million and the kingdom was sparsely peopled.

Catalonia had traditionally enjoyed a thriving commercial position in the Mediterranean, based on the export of textiles, and the prosperity of the coastal areas had provided benefits for the whole of Aragon. By the mid-fifteenth century the trading pre-eminence of Catalonia was in decay. This was partly due to serious visitations of the plague, partly to the challenge of Castilian merchants and sailors who were beginning to penetrate into the western Mediterranean and partly to the activities of the Genoese who took over much of the Catalan trade. The potential of Aragon was therefore much less than that of Castile and it is hardly surprising that Ferdinand and Isabella were preoccupied by Castilian problems and the need to mobilise the resources of Isabella's kingdom.

The three other states in the Iberian peninsula were Portugal, Navarre and Granada. Portugal had won her struggle to avoid Castilian domination in the late fourteenth century and by the middle of the next century was becoming increasingly preoccupied with exploration of the African coast *(see Chapter IV)*. This did not stop her interfering in the affairs of Castile when the opportunity arose. Navarre was a small kingdom but it straddled the Pyrenees and was therefore important in the rivalry between France and Spain. Granada was the last Moorish bastion in Spain, although an annual tribute was paid to Castile. It will be considered at length in a later section.

3. The Civil War in Castile

The death of Henry IV in December 1474 plunged Castile into civil war. Within 24 hours of the passing of her brother, Isabella had secured the royal treasury at Segovia and had been proclaimed Queen. She could not, however, feel secure while her rival, Joanna, remained at liberty. La Beltraneja was held in Madrid under the protection of the powerful Marquis of Villena, who rejected attempts by Ferdinand and Isabella to bribe him into handing her over. Joanna soon became a figurehead for those who genuinely believed in her right to the throne and those who merely wished to prolong the state of near anarchy in Castile for their own advantage. Across Castile, noble families ranged themselves behind one or other of the princesses, often because they could use the dynastic dispute to settle local scores.

Joanna's prospects of success were increased considerably by the support of Alfonso V of Portugal who sensed that intervention in Castile might bring the kingdom under Portuguese control. Thus, he declared his intention to marry Joanna and at the same time negotiated with Louis XI of France for an attack against Isabella from the north. Faced with imminent invasion, Ferdinand and Isabella reacted with an energy which was to be typical of their political and personal partnership. They confirmed the privileges of loyal nobles and attempted to buy the support of waverers, fortified strategic points, banned the export of money and precious metals, concluded a truce with the Moors of Granada in order to guard their southern flank and even made a somewhat spurious claim to the Portuguese throne. Propaganda played an important part in their campaign. Writs were issued to the nobles and cities of Castile, denouncing Joanna and her supporters as rebels 'against their natural lords' and 'foes of the fatherland' and accusing Alfonso of 'trying to create all ill and hurt in these our said kingdoms'.

In early summer 1475, Alfonso invaded Castile, betrothed himself to Joanna, claimed the throne and urged Castilian nobles to join him. Ferdinand challenged Alfonso to a duel to settle the matter, an offer which the ageing King of Portugal unsurprisingly refused, and then led an army to counter the invasion. Several months of inconclusive sparring followed but at the Battle of Toro in March 1476 *(see map on page 36)* Ferdinand defeated Alfonso and his Castilian supporters. This victory ended the threat of invasion from the west and illustrated the vital contribution of Ferdinand and the Aragonese military experts he brought with him. After Toro, other events helped to turn the war in favour of Isabella. Louis XI, more interested in conquering Burgundy than helping Alfonso, made peace with Castile. In 1478, Isabella gave birth to a son, thus providing a clear line of succession and attracting the support of many of the uncommitted nobles. The accession of Ferdinand to the throne of Aragon following the death of John II in 1479 increased his military resources and his prestige in Castile.

By September 1479, Alfonso was glad to make peace in a series of agreements generally known as the Treaty of Alcaçovas. The betrothal of Alfonso and Joanna was dissolved and in 1480 Joanna declared her intention to become a nun, living mainly in a Portuguese convent until her death in 1530. Alfonso gave up all claim to Castile and in return Isabella renounced Castilian claims to Portugal's possessions in the Atlantic and Africa.

Victory in the Castilian civil war was the first great achievement of Ferdinand and Isabella and it must be stressed that it was a joint achievement. The bulk of their army was Castilian but Ferdinand brought in siege and artillery experts from Aragon and the Aragonese navy played an important part in the war at sea. Ferdinand also negotiated support from a number of the Castilian nobles, including the powerful families of Alva, Mendoza and Enriquez. The defeat of Joanna and her adherents did not, however, mean an immediate restoration of political stability. The monarchs now faced the task of halting the disorder which had plagued Castile for decades.

4. The Pacification of Castile

The traditional view of Ferdinand and Isabella's actions following the civil war is that they ruthlessly suppressed any potential sources of opposition and extended the scope of royal power in Spain. There is some truth in this assessment. Certainly the monarchs were determined that there should be no repeat of the chaos which Castile had endured before their victory, but the degree of their success in destroying the forces which made for instability is questionable. All recent historians reject the notion of Ferdinand and Isabella consciously constructing a 'New Monarchy' in which their kingdoms were integrated, their cities and nobles brought under close control and their power exerted throughout Spain.

The first way in which the monarchs attempted to impose their authority was by travelling through Castile, meeting leading nobles and citizens and dealing with potential problems at first hand. For example, when revolt broke out in Galicia in 1485–86 both Ferdinand and Isabella travelled to this remote area to deal with the trouble. This 'peripatetic' style of kingship was medieval in origin and survived well into the sixteenth century. It was not until the reign of Philip II that Madrid was designated as the capital of Spain. Constant movement about Castile to some extent offset the difficulties of having only a small standing army available for internal security, very little bureaucracy in the provinces and an inadequate revenue.

Perhaps the most serious threat to the stability of Castile came from the nobility. The most powerful families of grandees collectively controlled economic and military resources far in excess of anything Ferdinand and Isabella could hope to muster. Moreover, the monarchs were obliged to look to their nobles to supply them with troops for foreign wars and to deal with internal rebellion. The aggressive instincts of the Castilian aristocracy were held in check by a subtle mixture of threats, pressure and bribery. As early as 1480, the monarchs attempted to buy support when, at the Cortes of Toledo, nobles were confirmed in possession of any royal land which they had managed to acquire before 1464 whilst the monarchs resumed ownership of Crown lands alienated after that date. There was no attempt to remove the nobility's exemption from taxation; nobles who remained loyal were not disarmed and privileges, honours and titles were granted as inducements to good behaviour. However, if Ferdinand and Isabella felt their interests to be prejudiced they acted decisively. The strategic port of Cadiz was confiscated from the Duke of Cadiz in 1492 and the Duke of Medina Sidonia was obliged to surrender Gibraltar in 1502. Nevertheless, in both these cases the aggrieved aristocrat was compensated with territories elsewhere. Henry Kamen has claimed that 'the taming of the Castilian aristocracy was an outstanding achievement of the Catholic kings. The great lords were taken into partnership with the Crown and confirmed in their estates and private armies'. It is true that many Castilian nobles served the Crown faithfully both in Spain and abroad but it must not be forgotten that, after the death of Isabella in 1504, considerable numbers rejected the authority of Ferdinand and supported the claim to the throne of the monarchs' daughter Joanna and her husband Philip of Burgundy.

To increase their military potential, Ferdinand and Isabella revived and extended the system of mounted militia provided by the *Hermandad* or association of Castilian towns. This institution dated from 1190 when four towns had agreed to patrol the roads and deter banditry as well as resolving trading disputes. Such associations became common during periods of instability in the Middle Ages and at the Cortes of Madrigal in 1476, the monarchs regularised them into the *Santa Hermandad* or 'Holy Brotherhood'. A Council of the Hermandad was established to administer it and the Hermandad provided substantial numbers of troops for the campaigns against Granada. In 1490, for example, the Hermandad was providing 10 000 men, approximately one-quarter of the total. The towns represented in the Hermandad met together in a *Junta* or assembly and this provided Ferdinand and Isabella with a useful method of consulting the cities and an even more useful method of levying taxation. In 1491–92, for example, the Crown received sixty four million *maravadís* (currency used before ducats) from the Junta of the Hermandad. This used to be seen as evidence of royal centralisation but, with the ending of the war against Granada, the Hermandad declined in importance and after 1498 reverted to its original role of rural police force.

Ferdinand and Isabella also brought under royal control the Military Orders of Santiago, Alcantara and Calatrava. These were medieval crusading corporations which had acquired massive landholdings during the Reconquest. They controlled considerable military might (they provided one-tenth of the infantry and one-sixth of the cavalry for the war against Granada) and the masterships of the Orders were highly prized by the grandee families. Ferdinand took control of the Order of Calatrava in 1487, that of Alcantara in 1494 and that of Santiago in 1499. A Council of the Military Orders was established in 1489 to take over the administration of the corporations.

The towns of Castile were another potential source of opposition. Crown intervention in the affairs of the municipalities was nothing new. In the fourteenth century royal officials called *corregidores* had been appointed in some Castilian towns to help decide local disputes and ensure that the interests of the Crown were upheld. In 1480, the Cortes of

Toledo agreed that corregidores could be despatched to towns where they did not already exist and by 1494 there were fifty four towns in Castile with a corregidor in residence. They dealt with public order and administrative matters and have traditionally been regarded as agents of government centralisation. However, although the corregidores were appointed by the Crown they were paid locally and were certainly subject to local pressures. Ferdinand and Isabella were prepared to arbitrate directly in conflicts in towns. In a number of cases they insisted that town councils should be chosen by lot and appointed for life rather than by the trouble-provoking method of annual elections. In addition, towns were consulted through the Cortes and the Junta of the Santa Hermandad. However, the policies of Ferdinand and Isabella cannot be seen as a total success in this area for it was the towns which revolted against their successor, Charles, in the Revolt of the Comuneros.

To maintain their hold on Castile the monarchs needed a sound financial and administrative base. Ferdinand and Isabella were not fiscal innovators. They relied on traditional taxes and did not significantly dent the noble and clerical exemption from taxation. Their main income derived from the *alcabala*, a sales tax first introduced in 1342 and providing up to 80 percent of the Crown's total revenue. The *servicio y montazgo*, a traditional tax on the sheep flocks of Castile, provided another profitable source of income, as did customs dues—another time-honoured royal right. The *cruzada*, a new tax on the Church granted by the Papacy during the Granada war, continued to be collected after 1492 and contributions raised from the Hermandad (which raised an average of 30 million *maravedís* per annum between 1485 and 1498) and granted by the Cortes were valuable additions to the monarchs' revenue. (In 1500–04 alone, the Cortes provided subsidies of 300 million *maravedís*.) The ordinary revenue of Castile rose from 73 million *maravedís* in 1474 (of which only 11 million were collected, owing to the civil war) to 320 million *maravedís* by 1510 and, when the 'extraordinary' revenue of the Hermandad and the Cortes were added, the Crown's financial position should have been healthy.

There were, however, huge expenses. The marriage of Catherine of Aragon to Prince Arthur of England, for example, cost 60 million *maravedís* whilst the second expedition to Naples cost 366 million *maravedís*. Grants and pensions were costing the Crown 112 million *maravedís* by 1504 (partly a result of the policy of buying noble support). The monarchs were obliged to resort to issuing *juros* or government bonds and the interest on these was taking up 131 million *maravedís* by 1516. Charles, the grandson of Ferdinand and Isabella, succeeded to a throne which was solvent but certainly not wealthy.

In administration, too, the monarchs preferred to adapt rather than innovate. A series of councils staffed largely by *letrados* (civil servants trained in law) administered the main areas of government. The Council of Castile spawned committees for foreign policy, justice, finance, the Hermandad and Aragon, and further councils were set up for the

Inquisition (1483) and the Military Orders (1489). It used to be thought that the reliance on *letrados*, who tended to be of middle class or gentry origin, was a conscious attempt by the monarchs to remove the nobility from government. Modern historians point out that the role of *letrados* was already well established by the reign of Isabella (Henry IV had insisted that at least eight of the twelve members of the Council of Castile be *letrados*) and that the monarchs were simply interested in obtaining the best possible administrative ability.

Thus the monarchs tended to pursue conservative policies in dealing with the problems of Castile. What made them successful was the close attention paid to the operation of the policies, backed up by the personal appearances of the peripatetic monarchs. Yet all this could be so easily threatened by a major crisis—such as the succession crisis after 1504 *(see page 56)*.

5. The Conquest of Granada

With the successful conclusion of the war against Portugal and the restoration of some degree of stability in Castile, Ferdinand and Isabella were able to turn their attention to the south. There, the Moorish kingdom of Granada bore constant witness to the incompleteness of the Reconquest. Several motives existed for the decision to destroy this last remnant of Muslim power in Spain. Ferdinand and Isabella supplied one justification in a letter to the Pope:

> We neither are, nor have been, persuaded to undertake this war by desire to acquire greater rents nor the wish to lay up treasure; for had we wanted to increase our lordships and augment our income with far less peril, labour and expense, we should have been able to do so. But the desire which we have to serve God and our zeal for the holy Catholic faith has induced us to set aside our own interests and ignore the continual hardships and dangers to which this cause commits us; and thus can we hope both that the holy Catholic faith may be spread and Christendom freed of so relentless a menace as abides here at our gates, until these Infidels of the kingdom of Granada are uprooted and expelled from Spain.

1 *According to this document, what were Ferdinand and Isabella's main motives for wishing to conquer Granada?*
2 *Given that the letter was written to the Pope, is it a reliable indication of the monarchs' aims?*

Fear of Islam was widespread in the late fifteenth century. The victories of the Ottoman Turks in the Balkans and the eastern Mediterranean seemed to signal an onslaught on Europe, an offensive in which the apparently wealthy and self-confident kingdom of Granada might play a leading role. The Ottomans had already made contact with the Moorish states of North Africa and with Granada, and a Muslim alliance would jeopardise Spanish trade in the Mediterranean, including the link with Ferdinand's own province of Sicily. By overcoming Granada the Spanish monarchs would not only improve the security of their own kingdoms but also win a significant local victory in the duel between Christendom and Islam.

A second, and perhaps more pressing, reason for the conquest was to provide the monarchs with land which could be distributed as patronage amongst the Castilian nobility. Those nobles who had fought for Isabella in the civil war had to be rewarded and those who still harboured doubts about her succession had to be bought. The conquered land could be disposed of as Ferdinand and Isabella wished and by 1492 over half the area of Granada had been granted to the Castilian aristocracy.

Linked with this was a third factor. Nobles who could give vent to their warlike inclinations in a potentially lucrative invasion of Granada would be less likely to revolt or engage in conflicts among themselves. Hernando del Pulgar described this as 'exercising the chivalry of the realm'. The Muslims were an easily identifiable enemy and war against them would unite all Castilian nobles under the banners of Christianity and Isabella.

The monarchs may also have been influenced by a fourth consideration: the wealth of Granada. The mountainous Alpujarras region was famous for its mulberry bushes on which silk worms were reared. Granada silk was a valuable luxury commodity to Christians and Muslims alike and would make an important addition to the prosperity of Castile. Moreover, the merchants of Granada had a share in the distribution of gold which reached the North African ports after being transported across the Sahara. European demand for gold was rising and access to this supply would be a useful windfall.

The occasion for war occurred in 1481. During the 1470s, a series of truces had barely restrained the skirmishing between Christians and Moors along the borders of Castile and Granada. In April 1478 the Moors attacked the Christian town of Cieza, killed eighty of the inhabitants and captured the rest. Heavily involved in the war against Portugal, Ferdinand and Isabella were in no position to retaliate, to negotiate the release of the prisoners or even to afford to ransom their luckless subjects. They may even have been obliged to give up the annual tribute traditionally paid to the monarchs of Castile by Granada. Once the war with Portugal was concluded, the monarchs were less willing to submit to such humiliations and began to make preparations for full-scale war. In 1479 they applied to Pope Sixtus IV for the coming conflict to be declared a crusade. The request was granted, conferring the status of martyr on those who died fighting and earning remission of sins for all who fought. Those who did not fight could obtain indulgence by contributing to war expenses. Tension heightened when the ruler of Granada, Mulay Hassan, refused to renew payment of the tribute. 'The coffers of Granada contain no more gold but steel', was his alleged reply to the demands of the Spanish. Alarmed by the Christian preparations, the Moors decided to strike first in order to improve their strategic position whilst there was still time. In December 1481, they seized a number of Christian strongholds on the border, including the town of Zahara. Ferdinand and Isabella welcomed this as a 'chance to put in hand forthwith what has long been in our minds' and prepared to invade Granada in 1482.

The ensuing war lasted for ten years and was fought with a bitterness composed of crusading zeal on the Spanish side and desperation on the Moorish. The Christians held the upper hand, deploying larger forces than the Muslims could muster (Spanish manpower exceeded 50 000 at times) and using cannon to reduce the castles and cities of Granada. Much of the credit for Spanish success can be attributed to Ferdinand who played an active part in the campaigns, directing strategy and leading armies in person. His Aragonese military experts possessed skills and technology (such as the new hand-held gunpowder weapons) which the Muslims could not match. Isabella was not the type of woman to sit meekly by whilst there was God's work to be done and she played a valuable part in the campaign by organising supplies and reinforcements. The practical partnership of the two monarchs was never seen to better effect than in the Granada war.

Militarily backward, Granada was fatally weakened by feuding within the ruling Nasrid dynasty. Mulay Hassan faced revolt by his son Boabdil and was then overthrown by his brother, al-Zagal, in 1485. During the following years Boabdil and al-Zagal fought each other, to the obvious satisfaction of the Christians. In 1489 al-Zagal surrendered to the Spanish, leaving Boabdil as ruler of a shrunken, devastated Granada. Appeals to the rest of the Islamic world brought no response and in 1491 Ferdinand's army closed in on the city of Granada. After an eight month siege, Boabdil capitulated and in January 1492 the Spanish entered the Muslim capital. This was perhaps the greatest moment of the reign: the culmination of several centuries of Reconquest and a rousing triumph for the joint monarchs.

The collapse of Moorish resistance had a number of important results. The international prestige of Ferdinand and Isabella was hugely enhanced. At a time when Christianity appeared to be on the retreat in the face of militant Islam, in Spain at least the tide had turned. In 1494 Pope Alexander VI accorded Ferdinand and Isabella the title 'Catholic Monarchs', describing them as 'athletes of Christ'. Spanish adulation was unbounded 'It is the extinction of Spain's calamities', crowed the scholar Peter Martyr and an observer of the fall of Granada wrote exultantly of the 'most distinguished and blessed day there has ever been in Spain.' The monarchs had temporarily united their kingdoms in a common cause, eradicated a persistent threat to the southern border of Castile, trained a formidable army in the techniques of modern warfare and assured their own supremacy in relation to the Castilian nobility. It may also have made the Castilians willing to support Ferdinand's campaigns in Italy after 1494, an area which had hitherto been an exclusively Aragonese preserve.

For the Muslims, the terms of the surrender were surprisingly generous. So generous, indeed, that it is possible Ferdinand was showing leniency to secure immediate compliance, with the intention of utterly crushing the Muslims at some convenient future time. Although the inhabitants of Granada became subjects of Ferdinand and Isabella, they were allowed to practise their own religions and customs, to trade freely, to own property and to emigrate in safety if they wished to do so. There was to be no forcible conversion to Christianity. Many of the élite of Granada preferred to cross to North Africa, carrying with them a desire for revenge and an ambition to liberate their co-religionists who remained under the heel of the Infidel.

The years after 1492 suggested that Muslims and Christians might live together amicably in Castile's new province. Areas depopulated by the wars were occupied by peasant settlers from Andalusia (35 000 to 40 000 immigrants moved south between 1485 and 1498) while Moorish farmers worked much as before, even if their masters were now Castilian rather than Moorish nobles. The Count of Tendilla was appointed Captain-General of Granada and pursued moderate policies, respecting the customs of the native population. Isabella's confessor Hernando de Talavera was created Archbishop of Granada. He, too, did not abuse the sensitivities of the Muslims and preferred to gain converts to Christianity by preaching and persuasion rather than harassment.

In 1499 all this changed. In Early Modern Europe it was regarded as a sign of weakness for states to permit more than one religion inside their borders, and the monarchs and their advisers must have been concerned that the Muslims in the south were a potential threat. With the intention of investigating the matter, Archbishop Ximenes de Cisneros of Toledo, primate of Spain, accompanied Ferdinand and Isabella to Granada. Appalled by what he saw as Talavera's leniency, Cisneros embarked on a programme of mass 'conversion'. It has been shown that this was not part of the surrender agreement of 1492 and, in November 1499, the Muslims of the Alpujarras rose in revolt. Ferdinand crushed the outbreak in an energetic campaign in 1500 and the Moors were offered the choice of conversion to Christianity or emigration. Most were too poor to leave. In 1502 the monarchs ordered the expulsion of all remaining adherents of Islam, with all those remaining automatically becoming Christian. These *Moriscos*, as they were known, were to be a source of anxiety for Spanish monarchs for decades to come. Unreconciled and unabsorbed, they remained a potential Muslim fifth column on Spain's strategic southern coast. Ferdinand and Isabella had created an intractable problem which was to last until the final expulsion of the Moriscos in 1609. Granada had been unified with Castile, but at the expense of a divided society.

6. The Economy of Spain under Ferdinand and Isabella

With the decline of the Catalan commercial empire, Castile moved into a position of economic domination of Spain. The most profitable product of Castile was wool, grown on the merino breed of sheep which had been introduced to Spain from North Africa in about 1300. Sheep farming enjoyed a favoured status and was encouraged by the monarchs for both financial and economic reasons. Considerable revenue was derived from the servicio y montazgo tax on sheep and the export of wool provided customs duties. There was a ready market for merino wool in Europe and large quantities were shipped to northern ports such as Antwerp, where it was sold for textile manufacture. The aristocracy also preferred pastoral agriculture as few workers and little capital investment were necessary for sheep farming. The number of sheep rose from 2.7 million in 1477 to 3.5 million in 1526 and huge areas of the Spanish interior were turned over to grazing. This expansion was a mixed blessing for Spain. Most historians believe that the emphasis on sheep led to the neglect of arable farming, inducing grain shortages in 1502–08 which necessitated large-scale imports in 1506 and aided the outbreak of plague in 1507. Moreover, the Mesta (the corporation of sheepowners) was granted privileges which were to the detriment of arable agriculture. In 1489 the *canadas* or migratory routes used by the sheep flocks were enlarged. In 1500 a royal councillor was appointed to the new post of President of the Mesta and in 1501 a new law stated that flocks could use for ever any land that had been used as pasture in preceding centuries. Preoccupation with the export of raw wool meant that Spain failed to develop her own textile industry. Much land was deforested and subjected to erosion, a further example of the imbalance between pastoral and arable farming which was a long-term legacy of Ferdinand and Isabella.

The monarchs' policy towards trade and industry was also not entirely beneficial. The harsh treatment meted out to the Muslims of Granada, the *conversos* (Jews converted to Christianity) and the Jews resulted in the flight from Spain of many skilled workers and some capital. To compensate for this, efforts were made to recruit foreign experts, especially from Flanders and Italy. A further handicap to development was the system of guilds. In most areas of Europe these were in decline but in Spain they retained their privileged position, discouraging innovation and initiative and perpetuating old-fashioned practices. A third factor hindering progress was that Aragon and Castile remained separate economic units with customs barriers operating between them. Catalan merchants were treated as foreigners at the great Castilian commercial fair of Medina del Campo.

Some measures were taken to encourage Spanish trade. Agents were sent to London, Bruges and other cities to facilitate the sale of wool and convoys were organised to ship Spanish wool to northern Europe. Navigation laws were passed to stimulate the carrying of goods in Spanish ships. In 1483 the trade fair at Medina del Campo was reorganised and some improvements were made to the dilapidated road system, although too much of the responsibility for this fell on the small settlements along the highways rather than on the major towns the repairs were intended to benefit.

By 1516, the Spanish economy was already in an unhealthy state due to lack of investment in home production, absence of commercial enterprise and an agricultural base too reliant on a single product —wool. The influx of gold and silver from the New World concealed these structural deficiencies for much of the sixteenth century but when this dried up it became clear that Spain had not developed an economy to match those of the Netherlands, England or France.

7. Cisneros and Church Reform

The condition of the Spanish Church in the mid-fifteenth century was regarded with concern by the monarchs, especially Isabella who was renowned for her piety. Most of the seven archbishops and forty bishops lived lives of ostentatious luxury and ignored their spiritual and pastoral duties. Absenteeism was rife. Several archbishops and bishops had participated in the civil war, drawing on their huge estates and revenues to finance their political ambitions. For example, Don Alfonso Carrillo, Archbishop of Toledo, fought with the Portuguese army at Toro and could command an army of a thousand men and the loyalty of 19 000 vassals. The state of the religious orders was widely regarded as a scandal and the parish clergy were frequently poor and uneducated.

Royal policy towards the Church had three main priorities. Firstly, the monarchs wished to obtain royal domination of the personnel of the Church. This meant wresting control of ecclesiastical appointments from the Papacy and ensuring that dependable and loyal men were appointed to senior posts. A second aim was to obtain a share of the vast wealth of the Church. The third priority was to reform the Church and raise its moral and educational standards.

In the aftermath of the civil war Ferdinand and Isabella carried out a number of measures to curb the political and military power of the Church, obliging it, for example, to hand over fortresses to the custody of royal appointees. This was followed by a determined royal offensive to gain control of the appointment of bishops, a power which was in the hands of the Papacy. At a gathering of Spanish clergy at Seville in 1478, the monarchs obtained support for the reduction of papal influence and a programme of reform. When the bishopric of Cuenca fell vacant in 1479, Ferdinand and Isabella asserted their right to nominate the new bishop and Pope Sixtus IV gave in after a prolonged wrangle. Following up this success, in 1486 the monarchs secured from Innocent VIII the important right of *patronato* or patronage over Church appointments in the newly occupied lands of Granada. Using Spanish support for the Papacy in the Italian wars as a lever, Ferdinand extracted further concessions, this time over the Church in the New World. In a bull of 1508 Julius II gave to the monarchs the *patronato* over all Spanish territory in America, including rights to dismiss churchmen, tax the Church and ignore papal edicts. The Papacy was thus excluded from influence in Spain's colonies, the Crown exercising a supreme headship. It was not until 1523 that Adrian VI admitted the power of Charles V to appoint to bishoprics in Spain itself, but the battle had effectively been won during the reign of Ferdinand and Isabella.

The monarchs were not slow to take advantage of their new rights by appointing reforming Spanish clergymen to the highest offices. The Queen's confessor, Hernando de Talavera, had constantly urged Isabella to improve the state of the Church and in 1492 he was appointed to the new archbishopric of Granada. There he practised what he advocated by preaching frequently, spending his revenues on the poor and providing work for the destitute. He abhorred idleness and even the poor blind were given employment blowing bellows for blacksmiths. Munzer, a German observer, recorded of Talavera that 'his continual studies, his constant labour and rigorous fasts had so debilitated his body that his bones were visible.' His place as the Queen's spiritual adviser was taken in 1492 by Cisneros, who was made Archbishop of Toledo in 1495. Cisneros proved to be the leading strategist in moves to improve the condition of the Church, setting a personal example of pastoral care and of poverty which led Pope Alexander VI to reprove him for not living in a state fit for a bishop.

With the active encouragement of Isabella, Cisneros set about improving the religious orders. This was a huge task as there were hundreds of monasteries and convents in Spain. At first, external visitors were used but when this proved unsuccessful attempts were made to discipline the orders from within. In Cisneros' own order, the Franciscans, those who believed in strict adherence to the rule of St Francis (known as Observants) gained ground at the expense of the Conventuals who enjoyed a more relaxed existence. When Cisneros died in 1517, there were no Conventual houses left in Spain. The Dominicans, Augustinians and other orders followed this trend. Of course, there were failures. Many remote houses were scarcely touched by reform and four hundred Andalusian friars showed what they thought of the reforms by settling in North Africa and becoming Muslims rather than give up their concubines.

Attempts to reform the secular clergy were also necessary. Talavera claimed that the Spanish bishops were guilty of absenteeism, simony and moral laxity. The lower clergy also left much to be desired. Isabella complained to the Bishop of Calahorra that, in his diocese, 'Most of the clergy are said to be in concubinage (living with mistresses) publicly and if our justice intervenes to punish them, they revolt'. In 1500 in Palencia the clergy had to be told not to 'gamble or fight bulls or sing or dance in public'. To combat such laxity, bishops were ordered to reside in their

sees and supervise their clergy. Parish priests were instructed to abandon their mistresses, preach sermons, wear appropriate clerical dress
and provide their congregations with religious instruction. Here, too, the
reformers ran into problems. The huge area of Spain made enforcement
of reform difficult and even cathedral chapters sometimes resisted
pressure to change their traditional modes of conduct. In 1496 the
chapters (cathedrals' governing bodies) of Castile appealed to the Pope
and Ferdinand and Isabella had to resort to kidnapping their representatives to prevent them leaving the country.

One of Cisneros' greatest achievements was the establishment of the
University of Alcalà, completed in 1508, which was intended to be a
theological and cultural dynamo for the Church in Spain. The university
offered a complete ecclesiastical education as well as specialising in
medicine, languages and literature at a time when most Spanish universities concentrated on the study of law. Cisneros encouraged the production of printed books on spiritual matters and sponsored the compilation
of the Polyglot Bible. Published in 1522, this was a five-volume edition
containing parallel texts of the Vulgate version and Greek and Hebrew
versions. Alcalà became one of the great centres of European learning in
the early sixteenth century, with scholars arriving from all over Europe
to use its library (which included Arabic works captured in Granada)
and participate in the stimulating intellectual atmosphere of the
university.

The overall impact of the reforms of the Church is disputed. Some
historians, notably Henry Kamen, have argued that improvements only
reached the religious orders and that the majority of the secular clergy
(those not in monasteries) were totally unaffected. Certainly, there is
little evidence that piety and morals were altered at a local level. Even
Cisneros' own cathedral chapter of Toledo could not be fully reformed.
In 1499, 25 of its members were reported to him for sodomy or concubinage and he seems to have taken no action. However, it can also be argued
that the changes ordered by Isabella and Cisneros were sufficiently
successful to protect the Spanish Church from the blast of anti-
clericalism and Protestant criticism later in the sixteenth century. It is
not surprising that it was Spanish theologians who led the counter-
attack against Protestantism. Due to the reforms, the Spanish Church
was better equipped than any other in Europe to face the challenge of the
Reformation.

8. The Inquisition and the Expulsion of the Jews

During the early Middle Ages, Spanish Christians, Jews and Muslims
had lived together in a state of mutual tolerance or *convivencia* as the
Spanish called it. During the fourteenth century, however, religious
tension had grown under the strain of economic depression and the
Christian majority had turned on the Jewish minority. In 1391

thousands of Jews were massacred in Seville, Toledo, Barcelona and other cities. Many Jews converted to Christianity to avoid a similar fate. These *conversos* or 'New Christians' were not safe from the virulent anti-Semitism which periodically gripped Spain in the fifteenth century. There were a number of reasons for the widespread hostility to the Jews and the *conversos*.

Firstly, Jews were identified in the popular imagination as Christ-killers and perpetrators of cannibalism and infanticide. Torquemada, the Inquisitor-Gereral, showed how they were classed with the worst enemies of the Church when he appealed to Ferdinand and Isabella for measures against 'Jews, blasphemers, deniers of God and the Saints, and equally sorcerors and necromancers'. Secondly, the Jews were hated for their role in Spanish society, being regarded as parasites and profiteers. Andres Bernaldez, a village priest, claimed, 'All their work was to multiply and increase. . . . They never wanted to take manual work, ploughing or digging or walking the fields with the herds . . . but only jobs in the towns, so as to sit around making money without doing much work'. To many Spaniards the typical Jew was a money-lender or a rent or debt collector. A third reason for prejudice was that the *conversos* were believed to have only adopted Christianity as a cloak to conceal their continued practice of Judaism. Hernando del Pulgar, writing of the *conversos* of Toledo in 1485, said that they 'neither kept one law nor the other' and Bernaldez suggested that 'the greater part were secret Jews'. Despite this hostility, many *conversos* rose through their own abilities to high positions in Church and state. The fourth, and increasingly important, reason for suspicion was the growing Spanish obsession with *limpieza de sangre* or purity of blood. This was the belief that only those Spaniards whose blood was untainted by Jewish or Moorish influence were worthy to hold office. Anti-Jewish riots in Toledo in 1449 led to a decree that no-one of Jewish ancestry was eligible for a place in the city government.

To combat the alleged problem of the *conversos* in Castile, the monarchs turned to an institution which had first been introduced to Aragon in the thirteenth century—the Inquisition. This organisation, which possessed authority to investigate and punish cases of heresy, had been under papal control when first established. It had not been extended to Castile and by the mid-fifteenth century, it was all but dead. When the monarchs decided to revive it and import it to Castile, they determined to make it independent of the Papacy and under royal supervision.

In November 1478 Pope Sixtus IV gave Ferdinand and Isabella the powers they sought by issuing a bull giving them authority to appoint Inquisitors. After two years' delay, Inquisitors were commissioned to operate in Seville and in February 1481 they claimed their first victims when six *conversos* were burned as heretics. Some *conversos* fled, others tried to resist but in the period 1481–88 Bernaldez recorded that 'the Inquisitors burnt over seven hundred persons and reconciled over five thousand and threw many into perpetual prison'. The harsh measures of the early Inquisitors caused such an outcry that in April 1482 Sixtus IV denounced the Spanish Inquisition and ordered that appeals to the Papacy be allowed. Ferdinand told the Pope that such interference was not acceptable and Sixtus had to admit defeat. This clearly marked another success for the monarchs in their struggle to control the Spanish Church.

It has been argued that the Inquisition was a device by which the monarchs could extend their general political control as it had powers which could over-ride any other jurisdiction. There is little evidence, however, of the political use of the Inquisition. It was employed to stop horse smuggling across the French border but, apart from isolated instances such as that, it kept to its religious functions. Nonetheless it was the only institution common to all of Ferdinand and Isabella's Spanish realms. Established in Castile at first, it was extended to Aragon after the murder of an Inquisitor there in 1485. Here at least was some unification of Spain.

The organisation and procedure of the Spanish Inquisition made it unique in both Spain and Europe. At the head of the structure stood the Inquisitor-General. The first of these was Tomás de Torquemada, appointed in 1483. Notorious for his implacable hatred of the *conversos*, Torquemada dominated the activities of the Inquisition until his death in 1498. Between 1507 and 1517 the post was held by Cisneros. Under the Inquisitor-General was a six-member Council of the Supreme and General Inquisition or *Suprema*, chosen by the Crown and directly responsible to it. The Suprema supervised the activities of local tribunals, of which there were eventually 13 in mainland Spain and others in Sicily, Sardinia and the Canaries. The main function of these tribunals was to seek out and punish *conversos* who still clung to Judaism. It must be stressed that the mission of the Inquisition was to combat heresy and therefore unbaptised Jews and Muslims were outside its sphere of influence. The procedure of the Inquisition involved the denunciation of heretics, the examination of the accused by the Inquisition (with the use of torture permitted) and, if found guilty, punishment by flogging, confiscation of property, service in the galleys or death by burning. It is not surprising that the Inquisition brought terror to many communities. In 1487 hundreds of *conversos* fled from Barcelona rather than face the rigours of the Inquisition's enquiries. However, as Kamen has made clear, the terror of the Inquisition was exaggerated by Protestant myth. Torture was used less than in ordinary courts and acquittals or mild penalties were far more common than floggings or burnings.

Even with the activities of the Inquisition, many Spaniards felt that a more drastic solution to the 'Jewish problem' was required. It was widely believed that the Jews encouraged the *conversos* to desert Christianity and return to their former religion. In addition, the war against Granada had engendered a spirit of militant crusade against non-Christian religions. In some areas there had already been attempts

51

to banish Jews, as at Seville in 1483. The climax of the anti-Semitic hysteria came in March 1492 at Granada when an edict was issued by Ferdinand and Isabella giving all Jews in Castile and Aragon the choice of converting or being expelled from Spain. Accurate statistical information is in short supply, but it seems likely that about 150 000 of the Jewish population of 200 000 chose to leave. Many of those who stayed must have been converts in name only. Perhaps the most significant aspect of the expulsion was the economic loss to Spain. The Jewish emigrants took with them their commercial skill and experience and the absence of their enterprise contributed to the lack of economic vitality in Spain in the sixteenth century. As for the Jews, they continued to regard Ferdinand and Isabella with loathing for decades. About 1575 an eastern Jew wrote 'Queen Isabel, the accursed, died weary of her life and half her body devoured by a cancer. God is just!'

9. The Foreign Policy of Ferdinand and Isabella

Until 1492 the commitments of the Castilian civil war and the Reconquest precluded the monarchs pursuing an active foreign policy. With the incorporation of Granada Ferdinand and Isabella could turn outwards and Spanish resources and troops were released for operations beyond Iberia. Foreign affairs were largely the responsibility of Ferdinand and he conducted relations with other states with an unscrupulousness which was remarkable even in the atmosphere of duplicity and treachery which surrounded European diplomacy in the sixteenth century.

It is perhaps dangerous to describe governments following a consistent foreign 'policy' in this period; rather they tended to act as circumstances dictated and opportunities arose. However, Ferdinand did have certain constant aims. Of over-riding importance was the need to check the growing power of France. A number of methods were used to achieve this: the construction of anti-French coalitions and marriage alliances (marrying his children to English, Portuguese and Habsburg royalty), the strengthening of Spain's northern border and military intervention to prevent French domination of Italy. In addition, Ferdinand followed a policy of cautious expansion onto the coast of North Africa and the reign of the monarchs also saw the beginning of the great Spanish colonial empire in America.

It was fortunate for Spain that the war with Granada was drawing to a close as Charles VIII of France reached adulthood and began to look for opportunities to fulfil his martial ambitions. Ferdinand was well aware that he could not hope to curb the French on his own and in 1489 he signed a treaty with Henry VII of England at Medina del Campo. A joint offensive was planned in which England would intervene to protect the independence of Brittany, which was being threatened by France, and Spain would recover Cerdagne and Roussillon. These two Catalan-speaking counties had belonged to Aragon until Ferdinand's father, John II, had been obliged to surrender them to the French in 1462 as a result of the civil war in Aragon. Both objectives failed: English forces (with some Spanish assistance) failed to save Brittany in 1492 and the Spanish were still too involved in finishing off Granada to make headway on the border with France. Charles VIII, however, did not seem to regard the retention of the two counties as a high priority and was prepared to barter them in exchange for Spanish neutrality during his projected invasion of Italy. At the Treaty of Barcelona in 1493, Cerdagne and Roussillon were handed back to Catalonia. This was a major success for the monarchs as it gave them control of the eastern ranges of the Pyrenees, denying France easy routes into the Iberian peninsula. The counties remained in Spanish hands until the Peace of the Pyrenees in 1659 when France occupied them once more.

The kingdom of Aragon had a long history of close involvement with Italy. A branch of the Aragonese royal house ruled Naples in the person of King Ferrante (1458–94), and Sicily was an important component of the Crown of Aragon. Thus, when Charles VIII invaded Italy and conquered Naples in 1494–95, Ferdinand could not stand idly by and see the French dominate the whole peninsula and then the western Mediterranean. A full account of the Spanish participation in the Italian Wars is given in Chapter III but there are several points which should be noted here. Firstly, Ferdinand's skilful diplomacy did much to counter the triumph of French arms. In 1495 he allied with Pope Alexander VI, Venice, Milan and Emperor Maximilian I to force Charles to retreat. Later in the wars, Spain joined with Pope Julius II, a number of the Italian states and the Swiss in the Holy League of 1511–13, an alliance aimed at destroying French power in northern Italy and which gave Ferdinand the chance to seize Navarre. A second feature of Spanish intervention was the success of her armies. Castilian and Aragonese troops had gained considerable battle experience in the long war against Granada. In 1495 a veteran of that war, Gonzalo de Cordoba (known as 'El Gran Capitan'), was given command of the expeditionary force dispatched to fight the French. Cordoba was a brilliant general with an excellent grasp of strategy, a talent for organisation and an ability to develop new tactics. His string of victories made Spanish troops feared throughout Europe. Cordoba was a Castilian and it is significant that, as Aragon had assisted Isabella in her war against Granada, so Ferdinand was able to mobilise the manpower and resources of his wife's realm for 'his' war in Italy. Indeed Castilian troops and Castilian money were used to such an extent that Aragon was replaced as the dominant partner in Italian affairs.

The outcome of the Italian involvement was highly satisfactory for Spain. At the Treaty of Granada in 1500, Ferdinand and Louis XII agreed to partition Naples but when war broke out soon after, Cordoba's victories forced the French to relinquish their claims to Naples at the Treaty of Blois (1505). Although France was still the strongest power in northern Italy at the time of Ferdinand's death in 1516, Spain was left in unchallenged possession of Sicily and Naples, territories which were to provide her with grain, revenues and recruits during the sixteenth century.

The wars in Italy also gave the Spanish a further opportunity to strengthen their border with France by gaining control of the small, nominally independent kingdom of Navarre. This state, like Cerdagne and Roussillon, had once been ruled by John II of Aragon. By 1494 Queen Catherine of Navarre and her French husband Jean d'Albret had been obliged to accept a Castilian protectorate over their territory but they retained close links with France. In 1498 one observer noted that Ferdinand and Isabella 'do what they please' in Navarre and it was clear that Ferdinand was only waiting for a favourable opportunity to take over completely. In 1512 the chance came; France was heavily involved in war against the Holy League in Italy. Ferdinand demanded that Spanish troops be allowed to pass through Navarre on their way to attack the French city of Bayonne. To permit this would mean Catherine and d'Albret losing their considerable estates in France and so they refused and signed a treaty with Louis XII. Claiming that this indicated aggressive intent (which was a complete fabrication) Ferdinand ordered an army of 17 000 men to occupy Navarre in the summer of 1512. It is typical of Ferdinand's extraordinary diplomatic skill that he persuaded Henry VIII of England to provide a diversionary action by sending a force to south west France to threaten the French while Navarre was occupied. The English army rotted with inactivity and achieved nothing for Henry. A dynastic pretext for this action was provided by Ferdinand's second wife, Germaine de Foix, who possessed a hereditary claim to Navarre. Pope Julius II agreed formally to depose Catherine and Jean and in 1515 the kingdom was integrated into Castile, although Navarre retained its own institutions of government, Cortes and coinage. The acquisition of Navarre was a triumph for Ferdinand: Spain dominated the Pyrenees, the whole Iberian peninsula with the exception of Portugal acknowledged his rule and, by transferring Navarre from the kingdom of Aragon to Castile, he cemented the relationship between them and involved Castile in the defence of the northern frontier.

To turn to the Mediterranean, for Ferdinand the war against Islam was justified as a religious crusade and as an extension of Spanish influence. In a letter of June 1509 he wrote that 'from my youth I was always very inclined to war against Infidels and it is the thing in which I receive most delight and pleasure.' There is even evidence that Ferdinand planned operations against Islam outside the obvious limits of Spanish national interest. In February 1510 he declared, somewhat ambitiously, that 'the conquest of Jerusalem belongs to us and we have the title of that kingdom.' However, it may well be that such statements are examples of Ferdinand's duplicity—he was endeavouring to prod the Cortes and the Pope into offering financial assistance for a crusade against the Turks when his true intention was to fight the French.

Following the conquest of Granada it seemed natural for the Spanish to carry the war across the Mediterranean into the Moorish states of Algiers, Morocco and Tunis in North Africa. The Portuguese had already seized important towns such as Ceuta and Ferdinand had no wish to be outflanked by his Iberian neighbours. By moving into North Africa Spain would protect her trade with Sicily and prevent the Moors from inciting or aiding disaffected elements in Granada. The emirates of North Africa seemed to provide an easy target, warring amongst themselves and lacking the modern powder weaponry which Ferdinand had employed so successfully against Granada. In 1494 Alexander VI granted crusading status to the projected offensive and in 1495 recognised Spanish rights in north eastern Africa. The conquest was begun as a private enterprise by the Duke of Medina Sidonia who occupied the city of Melilla, with the agreement of Ferdinand and Isabella, in 1497. The danger created by the revolt in Granada in 1499–1501 gave a fresh impetus to action against Islam. Following the conquest of Naples in 1503–04, Spanish troops were made available from the Italian theatre and an expedition sailed to North Africa in 1505. The town of Mers-el-Kebir was taken and in 1509 an army led by Cardinal Cisneros captured Oran. Tripoli fell to the Spanish in 1510 and Algiers had to accept a Spanish protectorate *(see map on page 36)*. Cisneros wanted to launch total war against the Muslims but Ferdinand understood the financial and military difficulties of prolonged campaigning in the African interior. Instead, he was content to garrison a limited number of coastal strongholds, sufficient to discourage aggressive intentions by the Moorish states. Although strategically valuable, these Spanish outposts proved to be expensive to maintain and dangerously weak when compared to the alliance of Ottoman Empire and Moorish emirates which Charles V faced in the late 1530s and 1540s.

The late fifteenth century and early sixteenth century witnessed the beginnings of Spanish exploration of the Atlantic and the foundation of the Spanish empire in the Americas. (Full treatment of this topic will be found in Chapter IV.) It must be stressed that Ferdinand and Isabella gave this aspect of policy a very low priority when compared with Italy or North Africa and the full significance of the discoveries was not appreciated until the years after the death of Ferdinand in 1516.

The Portuguese had been exploring the Atlantic for some decades and rivalry was an important motive in the development of Spanish interest in discovery. By the Treaty of Alcaçovas of 1479, the Portuguese acknowledged Spanish rights to the Canary Islands and a combination of royal and private initiative led to the conquest of Grand Canary in 1483, Palma in 1492 and Tenerife in 1493. The native populations of these islands were reduced by the fighting and by slave-raiding and Iberian colonists arrived to exploit the potential for sugar-cane production. The islands were eventually to become an important staging post on the route to America.

Ferdinand and Isabella were interested in breaking into the lucrative

Asian spice trade and it was to further this interest that they gave limited support to the plans of the Genoese navigator Christopher Columbus to sail westwards in search of an Atlantic route to the East. The successful voyage of reconnaissance of 1492 was followed by others and by 1516 a number of Caribbean islands (including Hispaniola, Cuba, Jamaica and Puerto Rico) had been settled by Spaniards and the central American coastline had been explored. Later in the sixteenth century Spain set about exploiting the wealth of America in earnest, but the origins of empire lie in the reigns of the Catholic monarchs.

It must be stressed that this was a Castilian empire with the Aragonese excluded from trade and settlement in America. Although Ferdinand was king of Aragon he exercised his power through his wife's realm of Castile given that it was far richer and more easily subject to royal authority. As a result even the possessions in Italy, which were officially attached to the realm of Aragon, were extended mostly by Castilian soldiers and exploited by Castilian office-holders. In the eyes of Europe, Spain was unified in its foreign policy—it is in diplomatic correspondence that the title 'King of Spain' first gained currency—but Ferdinand ensured that foreign policy was largely a Castilian matter.

10. The Succession Crisis

Ferdinand and Isabella had one son, John, and four daughters, Isabella, Joanna, Maria and Catherine. John married Margaret, the daughter of the future Emperor Maximilian in 1497, and within six months was dead of, it was rumoured, sexual over-indulgence. Margaret was pregnant at the time of her husband's death but she gave birth to a stillborn child. This left the monarchs' eldest daughter Isabella as heir. She was married to King Manuel of Portugal and they produced an heir, Miguel. However, Isabella died in 1498, leading the French observer Commynes to write of the 'miserable accidents which in a short space of time befell the king and queen of Castile, who had lived in so much glory and happiness to the fiftieth year of their age.' Worse was to follow. In 1500 the infant Miguel died, leaving the monarchs' second daughter, Joanna, as heir. Joanna was married to Philip 'the Fair', Duke of Burgundy and son of the Holy Roman Emperor Maximilian I.

This marriage had produced a son, Charles, in 1500. A Habsburg succession now seemed inevitable. Philip regarded Spain as something of a provincial backwater, disliked the Spanish and did not trust Ferdinand. Indeed, he joined Maximilian and Louis XII of France in an anti-Spanish alliance in 1504. In a will made shortly before her death in 1504, Isabella placed the government of Castile in the hands of Ferdinand until their grandson Charles should reach the age of twenty.

Isabella's death precipitated a prolonged succession crisis. Ferdinand announced the succession of Joanna, though with no mention of Philip. The latter set about constructing a party within Castile who would support him, led by the Marquis of Villena. The chronicler Bernaldez saw Villena and other such nobles as men who 'acted more out of greed for royal land than for the good of the kingdom.' However, English observers reported to Henry VII that Ferdinand was unpopular due to the high taxation for the war in Italy and that the people would welcome Philip.

In 1506, Philip landed in northern Castile and nobles rushed to join him. Ferdinand was obliged to withdraw from Castile and hand the government over to Philip and Joanna but the situation was transformed when Philip died at Burgos in September 1506 at the age of 28. Joanna's sanity, always fragile, now began to give way. She refused to leave Philip's lifeless body, having been informed by a monk that he would rise from the dead. In Castile a complete breakdown of government seemed likely. Nobles began to recruit and attack each other and without the strong hand of Ferdinand (who was engaged in reorganising the government of Naples) Bernaldez claimed 'men knew they were as sheep without a shepherd'. Ferdinand returned to Castile with an army in 1507 and soon crushed the dissident nobles. Ferdinand ruled as governor of Castile whilst the wretched Joanna, who could scarcely be persuaded to eat, wash or change her clothes, retired into mad obscurity. She survived until 1555, a pitiable inmate of the castle of Tordesillas.

Ferdinand had made a second marriage to a French princess, Germaine de Foix, in 1505 and still hoped for another heir. This did not materialise and when he died in 1516 all Ferdinand's possessions passed to his grandson, Charles. Charles was already Duke of Burgundy and when he was elected Holy Roman Emperor in 1519, Spain became inextricably involved in the politics of northern Europe. It was this international connection, rather than what had been a precarious dynastic union, which was to be of the greatest importance to Spain during the Early Modern period.

11. The Unification of Spain

By the time of Ferdinand's death in 1516, Castile and Aragon were scarcely more united than they had been in 1469. There was a measure of unification in terms of religion and foreign policy, and Granada had been absorbed, but Castile and Aragon were still undeniably distinct entities.

The institutions the monarchs had used to pacify Castile were confined to that realm. Ferdinand had tried three times to introduce the Hermandad into Aragon but three times he had failed. Rather than integrate Aragon with Castile, Ferdinand had neglected his own kingdom. He had settled some serious disputes there—a land dispute between nobility and peasants known as the *remensas*, for instance—but he had been acting as an arbitrator rather than as a continuously involved politician. This can be seen by the amount of time he gave to his kingdom in a period when personal kingship was vital. He spent under seven years visiting Aragon out of the thirty seven years of his reign. Aragon ran itself behind its protective hedge of liberties, the *fueros*.

The kingdoms of Spain retained separate institutions, laws, languages, coinage and economies. Aragon was in a political and commercial decline whereas the vigour of Castile was finding outlets in imperialist undertakings in the New World and Europe. That Castile and Aragon had not been united would hardly have been a cause of disappointment to Ferdinand and Isabella, for their priorities were different. Stability in the kingdoms, eradication of religious minorities, the destruction of Granada, the frustration of the expansionist ambitions of the French kings and the furtherance of Spanish power in the Mediterranean were their major aims and in these they were successful. They laid the foundations of the Spanish empire of the sixteenth century and won the admiration of contemporaries of all nationalities. In 1514 Ferdinand himself could remark, with some justification, that, 'For over 700 years the Crown of Spain has not been as great or as resplendent as it is now, both in the west and the east, and all, after God, by my work and labour'.

12. Bibliography

J H Elliott *Imperial Spain 1469–1716* (Edward Arnold, 1963). H Kamen *Spain 1469–1714* (Longman, 1983). J Lynch *Spain under the Habsburgs Vol 1* (revised edition, Blackwell, 1981). H Kamen *Inquisition and Society in Spain* (revised edition, Weidenfeld & Nicolson, 1985). J N Hillgarth *The Spanish Kingdoms Vol 2* (Clarendon, 1976).

13. Discussion Points and Exercises

A   *This section consists of questions or points that might be used for discussion (or written answers) as a way of expanding on the chapter and testing understanding of it:*

1   Why was the position of Isabella so insecure in 1474?
2   Why did Isabella and Ferdinand emerge victorious from the Castilian civil war?
3   Why were Ferdinand and Isabella such a successful partnership?
4   By what methods did Ferdinand and Isabella control Castile?
5   Why was the capture of Granada regarded as a high point of the reign?
6   Assess the economic thinking of Ferdinand and Isabella.
7   'Ferdinand and Isabella got what they most wanted in the way of Church reform.'
8   How important was the foundation of the Spanish Inquisition?
9   'It is in his foreign policy that Ferdinand reveals his greatest skills and ambitions.'

B *Essay questions*

1 What were the aims of Ferdinand and Isabella and how successful were they in achieving them?

2 Explain the causes and the consequences of the religious policies of Ferdinand and Isabella.

3 To what extent was the reign of Ferdinand and Isabella in the period 1479–1504 dominated by the policy of Reconquest?

4 'Ferdinand and Isabella joined Aragon and Castile in a dynastic but not a political union.' Discuss.

5 'Ferdinand was the most creative of politicians.' Do you agree?

C *Exercises*

Make a chart comparing the strengths and weaknesses of Castile and Aragon in the mid-fifteenth century. Then list the ways in which Castile had assumed a dominant position over Aragon by 1516.

Finally, write a paragraph assessing whether it is justifiable to talk about a Castilian empire rather than a Spanish empire.

14. Essay Writing—Planning

There are those who are so keen to finish an essay that they start to write it without planning it first. However, a good plan both saves time and leads to better results.

Take essay question 4 above as an example and then go through the following steps:

(a) Isolate first the key idea(s) contained in the wording. Here it is the idea of 'union'.

(b) Make a list of headings made up of all the issues in the chapter which are relevant to the question of unification. It would include 'foreign policy' and 'the Spanish Inquisition', for example.

(c) Take each heading in turn and review the relevant information. Jot down what strikes you as most important.

(d) Now you must relate the issues to the question. Write a sentence under each heading assessing the degree of unification involved in that issue.

(e) Number the headings so that they follow as logical a sequence as possible as you write the essay.

(f) Write the essay, with each heading in your plan providing the subject of a paragraph. The sentence you have written under a particular heading could be the first sentence of the relevant paragraph. The important information you have gathered can form your main evidence.

III The Italian Wars

1. Introduction

In 1537 a Florentine named Francesco Guicciardini retired to a villa in the countryside near his home city to write an account of events in Italy during the previous half century. Guicciardini had been a politician, diplomat, soldier and adviser to three popes. His experience of international affairs made him a perceptive commentator on the recent misfortunes of his homeland. His account of the Italian Wars was to form the basis of much future scholarship on the subject. Indeed, while many different aspects of the Wars have received critical attention, there has been no recent, standard general work on the topic.

The theme of Guicciardini's *History of Italy* was how the disunity and selfishness of the Italian states enabled foreign powers to invade the peninsula and turn it into an international battleground, inflicting 'innumerable horrid calamities' on the people of Italy. Yet before the wars began in 1494 the Italian states seemed to be at the height of their wealth and influence. This chapter will explore the inherent instability of the Italian political situation, the reasons why other states wished to invade and the factors which kept the wars going for so long.

2. The Condition of Italy in 1494

In 1454 the Peace of Lodi gave rise to the Italian League. The League was designed for two main purposes: to provide unity in the face of possible foreign attack (the Turks and the French were the main external threats), and to maintain a balance of power inside the peninsula so that no single state could achieve dominance. The League helped to give Italy nearly 40 years of comparative peace, leading Giovanni Bentivoglio, a citizen of Bologna, to praise it as 'this most holy League upon which depends the welfare of all Italy' *(see page 17 on Renaissance diplomacy)*.

The key to peace was the friendship between Milan, Florence and Naples, a coalition which restrained aggression amongst the smaller states and kept the peace among the larger. In 1482, for example, war broke out between Venice and the small neighbouring state of Ferrara.

The intervention of Milan, Florence and Naples terminated the conflict and preserved the independence of Ferrara. The guiding hand of the League was Lorenzo de Medici 'the Magnificent', ruler of Florence. Guicciardini commented that his name 'was held in great esteem all over Italy, and his authority influential in discussions on joint affairs'.

The general peace enjoyed by the Italians brought the following description from the pen of Francesco Guicciardini:

> Italy had never enjoyed such prosperity, or known so favourable a situation as that in which it found itself so securely at rest in the year of our Christian salvation, 1490, and the years immediately before and after. The greatest peace and tranquillity reigned everywhere; the mountains and arid areas as well as the fertile plains were under cultivation; she was dominated by no other power than her own and not only did Italy abound in men, merchandise and riches but she was also famous for the magnificence of many princes, the splendour of many noble and beautiful cities and as being the centre of religion. She flourished with men adept at administering public affairs and had the highest standards of knowledge in all the arts. According to the standards of the day Italy was not lacking in military glory as well. Blessed with so many gifts she deservedly held a celebrated name and reputation among all nations.

1   *Are there any ways in which Guicciardini might be a biased commentator?*
2   *Which features in the Italian situation described by Guicciardini might have encouraged European powers to invade?*

Although peace and prosperity seemed to be the most significant features of Italy in the second half of the fifteenth century, there were several factors which belied this appearance and rendered the Italian states vulnerable to external aggression. The first was that the Italian states failed to unite in the face of foreign invasion. In 1480 a Turkish army occupied the Neapolitan port of Otranto and King Ferrante of Naples requested aid from the other powers. This appeal met with no response. Although the danger passed when the Turks evacuated Otranto in the following year, it had been clearly shown that the states could not rely on each other for assistance. Indeed, the disunity of Italy in 1494 was to be the most important asset to Charles VIII of France in his invasion.

A second feature of the Italian political scene was the unpreparedness of the states for war with foreign powers. At a time when other nations, especially France, were constructing strong national armies, the rulers of Italian states tended to rely on mercenary bands led by professional commanders known as *condottieri*. The condottieri practised a formal and elaborate style of warfare in which the main objective was to suffer as few casualties as possible and merely outmanoeuvre, rather than defeat, the opposing army, which was likely also to be composed of mercenaries. Guicciardini made a telling comparison between the army of Charles VIII of France and those of the Italian rulers. Charles' army was, he believed,

'. . . formidable not so much because of the number as for the bravery of his troops. For, his men-at-arms were almost all the subjects of the king and not low-born persons but gentlemen whom the captains could not enlist or dismiss at will; in addition they were paid by the royal government and not by their officers. Their companies were at full strength, the men in good health, their horses and arms in good condition . . . Each one competed with his companions to serve honourably, driven on by the thirst for glory which noble birth encourages and also because they hoped their bravery would be rewarded as merit was rewarded with promotion. The officers, almost all of whom were nobles and subjects of the kingdom of France, had the same incentives . . . they had no other goal than to win praise from their king.

All these things were different in the Italian army, where many of the men-at-arms were either peasants or commoners subject to some other prince and completely dependent on the captains with whom they contracted for their wages, and who had the power to pay and dismiss them. Thus they had no incentive to serve well. The captains were very rarely subjects of the states which hired them . . . they did not hire the number of soldiers for which they were being paid . . . they frequently transferred from one state to another, sometimes tempted by ambition or greed to be not only unstable but disloyal.

Equally obvious was the difference between the Italian infantry and Charles', because the Italians did not fight in firm, well-organised units but scattered throughout the countryside, most of the time hiding in the cover of riverbanks and ditches. But the Swiss (who fought for Charles) . . . would face the enemy like a wall without even breaking ranks. . . . The French infantry fought with similar discipline.

1   *Explain the principal differences which Guicciardini saw between the armies of the Italian states and that of the French.*

2   *Why do you think the condottiere system was so popular in Italy before 1494?*

A third factor was the instability of the Italian state system. The 'concert of Italy' which existed after 1454 looked impressive but it concealed many unreconciled rivalries amongst the Italian states. And it was only the need to settle their own internal affairs which prevented other European powers from intervening before 1494.

The crisis of that year occurred through a combination of factors. In April 1492, the death of Lorenzo de Medici removed a stabilising influence, even though he was not quite the diplomatic genius portrayed by Guicciardini. More important was the unstable state of affairs in Milan. The Duke of Milan, Gian Galeazzo Sforza, reigned in name only with the real power in the state resting with his uncle the regent, Lodovico Sforza, who was known as 'Il Moro' (The Moor) because of his swarthy appearance. Gian Galeazzo was married to Isabella, the granddaughter of King Ferrante of Naples and daughter of Ferrante's aggressive son, Alfonso. Isabella sent a stream of complaints back to Naples that she and Gian were constantly insulted by Lodovico and his wife, Beatrice D'Este. Alfonso took this as an excuse to threaten Lodovico and by 1493 a Neapolitan attack on Milan seemed to be imminent. Fearful that Milan would lose such a war, Lodovico looked for a powerful ally. In April 1493 he declared himself to be an ally of France and invited Charles VIII of France to enter Italy, defend Milan and conquer Naples, to which the French king had a hereditary claim.

It is likely that Lodovico thought the mere threat of French intervention would be sufficient to deter Naples but Charles accepted the invitation. Thus it was Italians who opened the door to foreign action in Italy and in the following years mutual hostility among the Italian states was to give other rulers every opportunity and excuse to march their armies into the peninsula.

3. Charles VIII's Motives and Preparations for Invasion

The invitation from Lodovico Sforza was an unmissable chance for Charles VIII of France, providing him with just the pretext he needed to interfere in the affairs of Italy. And it came at a time when his kingdom had the resources and opportunity for foreign adventures. For much of the fourteenth and fifteenth centuries, monarchs of France had been beset by two major problems: the occupation of large tracts of their country by English troops during the Hundred Years War and the overweening power of some of the great ducal families who ruled their territories almost as independent states and even made war on their sovereign. By 1494 both these difficulties had receded. The English had been ejected from France (apart from Calais) by 1453 and had then lapsed into the confusions of the Wars of the Roses. The reign of Louis XI (1461–83) saw the danger from the feudal magnates diminish, especially after the death of Charles the Bold, Duke of Burgundy, who was killed by the Swiss at the Battle of Nancy in 1477. Louis was able to strengthen his eastern border by absorbing Burgundian territory. The power of the French monarchy was further augmented when Charles VIII married Anne of Brittany and took control of her duchy in 1491 despite an abortive, English-backed rebellion. Strong monarchy seemed to have returned to France and with it the possibility of an aggressive foreign policy.

The precise reasons why Charles VIII wished to invade Italy have been the subject of some debate. It is generally accepted that Charles' fanciful and erratic character played some part in the decision. He had succeeded to the throne in 1483 on the death of his father, Louis XI, but had been too young to rule personally. His sister, Anne of Beaujeu, capably held the reins of government during his minority. Charles seems to have possessed only limited intelligence—'very young, weakly, wilful, rarely in the company of wise men' was the scornful verdict of one contemporary observer, Philippe Commynes. His physical appearance also excited unkind comments: the Venetian ambassador described him as 'small and ill-formed in person, with an ugly face . . . shortsighted . . . and thick lips which are continually open. He stutters and has a nervous twitching of the hands'. Guicciardini cruelly pointed out that 'his limbs were so ill-proportioned that he seemed more like a monster than a man'.

Despite, or perhaps because of, these imperfections, the king fed his vivid imagination with the epics of medieval chivalry. He dreamed of winning glory for himself by advancing into Italy and then using it as a base to drive the heathen Turks out of Europe and re-establish the Byzantine Empire.

On a more practical level, Charles had a claim to the Crown of Naples. The French-descended House of Anjou had ruled in Naples until driven out in 1442 and Charles had inherited its claim. Given the ideas of the time, it was almost a duty as well as a matter of ambition to assert dynastic rights.

Italy was also the centre of European trade with the East and it has been suggested that Charles wished to advance the commercial interests of France in that area. This seems unlikely: fifteenth century kings were generally moved by considerations of honour and territorial ambition rather than economics.

Additional spurs to invasion were provided by a leading Italian churchman, Cardinal Giuliano della Rovere, and a powerful Neapolitan nobleman, the Prince of Salerno. In the papal election of 1492, della Rovere had been defeated by Alexander VI, head of the Borgia family. Determined to harass his hated rival, della Rovere joined the clamour for French intervention. Similarly, the Prince of Salerno, bitterly hostile to King Alfonso of Naples, encouraged the invasion plans. There was no Italian state, except perhaps for Venice, which did not have internal feuds acting to smooth the path of the invading French.

Aware that an invasion of Italy would be no small undertaking, Charles was careful to ensure that France was safe from attack during the operation. At the Treaty of Étaples in 1492, he promised an annual pension to Henry VII of England, and at Barcelona in 1493 he bought off Ferdinand and Isabella of Spain by returning the provinces of Cerdagne and Roussillon. In 1493, also, concessions were made to Maximilian of the Netherlands (who became Emperor Maximilian I in that year): at the Treaty of Senlis two areas on France's eastern border, Artois and Franche-Comté, were surrendered by France. Charles VIII was heavily criticised by some contemporaries for squandering the gains of Louis XI and, in the long term, weakening France's borders. Modern historians have tended to concur.

4. The French Invasion of 1494–95

It has already been shown that the Italian states were divided and militarily weak. Charles of France, in contrast, possessed the most formidable army in western Europe. The heavily armoured French

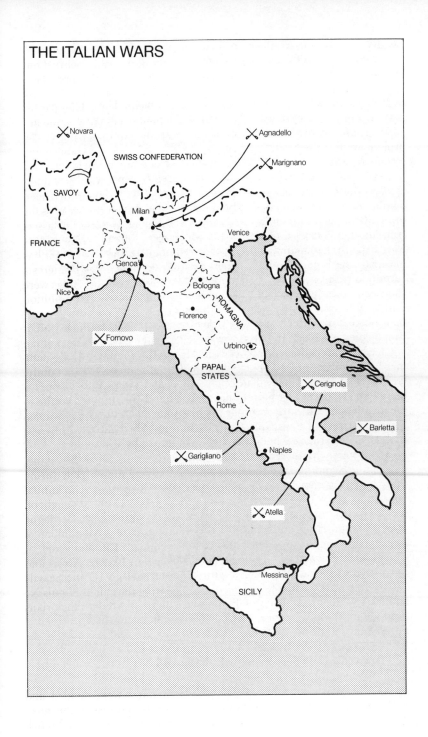

THE ITALIAN WARS

Novara

Agnadello

Marignano

SWISS CONFEDERATION

SAVOY

FRANCE

Milan

Venice

Genoa

Nice

Bologna

ROMAGNA

Florence

Fornovo

Urbino

PAPAL
STATES

Cerignola

Rome

Barletta

Garigliano

Naples

Atella

Messina

SICILY

cavalry were famous for their irresistible charges and Charles had hired a contingent of 8000 Swiss pikemen, the most feared and effective infantry in Europe. During the fifteenth and early sixteenth centuries, the Swiss cantons attempted to offset their lack of natural resources by hiring armies to any ruler who could afford them. The Swiss were to play a prominent part in the Italian Wars and the proximity of the battleground to such a recruiting source was one of the factors in the prolongation of the wars.

The decisive arm in Charles' 25 000 strong invasion force was, however, the artillery. Until the late fifteenth century, the typical artillery piece was a huge pipe of iron or bronze called a 'bombard'. This cumbersome instrument had to be transported about on a large waggon drawn by oxen and then lowered onto a solid block of wood for firing. Ammunition consisted of stone balls which were difficult to move and were expensive to manufacture as they required the expertise of skilled masons. The French military expert Jacques de Genouillac had made certain advances in the design of artillery by 1494. Barrels were shortened and lightened and mounted on a two-wheeled gun carriage pulled by horses, greatly easing the problem of mobility. Wrought-iron balls were fired which were to prove devastating against the high, thin medieval walls of Italian towns.

Charles marched his army over the Alps in the summer of 1494 and met his siege train of 40 guns, which had been transported by sea, in Genoa. The French passed through Milan and swept into Florence, the ally of Naples. The Florentines resisted and the military might of the invaders became apparent for the first time when they attacked the frontier fortress of Fivizzano. Guicciardini described the effects of the mobile siege artillery which was 'led right up to the walls and set into position there with incredible speed; and so little time elapsed between one shot and another and the shots were so frequent and so violent was their battering that in a few hours they could accomplish what previously in Italy used to require many days'. Moreover, the French introduced not only a new technology but also a new savagery to war in Italy. The garrison and many of the inhabitants of Fivizzano were massacred when the town fell, Guicciardini commenting that this was 'a thing unheard of and very frightening in Italy, which for a long time had been used to seeing wars staged with beautiful pomp and display . . . rather than waged with bloodshed and dangers.' Rather than experience similar treatment, a string of Florentine cities capitulated without a fight. The ruler of Florence, Piero de Medici, fled and the French king entered the city. The Medici had been growing less and less popular so Charles was actually welcomed as the protector of Florentine liberties and received a contribution towards the cost of the war against Naples.

The French then pushed on south, receiving the surrender of numerous cities as they went. Charles entered Rome on the last day of 1494 and Pope Alexander VI, 'oppressed by incredible anxiety and dread' according to Guicciardini, fled into the papal castle of Sant Angelo. The proximity and power of Charles forced Alexander temporarily to conceal his dislike for the French and he gave the French right of passage through his territory as well as control of a number of fortresses. After spending a month in Rome, Charles continued his march towards Naples.

Once again, terror was used as an instrument of war. The walls of the Neapolitan border fortress of Monte San Giovanni, which had once endured a siege of seven years, were battered down in eight hours. The French then slaughtered the garrison and fired the buildings of the town, 'induced by their innate fury, and also to warn others by this example not to dare to resist them', as Guicciardini remarked. Alfonso abdicated in favour of his son Ferrantino but the new king was forced to abandon the city of Naples, which Charles entered in triumph on 22nd February 1495. The French overran almost the whole kingdom and Charles seemed to have achieved his objective.

The French assault had been extraordinarily successful. In a few months their army had marched the length of the peninsula, forced the strongest towns to yield and so intimidated the Italians that little effective resistance had been offered. The rottenness of Italian political and military conventions had been exposed for all to see, and after 1494 there could be no return to the insularity which had existed before the advent of Charles VIII. For Charles, however, success was to bring problems, problems which would expose his victory as being as fragile as the Italian peace he had so comprehensively shattered.

5. The Holy League and the End of French Supremacy

Alarmed by Charles's domination of Italy, five powers formed a coalition in March 1495 with the aim of ejecting the French from Italy. Spain felt her grip on Sicily threatened and French occupation of Naples might well have serious strategic implications in the western Mediterranean. Hence, Ferdinand of Aragon was willing to commit troops to aid Ferrantino in the recovery of his kingdom. Also, he had long followed the policy of using his diplomatic mastery to restrict the French wherever he could. Pope Alexander VI and the Venetians both feared that permanent French control of Italy would inevitably weaken their own positions.

Even Lodovico Sforza was prepared to turn against his erstwhile ally. Gian Galeazzo had died in October 1494—it is uncertain whether this was due to Lodovico's poison or, as was commonly claimed in this period, sexual over-indulgence. Lodovico was recognised as Duke of Milan by the people and bought confirmation of his title from Emperor Maximilian. He felt secure and thus the powerful French presence in Italy was now potentially dangerous to him rather than reassuring.

Across the Alps in his Austrian territories, Maximilian was alarmed by the scope of Charles' ambition and his interference in a traditionally Imperial sphere of influence. Hence he too adhered to the Holy League, or League of Venice, as this rather motley collection of allies is sometimes known. Fear of France was certainly all that held the coalition together.

In the spring of 1495 Charles, concerned at the vulnerability of his lines of communication back to France and possibly bored with the whole enterprise, left a sizeable force to garrison Naples and returned north with the remainder of his army. The army of the League, made up largely of mercenaries provided by Milan and Venice and commanded by the condottiere Gonzaga of Mantua, moved to intercept the French. In July 1495 the two armies clashed at Fornovo *(see map on page 65)*. Although enjoying superiority of numbers, the Italians were badly mauled by the dash of the French cavalry and the firepower of their artillery. The battle marked another reverse for the formal, outmoded Italian style of warfare. Charles chose not to pursue his advantage but instead retired across the Alps. In October the Peace of Vercelli concluded the conflict between Charles and the League.

In the south, however, fighting continued. The Duke of Montpensier, Charles's viceroy in Naples, faced massive problems. His unruly troops soon became unpopular among the people, supplies were a constant problem and his force was seriously weakened by an epidemic of syphilis, known to the French as *le mal de Naples*. Ferrantino and the Spanish commander Cordoba gradually reconquered Naples, aided by local revolts against the army of occupation. In July 1496 at the siege of Atella *(see map on page 65)* Cordoba captured Montpensier and French resistance came to an end.

Thus the conquests of 1494–95 had proved transitory. Charles planned to return to the peninsula to re-establish his position but in April 1498, he died as a result of a stroke whilst watching a tennis match. However, this was not the end of French interest in Italy as his successor, Louis XII, also had ambitions in the peninsula.

6. The Campaigns of Louis XII

Louis XII was a very different character from Charles VIII but he came to share his predecessor's obsession with Italy. Peace-loving and cautious, Louis, Duke of Orleans, had become king when Charles his distant cousin, had died in 1498 without a son to succeed him.

Louis inherited the French claim to Naples and added a claim of his own to Milan. He traced this through his grandmother, Valentina, who was the daughter of a Visconti Duke of Milan. Milan, just to the south of the Alps, was wealthy owing to its position at the junction of trade routes and was also of great strategic importance, guarding the Alpine passes as the 'shield' of Italy. Louis was encouraged in his ambitions by his most prominent adviser, Georges d'Amboise, Archbishop of Rouen, whose immediate aim was to be raised to the cardinalate and whose ultimate aim may have been the Papacy.

Just as Charles had been invited into Italy by an Italian ruler, so Louis was given encouragement by Alexander VI who, according to Guicciardini, was 'pricked on by his own interests which he knew could not be satisfied so long as Italy was at peace'. Alexander was desperate to extend the influence of the Borgia family, especially by helping his son Cesare to win territory in central Italy. French assistance would be invaluable in obtaining this. In return, Alexander could promise Louis aid in divorcing his barren and deformed wife, Jeanne, and marrying Charles VIII's widow, Anne, whose hand carried with it the duchy of Brittany. In 1498, Cesare sailed to France, carrying the papal dispensation for Louis to marry Anne of Brittany and a cardinal's hat for d'Amboise. In France, Cesare married the sister of the King of Navarre and then accompanied the French army south into Italy.

Lodovico Sforza, who had betrayed his French allies by joining the Holy League and who now faced Louis' rival claim to his Duchy of Milan, was in an impossible position. His only firm ally in Italy was Federigo, the new King of Naples, who was also fighting for survival. When the French attacked in 1499, Sforza fled to the Empire where he was received by Maximilian I and where he hired 10 000 Swiss mercenaries to help him regain his duchy. He re-entered Milan in 1500 to a rapturous reception from the people who had rapidly grown tired of the financial demands of the pro-French clique who had taken power in his absence. The French responded to the challenge and at Novara in April 1500, Sforza's Swiss surrendered rather than fight their fellow countrymen in the French army. Sforza was captured and spent the rest of his life in comfortable retirement in the French Château of Loches. The French now had a secure grip on Milan and were encouraged to attempt the conquest of Naples as well.

Rather than try an outright attack on Naples, which would certainly bring a Spanish response, Louis decided to act through diplomacy. In November 1500, the Treaty of Granada partitioned Naples between France, which obtained the northern half (including the capital) and Spain, which annexed the south. It was typical of the duplicity of Ferdinand of Spain that he negotiated this agreement behind the back of Federigo, King of Naples since 1496. Disgusted by Spanish treachery, Federigo threw himself on the mercy of Louis XII who allowed him to stay in France and even installed him as Duke of Anjou.

Territorial disputes between the two powers occupying Naples soon reached fever pitch and in 1502 the French attempted a military solution by invading southern Naples. Cordoba, the Spanish commander, was forced to retreat into the port-fortress of Barletta *(see map on page 65)* where he was besieged during the winter of 1502–03. Supplied and reinforced by sea, Cordoba broke out in April 1503 and encountered the French at Cerignola. This battle was remarkable for being probably the first to be decided by hand-held gunpowder weapons: the French cavalry and Swiss pikemen attacked with their customary vigour but were driven back by Spanish arquebusiers occupying a carefully chosen defensive position and protected by a ditch and palisade. Cordoba followed up his victory by capturing the city of Naples and in December 1503 he surprised the French army defending the northern bank of the River Garigliano. Using secretly assembled bridging equipment, the Spanish crossed the river and routed the French forces. The victories at Cerignola and Garigliano mark Cordoba as one of the greatest generals of the sixteenth century.

Those victories also forced Louis XII to agree to the Treaty of Blois (1505) by which he gave up his claims to Naples and acknowledged Spanish control of the kingdom. From this point on, it was clear that the French had no hope of sustaining their claim to Naples. The problems of distance and lines of communication running through hostile states were overwhelming. In contrast, Spain could supply her forces in southern Italy from well-established bases in Sicily. For France, the key issue in the wars was whether she could continue to dominate Milan and conquer fresh territory in the north.

7. Papal Expansion in Central Italy

It has been stated earlier that one of the forces which helped to keep Italy in a state of war for so long was the political ambition of the Papacy. The campaigns of Louis XII in Milan and Naples gave Alexander VI an excellent opportunity, in the form of French diplomatic and military assistance, to further the interests of the Borgia family by building up a block of hereditary territory in central Italy. With French support, Cesare Borgia conquered the small states of the Romagna and established his own principality there. His government was harsh but efficient and Cesare became the model for Niccolò Machiavelli's manual of ruthless statesmanship, *The Prince*, His father remarked that 'Cesare is a good-natured man; he cannot, however, forgive offences'. He also had designs on other states, notably Florence, but the death of Pope Alexander VI in 1503 undermined his position. He lost his possessions and died in an obscure skirmish in 1507.

Alexander VI's successor, Pius III, survived his election only a few months. The papal tiara then passed to Giuliano della Rovere who took the title Julius II and held the Papacy between 1503 and 1513. Julius II was more of a soldier and a statesman than a cleric, revelling in the military and diplomatic battles of Renaissance Italy. Through administrative ability and personal energy, he succeeded in consolidating the Papal States in central Italy and at the same time made the financial structure of the Papacy more efficient. And his determination to assert the rights of the Papacy throughout Italy was to help drive the Italian Wars on.

8. The War of the League of Cambrai 1508–10

The next stage of the wars in Italy saw the construction of the League of Cambrai, an ill-assorted alliance of states which had nothing in common beyond the wish to crush Venice. Emperor Maximilian had quarrelled with the Venetians and had been heavily defeated by them at Friuli in 1508. The subsequent truce left Venice in control of territories such as Fiume and Trieste which the Habsburgs claimed. Eager for revenge, Maximilian allied with Louis XII, who saw the opportunity to enlarge his possessions in northern Italy. Julius II hoped to use foreign intervention for his own purposes: the Venetians had occupied a number of cities in the Romagna after the fall of Cesare Borgia and the Pope now demanded that they be handed over. A number of smaller Italian states hastened to join the League, intent on regaining land which they had lost to Venice in the past. The only military activity of any significance in the war was a battle between Louis XII's army and a Venetian force at Agnadello in May 1509. The French were victorious and in the south of Italy the Spanish gratefully accepted the chance to occupy a number of Venetian-held cities, thereby consolidating their position as the dominant power in the region. The Venetians had forfeited much territory although, as their lagoon city was secure and their real strength lay in their maritime empire, they were not facing a complete disaster. They regained most of their lost territory in a few years as part of the tortuous course of the Italian Wars.

Meanwhile, Julius II had used the opportunity presented by the French victory to regain the disputed cities in the Romagna. He then made a claim on the duchy of Ferrara, whose dukes were clients of the French. Thus a reversal of alliances took place, with the Pope constructing a new Holy League with the Papacy, Spain, Venice and Henry VIII of England as the main participants. Once again the chronic instability of Italian politics kept conflict in the peninsula simmering.

9. The War of the Holy League 1510–14

After a period of indecisive fencing between France and this next Holy League of Italian powers and Spain, founded in 1511, the military situation was transformed by the arrival of an energetic new French commander, the 21 year old Gaston de Foix. Moving his army with speed and precision, Gaston secured control of most of northern Italy and then marched south to besiege Ravenna (see map on page 65). A combined force of Spanish and papal troops moved to raise the siege and in April 1512 the two armies met outside the city. After a battle which was bloody even by the standards of the time (the Spanish lost 9000 killed out of an army of 16 000), the French emerged victorious but at the cost of their brilliant young commander, killed at the moment of victory. Just as the dismissal of Cordoba (for exceeding his orders) had deprived the Spanish of a general capable of winning decisive victories, so the death of Gaston de Foix robbed France of a soldier of genius.

Despite their victory at Ravenna, problems mounted for the French. Emperor Maximilian sent an army into Italy in 1512 and the Swiss turned against the French and occupied Milan in the same year. Unusually, they were acting on their own initiative rather than as mercenaries. Led by the formidable Cardinal Schinner, the Swiss were determined to take Milan to protect their southern boundaries and to secure their supplies of grain and wine. They defended their position in North Italy when they inflicted a heavy defeat on the French at Novara *(see map on page 65)* and installed Lodovico Sforza's son, Massimiliano, as Duke of Milan. However, the chronic instability of alliances in the Italian Wars now became apparent once again.

With France reeling from the defeat at Novara and Henry VIII's much vaunted triumph at the Battle of the Spurs during the English expedition to northern France in 1513, the time was ripe for a joint attack on the French by the League. Failure to formulate a combined strategy meant that the opportunity was lost and the Swiss concluded a separate peace with France in September 1513. The Papacy and Spain followed suit in December 1513, the Empire in March 1514 and England in July 1514. Nonetheless, France seemed to have failed in her bid for supremacy in northern Italy. But the death of Louis XII in early 1515 brought to the throne the young and aggressive Francis I who, just like Charles VIII and Louis XII, found that the disunity of the Italian states offered an excellent opportunity for military glory and territorial gains.

10. Francis I's Descent upon Italy

The main aims of the new king were to enhance his own and France's reputation through success in battle, to re-assert the French claim to Milan and, so his propaganda claimed rather optimistically, to deliver Constantinople from the clutches of the Turk. Following the expulsion of the French in 1513, the Italian states had wasted the opportunity to prepare to resist future external interference. The Venetians had openly supported the French. In Milan the Swiss ruthlessly pressed their demands for payment for ejecting the French and this, combined with Massimiliano's reckless expenditure on luxuries, alienated a population whose prosperity had already been ravaged by years of war. The Papacy was also playing its usual game of self-interest. Cardinal Giovanni Medici had been elected Pope as Leo X in 1513 and he set about promoting the interests of himself and his family. He was prepared to negotiate for French aid to further his ambitions in the peninsula but, in the event, opposed them when they invaded. Thus, the French and the Venetians found themselves primarily opposed by Swiss and Italian troops.

Francis commanded an army of about 30 000 when he crossed the

The Italian Wars

THE CONDITION OF ITALY
1454   Peace of Lodi
          ↓
Balance of power *but*
No unity
Instability of political system
Unpreparedness for major war

THE MOTIVES OF CHARLES VIII
Dynastic claim on Naples
Chivalric dreams of war
Wealth of Italy
Italian invitations to invade
(Domestic stability in France)

WAR—NAPLES
1494   Charles VIII's invasion via Florence and Rome
1495   French conquest of Naples
          Formation of Holy League v. France
          Battle of Fornovo—inconclusive
1496   French withdrawal from Naples

1500   (November) Treaty of Granada—Naples
          partitioned by French and Spanish
1502   War starts between French and Spanish
1503   Battles of Cerignola and Garigliano—Spanish
          victories
1505   Treaty of Blois—French recognise Spanish
          possession of Naples

WAR—MILAN
Louis XII's claim on Milan
Invitation to invade by Pope
Alexander VI
1499   French invasion
1500   (April) Battle of
          Novara—capture of Sforza
          Milan occupied by French

WAR—VENICE
1508   League of Cambrai—Emperor, Pope,
          French, Spanish etc. v Venice
1509   Battle of Agnadello—Venice defeated but
          League breaks up

1511   Another Holy League against
          France
1512   Battle of Ravenna—French
          victory but Gaston de Foix
          killed
1513   Swiss drive French out of
          Milan
1515   Battle of Marignano—Francis
          I's recapture of Milan
1516   Concordat of
          Bologna—recognition of
          French conquests by Pope

Alps into Italy in 1515. He scored an early success when he bribed nearly
10 000 of the Swiss defending Milan to return home. The French then
approached Milan and in September they fought a two-day battle at
Marignano against the 15 000 Swiss who had remained loyal to their
Milanese allies. The result remained in the balance until the Venetian
army threatened the rear of the Swiss, forcing them to retreat.

The Battle of Marignano had important results. Massimiliano was retired to a comfortable exile in France and the people of Milan were obliged to pay a heavy indemnity to Francis for 'their great rebellions and acts of disobedience'. Francis became the new Duke of Milan. The Swiss came to terms with Francis at the Eternal Peace of Fribourg in 1516 by which they agreed never again to serve against the French and were paid a subsidy in return. Leo X was also anxious for an agreement with the new master of northern Italy and the two settled their differences at Bologna in 1516 *(see page 220)*. Thus by 1516 the French seemed to have triumphed. They were firmly installed in Milan, the Swiss were happy to supply them with mercenaries, and the Pope was a pliable ally. However, the election of Charles of Burgundy and Spain as Holy Roman Emperor in 1519 greatly increased the strategic importance of Italy and the peninsula became the principal theatre of war in the Habsburg–Valois conflict which will be dealt with in Chapters VIII and IX.

11. Italy: the Prey of Foreign Powers

The internal weakness which had made Italy a prey to foreign states since 1494 continued into the nineteenth century. During the intervening centuries, the epithet of the Austrian statesman Metternich applied very well to Italy—it was just a 'geographical expression'. At various times France, Spain and Austria controlled parts of the country and it was not until 1870 that the last foreign troops were removed from Italian soil. Indeed, the eventual unification of Italy owed considerably more to the intervention of foreign powers than it did to the efforts of her own people. Guicciardini's despair at the failings of his countrymen proved to be not only an astute depiction of the events of his own lifetime but also an accurate prophecy of the future.

12. Bibliography

New Cambridge Modern History: Vol I Chapter XII (CUP, 1957). G Mattingly *Renaissance Diplomacy* (Jonathan Cape, 1955). J R Hale *War and Society in Renaissance Europe* (Fontana, 1985). M Mallett *The Borgias* (Bodley Head, 1969).

13. Discussion Points and Exercises

A   *This section consists of questions or points that might be used for discussion (or written answers) as a way of expanding on the chapter and testing understanding of it:*

1   What were the most important factors in the Italian political situation which caused the crisis of 1494?

2   What made Italy so attractive to foreign invaders?

3 'Charles VIII's invasion of Italy was just a chivalric adventure'.
4 Why was Charles VIII so successful in 1494?
5 Why was he unable to maintain this success?
6 Why did Louis XII become embroiled in Italy?
7 'Of all the Italian powers it was the Papacy which did most to prolong the Italian Wars'.
8 What were the motives and results of Francis I's invasion of Italy?

B *Essay questions*
1 Why did French armies invade Italy so frequently after 1494?
2 Why did foreign powers regard control of Italy as important between 1494 and 1529? See also Chapter VIII.
3 Explain why the French failed to make permanent conquests in Italy after 1494.
4 'It was the internal weakness of Italy which allowed foreign states to use the peninsula as their battleground.' Discuss.
5 Why did the Italian Wars last so long?

14. Essay Writing—Narrative and Analysis

The aim of an essay must be to provide an analysis rather than tell the story of what happened. However, it is particularly tempting to lapse into narrative when faced with a year-by-year series of events as in the Italian Wars.

Below are three narrative paragraphs, extracts from an essay written in answer to question 1 above: 'Why did French armies invade Italy so frequently after 1494?'. Criticise these paragraphs in detail and then rewrite them, converting them from narrative to analysis which is relevant to the question. Use the same information, but selectively and use it as evidence rather than just a sequence of facts. Following each paragraph are relevant analytical points which you should highlight.

(a) Charles VIII crossed the Alps into Italy in 1494. He was welcomed by the Duke of Milan, Lodovico Sforza. The French defeated the Florentine forces and the Medici ruler of Florence fled; Charles was then hailed by the Florentine people as the protector of their liberties. The French then arrived in Rome. The Pope, Alexander VI, persuaded them to pass through his lands quickly. In Naples the fortress of Monte San Giovanni was taken, King Alfonso abdicated and his son, who became King Ferrantino, fled. The powerful Neapolitan nobleman, the Prince of Salerno, was not sorry to see Alfonso and Ferrantino go.
Analytical points: *the ease of invading Italy owing to divisions amongst the Italians and the feebleness of their response.*

(b) Louis XII's grandmother had been a member of the Visconti family, formerly rulers of Milan. Milan lay just to the south of the Alps and was the centre for the main roads leading to the Alpine passes. Milan was a wealthy trading city, handling brocades, wines and grain. Louis crossed the Alps in

1499. He won the Battle of Novara, where the Swiss troops working for Lodovico Sforza would not fight their fellow countrymen in the French army, and he took firm control over Milan. Louis felt secure now in northern Italy and struck a bargain with Ferdinand of Aragon to partition the kingdom of Naples.

Analytical points: *the importance of Milan and the inadequacy of its defences.*

(c) Francis I became king in 1515 at the age of 21. He crossed the Alps in the same year. The Swiss had taken Milan from the French in 1513 and used one of the Sforza family as a puppet duke but Francis beat them in 1515 at the Battle of Marignano with the help of the Venetians. The French once again occupied Milan and the Pope, Leo X, made a settlement with Francis, the Concordat of Bologna, in 1516.

Analytical points: *the vulnerability of the French in Milan and their willingness/ capacity to strike back if defeated.*

IV The Age of Discovery

1. Introduction

At the beginning of the fifteenth century even educated Europeans had little notion of what territories lay beyond their own continent and the Mediterranean basin. The existence of Africa and Asia was appreciated but there was only the haziest knowledge of their shape and of the people who inhabited them. America was totally unknown, although there were persistent rumours of a mysterious land called Atlantis somewhere to the west of Europe. Yet by the end of the sixteenth century, most of the globe had been mapped and only Australia, New Zealand, Antarctica and the lands surrounding the North Pacific remained to be discovered.

The speed and extent of this 'Age of Reconnaissance', as it has been called, was unparalleled. Other civilisations had carried out voyages of discovery: the Vikings had explored the North Atlantic in the ninth century, in the early fifteenth century the Chinese admiral Cheng Ho sailed to Sri Lanka, the Indian Ocean and probably the north coast of Australia, and Arab ships had cruised the east coast of Africa. The unique feature of the European age of discovery was that a single culture intruded into all the major continents simultaneously and linked the oceans of the world with a single system of navigation. In one area of the globe, information about large numbers of other peoples was gathered for the first time and the process was begun by which the Europeans became the dominant military and economic force in the world.

The early explorers had little reliable factual knowledge to guide them. Some learning inherited from the classical world was becoming available. The *Geography* of Ptolemy, an Egyptian who wrote in the second century AD, was translated from Greek into Latin in 1406. This work gave an account of the state of geographical knowledge at the height of the Roman Empire and included material on North Africa and the western parts of Asia. A second author of the classical world whose works were known in the fifteenth century was Strabo, who lived in the first century BC and suggested that it would be possible to sail from Europe to Asia if the Atlantic was not so wide. The great respect with which ancient scholarship was regarded during the Early Modern period meant that Ptolemy and Strabo were given a rather uncritical acceptance, even when their findings were highly dubious. Ptolemy, for example, believed that it would not be possible to reach India by sea because the Indian Ocean was encompassed by a large mass of land to the south.

More recent information came from the writings of the Venetian Marco Polo who travelled across Asia to China in the late thirteenth century. He resided in Peking for 20 years and composed a largely accurate account of the wealth and splendour of the Mongol Empire under Kublai Khan. Polo's *Travels* was printed in the late fifteenth century, giving it a wide circulation in Europe, and it is known that Christopher Columbus possessed a copy. Polo was, however, unique and even his knowledge was beginning to go out of date by the time European navigators came within striking distance of Asia.

Competing for the attention of would-be explorers and the educated public in Europe were fantastic travellers tales which were believed with no less credulity than the account of Polo. The prime example of this genre was the *Travels of Sir John Mandeville*. This extraordinary fourteenth century work was packed with entertaining stories of men with eyes in their shoulders and mouths in their chests and giant ants which hoarded gold. It included almost no geographical information of any value but retained a quite undeserved popularity throughout the fifteenth and sixteenth centuries, even when reputable descriptions of newly dis-covered lands were being published. Other writers gave lurid accounts of the fate which would befall ships which ventured too far from Europe —falling off the edge of the world or boiling to death in the hot seas of the south. Mandeville and his imitators served only to obscure the truth about Asia and Africa.

Given this confusion between fact and fiction, it is not surprising that contemporary maps were of little help. The conventional depiction of the globe was the 'mappa mundi' which showed a disc-like world with Jerusalem at the centre and the known continents of Europe, Asia and Africa crudely arranged around it. The interiors of the latter two were filled with whatever the fertility of the map-maker's imagination pro-vided as appropriate. As a practical aid to navigation the 'mappae mundi' were useless.

Thus the explorers of the Early Modern period were taking a leap into the unknown in a very real sense. Whereas the space pioneers of the second half of the twentieth century have had a clear idea of their destination and been able to communicate with a base which can provide advice and assistance, men such as Columbus and Magellan left their home ports for months or years at a time with little navigational data and no prospect of aid if storms, reefs or hostile populations threatened the voyage. It is not surprising that losses of ships and men were heavy. The main questions which need to be considered in regard to the age of discovery are what motivated Europeans to face such hazards, what means they possessed which made their exploration successful, why it was that Spain and Portugal took the lead in the reconnaissance and what changes were brought about in Europe by the discoveries.

2. The Motives

The explorers and conquerors who sailed from Europe in the fifteenth and sixteenth centuries were driven by a mixture of impulses. The Spaniard Bernal Diaz acknowledged this when he wrote that it was his ambition to 'serve God and His Majesty, to give light to those who were in darkness and to grow rich, as all men desire to do'. In this remark, Diaz highlighted the two most significant motives: the urge to spread and strengthen Christianity and the prospect of national and personal profit. Although contemporary piety demanded that the religious element should be stressed, economic factors were of greater importance in almost every voyage and it is these which will be considered first.

It has been shown earlier that, at the end of the Middle Ages, Europe was in commercial contact with Asia. A highly profitable trade in luxury goods flowed from China, India and the East Indies (the latter being a convenient general term to cover Malaya, Sumatra, Java and Borneo) through the Indian Ocean, the Red Sea and the Persian Gulf and then overland to the ports of the eastern Mediterranean. There the goods were sold by Arab traders to the Venetian and Genoese merchants who conveyed them on to Italian ports for re-sale to the rest of Europe. By far the most important items in this trade were spices. Before the Agricultural Revolution of the eighteenth and nineteenth centuries, Europe was unable to grow sufficient feed to keep alive large numbers of livestock during the winter. Animals were therefore slaughtered in the autumn and the meat salted to preserve it for the coming months. Spices such as pepper (from India and the East Indies), cinammon (from Sri Lanka), ginger (from China) and cloves (from the East Indies) helped to flavour the putrescent flesh and also acted as a preservative. Apart from this very practical application, European palates were also acquiring a taste for seasoned foods, a craving which could only be satisfied by the imports from the East. Other high-value, low-bulk items which were shipped from Asia included silks from China, emeralds from India, rubies from Tibet and sapphires from Ceylon. Even the humble rhubarb (from China) was valued in Europe for alleged medicinal qualities.

By the fifteenth century, however, a number of factors were conspiring to threaten this long-established trade. The huge costs of transport, which were increased by the number of hands through which the goods passed and the tolls which were exacted along the route, made spices highly expensive by the time they reached the Mediterranean. Europeans longed for a method of supply which would reduce the price. Resentment had also built up at the virtual monopoly enjoyed by Italian merchants once the goods had reached the West, and other states began to search for ways of breaking this stranglehold. In addition, the expansion of Muslim influence in Arabia, and especially the threat from the aggressively inclined Ottoman Empire, rendered the route vulnerable. In short, a cheaper and more reliable method of obtaining the products of Asia was needed. It was this motivation which encouraged the Portuguese to sail south along the coast of Africa and into the Indian Ocean, and which prompted Columbus to sail west from Spain in his attempt to reach China by crossing the Atlantic.

The luxuries of Asia were not the only commodities over which Europeans wished to gain control: a shortage in the supply of gold meant that exploration of the gold-producing areas of West Africa might yield profitable pickings. The 'gold famine' in Europe was probably caused by two main factors. The expansion of trade inside Europe in the later Middle Ages created a need for more gold and silver coins and increasingly, European merchants were having to send gold and silver to the east in order to pay for imports from Asia. Silver could be supplied from the mines of Germany, Bohemia and Hungary but Europe lacked sources of gold sufficient to sustain her economic growth. Instead, gold was obtained from West Africa where it was extracted by surface mining and panning in the regions of the Upper Senegal River, the Upper Niger River and in Ghana (the 'Gold Coast'), regions given the collective name of 'Guinea'. From these areas the gold was moved across the Sahara Desert by camel and sold to Italian and Catalan merchants in North Africa. The Portuguese had captured the city of Ceuta in Morocco in 1415 and hence probably had information on the source of the Guinea gold, knowledge which almost certainly stimulated their reconnaissance of the African coast. The search for precious metals was also a consistent theme in the Spanish exploration and occupation of America. Columbus was obsessed by the belief that his American discoveries were in fact outlying areas of China or Japan and that mountains of gold lay just over the horizon. As he wrote, 'Gold is the most precious of all commodities; gold constitutes treasure, and he who possesses it has all he needs in this world, as also the means of rescuing souls from Purgatory, and restoring them to the enjoyment of paradise'. It is hardly surprising that the Spanish gave a high priority to looting the civilisations of America and then exploiting the silver mines of the region. Personal profit coincided with Spanish national interest. 'I came here to get gold, not till the soil like a peasant', remarked Francisco Pizarro, the conqueror of Peru.

The search for the sources of spices and gold were the most important economic motives but there were a number of other benefits which could accrue to the Europeans through exploration. Much of Europe was short of labour following the ravages of the Black Death in the fourteenth century. This was a particular problem for Portugal which had a population of about one million at the end of the fifteenth century. One solution to this problem was to recruit additional labour in the slave markets of North Africa. Negro slaves were transported across the Sahara with the gold caravans for sale to European and Arab buyers. Voyages down the African coast enabled the Portuguese to buy or capture slaves at source in West Africa and then ship them for use in the sugar plantations of Madeira and the Canaries or in Portugal itself. By the end of the fifteenth century, negroes may have made up as much as ten percent of the population of Lisbon. By 1540, about 10 000 slaves a year were being taken from West Africa, many of these being sent across the Atlantic to provide cheap labour in the Caribbean and Central America. The development of this profitable trade certainly encouraged Portuguese interest in Africa.

A less dramatic motive than the hunt for spices, gold or slaves was the urge to settle on land which was free from the obligations to a lord which were usual in Europe, and which could be farmed profitably. The second American voyage of Columbus in 1493,for example, consisted of 17 ships filled with 1200 settlers, attracted not only by the lure of gold but also the chance to acquire free land and a work force of local Indians who could be terrorised into submission. This process was repeated throughout the Spanish American possessions. On the Caribbean island of Hispaniola (modern Haiti and the Dominican Republic), for example, 24 mills were grinding cane sugar within a few years of discovery.

The following extract written by Columbus describes an encounter with Indians in the Caribbean:

> They had no proper weapons, and did not know what these were. When I showed them swords their ignorance was such that they seized them by the blades and cut their fingers . . . some wore a few grains of fine gold in their ears and noses which they gave us without difficulty . . . I must add that this island belongs to Your Highnesses as securely as the kingdom of Castile. It only needs people to come and settle here and to give orders to the inhabitants who will do what ever is asked of them. I myself, with the few men at my disposal, can travel all through these islands without risk. I have already seen three of my men land alone, and by their mere presence cause the flight of a whole crowd of Indians, although they had no intention of harming them. . . . They know nothing about the art of war and are so cowardly that a thousand of them would not stay to face three of our men. One can see that they are well able to do whatever is asked, and they need only to be given orders to be made to work, to sow or to do anything useful. They could build towns and get used to wearing clothes and to behaving like ourselves.

1 *In what ways would Columbus' description make the New World seem attractive to Europeans?*
2 *What does the passage reveal about European attitudes to newly discovered peoples?*

The second great motive for exploration was provided by religion. In the fifteenth century, Christendom felt under threat from Islam in eastern Europe and the Mediterranean. The fall of Constantinople to the Ottoman Turks in 1453 was the most obvious manifestation of this growing menace and throughout Europe demands were made for a counter-attack. The obvious location for this was Iberia. The Spanish and Portuguese had a long tradition of crusading against the Moors, both in the Reconquest of their peninsula and in fighting in North Africa. The important capture of the Moroccan city of Ceuta by the Portuguese in 1415, an event which greatly increased Portugal's awareness of Africa, was part of the centuries-old struggle in the western Mediterranean. It encouraged the Portuguese to sail south along the African coast in an attempt to outflank the Muslims and also to seek the aid of Prester John.

This legendary Christian king was believed to live in Africa and the explorers of the fifteenth century hoped to enlist his support in the struggle against Islam. Stories of his wealth and power were numerous. It was said that 30 000 guests could be seated at his table made of emeralds and that twelve archbishops sat at his right hand. Fantastic as such accounts seem today, to the embattled Christians of late medieval Europe they offered the prospect of deliverance from the shadow of Muslim might—if only Prester John's kingdom could be discovered. The search for Christians was a constant stimulus to exploration. When Vasco da Gama dropped anchor at Calicut in India he declared that he had come 'in search of Christians and spices' and at once mistook a Hindu temple for a church and a Hindu goddess for the Virgin Mary.

In 1492 the capture of Granada, the last outpost of Islam in Iberia, by the forces of Ferdinand and Isabella of Spain released Christian troops for service elsewhere. Some carried the struggle into the Moorish states of North Africa but others chose to take Christianity to the newly discovered lands across the Atlantic. As J H Parry has commented, 'the feelings which rallied Spaniards against Granada developed into a bold and methodical imperialism'.

The urge to defend Christendom was one element of religious motivation. Another was the genuine desire to bring the teachings of Christ to those who had not heard them. The obvious agency to lead such a mission was the Papacy but successive popes were preoccupied with European affairs and in any case lacked the resources or information to attempt mass conversion. Thus the responsibility tended to devolve on national governments, a situation recognised by a Papal Bull of 1493 which instructed Ferdinand and Isabella of Spain to send 'virtuous and God-fearing men endowed with training, experience and skill, to instruct the natives . . . and to imbue them with . . . Christian faith and sound morals'. When the Spanish occupied huge areas of Central and South America, priests accompanied them, smashing the idols and abolishing the practices of the native religions. They then set about building churches and converting the local inhabitants. In New Spain (Mexico) alone there may have been five million converts by 1536, with friars baptising up to fifteen hundred people in a single day. Of course, many of these could have had only the vaguest notion of the Christian message and the rituals and beliefs of the Catholic Church were often combined with those of pre-Conquest religions. Nevertheless, the establishment of the Christian faith in the New World is one of the most remarkable aspects of the era of discovery *(see page 324)*. In contrast, the Portuguese made less impact in Asia. This was because they did not destroy the existing cultures as the Spanish did in America and because they chose not to colonise large areas.

A third motive for participating in exploration is less easy to define. It has been argued that the spread of the values and ideas of the Renaissance *(see Chapter V)* contributed to the eagerness with which explorers and conquerors endured hardship and achieved almost super-human feats. The emphasis of the Renaissance on the importance of the individual and the fame which he could achieve provided a strong inducement to bold action. Hernando Cortés, who conquered the huge Aztec empire in Mexico with a few hundred Spaniards, gained a Renaissance education in Salamanca, one of the centres of the Spanish Renaissance. The theme of winning reputation runs through many of his recorded utterances: when he and his men landed on the coast of Mexico he urged them on with 'many comparisons with brave deeds done by heroes among the Romans'. This desire to emulate the achievements of the classical world was another feature of the Renaissance. Such is the theory. However, it seems far-fetched to believe that the Renaissance could work such a change in the basic patterns of human behaviour. Marco Polo had undertaken hazardous journeys without the benefits of a Renaissance education and there is no evidence that Francisco Pizarro read classical authors before taking Peru by storm. Another feature of Renaissance thought was the increasing desire for knowledge, even if this was at times somewhat uncritical and credulous. The invention of printing allowed the circulation of reports of voyages and discoveries and the diffusion of navigational information. For the first time monarchs, sailors, soldiers, churchmen and scholars co-operated in enterprises which were studied and commented on throughout Europe.

Different individuals had varying motives for seeking new lands across the sea. One person of great importance was the Portuguese prince, Henry the Navigator (1394–1460), who organised so many of the early voyages of exploration along the west coast of Africa. An account of his motives was written by Azurara, a Portuguese chronicler of the fifteenth century:

> You should note well that the noble spirit of this prince, by sort of natural constraint, was ever urging him both to begin and to carry out very great deeds. For which reason, after the taking of Ceuta he always kept ships well armed against the Infidel, both for war and because he had also a wish to know the land that lay beyond the isles of Canary and that cape called Bojador . . . he sent out ships to those parts, to have sure knowledge of them all . . .
>
> The second reason was that if there chanced to be in those lands some population of Christians, or some havens, into which it would be possible to sail without peril, many kinds of merchandise might be brought to this realm, which would find a ready market . . . and also the products of this realm might be taken there. Such trade would bring great profit to our countrymen.
>
> The third reason was that, as it was said that the power of the Moors in that land of Africa was very much greater than was commonly supposed,

and that there were no Christians among them, nor any other race of men; and because every wise man is obliged by natural prudence to wish for a knowledge of the power of his enemy, therefore the said Prince Henry exerted himself to cause this to be fully discovered, and to make it known definitely how far the power of those infidels extended.

The fourth reason was because during the 31 years that he had warred against the Moors, he had never found a Christian king . . . who for the love of our Lord Jesus Christ would aid him in the said war. Therefore he sought to know if there were in those parts any Christian princes, in whom the charity and love of Christ was so ingrained that they would aid him against those enemies of the faith.

The fifth reason was his great desire to make increase on the faith of our Lord Jesus Christ and to bring to him all the souls that should be saved . . .

But over and above these five reasons I have a sixth that would seem to be the root from which all others proceeded: and this is the inclination of the heavenly wheels.

1   *In your own words outline the six reasons Azurara mentions.*
2   *Which reasons seem to be the most plausible?*

3. The Means

The great voyages of discovery of the fifteenth and sixteenth centuries were not the result of any single technological breakthrough but rather the culmination of centuries of development in the skills of shipbuilding, navigation and seamanship. The details of these developments are sometimes complex but it is important to grasp them as, without maritime expertise, the Europeans could never have penetrated to every ocean of the globe.

The first requirement of any successful voyage of exploration is a ship capable of sailing long distances, investigating an objective and then returning safely to its point of origin. Until the late Middle Ages no vessel in Europe (with the arguable exception of the Viking longship) was capable of performing such a task. Mediterranean shipping was dominated by the galley—a sleek, fast vessel propelled by a combination of oars and sails and capable of manoeuvring in shallow or confined waters. Although favoured by the Italian states as both a merchant and naval vessel, the galley had definite limitations which made it unsuitable as a vessel of exploration. The large number of oarsmen meant considerable supplies of food had to be carried, severely limiting the range of the galley. The narrowness of the design restricted cargo space and the galley was vulnerable to the high waves of the open ocean.

The nations facing the Atlantic and the North Sea had evolved an entirely different type of vessel. These were broad, high-sided, stable ships, able to survive the pounding of heavy swells and carry large amounts of cargo in their holds. They were propelled by large square sails which made handling difficult in contrary winds and when delicate manoeuvring was required. Such unwieldy, clumsy vessels could be of little use in exploring unknown coasts. Instead, the Iberians developed a hybrid form of ship which borrowed features from Mediterranean and Atlantic designs and added rigging of Arab origin.

This vessel was the famous 'caravel', the most popular type of ship for voyages of discovery in the fifteenth and early sixteenth centuries. Originally used as a coastal trader and fishing vessel, the caravel had a shallow draught, light but seaworthy construction and the advantage of lateen sails. These are triangular sails whose design spread into the Mediterranean from the Red Sea during the Middle Ages. Lateen rigging gave an ease of handling in all winds which was crucial when sailing in uncharted waters. Sometimes square sails were also fitted to increase speed when sailing with the wind, this variation being known as a 'caravela redonda'. Small in size (about 60 to 80 tons) and crewed by 20 to 30 men, the caravel was sufficiently fast, nimble and sturdy to be favoured by explorers such as Columbus who included two in his fleet of three ships for the first Atlantic crossing in 1492. (It is significant that his only non-caravel, the square-rigged *Santa Maria*, foundered on a reef and had to be abandoned.)

The limited size of the caravel made it unsuitable as a cargo carrier and, once trading links with a newly discovered area had been established, merchant ships of a larger size were operated. These 'carracks' were broad, heavy ships with considerable carrying capacity in their three or four decks. By the mid-sixteenth century carracks of over a thousand tons were routinely plying between Europe and the Indian Ocean and America.

Medieval seamen had few navigational aids available to them. They relied on coastal landmarks and accumulated knowledge of natural phenomena such as cloud formations, flocks of birds, sandbanks and shoals of fish. Simple observation of the sun and stars was probably also used. Thus navigation tended to be by instinct and experience rather than through scientific means.

This rather primitive situation was improved by the advent of the magnetic needle in the Mediterranean in the twelfth century, allowing a reasonably accurate estimation of the direction of north. Attached to a card showing the main points of the compass and housed in a box for protection, the magnetic needle had become the principal method of navigation in the Mediterranean by the fifteenth century and was to be a vital tool for the early explorers. For measuring the latitude of a vessel it was possible to use an instrument called an astrolabe but very calm conditions were required for effective use and thus it was of dubious value in the rough waters of the Atlantic. Most medieval seamen preferred to use the technique of 'dead reckoning' to plot their position. This involved estimating the speed, direction and length of voyage elapsed and then working out the location on a chart. However, in 1484 a body of astronomers advised John II that latitude might be calculated by measuring the height of the midday sun and then comparing it with a set of tables which had been worked out by a Portuguese named Zacuto in

1478. It was typical of the highly organised nature of Portuguese exploration that a ship was despatched south to check the practicality of the calculation. Navigators could now arrive at the correct latitude and then sail east or west to their destination. (An accurate method of measuring longitude was not developed until the eighteenth century.)

This improvement in navigational techniques also enhanced the quality of maps and charts. In the Middle Ages sailors in the Mediterranean were able to make use of 'portolans' or maps showing the coastline with main ports, natural features and hazards such as reefs. Lines of direction radiated from important points on the map and thus with a compass, a portolan and an idea of his speed, the mariner could judge his location with reasonable accuracy. In northern European waters the 'rutter' was more common: written sailing directions with information on tides, shallows and currents. Portolans were, of course, no use when a ship was sailing outside European waters and so the new methods of navigating were important in increasing the confidence of explorers.

Another important technical advance which improved chances of success was the development of powder weapons. The caravels of the early explorers tended to be lightly armed, but once contact had been made with potentially hostile populations, ships sailed with greater firepower. In the fifteenth and early sixteenth centuries artillery on ships was of small calibre, useful mainly for killing enemy crew and bringing down rigging but during the sixteenth century naval cannon became heavier and capable of sinking opposing vessels. These guns were mounted along the sides of a ship in 'broadsides' which could deliver a formidable weight of shot. European armaments technology made Portuguese and Spanish fleets almost invulnerable to attack by less developed ships. On land, too, gunpowder weapons often gave Europeans a significant advantage over more numerous but less well-armed peoples. However, this superiority should not be exaggerated, at least in regard to the early phases of discovery. Cortés marched into Mexico with only a few small cannon and thirteen hand-held firearms. Just as decisive in European victories were high quality steel swords and armour and sometimes, in America, the horses of the Spanish, which were unknown to the local populations. The conquistador attributed Spanish victories 'under God, to the horses'.

4. The Portuguese Experience

It is one of the most remarkable features of the age of discovery that the lead in exploration was taken by the small and economically backward kingdom of Portugal. With a population of about one million in the fifteenth century, a dearth of fertile agricultural land, no tradition in long sea voyages and few good harbours, Portugal seemed to have little to recommend it when compared with, for example, the rich and commercially sophisticated Italian states. Virtually its only contributions to European trade were fish, salt, cork and olive oil. Appearances were, however, deceptive: Portugal possessed assets which made her unique.

Firstly, the geographical position of Portugal was a great advantage. Situated at what J H Parry has graphically described as the 'street corner of Europe', Portugal absorbed influences from both the Mediterranean and northern Europe, leading to the evolution of the caravel, for instance. The Portuguese also possessed a considerable inshore fleet to take advantage of the fishing grounds just off her coast. Only a small proportion of the population was involved in this activity but it did give Portugal a nucleus of tough, trained sailors manning handy, seaworthy craft. The caravels were small enough not to require much capital expenditure—an important point when the comparative poverty of Portugal is considered. Perhaps most important of all was the location of Portugal in relation to the wind systems of the North Atlantic. In summer the prevailing winds off the Portuguese coast blow from the north and north east, driving ships down the coast of Morocco and out into the Atlantic. These 'north east trades' provided favourable sailing conditions for at least 1500 miles, as far south as the Cape Verde islands. By turning north, ships could then use the prevailing westerly winds to return to Europe on a more northern route. Iberia was thus an ideal starting-point for voyages south and west into the Atlantic.

A second advantage enjoyed by the Portuguese was political stability during much of the fifteenth and early sixteenth centuries. Moorish resistance had been overcome by Alphonso III (1248–79) and in 1385 Portugal, assisted by English forces, defeated her larger, expansionist neighbour Castile at the Battle of Aljubarrota. A permanent peace was established in 1411 and for much of the rest of the century, Castile's energies were taken up in civil war. Secure from external threat, prevented by geography from expanding in Europe and with the capable Avis dynasty providing firm government at home, Portugal could devote men, ships and money to exploration. Many of the early Portuguese expeditions were led by members of the nobility, who combined a thirst for personal glory through war and conquest, a chivalric desire to serve their lord, the king, and a hatred of non-Christians in roughly equal measures.

A third point to consider is that Portugal had several powerful motives for embarking on a period of exploration. It has already been shown that the Iberians were heirs of a crusading tradition. In addition, economic factors seem to have been especially strong. The gold famine hit Portugal particularly badly, with no gold coins being minted between 1383 and 1435, and thus the need to reach the sources of Guinea gold was pronounced. Success was apparent when the Lisbon mint began to issue a new gold coin, the *cruzado* (or 'crusade') in 1457.

A final reason for Portuguese leadership in the era of discovery was the

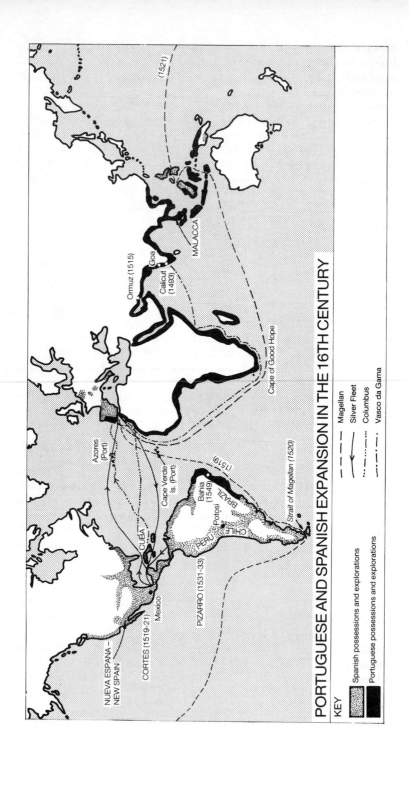

PORTUGUESE AND SPANISH EXPANSION IN THE 16TH CENTURY

NUEVA ESPANA – NEW SPAIN

CORTES (1519-21)

Mexico

CUBA

PIZARRO (1531-33)

PERU

Potosi

CHILE

BRAZIL

Bahia (1549)

Strait of Magellan (1520)

(1519)

Azores (Port)

Cape Verde Is. (Port)

Cape of Good Hope

Ormuz (1515)

Calicut (1493)

Goa

MALACCA

(1521)

KEY

Spanish possessions and explorations

Portuguese possessions and explorations

- - - - Magellan

——— Silver Fleet

·–·–· Columbus

·–··–·· Vasco da Gama

Portuguese royal family. A succession of kings and princes, of whom Prince Henry the Navigator (d.1460) is the most famous, acted as patrons of the Portuguese seamen, giving an organisation and discipline to the exploratory voyages. Prince Henry was appointed governor of the Algarve in southern Portugal in 1419 and from his base at Sagres he financed and supervised the discovery and occupation of Madeira and the Azores and encouraged the reconnaissance of the African coast. Although the traditional picture of Henry as a Renaissance scholar who surrounded himself with the foremost geographical experts of the day has long been discarded, his contribution was certainly significant. Perhaps of greater importance was the work of King John II (nicknamed 'the Perfect') who ruled Portugal between 1481 and 1495. In the mid-1480s, John despatched meticulously planned expeditions to search for Prester John and a route to the Asian spice sources. Not only did Bartholomew Diaz reach the southern tip of Africa whilst under his patronage but John also sent Pedro de Covilha to India by an overland route to gather information which might be useful on future voyages. John even ordered his captains to erect limestone pillars at intervals along the African coast to claim the continent for Portugal. Such personal royal involvement was an important component in Portuguese achievement.

Having established why Portugal was in the forefront of European exploration, it is now necessary to consider the extent of the empire which Portugal acquired and what benefits and problems it created. It is convenient to divide the empire into four areas: the Atlantic islands, Africa, Asia, and Brazil.

There are four main groups of islands off the African coast: Madeira, the Canaries, the Azores and the Cape Verde Islands, Europeans had sailed to all except the Cape Verdes in the fourteenth century but active colonisation only began in the fifteenth century. Madeira (settled about 1420) was at first renowned for its quality timber but soon became more important for sugar production. Sugar-cane was imported from Sicily at the instigation of Prince Henry, who in 1452 supplied capital for the first sugar-crushing mill. Madeira soon became a major supplier of the voracious European sugar market. The island also became the home of a profitable wine trade as a result of Prince Henry's introduction of the Malvoisie grape from Crete. Attempts were made to settle the Canaries in the 1420s but these were met with a hostile reception from the native inhabitants and from the Castilians who also claimed the islands. At the Treaty of Alcaçovas in 1479, Portugal gave up her claim to the Canaries in return for Spanish recognition of her rights in the other three groups of islands. The Azores were explored in the 1430s and by the late fifteenth century produced considerable quantities of grain, grown on the fertile volcanic soil. The Portuguese began the settlement of the Cape Verdes in the 1460s, sugar becoming the main agricultural product of the islands. The Atlantic islands had another function, that of staging-posts in the long oceanic voyages to the Americas and Asia. Ships would put in for supplies of food and water and other necessary stores, increasing the economic and strategic value of the islands.

The Portuguese made no comparable attempts to colonise the mainland of Africa due to the inhospitable climate, the vast scale of the continent and the tropical diseases which afflicted Europeans in the sweltering jungles of the west coast. Instead, forts and trading-posts were established as they made their way south, the first probably being established on the orders of Henry the Navigator at Arguin Island in the 1440s. From these secure bases the Portuguese traded European textiles, weapons and trinkets for gold and slaves. By the late fifteenth century, an average of 400 kilograms of gold a year was being shipped to Portugal, whilst between 1450 and 1500 about 140 000 slaves were captured or purchased. As America was opened up in the sixteenth century, the demand for slaves increased and by 1600 about 60 000 negroes had been sent to the Portuguese colony of Brazil. Other destinations for this profitable trade were the Spanish possessions in the Caribbean and Central America. It was only in the 1560s that the Portuguese monopoly on this trade was challenged by the English trader John Hawkins. In addition to gold and slaves, other items of value obtained from Africa included ivory and pepper. After 1500 forts were also built on the east coast of Africa, these acting mainly as ports of call for shipping sailing to or from Asia.

Vasco da Gama's trail-blazing voyage to Calicut in India in 1498 *(see map on page 88)* was the signal for the start of a Portuguese maritime offensive to take control of the trade routes of the Indian Ocean. Da Gama was able to take advantage of the mutual hostility of the Indian states to gain political advantage and any opposition could be dealt with by a crude application of European firepower. The Portuguese strategy was based around the destruction of rival fleets at sea and the seizure of strategic points on land to provide naval bases and trading-posts. The victory over an Egyptian fleet at Diu in 1509 secured mastery of the Indian Ocean and was followed by the capture of the port of Goa in India in 1510 and of Ormuz at the mouth of the Persian Gulf in 1515. A fort was established in Sri Lanka in 1518. Further east, Malacca, the collection point for spices from all over the East Indies, was occupied by the Portuguese in 1511 and in 1557 they began the creation of a city at Macao in southern China. By 1600, Portugal owned a network of fifty fortified points between southern Africa and Japan which, together with her naval power, allowed her to plunder, tax and monopolise certain trades almost at will.

Spain might have challenged this dominance but in 1529 Charles V sold his claim to the spice islands to the Portuguese for 350 000 ducats. The Portuguese derived considerable profit from importing spices, especially pepper, to Lisbon and then selling them on to the rest of Europe. They also became the carriers of Asia, trading Chinese silk to Japan and Indian cotton to Africa, for example. However, the Portuguese position in the Indian Ocean was always rather precarious due to a shortage of manpower (the tiny Portuguese population could not meet the demands of her far-flung empire in Asia, Africa and Brazil), a lack of ships (Portugal produced little timber and ship losses on the long voyage between Lisbon and Asia were frequent) and a tendency to alienate local populations by unnecessarily harsh treatment. By the end of the sixteenth century, the empire in the east was in decay with the Dutch preparing to oust the Portuguese as the leading European power in the region.

The final component of the Portuguese overseas empire was the South American possession of Brazil. Discovered by Pedro Cabral in 1500 (after his fleet had been blown off course in the Atlantic when bound for India), it lay in that portion of the Atlantic assigned to Portugal by Pope Alexander VI at the Treaty of Tordesillas in 1494. (In an act of arbitration between the rival Portuguese and Spanish explorers, the Pope had decreed a line 270 leagues west of the Azores—territory discovered to the west of the line was to be Spanish, leaving territory to the east to the Portuguese.) At first Brazil seemed to possess little of economic attraction apart from red wood useful for dyeing. When the French began to show an interest in the area in the 1530s, John III of Portugal decided to encourage settlement of the coastal strip and sugar-cane was introduced from Madeira. As the local Indian population proved inadequate to labour in the sugar plantations, African slaves were shipped to Brazil. By 1580 the Portuguese population of the colony numbered about 20 000 and sixty sugarmills were at work to supply Europe. As in Asia, the Portuguese in Brazil came under increasing pressure from the Dutch in the following century.

The rise of the insignificant nation of Portugal to the status of a global power is one of the most surprising developments in Early Modern Europe. That the Portuguese could not sustain their expansion is hardly surprising, especially when comparison is made with her larger and more populous neighbour, Spain.

5. The Spanish Experience

The Spanish were slower than the Portuguese to take advantage of their favourable geographical position, facing the Atlantic, but once they had started they displayed a ferocious commitment to discovery and exploitation of new lands. There are several reasons why it was the Spanish who followed the Portuguese lead so enthusiastically. Spain was a recently united country in the late fifteenth century. The traditionally hostile kingdoms of Castile and Aragon had been brought together in an uneasy association by the marriage of Isabella of Castile and Ferdinand of Aragon *(see Chapter II)*. Energies previously dissipated in competition could now be harnessed and turned outwards.

Ferdinand and Isabella were determined that their state should not miss opportunities which their Iberian neighbours were taking. As the

Portuguese slowly navigated the African route to the East, the Catholic Monarchs and their subjects began to consider the possibility of a western route to the Indies. The discoveries of Columbus stimulated this race.

A second reason has to do with the nature of Spanish society. For centuries the Spanish had battled against the Moorish occupiers of their country. In the atmosphere of the Reconquest, bravery, ruthlessness and Christian fervour were virtues to be admired and emulated. Although internal wars and then the assault on Granada occupied the Spanish for most of the fifteenth century, these conflicts continued to foster an aggressive militarism in the Spanish, and especially Castilian, nobility. After 1492 new outlets were needed for these urges and the prospect of fame, land and gold ensured that a steady stream of hidalgos (noblemen) were available to lead expeditions in newly discovered lands. Extended contact with a different culture, that of North African Islam, helped to equip the Spanish to deal with the civilisations which they would encounter beyond Europe.

The nature of Spanish exploration differed markedly from that of the Portuguese. The Portuguese knew even before their voyages commenced that India, China and the spice islands existed. Their knowledge of the location of these areas was imperfect but they had clear objectives; the problem was how to reach them. Once they had reached the East they were content to capture strategic points and use these to control trade. The early Spanish voyages, too, started with a clear aim: to reach the East by sailing across the Atlantic. It soon became apparent, however, that the discovery of América opened up territory completely unknown to Europeans. The Spanish then began to establish colonies in the new lands in a manner never attempted by the Portuguese.

The establishment of the Spanish empire in America took a remarkably short time, little more than a generation. The process began with perhaps the most famous voyage of exploration of all, the trans-atlantic passage of Christopher Columbus in 1492. Columbus, a Genoese by birth, was an experienced navigator who in 1484 approached John II of Portugal with a plan to reach China by sailing westwards. As the Portuguese were putting all their resources into the exploration of the African route to the East, Columbus was unable to secure the necessary financial backing. He then turned to the court of Ferdinand and Isabella and, after a long delay, obtained financial support. The voyage of 1492, made with three ships and less than a hundred men, convinced Columbus and the Spanish court that a short-cut to the wealth of the East had been discovered. In fact, he had touched on various Caribbean islands as far west as Cuba *(see map on page 88)*. Nevertheless, the gold and placid Carib Indians he brought back stimulated a rush of volunteers in search of riches and an easy life. Columbus made further voyages to America but he never found the route to China for which he searched so desperately and he died, a disappointed man, in 1506.

Columbus had shown that there were lands worth exploring to the west and in the early sixteenth century, a number of expeditions vastly increased the geographical knowledge of Europe. Amerigo Vespucci, a Florentine who was sponsored at different times by both Spain and Portugal, sailed along the coast of South America in 1499 and 1501 and received such acclaim in Europe that the new continent was named after him. It was now clear that the lands in the west were a formidable barrier across the route to the East and not outlying islands of Asia. This was confirmed in 1513 when a Spaniard named Balboa, searching for gold on the American mainland, crossed the isthmus of Darien and became probably the first European to see the Pacific. The huge size of this hitherto unknown ocean only became apparent when a Portuguese in the service of Spain, Ferdinand Magellan, sailed a small fleet around the southern tip of South America in 1519. Suffering appalling privations, Magellan struggled across the Pacific, only to be killed by hostile natives in the Philippines. However, one of his ships, commanded by Sebastian del Cano, limped back to Spain—the first expedition to circumnavigate the globe.

At the same time as these voyages were taking place, the Spanish were exploring and colonising the islands of the Caribbean and investigating the coastline of Mexico. Rumours of a vastly wealthy empire in the interior of Mexico soon reached the Spanish. In 1519 an expedition of about six hundred Spaniards led by Hernando Cortés set out to find the source of these rumours. Cortés, an inspirational commander, marched into the heart of the huge Aztec empire, killed its ruler, Montezuma, and captured and destroyed its capital, Tenochtitlan. The Spanish advantages over the Aztecs had been the horse, well-made steel swords, cannon, help from local enemies of the Aztecs and considerable good fortune in that the Aztecs thought Cortés was the god Quetzalcoatl returning from exile in the east. Nonetheless, this was a staggering achievement for such a small force. The gold and silver of the Aztecs was looted and their lands occupied by the conquistadores. Mexico City arose on the site of Tenochtitlan. In 1522 Cortés was given the title of Governor of New Spain by Charles V and a fresh province had been added to the Spanish empire in the New World.

Encouraged by this success, other Spanish adventurers set out to explore the interior of America. By the early 1530s, another empire ripe for conquest had been discovered: that of the Incas, located high in the Peruvian Andes. In 1532 about 180 Spaniards led by Francisco Pizarro attacked the Incas, who were fortuitously weakened by civil war, captured and in 1533 killed their emperor, Atahualpa, and plundered the empire. Although the Incas revolted in 1536 and the Spanish almost ruined their position through internal feuding, Peru became another colony.

The conquests of Mexico and Peru opened huge areas for exploitation by the Spanish. As in the Caribbean islands, Spanish settlers allocated themselves vast estates or *encomiendas* which were usually confirmed by royal grant. The holder of each *encomienda* owed military service to the

Crown and in return was permitted to force the native population to work for him. The nature of this labour was mainly agricultural: natives were employed on plantations of sugar, cotton, vines and olives and in fields of barley, maize and wheat. Cochineal was regarded as being as valuable as gold as it was used as a dye in the European textile industries. Cocoa was grown as chocolate became an increasingly fashionable drink. European domestic animals flourished in the lush and ungrazed grasslands of the New World. Huge flocks of sheep and herds of cattle provided the settlers with all the meat they needed. Hides from the vast numbers of cattle in Mexico became the largest item by volume to be shipped back to Spain, providing a cheap and plentiful raw material for the leather industry there.

The impetus for the Spanish advance into the Americas was not, however, provided by profits from agriculture but rather the search for precious metals which could be sent to Spain at a great profit. Although the conquistadors had hoped for cascades of gold they were sadly disappointed. The native inhabitants of Hispaniola were early on stripped of their relatively small supplies of gold ornaments and then put to work panning for gold in the rivers of the island. The diminution of the work force and the decreasing returns of this source meant that Hispaniola was no longer a significant producer after 1530. The plunder of the Aztec and Inca empires provided windfalls of gold but finds in Chile and Colombia proved difficult to operate due to shortage of labour and inaccessible seams. Between 1500 and 1660 it is probable that about 300 tons of gold were transported from the New World to Spain.

Silver was a far more plentiful commodity. Once again, the native empires were a fruitful source of loot and northern Mexico yielded considerable quantities of ore. The major finds were, however, in the central Andes, especially at Potosi where whole mountains of silver ore awaited excavation. This site was opened up in 1545 and although it was remote and difficult to reach (5000 metres above sea level), soon there were some 13 000 workers (mostly Indians) on the site. The development of refining techniques using mercury, a method which was first used at Potosi in 1573, allowed more rapid exploitation of the silver. As much as 25 000 tons of silver were despatched to Spain in the period 1500 to 1660, with large amounts also being retained for use in the New World. These shipments were of the highest importance to Spain, allowing her the financial strength to dominate Europe but also providing her with the strategic problem of how to protect her silver convoys against envious enemies. Spain was not the only overseas market for New World silver. From the late sixteenth century, considerable quantities were sent from Acapulco in Mexico to Manila in the Philippines and from there distributed to China and other states in Asia. This trade made Manila an important commercial centre as silk, pearls and (ironically) gold were obtained from Asia and shipped back to America.

The profits from the export of silver and other goods and the affluence of many of the settlers engaged in farming allowed the construction of an impressive colonial structure. The Spanish founded new cities such as Lima in Peru and also adopted former Indian locations such as Mexico City. Buildings in the Spanish style were put up and the settlers took a pride in the prosperity and size of their new municipalities. A number of vigorous industries began to grow. Shipbuilding became a prominent activity in the Caribbean and on the Pacific coast of America, meeting the need for coastal traders and even warships. Another area of economic growth was textiles. The merino sheep was introduced to Mexico and by the end of the sixteenth century there were 25 cloth factories in the vicinity of Mexico City. Once again the unfortunate Indians provided slave labour in the textile factories.

The Spanish government was determined not to let the unruly conquistadores exist in a state of near-anarchy. The ruling oligarchies in the towns and cities of the New World proved to be a powerful obstacle to central authority but the power of the Crown's representatives gradually grew. Each province was under the control of a governor who was advised by an *audiencia* or court of appeal, who also watched for signs of disloyalty or incompetence. The *audiencia* was staffed by lawyers who acted not only as judges but also professional civil servants and provided the Spanish government with a competent and loyal bureaucracy.

Despite the problems of Spain in Europe, the Spanish colonies in the New World were to survive into the nineteenth century until the urge for independence could be held back no longer.

6. Europe and the World

It can be argued that the opening up of the rest of the world by European explorers in the fifteenth and sixteenth centuries was the single most important development in Early Modern European history. It is true that the discoveries of the Portuguese and Spanish had little immediate impact on the vast mass of the European population; new goods from America such as peanuts, tomatoes, turkeys and tobacco being regarded as mere curiosities for decades and the trade in luxuries from the East remaining the preserve of the rich. The most important developments were in the political and cultural spheres. Spain rose to a position of European pre-eminence owing to the flow of American silver and the credit which this enabled her to enjoy. For over a century she was the most feared power in Europe thanks to her empire and its resources. In terms of European civilisation, accepted views on history, geography and theology were challenged and revised. The Europeans gained a new self-confidence and a belief in their own superiority, summarised neatly by the remark of Hernan Perez de Oliva when he wrote in 1528 that 'Columbus set sail to unite the world and give to these strange lands the form of our own'. This arrogance was to grow in subsequent centuries and allow the numerically small peoples of Europe to assert their dominance in every continent on earth.

In the short term, apart from some examples of enlightened adminis-tration *(see page 325)*, this dominance was to bring the peoples subject to Europeans little more than interminable labour, a new religion variously assimilated and new diseases to which they had no resistance. In the long term there was to be the cultural and economic legacy of imperialism which played so great a part in shaping the modern world.

7. Bibliography

J H Parry *The Age of Reconnaissance* (Cardinal, 1973). J H Parry *The Spanish Seaborne Empire* (Hutchinson, 1976). C R Boxer *The Portuguese Seaborne Empire 1415–1825* (Hutchinson, 1969). G V Scammell *The World Encompassed* (Methuen, 1981). D Arnold *The Age of Discovery 1400–1600* (Lancaster Pamphlets, 1983). D O'Sullivan *The Age of Discovery 1400–1550* (Seminar Studies, Longman, 1984). J H Elliott *The Old World and the New* (OUP, 1970).

8. Discussion Points and Exercises

A *This section consists of questions or points that might be used for discussion (or written answers) as a way of expanding on the chapter and testing under-standing of it:*

1   Why was the geographical knowledge of the Europeans so limited at the start of the fifteenth century?
2   What problems did the explorers of the Early Modern period face?
3   'The motives which really mattered in leading to exploration were primarily economic.'
4   What were the main developments in ship design and navigation in the fifteenth and sixteenth centuries and how important were they?
5   What other factors allowed the European expansion to be so successful?
6   'Portugal's position was all-important in her taking the lead in overseas exploration.'
7   What form did Portugal's empire take?
8   Were Spain's reasons for embarking on discovery similar to those of Portugal?
9   Why did the Spanish engage in exploration later than the Portu-guese?
10   Why were the conquistadors so successful?
11   How did the Spanish empire differ from that of Portugal?

B *Essay questions*
1   What technical developments aided the Europeans in their voyages of discovery?

2 Why did so many of the voyages of discovery start from Portugal and Spain?

3 Why did Europeans make voyages of exploration in the fifteenth and sixteenth centuries?

4 What benefits did Portugal and Spain receive from their overseas empires?

5 How did the discovery of the New World affect Europe in the sixteenth century?

C *Exercise*

It is the year 1490. You are an explorer who is planning a voyage to open up the route to Asia. As part of your planning you are seeking sponsorship from a European monarch who is a rival to both the Spanish and the Portuguese.

Write two briefs, one describing the advantages of the African route and one the advantages of a western route.

Then write a concluding document explaining which route you would recommend.

V The Renaissance

1. Introduction

Many people have traditionally seen history as just a series of events. Nowadays in schools, there is much greater concern with empathy, the attempt to take on a past way of thinking in order to understand events from the inside and to see life as it would have been seen by a contemporary. Some cultural and social historians go further, feeling that trends in thought are far more important than superficial 'events' and that the study of them can reward us not just with a better, more human understanding of the past but also with a greater sense of the possibilities within ourselves.

This is not a new approach. A nineteenth century historian who preferred to study the way people thought rather than the political narrative was Jacob Burckhardt. He often relied on his intuition more than the primary sources and he made sweeping generalisations but he is still recognised as having written the classic work on the Renaissance. For Burckhardt, the political and social conditions in late medieval Italy, with the revival of classical learning as a catalyst, led to 'the discovery of the world and of man'. He meant that, instead of all eyes tending to heaven, men became determined to explore their environment and their own potential, concerns which have been taken to characterise the modern era up to the present day. This majestic view has been much disputed and refined by recent historians but the issues Burckhardt raised are still at the centre of debate and the Renaissance is still seen as the major cultural influence at the opening of the Early Modern period.

2. The Italian Humanists and the Origins of the Renaissance

The term Renaissance is derived from the Italian word *rinascita* meaning 'rebirth'. The sixteenth century art historian, Vasari, coined it to describe how what he saw as the stereotypes of medieval art had been done away with by about 1400 and replaced by a new, more vigorous and freer creativity based on a 'rebirth' of Roman and Greek classical principles. It is Vasari's depiction of artistic genius which has been passed down to us in familiar images of the Renaissance, such as Leonardo da Vinci and his *Mona Lisa*. The true origin of the Renaissance as a movement, however, was to be found in classical scholarship.

Around 1400 there began a craze for book collecting, following on a renewal of interest in classical literature led by the great poet Petrarch in the fourteenth century. Scholars mainly based in the central Italian city of Florence, such as Poggio Bracciolini, scoured monastic libraries to find older, more authentic versions of the texts of Latin authors or, where they were really lucky, to rediscover classical texts which had been lost altogether. This was not just a fad. Those enthusiastic scholars saw themselves as overthrowing the errors of centuries. Generations of their predecessors had relied on corrupt texts which had been copied out wrongly by scribes; or their way of thought had been cramped by medieval scholasticism, a Christianised version of the philosophy of the Greek Aristotle *(see page 24)*. Turning away from such scholastic philosophy, the critical scholars of early fifteenth century Italy were known as humanists because they taught that the humanities in the form of classical literature are the basis of civilised life.

It was the humanists' belief that, before any understanding could develop, there had to be a good grasp of pure and elegant Latin. Matteo Palmieri, writing in 1432, rejoiced in 'seeing our youth entering on the study of Latin by such order and method that in a year or two they come to speak and write that language with a fluency and correctness which it was impossible that our fathers could ever attain to at all'. This celebration of a classical language may seem odd for us with the current emphasis ever more on modern languages. But around 1400 Latin was of enormous importance as the international language and the medium of all scholarship. If you wanted to communicate you had to be effective in Latin. So the humanists studying Latin were concerned with rhetoric (the ability to express yourself) and with the moral problems involved. The subject which serves similar purposes today would be English.

Just as one can see a modern equivalent for the study of rhetoric, so it has been pointed out that this concern for classical literature was older than the fifteenth century Renaissance. Historians have busied themselves looking for the 'original' Renaissance. It has been sighted in the twelfth century or even as early as the reign of Charlemagne around 800 AD. The work of P O Kristeller has clarified the debate somewhat. He suggests that there have always been rhetoricians, professional men, scholars and teachers, concerned with expression as opposed to the logic of the philosophers. He sees the influence of the rhetoricians rising and falling throughout western history and he identifies the Italian Renaissance as just another phase when their profession was dominant. While this 'long view' is useful it is also necessary to find out what renewed the influence of rhetoricians in the particular Renaissance we are considering.

The career of Coluccio Salutati (1331–1406) provides some possible answers. He was a lawyer and a public servant as well as being a leading humanist. He worked as Chancellor (in effect, head of the civil service) in three Italian cities, culminating in Florence where he held office from 1375 to 1406. Salutati did not just pursue his humanist study of Latin as a private hobby, he introduced it into his public service. He particularly admired Cicero, the great writer from the age of Caesar, and he modelled his diplomatic correspondence and speeches on Cicero's fine rhetorical Latin. In doing this, Salutati set a trend. His rivals in other cities and his successors in Florence competed in writing the best, most classical Latin. And the rulers of Italy, appreciating the prestige and the subtleties of humanist diplomacy, encouraged that competition. Humanist scholarship and power politics could come together in a fertile relationship.

Salutati did not just provide the practical model of the humanist in political work; he also found in Cicero a justification of what he was doing. Cicero promoted the principle of *negotium*, the idea that scholars should not hide in their ivory towers but should be active in the world, letting their learning influence their public life and be influenced by it. While there had previously been politically active scholars, Petrarch, who had dominated attitudes towards classical Latin in the mid-fourteenth century, had not known all of Cicero's writings and was anyway committed to the principle of *otium*, retreat from the world into neutral and undisturbed pursuit of the truth. Now that semi-monastic ideal was discarded; the fifteenth century humanist was dedicated to public life, to *negotium*.

A cynic might point out that *negotium*, in the form of government service, paid better than *otium* but there are historians who cannot believe that the burst of Renaissance creative energy which followed was mercenary. Hans Baron in particular has argued that the Renaissance grew from *civic* humanism, that is, not just professional government service but the humanist's patriotic dedication to his community. For Baron, the model humanist was Leonardo Bruni (1370–1444) who was Chancellor of Florence for seventeen years from 1427. He not only believed in *negotium*, he saw his adopted city, Florence, as the most advanced form of community, a republic to be contrasted with the petty despotism of most Italian city-states. His views were clear in all his writings, particularly in his *History of the Florentine People* which glorified the republic and confirmed the Florentines in their growing conviction that, owing to their ideals and their skills, they were entitled to be regarded as the New Romans. So political conviction as well as political activity may have been crucial to the achievements of the Renaissance humanists.

The Baron thesis certainly clarifies the origins of the Renaissance. It tells us where it had to begin—Florence, set apart by its vigorous republican institutions. It even tells us more precisely when it began —civic humanism was galvanised in the 1390s when Florence was threatened by the aggressive dictator, Gian Galeazzo Visconti, Duke of Milan. There was a display of patriotic rhetoric which continued even after the threat to Florence was removed by the death of Gian Galeazzo in 1402. According to Baron, Bruni and other civic humanists found their inspiration, and therefore the inspiration of the Renaissance, in the liberty of Florence.

There are problems with the Baron thesis. Bruni was not exclusively dedicated to the republic of Florence—he spent part of his career working in the Curia, the papal civil service in Rome which provided jobs for many humanists. Bruni's writings do not all coincide neatly with the political events which are supposed to have stimulated them. And the liberty of Florence which lay behind civic humanism may have just been a rhetorical invention itself, used to disguise the narrowing oligarchy, the small group of influential men, which really controlled Florentine affairs.

Perhaps Florence needed the humanists, with their classical dignity and reassuring rhetoric, not to express an authentic republicanism but to hide just how precarious the city's republican institutions had become. From failed popular revolt (the Revolt of the Ciompi in 1378) to unofficial monarchy (discreet dominance by the Medici family from 1434), Florence passed through a period of profound transformation. The humanists with their optimism and eloquence could make the transition smoother. Likewise a little later in Rome the popes were seeking to re-establish themselves after the Great Schism *(see page 5)*; it was logical that the reassurance and persuasion of the humanists' commanding Latin could be employed there as well. Bruni was not the only humanist to move between Florence and Rome in search of employment. And so with the trend established, the other princes of Italy started to compete for the services of the best humanists and the Renaissance gradually spread. It is still the case, though, that the best in the early fifteenth century remained mostly in Florence. That may well be because it was there, in that precariously republican city, that they were most needed.

The cynic might still object that the humanists were nothing more than unusually plausible frauds, pumping out propaganda on political demand. This would be to ignore their genuine response to the classical world they studied and the intellectual innovations stimulated by it *(see page 108 on the developments in Renaissance thought)*. It is also the case that if the humanists had ignored political opportunities, their cultural field would have been much smaller—they would not have had the political élite as the builders of their libraries and the readers of their works. Rhetoric had to be kept in touch with political reality if the humanists were to have any social purpose.

The humanists did have social purpose; rhetoric is not necessarily the same as propaganda, it can express something more than what is called for by passing political interests. The patrons of the humanists had broken free from many of the medieval conventions and were looking for new values. In medieval thought poverty was an ideal; the humanist Barbaro, in contrast, was one amongst many who argued that wealth was necessary for the exercise of virtue in supporting your family and your community. There had been much wealth amassed in medieval Italy but there had been guilt to go with it. Now the Renaissance offered the idealisation of wealth. There was a Renaissance debate about nobility. The Italian élite, dependent on urban wealth, could not rely on ancient titles tied to the land to guarantee them their social identity, as aristocrats could elsewhere in Europe. The humanist Poggio argued that it was virtue, not ancient lineage, which made a nobleman. Other humanists did stress the breeding which came from belonging to a noble family but they meant the nobility derived from wealth and power in the cities, not feudal titles. The humanists were not just propagandists but also idealists and educators. For better or for worse, they liberated the conscience of the Italian ruling class.

The humanists did not just debate issues relevant to the moral and social dilemmas of their employers. They helped to develop a new moral vocabulary. For instance, the word 'virtù' in the Middle Ages carried more or less the sense of what we mean by virtue or sometimes manliness. In the hands of the humanists, 'virtù' became the moral duty to develop all your individual potential to the full, including your political potential. The humanists were idealising the pursuit of power. Lauro Martines has developed this theme fully in his recent book *Power and Imagination*, in which he shows how closely inter-related those two aspects of the Italian Renaissance were.

The Renaissance was neither just an event amongst scholars nor a style of propaganda. We have seen how much the humanists had to offer to Florence in particular and to the Italian élite in general. We must turn now to the unique environment in Italy which made sure that the Renaissance was not just a local or a passing fashion; an environment which made the relationship between patrons and humanists, power and imagination so fertile.

3. The Italian Environment

That Italy was characterised by the sharpest, most constant political competition has already been established *(see above and Introduction page 5)*. This arose from Italy being at the forefront of Europe in urban development. The cities of the north and centre of the peninsula had emerged in the form of communes, self-governing groups of citizens, having grown rich from the trade which started to 'take off' again in Italy from the eleventh century onwards. These communes over the next two or three centuries forced the feudal nobility of the countryside to integrate themselves into the political life of the cities and they struggled with their local bishops until they had reduced much of their power. There were independent cities elsewhere in Europe, especially in the Rhineland and in the Netherlands, but there were few which were as wealthy as their Italian counterparts or as politically precocious. The city was the centre of everything. As one Remigio put it around 1300: 'Destroy his city and a citizen is like a painted or a stone image, because he is thereby shorn from the vigour and work that he once had.' The obvious exemplar for such dedication to the city was that greatest of all city-states, ancient Rome. When the humanists proclaimed the values of ancient Rome to willing listeners, and when Renaissance artists, sculptors and architects offered their services, the cities, and not just Florence, supported their 'vigour and work'. There had to be some measure of stability, though, before the men of the Renaissance could get their message across.

The trouble with the medieval Italian cities being a law unto themselves was that their citizens could not always agree on what that law should be. There were struggles between the various families or neighbourhoods or guilds within the cities. It was quite normal for a home to incorporate a watchtower, patriotism not always extending to your street let alone the city. (In one town square, the inhabitants would gather to let off steam by throwing rocks at one another, a practice not unknown today but rarely accepted as an official sport.) With the faction fighting being so violent, it was always likely that any politically active intellectual would end up in exile for his pains, as happened to the great poet and philosopher, Dante, driven out of Florence in 1301. However, this served to make civic unity an even more desirable, if elusive, ideal. As Waley has put it, 'As hungry men dream of food and frozen men of warmth, so the men of the Italian republics dreamed of concord.' By 1400, the vitality of the communes was declining but so was the extensiveness of their internal struggles. A point of equilibrium was approaching where the humanists could give a gloss of concord and even greatness to the cities—the political reality underneath was still uncertain but by 1400 not so uncertain as to give the lie to the rhetoric or spoil the dream.

The decline of the communes meant that the republics became *signorie*, that is, despotisms. There were exceptions, primarily Venice and Florence, but the former was still more a maritime empire than an Italian city-state and, as we have already seen, the Florentine republic was sliding towards rule by one family, the Medici. Despotism had become the norm by 1400. For Burckhardt these despotisms were the seedbeds of the Renaissance and, through that, the modern world. The despots judged the world in terms of their own interests—modern individualism was born. They saw 'the state as a work of art . . . the fruit of reflection and careful adaptation'—that was the origin of rational constitutional development. These generalisations have been much qualified by Burckhardt's successors, but it is true that despots provided a working environment for humanists, once the fashion to employ them had caught on. The despots needed humanists to adorn their courts to give them an air of legitimacy.

Elsewhere in Europe, princes found security in inheritance of their title, with land as the measure of status and authority. In Italy it was more political skill which counted, with money as the measure of power; but neither gave sufficient security. (An exception was feudal Naples but that was the part of Italy least affected by the Renaissance.) A humanist Chancellor and a programme of general spending on the arts could give a despot some dignity to bolster his position. Sigismondo Malatesta, the vile dictator of Rimini, was the patron for one of the most perfect of Renaissance buildings, Alberti's Tempio Malatestiano. Sometimes the desire to express power could grow rather vulgar—Borso d'Este of Ferrara decided to have a mountain constructed in order to improve the view. More significant was to be the attitude of Lorenzo de Medici, the ruler of Florence from 1469 until 1492. He knew how he had earned his nickname, 'Il Magnifico'. He commented on the 663 755 gold florins he had spent on the arts, charity and in taxes (it is not odd that he made no distinction as they were all seen as being of public benefit): 'I think it casts a brilliant light on our estate and it seems to me that the monies were well spent and I am very well pleased with this'. So there was certainly the need and the will to spend on Renaissance culture, and there was the money.

Italy was already immensely wealthy by the early fourteenth century owing to its trade with the East. If anything, it started to decline from that time, a situation worsened by the onslaught of bubonic plague after 1347 with no preventive measures possible. The population of Florence, around 95 000 in 1338, had dropped to 40 000 by 1427. Economic and demographic downturns do not seem propitious for a great cultural movement but actually they may have helped. The fewer people to inherit accumulated wealth, the greater amount there was to inherit per capita—to spend on culture. And while there were fewer trading opportunities, this allowed for more idle money to be invested in culture. In general, Italy's wealth had accumulated sufficiently during the earlier Middle Ages to afford cultural extravagance during the period of its relative decline.

It was not just the quantity of Italian wealth that affected the Renaissance but also the techniques by which it was controlled. For instance, with their innovation of double-entry book-keeping (it sounds very dull but it can stop you going bankrupt), the Italians had developed one of the basic, rational devices of modern capitalism. The minds behind such a device could appreciate the down-to-earth, rational ethos of the ancient Romans and the humanists who imitated them. Urbanisation and commerce had given the Italian élite a worldly outlook which favoured the Renaissance and its secular, even pagan, values of the classical world.

Talk of secularism and paganism makes it seem as though the Renaissance displaced a weakened Christianity in Italy. Buckhardt suspected that this was so but he ignored the fact that the vast majority of Italians were entirely traditional in their Christian devotions and he underestimated the capacity of the Renaissance élite to reconcile their secular interests with religious beliefs. One Florentine businessman gave a regular percentage of his takings to charity, marking 'to God' in his accounts. It was in line with this attitude to commission a religious painting by a Renaissance artist and donate it to the parish church, thereby earning prestige, of course, as well as religious merit. A modestly clad Virgin Mary was still a far more common figure in Renaissance art than a naked Venus and it has been estimated that 90 per cent of Renaissance paintings were of Religious subjects. The social and intellectual context of Renaissance art was still Christian. In literature, too, the values of the Renaissance did not seem necessarily to contradict Christianity; even the pagan philosophy of Plato was to be reconciled with Christianity by Marsilio Ficino, as we shall see. The Renaissance was to flourish in an environment which was not demonstrably less Christian than other parts of Europe.

The maintenance of Christian belief in the environment of the Renaissance did not stop Italian churchmen being worldly in many of their interests. The Marquis of Mantua showed the tone of Italian ecclesiastical life in the 1460s in a comment to his son: '*Although* you are a cardinal, be religious and observe your obligations'. With the Pope in Rome and as many dioceses in Italy as the rest of Europe put together, the Church provided rich pickings for the Italian élite. For example, the Medici began as rulers of Florence but in the early sixteenth century they were to provide two popes. Bishops were as interested as secular rulers in the wordly glory that could come through learning and the arts. The Italian Church, as much as the chancelleries of Italy's cities, was to give employment to humanists like Bruni and to artists, and thereby provide an institutional basis for the Renaissance.

It was not just the social and institutional environment in Italy which fostered the Renaissance. Pevsner, the historian of architecture, even comments on the Florentine climate being 'clear, keen and salutary' and suggests that this was significant in the clear rationalism of the Renaissance vision. Easier to establish as a stimulus to the Renaissance vision are the classical remains which abounded in what had been the heart of the Roman empire. Much of what the tourist sees today has been dug out of the ground since the Renaissance but the great landmarks, such as the Colosseum, were magnificently visible even then and challenged the men of the Renaissance to look closely at the culture which had produced them. And there were numerous reminders of that culture in objects such as the sarcophagi, Roman marble tombs decorated with relief sculpture, which had often been taken over for Christian burials and so were conveniently situated for study in cloisters and quiet churchyards. Given these plentiful remains, it is surprising that Italians had not tried to copy their Roman ancestors earlier. But having something in view is one thing, taking the trouble to look is another. It was the literary inspiration of the humanists which caused Italians to appreciate the classical remains around them. Clearly the development of Italy, in its urban society and politics, its economics, its religion and its culture, created an environment favourable to the Renaissance. This does not mean that it

105

was an inevitable cultural event. It depended much for the form it took on the work of those key humanists in Florence around 1400. However, once established, the Renaissance could spread relatively easily through the rest of Italy. And its message of classical revival could spread through every aspect of the culture of the Italian élite, especially the visual arts.

4. The Visual Arts in the Early Renaissance

Words in a textbook can only inadequately describe the changes in the arts which came about during the Renaissance. It is necessary to go to an art gallery to look at a Renaissance collection or, best of all, to go to Italy to experience the variety and exuberance of what Italians painted, sculpted and built in the period after 1400. All a textbook can do is to suggest some of the social conditions in which creativity flourished and some of the breakthroughs made by key artists.

Artists in the Middle Ages did not have a distinct social status. They were classed as craftsmen. The value of their paintings was usually determined by the costs of the materials rather than the artistic quality; the most valuable painting was the one most laden with gold leaf. Even when they created what today would be thought of as a masterpiece, they won no more fame for it than their fellow craftsmen did for making cloth or nails. In contrast, there was to be nothing anonymous about Renaissance artists. The greatest of them developed distinct styles and were recognised for it, sometimes to the extent of being seen almost as heroes. Gradually artists ceased to be ordinary craftsmen and rose in social status, as members of the Italian social élite competed for their services.

This was a feature of the individualism which Burckhardt emphasised but it should not be confused with the romantic image of the artist working in heroic isolation. All Renaissance artists were trained in a *bottega*, a workshop. As apprentices they would learn basic techniques from their master who would then employ them in the painting of background detail. The workshop of the medieval guilds had not been entirely abandoned. However, the aspiring Renaissance artist would leave his workshop and look at the work of other masters. He would learn from the style of other artists in order to create his own. It is this combination of individualism and co-operation which made Renaissance art so fertile in new ideas. We shall consider some of these new ideas in relation to painting first, then sculpture and finally architecture.

It was the work of Masaccio (1401–28) which was the model for Renaissance painters. Even the confidently individual Leonardo da Vinci (1452–1519) acknowledged that he took much inspiration from the Brancacci Chapel in Florence which contains Masaccio's most famous work. He was not the first to break away from medieval conventions—a hundred years earlier Giotto had won fame for introducing into painting the movement and emotion of a dramatic situation with some space for the action. But Masaccio was the first systematically to paint everything as seen from a one-point perspective, with the size of the objects portrayed depending on whether they were close to the viewer or far away. This technique enabled the artist to model images in three dimensions and to get away from the flat stereotypes of medieval art; it gave the space in which the image of living people could be created. Such a technique might, however, just allow for clever illusion. Masaccio offered something more. He peopled the space his technique created with beautifully composed figures expressing human dignity. This was the same dignity found in classical sources and celebrated by the humanists. Indeed, Masaccio took inspiration direct from classical sources; he looked at Roman statues as well as at living people when he was designing the figures in his painting. For all the fame of his successors, he was the original Renaissance artist.

There are more contenders for the title of original Renaissance sculptor. In 1401 in Florence, there was a competition to decide who should create the sculpture which was to adorn some new doors for the Baptistery, that prominent building next to the Cathedral which was thought by many to be Roman. The winner against stiff competition was Lorenzo Ghiberti (1378–1455). One of the doors he created was to be called by Michelangelo the gate of Paradise. He worked to themes suggested by the humanist Bruni and he used perspective to give an appearance of depth to the sculpture which was in relief, that is, fairly flat up against the doors. He was even the first artist to announce his individuality by writing about himself. So Ghiberti has some claim to being the originator of Renaissance sculpture.

He was, however, rapidly surpassed by his pupil, Donatello (1386–1466) who went on to look more closely at classical examples and at the human body and then, with unique skill in handling stone or bronze, created masterpiece after masterpiece. He was to break much more completely from the stiffness of medieval sculpture, incorporating into his work dramatic expression and a sense of fluid human movements. Donatello's study of David after the slaying of Goliath was the first nude statue since classical times. His portrayal of the mercenary Gattemalata astride his horse was the first equestrian statue since that of Marcus Aurelius 1100 years before. As well as completing much fine work himself, he established many of the possibilities which later Renaissance sculptors were to explore.

More extraordinary perhaps than any other in his contribution to the Renaissance was Filippo Brunelleschi (1377–1446). It was he who first developed the systematic perspective which was to be employed in such a significant way by Masaccio. It was he who was Ghiberti's closest challenger in the competition over the design of the Baptistery doors. He even sculpted a crucifix in a way that Donatello had said could just not be done. But he is remembered most often as the first Renaissance architect.

He accompanied Donatello in his study of classical remains and he learnt not just the classical details, but the rules of proportion which had given Roman architecture a sense of harmony as well as grandeur. In, say, the Pazzi Chapel by Brunelleschi the columns are just the right height and breadth and the arches are at just the right elevation to fit the rest of the building perfectly. Even for those citizens who might not appreciate a refined sense of proportion, Brunelleschi had something to offer. A century earlier the Florentines had begun to build a magnificent cathedral but they had not completed it. Brunelleschi provided the solution to the problem of covering the central space. He designed a dome which surpassed the engineering even of the Roman Pantheon. When they were homesick, Florentines started to say they longed for the cathedral and its dome. Bunelleschi had originated Renaissance architecture by learning from Roman techniques and architectural values. He also brought to his fellow Florentine citizens something of Roman greatness.

Masaccio, Ghiberti and Donatello, Brunelleschi—in their careers can be found much of what characterised the artistic Renaissance. It is hard to explain how such a cluster of genius arose in one generation after 1400 and in one city, Florence, with a population rather smaller than modern Surbiton. Some would put it down to extraordinary fortune. Some art historians see it as the logic of art's internal development, one idea stimulating the next. But the intellectual atmosphere created by the Florentine humanists with their call to revive Roman culture both helped the artists to develop their own ideas and conditioned an audience to welcome their innovations. In the end that audience counts almost as much as the creators. It was the ruling class of Florence, or at least part of it, which was to make the decision over the Baptistery doors. It was the ruling élite, first of Florence and then of Italy as a whole, which was to pay for Renaissance art and was therefore in a position to make the final choice as to its direction. Happily the Italian patrons seemed to see themselves in the dignified figures and harmonious spaces of Renaissance painting, sculpture and architecture. With these patrons looking on them with tolerance, and sometimes even sympathy, and added to this the general advantages of the Italian environment noted earlier, the artists of the Renaissance were able to develop their remarkable talents freely and fully.

5. The Development of Renaissance Thought

A discussion of the humanists and the artists of the early Renaissance should give a sense of the values of the movement that was going to affect the whole of élite culture in Early Modern Europe. Those values, however, were not fixed. Apart from innovative thinkers and artists stimulating each other, the gradual retrieval of the classical past proved a continuing source of inspiration.

More and more classical texts were collected, edited and made available to those educated enough to read them. They could be consulted in new libraries, such as the St Mark's Library founded by Cosimo de Medici in 1437 and the first one to be endowed by a layman since Roman times. Scholars' use of different versions of classical texts enabled them to arrive at more accurate editions. The works of the Roman poet Virgil, for instance, had been known throughout the Middle Ages but it was not until 1470 that an edition came out that was reliably close to the original. Artists as well as scholars could be inspired by what they found in libraries. Painters could read the Roman author Pliny on the theory of art, which partly made up for the fact that no original Roman painting had yet been unearthed. Architects could read Vitruvius whose writings, largely forgotten for 1500 years and then brought to light in an Alpine monastery around 1410, became the standard textbook of classical architecture. But the most significant fertilisation of Renaissance thought came from the rediscovery of Greek.

In some ways Greek thought, at least that of the great philosopher Aristotle and the mathematician Euclid, had never been lost. It had been absorbed into medieval thinking but only through Arabic translations and it had been overlaid by the logical intricacies of scholasticism. The original Greek texts were available in the Byzantine Empire but the Christians of the Church of Rome in western Europe put up a sort of cultural wall against the Greek Orthodox Church of the Byzantine Empire in eastern Europe. Then around 1400, the Italian humanists reacted against what they saw as the obscure thinking of the scholastic philosophers and saw the necessity of reviving Greek thought as well as Roman. The trouble was, while Latin was in use although waiting to be purified, no-one understood Greek. Petrarch had a copy of Homer's poetry and he would kiss it to acknowledge its greatness but he could not read it. He hired a monk called Pilatus to translate it but the monk, ill-advisedly standing too near to a ship's mast in a storm, was killed by lightning and no successor could be found. It was not until 1396 that a scholar from Constantinople, Emanuel Chrysoloras, became the first Professor of Greek at Florence and began the gradual process whereby the Greek language and Greek thought were re-introduced into western Europe during the fifteenth and sixteenth centuries. Texts were brought from Constantinople and after the fall of that city to the Ottoman Turks in 1453, refugee scholars came as well. The cultural effects were enormous. The Greeks had been the originators in western thought of science, of medicine, of drama (tragedy and comedy), of history, of geography. The insights of that classical world opened up a new world of ideas as the Renaissance developed. And it seemed to many that the greatest insights came from Plato.

We think reality is the world we see around us. Plato, writing about 400 BC, thought that the world we see is just the shadow of what is real and that the job of a philosopher is to see through this world to the reality of perfect forms beyond. Modern science makes it hard for us to appreciate this but Marsilio Ficino (1433–99) did; he established a group of neo-Platonists in Florence who were to turn the Renaissance into a philosophical as well as a literary and artistic movement.

Ficino and his fellow neo-Platonists influenced all the men of Renaissance culture around them. Both Cosimo de Medici and his grandson Lorenzo Il Magnifico, those unofficial rulers of Florence, were friends as well as patrons to Ficino. Botticelli developed the symbolism of his painting from Ficino's ideas, especially in his masterpiece known as *Primavera*. Poets such as Poliziano absorbed the ideal of Platonic love —not just non-sexual affection as it is thought of today but the neo-Platonists' vision of spiritual love transcending the merely physical. Theological debate was sharpened by the neo-Platonic ideas about the soul as the immortal essence of man.

One of Ficino's main aims was to explore such ideas in order to reconcile Platonic philosophy with Christianity. One of the most remarkable of Ficino's disciples, who went too far with the theology at least for the Pope's liking, was Pico della Mirandola (1463–94). He also gave a definition of man which seemed to sum up and go further than the earlier views of the Renaissance humanists on the dignity of man. In 1486 he wrote as if God were speaking to newly created man:

> The nature of other creatures, which has been determined, is confined within the bounds prescribed by Us. You, who are confined by no limits, shall determine for yourselves your own nature, in accordance with your own free will, in whose hand I have placed you ... We have made you
> 5 neither heavenly nor earthly, neither mortal nor immortal, so that, more freely and more honourably the moulder and maker of yourself, you may fashion yourself in whatever form you shall prefer. You shall be able to descend among the lower forms of being, which are brute beasts; you shall be able to be reborn out of the judgment of your own soul into the higher
> 10 beings which are divine.
>   ... Whatever seed each man cultivates will grow and bear fruit in him. If the seeds are vegetative, he will be like a plant; if they are sensitive, he will become like the beasts; if they are rational, he will become like a heavenly creature; if intellectual, he will be an angel and a son of God ...

1   *What distinguishes man from the beasts (lines 1–4)?*
2   *All humanists regarded man as being able to improve himself in some way. In what way is Pico going further in this optimism than the civic humanists of the early Renaissance (lines 4–10 and refer back to page 101)?*
3   *There is a view that the Renaissance became increasingly élitist. Is there any evidence from Pico's writings above to support that view or to contradict it?*

During the fifteenth century, the subject of the Renaissance seemed to have become Man rather than men, the ideal or perfect form of humanity rather than the citizens of ancient Rome or contemporary Florence. At the start of the century the status of artists had risen; by the end of the century some were thought of as geniuses. They were men like Leonardo da Vinci, Raphael and Michelangelo—the heroes of what is known as the High Renaissance at the end of the fifteenth century and the beginning of the sixteenth century.

6. The High Renaissance

Leonardo da Vinci (1452–1519) is still the model of 'a genius'. Although he often failed to finish what he started, he always did enough to show his unique insight whether it was in military engineering or the anatomy of the human body, in his theoretical grasp of the principle of the helicopter or in his painting. The people he portrayed in art were created with techniques such as the clever use of light and shade and newly introduced oil painting, but Leonardo's people are more than that—even when armed only with a piece of charcoal Leonardo could make his subjects seem full of complex meaning and beauty. He was so highly regarded in the end that Francis I saw it as a coup in terms of cultural prestige to tempt Leonardo to come and live near him at Amboise.

One of the few artists to rival Leonardo was Raphael (1483–1520). He spent most of his career in Rome where he decorated the Papal apartment with frescoes (painting onto fresh plaster). His subjects included 'The School of Athens' showing Plato and other Greek philosophers, illustrating the Greek emphasis which the Renaissance had acquired. Raphael painted many versions of the Madonna and Child—his Mary and Jesus were so ideal as to be almost too sweet but for the firmness of his composition. With Raphael, there was no sense of ordinary citizens featuring in his art, even though his portraits were unsentimental and full of vitality.

Michelangelo (1475–1564) felt even less for the ordinary citizen in his art. He was consumed by the ideal, expressing contempt for Flemish art which, for all its brilliant technique, was far too concerned with realism. When Michelangelo sculpted he did not just copy from nature; he felt that there was a figure already in the block of marble struggling to free itself. Like the neo-Platonists, he saw his role as seeking a reality beyond what was ordinarily visible. On the ceiling of the Sistine Chapel in the Vatican, he depicted the Creation of Man itself, the most familiar image since then of divine and artistic inspiration. Around the Bible stories shown on the Chapel's ceiling, Michelangelo painted characters from mythology and a series of heroic male nudes which were thought to be unsurpassable as portrayals of the human body. And being unsurpassable was the problem—for all the glory that Michelangelo had brought to art he made it difficult for lesser artists to find new things to express within the Renaissance tradition. He and the other great artists of the High Renaissance had, as it were, said it all. Apart from the Venetians, who were developing their own tradition, the artists of the Italian Renaissance gradually turned to Mannerism, imitation or exaggeration of the *maniera* or style developed in the High Renaissance particularly by Michelangelo.

7. History and Political Thought

The neo-Platonists dominated later Renaissance thought but not exclusively. The development of humanist ideas in a rather different direction can be seen in the writing of history. The later Renaissance historians, such as Francesco Guicciardini (1483–1540), continued, like Bruni before them, to imitate classical historians such as the Roman Livy and to look for reality in the world around them and its past rather than searching for an ideal reality beyond. Although they often had a political or moral motive for writing history, historians like Guicciardini used their sources with some discrimination and excluded what was most obviously myth from their analysis. Rather than speculating a great deal about the intervention of God or the Fates, they wrote about down-to-earth causes and human motivations. Although not as scientific in their methods of research, they resembled modern historians more than they did their medieval predecessors, the usually superstitious and uncritical monastic chroniclers. And rather than fleeing everyday reality like their contemporaries the neo-Platonists, they tried to meet it head on—ever more unpleasant though this became with the onset of the Italian Wars after 1494.

When he came to write his *History of Italy* in the 1530s Guicciardini, for all that his account was minutely detailed, was not engaged in scholarship for its own sake. He was trying to explain why Italy, once great, had collapsed in the face of foreign invasion and internal disorder after 1494. A friend of his was to employ history in a more radical way as part of an early type of political science, designed to show how the disorder might be reversed. He was a Florentine named Niccolò Machiavelli (1469–1527).

Machiavelli had been an earnest politician but also a failed one. From 1498 he had taken part in the republican government of Florence, renewed after the Medici had fled in 1494. However, in 1512 the Medici returned, with Spanish help, as Dukes of Florence. The Republic was no more and Machiavelli was forced into retirement at his country farm. He was bored by the rural routine and was only happy when he could shut himself away in his study, put on his robes of state and, through his books, converse with the classical authors about history and politics. For him, it was through his humanist imagination that the doors of power could once again be opened. This is in contrast to the humanists, such as Bruni, of a century before. Their classical learning had opened to them the doors of power in reality, not just in imagination.

Machiavelli did not, however, intend to remain only in the realm of imagination. He was quite prepared to work for the Medici and so in 1513, almost as a job application, he wrote a manual on how to be a successful ruler, calling it simply *The Prince*. The Medici ignored it and it was not published until 1532 but it then came to be regarded as the most scandalous product of the Renaissance. Most writing on politics had told a prince how to be good, Machiavelli told him how to win:

. . . since my intention is to say something that will prove of practical use to the inquirer, I have thought it proper to represent things as they are in real truth, rather than as they are imagined. Many have dreamed up republics and principalities which have never in truth been known to exist; the gulf
5 between how one should live and how one does live is so wide that a man who neglects what is actually done for what should be done learns the way to self-destruction rather than self-preservation. The fact is that a man who wants to act virtuously in every way necessarily comes to grief among so many who are not virtuous . . .
10 . . . there are two ways of fighting: by law or by force. The first is natural to men, and the second to beasts. But as the first way often proves inadequate one must needs have recourse to the second . . .

. . . as a prince is forced to know how to act like a beast, he should learn from the fox and the lion; because the lion is defenceless against traps and a
15 fox is defenceless against wolves. Therefore one must be a fox to recognise traps, and a lion to frighten off wolves . . .

The most prominent example in *The Prince* is Cesare Borgia, the son of Pope Alexander VI. He conquered an anarchic and violent region known as the Romagna and appointed one Remirro de Orco to restore peace and stability. Machiavelli describes how Cesare reviewed the situation once that was done:

Knowing also that the severities of the past had earned him a certain amount of hatred, to purge the minds of the people and to win them over completely he determined to show that if cruelties had been inflicted they
20 were not his doing but prompted by the harsh nature of his minister. This gave Cesare a pretext; then, one morning, Remirro's body was found cut in two pieces on the piazza at Cesena, with a block of wood and a bloody knife beside it. The brutality of this spectacle kept the people of the Romagna for a time appeased and stupefied.

1 How does Machiavelli justify his approach (lines 1-9)?
2 For Machiavelli, 'virtù' (see early Renaissance definition on page 102) involved acting like a lion or a fox as necessary (lines 10–16). What political characteristics did these animals symbolise?
3 How does Cesare's disposal of Remirro (lines 17–24) illustrate those political characteristics? What might have happened if such brutal action had not been taken?
4 Compare Machiavelli's view of mankind as expressed above with that of Pico della Mirandola as quoted on page 110.

Machiavelli cannot be judged by *The Prince* alone. He developed a much more complete philosophy in a substantial work known as *The Discourses* inspired by the writing of the Roman historian, Livy. He made clear his cyclical theory of history—all states move from rule by a prince through rule by an aristocracy to rule by the people. The last stage necessarily degenerates into anarchy until a leader emerges, ruthless and effective enough to make himself prince, and the cycle begins again. Given this theory, a prince acting like Cesare Borgia was an antidote to anarchy, perhaps an evil but a necessary evil.

From one point of view, Machiavelli was the first political scientist. He developed his theory quite systematically, backing it up with evidence drawn from history and from contemporary affairs, and trying hard to exclude any prejudices. This does not mean that his conclusions would all be accepted today but a refined version of his method is.

From another point of view Machiavelli signalled the end of the Renaissance in Italy. The tremendous Renaissance optimism, culminating in neo-Platonism, was turning to the pessimism about mankind contained in *The Prince*. And Machiavelli's little manual was to win him nothing but condemnation. However realistic he might have tried to be, he was in the end powerless. That was to be the fate of other Renaissance men as their social and political context changed out of all recognition.

8. The Changing Social and Political Context of the Renaissance

From its beginning, the Renaissance had been associated with the ruling élite in Italy rather than with the people as a whole. However, that élite had been quite broadly based. In Florence, the Medici became the major patrons but there were other bankers besides them, and merchants made rich by the *arte della lana*—the Florentine cloth industry—and powerful guilds, all of whom could support scholars and artists. However, as society became ever more stable and economic opportunities diminished there was less social mobility and the Renaissance élite grew more exclusive. Even more exclusive were the smaller courts to which the Renaissance spread and where so much depended on the whims of individual rulers. Nevertheless, while the ruling élites retained their tradition of patronage and while the individual princes were discriminating and in control of their own destinies, the Renaissance continued to develop. But the Italian social and political environment was not secure against foreign invasion.

In 1494, the French invaded Italy and from then until 1559 the peninsula was the battleground of the great powers of Europe *(see Chapters III, VIII and IX)*. In Florence the effects were devastating. The then head of the Medici family, Piero, was forced to flee in 1494, having bungled the diplomacy with regard to the invasion. In his place a Dominican monk named Savonarola came to dominate the Florentines through his powerful preaching. He told them that the invaders were the scourge of God punishing them for their sins. Amongst their sins could be numbered those editions of pagan authors and those paintings which were not austerely religious enough. Savonarola organised bonfires of such vanities and converts to his exclusively religious cause included Pico della Mirandola and even the painter of that pagan nude in *The Birth of Venus*, Sandro Botticelli. It seemed as though the era of the Renaissance had ended and the era of repentance had begun. This was not yet so. Savonarola eventually lost his influence and was burnt in

1498, and the republican government which succeeded him not only employed Machiavelli but also commissioned that great symbol of republican defiance, Michelangelo's statue of *David*, the giant slayer. The trouble was that the republic could not slay giants and, as we have seen, it succumbed to Spanish dominance and the restoration of the Medici, their power now openly ducal rather than disguised by republican forms. After one brief outburst of renewed republicanism in 1527–30, Florence settled down into a dull stability. The city became essentially provincial. The Florentine Renaissance was over.

The Italian Wars brought internal disruption and domination by either the French or the Spanish to many other city-states besides Florence. For a while, the Italian princes had formed leagues and tried to play one power off against another but their famed diplomacy proved to be no protection *(see page 61)*. Those princes had used culture to express their power; during the Italian Wars it gradually became a substitute for it. A Spanish-style rigidity set into court life which inhibited innovation. Princes, compensating for their diminishing power, wanted to control artists rather than to befriend them and sympathise with their aims. This can be seen in the way that the free atmosphere of the open *bottega* or artistic workshop of the fifteenth century turned into the rule-bound formality of the private academies, many of which were organised for the princes of the sixteenth century. There was less wealth to pay for culture as the wars took their toll on the Italian economy. The rhetoric which had joined the early humanists with the ruling élite degenerated into servile praise or vicious satire, both of which were well exemplified by one Aretino (1492–1556) who was avidly read or lividly banned all over Italy. As the princes' foreign policies became futile the chancelleries, which had fostered the talents of the early humanists, became far more concerned with just keeping the people under control. And in the end that needed guns not rhetoric.

At first Rome, with the wealth and prestige brought to it by the Papacy, seemed immune from this. It had maintained that immense confidence in which the Renaissance flourished. While wars raged across Italy, the artists of the High Renaissance, such as Raphael, worked in Rome and humanists could still find employment for their talents as in the case of the great linguist and philosopher Pietro Bembo, who became the Pope's secretary in 1521. This atmosphere was not to last. The confidence became diplomatic over-confidence and Rome was sacked in 1527 by a mutinous imperial army. The atmosphere thereafter was one of pessimism. Michelangelo, for instance, did not abandon Rome, but around 1536 he painted his sobering vision of the Last Judgement in the Sistine Chapel, contrasting sharply with the hope in his image of the Creation painted before the Sack of Rome. Political circumstances cannot entirely determine what may have been a fundamental change in artistic values but they can confirm a trend.

Only in Venice did the Renaissance outlast the middle of the sixteenth century. That republic was ruled by a closed group of aristocratic families but scholars and artists tended to work in harmony with them rather than being controlled by them, as was the trend elsewhere in Italy by that time. And there was that necessary degree of freedom to allow for innovation. The maritime republic escaped foreign domination. Also the Counter-Reformation was limited in its impact there—that is best illustrated by the case of Veronese who was prosecuted for painting the Last Supper as an entertaining, lavish dinner party: he merely changed the title to *the Feast in the House of Levi* and all was well.

It was not just the more creative environment in Venice which helped to prolong the Renaissance there. The city's artists also had a distinct contribution to make owing to their tradition of *colore*, expressing much more through colour than through the drawing or *disegno* which characterised earlier Renaissance art. The artist who dominated in Venice, and indeed the European art world of his day, was Titian (1489–1576). He painted masterpieces right up to his death at the age of 87. But by then even the Venetian Renaissance was on the wane.

The Serene Republic, as it was known, had entered into its period of relative decline by the end of the sixteenth century. The economy was being hit by foreign competition. The Venetian aristocrats were turning their attention away from the city and towards the villas they were building as rural retreats, 332 of them constructed in the seventeenth century. Machiavelli had hated his rural retreat, craving the excitement of power. The Venetian élite seemed to be happiest away from the strains of the city. The Renaissance, which had thrived amidst urban life and its politics, was no longer an Italian phenomenon.

The Renaissance did not just expire, though, as it came to an end in Venice. Ways of transmitting it had been developed as it spread through Italy and it was carried across the Alps, albeit in a modified form, beyond the social and political environment in which it had originated.

9. The Transmission of the Renaissance

The Renaissance was transmitted through education. That made it durable despite the changes in its social and political context. The earliest humanist educators included Vittorino da Feltre who founded a school in Mantua in 1423 and Guarino da Verona who founded his school at Ferrara in 1436. These schoolmasters provided the model of Renaissance education. The curriculum was based on the study of classical texts, mainly Latin authors but Greek was introduced as well. To some this might not sound exciting but the subject matter—the speeches, the history, the poetry—was well adapted to the needs of a wide range of pupils, medieval education having been directed mostly towards would-be churchmen. And the Roman ideal of 'a healthy mind in a healthy body' was adopted, games being an important part of the curriculum. In Vittorino's school, girls as well as boys were admitted and poor students who showed promise studied in the school on an equal basis with the children of the rich and even with the Gonzaga family which ruled the city. It was, however, more normal as the Renaissance developed for the majority of pupils to be boys and to be drawn from the wealthier section of society. Privilege did not mean that the boys were always pampered. Some teachers taught through encouragement but many were to regard regular corporal punishment as a more effective teaching aid than gentle words. Still, most of the pupils who left such schools carried with them a respect for humanist learning, however painfully acquired, which kept the Renaissance alive.

Humanist schools originated in Italy but they were not confined to the peninsula. The Renaissance educational ideal spread all over Europe. In England, for instance, it was embodied in the grammar schools which were set up in the sixteenth century. (And, even though the study of classics has declined, the humanist ideal of a balanced curriculum survives in modern schools.) All over Europe in the Early Modern period the ruling classes, from those who ran the shires in England to the nobility of Poland or the burghers of Swiss cities, came to experience the Renaissance through their education.

Critical to the success of these Renaissance schools was the fact that they had an increasing number of books available. This was due to printing (see page 25). It can be argued that printing, developing from the second half of the fifteenth century, was vital for the Renaissance both to last and to spread. The movement had begun in part as a reaction against the errors of medieval scribes. Before printing, there had been the danger that once the generation of energetic early humanists had passed there would have been a lapse back into the old ways of copying errors. And without printing, the libraries, those storehouses of Renaissance knowledge, would not have become so widespread or have been built up so quickly. In the scriptorium where scribes toiled the Renaissance could have been worn away. It could flourish in the printer's workshop in any part of Europe.

The spread of the Renaissance was not just a technical matter of educational systems and movable type. It represented an ideal. In its early form of civic humanism, it had been confined to the urban élites of Italy. The feudal aristocracy north of the Alps had very different interests and clung to their own Gothic culture rather than import the Renaissance from Italy. However, the Renaissance ideal in Italy was not static. In succession to the civic humanist came 'the Renaissance man', a character much more likely to be international in his appeal.

The Renaissance man is the archetypal all-rounder. He is learned and courteous, poetic and well-dressed, but he can also run, jump, swim, ride and fight, all to perfection. The model of this universal man, if he can ever have existed, was Leon Battista Alberti. Modesty was not one of his qualities, as he showed when he wrote in the 1460s about the extraordinary variety of qualities he did possess. Alberti could not be directly imitated—he was a great architect and a leading theorist of painting amongst his other attributes—but the ideal of versatility appealed to competitive men of many European élites. The ideal was embodied in what amounted to a textbook for the aspiring Renaissance man, *The Book of the Courtier* by Baldassare Castiglione.

Castiglione was a diplomat and a government adviser who worked for various princes and finally for the Pope. He was admired by many of those with whom he came into contact, including the Emperor Charles V. He was an international figure and so when *The Courtier* was published in 1528 it was greeted with much interest. It was based on Castiglione's experiences at the court of Urbino, a tiny principality in central Italy sustained mainly by what its Duke could earn as a leading mercenary. Those earnings were good and paid for the construction of one of the finest palaces in Europe in which a refined court of noblemen and intellectuals was assembled. Castiglione claimed to be describing how those courtiers related to one another, what they did and what they talked about in their debates:

> Noble birth is like a bright lamp that makes clear and visible both good deeds and bad, and inspires and incites to high performance as much as fear of dishonour or hope of praise; and since their deeds do not possess such noble brilliance, ordinary people lack both this stimulus and the fear of
> 5 dishonour . . .
> I have very seldom known men who are good at anything who do not praise themselves. It seems to me that it is only right to allow them to do so, since when a man who knows he is of some worth sees himself being ignored, he grows angry at the way his qualities are hidden from sight . . .
> 10 There are also many other sports, although they do not directly require the use of weapons, are closely related to arms and demand a great deal of manly exertion. Among these it seems to me that hunting is the most important, since in many ways it resembles warfare; moreover, it is the true pastime of great lords, it is a suitable pursuit for a courtier . . .

1   *The above extracts of dialogue identify three of the distinguishing features of a courtier. What reasons are given for including noble birth (lines 1–5), self-praise (lines 6–9) and an appreciation of hunting (lines 10–14)?*

2   *How might such dialogue make* The Courtier *acceptable in aristocratic circles anywhere in Europe?*

The Courtier did not say anything startlingly new; it summarised the attitudes of the early sixteenth century Renaissance with regard to the arts, learning and neo-Platonic philosophy. Although it was set in the real court of Urbino, the atmosphere was more of a fantasy world of wit and wisdom which was not rooted in any one place. *The Courtier* was a package of ideas easily exported to the rest of Europe, especially given its endorsement of aristocratic principles. By the end of the century it had been translated into all the major European languages and it had inspired a number of imitators such as one in English called *The Governor* by Sir Thomas Elyot. The Renaissance man was very much the fashion.

The northern Renaissance was not just a copy of the Italian Renaissance. In many respects northern Europe retained its own traditions. The

Flemish school of painting, for instance, had developed independently of the Italian Renaissance and was to continue as an influence throughout the Early Modern period. In architecture, decoration was often classical in the Italian fashion in the sixteenth century but on the whole the plans of buildings, their basic structure, remained true to native styles. In the realm of learning the northern Renaissance was characterised by Christian Humanism, the use of humanist techniques to edit and interpret the Bible and other religious texts. One man more than any other merged northern piety with Italian learning to create Christian Humanism —Erasmus of Rotterdam. He deserves special attention as he came to represent the northern Renaissance as a whole, his achievements showing how the Renaissance could be transmitted and how it was transformed as it passed north of the Alps.

10. Erasmus and Christian Humanism

Erasmus (c1466–1536) was the greatest of the Christian Humanists. He was born in Rotterdam around 1466, the illegitimate son of a priest, and was educated at a school in the Dutch town of Deventer where most of the teachers belonged to the Brethren of the Common Life, a group of laymen who did not take monastic vows but who cultivated monastic ideals of prayer and poverty. Although Erasmus later criticised his teachers he had permanently absorbed their devotion to a simple piety.

At first, Erasmus seemed destined to be a monk and, under pressure from his guardian, entered the monastery of Steyn. He found life there intolerable. He hated the rigid formality and the excess of ceremonies which he felt obstructed religious devotion rather than inspired it. Above all he needed freedom and he leapt at the opportunity to leave the monastery in 1494 to act as a bishop's secretary. From then on, as he grew more famous, if not richer, through his writings, Erasmus was to wander Europe, never settling down for long, refusing offers of professorships or rich bishoprics rather than risk being tied down. He journeyed between the Netherlands, France, Italy, Germany, Switzerland and England. He was the most truly international scholar of his day.

Just as he travelled from country to country so Erasmus rejected any fixed system of ideas and sought continually to extend the frontiers of his knowledge. From his youth he could not accept what he saw as the sterility of scholastic theology and he commented that the theology lectures he attended at Paris in the late 1490s were the time to catch up on his sleep. He saw the light of clear reason instead in the classical texts which had been collected and edited by the humanists of Italy. He imitated the classical authors in his own writing although making Latin alive and energetic again rather than in pure mimicry. As Mann Phillips put it, 'He felt more at home with antiquity than the world into which he was born'. However, the classics he valued were always those which illuminated Christian thinking. When he jokingly referred to 'St Socrates' he was not sanctifying the pagan ways of the Greek philosopher but commenting on how much Socrates' thought prefigured Christianity.

The fruit of Erasmus' extensive survey of classical literature was the *Adages* published in 1500. The *Adages* were quotations culled from classical Roman authors to illustrate all that was best in Latin style and thought. If Erasmus had never published anything else, he would still have been famous for the *Adages* as, more than any other single work, it introduced educated northern Europeans to the classical learning of the Renaissance.

For Erasmus himself this was of secondary importance. However highly he valued reason and classical learning, they were just the means to an understanding of virtue which in turn would reinforce faith. This was Christian Humanism. Erasmus never gave up reading and editing classical texts but his primary concern was clear from 1504 when he published the *Enchiridion Militis Christiani*, the *Handbook of a Christian Soldier*. He was arguing for a simplified Christian life, getting to know Christ as a person through reading the Gospel, interpreting charity as love for one's neighbour rather than merely participation in the externals of religious ritual. This personal, ethical approach to religion was termed the 'Philosophy of Christ' but, while 'philosophy' sounds intellectual and exclusive, Erasmus expressed the hope that education would lead to the participation of everyone through knowing the Gospels, such that 'Out of these the farmer should sing while ploughing and the weaver at his loom'. Erasmus had absorbed some of Pico della Mirandola's ideas about man's divinely granted capacity for self-improvement but he saw himself as working for the potential of all mankind rather than just for a humanist élite.

For all his emphasis on personal religion in the *Enchiridion*, Erasmus did not attack Catholic doctrine or the main religious services such as the Mass—he respected tradition and saw the need to treat it with a sense of proportion and to purge it of abuse rather than to abandon it. But the alternative to 'handbook' as a translation of *Enchiridion* is 'dagger' and that was an intentional ambiguity. Erasmus was not just setting out the personal approach to religion but also fighting against the ignorance and profiteering which he saw as being so prevalent in the Church and so burdensome to the faithful. A demand for reform was a consistent theme in his career, although rather than using protest as a weapon he generally chose wit and satire. His most popular satire was his *Encomium Moriae*, the *Praise of Folly*, which he wrote in 1509 as a joke for the friend he was staying with at the time, Sir Thomas More.

The middle section of the book consists of Folly personified as a preacher describing the foibles and feebleness of different types of people. Folly encourages sympathy for some such as teachers; 'surely a tribe whose lot would seem most disastrous, the most wretched, the most godforsaken, if I did not soften the horrors of that miserable profession with a sweet touch of madness'. With regard to others the satire was more biting:

> ... In the first place, (monks) believe it's the highest form of piety to be so uneducated that they can't even read. Then when they bray like donkeys in church, repeating by rote the psalms they haven't understood, they imagine they are charming the ears of their heavenly audience with infinite delight ... But nothing could be more amusing than their practice of doing everything to rule, as if they were following mathematical calculations which it would be a sin to ignore. They work out the number of knots for a shoe-string, the colour and number of variations of a single habit, the material and width to a hair's breadth of a girdle ... Yet another monk will produce such a pile of church ceremonies that seven ships could scarcely carry them ...'

1 *What does Erasmus' satire imply is wrong with this type of religious life?*
2 *Why might such satire have been so popular amongst Erasmus' readers?*

The *Praise of Folly* was not so remarkable just because of the impact of its satire. Folly was personified to show not only how people might degenerate for want of reason but also how they need more than reason to be fully human. Humour, joy, love, all irrational emotions which make life worth living are aspects of Folly. And the final section of the book deals with that most sublime foolishness, the necessary transcendence of reason which is faith. Erasmus' humour and satirical outrage, just like his classical learning, were brought into the service of the Philosophy of Christ.

When Erasmus wrote the Praise of Folly in a few days, he was just taking time off from his major labour which was his work on the Bible and other religious texts. In 1499 on one of his visits to England, he had noted the work of the humanist John Colet on the writings of St Paul. Colet had suggested similar work to Erasmus but the great Latin scholar declined on account of his ignorance—he knew no Greek and that was necessary to read Scripture in the original. The seed was sown in Erasmus' mind, however, and he set himself the task of learning Greek even though, as he complained in one of his letters, it nearly killed him. By 1504 he had read the *Annotations* on the New Testament by the great Italian scholar of half a century earlier, Lorenzo Valla, and he decided that he would complete the great task which Valla had begun. He published a series of commentaries on books of the New Testament which emphasised the simple lessons to be learned as against the allegorical complexities created by the scholastic commentators of the Middle Ages. But his most important task was to purify the text of the New Testament itself.

In 1516 Erasmus published his version of the New Testament in its original Greek. This Greek New Testament was no perfect work of scholarship, having been rushed in the end, but it had a revolutionary impact equalled by little else published in the Early Modern period. For centuries the Church had based its doctrines on the authority of the official version of the Bible, the Latin Vulgate. Over those centuries of scribal copying, many errors had crept into the Vulgate until, in 1516, Erasmus proposed to correct them through employing humanist techniques on the Greek original. He saw it in terms of the sweet light of reason. His preface to the Greek New Testament anticipated 'the easy triumph of pure knowledge and Christian meekness' (Huizinga). Instead, the Protestant reformers were going to use the Greek New Testament in their attack on the doctrinal authority of the Church of Rome and so usher in centuries of religious strife.

Through works such as the *Praise of Folly*, Erasmus had become the leading critic of the abuses of the Church, of idle monks and false relics, of all the paraphernalia which were involved in the exploitation of the faithful. He had no automatic respect even for the Pope—in 1513 he had written *Julius Exclusus* in which he pictured the warlike Julius II being turned away from the gates of Paradise by St Peter. He had done his best to use humanist scholarship to strip away the errors of centuries in the name of Christian truth. But, although he had inadvertently prepared the way for the Protestants, he had assumed that reasoned argument and lively wit would lead to gradual, peaceful reform and the last thing he wanted to do was to threaten the unity of the Church.

Erasmus' position was one of moderation but once the storm of the Reformation had broken after Luther's protest in 1517, there was little understanding of that. He believed in civility, containing argument within courtesy, and he was reluctant to consider divisive religious questions beyond the capacity of man to answer. Such beliefs gained him no respect amongst the religious combatants. In the 1520s and 1530s, the Protestants vented their fury on him for his refusal to side with them, whilst many Catholics blamed his satires and scholarship for helping to set off the Reformation in the first place. Even when Erasmus did openly oppose Luther in 1524 over the issue of free will *(see page 140)*, he was still attacked by Catholics for being too timid. In the early years of the century, the best days of Christian Humanism, Erasmus had regularly prophesied the dawning of a Golden Age. There were no more such prophecies once the Reformation crisis had taken hold.

Although some historians, especially Huizinga, have criticised Erasmus for his indecisiveness when faced with Protestant rebellion and Catholic reaction, he was determined in sticking to his own moderate course however the religious zealots reacted. Starting in 1519, he published regular editions of his *Colloquies*, dialogues in which he continued to contrast the ridiculous and the worthy sides to human behaviour in all their social as well as religious forms. The *Colloquies* expressed Erasmus' belief in the value of liberty and its responsible use. His message and his style may have affected little the controversies of his own age but they have had an enduring effect on authors through succeeding generations.

Erasmus spent his last years in Basle and in Freiburg, seeking to preserve his freedom, which seemed increasingly threatened, and feeding ever more works to the printing presses which had spread his fame wherever Latin was read. His capacity for friendship and his endless, elegant letter-writing maintained a cultural network which covered half Europe. Huizinga described him as 'the international pivot on which the civilisation of his age hinged'. However, in many ways his age had already passed before he died in Basle in 1536. In England his old friends the Christian Humanists, Thomas More and John Fisher, had been executed for their loyalty to the Church of Rome whilst on the other side his fellow Christian Humanist and sparring partner in France, Lefèvre d'Etaples, had been forced to flee on suspicions of heresy. By the time of Erasmus' death the Christian Humanists were no longer the dominant intellectual force they had once been. In aspects of education and style the humanist influence survived but the Age of the Renaissance had given way to the Age of the Reformation.

11. Bibliography

J Burckhardt *The Civilization of the Renaissance in Italy* (Basle, 1869. English translation, Phaidon, 1944). P Burke *The Renaissance* (Macmillan, 1987), an inexpensive pamphlet. L Martinez *Power and Imagination* (Knopf, 1979). J Plumb (ed.) *The Pelican Book of the Renaissance* (2nd edition, Penguin, 1982). M Mann Phillips *Erasmus and the Northern Renaissance* (Hodder & Stoughton, 1949). J Huizinga *Erasmus* (New York, 1924. Princeton paperback, 1984).

12. Discussion Points and Exercises

A   *This section consists of questions or points that might be used for discussion (or written answers) as a way of expanding on the chapter and testing understanding of it:*

1   Why has Burckhardt's view of the Renaissance been at the heart of historical debate?
2   Why was it thought to be so important to collect and edit Latin texts?
3   Was civic humanism anything more than propaganda?
4   'Renaissance patronage was the product of political chaos in Italy'.
5   'The Italian environment was uniquely favourable to the Renaissance'.
6   What was so radically new in the visual arts of the early Renaissance?
7   Why did the study of Greek lag far behind the study of Latin and why was it so important to the development of the Renaissance?
8   In what ways did neo-Platonism affect the Renaissance?
9   Why was Machiavelli so controversial?
10   Why and when did the Italian environment cease to be favourable to the Renaissance?

11 What was most significant in helping to transmit the Renaissance to countries beyond the bounds of Italy and to future generations?

12 In what ways did Erasmus' Christian Humanism differ from the Italian humanism of the preceding hundred years?

13 What made Erasmus so successful in the first two decades of the sixteenth century?

14 Should Erasmus be judged a failure towards the end of his career?

B *Essay questions*

1 What was the Renaissance?

2 What was Renaissance humanism?

3 Why did the Renaissance develop in Italy and only slowly spread to the rest of Europe?

4 Assess the significance of two of the following: Marsilio Ficino, Castiglione, Machiavelli.

5 What did the northern Renaissance owe to the Italian Renaissance?

6 'Erasmus' greatness was as a scholar and a wit rather than as a reformer'. Discuss.

C *Exercise*

You are to take on the role of an Englishman, a young relative of Lord Mountjoy, a friend and admirer of Erasmus. You have been studying law in Italy and travelling as much as you can. It is early 1509 and you have just visited Erasmus in Venice where he has been working with the great Venetian printer, Aldus Manutius. Erasmus has complained about the food he gets at his lodgings and about the pains of his advancing age but he has also impressed you with his talk of the dawn of a Golden Age.

Write a letter home reviewing the evidence for this emerging Golden Age. Consider the achievements in the visual arts in Italy which have impressed you even though they have virtually been ignored by Erasmus. Comment on the advances in learning during the previous century. Show your appreciation of Erasmus, although you might dare to be critical in some ways. Finally, remembering that your vantage point is Italy in 1509, give your opinion as to the likelihood of such a Golden Age developing in the century to come in Italy or beyond the Alps.

VI The German Reformation

1. Introduction

The German Reformation has traditionally been seen as the most important topic of the Early Modern period. For centuries the Roman Catholic Church had been fighting off the heresies which periodically threatened to undermine it. The reformers of Germany, or Protestants as they became known after 1529, were the first to defeat the established Church. They attacked the corruption of the old Church, following the Christian Humanists in this *(see page 120)*; but they also attacked much of its doctrine, its basic religious teachings. It was on the basis of a renewed doctrine that the Protestants established breakaway churches, first in Germany and then all over northern Europe, fracturing the unity of western Christendom.

This was not just a blow to the authority of the Pope or a quarrel amongst academic theologians. As Steven Ozment has illustrated in his recent general survey *The Age of Reform*, 'The Reformation was an unprecedented revolution in religion at a time when religion penetrated almost the whole of life'. From its roots in late medieval religious thought, the Reformation grew into a movement affecting all aspects of learning, the arts, family life, the economy and, of course, politics.

For German princes, the Reformation offered an opportunity to defy the authority of the Emperor as well as the Pope, a crucial move in the formation of the independent territorial state. Their power was also reinforced by the taking over of Church lands and revenues in the name of Protestantism. This princely ambition used to be seen as the power-house of the Reformation in Germany. Historians, such as A G Dickens, now look more to the great German cities for 'the creative and irrevocable events' in the development of Protestantism, especially in its early stages. It was to cities that ordinary people came to hear about and argue through the new religious ideas. It was their clamour which then forced the Reformation on their city councils and it was the cities' printing presses which spread Reformation ideas throughout Germany and beyond.

Those presses were not just printing pamphlets for the literate. They also turned out woodcuts by the thousand which, as Robert Scribner has shown, were essential in adding to the words of popular preachers, modifying and transmitting the ideas of the Reformation to a largely illiterate population in the countryside as well as in the cities. The history of the Reformation is not just concerned with religious reformers but also with the peasants who adapted it to meet their own ideas and needs.

The Reformation affected every issue, every level of society, often with dramatic results. It clearly could not be controlled by any one man. But, for inspiration, many Protestants in Germany turned to the man who had launched the whole movement after 1517—Martin Luther. Some, such as Gerhard Ritter, see Luther as being essential for the success of the Reformation given that 'he walked onto the stage of history in a role for which he alone had the strength'. Even if this view of Luther's personal contribution seems exaggerated against a background of other reformers' work and a rich variety of popular beliefs, his writings and his example were certainly seen by contemporaries as being of vital importance for the Reformation.

2. Martin Luther (1483–1546)

Luther was born in Saxony in north eastern Germany. His father was a miner, eager to make himself a successful businessman and to make a professional man, a lawyer, out of his son. Martin certainly had every educational opportunity, despite the financial struggle involved, finally taking his Master's degree in law at the University of Erfurt in 1505. But he was not to be a lawyer; another event in 1505 was far more significant than Martin's law degree, at least according to his own later reminiscences. When on a journey, he was caught in a thunderstorm so dramatic that he feared for his life. He fell to his knees and vowed that if he survived he would dedicate his life to God by becoming a monk. Shortly afterwards he entered a branch of the Augustinian Order.

Martin's life as a monk was one of constant struggle. He felt he could only satisfy the implacable God, whose terrifying power had taken physical form in that thunderstorm, by purging himself of sin. He tried everything the Church offered to achieve that—constant prayer, devotion to Church services and especially the Mass, penance in the form of self-denial practised to the extent that he damaged his health by not eating or sleeping enough. And it did no good; his sense of sin was overwhelming. The constant emotional strain made him a most unusual monk: he came to a point where he even felt hatred for God.

In 1508, he joined the Faculty of Theology at the recently founded University of Wittenberg. He read extensively in the theology of the previous hundred years and came under various intellectual influences. Biel, the 'nominalist' philosopher who stressed the unknowable majesty of God; Tauler, the mystic who wrote of loss of personal identity in total surrender to God; and the 'Augustinisers' who laid a renewed emphasis

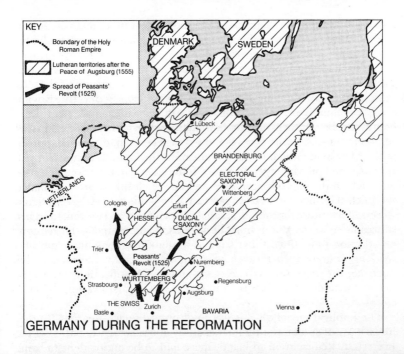

KEY

- Boundary of the Holy Roman Empire
- Lutheran territories after the Peace of Augsburg (1555)
- Spread of Peasants' Revolt (1525)

DENMARK
SWEDEN
Lübeck
BRANDENBURG
ELECTORAL SAXONY
Wittenberg
NETHERLANDS
Cologne
Erfurt
Leipzig
HESSE
DUCAL SAXONY
Trier
Peasants' Revolt (1525)
Nuremberg
Strasbourg
WÜRTTEMBERG
Regensburg
Augsburg
THE SWISS
Zurich
Basle
BAVARIA
Vienna

GERMANY DURING THE REFORMATION

on aspects of the writings of St Augustine which stressed faith and Christ's freely given grace as against the merits of human works. Luther read St Augustine for himself and, encouraged by the spiritual advice of his monastic superior, Johann von Staupitz, he pondered much on the overwhelming power of God and the nature of faith as against all those good works and devotions which seemed to get him nowhere.

In the ten years after he became a university teacher at Wittenberg, Luther found his ideas growing clearer as he expounded them to his pupils. In preparing his lectures, he turned to the Epistles of St Paul, letters written to the congregations of the early Church advising them on the essentials of Christian belief and practice. This was just what Luther needed—a return to the sources of Christian thought as against the accumulated doctrines of centuries of scholastic argument which muddled him and offered him no hope. When studying St Paul's Epistle to the Romans he lighted on the sentence, 'He who through faith is righteous shall live'. Suddenly he realised that all his attempts to purge his sins and be righteous were useless because righteousness can come only through faith and faith comes freely given by God. Luther no longer hated God. He wrote later of his experience, 'I felt that I was altogether born again and had entered paradise itself through open gates'.

This came to be known as the 'tower experience', Luther's flash of insight while shut away in his study. Historians now debate when it occurred, agreeing only that it was between 1513 and 1519. And some

127

also doubt that it was as dramatically sudden as Luther later made out. But the implications of Luther's insight were dramatic enough to shatter the religious unity of western Europe.

Luther had developed the central doctrine of what was to be called Protestantism. It has a formal Latin name, *sola fide*, meaning that 'by faith alone' can God be satisfied. Its consequences for the Roman Catholic Church, of which Luther was still very much a member, were enormous. For Luther, justification, that is when you are free of sin and righteous enough in the eyes of God to enter Heaven, depended only on faith. That made much of the apparatus of the Church redundant. All the relics and pilgrimages and saints' festivals and multifarious services, all of which the Church promoted and on which the Church depended for much of its income, were threatened. These things the Church offered were opportunities for the Christian to work his way to Heaven, to secure salvation by works, not, it must be said, as an alternative to faith but as an addition to it. But Luther's life as a monk had convinced him that working your way to Heaven was impossible and, according to his doctrine, the attempt was irrelevant anyway. Justification 'by works' became meaningless when seen in contrast with justification 'by faith *alone*'.

The implications of all this were not immediately apparent. Luther himself saw it as a matter for further study and scholarly debate. For the Protestant Reformation to begin, there had to be an incident to bring Luther and his ideas to the attention of the Church authorities and the people at large beyond the cloisters of Wittenberg University. That incident was to be the Indulgences Controversy.

3. The Indulgences Controversy

In 1517 there appeared on the borders of Saxony a Dominican preacher named Johann Tetzel who displayed more of the character of a salesman than a friar. He was selling indulgences which were, in effect, much sought-after passports to Heaven. According to the doctrine of the Church, these indulgences worked by the Pope drawing on the 'Treasury of Merits', the accumulated good works of saints through the ages, which could make up for the ordinary person's lack of righteousness. Such an indulgence was attractive because it could save you many agonising years in Purgatory where your impurity would normally have to be burnt out of you before you were fit to enter Heaven. And developments of the doctrine of indulgences as recently as 1476 had meant that they could be bought on behalf of someone already dead, who would then gain instant access to Heaven as well. In between his vivid impressions of the groaning of his listeners' parents in Purgatory, Tetzel would chant, 'As soon as the gold in the basin rings, right then the soul to Heaven springs'. Although it was not publicly known at the time, the money raised was to be spent on the rebuilding of St Peter's in Rome and to pay off the debts of the Archbishop of Mainz who had spent much to buy his archbishopric.

The ruler in Wittenberg, the Elector of Saxony, had banned Tetzel from his lands, not because of any religious qualms, but because he wanted no competition for the funds he could raise through his own relics collection. But the people were prepared to travel to buy indulgences and Luther, for one, watched them go with dismay. He was by no means the first to suggest that this sale of indulgences was an abuse, but his assault on them was to develop into an attack on the fundamental doctrines of the Church at that time.

On October 31st 1517 in Wittenberg, Luther published his *Ninety Five Theses* (debating points) on the subject of indulgences, perhaps doing so in the traditional manner by nailing them to the church door. Some of the theses engaged people's support in a fairly simple emotional way. For instance, Luther wondered why the Pope, if he had the power to release souls from Purgatory, did not do so out of charity rather than charging for it. This made Tetzel's offer seem less of a bargain and more like just another stratagem by which the Church squeezed money out of its overburdened members. But the more important underlying point, which Luther made clearer later, was that the Church was not just abusing its right to issue indulgences—it probably did not have that right in the first place, even if its purposes were moral and the indulgences were free. For Luther, no action or works by a mortal, whether the Pope or the recipient of an indulgence, could affect God's decision on whom to admit to Heaven.

The impact of the *Ninety Five Theses* was immediate. Through the recently established printing presses they became known throughout Germany and beyond. They caught the popular imagination, being discussed in taverns and market-places as well as universities and cloisters. To many Germans it was as though Luther, that hitherto obscure professor, was a David challenging the Goliath which was the corrupt Roman Church intent on exploiting Germany. Clearly the Church had to stop Luther before that valuable source of income, indulgences, was lost forever amidst the popular furore. And, as Luther clarified his ideas during 1518 and 1519, it became clear that what he was saying posed a threat to the structure of the Church as a whole.

The problem for the Church was that Luther acquired influential protectors from the start. In the spring of 1518 he won over the support of some of his own superiors in the Augustinian Order. More importantly, the Elector Frederick of Saxony was proud of the university he had established at Wittenberg and he was not going to allow any foreign Church authorities to suppress one of his professors. Also he was under the influence of a close adviser, Georg Spalatin, who had much sympathy for Luther.

The Church authorities, being unable to move against Luther directly, decided to try a mixture of persuasion and threats. Luther was summoned to Augsburg in October 1518 to meet with the papal legate (ambassador) in Germany, Cardinal Cajetan. The Cardinal appealed to Luther not to disturb the peace of the Church with his dangerous ideas. And he reminded Luther of the danger of opposing the Pope and being judged a heretic. But such a threat was an error. Luther's first instinct when the controversy began had been to apologise to his bishop for any disruption he had caused. He had even written to the Pope in May 1518, '. . . I fling myself at the feet of your Holiness . . . I shall acknowledge your voice as the voice of Christ. . . .'. Now he saw that he was being forced to make a choice between his vision of the truth and his personal safety. From his early days as a monk Luther had not been one for the easy way out. He was no revolutionary by temperament but he was obstinate. He refused to deny what he saw as the truth and so he defied Cajetan. He even attacked the Pope's right to decide issues of doctrine without clear Biblical proof.

1519 was no easier a year for the Church authorities. In January the Emperor Maximilian died. The Pope, Leo X, wished to prevent Maximilian's grandson Charles, who already ruled the Netherlands and Spain, from becoming Emperor and thus the dominating power in Europe. A critical voter in the forthcoming Imperial election, and even a possible candidate, was the Elector Frederick of Saxony. The Pope sent the Elector a Golden Rose, the highest sign of papal favour, and certainly did not choose to cause irritation by pressing too strongly for the arrest of Frederick's protégé, Martin Luther. Political force clearly could not succeed. It was hoped that intellectual force in the form of the Dominicans would prevail instead.

Since their foundation in the thirteenth century, the Dominicans were the religious order which had staffed the Inquisition. They were the most relentless hunters out of heresy, symbolised by a Latin pun on their name meaning 'the dogs of the Lord'. They distrusted rival orders, such as the Augustinians, whom they were ready to accuse of harbouring heresy and, in particular, they were eager to defend their own member, Tetzel. They felt confident that their champion, Johannes Eck, could discredit Luther in a disputation, a public debate.

The two sides met in the summer of 1519 in Leipzig. At first Luther, trying to keep a low profile, was represented by his University superior and now follower, Andreas von Karlstadt. But Karlstadt could not stand up to Eck's rigorous cross-examination. Luther had to speak for himself as only he had the certainty of basic principles necessary to refute aged dogmas being presented by Eck as obvious truths. With the atmosphere now heightened by Luther's intervention, Eck played his trump card. He exposed the likeness between some of Luther's ideas and those of Jan Hus, the Bohemian burnt as a heretic a century before. In disputing the authority of the Pope, Luther had earlier appealed to a General Council of the Church, viewed by many as the highest ecclesiastical authority. This did not help him now—Hus had been condemned in 1415 by a General Council at Constance and, by implication, Luther's ideas stood condemned as well.

It looked as though Luther would have to give in or deny the authority even of a General Council. He chose the latter course, as certain as ever that it was his duty to uphold the truth as it was revealed to him by God through the Holy Scriptures. Luther had been forced into a position where he would recognise only one authority with regard to religious belief—not the Pope, not a General Council but Scripture alone. *Sola scriptura* (by Scripture alone) was to take its place alongside *sola fide* (by faith alone) as a foundation of Protestant belief.

Luther had not planned to subvert the established order of the Church. It was the authorities' reactions to his views which had forced him to develop his arguments in debate with Cajetan and Eck to the point where he denied the tradition and the hierarchy of the Church. He was now reliant solely on Scripture—not the faulty, official version, the Latin Vulgate, but the Greek New Testament published by Erasmus in 1516 which, in his view, showed up the errors of Catholic theology. Luther had not been a willing revolutionary but he now took the initiative, publishing pamphlet after pamphlet on what was wrong with the practice and the teaching of the Church and how these could be put right. In particular, there were three pamphlets from 1520 in which he worked out the implications of *sola fide* and *sola scriptura* and launched the Reformation.

4. The 1520 Pamphlets

(a) *Address to the Christian Nobility of the German Nation*
Luther asserted that 'the Pope almost seems to be the adversary of Christ called in Scripture the Antichrist'. Not only had the popes failed the Church, they had also brought the world near to chaos by claiming the authority of secular princes as their own. According to Luther's doctrine of the 'Two Kingdoms', the Church wielded only the spiritual sword concerning matters of faith whereas the princes wielded the secular sword concerning all affairs of this world. Luther regarded the worldly corruption of the Church as a secular matter so he appealed to those princes to lead the Reformation. His protest was necessarily bound up with politics.

The politics, however, was not Luther's first concern. The greater part of the pamphlet was devoted to moral outrage at the abuses of the Church, the sexual permissiveness, the luxury, the exploitation. Attacks on abuses were nothing new but Luther went on to attack the Church at its doctrinal roots.

Luther denied that priests were any more sacred than ordinary men, or that they could act as intermediaries between their congregations and God. Instead Luther wrote of 'the priesthood of all believers'—any man who had faith could be saved and consequently he was his own priest. This did not make ministers redundant in Luther's eyes, but it did mean that they acted as representatives of their congregations rather than superiors. With the priests' role so diminished it was as though a religious revolution was being launched on behalf of laymen. More of the doctrinal details of this revolution were to be made clear in Luther's next major pamphlet.

(b) *The Babylonish Captivity of the Church*

The title refers to the enslavement of the Jews by the Babylonians described in the Old Testament, the implication being that the true Christians of the Church had been enslaved by the Roman tyranny of the Pope. Luther's purpose was to show how it had all been achieved through what he saw as fraud. In doing so he attacked Catholicism at its heart, the seven sacraments. It was this pamphlet which was most controversial and which shocked moderate Catholic reformers like Erasmus into realising that Luther was not just a reformer of abuses but a religious revolutionary.

The most important function of the Church had been to administer the seven sacraments *(see page 23)* which took the believer through a series of rituals from birth to death. Luther believed these had been used to make believers reliant on priests; and for four of the sacraments he could find no basis in Scripture at all. He claimed that there were only three genuine sacraments—baptism, the Eucharist and penance—although he later reduced the figure to two when he dispensed with penance.

Most controversial was Luther's doctrine of the Eucharist. He retained the Eucharist as a sacrament but he condemned the theory of transubstantiation *(see page 24)* and the idea that the priest was miraculously re-sacrificing Christ during the ceremony. For Luther, Christ's sacrifice had taken place once and for all upon the Cross, the priest was no miracle worker and the bread and the wine remained bread and wine.

Luther, however, did not break so free from Catholic tradition that he thought that the Eucharist was purely a symbolic act. He believed that Christ was physically present in the Eucharist, not replacing the bread and wine but entering into them. He explained the physical presence of Christ in the bread and wine as being like the presence of heat in hot iron. This view he justified with the theory of the 'ubiquity' of Christ, that is the capacity of Christ's crucified body miraculously and invisibly to cut across space and time and so be present in the Eucharist as a renewed experience of the original physical sacrifice.

Many today find this hard to grasp and so did many of Luther's contemporaries. Not only Roman Catholics condemned his view but some Protestants were to see the notion of the physical presence of Christ in the Eucharist as the superstitious nonsense of someone who had not broken cleanly away from the corrupt beliefs of the medieval Church. Luther's own followers were later to feel the need to clarify his doctrine philosophically and call it 'consubstantiation'. But, for Luther, the words of Christ at the Last Supper clearly supported him and, to understand his emotional conviction, think back to his story of God's power in that thunderstorm which made him vow to enter a monastery —he always had a strong sense of God's physical intervention in the world.

What Luther had lost was his terror of that awe-inspiring power of God. He expanded on how such terror could be transformed into joy in the last of his major 1520 pamphlets.

(c) *The Freedom of the Christian Man*

Without compromising any of his beliefs, Luther was to make this work one of his most uncontroversial in tone. Rather than attack any of his opponents, he was trying to share his sense of liberation. The freedom he celebrated was freedom from those laws of God which no mortal could satisfactorily obey. This did not mean that Luther expected the faithful to stop trying to obey the laws of God—they would naturally go on doing so owing to their love for God and their awareness of the imperfection of the world and themselves—but they could rest assured that, insofar as they failed, Christ would make up for it. This was a freedom from the consequences of human inadequacy.

Luther was even conciliatory towards the Pope, perhaps as an idealistic gesture or because Elector Frederick was worried by the violence of the controversy. Still, Luther's conciliation was strictly limited. He sympathised with Pope Leo X as being amongst evil counsellors, like a Daniel amongst the lions, but he also made clear that he expected Leo to abandon his former position completely and join in the Reformation. Such a notion was, of course, laughable in Rome. Indeed Pope Leo, preoccupied by politics closer to home, gave little attention to the Luther affair and is unlikely to have had any perception of the new theology which was being expounded in the 1520 pamphlets.

By the end of 1520 that new theology was near completion. It was unsystematic as Luther responded spontaneously to ideas and events, and there were many details to be argued over, but the essentials were there. And in 1521 Luther's teaching was brought together in *Loci Communes*, a textbook written by Philip Melanchthon, Luther's close supporter in Wittenberg.

From the basis of *sola fide* and *sola scriptura* Luther had worked out the priesthood of all believers, the need for only three (later two) sacraments, the rejection of transubstantiation and the meaning of Christian freedom. He was not simply revolutionary, as his cautious treatment of baptism and the Eucharist show, but he had been sufficiently radical to destroy much that had underpinned the structure of the medieval Catholic Church. The question became whether Luther would have the chance to preach his theology further or whether he would be crushed by the authorities of Church and Empire.

5. Under the Ban of Church and Empire

'Arise, O Lord, and judge Your cause. A wild boar has invaded your vineyard. . . . Arise all ye saints, and the whole universal Church, whose interpretation of Scripture has been assailed. . . .' These were the opening words of a Papal Bull named *Exsurge Domine* which threatened Luther with excommunication if he did not repudiate his heresy within sixty days. But Luther was to demonstrate how little he respected or feared papal authority when his time was up on 10 December 1520. He staged a bonfire on which he burnt the Bull and then he fuelled the flames further with the books of Canon Law which defined the legal powers of the Church. Luther's words soon became more fiery as well: 'The Emperor and princes must take up arms against the Roman Antichrist and the Roman Sodom. We must wash our hands in their blood'. But the greater likelihood at this stage was the reverse, that Luther's enemies would wash their hands in his blood.

Here again the steadfast protection of Luther by Elector Frederick was critical for the beginnings of the Reformation. Hoping to ensure a favourable hearing for Luther and to forestall a final excommunication, he arranged for his controversial professor to put his case before the Emperor at the meeting of the Imperial Diet at Worms in April 1521. Luther went willingly—he said that he would not refuse to go if there were as many devils at Worms as there were tiles on the roofs. He no doubt had it in mind that this was the big opportunity for his plain speaking of God's Word to win over the young Emperor Charles V and assembled princes. And he may well have put some trust in the safe-conduct granted by the Emperor.

At Worms, however, even Luther's confidence faltered. He was shown a pile of his own books and asked whether he stood by all of them—he was being tempted to give way on his most controversial views on the assumption that he could then be brought to modify the rest. Faced by the ritual and the challenge of the occasion Luther wondered whether he alone could be right. He asked for a day to think things over. When he came back to face all the powers of Germany his resolve was as strong as ever: '. . . my conscience is captive to the Word of God, I cannot and I will not recant anything, for to go against conscience is neither right nor safe. So help me God. Amen.' The safety he was thinking about was not of this world. That made him all the more difficult for ordinary politicians to deal with.

The Emperor had listed patiently to Luther but he was not moved by what he said. Charles V had a high sense of duty both with regard to the faith of his ancestors and to his Imperial role as defender of the Church. Ironically he could also score a propaganda point against the Pope by being first to act decisively against the rebellious monk. Luther was put under the Ban of the Empire, that is to say, outlawed. But before this was formally decided the princes had already turned to business more pressing than complex theological disputes—making complaints against papal taxation. Elector Frederick had tactfully withdrawn from the Diet and Luther himself had started to travel home, free to do so owing to his Imperial safe-conduct. It was all very well for the Emperor formally to condemn Luther but he had no practical means of stopping him writing and preaching. It looked as though Luther was going to slip through the political holes in the German constitution.

On the way home from Worms, however, it looked more as though Luther had slipped into the hands of his enemies. A group of mysterious horsemen kidnapped him and the rumour spread rapidly that he had been assassinated. As it happened, it was the Elector Frederick being cautious again. He had had Luther abducted for his own safety and he was installed in a castle of the Elector's called the Wartburg. There Luther grew a beard and was known as Junker George. It soon became clear that Luther had not been assassinated—he started to translate the Greek New Testament into German and to turn out anti-Catholic pamphlets at the rate of about one a fortnight.

Those pamphlets were bought up as fast as they could be printed. We must now turn to the reasons why Germans were so ready to listen to this dissident intellectual.

6. Germany's Grievances and Prophecies

When the princes at Worms turned away from the Luther affair, they compiled a list of no less than a hundred and two complaints, known as *gravamina* or grievances, against papal extortions and abuses. One grievance complained of the Pope appointing to Church offices the unqualified and the unlearned, such as bakers and donkey drivers, even when they could speak no German. Another grievance stated: 'We also regard it in the highest degree objectionable that His Holiness the Pope should permit so many indulgences to be sold in Germany, a practice through which simple-minded folk are misled and cheated of their savings'. The princes at the Diet of Worms might have accepted the Imperial ban on Luther for heresy but they were by no means hostile to everything that he stood for.

Grievance lists had been compiled as early as the Diet of Frankfurt in 1456. They were reactions to the renewed vigour of the Papacy in its recovery from the Great Schism and they expressed the frustration caused by Germany's constitutional weakness in facing up to papal demands. Other countries—France, England, Spain—had long since limited papal control over their national Churches but Germany did not have a central authority with sufficient strength to do so. There had been an attempt in the Concordat of Vienna of 1448 to restrict papal authority but it only applied to Habsburg lands. The same slackness in the Imperial constitution which made it so difficult to suppress Luther had, ironically, allowed the Papacy to extend its powers in the first place. The people as a whole bitterly resented papal taxation and, well before

Luther, they welcomed parodies of the Papacy in carnival displays and woodcuts, their equivalent of cartoons. This anti-papalism did not automatically mean the rejection of Catholic doctrine. But it did mean that the enemy of the Pope might well be seen as the friend of the German people.

It was not just the Papacy that was an object of resentment. The whole German clergy came under fire for living a luxurious life at the expense of ordinary lay people. For educated people Erasmus' satire represented a refined anti-clericalism *(see page 120)*. It was not confined to Germany but it was at least as popular there as elsewhere. In towns, the clergy could be disliked for living a privileged life distinct from the rest of the community. The grievances of the craft guilds of Cologne in 1513 included: 'Clerical persons should from now on bear the same civic burdens as burghers . . . Let the clergy pay taxes on the wine they tap for themselves . . . The council should instruct the preachers of the four regular orders to preach nothing but the true word of God and to utter no lies or fables . . .'. Preachers who criticised the clergy received a favourable hearing in towns and cities all over Germany.

For peasants, the money they had to pay to the Church, the tithe, was a burden they found it difficult to shoulder, given ever greater efficiency in the collection of other dues they owed to lords and princes. Peasant protest had already begun before 1521. For instance, in 1476 Hans Böhm, the so-called Drummer of Niklashausen, had attacked the established clergy and at the same time demanded that 'it must come about that the common people have enough to give all an equal sufficiency'. Böhm and his movement were exterminated by the Bishop of Würzburg but it was still the case that the sign of peasant protest, the *Bundschuh* or clog, was to be seen at Worms when Luther was defending himself there and there was popular clamour in support of him. Those who were anti-clerical, or whose general social protest included anti-clericalism, did not necessarily understand Luther's doctrine but they would voice support for a man who appeared to be cutting the clergy down to size.

Social and economic problems were of great importance but they did not automatically lead to the German people becoming rebels, religious or otherwise. Their reactions were fashioned by popular beliefs. The Drummer of Niklashausen, for instance, did not begin his campaign with a programme of social reform but with his claim that he had had a vision of the Virgin Mary. As his peasant followers approached Würzburg they responded to the threat of the bishop's cannon by saying, 'Our Lady will protect us from harm. You cannot hurt us.' Luther had no visions of the Virgin Mary but he was seen by many as a man inspired by God, whose religious imperative could overturn the normal order of things.

That overturning of the normal order of things was not just thought to be possible owing to divine intervention: it was expected. Prophecy was a central element in popular belief. The prophecies of Joachim of Fiore (1132–1202) were still popular in the sixteenth century. He believed that the world was in the 'Age of the Son' but would pass into the 'Age of the

Spirit' which would be an era of full and genuine freedom when the old order would pass away. More specifically, for several generations before the 1520s, a 'holy man' had been expected who would begin the reform of the Church. This inspired reform literature, amongst which was the *Reformatio Sigismundi*, written in c1438 but published in eight editions between 1476 and 1522. It combined warnings with recommendations of what needed to be done:

> The hour will come for all faithful Christians to witness the establishment of the rightful order. Let everyone join the ranks of the pious who will pledge themselves to observe it. It is plain that the Holy Father, the Pope, and all our princes have abandoned the task set them by God. It may be that God
> 5 has appointed a man to set things right. Let no one, neither princes nor cities, make excuses for not heeding God's warnings . . .
> Take a good look at how bishops act nowadays. They make war and cause unrest in the world; they behave like secular lords, which is, of course, what they are. And the money for this comes from pious donations that ought to
> 10 go to honest parish work, and not to be spent on war. I agree with a remark made by Duke Frederick of Austria to the Emperor Sigismund in Basel: 'Bishops are blind; it is up to us to open their eyes' . . .
> It seems to me that great evils have arisen in the western part of Christendom since Pope Calixtus imposed the rule of celibacy. It may be a
> 15 good thing for a man to keep himself pure, but observe the wickedness now going on in the Church! Many priests have lost their livings because of women. Or they are secret sodomites. All the hatred existing between priests and laymen is due to this. In sum: secular priests ought to be allowed to marry. In marriage they will live more piously and honourably, and the
> 20 friction between them and the laity will disappear . . .'

1   How might the Reformatio Sigismundi *have affected attitudes towards Luther and his enemies (lines 1–6)?*
2   What does the second paragraph above (lines 7–12) have in common with Luther's Address to the Christian Nobility of the German Nation *(see page 131)?*
3   Why should hatred between priests and laymen be due to celibacy (lines 13–20)? How might this attack on clerical celibacy have helped to prepare the way for Luther?

The *Reformatio Sigismundi* fitted in to the popular tradition that reform must come but its appeal was largely confined to the literate (between five percent and ten percent of the population), although it could reach others through being read aloud. More important were the oral tradition and the pictorial representations in woodcuts which adapted and popularised Bible stories and sustained beliefs in prophecy. In this tradition, the 'holy man' would be the new Elijah who would identify the Antichrist, launch the last battle against Satan and announce the Second Coming of Christ and the Last Judgement. There was a feeling that the end of the world was at hand. When the image of Luther appeared in woodcuts as a 'holy man', in the robes of a doctor of theology or a monk, sometimes with the halo of a saint or the dove of the Holy Spirit above his head, the response to him could be rapid and dramatic.

Despite this mood of expectation, however, Germany's grievances and prophecies did not amount to a reform movement which Luther simply had to take over. For all the criticism of it and the hopes for future reform, the beliefs and rituals of the Catholic Church were still seen as the only route to salvation. Luther did not build on a tradition of dissent: there had been virtually no heresy trials in Germany since the 1470s. Instead there were many examples of a growth in orthodox religious enthusiasm. Since the fourteenth century, laymen in the Netherlands and north-west Germany had been joining the Brethren of the Common Life (a religious association fully Catholic in its doctrine) and reading devotional literature such as Thomas à Kempis' *The Imitation of Christ*. In Upper Austria the number of Masses endowed to be said for the dead increased greatly, reaching a peak in 1517. There were mass pilgrimages such as one to Mont St Michel in 1457 made up mostly of children from southern Germany. For all that the Imperial Diet complained about the selling of indulgences, they only sold because there was a ready market for them amongst the people of Germany. Bernd Moeller has suggested that 'the late fifteenth century in Germany was marked by greater fidelity to the church than in any other medieval epoch'.

This does not seem to fit into the picture of a Germany ready for the Reformation owing to grievances and prophecies. However, both the devotion to the beliefs and rituals of the Church and much of the criticism of its personnel sprang from an underlying spiritual anxiety. Laymen were increasing their spiritual demands on the Church which, with its poor intellectual and moral standards *(see page 20)*, was unable to meet them. That caused laymen to try even harder in their Catholic devotions until Luther arrived on the scene, writing pamphlets, standing defiant at Worms and appearing in woodcuts. He was the 'holy man', armed with his Bible, who could relieve spiritual anxiety and offer an alternative route to salvation. His impact is graphically illustrated by one German who had collected a whole pile of indulgences, showing both his fidelity to the Church and his spiritual anxiety. Responding to Luther's message, his anxiety disappeared and he made much of the fact that he was using the indulgences as toilet paper.

Amongst the various sources of support which emerged from a spiritually anxious population, one source was crucial in turning Luther's popular protest into the Reformation movement—the humanists. They were the first to close ranks in support of Luther and most of the early Lutheran preachers were of a humanist background. As the officers of city councils or as counsellors to princes, they were to give the Reformation much of its political force. However, while it was of critical importance, the relationship between Luther and the humanists was not clearcut.

7. Luther and the Humanists

The Christian Humanists had many reasons for rallying to Luther's cause. They saw Luther's ideas pitted against scholastic theology which they already despised as being barbaric and futile. One humanist, Mosellanus, wrote in 1519 that Luther had 'hissed the Aristotelian theology off the theological stage'. The Christian Humanists had had immediate sympathy with Luther's doctrine of *sola scriptura* which was akin to their own intellectual ideal of going *ad fontes*, back to the original sources to seek understanding, which meant the Scriptures with regard to religious thought. As we have seen, Luther relied on Erasmus' Greek New Testament of 1516 and much of what he had to say about inner faith seemed to correspond well with Erasmus' Philosophy of Christ *(see page 120)*.

There were reasons other than religious ones for humanists to support Luther. When he wrote of Germany 'which nation with its noble nature is praised for its constancy and faithfulness in all history', some humanist nationalists welcomed his protest as another blow struck on behalf of German pride. One of their number, Conrad Celtis, had in 1500 republished an ancient Roman text, Tacitus' *Germania*, which had rapidly become a cult work and had detailed the resilience of the Germans 1500 years before. Elsewhere Celtis wrote, 'Resume, O men of Germany, that spirit of older times wherewith you so often confounded and terrified the Romans'. Clearly such nationalism could reinforce Luther's cause. However, its influence should not be over-estimated. This nationalism was not the modern sort which is concerned with political unity and national self-determination. German nationalism in the time of Luther would perhaps be better termed national senti-ment—it was made up of a literary mythology about inherent German greatness and was not a practical programme of national political unity. Still, those who read the works of the German nationalists had been made more receptive to a stand against a foreign power such as the Papacy. All they needed was a controversy to make their suspicion of the power of the Church yet more intense.

For the humanists that controversy was not in the first instance about indulgences. The Church was already being rocked by the Reuchlin affair. Johann Reuchlin was a scholar specialising in the study of Hebrew as a way of furthering understanding of the Old Testament. But in 1510 he had been attacked, on the grounds that he was slipping into Judaism, by Pfefferkorn, a new Christian eager to prove that he really had put behind him the beliefs of his own Jewish ancestors. The controversy grew in proportion as the theologians of Cologne weighed in on the side of Pfefferkorn while some humanists, although not the cautious Erasmus, backed Reuchlin, seeing the attack on him as an attack on the whole *ad fontes* way of intellectual enquiry. The humanists had the better of the argument in terms of propaganda. Their *Letters of Obscure Men*, written by Crotus Rubeanus and Ulrich von Hutten in 1515 and 1517, made a mockery of their opponents. They even gave us a new word, obscurantism, to describe the sterile thinking of closed minds. When Luther made his stand there were plenty of humanists, especially the younger, more radical ones, who were prepared to see him as another Reuchlin in need of defence against a Church which might suppress any new, critical thinking.

It was the younger and more radical humanists who were to provide not just a sympathetic reception to Luther but practical action on his behalf. They were the group from which were largely drawn the pamphleteers, the preachers and finally the pastors who were to campaign for him and establish Lutheran congregations far and wide across Germany. Moeller has laid great stress on their importance: 'Without them (Luther) would have failed as did many before him who had tried to stand up against the old Church. One can state this pointedly: no humanism, no Reformation.'

These enthusiastic young humanists were men like Philip Melanchthon who became a leading Lutheran in Wittenberg itself and who used his humanist training to give more shape to Lutheran theology in his *Loci Communes* published in 1521. But even Melanchthon, along with others who came to Luther from humanism, retained a faith in human rationality which Luther never had. This leads A G Dickens to comment that 'without undue cynicism it has been suggested that Lutheranism arose from a series of misunderstandings'. The nature of these misunderstandings became increasingly apparent the more that Luther wrote and argued. Some of the radical humanists felt that Luther had not abandoned medieval superstition in his belief concerning the physical presence of Christ in the Eucharist: they were to gravitate towards the Swiss Reformation *(see Chapter XI)*. Others, especially the older, more conservative humanists, came to feel that Luther was not going to purify the Church but to wreck it.

Before 1517 the humanists had been critical of the clergy and scholastic theology, but they had been fundamentally Catholic in their beliefs and many remained so. Even Reuchlin, the victim of the Cologne theologians, was shocked by Luther's attack on the seven sacraments. Many humanists, used to the civility of intellectual debates, were appalled by the violence unleashed by the Reformation. Mutianus wrote, 'I for one do not love the fanatic stone throwers'. And a central element in humanist thinking was the possibility of man's self-improvement; that contrasted with Luther's belief in man as being totally worthless in himself and entirely dependent on God's grace. Erasmus for one could not resolve that conflict.

Erasmus tried to remain detached from the Reformation debate although he at first suspected that the attack on Luther was an attack on Christian Humanism. He grew increasingly distressed, however, as he saw Luther 'rending the seamless robe of Christ' in threatening the unity of the Church, especially with his revolutionary attack on the seven sacraments in *The Babylonish Captivity of the Church*. In 1524 Erasmus at last committed himself in a diatribe against Luther on the issue of free will, which he argued it was vital to believe in if man was to have any purpose on earth. In his reply Luther praised Erasmus' eloquence but condemned his argument: 'it is as if rubbish, or dung, should be carried in vessels of gold or silver'. He argued that all things are decided according to God's 'immutable, eternal and infallible will. By this thunderbolt free will is thrown prostrate and utterly dashed to pieces'. This debate on free will showed clearly the gulf between the optimism of the humanist and the pessimism of the Lutheran vision of man.

The humanists were split, some, like Erasmus, rejecting Luther's vision and others being converted to it. Luther had gained much from the humanists but he had not compromised with them. He retained his distinctive view of what the Reformation meant. The question after 1521 was whether all those flocking to the cause of the Reformation would continue to share his view.

8. The Crisis in Wittenberg

Luther was uncompromising over what he saw as essential doctrine but he was quite prepared for the details of Catholic religious practice to change only slowly, if at all. However, there were those in Wittenberg who wished to hurry the Reformation on and make a cleaner break with the Church of Rome. While Luther was in the Wartburg there was little he could do about it.

In the autumn of 1521 the changes in Wittenberg began. First of all the laity were given Communion in 'both kinds', which means that they received both bread and wine, instead of just the bread with only the priests receiving the wine. This followed through on the logic of 'the priesthood of all believers'. Monks began leaving their monasteries, their vows being made redundant by the doctrine of *sola fide*. These changes Luther could accept although he was concerned when they did not have the agreement of the secular authorities. But events took a more radical turn with the arrival in December of the Zwickau prophets.

In 1520, the town of Zwickau had witnessed an extraordinary experiment led by Thomas Müntzer who had declared there a Kingdom of Christ to replace all authorities, secular as well as religious. The magistrates had acted against Müntzer, who fled. Three of his followers became the Zwickau prophets who appeared in Wittenberg. They accused Luther of being cowardly and demanded a complete cleansing of the churches. This involved the removal of all statues and paintings of saints which might be worshipped idolatrously instead of all worship being focused on Christ. This removal of images, known as iconoclasm, threatened to take a hysterical turn and degenerate into iconoclastic riots. And even peaceful iconoclasm was serious as an attack upon property and not just upon doctrine.

Andreas von Karlstadt, Luther's university superior and failed debater against Eck, was carried along in the mood of exultation created by the Zwickau prophets. Philip Melanchthon, closer to Luther and of a more moderate disposition, just did not know what to do. There was the danger of Elector Frederick using force to stop the attacks on church property. Luther had to intervene personally. He wrote from the Wartburg in January 1522: 'Without spilling blood or drawing the sword, let it not be doubted that we shall gently extinguish these firebrands'. Luther returned to Wittenberg in March 1522 to extinguish the firebrands with his preaching.

On eight successive days he preached what were known as his *Invocavit* sermons. Here are some extracts from one of them:

> We must first win the hearts of the people. But that is done when I teach only the Word of God, preach the gospel, and say: Dear lords or pastors, abandon the Mass, it is not right, you are sinning when you do it; I cannot refrain from telling you this. But I would not make it an ordinance for them
> 5 or urge a general law. He who would follow me could do so, and he who refused would remain outside. In the latter case the Word would sink into the heart and do its work. Thus he would become convinced and acknowledge his error, and fall away from the Mass; tomorrow another would do the same, and thus God would accomplish more with His Word than if you and
> 10 I were to merge all our power into one heap . . .
> Take myself as an example. I opposed indulgences and all the papists, but never with force. I simply taught, preached and wrote God's Word; otherwise I did nothing. And while I slept or drank beer with my friends, the Word so greatly weakened the Papacy that no prince or emperor ever
> 15 inflicted such losses upon it. I did nothing: the Word did everything.

1 How might this sermon have curbed the Zwickau prophets or at least those who had responded to their message?

2 Why did Luther want to avoid making ordinances or general laws (lines 4–5)?

3 What problem did the very existence of the Zwickau prophets indicate with regard to relying solely on the Word of God for authority?

The *Invocavit* sermons worked. For a time, at least in Wittenberg, Luther had taken back control of the Reformation. The influence of the Zwickau prophets was brought to an end. Karlstadt left Wittenberg and was to wander Germany in peasant clothing, rather ineffectively preaching a simple, spiritual religion.

Luther always emphasised the importance of sermons and he himself produced at least three thousand of them. In 1518 he had described the 'ears alone' as the organs of the Christian. Lutheran preachers all over Germany reached the illiterate as well as the educated and, even for those who could read, they added that extra emotional charge which established the Reformation. However, the direction of the Reformation, and Luther's own role in it, owed much to what he called 'God's highest and ultimate gift of grace by which He would have His Gospel carried forward'—the printing press.

9. The Reformation and the Printing Press

It has been argued by Elizabeth Eisenstein that printing did not just spread Protestant ideas but helped to shape the Reformation in the first place *(see page 26)*. Printing ended the scribal corruption, the copying errors, of the Middle Ages. The new accuracy made it easier to define theological positions exactly and easier for Luther to attack the corruption of doctrine. With regard to *sola scriptura*, an appeal to the Bible as the sole authority had been made before Luther by other reformers such as Wycliffe; but an evangelical, i.e. Bible based, religion only became possible once the Bible could be mass produced. In September 1522 Luther published the *September Testament*, his translation into ordinary German of Eramus' Greek New Testament. (Other translations of the Bible had been on the market for some time but they were based on the corrupt official version, the Vulgate.) Within twelve years 200 000 copies of the *September Testament* had been sold and by then, in 1534, Luther had completed his translation of the Old Testament as well.

The Church had faced heresy before and had generally contained it slowly but surely. The printing presses gave it no time. Luther said that it had taken a fortnight for his *Ninety Five Theses* to spread across Germany. In the 60 years since printing had been invented, literacy had grown to a rate of perhaps 20 percent in towns. The literate layman's appetite for books was inflamed by the Reformation controversy and the output of books was to increase by six or seven times between 1518 and 1524. There were Catholics writing against Luther but they were outnumbered twenty to one by those writing in favour of him. Luther himself used the press as a weapon in personal contests with his opponents and it was not all a matter of theology—he caricatured Dr Eck as Dreck (dirt) while Johannes Cochlaeus became Rotzleffel (snot spoon). The demand for what Luther wrote was immense. The 30 tracts published by Luther between 1517 and 1520 amounted to some 300 000 copies. In the early years of the Reformation, the Lutherans won the battle of the books hands down.

Through the press Luther could also give shape to the services and methods of the new Church which was emerging. In 1523 he published a reformed Mass, the *Formula Missae et Communionis*, and in 1526 his German Mass, the *Deutsche Messe*, appeared. Other reformers, starting with Karlstadt in 1521, had adapted church services in their own way but, through the printing press, Luther was able to issue the authentically Lutheran version. He also published many hymns which were to characterise Lutheran worship. Vital for less able preachers, who might get things muddled, he wrote the *Kirchenpostille*, a series of textbook sermons. By 1529 he had completed his *Small Catechism*, a question and answer instruction manual for use in the home, and his *Great Catechism* for more thorough education. Luther did not just drink beer with his friends while the Word did it all, as he claimed in the *Invocavit* sermons. He wrote down what he was convinced the Word was and got it printed.

Printing did not ensure Luther's total control over the Reformation. The press could spread the ideas of one man more quickly and certainly than ever before, but it also magnified the explosion of differing ideas which resulted from the break-up of the medieval Church. Luther had calmed the radicalism in Wittenberg but there were restless radicals elsewhere who would not conform and there were other reformers, particularly in southern Germany and Switzerland, who had independent minds. Also, it was not so much what Luther published which counted but the varying reactions to it. We must now look at the impact of the Reformation upon the different types of people who made up the German nation.

10. The Reformation and the Imperial Knights

The papal ambassador, Aleander, wrote of his disturbance just before the Diet of Worms when he saw a woodcut showing Luther holding a book and Ulrich von Hutten, an Imperial Knight and a humanist, holding a sword. The inscription read *To the Champions of Christian Liberty*. Luther valued von Hutten's support but the militancy in the woodcut implied by the sword represented a more extreme political stance than Luther intended.

The aim of von Hutten was not so much to renew the Church as to renew Germany and, if necessary, through war. His humanism was of the nationalist variety. He wanted to stop papal taxation and use the money saved to finance Imperial armies which would be the German spearhead of a new European crusade. Luther emphasised the primitive piety of early Christians; von Hutten identified that with the virtue of early Germans. He merged Luther's religious teaching with his own political vision of a peasant society ruled over by humanist aristocrats, uncorrupted by clergy, merchants or foreigners. And the aristocrats who would revive Germany were the Imperial Knights.

The Imperial Knights, owing allegiance directly to the Emperor rather than to a prince, were lords of all they surveyed, which in most cases was a few square miles around a dilapidated castle. Ulrich von Hutten idealised his fellow knights but they were in reality a decaying class hard-pressed to maintain their independence against neighbouring princes and cities. However, they still had some fight in them, as was shown by Hutten and his ally, Franz von Sickingen, in the Knights' War of 1522. They attacked the Archbishop Elector of Trier in the name of the Reformation and their own independence. They were defeated, von Sickingen was killed and von Hutten fled to Switzerland where he died in 1523. Their uprising merely hastened the decline of the Imperial Knights as a class but they had shown both that the Reformation could become a military as well as a theological threat and that Luther's religious protest could all too easily merge with social and political discontents. And this could happen even though Luther himself disapproved. Much of his popularity arose because Germans could make of his words what they wanted to hear. A far more dramatic consequence of this was to be the Peasants' War of 1525.

11. The Reformation and the Peasants

Luther recognised the need to communicate through woodcuts 'for the sake of simple folk' and we have seen *(page 135)* how there was already a tradition of anti-papalism in these cartoons. Scribner has described these woodcuts as being like 'homemade gin: cheap, crude and effective.' However, he has also shown that much of the message that got through to the peasants was a negative view of the Papacy rather than a positive representation of Luther's teaching. For example, the depiction of Christ on the Cross might indicate *sola fide* but this could not be an unambiguous image as the Crucifixion was also important in Catholic devotion. Luther was the 'holy man' and his fellow ministers might be seen as worthy preachers but in many woodcuts an even more dynamic image would be that which showed the Pope and his supporters in all their viciousness. The Pope was pictured as the Antichrist heralding the end of time and the Last Judgement; he was to be seen as the seven-headed beast of the Apocalypse or the Whore of Babylon. Another favourite image was the Wheel of Fortune, or 'the world turned upside down', showing the mighty being overthrown and the meek being raised up. There was an air of expectancy that, with papal power being overthrown, society would be transformed. Lutheranism was thought of by many peasants in terms not of theology but of godly rebellion.

We have already seen how religious and social discontents could merge *(see page 136)* and how this could add to Luther's popular appeal. By 1524 not only was the Reformation shaking Germany but also the grievances of peasants against their lords had reached a new intensity such that rebellion, when it came, was devastating. Particularly in the south and south west of Germany, peasant communities in the course of the previous century had been losing their freedom. It was made difficult to move from one estate to another. Especially controversial was the use of the forest which the peasants regarded as free territory and which the lords were trying to regulate, inventing the crime of poaching. The labour services which the peasant had to give to his lord in return for land were not legally specified and so could be gradually stepped up. The peasant of southern Germany, who had been in most respects free, was being turned into a serf.

This departure from customary freedom was a long-term trend. What made it unbearable by 1524 was that the population was rising by as much as 0.7 percent a year so that there was an increasing demand for fertile land which could not be met, whilst recent harvests had been failing at the rate of about one in four. Added to this was an increased burden of taxation to pay for the wars against the Turks.

The growing resentment of the peasants found a particular object in the ecclesiastical landlords, mainly abbots, who took tithes as well as rents. In 1525 one grievance against the Abbess of Buchau asserted that every peasant should be 'as free as a bird on a branch and may move to and live in towns, markets and villages unhindered by any lord. She (the Abbess) has forcibly squeezed our freedom from us and has monstrously burdened us with ruin, death taxes, marriage restrictions and serfdom, defying God's decree and all reason and even her own edict of freedom'. Luther's protest seemed like a manifesto of liberation against such ecclesiastical oppression. His call for spiritual equality given 'the priesthood of all believers' was readily extended by the peasants to a demand for social equality.

The Peasants' War began with an uprising near Schaffhausen on the Swiss border. It spread rapidly, reaching its peak in the spring of 1525 with all of southern Germany in turmoil, except for Bavaria where the dukes had kept lords more under control and the status of the peasants more stable. The uprising, although it seemed so general, was not one organised revolt but a series of provincial rebellions sparking others off, but each with its own character and its own independent peasant army. In a region where petty lordships dominated, the peasants tended to organise as a federation of several bands. Where a prince had consolidated his lands into a territorial state, there was more likely to be an attempt to act through the local parliament, the Estates.

Despite regional variations one set of peasant grievances gained particularly wide circulation—the *Twelve Articles of Memmingen*, adopted by a peasant parliament in Memmingen in March 1525. The bulk of the articles were demands for the peasants' rights to be restored and the drift into serfdom halted. This was in line with earlier peasant demands based on an appeal to custom. However, the mark of the Reformation was clearly visible. One article called for congregations to elect their own ministers, which indeed had been an early reform favoured by Luther. But, more than that, instead of an appeal solely to customary law there was an appeal to godly law. The preamble to the *Twelve Articles* began: 'There are many antichrists who, now that the peasants are assembled together, seize the chance to mock the gospel'. It continued with the point that the peasants seeking Christian justice could not be rebels but those who opposed them were the rebels against God. The peasants had seen the woodcuts where the Pope as Antichrist had been cast down and now they were going to cast down antichrists as well.

Peter Blickle has recently emphasised the significance of this appeal to godly law. Peasant demands were no longer limited by custom; the social and political order became an open question. Godly law could form an ideology which united townsmen and miners, all the unprivileged, with the peasants. As the uprisings spread northwards more and more cities became involved, while to the east the miners of the Tyrol joined with the

146

peasants. Blickle has argued that, rather than the Peasants' War, the uprisings should be termed the Revolt of the Common Man. When Michael Gaismair, a rebel leader, wrote his *Tyrolean Constitution* he envisaged a Christian democratic republic. All social privileges were to disappear, as were all barriers between people, meaning literally the destruction of castle and city walls. The economy was to be self-sufficient and controlled by locally elected officials. All that was to be left of the social order was the Common Man.

The *Tyrolean Constitution* and all similar rebel programmes were utopian. In some regions, however, the peasant mood was simply that of destruction, generally where there was inadequate leadership or where the rebels were in the grip of religious hysteria. In Thuringia on the borders of Saxony, the latter was the case as Thomas Müntzer, who had earlier inspired the Zwickau prophets, was in control there. He advocated a form of communism ('Everyone should properly receive according to his need') and swift justice for any lord who did not co-operate ('He should be hanged or have his head chopped off'). But this was not demanded in the name of a fair society; it was in preparation for the Second Coming of Christ on earth. Lords had to be disposed of because they had forced the peasants to concentrate on material existence and had prevented them from learning how to read the Bible. Müntzer was so confident of victory that he just made the defeat of his peasant army and his own destruction at the hands of Landgrave Philip of Hesse and Duke George of Saxony all the more certain at the Battle of Frankenhausen in May 1525.

Some peasant armies of up to 15 000 strong held out until the following year but they were picked off one after another by better organised forces such as the Swabian League, a regional defence association of cities and princes. It had not been entirely a disaster, however. Many landlords, even Georg Truchsess von Waldburg who had emphasised a victory by having one rebel leader roasted, were more cautious and recognised their peasants' freedoms. There was also some sympathy for the peasants. The Elector Frederick of Saxony commented just before he died in 1525, 'the poor people had cause for their revolt'.

Unlike his protector, the Elector of Saxony, Luther had lost all sympathy with the peasant rebels. He claimed that his message had been wickedly misinterpreted. He had preached only spiritual equality and he had consistently opposed rebellion against princes who, even if they were tyrants, had been appointed by God to keep sinful men in order. He had some justification for his claim that his words were twisted, but he had helped misinterpretation to occur. His fighting talk encouraged rebellion. He had criticised lords and princes, calling them the 'biggest fools or the worst scoundrels on earth'. He used the rhetoric of freedom and communal solidarity which had far more explosive effects in southern Germany than Luther had anticipated from his vantage point in the north. He tried to halt the revolt, publishing his *Friendly Criticism* of the *Twelve Articles of Memmingen* in April 1525, but he could not control disturbances which had been set in motion by mounting peasant grievances and the new impact of the Reformation and the 'godly law' it inspired. Frustrated, he published a furious tract in May 1525 entitled *Against the Thieving, Murdering Hordes of Peasants* in which he invited the princes to destroy the peasants and show no mercy until they submitted. It seemed as though the popular Reformation had ended in disaster and only a princely Reformation would be possible for the future.

This view that the popular Reformation came to an end in 1525 was put forward by those historians who preferred to concentrate on the high politics of the princely Reformation and also by some Marxist historians who followed Engels in regarding the Peasants' War as being doomed to failure given the undeveloped proletariat and the 'bourgeois nature' of the Reformation. However, it is now recognised that the Reformation remained very much a popular force even after 1525 in the great cities of Germany, even though illiteracy was a barrier to Luther's ideas being accurately transmitted to the peasants.

12. The Reformation and the Cities

In 1521 there were 65 Imperial cities, that is free cities, not under the control of any prince and owing allegiance direct to the Emperor. Of those 65, 51 became Protestant at some stage. And the Reformation was not imposed in those cities just by merchants or magistrates; in nearly every documented case popular support was registered. For instance, in Ulm in 1530 when the citizens were asked to vote on whether to maintain the Reformation or return to Catholicism, 87 percent of the votes were in favour of the Reformation.

It was in cities that the growth in late medieval piety had been concentrated. The cities themselves and institutions within them were regarded not as secular but as sacred societies. In Ulm in 1508, for instance, a blasphemer had been banished for fear that God would punish the whole community if he stayed. The guilds and confraternities within cities had their chapels and their patron saints. So the Church was not a purveyor of religion to passive laymen; the views of the laity counted. And, as earlier noted *(page 136)*, the clergy were not always regarded as the finest examples of sound religion. Anti-clericalism was common, given the money paid over to the clergy who were often regarded as parasites and, being unmarried, disturbingly alien from the ordinary community.

People in the cities were able and willing to respond to Luther's message. There was a relatively high degree of literacy and the printing presses producing Lutheran literature were to be found in the cities —books and pamphlets were readily available.

Print in many ways, though, was a supplement to preaching. A characteristic of city life has been termed 'sermon addiction', given that some would sit through sermons of four hours length. Many cities and towns endowed preacherships—31 percent of the towns in Württemberg, for instance—in order to satisfy the public demand. This fitted in well with the Lutherans' greater emphasis on preaching.

Some specific preachers prepared the way for Lutheranism. In Nuremberg in 1516 Johannes von Staupitz, Luther's monastic superior, preached on the powerlessness of man to find the route to salvation for himself. This was not fully Lutheran but it was an important element in the reformer's thinking which was thus current in Nuremberg even before the Indulgences Controversy. While Staupitz preached largely to an élite, in Strasbourg from 1478 to 1510 there had been an enormously popular preacher called Geiler von Kaisersberg who had attacked abuses in Church and state and who had based all his arguments on the Bible—the Lutheran reformers did not invent the evangelical approach.

Not only were the cities of Germany sensitive to religious ideas, they were also growing in political awareness. Most cities had had to struggle with the authority of a local bishop. By the 1480s not only had those struggles been won but the cities, in order to protect themselves against the power of territorial princes, had won the right to attend the Imperial Diet and even to meet as a separate Estate of the Empire. Many city councils had acquired sophisticated civil servants working in chancelleries, in many ways the model for modern bureaucracy. And those civil servants were often humanists. The cities were independent enough to decide religious issues for themselves and, where there were humanists, they had the men capable of presenting the arguments.

As well as political awareness, the cities' attitude towards the Reformation was also affected by social change. The development of trade had damaged the medieval ideal of unity and had led to increasing divisions between rich and poor. The result was social tensions but also a greater chance of movement between classes. This led to the emergence of groups which Steven Ozment has described as 'the ideologically mobile', that is people made more receptive to new ideas by social change. This could be because of social grievance (workers or the poorer clergy), ambition (certain guilds, newly rich merchants) or ideals (university students, humanists). These groups were the most enthusiastic when Lutheran preachers arrived in town.

City councillors were less enthusiastic about reform, fearful of innovation and also of the wrath of the Emperor or Catholic princes. However, in few cities was there a concerted attempt to crush the Reformation. Over-riding any question of religious zeal was the determination amongst most city councils to maintain the peace and their own positions. Lutherans were generally permitted to preach, as an attempt to prevent them could risk a riot.

When an attempt was made to replace Lutheran preachers, there could be difficulties other than popular opposition. In Strasbourg in 1523 the preacher Matthew Zell was dismissed, but only other Protestants could be found to replace him. Similarly in Lubeck the council gave in to popular demands for preachers but could find no Catholic priests to fill the posts. There was little the city councils could do to help the Catholic Church when it was unable to help itself.

Gradually one city council after another gave in to popular pressure, not just tolerating Protestant worship but declaring the whole city reformed and banning Catholicism. This occurred even in Nuremberg, the most stable and authoritarian of cities, because, although there was little social tension, it was feared that the precious unity of the city might finally succumb to religious strife. The formal occasion for the adoption of the Reformation was usually a disputation when leading reformers and Catholic theologians would debate in front of the city magistrates —who would then declare that they had been convinced by the weight of the Protestants' arguments. The time-scale for this did differ considerably. Nuremberg's calm Reformation was one of the earliest, established in 1525. The Council of Augsburg finally decided that it had more to fear from its own citizens than from Catholic reprisals and declared the city reformed in 1534 after rioting had occurred. In Regensburg, even though Protestant ideas were widespread there as early as 1522, there was no formal Reformation until as late as 1542, for fear of neighbouring Catholics, the Dukes of Bavaria.

The city councils were pushed towards Reformation by popular pressure but there were also advantages for them in giving in to it. It saw the completion of civic control of ecclesiastical affairs which had been developing during the Middle Ages. For example in 1523, the city of Leisnig established a 'common chest', a treasury which handled the income from Church property and devoted it to charity. As well as these practical powers, Protestant preachers also reinforced the theoretical powers of the magistrates, quoting Scripture on the sanctity of the magistrates' office. The public image of city councils was much enhanced when they had accepted the Reformation, as they were then revered as the guardians of it.

Although the Reformation was established in this way in the majority of German cities, there were differences in the forms it developed, along roughly a north–south divide. In the north of Germany, in such cities as Stralsund, religious change was part of a democratic movement with citizen committees trimming the powers of the oligarchic councils as well as forcing the introduction of the Reformation. The nature of the Reformation there was strictly Lutheran with few independent-minded reformers.

In the south, although it is more difficult to generalise there, there seemed to be much greater emphasis on the solidarity of the community with a strict religious discipline and organised charity. This is possibly because, as Thomas Brady has suggested in *Turning Swiss*, the cities of southern Germany were following the Swiss model. There were also reformers in the south who were not always prepared to toe the Lutheran line. For instance, Martin Bucer, active in Strasbourg from 1523, established not just a corps of Protestant preachers and teachers but also lay elders to discipline the faithful and deacons to look after social welfare. He was taking much more social and political initiative than Luther allowed in his doctrine of the 'Two Kingdoms' concerning the separateness of Church and state. These reformers in the south were also influenced by the Swiss Zwingli *(see Chapter XI)* who rejected various Lutheran doctrines, especially the idea of the physical presence of Christ in the Eucharist.

This variety and vitality in the urban Reformation was not to last. The cities found themselves caught between the Lutheran princes of the Schmalkaldic League *(see page 154)* and the Catholic princes led by the Emperor. With the victory of the Emperor at the Battle of Mühlberg in 1547, many cities lost their freedoms—Charles V abolished 28 city constitutions and introduced 'trusty' Small Councils. When the Emperor was in turn defeated, the cities which did not remain Catholic found that they had to toe an orthodox Lutheran line instead. The popular element in the Reformation had finally given way to mass conformity as the age of the free city came to an end.

While it had lasted, the urban Reformation had followed a fairly consistent pattern—the arrival of a Protestant preacher and the circulation of Protestant literature, an enthusiastic popular response, the acceptance of the Reformation sooner or later by the city council making it official after a disputation. There were broad variations in the pattern, as we have seen in the north-south divide. However, each city followed its particular path to the Reformation and indeed, a few cities, such as Cologne, remained Catholic. There is an exercise on page 158 to test generalisations about the urban Reformation against individual case studies. And it must also be remembered that, while the Imperial cities have been extensively researched, there were also two thousand territorial cities, many of which may have seen lively variations in the people's experience of the Reformation, albeit under princely control.

13. The Reformation and the Princes

Before the recent growth in studies of the cities, the princes of Germany were given the credit for introducing the Reformation. While they were of increasing importance in later years, they were slow to dedicate themselves to the cause in the 1520s. Even Frederick the Wise of Saxony, Luther's protector, did not clearly adopt Lutheranism himself until on his deathbed in 1525. And the non-committal Frederick had been Luther's only princely supporter in the first seven years of the Reformation.

This does not mean that princes were necessarily hostile to Luther and all he stood for. We saw earlier *(page 134)* how the princes at the Diet of Worms turned as rapidly as possible from the Luther affair to their grievances against the Papacy. At the Diet of Nuremberg in 1523, they demanded more national control and 'the preaching of the pure Gospel according to true Christian understanding'. But they nearly all remained Catholic, unwilling to break completely from tradition or to risk conflict.

There were just three notable exceptions to this. In 1524 Luther's close associate, Philip Melanchthon, had managed to convert the 20 year old Landgrave (i.e. Count) Philip of Hesse who was to be the most dynamic of Lutheran politicans. In 1525 the Elector Frederick's successor, John of Saxony, declared himself a firm Lutheran and the Electors of Saxony were to remain so for over two centuries. Also in 1525 the Grand Master of the Teutonic Order, a crusading order of knights in north east Germany, converted to Lutheranism, secularised the Order's estates and declared himself Duke Albrecht of Prussia. Eventually, over half of Germany was to be ruled by Lutheran princes—but it was nearly 30 years before that came about.

It is impossible to be completely certain why a prince converted to Lutheranism—faith is a private thing. However, some historians have stressed the material gains involved. When a prince became Lutheran he would take over Church lands and use them for his own purposes. This does not necessarily indicate simple greed. Philip of Hesse used former monastic revenues to finance a new university at Marburg and to set up a hospital for the poor and sick at Haina. In all, 60 percent of the revenues he acquired were spent on such charitable endeavours and much of the rest of it went on the upkeep of the Lutheran Church. In any case, an acquisitive prince could take over ecclesiastical revenues and yet remain a Catholic, as Ferdinand and Isabella demonstrated when they took control of the crusading orders of Spain.

Alongside the 'church lands' motive there was the expansion of the prince's sovereign powers. When a prince adopted Lutheranism he no longer had to share his authority with Pope or bishops, and his defiance of the Catholic Emperor further demonstrated his independence. This was part of the development of the Early Modern state, not yet the secular state of modern times but no longer the medieval state with its recognition of universal authorities such as Pope and Emperor. The princes of Germany were not to make themselves completely free of Imperial authority but Luther had assured them of their sovereign importance when it came to religion in his *Address to the Christian Nobility of the German Nation* in 1520. Luther's doctrine of the 'Two Kingdoms' did declare that Church and state were separate but in fact that served the prince's authority. The Church had no right of interference in temporal affairs while the prince had a duty to maintain good order in the Church and supervise its activities as a matter of paternal concern for his subjects.

The duty of supervising the Church, and the power it brought the prince, was a positive inducement to convert to Lutheranism. Something more negative was fear of religious strife. In the sixteenth century, toleration was regarded as a sign of weakness rather than a virtue —heresy was tantamount to treason and could easily lead to civil war. To maintain civil peace it was felt that the people had to be of one religion, the prince's religion. This led to conservatism, a reluctance to adopt what might be heresy. However, as Protestantism spread amongst the people of Germany, and Catholicism seemed incapable of standing up to it, the balance shifted and it became the safe policy for many princes to become Lutheran. There was an alternative, the systematic suppression of Protestantism as undertaken by the Dukes of Bavaria, but it often seemed riskier than defying the Emperor, given the threat of popular disturbances.

It was not difficult to defy the Emperor as he was regularly distracted by his commitments in other parts of Europe and the Mediterranean. He could not be present at the Diet of Speyer in 1526 as he was in Spain, concerned with the new hostile League of Cognac led by France. Even his brother, Ferdinand, who had special responsibilities in Germany, was keeping an anxious eye on the Ottoman invasion of neighbouring Hungary. This meant that Philip of Hesse and John of Saxony could attend the Diet of Speyer in 1526, sporting Lutheran lapel badges with impunity. The princes as a whole could not agree to enforce the Edict of Worms against Luther so the only conclusion was that each prince should conduct himself 'as answerable to God and to His Imperial Majesty'. This gave no right to reform but it was a great encouragement to it none the less.

Despite this lack of decisive action by the Emperor, however, the reformed princes were worried about possible aggressive action by Catholic princes. In 1525, the League of Dessau had been set up bringing Catholic princes together, including Duke George of Saxony, the cousin and rival of the Elector. In response, in 1526 Philip of Hesse and John of Saxony joined the Lutheran League of Torgau along with princes from Brunswick-Lüneburg, Brunswick-Grubenhagen, Mecklenburg, Anhalt-Zerbst and others. Unfortunately these minor princes rejoiced in long names rather than powerful armies so the Lutherans felt no security. In 1528 war almost broke out owing to the Pack affair—Pack, Duke George's Vice-Chancellor, leaked false details of a Catholic attack and that prompted a pre-emptive strike by Philip of Hesse and John of Saxony. When the error was realised, Philip got the blame as it was thought that he had been trying to force John into an attack in spite of the latter's wish to restrict the League of Torgau to a defensive purpose. And the Catholics were outraged. Their fears that Lutheranism could only lead to conflict seemed to have been confirmed and they demanded that it be eradicated.

In 1529 at the Diet of Speyer the princes called for a halt to reform and for Catholicism not to be hindered anywhere, although they saved their most aggressive words for the Zwinglians *(see Chapter XI)* and other 'debasers of the sacraments'. The response to this was the Protestation, from which Protestantism took its name: 'In matters relating to God's honour and the soul's felicity each must stand before God and answer for himself'. The Protestants on this occasion were Philip of Hesse, John of Saxony, four other princes and the delegates of 14 cities.

The Emperor's response to the Protestation was initially muted. He was on his way back to Germany and a far more immediate problem in 1529 was the fact that the Ottomans, who had destroyed the kingdom of Hungary in 1526, were now at the gates of Vienna. However, his position was stronger in 1530. The Ottoman siege of Vienna had been unsuccessful, peace with France had been renewed in 1529 and in 1530 the Pope had submitted so far as finally to crown Charles as Emperor *(see page 194)*. On the Protestant side Philip of Hesse's grand vision of an alliance stretching from France to Transylvania had come to nothing while John of Saxony continued to insist on a defensive stance only. Some Protestant powers, especially Nuremberg, declared that they had no right to resist the Emperor at all. Charles had decided that the time had come to settle the Lutheran question once and for all.

The fair-minded Charles invited the Lutherans to present their beliefs to a Diet at Augsburg in 1530. It was the diplomatic Melanchthon who prepared the Lutheran statement of belief which was called the Confession of Augsburg. Melanchthon steered clear of contentious issues, such as Purgatory or the status of the Pope, and concentrated on points such as Communion in both kinds and clerical marriage, on which he hoped there could be agreement. But however impressive the common ground, the two sides were not to be reconciled. Luther, observing the Diet from a place of safety a few miles away, did not approve of compromise, as for him it was a matter of truth pure and simple. Likewise the Catholic theologians were not going to paper over the cracks—their rejection of the Confession, known as the Confutation of Augsburg, was accepted by the Emperor. It looked as though the question could only be resolved by war.

In 1531 the Protestants prepared themselves by forming the Schmalkaldic League. Luther, always reluctant to oppose a secular ruler, at last gave his personal approval to resistance to the Emperor. However, there was to be no war as yet—the Emperor once again found himself preoccupied by the Ottoman threat and a truce (the Nuremberg Standstill) was agreed in 1532. For the next twenty years *(for details of which see Chapter VIII)* there was to be much jockeying for position between princes and Emperor until the final reckoning of the Peace of Augsburg in 1555. There the princes won the right to decide whether their territories were to be Lutheran or Catholic, a principle known by a Latin phrase *cuius regio . . . eius religio* (his territory, his religion). The Reformation was by now definitely princely rather than popular. How far this could foster genuine Lutheranism will be examined in the next section. However, it is clear that Lutheranism could not have survived without princely protection against hostile forces. There again, as Fischer-Galati has shown, the Ottoman threat conditioned the success of the Lutherans, taking the pressure off them at nearly every critical moment. This did not escape Luther's notice—the cause of God could be served by the unwitting Infidel as well as by Christian princes.

14. The Lutheran Church

In the end Luther had to rely on the princes to organise and protect a new, reformed Church. This involved a double disappointment for him. He had assumed that the changes he had demanded would entail the reform of the old Church rather than the creation of a new one. By the end of the 1520s it was clear that the Church was in schism (split) for the foreseeable future—a new Lutheran Church now existed in rivalry with the old Church of Rome and later in rivalry with other Protestant Churches. The separate Lutheran Church had come into existence almost by default.

The other side to Luther's disappointment related to the organisation of the Church. At first Luther had laid down that 'a congregation which has the Gospel must and should choose and call from amongst itself someone to teach the Word on its behalf'. However, in too many cases the people clung to their old ways and their old, unconverted Catholic priests. Or, more immediately dangerous to the Lutheran Reformation, the people went too far, turning to the *schwärmerei*, the 'dreamers' or extremist sectarians who seemed to Luther to be about to destroy the Reformation before it became established. *(See page 142 for Luther's early responses to this problem.)* And even where a minister was doctrinally reliable, he sometimes demanded too much independence from the secular authorities, as was shown by complaints from city councils such as Speyer where Lutheran ministers were seen to be as arrogant in asserting their authority as Catholic priests. (Indeed, amongst a sample of 176 Lutheran ministers investigated by Scribner, three-quarters had formerly been Catholic priests.) Where Luther had hoped there could be freedom and spontaneous Christian brotherhood, there had to be discipline.

The first step was to organise visitations, inspections of parishes to check up on preaching and the conduct of services. Also, the people were questioned on articles of faith to see how much they understood. The first visitation to be carried out in Saxony was under way by 1527. The results horrified Luther. In 1529 he wrote, 'Men have been hearing the pure Word for ten years now but they act as though nothing had changed'. Steps were taken to remedy this. Officials known as superintendents were appointed to act as permanent inspectors. In 1532 church authorities were formally established in Saxony with most responsibility vested in visitation committees made up of theologians and lawyers appointed by the prince and given the job of examining ministers and their progress in the parishes. This system was adopted in most Lutheran principalities.

Discipline was established but it seemed neither to inspire greater zeal nor remedy the problems Luther saw in 1529. In comparison, the Calvinist system *(see page 283)* was to be much more dynamic, bringing ministers closely into co-operation with each other and with the lay elders, the leaders of their congregations. Another contrast was to be seen in Denmark and Sweden where the Lutheran Reformation was firmly established by the 1540s. There it was found necessary to retain bishops for Church government to be properly managed—and, of course, to serve the interests of the state.

Neither Calvinist organisation nor Lutheran bishops could maintain perfect unity in their Churches but the loosely organised Lutherans of north Germany were to split into factions in the generation after Luther's death in 1546. The Philippists, the followers of the more liberal Philip Melanchthon, were bitterly opposed by the Gnesio-Lutherans, the followers of the much more dogmatic Flacius Illyricus. As one faction gained the upper hand over the other, Lutheran ministers were required to show their understanding and acceptance of the 'correct' position or face disciplinary action. This factional competition much disrupted the work of the Lutheran clergy and, even when a compromise was reached in the Formula of Concord of 1577, there was little renewal of the sense of common purpose which had been so strong in the early years of the Reformation.

The various visitations and inspections of the Lutheran Church were not just concerned with the conduct of the clergy but also with the knowledge of the people. Lutheran schools had been set up to spread literacy so that the Scriptures could be read and the main articles of the faith understood. Gerald Strauss has recently shown how limited in effect Lutheran teaching methods were. The visitation records for later in the sixteenth century show little optimism about the impact of Lutheran ideas upon ordinary people. In Geislingen the people showed 'contempt for the sermon, catechism and the Lord's Supper, also sacrilegious behaviour on the Sabbath . . . they open their shops on Sunday and do their buying and selling as though we had no divine and secular laws against these sins'. In the countryside around Hamburg the inspectors found 'unbelievable self-indulgent wickedness and contempt for preaching, for the holy sacraments'. At the time of the Peasants' War many of the people had adapted Lutheranism to their own needs. Later on in the sixteenth century they were more prone to distance themselves from it. Strauss concludes that Lutheran indoctrination of the people was a failure.

Like so many other movements Lutheranism suffered from 'routinisa-tion', the exhaustion of early enthusiasm and its replacement by dull routine procedures. However, despite all the weaknesses of the Lutheran Church as an institution, Lutheranism had made an indelible impact on the history of Early Modern Europe. The medieval Church had been undermined. By the later sixteenth century, seven out of every ten inhabitants of the Holy Roman Empire were at least officially Lutheran. Even though Lutheranism itself was largely confined to Germany and Scandinavia the initial split in the Church led to the development of other Protestant churches and reactions within Catholicism *(see Chapters XI and XII)*. The Lutheran protest had contributed to popular turmoil in Germany in the 1520s and substantial changes in the cities. The constitution of the Holy Roman Empire, the looseness and tensions within which had allowed for the spread of Lutheranism in the first place, was permanently affected by the religious divisions amongst princes and cities. And in Europe as a whole, little in the way of intellectual attitudes, diplomacy, ecclesiastical or social policy was left unaffected by Luther's challenge.

15. Bibliography

S Ozment *The Age of Reform* (Yale, 1980). A G Dickens *Reformation and Society* (Thames & Hudson, 1966); *Martin Luther and the German Nation* (Edward Arnold, 1974). L W Spitz *The Protestant Reformation* (Harper & Row, 1984). M Mullett *Luther* (Lancaster Pamphlet, 1987). R W Scribner *The German Reformation* (Macmillan, 1986). R W Scribner 'The Reformer as Prophet and Saint' in *History Today*, November 1983.

16. Discussion Points and Exercises

A *This section consists of questions or points that might be used for discussion (or written answers) as a way of expanding on the chapter and testing understanding of it:*

1 Why was the Reformation not purely a religious event?
2 What was at the heart of Luther's rejection of medieval Catholicism?
3 'It was not Luther but his opponents who created the Reformation crisis.'
4 In what ways were the 1520 pamphlets most radical?
5 Why did Charles V choose not to lead the German Reformation?
6 How significant were anti-papalism and anti-clericalism in preparing the way for the Reformation?
7 How did popular beliefs encourage the spread of Lutheranism?
8 Why did the humanists support Luther but only in part?
9 How effectively did Luther deal with the crisis in Wittenberg in 1522?
10 How crucial was the printing press to the development of the Reformation?
11 How far was Luther's protest responsible for the Knights' and Peasants' Wars?
12 'Only in the cities was the Reformation truly popular.'
13 How far did the Reformation become purely a political issue once the princes had taken over?
14 'The Lutheran Reformation had all the advantages and disadvantages of being unplanned.'

B *Essay questions*
1 How revolutionary was Luther?

2 'Luther lost control of the Reformation almost as soon as it had begun.' Discuss.

3 How far was the Reformation more a princely than a popular movement?

4 'Without the work done by Erasmus and other humanists, Lutheranism could never have developed.' Do you agree?

5 Why did the Reformation begin in Germany?

6 Why was the Reformation in Germany only a partial success?

C Exercise

The aim is to use case studies to analyse some of the factors causing the Reformation to be adopted quickly, slowly or not at all in various German cities. You will need a copy of A G Dickens' *The German Nation and Martin Luther*.

Read Dickens' short accounts of the Reformation in Nuremberg, Strasbourg, Augsburg, Erfurt and Cologne. Then make out a list of headings for the factors which appear to be important. You should include 'Location' *(see map on page 127)*, 'Social Tensions', 'Trade', 'Constitution' and any others which occur to you.

Under each heading note down the relevant information relating to the individual cities and note how that factor affected the adoption of the Reformation.

Finally, assess the overall importance of each factor in determining how the Reformation was received in these cities. You might find it best to set out your notes in a box as follows:

	Location	Social Tensions	+ other headings
Nuremburg			
Strasbourg			
Augsburg			
Erfurt			
Cologne			
Overall importance of factor:			

17. Essay Writing—Constructing an Argument

It is important to construct an argument before you start writing an essay. It will help you to avoid lapsing into the sort of narrative criticised on page 75 and it will give your essay a clear sense of direction. Your argument should build from relevant point to relevant point without contradiction or repetition.

Consider the question 'How revolutionary was Luther?'. At first sight that is not an easy question because 'revolutionary' is not a word with one precise meaning. You might be tempted to write an answer which just summarises what Luther did and leaves the reader to make up his or her own mind. However, an essay is a test of your judgement. If you are methodical it is not so difficult to develop your own case. Try the following procedure:

(a) Break down the question into component parts which could form the basis of your plan. In this case they might include:

How revolutionary was Luther with regard to doctrine?
government of the
church?
politics?
society?

(b) In just a couple of sentences, jot down a summary answer to each of the component questions.

One sentence could state whether Luther *intended* to be revolutionary in the sense of breaking away from medieval tradition.

Another sentence could suggest whether or not he had a revolutionary *effect*, whatever his intention.

Take into account how far Luther's position changed as the Reformation developed.

(c) You can sharpen your argument through comparison. Think through what your answers to the component questions would have been if the subject had been Erasmus or Müntzer. By reference to other reformers you can put Luther into perspective.

(d) Now review your short answers in order to come up with your overall argument.

A good argument has to be clear and consistent but it does not need to be dogmatic. You might take the view that Luther was revolutionary in some ways and not in others. You could argue that his protest had far more revolutionary effects than he had ever intended. Remember that element of change—it could be that Luther became more or less revolutionary as the years went by.

(e) As you write your essay bear in mind the following:
i) The first sentence of each paragraph should be a point relating directly to the question and advancing the argument which you have thought out. In the rest of the paragraph you can then present the evidence which supports or extends your point.
ii) As you write you should be refining your argument, dealing with any exceptions or differing points of view.

VII Popular Culture and the Witch Hunts

1. Introduction

Popular culture is one of the newer areas of research by historians. There has been academic interest in folklore since the eighteenth century but customs or tales of the past were then studied for their romantic cultural value or, at worst, just for their quaintness, rather than to find out their original meaning. Since earlier this century, historians have been examining popular culture as the key to past ways of thought. Some social historians are still sceptical; for them it is the material conditions of life which really matter. However, with borrowings from the ideas of anthropologists who are used to studying societies with ways of thought alien to our own, more and more has been done to piece together the beliefs, values and basic concepts of ordinary people in the past. These all-embracing ways of thought of past peoples are generally known by the name given to them by French historians, *mentalités*.

A problem with the study of *mentalités* is the difficulty of being precise. It is hard to categorise *mentalités*, saying where one ends and another begins through the years or from one region to another. There are problems with the evidence—a folk tale known in 1700 may well have been already current in 1500 or earlier, but it is uncertain. And there are 'middle-men' to beware, the literate observers who reported the visual events of a sixteenth century carnival or wrote down a tale which may have circulated orally for centuries. They may not have understood what was going on and so garbled the evidence. The historian has to try and reconstruct the way of thought of a largely illiterate society through literary means. That is why many judgements are less certain and generalisations more tentative than in other areas of historical study.

Debates about many specific aspects of popular culture thrive but the central issue for many historians is that of class. Robert Mandrou has studied the stories and songs in cheap booklets which were read by the minority of literate peasants but presumably also read aloud in taverns. He reckons that it was an escapist culture full of futile beliefs and miraculous occurrences imposed by the dominant classes in order to keep the people quiet. For Geneviève Bollème this same literature shows the basic concepts of the people with regard to life and death, freedom and oppression; in her view the people developed their own culture.

Peter Burke in his *Popular Culture in Early Modern Europe* stresses that élite culture and popular culture were not in watertight compartments. A courtly display, such as the masque, could have its origins in popular entertainment. Classically inspired poets such as Ariosto were published in shortened versions for popular consumption. And anyway, the ruling classes joined in popular culture, singing the songs, telling the tales and processing in the carnival until the eighteenth century, when the idea of what was 'vulgar' and to be avoided really took hold.

Even if we accept that there was genuine cultural interaction between the classes, that does not take away the stresses and strains of class and culture in the sixteenth century. Le Roy Ladurie has shown us how a carnival could be used for upper-class plotting at Romans in 1580. And the Witch Craze which had swept across much of Europe by the end of the sixteenth century, which we shall look at in some depth, is a dramatic example of how the culture of the learned could absorb that of the people in creating the stereotype of a witch.

Much of popular culture, however, concerns communities coming together and expressing their solidarity. The locations for shared ideas and entertainments might be the church, the tavern or the home, and the streets.

2. Popular Culture in the Church

The Church might seem the classic example of the learned élite imposing its culture on the people. However, the people in many ways used the church physically and symbolically for their own purposes.

The church was frequently adorned with gargoyles. They could be functional as part of the guttering but they also served to ward off the malevolent natural spirits which inhabited the mental universe of the people. The graveyard around the church was not just consecrated land where the dead could lie in peace. It was an open space which could be used for dancing and for sports, a practice condemned by sixteenth century reformers. Within the church there was not necessarily the reverential hush which we might expect today. There were no pews and angry reformers have again left us a picture of a congregation wandering around, gossiping and even playing with their dogs during a service. A congregation then did not see itself as simply disciplined and passive.

This does not mean that the people discounted religion. There is no evidence of widespread atheism and, indeed, Lucien Febvre in *The Problem of Unbelief* doubted whether atheism was conceptually possible in the sixteenth century. We saw on page 22 how church services gave an identity and security to the community. But what is most revealing is the way official Church teaching was given a twist by popular inter-pretation.

In the fifteenth century, the Holy Family had been much promoted as an object of veneration. However, Joseph was popularly viewed as a figure of fun. He was seen as a cuckold—Jesus was not his child—and many a joke was cracked about his lack of virility. What was being reinforced in this popular humour was the biological and social role of the father. In the decoration of a crib at Christmas, a practice growing in popularity since the twelfth century, the vulnerability of the baby Jesus at his birth was emphasised and along with it the need to care for the young. The cultural trappings of the Holy Family served to reinforce the norms of family life.

The saints in general gave expression to popular culture as well as to official theology. The Feast of St John falls in midsummer and was celebrated with great bonfires, the Fires of St John, especially in northern Europe where the lengthened days of the season were of such importance. The night before a saint's festival there was an opportunity for eating and drinking which could last the whole night through. These were called wakes, when time was turned around and night became day. Such celebrations were part of the making of holy days into holidays which acted as markers amidst the ordinary time of the year. Given Sundays as well as the number of such markers, there was limited ordinary time for working, just two hundred days during the year.

Churchmen were not separated off from popular culture. They exploited it, as in the church at Augsburg where popular drama was used which even included stage machinery with an angelic figure being lowered through the roof. Churchmen also shared popular culture. A variant of their own was the Feast of Fools when they would perform mock church services leading an ass around the church dressed up in holy vestments. Such a performance was not intended as a mockery of church services but as comic relief which would allow due seriousness to be sustained for the rest of the year. When the Feast of Fools came under attack during the fifteenth century, one French cleric defended it using the metaphor of a wine barrel which needs air holes to stop it exploding.

Popular culture in the church was made out of the materials of official religion but something new was created. The norms of traditional society were reinforced and celebrations, like a safety valve, could make ordinary life that much more acceptable and stable. This was so at least until the reformers, both Catholic and Protestant, took control in the sixteenth century.

3. Tales in the Tavern or the Home

Inside the tavern or the home, or at the *veillée* in France when women sewed and men sharpened their scythes, there was the joking and the gossip which is lost to the historian. However, there were also the bards or ballad singers, some of whose traditional stories, variations on stock characters and situations made recognisable by standard phrases about dying heroes or forlorn lovers, finally found their way into print. Such stories can tell us much about the values and fears of the society which responded to them.

162

One such tale, transmitted in taverns or simply retold at home or at the *veillée* and known in over a hundred versions in Germany, France and elsewhere, is that of Aschenputtel, or Cinderella as she has become known. The story is made up of five standard elements: abuse by relatives (the wicked stepmother and stepsisters); supernatural assistance (the fairy godmother); meeting with the hero (the prince); the recognition test (the fitting of the slipper); and marriage to the hero. These elements could be varied according to the creative skill of the performer and the liking of the audience. The recognition test, for instance, could be the fitting of a slipper, the wearing of a ring or the plucking of an apple. The idea of a recognition test itself floats from story to story, turning up in King Arthur and the Sword in the Stone, for example. In Cinderella, the recognition test, however, shows some of the anxiety about a woman being matched up with a suitable husband, which is why matchmakers were to be found in primitive societies. In the variation where only Cinderella could pluck the apples, having been starved by her stepmother, there surfaced the peasant fear of malnutrition. Remarriage was frowned upon in Early Modern society—hence the 'wicked stepmother and stepsisters' element. Involved in that is a universal emotional problem of the stepmother being seen as an intruder into the family circle. But it was also a matter of property settlements and dowries and deciding who should have precedence. Behind every fanciful tale there were the emotional and material realities of life.

Robin Hood, one of a number of outlaw heroes in the different regions of Europe, was already popular enough by 1405 for a Franciscan friar to complain then about people listening to rhymes about him in preference to going to Mass. Historians have debated as to whether he actually existed. He may have just been an offshoot of courtly romance or he may have been a historic outlaw, a primitive social rebel acting as a nucleus, rather like Jesse James in America, for a series of legends which grew in the re-telling. If he did exist, it is likely he operated in Barnesdale in the early fourteenth century rather than Sherwood Forest in the late twelfth century where later tradition and modern films have placed him. But the reality of Robin Hood is of less importance than his impact on the popular imagination.

Robin's adventures took place in the greenwood. The contrast of his life there with that of a settled village or town was the eternal contrast of nature as against culture. In this he merges with 'the green man' the personification of nature, who, however, suffers the fate of culture re-asserting itself over nature when his image is caged and then burnt. Robin's representation of nature also helped him to acquire Maid Marion as the legend developed, her role being identified with that of the Queen of the May. More specifically, Robin Hood was free of legal restraints, flouting the strict forest laws which prevented peasants from hunting and taking advantage of the abundance of nature.

In *Robin Hood and the Monk* a religious element is added. Christ is referred to as 'hym that dyed on a tre', identifying him with the forest, and Robin, relying on the 'myght of milde Marye', risks all in showing his outlaw's face in church in order to attend Mass. Religion seemed to be the property of the Church rather than the people and that could always breed resentment, if only occasionally heresy. In his guise as a social rebel Robin also stood up to financial exploitation by the Church. The earliest villain was not Prince John or the Sheriff of Nottingham but the Abbot of St Mary's.

With 'Robin Hood' showing us the general concerns of a primitive society and social issues concerning the peasants, it would seem to offer clear insights into popular culture. Historians, however, are uncertain as to the original audience and authorship for these ballads. There are aristocratic elements in the tales but it seems likely that yeomen and their minstrels were responsible for them, that is, small landowners rather than the peasants who made up the mass of people. This is another case where the boundary between popular and élite culture is blurred.

Whether peasants or small landowners, those who shaped popular culture were responsive to the events of the larger world. When Gaston de Foix was killed at the Battle of Ravenna in 1512 ballads sprang up about him which transmitted the news of his life and death. However, when news was assimilated into popular culture a pattern was often imposed on it. The ballads about Gaston de Foix were reworkings of those about King Rodrigo, the heroic fighter against the Moors of centuries before. Likewise, Louis XII of France was celebrated for his relatively peaceful, prosperous and just reign in the early sixteenth century; but Louis XII was also benefiting from the favoured place in ballads of St Louis, a predecessor as King of France. In popular culture, names carried a magnetic quality. The Emperor Frederick had inspired many tales of his return from sleep in a mountain in order to save Germany (another theme which crops up in the King Arthur legends); the name Frederick was seen in a prophetic way with regard to Luther's protector, the Elector Frederick of Saxony, who could then be regarded as a saviour of Germany. The mass of people were aware of current events and politics but through the matrix of popular culture.

If anything was to alter that matrix of popular culture, concerned as long as peasant society existed with the fertility of nature and the saviours of customary justice, it was printing. Printing fixed tales in a permanent form when they had before gone through the variations of oral transmission. Alien ideas, whether from another class or another region brought in by the colporteurs, the travelling salesmen of cheap booklets, could weaken the local tradition. But popular culture survived. Even into the twentieth century, folklorists have collected tales quite distinct from any printed versions.

4. Performances on the Streets

When a gang of youths appeared on the streets of a town or village around 1500, yelling and beating drums or anything else they could find in order to make 'rough music', they were not necessarily just drunk. It was quite likely that a *charivari* was under way.

A *charivari* was the ceremonial mocking of those who had offended the norms of a community. It was often provoked by great disparity in age between marriage partners, the elder usually being a widow or widower. This was disliked because a young person was being removed from the pool of eligible partners. In the case of re-marriage, there was the 'Cinderella syndrome' again—the rights of the children of a previous marriage were not guaranteed. So while the *charivari* might appear riotous, letting off steam and just acting as a sort of social safety valve, it was in fact seeking to re-assert the traditional order of things.

The youths who took part in a *charivari* were organised in Abbeys of Misrule. They were quite elaborate youth groups, even possessing their own judges and mock coinage. Their function was not just the *charivari* but the bearing of burning brands in procession and dancing for the fertility of the land and the people. The Abbey of Misrule in Romans was responsible for the maypole and it taxed and policed all weddings. An essential part of a marriage was the 'bedding' of the couple. In Artigat the village youths burst into the bedroom of the newlyweds Bertrande de Rols and Martin Guerre at midnight in order to serve the couple with *resveil*, a drink full of herbs and spices to ensure ardent and successful love-making. Whatever their different functions, the Abbeys of Misrule and other organised gangs of youths channelled the energies of the young, who were not settling into family life until quite late on in their mid-twenties in the sixteenth century. Youths in between puberty and marriage, a potential source of disorder, were thus tamed and made useful.

A *charivari* might take place at any season but the most important performance on the street, in southern Europe at least, took place in the run up to Lent, the period of compulsory fasting before Easter. This was the carnival—or *carnevale*, farewell to flesh. It was a time of riotous good living before the repressive season of abstinence from meat and sex. It was an occasion for ordinary hierarchy to cease to exist, for the world to be turned upside down.

The carnival might begin with a masquerade, dancing with faces painted or masked so that ordinary time and society would be suspended. In the carnivals of southern France the *reynages* would then take over, mock kingdoms like the Abbeys of Misrule, complete with mock kings, queens, ministers and laws. These reynages would take on animal emblems, possibly totems of ancestors but also with a social point to make; an earthbound animal such as a sheep being suitable for a largely lower class *reynage*, a bird such as an eagle fitting the social pretensions of a more upper class *reynage*. There would be feasts and sports, running

165

and horse races or tilting at rings with their suggestive sexual imagery. But it was not just a period of licence to have a wild time.

This was a time when norms would be reinforced with much hilarity. A cuckold or a husband beaten by his wife would be led through the streets seated backwards on an ass. If sex roles were to be re-affirmed, though, they first had to be reversed. In the processions through the streets there would be transvestitism, men in particular aping the 'unruly woman' who would threaten to disrupt the male ordered society. As well as sex roles, food had to be put in its place by first inverting it. An 'official' price list might be issued with strawberries costing nothing and hay or rotten herring as the most expensive. Violence as well was brought into the open—only in play unless something went wrong or there was malicious disruption. It would culminate in a duel between Carnival, in the shape of a self-indulgent, fat old man, and Lent, in the form of a crabbed old woman.

All this was not anarchy, despite all the tension and joy and fear. It was the logical, quite strict inversion of what was normal which could imprint onto people's imagination the structure of normality. And the world would be turned the right way up again come Ash Wednesday. Lent, the crabbed old woman, always won her duel or Carnival might be tried and symbolically executed. Built into every carnival was its own ending. It could only exist in extra-ordinary time, which served to highlight the nature of ordinary time and society.

Carnival was the occasion when sin was brought out into the open in order to be banished before Lent. There was a focus on excess in food and sex (the deadly sins of gluttony and lust) but sin also included anything which disrupted the customary order of things. That is why the carnival at Romans in 1580, studied by Le Roy Ladurie, became both an occasion for protest at new nobles seeking tax exemption and a response from the authorities who used the tension of mock violence to breed a fear of real anarchy in order to justify crushing, and even massacring, the protesters. When mixed with politics, the functions of carnival could be manipulated but Keith Thomas has pointed out carnival's importance in more primitive rural communities with no experience of politics as such. Carnival was a safety valve, releasing the tension which could build up in a hierarchical society where the people had no outlet through politics. And, for all its inverted references to everyday life, carnival had a value as an experience of sheer exhilaration, a second life in itself distinct from hierarchy and the dull grind of ordinary, ordered existence.

5. Identities

Popular culture could be quite unspecific. Tales or customs could be current across the whole continent and might have lasted, albeit in many variations, through the centuries. That reflects the features common to all of pre-industrial society in Europe. But popular culture could also be distinctive to different regions or communities and could express the identity of a group within the community. We have seen how different classes could concentrate in different *reynages*. There were also occupational groups who had their own stories and rituals. Apprentices in different trades might gather together in clubs, *compagnonnages*, with their own initiation rites, often variants of baptism. In Germany and other parts of Europe, it was compulsory for apprentices to spend some years travelling the country. That way they picked up new skills and enhanced solidarity between the scattered workers in the same trade.

This differentiation in popular culture was most likely to occur in towns but there were groups whose occupation separated them off from the culture of both ordinary towns and villages. Mariners lived for long periods in small, claustrophobic communities on board ship. They developed their own styles of dress, speech and music in the form of sea shanties. Shepherds were closer to ordinary communities but they were often on the move up in the hills and so developed their own distinctive culture, the pan-pipes in their music, for instance. The hundred thousand miners at work around 1500 lived in their own settlements and, working for wages, were the closest approximation at the time to a proletariat. They not only developed their own culture but were allotted a not quite human place in the imagination of the larger society—the idea of dwarves toiling in the mines is present in the tales of this period and was not invented by Disney or Tolkien.

The cutural symbols of a group could give it identity in its own eyes or in the eyes of others, but by the same token they could encourage conflict. When the Reformation came, it was not just beliefs which changed but also the religious practices which had helped to give a community its identity. There then began what Natalie Zemon Davis has identified as 'the Rites of Violence' with Protestants and Catholics being outraged by displays of the opposing group's culture and rituals. A funeral could lead to the snatching of the body by those of the rival religion. A baptism could lead to kidnapping. Protestants might trample on the Catholics' consecrated bread, the Host, while Catholics might burn Protestant bibles. Both sides would kill in order to purify the community. Religion and popular culture were closely integrated. That could serve the solidarity of the community but, when there was religious conflict, the associated cultural symbols signalled the split in the community rather than its unity.

There was one way, however, whereby religion and popular culture, the learning of the élite and the beliefs of the people, could come together to enhance solidarity. Individuals on the margins of society could be used as scapegoats once they had been given the religious/cultural identity of a witch.

6. Witches

We know about witches in this period largely from the records left behind by witch hunters. Margaret Murray, working on this evidence half a century ago, argued that the witch hunters of the Early Modern period were trying to crush a surviving pagan religion, its main ceremony held at the witches' sabbath and its horned god identified by Christians as the Devil. That theory has largely been discredited given the lack of evidence of a sabbath ever having taken place outside the imaginations of the witch hunters and their victims, who, broken down by torture, would admit to anything. There were magical practices amongst the people of Europe but nothing so systematic as a pagan religion.

The witch hunters were the believers in devil-worshipping witches, as we shall see, but that does not mean that they invented witches. Popular witch beliefs were prevalent in Early Modern Europe. The image of the Ancient Roman witch, the *striga*, seems to have survived in the form of the follower of the goddess Diana (or Holda in Germany) who would leave her home and fly out by night across towns or villages. It is hard to tell whether this is just a myth preserved in popular tales or whether some women convinced themselves that they were able to fly. It could be that the sensation of flight was brought on by applying special unguents—the recipes of some of these have been analysed and at least one ingredient, toad excrement, can apparently have a hallucinatory effect. Whatever the psychological realities of these beliefs, witches were not thought of in the popular mind as being worshippers of the Devil. Magic, good or bad, seemed generally independent of official Christian theology.

Only one group of witches has been properly documented, in Friuli in northern Italy, and they saw themselves as the opposite of evil-doing witches. They were the *benandanti*, 'good-walkers', who claimed that they left their bodies by night in order to battle against evil. They became *benandanti* if they were born with the caul (the membrane around the embryo) intact. They told the Inquisition how, when they were in their early twenties, they were summoned to battle by a mysterious captain and had no choice but to go. They saw their magic as specifically serving Christ. However, that did not fit in with the official theology of the Inquisition which judged all magic to be evil.

In 1580 one of the *benandanti*, Moduco, told the Inquisition this, shortly after investigations had begun:

> I am a benandante because I go with the others to fight four times a year, that is during the Ember Days, at night; I go invisibly in spirit and the body remains behind; we go forth in the service of Christ, and the witches of the Devil; we fight each other, we with bundles of fennel and they with sorghum stalks . . . In the fighting that we do, one time we fight over the wheat and all the other grains, another time over the livestock, and at other times over the vineyards. And so, on four occasions we fight over all the fruits of

the earth and for those things won by the benendanti that year there is abundance.

By 1649 another of the benandanti, Michele Soppe, was telling a different story to the Inquisition:

> The place was in the country near Malisana during the dance and convent-icle of the witches, in that field where they gather, about two years after I began to go to the ball, in the presence of all the witches and warlocks who were assembled there. It happened like this: the devil asked me if I wanted to give my soul up to him; in exchange he would grant me all the favours that I desired. At the devil's request I replied that I surrendered my soul to him . . . Also, at the request of the devil I twice denied Jesus Christ and his holy faith; every time I went to the witches' ball I kissed the devil's arse, just like all the witches and warlocks, and I did all the things the others did.

1 *Originally how did the* benandanti *see themselves as serving the community?*
2 *What had changed by 1649 in the image they presented of themselves?*
3 *How might such a change of image have come about?*

The *benandanti* were specific to one small region but all over Europe there were 'cunning' women, healers and diviners, people who had supernatural powers which could serve the community. But whoever could cure could also kill. When someone used magical powers to harm people, livestock or the soil, he, or more usually it was thought to be she, was guilty of what was called *maleficium*, the casting of harmful spells. It was *maleficium*, not devil worship, which was an idea originating in popular culture.

After 1500 there were an increasing number of accusations of *male-ficium* against neighbours and even members of the same family. Each accusation had its specific cause, a personal quarrel, a mysterious death, a wild old woman prone to dangerous cursing. But there are also more general causes. The plague continued to strike sporadically so the threat of devastating misfortune was always present and could make people readier to accuse others of the evil arts. More specifically, sixteenth century communities were disrupted by the growth of the population and by changes to family and commercial life. This gave rise to elusive anxieties which could be relieved by finding a scapegoat in the form of a witch.

The Reformation had its effect. Alan McFarlane sees the decline of Catholic almsgiving as a source of guilt: that guilt could be relieved by labelling the beggar turned away from the door as an evil-doer, even a performer of *maleficium*. Keith Thomas has shown how the Catholic Church, with its many sacramental practices, was a source of counter-magic whereas the law was the only recourse for Protestants. This does not explain why accusations of *maleficium* also increased in Catholic countries but in those cases there was the Counter-Reformation, not just the counter-attack on Protestantism but also a drive to impose official religion more firmly on the masses, leaving less scope for either magic or counter-magic *(see Chapter XII)*. And, while accusations of *maleficium* were natural to a peasant society and perhaps intensified by religious changes, they were also encouraged by the way they fitted in to the panic amongst churchmen and judges about the devil being loose in the world. Popular culture and learned demonology merged in the witch craze.

7. The Witch Craze

Up to the eleventh century, Christian writers had dismissed witchcraft as an illusion but through the succeeding centuries, details were added to what Levack has called a 'cumulative concept of witchcraft'. Witches were clearly capable of *maleficium* but many other features were added to their original image amongst the people.

According to these developing academic beliefs, witches were supposed to commit the most heinous crime of killing and eating babies. It was asserted that they could change themselves into the shapes of different animals. From the followers of Diana, they acquired the power of flight on a broomstick or perhaps a goat. They were thought to fly to a sabbath and worship the devil in an inverted form of Christian worship, as the *benandanti* were supposed to do once the Inquisition had finished with them. Later on, the image of witches was joined by that of familiars, animals who would do their bidding and who would leave a tell-tale sign, the mark, a spot of insensitive skin where the familiars could suckle the witch's blood. By the mid-fifteenth century inquisitors were finding most of these characteristics, or persuading themselves they were, in their witch hunts in mountainous regions. One inquisitor at Como at the foot of the Alps in northern Italy claimed 41 victims in one year. For him and his like, *maleficium* was not just one brand of popular magic; it was an indication that a sabbath-attending servant of the Devil was at work.

There was nothing amongst the dominant ideas of the time which could erode the concept of the witch. Such supernatural malice and service to the devil contradicted nothing in scholastic philosophy. Some Platonic philosophers of the Renaissance, who believed in harmonious natural forces dominating the world, good demons in a sense, criticised the beliefs about witches but their voices were in a minority. Another intellectual trend of the time was a re-examination of the thought of St Augustine, which would inspire Luther but also contained within it a demonology which just reinforced the concept of the witch. Stuart Clark has shown how there was an increasing obsession during this period with inversion—if Christ inspired reverence then His inverse, the Devil, along with his servants the witches, consequently inspired all the greater fear.

Given such ideology it is not so surprising that two particularly enthusiastic witch hunters, Heinrich Krämer and Jakob Sprenger, managed to panic Pope Innocent VIII into issuing a Papal Bull in 1484 empowering them to pursue witches with all vigour in Germany and, by implication, making general what had hitherto been local hunts. They followed this up in 1486 with the publication of *Malleus Maleficarum*, an encyclopaedia of what inquisitors could expect witches to get up to. Some details, about the sabbath for instance, were actually left out but with the addition of the work of Paulus Grillandus, published in 1524, the picture of the witch was more or less complete. Again printing had played a vital role. The inquisitor and the judge could now run a trial according to the textbooks, and the realities of the crimes being investigated mattered less and less.

The Church had provided the image of the witch but the judges had added to it. They had teased out new details during trials which could be fed back into the textbook image. And there was no shortage of details given that witchcraft was the *crimen exceptum*, the exceptional crime warranting the suspension of normal procedures. Rules on evidence, disinterested juries and the reliability of witnesses were ignored. The unsupported testimony of hysterical children could identify someone as a witch and bring them to the stake. But in many cases there were no witnesses, just circumstantial evidence, and there was always the need to find out the names of other witches. Torture, which had been introduced into ordinary legal procedures since the thirteenth century, would be applied and confessions extracted from those accused of witchcraft.

The full range of torture instruments was used—thumbscrews, racks, the strappado where the body was suspended from a pulley and jerked violently in mid-air—but the *tormentum insomniae*, sleep deprivation, was the one guaranteed to make the suspected witch break down, supply any details of her attendance at the sabbath which might satisfy the relentless interrogator, and provide a list of names of others who could be tried for witchcraft and tortured in turn. With torture forcing confessions, it is not surprising that judges found their worst fears were realised. The answers to their leading questions confirmed for them the truth of the textbooks such as the *Malleus Maleficarum*. Where the victim had a lurid imagination, and many were accused in the first place because they were old and confused or were displaying symptoms of psychosis, new details could emerge on, say, the consumption at sabbaths of fried bats, a witches' delicacy in Alsace. Such detail could be used to amplify the theologians' theory of witchcraft. And there were those names of other witches which showed conclusively that Satan had a legion of followers who could overwhelm Europe unless they were mercilessly crushed. There was no room for doubt. In cases where torture was used, the conviction rate was around 95 percent.

The conviction rate in England's secular courts was much lower than was general on the Continent, being around 50 percent or below. This seems to have been due less to English scepticism than to differences in legal procedure. In secular courts on the Continent there had been a judicial revolution. Restorative justice, whereby the injured party had to sue for justice and suffer penalties if he could not prove his case, gave way to retributive justice with the state prosecuting the criminal. That meant that victimless crimes, such as simply being a witch even without any evidence of harm to others, could be prosecuted on the Continent whereas in England one individual had to accuse another and provide evidence of actual injury. And torture was not a part of ordinary legal procedure in England. This did not exclude witch scares altogether in England but they were fewer and quicker to end than on the Continent. In Scotland, which shared some of the Continental procedures such as torture, three times as many were executed for witchcraft as in England.

Spain was another country where the witch hunts were few and relatively controlled. Given its reputation for religious bigotry in the Early Modern period, this has puzzled some historians. H R Trevor-Roper has suggested that the Spanish were well supplied with scapegoats in the form of Jews and so they had less use for the stereotype of the witch. This explanation is problematic given that the Rhineland was a centre both of intense anti-semitism and some of the most savage witch hunts. Brian Levack has emphasised that witch hunting hysteria grew in the most uncontrolled fashion where the courts concerned were both secular and local. In Spain the highly centralised, ecclesiastical courts which made up the Spanish Inquisition handled witchcraft cases and kept hysteria under control. Indeed, there were Spanish Inquisitors among the sceptics concerning witchcraft. In 1610, the witch craze broke out in the Basque country. Inquisitor Salazar, sent to investigate it, reported that 'there were neither witches nor bewitched until they were talked and written about.' This scepticism was fostered by the Spanish Inquisition's long experience of false denunciations for heresy; with its own, more sophisticated measures for dealing with religious deviance, it was less prone to panic.

A witch-believing peasantry ready to make accusations; a learned demonology which absorbed the popular idea of *maleficium* into Devil worship; the dissemination of that demonology through printing; a judicial revolution and the use of torture, with local, secular courts ready to be caught up in hysteria—these were the preconditions for the witch craze and countries, such as England and Spain, which did not share them all, escaped more lightly. But these preconditions were established by the early years of the sixteenth century and yet there was a lull of nearly half a century before witch hunts started to spread like epidemics across Europe from the 1560s onwards. Trevor-Roper has argued that the precipitant of these witch hunts was religious conflict in Europe: 'The recrudescence (outbreak) of the absurd demonology of the *Malleus* was not the logical consequence of any religious idea: it was the social consequence of renewed ideological war and the accompanying climate of fear.' By the 1560s some Protestants, and in particular the Calvinists, were becoming more evangelical and more expansionist. Also by then the Catholic Church had started to re-organise itself and the Counter-Reformation was under way. Particularly hard hit by witch hunts were the border lands of France, Germany and Switzerland and these were the areas most disputed by Catholics and Protestants. Johann von

Schöneburg, the Archbishop-Elector of Trier, for instance, was a militant supporter of the Counter-Reformation, first hammering the Protestants after he began his reign in 1581. Then between 1587 and 1593, he had 368 witches burnt, leaving two villages with only one female inhabitant apiece. When one of his judges proved too lenient he had him tried for witchcraft, tortured, strangled and burnt. Such intensive witch hunts reached a peak in both Protestant and Catholic lands in the 1620s when the Thirty Years' War had brought with it renewed religious conflict. The worst was over in western Europe by 1650, when religious conflict in Europe was dying down.

Although religious conflict helps to explain much of the timing of the witch hunts it does not work in all cases. In Scotland, for instance, Christina Larner noted that although the passing of legislation against witchcraft in the 1560s coincided with the campaigns against Catholicism led by John Knox, the first major period of witch hunting was not until the 1590s. That was sparked off by James VI when he put the Earl of Bothwell on trial, accusing him of treachery and witchcraft. For James, the two crimes were closely allied, witchcraft being a form of treachery. As the *Malleus* put it: 'For witchcraft is high treason against God's majesty . . . Any person, whatever his rank or position, upon such an accusation may be put to the torture.' James, with the theory of the divine right of kings developing at the time, thought that any rebellion against the king must also be a rebellion against God and vice-versa. Those at the centre of such plots might be of high rank but their supporters could be anywhere and everywhere. So the hunt for witches was given a political boost.

Politics had always been an aspect of witch trials. In the fifteenth century the Duchesses of Bedford and Gloucester had been accused of witchcraft in the midst of political intrigues. In France, Joan of Arc's claim of supernatural inspiration had laid her open to charges of witchcraft by her political enemies. But by the late sixteenth century, the politics had changed. No longer were leading politicians just seeking to overcome opponents. With the decline of the Church as an independent institution in the Early Modern period, politicians sought to exercise an increasing moral authority. Larner has shown how witchcraft legislation was often accompanied by measures to regulate morality. Witch hunts were part of a general moral panic which included fears about infanticide, incest, adultery and sodomy, as efforts were made to regulate the lives of the peasantry and the unrespectable hordes of the towns. The witch craze was in part a feature of the emerging Godly state, taking on the moral authority formerly exercised by the Church.

Witch hunting did not end completely once the Godly state had established itself or when religious conflict died down in the mid-seventeenth century. In Poland where the Counter-Reformation did not become militant until the late 1600s, the witch craze was delayed and lasted from 1680 to 1750. But this was exceptional because by then educated Europe had dropped the late medieval demonology which justified the craze. This was not because of the reasoning of critics. In the sixteenth century Johann Weyer had put forward strong arguments for apparent cases of witchcraft being the product of torture and psychological delusion. James VI's retort was all too typical in suggesting that Weyer himself must be a witch. The disappearance of the demonology resulted from the triumph amongst the educated classes of a scientific, mechanistic world view which took hold in the Enlightenment of the eighteenth century. There was no room for Devil-worshipping witches in a universe which God had made to run like clockwork according to scientific laws.

But this brings us back to where we started—the relationship between popular culture and the learning of the élite. We have seen how the prevalent popular belief in *maleficium* was fitted in to the devil worship which was worked out schematically by theologians and amplified by judges. In the process, popular belief was itself transformed. The people started to believe in devil-worshipping witches as portrayed in the *Malleus Maleficarum* and they were not quickly convinced that they did not exist just because a scientific world view had taken hold of the upper and middle classes. There were still witch prickers ('brodders' in Scotland) who specialised in finding the Devil's mark. Suspected witches were still subject to the 'swimming' test—when they sank they were innocent, if also possibly drowned. One Ruth Osborne did die as a result of such a test at Tring in Hertfordshire as late as 1751. The witch beliefs completed in sixteenth century Europe had staying power as part of popular culture until improved communications and widespread urbanisation eroded their rural environment.

8. Witchcraft and Women

Witchcraft raises one last issue with regard to popular culture and society—the place of women. A man could be a witch but around 80 percent of those accused were women. This reflects an enduring fear of women, particularly old women, marginal to society. And there were strains as a woman's place in society deteriorated in the Early Modern period.

Women were suspect in the first place because, just as they had power over life, so it was feared they had power to bring death. On the whole, they were the healers who gathered herbs, made up the medicines and perhaps muttered the incantations taught to them by their mothers. Such a woman could kill as well as cure by use of her skills.

Women were sexually stereotyped as having only a fragile control over insatiable lust. This threatened order in the community and the family in particular. And the stereotype fashioned fantasies about the orgies of perverted sex to be experienced with the Devil at the sabbath.

While women were perceived as a threat, their real position might be one of defencelessness. Not having the social or legal standing of a man, a woman might turn to spells in her own defence, attempting *maleficium*. If she was brought to court, even when she had not attempted *maleficium*, her word would be treated as of much less value than that of a man.

In particular, old women (at that time those over 40 or 50) were subject to witchcraft accusations. They were thought to be useless to the community in general, marginal and therefore dangerous. A fear might have been that they would prey sexually on young men—if a *charivari* did not scare them away from doing so. If they were widows there might be property disputes regarding their inheritance. In a dispute with neighbours an old woman, made strange by senility, might mutter curses and pay for it dearly when she was brought to trial as a witch.

This fear of women was not confined to instances of witchcraft. On the streets during a carnival there were men imitating 'unruly women' as we saw earlier. These 'unruly women' would not play the sex role allotted to them and submit to male domination. And the demand for such submission was growing as society became ever more patriarchal during the Early Modern period. Marriage laws were restricting women further. Their role in guilds, in commerce and in farm management dwindled. By 1600 the differential between the wages of men and women had increased sharply.

Witchcraft accusations were the most savage assaults on the position of women as it deteriorated during the sixteenth century and beyond. This does not mean that all the accusers were men. Women too would spread rumours about a suspect neighbour and act as witnesses in courts. This is in part due to the fact that they, as well as men, were subject to all the demographic, economic and religious changes which disrupted communities and they were therefore prone to accept the stereotype of a female witch offered by male theologians and judges. Also, women might have felt the need to prove their own normality, their own willingness to accept the assumptions of a patriarchal society. Their collaboration in witchcraft trials does not stop the witch craze being an important historical example of the repression of women.

9. Bibliography

P Burke *Popular Culture in Early Modern Europe* (Temple Smith, 1978). E Le Roy Ladurie *Carnival in Romans* (1979. Penguin, 1981). N Z Davis *The Return of Martin Guerre* (Harvard, 1983). (Daniel Vigne's film about Martin Guerre is also well worth seeing.) R Darnton 'Peasants Tell Tales' in *The Great Cat Massacre* (Random House, 1984). H R Trevor-Roper *The European Witch-Craze* (Pelican, 1969). C Larner *Witchcraft and Religion* (Blackwell, 1984). B Levack *The Witch Hunt in Early Modern Europe* (Longman, 1987). C Ginzburg *The Night Battles* (1966. Routledge & Kegan Paul, 1983)—about the *Benandanti*.

10. Discussion Points and Exercises

A   *This section consists of questions or points that might be used for discussion (or written answers) as a way of expanding on the chapter and testing understanding of it:*

1   What problems do historians face in analysing popular culture?

2   How far was the Church responsible for forming popular culture?

3   What insights can peasants' tales give us into their concerns and priorities? In what ways must the historian be cautious in his analysis?

4   What counted most in a *charivari* or carnival—the joy of licensed anarchy or the social meaning?

5   How could popular culture sometimes help to unite a community and sometimes help to destroy it?

6   In what ways were witches real?

7   How did the cumulative concept of the witch as devil worshipper arise?

8   How did the courts react to peasant beliefs in *maleficium* and how did judicial procedures encourage a witch craze?

9   Why did witch hunting become so intensive in the later sixteenth century?

10   What place does witchcraft have in the history of women?

B   *Essay questions*

1   What are the significant features of society in Early Modern Europe which a study of popular culture reveals?

2   'Popular culture at the time of the Reformation did not exist in its own right. It was dependent on the culture of clerical and noble élites'. Discuss.

3   How important was the religious element to popular culture in the Early Modern period?

4   'The witch craze was like a disease in Early Modern Europe, always present and ready to break out in devastating epidemics.' What made 'epidemics' of witch hunting possible?

5   How had the stereotype of the witch developed and become so firmly established in Europe by the beginning of the sixteenth century?

6   Whose interests, if any, did the witch craze serve?

C   *Exercise*

For each of the following statements, find two or more pieces of evidence, at least one example of which supports and one of which qualifies, the generalisation made. The material can be drawn from this chapter, other chapters or general reading. The evidence can then be collated and considered in group discussion to decide what can be stated with some certainty and what needs to be tentative.

a) 'Popular culture could not escape control by official religion.'

b) 'The main purpose of popular culture and the witch craze was to crush any deviance from social norms.'

c) 'Printing ended the autonomy of popular culture.'

d) 'Popular culture consisted of ways of letting off steam. It kept society stable by acting as a safety valve.'

e) 'Popular culture is, in many respects, just another term for popular superstition'.

f) 'Women were inevitably subject to men in pre-industrial society.'

The material discussed in this exercise could then be used in answering essay question 1 above.

VIII Charles V

1. Introduction

'Roman King, future Emperor, semper augustus, King of Spain, Sicily, Jerusalem, the Balearic Islands, the Canary Islands, the Indies and the mainland on the far shore of the Atlantic, Archduke of Austria, Duke of Burgundy, Brabant, Styria, Carinthia, Carniola, Luxembourg, Limburg, Athens, and Patras, Count of Habsburg, Flanders and Tyrol, Count Palatine of Burgundy, Hainault, Pfirt, Roussillon, Landgrave of Alsace, Count of Swabia, Lord of Asia and Africa.'

Thus ran the titles of Charles I of Spain, more commonly known as Charles V, the Holy Roman Emperor. The list conveys the extent of Charles' territories, stretching from Spain to Italy, Austria, the Netherlands and Franche-Comté and, across the ocean, the vast, only partly discovered bulk of the New World. Some of the titles are purely honorific, such as Lord of Africa and Asia, while the title 'Roman King, future Emperor' conveyed great prestige but no territory. The latter is very important. By virtue of his titles Charles could legitimately see himself as the leader of Christendom with all that would entail in the fight against the Infidel and heresy; but the support for such a claim to leadership came from a strictly limited territorial base, albeit one that dwarfed the possessions of any other European ruler.

The key to Charles V's empire lay not in conquest but in dynasty. It was an accident of inheritance that indicates the second vital point about Charles V's empire, which is also revealed in the list of his titles. The only link between the territories was the person of Charles himself. In each dominion he had a different position (for instance, King of Spain, Archduke of Austria, Count of Swabia) and there was no unity between them, hence the more accurate and contemporary term to describe his empire— 'monarchia'. Charles respected the individual traditions and privileges of his territories. This was unavoidable given the impossibility of fighting sustained opposition had he done otherwise, but it meant that no imperial institutions or financial systems were created which would have made his empire more manageable.

Charles was the eldest son of Philip of Burgundy and Joanna of Spain, sometimes called Joanna the Mad. He spent his entire childhood in the Netherlands and became Duke of Burgundy at the age of six. The

THE EMPIRE OF CHARLES V

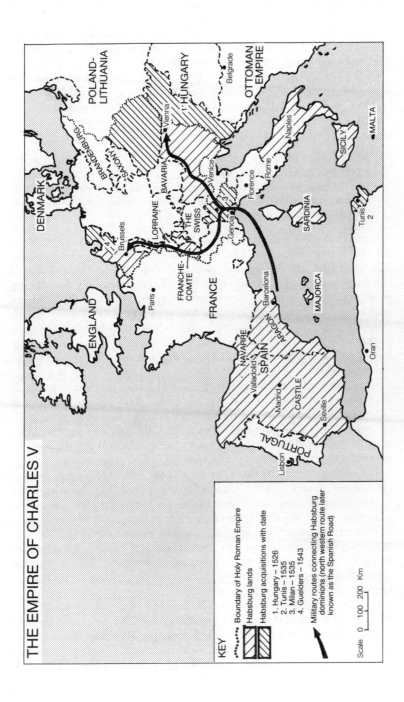

KEY

- Boundary of Holy Roman Empire
- Habsburg lands
- Habsburg acquisitions with date
  1. Hungary – 1526
  2. Tunis – 1535
  3. Milan – 1535
  4. Guelders – 1543

- Military routes connecting Habsburg dominions (north western route later known as the Spanish Road)

Scale 0 100 200 Km

Burgundian court had an elaborate code of chivalry expressed in the order of the Golden Fleece and this heavily influenced Charles. He believed strongly in the idea of knightly honour and fighting for the Christian faith and this sometimes led him into naive behaviour, as in 1528 when he challenged Francis I to single combat for breaking his word over the Treaty of Madrid *(see page 193)*.

Charles believed he had received his inheritance from God as a sacred trust and it was his responsibility to maintain the unity of Christendom and to fight the Infidel. This view was shared by Mercurino Gattinara, his Imperial Chancellor from 1518 to 1530, who wrote to Charles immediately after his election as Emperor in 1519:

> Sire, God has been very merciful to you: he has raised you above all the Kings and princes of Christendom to a power such as no sovereign has enjoyed since your ancestor Charles the Great (i.e. Charlemagne). He has set you on the way towards a world monarchy, towards the uniting of all Christendom under a single shepherd.

Unfortunately for Charles, the rest of Europe did not want a single shepherd, certainly not one who had the power to make the idea a reality. The emerging nations of England and France and the princes of Germany saw Charles' claims to overlordship as potentially threatening while the Pope, whose duty it was, according to Charles, to support him, could tolerate neither Charles' claim to be the arbiter of Europe's religious problems nor his pretensions to power in Italy. 'Successive popes were not sorry to see Charles V ruined by the problem of heresy whose resolution might have greatly increased his power' (N M Sutherland).

Thus the uniting of Christendom eluded Charles precisely because of the extent of his world monarchy. His power held out the prospect of success and yet at the same time snatched it away. However genuine his religious ideals, his potential allies in the struggle against the Protestants, the Pope and Catholic princes, were reluctant to give him the necessary support to ensure success because of his political role.

It has been suggested that Charles was the victim of his inheritance, condemned to seek a prize that would always elude him because of the forces ranged against him. This is too simple a view; religion was not the only motive behind Charles' actions. The war against France always took precedence over defence of the Danube against the Turks and over the struggle against the German Protestants. It is important to consider whether this was putting his dynasty and inheritance first or whether Charles could legitimately justify his actions by putting the security of his frontiers above all other considerations.

Charles V had great power but this brought awesome responsibilities and the suspicion and potential hostility of the other powers of Europe. In general, Charles failed when the forces ranged against him were too great. But much depends on how Charles is viewed. The great biography by Karl Brandi which is the foundation of modern studies of Charles V focuses attention on Charles in northern Europe, where his setbacks were greatest. He might be thought more of a success if he is viewed as a Mediterranean monarch rather than as a world emperor.

2. Charles in Spain

In January 1516, Ferdinand of Aragon died and Charles became King with his mother Joanna the Mad, who lived on as a shadowy figure at Tordesillas until 1555, technically sharing the Crown. It was not until September 1517 that Charles arrived in his new kingdom because first the Netherlands had to be safeguarded from attack by offering concessions to the French in the Peace of Noyon. Cardinal Cisneros, the regent of Spain after Ferdinand's death, had been urging Charles to arrive as soon as possible because of widespread discontent in the country.

The nobility sought to take advantage of the power vacuum before Charles' arrival to re-establish the control they had lost under Ferdinand and Isabella, and the towns were ready to fight to defend their privileges. Cisneros' attempt to raise a permanent army was defeated by both towns and grandees, who saw that it would have made the Crown militarily independent and Cisneros had to give way to prevent serious trouble.

The young, ugly and awkward king did not make a favourable first impression and his actions soon confirmed the Spaniards' worst fears. Cisneros was dismissed but he died before the letter could reach him. Worst of all, Burgundians were installed in key positions. To avoid breaking his promise not to give offices to foreigners, Charles issued them with letters of naturalisation, a device which caused widespread resentment. The most glaring affront was the appointment of a seventeen year old Burgundian as the Archbishop of Toledo.

In spite of the tension, the Castilian Cortes (parliament) was persuaded to vote an exceptionally large *servicio* (tax) of 600 000 ducats payable over three years. Charles immediately left for Aragon where the more entrenched nature of the Cortes' privileges, the *fueros*, delayed his recognition as king and a grant of 200 000 ducats for eight months. In Catalonia, the process took a year and produced 100 000 ducats. Before he could visit Valencia in 1519, Charles received news which meant he had to leave for Germany to ensure his succession as Holy Roman Emperor. Such a journey required ready cash.

To provide this money, the Castilian Cortes was summoned, in defiance of tradition, to the northern town of Santiago to vote a second *servicio* before the expiry of the first. The town of Toledo refused to send anyone and the instructions given to the deputies of Salamanca summed up the feelings of the Cortes: 'adjourn the Cortes . . . stop offices going to foreigners . . . do not agree to any servicio . . . the king's duty is to govern . . . by his presence, not by his absence.' It was only by the most intense pressure, and by adjourning the Cortes to La Coruna where

Charles was preparing to set sail, that the court managed to secure a subsidy. The money was never collected and the alienation of Charles' Castilian subjects was now complete.

3. Revolt: *Comuneros* and *Germania*

Charles abandoned his Spanish kingdoms as they flared into revolt. The causes of the rebellion did not lie merely in his tactless handling of the Cortes or appointment of foreigners. Resentment had been growing in the towns for years as a result of the Crown's failure to protect them against the attacks of the great aristocratic families. A myth developed of a golden age under the Catholic Kings and Charles was urged to 'act in everything like the Catholic lords, King Ferdinand and Queen Isabella'.

The accession of a foreign king and Emperor was unwelcome in three respects: he would be absent for much of the time; his empire was centred on distant north Europe; his advisers treated the Castilians 'as Indians'. Thus the *Comunero* movement which developed in the towns was essentially reactionary, united in a hatred of present conditions and groping after a previous, more satisfactory state. The demands issued in November 1520 asked that Charles return to Spain and marry soon; he should remove foreigners from his entourage; the Cortes was to be given a major role in government and to meet every three years; taxes and the expenses of the court should be reduced. None of these demands was revolutionary but even so Charles' position in Castile was soon in grave danger.

Following the lead of Toledo, riots broke out in most of the major towns of Castile. In Segovia the deputies who had voted for the new taxes were murdered. Royal authority broke down and the *grandees*, further angered by the appointment of Adrian of Utrecht as Regent despite Charles' promise to appoint no more foreigners, did nothing to help the royal cause. The rebels found leadership in men such as Juan de Padilla, members of the lesser nobility of the towns, from whom the deputies to the Cortes were drawn.

A crisis was reached after the accidental burning of the great centre of Medina del Campo, which was blamed on government forces. In outrage, fourteen of the eighteen cities represented in the Cortes set up a Holy Junta and in September 1520 their forces seized Tordesillas and Joanna, the legal Queen. If she had been persuaded to support the *Comuneros* in writing, it would have legitimised the rising and made the loss of Spain a real possibility. This was the climax of the rebellion but Joanna would sign nothing and the *Comuneros* could not agree on a common course of action. At this opportune moment, Adrian of Utrecht made some skilful concessions to win over the *grandees*. The Constable and Admiral of Castile were appointed co-regents; the collection of the *servicio* was to be suspended and no more foreigners would be appointed.

These concessions, combined with the increasingly radical nature of the revolt as it spread to the estates of the *grandees* and threatened their

182

privileges, brought them over to the government's side. Old antagonisms between the towns and the nobility surfaced and at Villalar in April 1521, the Castilian nobles and their retainers destroyed the *Comunero* army and executed Juan de Padilla and other leaders. The revolt was stopped just in time to prevent its exploitation by Francis I who had invaded Navarre. Castilians joined Aragonese in repelling the invader who was crushed at the battle of Pamplona in June 1521.

The revolt of the *Comuneros* was over but Charles could not take the credit. His inability to make quick decisions and the problems of ruling a country from the other end of Europe had brought his reign close to collapse. It was the transformation of the revolt into a social protest rather than a political one which mobilised the forces of the nobility on his side. Despite this, Habsburg power was never seriously challenged in Castile again. The ceremony of swearing the *fueros*, liberties and privileges, at the start of each reign became a mere formality. The towns retained their privileges but the *corregidores* were re-established and the Cortes became little more than a tax-voting assembly. The deputies' salaries were paid from the taxes they voted and Charles refused to consider 'grievances' before supply (of taxation).

The nobles who had saved Charles were rewarded by being confirmed in their social position and privileges, above all in their exemption from taxes, but they were increasingly excluded from the government of Spain. With a compliant Cortes, Charles could now afford a standing army and therefore he was less dependent on the power of the nobles.

The fragmented nature of the Spanish peninsula had been clearly illustrated in the revolt of the *Comuneros* not only by the failure of the Castilian towns to overcome their rivalry but also by the failure to link up with a major rebellion which broke out simultaneously in Valencia. This revolt of the *Germania* (brotherhood) never posed as great a threat to Charles because it was a class conflict which was dealt with by the nobility.

The *Germania* had been set up to repel attacks by Barbary pirates but its leaders took the opportunity of a plague outbreak in Valencia in 1520 to seize control of the city and the surrounding countryside. The violence of the rebels ensured their eventual defeat at the hands of the nobility even though the rebellion spread across the whole kingdom and over into Majorca. The main forces of the *Germania* were defeated in October 1521, but resistance continued into 1523 and it was not until December 1524 that a general pardon was finally issued after the execution of hundreds of rebels.

The revolt was allowed to continue for so long because the government attached less importance to Valencia. A challenge to royal authority there lacked the force of a similar challenge in Castile and the nobles could therefore be left to control the revolt themselves.

The revolt of the *Germania* did not affect the privileges of the Aragonese. The nobility continued to exercise great power over their tenants and, in contrast to Castile, the Cortes maintained the right to discuss grievances before taxation, a privilege it was not worth the Crown contesting given the poverty of the eastern kingdoms. Aragon kept its liberty at a price, however. As J H Elliott saw, the history of Spain became in fact the history of Castile. Castilians became reconciled to the new, alien regime by the opportunities it opened up and by Charles' increasing attachment to his eventual homeland, while the Aragonese found themselves ever more isolated from affairs of state, especially after Charles' death.

4. The Government of Spain

Charles returned to Spain in July 1522 and remained there until 1529, his longest stay in the country. During those seven years he married, remodelled the administration and underwent a decisive shift in outlook. When Charles left Spain again he was no longer a foreign monarch; he had adopted it as his spiritual home even if he was present there for only eight of his remaining 29 years. Spain had become the centre of his empire and the home of his family. In choosing Spain, Charles tied the interests of his dynasty to the Mediterranean and Atlantic, leaving the Austrian homeland of the Habsburgs, and therefore the Imperial crown, to his younger brother Ferdinand.

The other major feature of these years is the decisive relegation of Aragon to a secondary role. Charles continued the policy of Ferdinand in regarding Castile as 'the head of all the rest' because it was wealthier and more populous and also because it was easier to extract revenue from it.

Charles returned to a country that was still seething with discontent. It was vitally necessary to rebuild support for the monarchy rapidly because the treasury was in ruins: the Comuneros had taken the Crown's ordinary revenue for 1521–22 and the *servicios* had not been collected. Charles had to reduce popular hostility to his government and thus gain acceptance for his new taxes. A number of reforms were therefore adopted including the replacement of unpopular or corrupt officials. The Cortes was allowed into partnership with the Crown. In return for taxes, it was responsible for handling revenue which provided opportunities for members of the Cortes to enrich themselves.

A partnership was also effected with the nobility. As the price for their exclusion from central government except on the king's terms, the nobility were allowed to govern the countryside with very little interference. Peace was brought to Spain but at considerable cost, with severe limitations on central policy and on the Crown's ability to make changes.

The Spanish empire had no institutions in common and no imperial bureaucracy. Any attempt at reform of the administration had to take account of the privileges of each territory and also the prolonged absence of the Emperor. But throughout Charles' huge empire there was a need for central direction and co-ordination of policies. Gattinara, the

Imperial Chancellor, therefore developed the conciliar system of Ferdinand and Isabella by reforming the Council of Castile, creating the Councils of Finance and the Indies and remodelling the Council of War. Later, in 1555, a Council of Italy was created which completed the system. The councils were bureaucratic committees composed mainly of *letrados* (university trained lawyers) for the administration of royal policy. They communicated with the Emperor through a secretary who thereby acquired considerable power. The most important of these was Francisco de los Cobos, secretary of the Council of Finance, who was largely responsible for the administration of Spain in Charles' absence. An Andalucian of humble origins, he amassed a vast fortune but he was a reliable and efficient servant and as such enjoyed Charles' fullest confidence. Cobos was a rival of Gattinara's and this led to a decline in the latter's influence from about 1527. After Gattinara's death, Charles became his own Chancellor with Cobos responsible for Spanish and Mediterranean affairs and Nicholas Perrenot, Lord of Granvelle, his leading adviser on the Netherlands and the empire.

The secretaries acted as filters for incoming correspondence and decided whether a dispatch should go direct to the Emperor or first to the appropriate council for discussion. The system also gave council members, and especially the secretaries, enormous patronage as they controlled acccess to the Emperor. Corruption was rife and the bureaucracy grew to parasitic proportions. Although it worked adequately in ordinary circumstances, the conciliar system found it hard to respond to crises. This is clearly seen in the council of Finance.

5. Finance

The Council of Finance was created in 1523 to supervise and control all income and expenditure, and to establish regular and efficient means of raising money. In fact the enormous scale of Charles' commitments meant that all the Council could do was to stave off bankruptcy by a series of desperate measures, such as the sale of offices or the seizure of private shipments of bullion. The government of each of Charles' territories was in theory self-supporting but in practice by the end of the reign several, such as the German territories, were reliant upon the subsidies of other areas. In addition, there were the constant wars against France and the Turks which were an impossible burden (as Phillip II's bankruptcy in 1557 was to show).

Castile came to play an increasingly vital role in the financing of the empire, not because it was particularly rich, rather the reverse, but because of the ease with which money could be extracted from it once the Cortes of Castile had been humbled. The influx of bullion from the New World, although not significant until the end of the reign, was channelled through Castile and this was a readily obtainable source of wealth. For this reason, above all, Castile became the centre of Charles' empire and the most frequently tapped supply of funds. The results for Castile itself were not entirely favourable *(see page 187)*.

Initially, Charles relied most heavily upon the Netherlands and Italy for money as these were the wealthiest parts of his empire. However the scale of the tax demands placed upon them led to revolt in Ghent in 1539 and to the viceroy of Naples complaining that further claims would be 'to squeeze juice from a stone.' In 1540 Charles wrote to his brother, Ferdinand, 'I cannot be sustained except by my realms of Spain', and in effect this meant Castile, which henceforth bore the brunt of imperial expenditure. This was done with the agreement of the nobility as they were exempt from taxation. The Cortes invariably voted the huge sums demanded of them because they were unaffected. The unevenness of the tax burden was recognised by the rulers. In 1545 Philip wrote to his father: 'The common people who have to pay the servicios are reduced to such distress and misery that many of them walk naked'. Charles had made an attempt to spread the distribution of taxes more widely in 1538 when he summoned the nobility and clergy to attend the Cortes and proposed the introduction of a new tax on foodstuffs, the *sisa*, which would be payable by all. The nobility refused to abandon their tax-free status and as a result were never again summoned to the Cortes, which found itself powerless to refuse the increasingly arbitrary demands of the Crown. The nobles' financial privilege had been bought at the expense of their political influence over government policy.

Instead Charles relied more heavily on *servicios*, non-noble taxes, and on a number of more dubious expedients such as the sale of *juros*, government bonds which carried a fixed annual interest and which meant mortgaging future revenues for present gain. He also used the services of foreign bankers whose interest rates climbed steeply as the reign progressed. To pay this interest, specific items of revenue were assigned to each debt and thus it was that by 1554 all revenue had been anticipated (earmarked for debt repayment) up to 1560. Castile's resources were swallowed up to meet expenses, most of which had little to do with Spanish interests.

6. The Economy

Charles presided over the start of Spain's 'golden age' when it became the most powerful state in Europe with an admired and feared army, a vigorous cultural life and an expanding overseas empire that produced unimagined wealth. But he has also been criticised by historians such as Koenigsberger for distorting the Spanish economy and failing to provide the right circumstances for growth with the result that eventually Spain became an economic backwater from which it is still struggling to emerge.

His over-riding need for money made it impossible for Charles to develop a coherent economic strategy. The opportunities afforded by the opening up of the New World ought to have given Spanish, and especially Castilian, trade and industry a great stimulus. In fact it proved totally unable to cope with the demands of the colonists and it was foreign merchants who benefited the most.

There was little understanding of economic forces and at one stage Charles agreed to a ban on all exports of cloth except to the Indies in an effort to keep domestic prices down. That caused such a depression in the textile industry the ban had to be lifted after five years.

The reasons for the high prices which prompted the export ban are uncertain *(see page 31)*, but it has been claimed that the influx of bullion was partly responsible. Bullion helped to finance Charles' wars and to provide an extravagant lifestyle for the nobles but it was not used for investment in industry and provided no lasting benefit to the economy. Heavy taxation discouraged industrial investment, which was despised, and the greatest financial return was to be obtained by buying *juros*. It was the pressing demands of warfare that led to the failure to develop an economy in the New World to complement Castile's, or to build up the Castilian economy for future benefit. Money was always required immediately and this effectively prevented any long-term strategy.

Some parts of the Spanish economy did flourish in Charles' reign. Seville and its hinterland enjoyed the fruits that a monopoly of the Atlantic trade gave them; the ironworks of the Basque region flourished; ceramics, leather and silk were all in demand. However, Spanish agriculture was neglected and backward. Too much emphasis was placed on the rearing of sheep, encouraged by the government because of the taxes it produced, but this meant that, with an expanding home market as well as the Indies, Castile was regularly importing wheat by 1560. Increased demand led to higher prices and the consequence of the empire for the ordinary Spaniard was a decline in living standards.

In general it can be said that opportunities were missed to put the Spanish economy on a sound footing that would enable it to meet the demands of imperialism. That Spain managed to maintain an illusion of strength as Europe's greatest power until 1660 says more for the long-suffering of the ordinary people than it does for the inherent strength of the economy. Decline, when it became evident, was swift and almost irreversible.

With hindsight, it is easy to see Charles' handling of the Spanish economy as his greatest failure. Henry Kamen points out how other countries profited from Spain's failures. Armaments were imported from Italy and textiles from England to provide for Spanish colonists' needs. The Cortes of Valladolid complained in 1548: 'Spain has become an Indies for the foreigner'. And by the seventeenth century five-sixths of the trade from Cadiz was not in the hands of Spaniards. In criticising Charles' lack of imagination, however, we must bear in mind the very imperfect understanding of economic forces and his desperate need for ready cash. Investment in industrial enterprises was a risky business with a slow and uncertain return. On the other hand, bullion was very acceptable to foreign financiers who would lend large sums on the security of future shipments. As is often the case with governments, short-term expediency triumphed over long-term planning.

The 1520s and 1530s saw both the circumnavigation of the world by Magellan's expedition and the conquest of Mexico and Peru by Cortés and Pizarro *(see Chapter IV)*. For the Indians the effect of conquest was devastating: the cruelty of the Spaniards, their diseases and their labour demands combined to reduce the native population of Mexico from about 25.2 million in 1518 to 2.65 million in 1568. The belated recognition by the government that the labour force was being destroyed led to the decision to import black slaves from Africa, with incalculable results. It also led to the passing of the New Laws in 1542 which freed, at least in law, all Indian slaves in the New World and set up an organised system of *audiencias* (courts) and officials under a viceroy. Despite its imperfections, this system worked reasonably well and can justifiably be seen as one of Charles' successes.

Spain achieved its greatest glory under Charles and his descendants. For 150 years the rest of Europe feared and respected its power. The foundations of this power were, however, less solid than they appeared. The enormous scale of Charles V's commitments, above all the struggle in Germany and Eastern Europe, led to a distortion of the Spanish economy for reasons which had no connection with Spain. The country was saddled with an intolerable burden of debt which led to successive bankruptcies in future decades. Specifically Spanish interests, above all in the Mediterranean, were neglected for problems in the rest of the monarchia, so that Spain's glory was also her weakness. The privileges of empire could not be divorced from the burdens.

7. Charles' Empire: The Monarchia

The seven years that Charles spent in Spain from 1522–29 was the most settled period of his reign. Charles declared, 'My life has been one long journey'. One quarter of the days of his reign were spent in travelling at a time when this was often extremely hazardous. On his first journey from the Netherlands to Spain, apart from long delays and a storm which forced him to land on an inhospitable part of the Spanish coast, the ship carrying his horses caught fire and all 160 on board were lost.

This constant travel was necessary because of the fragmented nature of Charles' empire. Because it had no centre and no one territory took precedence over another, at least in theory, Charles continued to rule each part as if he were present in person. To maintain this fiction, he had to make an appearance as often as possible, so Charles visited Germany nine times, Spain six times, the Netherlands on ten occasions and Italy on seven. Despite this level of activity, Charles was only able to maintain his system of government through the good offices of his family who acted as his regents. Only Italy and the Indies had to make do with non-royal viceroys. The Netherlands were well governed by first Margaret of Austria and then Mary of Hungary, Charles' sister. Ferdinand was in charge of the Empire in the absence of Charles, and later Philip his son ruled Spain. The use of royal governors helped to suppress unrest but even so there was widespread dissatisfaction in most areas at Charles' continual absences, and some problems only he could solve. Thus the German Protestants were able to flourish until Charles could deal with them himself.

One reason for the desire to have Charles present was that he controlled all patronage and the benefits of advancement it could bring. This could hamper the regents as they were unable to buy support for a royal party. Charles insisted on taking all major decisions himself despite the inefficiency this led to, but no central administration was created nor was a unified tax system developed. The only central institutions were the councils which travelled with Charles and this is why the role of secretary was so important.

Gattinara had a vision of a true union of all Charles' territories, hoping that he would eventually be the legislator of the whole world, but nothing came of this idea. Gattinara himself was the only link between the territories (apart from Charles) because he exercised jurisdiction over all of them and presided over all councils. He saw Italy as the centre of Charles' empire and the struggle for Milan as therefore of the first importance. If Charles could win Italy and the friendship of the Pope, he would be able to dominate Europe. Gattinara died in 1530 at an auspicious moment when it seemed as if his dream was realised. Charles did not appoint another chancellor, taking on the duties himself, but he had absorbed much of Gattinara's outlook.

However, the concept of a universal empire had to come to terms with political realities. The Holy Roman Empire from which Charles derived his prestigious title was where he in fact enjoyed least power. The size of the monarchia and the threat it posed to other states meant that Charles was engaged in a constant struggle with hostile forces and his twin aims of defeating the Infidel and eradicating heresy would remain unrealised. Charles drew his main strength from Spain and the Netherlands. The rest of his territories in Europe were a drain on his resources because of the conflicts they were involved in, either with France, the Turks or the Protestants.

8. The Netherlands

Charles' ancestral home, the Netherlands, where his reign began and ended, provided crucial resources for the Emperor's wars in the first part of his reign. Charles made relatively frequent, but brief, visits to the Netherlands (ten visits totalling twelve years) and he relied heavily on the capable services of his aunt, Margaret of Austria, and sister, Mary of Hungary.

The Netherlands were the most urbanised part of Europe. They were the richest of Charles' territories with a flourishing cloth industry and enterprising merchants. For many years Charles was dependent on the subsidies they granted him. In 1559 Soriano, the Venetian ambassador, wrote 'These lands are the treasuries of the King of Spain, his mines and his Indies, they have financed the enterprises of the Emperor for so many years in the wars of France, Italy and Germany.' Already, however, this was no longer true. As in Spain, Charles taxed his subjects until they would pay no more. In so doing he provoked serious opposition, especially in Ghent, and, more seriously, stirred up hostility to the notion of foreign rule. This was kept in check during his reign because of his personal popularity as a Burgundian but it surfaced with great vigour when his son, a complete Spaniard, took over. The Low Countries resented the fact that the money they voted was not always spent in their interests. In particular, they disliked the war with France.

Charles was eager to bring the provinces of the Netherlands into a closer union and provide them with a more efficient and centralised government. Each province had its own Estates (parliament) and this made effective control more difficult. In 1531 the Council of State set up a Council of Finance to co-ordinate the collection of taxes, and a High Court of Appeal. Both were strongly opposed, as was a plan in 1534 to create a standing army paid for by each province, for if we accept the proposal we shall undoubtedly be more united, but we shall be dealt with in the manner of France' i.e. with a loss of local liberties (Spain and Germany also resisted similar proposals for the same reason).

Charles realised that to insist on reforms might jeopardise his sources of revenue and therefore refrained from pushing his claims too far. He was forced to concede the redress of grievances before supply and to watch every demand for money being haggled over and whittled down. The Provincial Estates were even allowed to build up their own administrative machinery to control the collection and expenditure of the taxes they voted. The government derived one major advantage from its failure to centralise and that was the continuing localism of the Estates. Whilst there was no political unity, there would be no concerted opposition to challenge the position of royal authority.

This became increasingly important as the government increased its demands for money against a steadily rising tide of discontent. War disrupted trade and was therefore damaging to the economy and the Netherlands were very vulnerable to attacks from France, so there were constant demands for peace. These were ignored by Charles and as a result there were riots in Bois-le-Duc in 1525, Brussels in 1532 and in 1537 Charles' birthplace Ghent began a tax strike that had flared into open rebellion by 1539.

Ghent was a city in decline and the demands for subsidies in the French war of 1537 had been too much. The whole of Flanders was equally dissatisfied but the revolt failed to become general because the guilds set up a democratic dictatorship and terrorised the government's supporters in the upper classes, thus frightening potential leaders in other areas. Charles took the revolt seriously enough to come in person in 1540 to crush it. Ghent lost its charter, was forced to pay a heavy fine, a quarter of the town was pulled down to make a fortress and representatives of all classes had to beg pardon barefoot and on their knees. Such harsh punishment was intended to deter potential imitators, and the excessive tax demands continued. The Netherlands claimed that in five years they had given Charles extraordinary grants of eight million ducats, yet he still left his son Philip with a sizeable debt.

In religion, Charles acted with severity. The laws against heresy ('Placaten') became increasingly harsh throughout the reign although already Lutherans were being burnt in 1523. Despite this, Lutheran and radical preachers found a ready audience among the artisans of the towns and heresy continued to spread and flourish.

Superficially, Charles' reign was successful in the Netherlands. Certainly he extended its territory by annexing Tournai (1521) and Cambrai (1543) from the French and creating six northern provinces by the defeat in 1543 of William, Duke of Cleves, the successor to Charles of Egmont, Duke of Guelders. The Netherlands thus became a coherent unit, at least in geographical terms. However, there was no political union and little sense of a common identity as the course of the Revolt of the Netherlands in the latter half of the century was to show. Charles detached the Netherlands from the Empire, with which it had little in common, and created the prospect of a powerful North Sea empire by the marriage of Philip to Mary Tudor in 1554. The frustration of this hope by Mary's childless death in 1558 left the Netherlands as an isolated outpost of a Spanish empire that was firmly centred on the Mediterranean. In such a context, with a foreign king as ruler, the latent discontent which had scarcely been suppressed under Charles would surface with explosive force that would require great tact to manage. Charles' legacy to Philip in the Netherlands was potentially a powder keg.

9. Habsburg–Valois Rivalry 1521–29

Any consideration of a map of Europe in 1520 will show that one power would be constantly threatened by the encircling wings of Charles V's empire. This power was France, which engaged in a series of wars against Charles, mainly in Italy, to prevent his domination of the peninsula and the completion of the circle which Charles' capture of Milan would represent. Charles had begun his reign at a disadvantage compared to the already victorious Francis I. He was forced to sign the Treaty of Noyon (1516) in order to ensure French neutrality while he went to Spain to claim his inheritance. This involved, amongst other humiliating clauses, paying France an annual tribute of 100 000 ducats. Three years later, however, the tables were turned when Charles became

Holy Roman Emperor and immediately took precedence over his rival.

This rivalry with Francis I was at the heart of Charles' problem as Emperor. Francis would never accept his claim to leadership of Christendom, and French interference in Italy and support for the Pope could prevent Charles from dominating the Papacy and securing the alliance he hoped for, which would be essential if he was to make his dream of leadership a reality. The threat to Francis was more of a psychological one than a reality. Charles had no desire to conquer France, and no hope of doing so. However, Francis had to maintain his prestige by constantly diverting Charles from problems in the Empire and against the Turks, by forcing him to engage in costly wars over Italy.

Northern Italy, and specifically Milan, was crucial to Charles because it provided a route from Spain to Austria along which troops could pass when necessary. It was also important to have a safe overland route to the Netherlands. Milan was the key to this too. (The 'Spanish Road' was to increase in importance under Philip II.) If Charles lost control of Milan to France, the different elements of his empire would be isolated and effective action would become extremely difficult. The only alternative route to the Netherlands was by sea, which was also vulnerable to the French, and it therefore became important to secure the co-operation of England which was forthcoming in the early 1520s at least.

Not only was Charles a threat to Francis but also the reverse was true. Charles had the difficulty of co-ordinating men and money from scattered territories, with France eager to exploit any weakness in the chain. Meanwhile, France as a unitary state did not experience the same logistical problems and could strike at whichever part of the empire seemed vulnerable. Charles was a man of integrity and he found the unscrupulous Francis very hard to deal with, especially when the latter allied with the great enemy of Christendom, the Ottoman Empire.

There were also other irritants to drive the two sides apart. Italy had been a battleground since the fifteenth century and only domination by one side would end the conflict there. Charles wished to regain Burgundy, the ancestral home of his dynasty, annexed by France in 1477. Similarly, the incorporation of Navarre into Castile was not recognised by France. These old disputes could be revived whenever circumstances seemed appropriate (so France tried to take advantage of the revolt of the *Comuneros* by reasserting claims to Navarre).

Ultimately, Francis I could not tolerate Charles' claim to dominance. The latter might protest, as he did in 1536, 'There are those who say that I wish to rule the world, but both my thoughts and my deeds demonstrate the contrary'. But this was hardly enough to dissuade Francis from plotting the downfall of his great rival.

The effect upon Charles' policies was immediately apparent. Decisive action against the emergent German Protestantism had to be postponed and, not for the last time, the internal needs of Charles' empire were sacrificed to the struggle against 'the most Christian' King of France.

Trouble flared up in 1521; to distract Charles from interference in

Italy, French troops invaded the Netherlands and Navarre. Both campaigns went badly. Charles seized Tournai, the Spanish united against the French threat and, in Italy, Imperial troops took Milan, defeating a Franco-Swiss army at Bicocca in 1522. Charles had also secured alliance with the Pope and England for a joint attack on France. When Adrian of Utrecht succeeded Leo X as Pope in January 1522, it looked as if Gattinara's two conditions for the success of Charles as Emperor—the domination of Italy and alliance with Rome—had been fulfilled.

It was to be a shortlived illusion. Adrian died in 1523 and a combined attack upon France by Charles and Henry VIII was a miserable failure. In 1524, Francis I invaded Italy in person and recaptured Milan, and the new Pope, Clement VII, abandoned the Imperial side. Charles gloomily committed his thoughts to paper: 'I cannot support my army let alone increase it, if that should be necessary . . . My friends have forsaken me in my evil hour; all are equally determined to prevent me from growing more powerful and to keep me in my present distressed state . . . A battle in which I shall be either victorious or wholly defeated cannot be postponed for much longer . . .'

The decisive battle in fact came as Charles wrote. Outside the city of Pavia on February 24 1525 (Charles' twenty-fifth birthday), Francis I was captured and his army suffered a crushing defeat. This unexpected victory did not bring Charles much advantage: it increased Italian fears of Habsburg power and led to a split with Henry VIII. Charles was also determined to win back the old Burgundian lands, an impossible condition for Francis to fulfil and one which the French nation would probably have resisted. As a result, negotiations with the royal prisoner, who was taken to Madrid, made no progress. Meanwhile the Regent of France, Francis' mother Louise of Savoy, was making alliances with Italian cities, Henry VIII and the Turks. Eventually the stalemate was broken. Francis made a secret vow to declare his promises null and void on his return to France and he was then ready to sign the Treaty of Madrid in January 1526. This bound him to seek the permission of the Estates General for the return of Burgundy to Charles; to renounce claims to territories held by Charles in Italy and the Netherlands; to reinstate Bourbon; to marry Charles' sister, Eleanor, and to join a crusade against the Turks.

Charles had won a battle but he had not won the war and the treaty brought Charles nothing. The holding hostage of the two eldest French princes was not enough to prevent Francis I from denouncing the treaty and forming the League of Cognac. Francis then made an alliance with Suleiman I, the Ottoman Emperor, which contributed to the latter's victory at Mohacs *(see page 198)* by diverting possible aid that Charles might have given to the Hungarians.

The Turks now directly threatened the hereditary Habsburg lands in Austria but, for Charles, war against France took priority and he continued to demand troops for Italy from his brother Ferdinand, a request which was met but which strained the younger man's loyalty. In

Germany, the Lutherans were offered an amnesty in return for their support of the Empire and to relieve the pressure on Ferdinand. As before, the struggle against France in Italy took precedence over other concerns.

Charles' troops in Italy now took matters into their own hands. They had been short of money since Pavia and the idea grew at the end of 1526 that the Pope was to blame for all their distress. In 1527 the starving, leaderless soldiers moved inexorably south and sacked Rome in an orgy of looting and destruction that appalled the rest of Europe. Although unintended by Charles, he could hardly ignore the imprisonment of the Pope, but passed the summer in a state of indecision while his enemies seized the upper hand.

The problem for Charles was that he regarded alliance with the Pope as his right, but the popes were unreliable and unco-operative. As with Francis I, however, Charles could not see how to exploit the fact that he held the Pope prisoner. In 1528, it seemed as if Imperial troops might be pushed out of Italy altogether. Things were going badly in the north, while Naples was besieged on land by the French and blockaded at sea by the Genoese. This desperate situation was transformed by the sudden defection of the Genoese naval commander, Andrea Doria, to Charles' side because of insensitive French treatment. This event was crucial both for Habsburg control of Italy and in the coming struggle for the Mediterranean with the Turks. Communications between Italy and Spain were safeguarded and Charles came to rely increasingly on Genoese money and soldiers.

In the short term the Genoese alliance saved Naples and, after defeat at Landriano the following year, Francis I was ready to make peace. Charles made peace first with the Pope in the Treaty of Barcelona. Clement recognised Charles as ruler of Naples, granted him the *cruzada* (a Spanish tax paid for a Bull of Indulgence granted every three years), and agreed to crown him Emperor. In return, Charles promised to uphold the rights of the Pope's relatives, the Medici, in Florence. The Treaty of Cambrai (1529) signed with France repeated the Treaty of Madrid without the claim to Burgundy.

10. From Victory to Defeat 1530–59

Charles was now at the height of his power; he had secured a very favourable treaty with France and in 1530 he was crowned Holy Roman Emperor by the Pope in great splendour at Bologna. Attention could thus be given to the other pressing problems of his reign, the Turks and the Lutherans. Francis I recognised the futility of direct action against Charles but continued to intrigue with his enemies, making alliances with the Duke of Cleves, Henry VIII, Suleiman and the Pope (whose niece, Catherine de Medici, married Francis' son, Henry).

The chance to re-open the war came when Francesco Sforza, Duke of

Milan, died childless in 1535. As a preliminary to claiming Milan, Francis marched into Savoy, the gateway to Italy, in 1536 and occupied Turin. This was an act of pure aggression caused by the fear of direct Habsburg rule in Milan and enabled Charles to pose convincingly as the responsible protector of Christendom, but even so he was unable to win the active support of the Pope (Paul III since 1534) and had to be content with his neutrality.

The war went badly for Charles who made the mistake of attacking France itself, but the French were also unable to make headway and, after a year's inconclusive fighting, the Pope negotiated a ten year truce at Nice (1538). This solved nothing; Francis remained in possession of Savoy and Piedmont, but it allowed Charles to pursue grandiose dreams of a crusade against the Turks while on a more mundane level it gave his hard-pressed treasury some relief, although in Castile all revenue was anticipated up to 1540.

The truce was not destined to last ten years. Francis was ready to use any pretext to resume the conflict and was eager to take advantage of Charles' weakness after the failure in Algiers *(see page 198)*. The excuse was the murder of two French envoys in Milan. Francis I declared war in July 1542. Fighting took place on three fronts, in Milan, the Pyrenees and the Netherlands. Only the latter was under real threat. The French were in alliance with the Duke of Cleves who had a claim to Guelderland and large parts of the Netherlands were devastated. However Francis lost support by his open alliance during this war with the Turks, the enemies of Christendom, and Charles had been able to increase his revenues by the dowry for the Portuguese Infanta who married his son Philip. Charles left Spain for the last time as ruling monarch and crushed the Duke of Cleves before winning Cambrai from the French. The unification of the Netherlands was now complete with the encroaching territories of Guelderland, Utrecht and Cambrai all under Charles' control.

Charles now took the offensive and invaded France, causing panic in Paris while Henry VIII, his ally, captured Boulogne. Francis I was forced to come to terms and in the Peace of Crèpy, 1544, all conquests made since 1538 were restored. France agreed to support the calling of a General Council of the Church and to help against the Turks and the German Protestants. The Duke of Orleans was to marry either Charles' daughter or his niece who would receive the Netherlands or Milan as a dowry. This came to nothing because the Duke died in 1545, 'just in time' as Charles admitted in his memoirs.

In 1547 Francis I died, shortly before Charles' great triumph at Muhlberg *(see page 202)*. It looked as if the Habsburg–Valois struggle had been decided in favour of the former. Charles had no equal in Europe and the stranglehold on France was tighter than ever; yet within six years Charles was a broken man, seeking only to escape from the trials of the world.

Francis I was succeeded by Henry II whose anti-Habsburg feelings had been encouraged by his years as a captive in Spain. He abandoned the struggle in Italy in order to concentrate on Charles' weakest spot by allying with the German Protestants. In the Treaty of Chambord of 1552, the Protestants agreed Henry should have the key Rhine bishoprics of Metz, Toul and Verdun in return for his support in the war against Charles. After coming to terms with the Protestants, which he found deeply humiliating, Charles made a valiant but unsuccessful attempt to recapture Metz, which, as he wrote to his sister Mary, gave the French 'a clear road to the Rhine and so they will be able to cut off my communications from South Germany to the Netherlands and Franche-Comté.'

His failure at Metz in 1553, coupled with the victory of the Protestants, convinced Charles that God had deserted him and he began to seek the best way to abdicate. The siege of Metz had been ruinously expensive (it had cost two million ducats) and money could no longer be raised, even at interest rates of nearly 50 percent. Charles decided a younger man must tackle the problems and his reign ended with the final phase of the conflict with France unresolved.

Charles' son, Philip II, began his reign with a five year truce with France. This lasted barely a year before Pope Paul IV, who nursed a fanatical hatred of the Habsburgs, re-opened the conflict by trying to oust Philip from Naples, and summoning the French to his aid. Fighting resumed on all fronts and the Spanish won a major victory at San Quentin but they were unable to follow this up because of lack of funds. Both Philip II and Henry II were forced into bankruptcy in 1557 and exhaustion prompted both sides to peace. Two factors combined to improve the prospects of a lasting peace. The break-up of Charles V's inheritance removed the irritant of encirclement from France, and the death of Philip's wife, Mary Tudor, in November 1558 broke the Spanish–English alliance which was so dangerous to France.

The Peace of Câteau-Cambrèsis (1559) was a triumph for Charles V's southern struggles against the French. Italy, with the exception of Venice, became almost a Spanish province. Spanish dominance in the peninsula was secured and with it the 'Spanish Road' to the Netherlands. All France retained were five fortresses in Savoy. In the north, the advantage was with the French. Henry II retained Metz, Toul and Verdun and did not restore Calais to the English, while Philip withdrew from occupied towns in northern France. Many of the provisions of the treaty lasted for a century as France was riven by forty years of internal strife, allowing Spain unchallenged dominance of western Europe.

11. The Struggle with the Ottomans

For centuries Christendom and Islam had co-existed with uneasy relations on the frontiers. Islam had come closest in Spain, where the Moors were only finally defeated in Granada in 1492. Then the main threat came from the Barbary pirates and their raids on shipping and the coast. But this was no more than an irritant for a long time. This secure state was shattered by the emergence of the aggressive Ottoman Empire which was committed to conquest and expansion *(see Chapter X)*. The fall of Constantinople in 1453 opened the way to the Mediterranean and in 1522 Rhodes fell—the last bastion of Christian power, except for Cyprus, in the eastern half of the sea. The previous year had seen the conquest of Belgrade, exposing the Danube, a route that would take the Turks deep into Europe and enable them to threaten Vienna, at the heart of the hereditary Habsburg lands.

Thus, within a few years of assuming power, Charles V was faced with the task of preventing further incursions by the Turks. He was in the front line of any attack and inevitably the activities of the Sultan were a cause of constant concern. Ferdinand bore the major responsibility for defending central Europe, although Charles assisted him when he could; it was in the Mediterranean that Charles was more closely involved. One of his most cherished wishes was to lead a crusade against the Turks, but the politics of Christendom never allowed this. Instead, Charles was denied the opportunity to take decisive action against the Turks in his home territory of the western Mediterranean by the scale of his commitments elsewhere. The reverse was also true. The pressure of the Turks on his eastern flank prevented harsh measures against the German Protestants until it was too late.

For Charles' Spanish subjects in the south, firm action against the Turks was essential if they were not to be in continual fear of attack from Barbary pirates who became immeasurably more threatening in alliance with the Turks and with the possibility of internal revolt by the *Moriscos*. In 1516, the pirate Barbarossa had established himself in Algiers and become a vassal of the Sultan. In 1532 he became grand admiral of the entire Turkish fleet. This exposed the coasts of Italy and Spain, which suffered constant raids, and seriously threatened Charles' communications. This was especially serious in Sicily which acted as a granary for other parts of the empire. Charles was unable to take action against Barbarossa until the 1530s when he had the help of the Genoese. There was no Spanish fleet which could compare with that of the Turks and no effort was made to build one. However, when Charles arrived back in Spain in 1533 after an absence of four years, he was anxious to fulfil his religious mission and to please his Spanish subjects by striking a blow at the Turks.

This became more urgent after 1534 when Barbarossa made a daring attack on Italy that brought him close to Rome, and on his return captured Tunis. This was too serious to be ignored and Charles decided to lead in person an expedition to conquer Tunis, the gateway to the western Mediterranean, thus winning glory for himself as well as protecting the western Mediterranean. La Goletta and Tunis were taken in 1535 and 85 of Barbarossa's galleys—the bulk of his fleet—were captured. Although spectacular, the victory did not alter the balance of power. Barbarossa escaped to Algiers and within a few weeks had organised an attack on Minorca. Charles lacked the naval strength to follow up his acclaimed triumph and in 1536 the French entered into open alliance with the Sultan, which opened French ports to his ships.

War with France (1536–38) prevented a continuation of the Mediterranean campaign until after the Truce of Nice *(see page 195)*. Charles then arranged an alliance with the Venetians and the Pope but distrust between these allies led to their defeat by the Turks at the Battle of Prevesa off the Greek coast in 1538. The Venetians made a separate peace with the Turks and without their galleys it was impossible for the western alliance to offer effective resistance to the Turkish fleet. Charles decided to strike at the heart of Barbarossa's power—Algiers. He regarded his mission as a Holy War and again led his troops in person. Unfortunately the campaign in 1541, which started out too late in the year, was a disaster. One hundred and fifty ships were lost in a storm and Charles was forced to retreat with his army almost intact, partly because his own captivity or death could not be risked. This was a great blow to his reputation and put an end to serious moves against the Turks in the Mediterranean.

In 1543–44 the Turkish fleet wintered in Toulon and Christian slaves were sold in the market. In 1551 Tripoli was taken with ease by the new leader of the Turkish fleet, Dragut, providing another useful link in the chain with Algiers. Alarmed by the threat to Sicily, Charles removed Spanish and Italian troops from Württemberg, thus directly encouraging the German rebellion of 1552. What saved the western Mediterranean from complete Turkish domination was its distance from Turkey, the internal dynastic problems of Suleiman, and war against Persia. Charles V and Suleiman I faced similar problems. Their empires were too big to make concerted action in one area a possibility for long. Both linked up with the other's enemies but in the end the empires were too far apart for a decisive confrontation between them. Charles had dreamed of a crusade against Constantinople. Instead he had been unable to safeguard even his own territories.

The naval power of the Turks was worrying but posed a less serious threat than the huge armies which Suleiman could muster for attack on central Europe. While German attention was focused on the Diet of Worms in 1521, Suleiman was capturing Belgrade and thus exposing Hungary to his attacks. The challenge was delayed for four years, but in 1526 he returned in force and wiped out the Hungarian army, together with its king, Louis II, at the battle of Mohacs. As brother-in-law to the childless Louis, Ferdinand claimed the crowns of Bohemia and Hungary despite the opposition of the powerful noble John Zapolyai who wanted the throne himself. Zapolyai won the support of Suleiman by swearing allegiance to him, presenting Ferdinand with a double threat. In 1529, the most serious attack on Habsburg power was launched. Vienna was besieged for three weeks until the onset of autumn forced the Turks to withdraw. It was the immense distances involved which saved the Habsburg lands because the campaigning season was eight to ten weeks long. The further the Ottomans penetrated into enemy territory, the longer were their lines of communication: the campaigning season became progressively shorter and the likelihood of further conquest more remote. Charles also made diplomatic contact with the Shah of Persia as a way of pressurising their common enemy.

In 1529, Ferdinand's pleas for aid had been largely ignored as Charles concentrated on securing his coronation before tackling the German problem. By 1532, when there was news of the approach of another large Turkish army, he was ready to show more positive support. A large army was assembled which confronted the Turks at Guns and forced them to retreat. The advantage was not followed up because the German troops refused to cross the frontier into Hungary. This failure was deeply disappointing to Ferdinand: inevitably his interests lay in central Europe and his devotion to Charles' wishes was often strained as the latter's attention was heavily concentrated on the western Mediterranean. For his part, Charles had not welcomed Ferdinand's election as King of Bohemia and Hungary because of increased conflict with the Turks and he was most concerned to ensure peace on his eastern flank so he would be able to deal with other matters. Ferdinand's negotiations with Suleiman were therefore not unwelcome and the latter part of the reign saw a diminution of the Turkish threat, with the exception of the early 1540s when a fully Turkish administration was established in eastern Hungary. Uneasy co-existence could bring trouble. As late as 1683 the Turks were besieging Vienna. The problem was contained in the sixteenth century, not solved.

The most serious effect of Turkish activity in central Europe was seen in Germany. Distraction by the Infidel was to cost Charles dear in his dealings with the heretic Lutherans.

12. The Holy Roman Empire and the Protestant Threat

Charles was unanimously elected Holy Roman Emperor in 1519 in succession to his grandfather Maximilian. The title remained in the Habsburg family until it died out and therefore it is easy to regard Charles' election as a foregone conclusion. This was not the case. The seven electors (Cologne, Mainz, Trier, Bohemia, the Palatinate, Brandenburg and Saxony) guarded their independence and the issue was in doubt to the end. The electors were persuaded to choose Charles by a combination of factors: he was prepared to spend most money in bribes—the election cost him nearly one million gold gulden; the Pope supported his main rival, Francis I, and Charles was unlikely to be able to interfere too much with the privileges of the princes given the scattered nature of his territories.

Thus Charles became the pre-eminent ruler in Christendom. It was a dubious honour. The Empire entailed far more responsibilities than privileges since the title brought with it no actual power, only prestige, and it was in the Empire that Charles was to be defeated.

Germany was the largest nation in Europe, with great resources. However it was impossible to use these for common political objectives because of its internal disunity. There were more than 2500 different authorities, mainly knights but also great princes, Church leaders and cities, which acknowledged no overlord except the Emperor. The Emperor was limited by the Diet which represented the electors, the princes and the free Imperial cities. Without the co-operation of the Diet, the Emperor was powerless unless he could muster troops of his own to enforce his will—this was very seldom possible and even then he relied on the support of at least some of the Diet's members. In the early sixteenth century, both Maximilian and Charles made attempts to reform the Empire to make it a more coherent unit but these plans came to little, mainly because the princes were unwilling to surrender any of their power. There was a general desire for a united Germany in theory, but not at the expense of anyone's privileges. The development of a religious split in the Empire made an already difficult situation impossible for its ruler.

Charles was deeply hurt by the appearance of heresy within his territories and pledged himself in 1521 to its eradication: 'To settle this matter, I am determined to use my kingdoms and dominions, my friends, my body, my blood, my life and my soul'. Unfortunately for him, it was politically expedient for many of the princes to adopt Lutheranism and without their active support, Charles could do little. The crucial middle years of the 1520s were devoted to settling Spain and by the time Charles turned his full attention back to the Empire, the Lutherans had established themselves too firmly to be easily dealt with. Charles' desire to give them a fair hearing and win them back by compromise through the action of a General Council also played into the Protestants' hands because it gave them over twenty years to build up their strength before an open confrontation took place.

Charles returned to Germany in 1530 for the Diet of Augsburg, fresh from his coronation as Emperor by the Pope and at the peak of his power. Peace had been secured with France and he was now anxious to settle the religious problem so that a united Empire could face the Turkish threat. It was not to be so simple. The Catholic majority in the Diet was not prepared to use force against the Protestants until a General Council of the Church had met, something Pope Clement VII was resolutely opposed to. Despite a desire for compromise on both sides, the conciliatory Augsburg Confession was too much for Charles to accept. When the Protestants withdrew from the Diet, it was decided to return to the Edict of Worms after a delay of six months. In response, the Protestants formed the Schmalkaldic League in 1531.

Further action against the Protestants was postponed by the approach of a huge army under Suleiman. A religious truce meant that all the Estates sent help to Charles which enabled him to halt the Turks at Guns. This was the first of a series of temporary truces granted to the Protestants as Charles required all his strength for the international situation. In 1534 Charles acquiesced in the loss of Wurttemberg to the Protestants because he was preparing to attack the Turks in the Mediterranean.

The Schmalkaldic League grew in power throughout the 1530s. It established contacts with France, England and Denmark, while carefully preserving an appearance of loyalty to the Emperor. Charles was more concerned about relations with France and the Turks and, as a result, his policy in Germany throughout the 1530s consisted of periodic denunciations of heresy combined with toleration in practice, while a solution was left to the General Council he repeatedly pressed upon the Pope. This absence of direction meant that the Protestants were able to make steady gains. By 1545 all of north east and north west Germany was Protestant, as well as large parts of the south. In 1544 Frederick II of the Palatinate became a Protestant. With all the secular Electors favourable to Protestantism and the Elector Archbishop of Cologne leaning in the same direction, the possibility of a Protestant Empire could no longer be ignored. It was time for Charles to take positive action. Fortunately for him, events had been moving in his direction for some time.

The Schmalkaldic League began to break up after 1540. From 1541 Landgrave Philip of Hesse, its most dynamic leader, was at the mercy of Charles V after he made a bigamous marriage (with the support of Luther) to avoid the sin of adultery! Bigamy carried the death penalty and so Philip was forced to support the Emperor. This gave rise to hopes for peace at the Diet of Regensburg in 1541. Two months of amicable talks between theologians of both sides failed to secure a compromise that either would accept *(see page 307)*. This was a turning point for Charles; he had based his whole policy on the idea of peaceful compromise and its failure left him bitterly disillusioned. Charles did not understand how strong religious passions were, especially on the question of the Eucharist. Issues that might have been peacefully settled by compromise twenty years before were now too deeply entrenched; only military victory or toleration would solve the problem now. As the latter was unacceptable in the long term to Charles, it left force as the only option.

Accordingly, Charles began to look for allies among the princes, but in the meantime he remained outwardly conciliatory in order to secure the help of the Protestants for the last war against Francis I. In the Peace of Crèpy (1544), Francis not only agreed to co-operate over the calling of a General Council but also not to form alliances with the German Protestants. Suddenly they were isolated and Charles increased his advantages by making important alliances. The support of Bavaria was secured by promising Ferdinand's eldest daughter for Duke Albert's eldest son. Most important of all, the Protestant Duke Maurice was promised the Electorate of Saxony if he went over to Charles. For once the Pope (Paul III) was in full support of the Emperor and was generous with troops and money. All was now prepared for full-scale war against the heretics. Already, in 1543, a campaign against the Duke of Cleves had forced him to abandon the reformation of his territories.

A Venetian ambassador at the court of Charles V reviewed the situation in July 1546:

> Concerning the Emperor's disposition towards the States of Germany, every one is at present certain that war is in contemplation . . . The causes which are said to have moved the Emperor to this, are: first, the little regard which the German States have for some years past shown to his orders, by not attending the Diet; and secondly, the fear that the heresy which infects some of them, should spread over them all, and finally pervert his dominions in the Low Countries, which are the chief sources of his greatness. . . . The Princes of Germany have never liked Charles V; probably because he continually avails himself of their counsels, without treating them in the deferential and considerate manner, which Maximilian and all the former Emperors accustomed them to expect.
>
> They complain that he has wasted power in disputes with his fellow Christians, instead of turning it to account against the Turk, as was his duty; that he is now about to make war upon themselves, and that under the pretence of religious zeal, he intends to conduct a foreign army into Germany, to trample on their ancient liberties.

1 *What distinction can be drawn between the motives for war attributed to Charles V and what the princes believed to be the case?*
2 *From your reading on Charles V so far, do you think the princes' fears were justified?*

13. Resort to Force

The Schmalkaldic League was slow to realise that Charles had changed his policy. This was partly because they had no wish to fight the Emperor. Luther's insistence on obedience to secular rulers was part of his appeal to the princes but also made it harder for them to challenge their own overlord. The Emperor's troops were being assembled from the middle of 1545, but it was not until September 1546 that his army from the Netherlands, Hungary, different parts of the Empire and Italy was united. The failure of the League to win a quick victory before the armies united demonstrates their lack of effective leadership. There was no common ultimate objective and considerable distrust existed between the cities (who refused to pay for the troops) and the princes.

Charles won control of south Germany with little difficulty. Then in April 1547 he took the Lutherans by surprise and at the Battle of Mühlberg he crushed the army of the League, captured Elector John Frederick and gave his electoral title and the land which went with it to Maurice of Saxony. Mühlberg gave Charles control of the whole of

Germany and his triumph was completed when Philip of Hesse surrendered in June. Germany was at his mercy; Francis I, Henry VIII and Luther were all dead. It seemed as if Charles could do as he pleased.

Paradoxically, the very completeness of his triumph ensured that it would be temporary. The Pope had already withdrawn his support and the Catholic princes were not prepared to see Charles consolidate his position at the expense of the Protestants if it would also adversely affect their own power. Charles had shown his strength in combination with a number of the princes but if they all combined against him, he was powerless to enforce his will. Charles' position had been untenable from the start. An alliance with the Protestant Duke Maurice in a religious war was always bound to break down.

A Diet was summoned to Augsburg in the autumn of 1547 and the Emperor proposed the formation of a league of princes with himself at the head, in which each member would contribute to the cost of a standing army to enforce the laws of the Empire. This was not a new idea—it was based on the earlier Swabian League—but it was defeated by the opposition of the princes who recognised how much Charles would be strengthened. The Elector of Brandenburg summed up their feelings: the Empire 'would be reduced to servitude'.

The religious question was also unresolved. The General Council at Trent, which first met in 1545, was a disappointment for Charles because it was not seeking a compromise solution to the Protestant problem, but a restatement of the Catholic faith in opposition to Protestantism. Charles attempted to solve the German problem himself by drawing up the 'Interim', a compromise which allowed clerical marriage and communion in both kinds; but there were no substantial concessions and the Interim was disliked by everyone. The Pope saw it as an attack on his own position and rights, while for the Protestants it was a wholly inadequate address to the depth of their religious convictions.

This double failure by Charles to resolve the political and religious problems of the Empire made him consider the future in a new light. The victory at Mühlberg had only been possible with the help of money and troops from the Netherlands and Spain. Any future Emperor deprived of these resources would find governing the Empire even more impossible than Charles himself. Such reasoning led Charles to question the position of his brother Ferdinand and, in so doing, to split the Habsburg family down the middle.

14. Dynastic Quarrels

Ferdinand had been granted the hereditary Habsburg lands in Austria and the Empire in 1522 by the treaty of Brussels, although Charles retained nominal rights in them. At the same time Charles had promised to work for Ferdinand's election as King of the Romans which would give him the right to succeed Charles as Emperor; a promise that was fulfilled in 1531 after Charles' coronation as Emperor. Since then, Ferdinand had been Charles' devoted regent, putting his brother's interests above his own even when there was serious danger, especially from the Turks. This was not easy for a proud and ambitious man but Ferdinand recognised that his power had come from Charles and that he gained from the latter's prestige as Emperor. Relations between the brothers had been especially good during the 1540s and in the Schmalkaldic War. It therefore came as a great blow to Ferdinand when Charles proposed that his own son, Philip, should succeed Ferdinand as Emperor instead of the latter's son, Maximilian. In this way Charles felt that the two sides of the dynasty could be kept closely linked and Spanish resources could be made available for Imperial purposes.

This provoked a bitter family quarrel. Eight months of negotiations at Augsburg, 1550–51, eventually produced the Augsburg agreement in which Ferdinand accepted the idea of alternating the succession in the Empire between the two branches. The agreement did not please Maximilian or the princes, who felt their rights as Electors were being ignored and who were not prepared in any case to accept the succession of Philip who was a foreigner with no knowledge of Germany. The level of opposition was such that eventually Philip renounced his right to succeed Ferdinand. In return, Milan was detached from the Empire and added to the Spanish kingdoms. Charles had alienated his brother to no purpose and at a time when he was to face the most serious challenge to his power.

15. The Revolt of the Princes

Charles' cavalier attitude to the rights of the Electors and his humiliating imprisonment of John Frederick of Saxony and Philip of Hesse produced fears about the future liberties of the princes which sparked off revolt. The northern princes formed themselves into a league in 1550, for the defence of Lutheranism and the liberation of Philip of Hesse. This became much more dangerous for Charles when Maurice of Saxony joined, having not received the bishoprics of Halberstadt and Magdeburg which he had been promised. Also the Protestant princes secured the alliance of Henry II of France in return for the bishoprics of Metz, Toul and Verdun *(see page 196)*. Such a combination had always been Charles' greatest fear but for a long time he refused to take seriously the reports of a movement against him. His contempt for the princes after Mühlberg convinced him that they would never dare to attack him.

Accordingly he left any preparations for war much too late. Maurice took the city of Magdeburg and Henry II walked into the Rhine bishoprics with no effective opposition. Charles was nearly captured in Innsbruck in May 1552 and the humiliation of flight gave him a shock from which he was unable to recover, although in the short term he showed great resolution in mustering resources from the one territory that could supply them—Spain. Charles now distrusted Ferdinand but had no-one else to rely on to negotiate with the princes. Peace within Germany became vital as the external threats mounted. The pirate Dragut was terrorising Naples, Ferdinand became involved in another Turkish war in Hungary, with French help the Imperial garrison was driven out of Siena and there were hostilities on the Flemish border.

Maurice of Saxony was also ready to negotiate because he lacked the resources to follow up his victory over the Emperor. In August 1552 temporary agreement was reached in the Treaty of Passau. Charles was not prepared to accept the existence of Lutheranism as inevitable and permanent; the furthest he would go was to offer a truce in religious matters until the next Diet. Maurice and his allies were compelled to make do with this and attention could then be turned to the French.

The failure of the siege of Metz (November 1552—January 1553) was a bitter blow to Charles. He had hoped to drive the French out of the Empire and then resolve the problems in Germany by force. This was now impossible and the scale of his problems outstripped his resources. Even the long-suffering Castile could do no more—its revenues were already anticipated for the next three years. In the Empire the rule of law had broken down and Albert Alcibiades of Prussia, described as 'an enormous, insane, wild beast', was able to terrorise the country. Deeply disillusioned and with a feeling that God had deserted him, Charles decided that he was unable to solve the problems of the Empire and he must withdraw from it. In January 1553 he went to the Netherlands and never returned to Germany. The final acts of the reign were to be Ferdinand's although Charles' abdication was not accepted by the Electors until 1558.

16. The Peace of Augsburg

The first priority was to restore order. Leagues were formed which included both Catholic and Protestant princes. In July 1553 Albert Alcibiades was defeated at the battle of Sievershausen by Maurice of Saxony who was fatally wounded. Order was restored but only because the princes had wanted it. The reliance of the Emperor on the power of the princes was made plain, but so was their commitment to the continuing existence of the Empire and their willingness to preserve it. Ferdinand recognised that he could not coerce the princes within their own territories and this acceptance of political reality made the solution of the religious problem a possibility.

The Diet met at Augsburg in February 1555. Charles refused to attend: 'My reason is only this question of religion, in regard to which I have an unconquerable scruple'. In April 1555 he repeated his opposition to compromise, protesting against anything which 'could infringe, hurt, weaken or burden our ancient true Christian and Catholic faith'. In theory, this absolute stand was the position of both sides at the Diet. The ultimate aim was Christian unity but in the meantime, peace was a temporary necessity. The Catholics recognised they could not subdue the Lutherans by force, while the latter felt that their faith would become universal once it was freed from persecution.

The final solution was not tolerant in any real sense. It made provision only for Lutherans and Catholics, ignoring the growing strength of the Calvinists. Each prince was allowed to choose his own religion and thus determine the faith of his subjects—summed up in the formula *cuius regio, eius religio* (his territory, his religion). There was to be no missionary activity or protection of co-religionists in other territories. No territory ruled by a bishop which was Catholic in 1552 was allowed to become Protestant.

This pragmatic solution subordinated religion to politics. It was only possible in a nation such as Germany which had little real unity. Religious unity was preserved—but only within the bounds of each principality. More than anything else, this destroyed the medieval concept of the unity of the Empire and opened the way for the destructive conflicts of the next century.

Charles regarded his defeat in the Empire as his greatest failure and, on his own terms, it was.

17. The Abdication of Charles V

After his defeat at Metz, Charles sank into apathy and despair. He was aroused by the death of Edward VI in July 1553 and the succession of the still unmarried Mary. This gave rise to the possibility of leaving Philip with an empire that would revolve around Spain, England and the Netherlands, effectively strangling the hated France. This was a worthy inheritance for his beloved son and Charles felt he could then abdicate with a clear conscience. His plans had to be postponed for a time, however, because Henry II launched a savage attack upon Hainault in 1554. But then events in 1555 convinced Charles he must go. His mother died in April, Mary turned out to be barren, the religious peace of Augsburg was agreed in Germany and the new Pope, Paul IV, was fanatically anti-Spanish. To Charles, it seemed as if the same problems were reappearing and that he had failed in all his objectives.

On 25th October 1555, in the great hall of the castle at Brussels where he had begun his reign, Charles V abdicated with great solemnity: the crowd 'could not restrain their tears and sobs'. In a private ceremony in January 1556 he renounced his rights to Spain. He continued as Holy Roman Emperor in name only until February 1558 when the Electors agreed to choose Ferdinand instead.

Charles retired to Spain with his sisters Mary and Eleanor. He built himself a modest house near the remote monastery at Yuste and there he died in September 1558.

18. Charles V—A Failure?

Charles V was one of the great figures of his time. 'His personal moral character towered far above that of the princes of his age.' (H Holborn) He took the highly unusual step of abdicating voluntarily, feeling that his reign had been a failure, which in itself shows his integrity. Charles undoubtedly did fail in his two main objectives of suppressing heresy and leading a crusade against the Turks but this should not blind us to his achievements. The Turkish menace was withstood; Lutheranism had to be accepted as permanent but German Catholicism was saved at a crucial moment and revived in the latter part of the century; the Papacy was saved partly by Charles' vision of Emperor and Pope leading a

Charles could rarely concentrate on one problem at a time. The following shows some key years of the reign when he particularly suffered distractions from one problem to another.

Revolts of the *Comuneros* and Germanias

Diet of Worms— | 1521–22 | —War against Francis I in the regions of the Netherlands, the Pyrenees and N Italy

Turks take Rhodes and advance in the Balkans

Battle of Landriano against the French

Diet of Speyer—the Protestation— | 1529 | —Turks besiege Vienna

---

Protestants take Württemberg— | 1534–36 | —Charles takes Tunis

Francis I invades N Italy

Charles fails to take Algiers

French attack in alliance with Ottomans——— | 1541–43 |

Charles takes Guelders

Turkish-backed pirates take Tripoli

| 1551–53 |

Henry II invades Germany   Revolt of the German princes united Christendom together, despite the bad relations that often existed between them. 'His weaknesses do not diminish the genuineness of that gesture which was of a piece with his lifelong attitude to his work. Charles' own attitude towards his office revived respect for the religious side of the imperial dignity.' (Frances Yates)

Charles' real failure as a ruler lay not in the inability to achieve his ideals, which were unrealisable, but in the legacy he left to his successors. He aimed for peace but the nature of his empire was such that the other powers in Europe could not tolerate it. Peace could only be obtained by unity or a balance of power. The resultant warfare, which was an almost constant backdrop to the reign, distorted the economies of Spain and the Netherlands and in the latter caused serious unrest. In Germany the Imperial title was preserved but only with the failure to gain real power and the effective fragmentation of the Empire.

Charles was a man of ideals with a deep sense of religious calling and purpose. He told Philip to 'exterminate heresy, lest it take root and overturn the state and social order' and he sought for peace so that he could purge the stain of heresy from his lands. Throughout his reign, the prize of victory seemed to come within his grasp (e.g. in 1525, 1530 and 1547) only to be snatched away by a new combination of forces working against him, fearful of his power.

The tragedy of Charles V was that he had a vision of Christendom united under one Pope and one Emperor working in harmony, which the extent of his dominions appeared to make a real possibility. In reality, the very power that he wielded was so threatening to others that it led to constant division and warfare, precisely what Charles sought to avoid. Vision and failure were inextricably interwoven from the start and it was no disgrace when Charles realised this and abandoned the struggle to men whose responsibilities were less and whose vision was narrower.

19. Bibliography

A F Alvarez *Charles V: Elected Emperor and Hereditary Ruler* (Thames & Hudson, 1975). H G Koenisberger *New Cambridge Modern History Vol. 2* (Chapter X) (CUP, 1959). Karl Brandi *The Emperor Charles V* (Harvester, 1980). J Lynch *Spain Under the Habsburgs Vol. 1* (2nd edition, Blackwell, 1981). H Kamen *Spain 1469–1714: A Society of Conflict* (Longman, 1983). H Holborn *A History of Modern Germany: The Reformation* (Knopf, 1959).

20. Discussion Points and Exercises

A *This section consists of questions or points that might be used for discussion (or written answers) as a way of expanding on the chapter and testing understanding of it:*

1 Why is 'monarchia' a more accurate name for Charles' territories than 'empire'?

2 What mistakes by the young King prompted the revolt of the *Comuneros*?

3 What were the results of the *Comunero* revolt for a) the Cortes, b) the nobility?

4 Draw up a balance sheet of the gains and losses for Spain resulting from Charles' rule.

5 Could Charles be held responsible for the long series of wars against France?

6 Why was the Genoese alliance so important to Spain?

7 Why were the Turks such a problem for Charles V?

8 'More of a burden than a privilege.' Is this a reasonable view of the Imperial title?

9 Why did Charles wait so long before taking decisive action against the Protestants?

10 Explain why the victory at Mühlberg led to the revolt of the Princes.

B *Essay questions*

1 Why did Charles V encounter opposition within the Holy Roman Empire? How successful was he at overcoming this opposition?

2 To what extent were Charles V's problems of his own making?

3 'A resounding success.' Is this a fair judgement of Charles V's rule as King of Spain?

4 Why did Charles V never create a unified administration for his empire?

5 Was Charles' conception of his role as Emperor unrealistic in the sixteenth century?

6 What were Charles V's aims against the Turks and how far did he realise them? *(See Chapter X to help with this answer.)*

21. Essay Writing—Discussion Essays

Many A-level essays have the word 'discuss' before or after a statement or quotation. Variants include 'comment' or 'do you agree?' but they are all the same type of question and are inviting a 'yes/no' answer. If a one-word answer makes sense, it is a discussion essay, e.g.: ' "A resounding success". Is this a fair judgement of Charles V's rule as King of Spain?'. Note that in this example 'discuss' or 'comment' is not included in the title.

You may have strong views on the question asked but the examiners would not have asked the question unless there was an opposing case, so even though you should express at least qualified support for one side or the other, it is essential to look at both sides. To put it another way, you must do the 'yes' and the 'no' side.

For this type of question, examiners often choose areas of current controversy among historians. If you have familiarised yourself with recent interpretations on a topic and can demonstrate your knowledge of leading ideas, this will be a great advantage.

Planning a 'yes/no' essay is relatively easy as a structure is already provided since you must consider each side in turn. If the question is in two parts, each of these must also have a 'yes' and 'no' side. In your conclusion you should then explain which side of the argument you favour and why.

Consider this question: '"More a Mediterranean Monarch than a European Emperor" Discuss this view of Charles V.'

(a) To plan the essay, first assemble arguments with supporting evidence in favour of the statement.

(b) Next, assemble arguments with supporting evidence against the statement.

(c) Having assembled your arguments, you must arrange them in order. There are two ways of approaching this. *Either* put the 'yes' case first with arguments ranked in order of importance and then do the same for the 'no' case; *or* weave the two together—this can be more difficult as there are seldom times when there is a straight alternative but if you can link the contrasting views throughout the essay, it will make more effective reading.

(d) Finally you come to the writing of the essay. Use your introduction to explore the difference between a Mediterranean Monarch and a World Emperor, i.e. what it is the examiner wants you to contrast. Then follows the bulk of the essay with the argument for each paragraph clearly stated in the first sentence and followed by some selected supporting evidence (you are not giving Charles' life history). From your weighting of the essay, one should be able to tell which side you are favouring. In your conclusion you must then state what your answer to the question is, with any reservations.

IX Francis I

1. Introduction

New Year's Day, 1515, heralded the accession of a new king of France, later in the sixteenth century wistfully remembered as *le grand roy Francoys*. In an age of personal monarchy, the fate of the country rested to a tremendous extent on the character of the king. The young king, Francis I, was every inch a Renaissance figure, not only in his handsome, powerful physique (apart from his bandy legs below the knees), but also in his personal charm and tastes. Although he lacked a classical education he loved books and built up one of the finest libraries in Europe. Like his contemporary and great rival, Henry VIII of England, he blended a love of poetry, art and architecture with an obsession for sport and his court was bursting with life and lavish entertainments. Most biographers have concentrated on this personal life of the King. Yet Francis also worked hard; each morning was devoted to matters of state and, right up to his death, he took all the major decisions concerning policy. His role has been more fully appreciated of late owing to the recent definitive biography by R J Knecht.

In 1515, few Frenchmen would have been able to visualise their country as a whole. Many of the great frontier provinces had only recently been assimilated, for example, Brittany in 1491. Aristocratic families still held sway over their lands and threatened the security of the king, regional differences abounded and Frenchmen did not even share a common language. The population probably stood at about 15 million but, as France recovered from the ravages of the Hundred Years' War, this began steadily to increase. This, in turn, stimulated French agriculture, urban development and trade.

The kings of the late fifteenth century had concentrated on consolidation after the long war with England and firmly established the authority of the Crown after the period of civil war. Charles VIII (1483–98) brought Brittany to the Crown, the last great fief to remain aloof. He sought to reduce dependence on his nobility by introducing professionals of lower status to sit alongside them on the council. And he began the Valois intervention in Italy *(see Chapter III)*. Louis XII (1498–1515) kept the *taille* (the main tax) at a standard rate to ease the burden on the poor and encouraged the codification of the various provincial laws. Because of the strains of war, Louis began to levy taxes without even the formality of consultation. This then was Francis's inheritance: the beginnings of centralisation, lack of ready cash, little consultation with his subjects, interwoven with the Italian question. These themes were to be repeated frequently in the reign of Francis I.

2. Domestic Policy

(a) Central government: institutions
In order to govern the whole of France efficiently, Francis needed the support of the central government and local administration developed by his predecessors.

By the early sixteenth century, there were three organs of central government that were particularly important: the king's Council (*Conseil Etroit*), the Grand Conseil and the Parlement of Paris. These institutions had once formed part of the medieval Great Council, the *Curia Regis*, but they now enjoyed very different functions and were to develop even more under the administration of Francis I.

The king's Council was the most important, consisting of the monarch and his advisers. In the past, these had been royal princes, the higher nobility and the most important officers of state, but now membership was usually by royal invitation. By the fifteenth century, and Francis continued in this, the king was anxious to prevent any aristocratic domination of the Council. The value placed on the *maîtres des requêtes*, who were trained lawyers, shows this concern. Under Francis an inner circle also developed, known as the *conseil des affaires*, which was consulted over crucial issues. Since 1497 the Grand Conseil had taken over part of the judicial business transacted by the king's Council. It acted as a court of appeal, intervened in (jurisdictional) conflicts between courts and checked on complaints against royal officials. Although relatively inexpensive, suitors found it frustrating to use because, like the king's Council, it followed the monarch on his travels round the kingdom. However, this proximity was to the king's advantage and made it more attentive to his wishes than the Parlement.

The Parlement of Paris was the highest court of law, its jurisdiction covering two-thirds of France. *Parlementaires* were the magistrates who served in the Parlement. It had remained in Paris since the thirteenth century but was still considered a part of the king's Council.

The Parlement's jurisdiction had once covered the whole kingdom but as France had extended her boundaries, a number of provincial parlements were added. As a court of law, the Parlement judged all offences concerning the king's person, his rights and his lands, from treason to rape and highway robbery. It also acted as a court of appeal from less important royal tribunals. But its powers also embraced social, economic and ecclesiastical matters, from ensuring that Paris received enough corn and fuel, public hygiene and upkeep of roads to controlling the price of bread, fixing wages and academic matters. No Papal Bull could take effect in France until it had been registered by the Parlement. Probably its most influential role, in a political sense, was in ratifying royal legislation.

It is important to remember that this institution was very different from the English Parliament. The Parlement was made up of royally appointed judges, not elected MPs. Historical precedent, however, allowed the Parlement to resist the monarch on occasion. When this occurred it would submit remonstrances to the king who would either modify his suggestions or issue a *lettre de jussion*, which was an order to register his edict without any more delay. This could lead to further remonstrance and *lettres de jussion*, only terminating with the king appearing in person to register his enactment. Such an event was known as a *lit-de-justice*, meaning that the king was temporarily assuming the power he had delegated to Parlement. (As you read this chapter note examples of the clashes between Parlement and the King.)

The Estates General was the closest equivalent to the English Parliament. Composed of delegates representing the three orders of society (clergy, nobility and commoners known as the third estate), it claimed the right to ratify treaties and approve taxation. The fact that the Estates General was not summoned under Francis 1 is another example of the growth of royal power at this time. The Crown made treaties and raised taxes on its own authority.

During the reign of Francis, the bureaucracy became more extensive and it was more sophisticated and complex than the machinery of government in England. The Chancery, headed by the Chancellor, turned the Council's decisions into laws. Chancery secretaries were assisted by the *maîtres des requêtes de l'hotel* (trained lawyers under the Chancellor's control). There were 50 *maîtres* under Francis and they proved to be a vital link between senior departments of state. They benefited socially, many being ennobled. Francis increased the number of people holding office under the crown; it has been estimated that there was an average of one office-holder to every 3000 inhabitants in his reign.

Francis also increased central administration by creating offices and then selling them, thereby increasing his revenues, a practice known as venality. An office in this sense had a definite meaning: it was a permanent government post. Whereas Francis was quite restrained in selling titles of nobility, it was he who turned the sale of offices into a system. He sold offices to those anxious to acquire social status or gave them away as rewards so that the recipients were then free to sell them if they wished. This created serious problems for his immediate successors, as offices tended to become the property of a limited number of families. However, in the short term it was financially advantageous and resulted in loyalty to the King as well as increasing the specialisation of central government.

(b) Provincial government
In contrast to this increasingly bureaucratic central authority, local

government in early sixteenth century France was irregular and re-
gionalised. This did not prevent it, however, from playing a vital role in
the development of royal authority.

As well as the one in Paris, there were six provincial parlements in
1515 which had developed since 1443: Toulouse, Rennes, Bordeaux,
Dijon, Rouen and Aix-en-Provence. They had similar powers to the
Parlement of Paris and each one had to register royal enactments. A
law registered in Paris could not become law in, for example,
Provence without first being registered by the Parlement of Aix-en-
Provence. They were viewed with suspicion by their parent body in Paris

SIXTEENTH CENTURY FRANCE

KEY

Rennes ■   Towns with parlements

BRITTANY   Provinces with estates

Scale 0   100   200   Km

because, rather than acting as one sovereign judicial body, they tended to defend provincial interests against royal governors or the central power.

Much responsibility for provincial administration lay outside the direct control of the Crown. For example, most of the great provinces, which had formerly been independent political units, retained their Estates which were the provincial parliaments. Unlike the Estates General, the provincial Estates still played an important role in the life of the country. Although they only met once a year for a week or less, many Estates had succeeded in gaining control over the levying of money within their areas and were able to play a leading part in the life of the province by constructing roads and public buildings, fixing and levying customs duties and sometimes by organising a rudimentary police force for the countryside.

Of all the positions in the structure of local government, the provincial governors were the most important. Their jurisdiction did not cover all the country but they were active in the border provinces. They were usually of the higher nobility and under Francis included his sons, uncle and favourites (including the husbands of his mistresses!) but their posts were revocable at the whim of the king. The patronage which the position of governor involved, both at court and in the province, made him potentially dangerous to the Crown. In 1542 Francis annulled the powers of all governors saying they had become too excessive. In this way he removed one of the governors, Montmorency, who was out of favour and later restored the powers of the other governors. The King had shown who was ultimately in control. The office of governor was both useful as a means of extending royal authority and dangerous as a way of preserving noble interests.

Below the rank of provincial governors were the *baillis*. They staffed the *bailliages*, of which there were about 86, which can best be described as mini-parlements in their spheres of activities but acting on a much smaller scale and within a vastly reduced area. The officials working within the *bailliages* were not well paid and had to rely on fees and gifts. The king thus ensured an active, if corrupt, system of local government.

The *maîtres des requêtes de l'hotel*, who helped the Chancellor of France run his departments, were a link between the *bailliages* and central government. They were sent on tours of inspection around the provinces, dealt with complaints against royal officials and if they found anything amiss they were supposed to report back to the king's Council. Their role was important in the development of centralised government in France, although they were not permanent inspectors like the *intendants* to come in the seventeenth century.

Francis made no startling innovations in central and provincial government, probably because foreign and religious problems seemed more pressing. However, we can identify a move towards centralisation and specialisation, the use of trained expert officials, and increased efficiency.

(c) Financial administration

Francis had a significant advantage over his contemporary rulers and this was the power to tax at will. Ever since Charles VII had managed to turn a limited concession by the Estates into an established right, kings of France had collected the *taille*, the main direct tax, on this basis, and it was later extended to include the *gabelle*, a tax on salt which was vital for the preservation of food. This enormously increased the king's revenue. With all its inconsistency the *taille* represented the greatest single source of revenue for the Crown. At the beginning of Francis's reign, it amounted to 2.4 million livres out of his total revenue of 4.9 million livres (1 livre = 2 English shillings). The sales tax known as the *aides* brought in about a third as much as the *taille* and the *gabelle* about a sixth.

Indirect taxes were collected by the practice of tax-farming. By this system the king authorised an individual, often the highest bidder, to collect and keep a particular royal tax after prior payment to the king of a fixed sum. This pleased both financier, because he could make a profit, and king, because he received the money without any administrative problems and expense. A different method was used for the *taille*. An assessor and collector were elected from a parish. When the parishioners had been assessed the amounts owed were read out in church and the following Sunday taxes were paid. Few escaped, as the assessor would suffer if the expected amount did not reach Paris. So, although the system seemed corrupt and in need of reform, it did work.

Francis was extravagant in every sphere of life but it was his foreign policy and wars that were the single heaviest item of expenditure. His first campaign into Italy leading up to Marignano cost 1.8 million livres. By 1517 Francis's debt equalled his regular annual income but he continued naively to pay out huge sums such as the 200 000 livres he spent in 1520 on entertaining Henry VIII at the Field of the Cloth of Gold.

In order to begin to meet the huge expenses he was incurring, Francis embarked on a programme of fiscal reform. He aimed to cut down on corruption in the administration and increase its efficiency to give him the greatest profit on which to fall back when the occasion arose. In 1523 Francis established a new central Treasury, the *Trésor de l'Epargne* (headed by the *Trésorier*) into which all his revenues, whatever their origin, were deposited. This innovation gave Francis supreme control of financial matters but money still did not reach the *Trésorier* as plentifully or swiftly as the King would have wished.

Francis tried again in 1542 when he was once more at war with the Emperor. This time he established 16 *recettes générales* which were financial and administrative regional offices which collected all forms of royal income previously collected separately.

It had taken Francis 20 years, in a rather staccato way, to implement his financial reforms but he did accomplish his aims. Centralisation by the subordination of all the royal 'receivers' to the *Trésorier* who in turn had to refer to the king, uniformity by fusing ordinary and extraordinary revenue, and simplification by more efficient methods of collection. The system was by no means perfect but the framework for the future had been established.

Nevertheless, because of his constant need for ready cash Francis resorted to several expedients to see him through a crisis. He practised venality, the sale of offices *(see page 213)*. He borrowed heavily from the Italian bankers of Lyons, requested forced loans from towns exempt from the *taille*, borrowed from his own tax officials and, much to the horror of the Parlement, sold Crown land.

The financial crisis of 1521–23 showed Francis' powers of ingenuity. War with the Emperor proved expensive and France's revenues were stretched beyond their limits. The King's chief financial minister was Jacques de Beaune, Baron de Semblançay, who sensibly warned his master in September that the money left in the Treasury would only last for another month. The war continued over the winter into 1522, with Francis moving from one expedient to another. Finally, the following September, the scheme known as the *rentes sur l'Hôtel de Ville de Paris* was established. This was an early type of public credit. Francis borrowed 200 000 livres from Paris against the security of the municipality's revenue and each contributor was assured of a life annuity or *rente* at eight and a half percent. It was an ingenious idea for the time—in total it brought in 725 000 livres, other *rentes* being sold in 1537 and 1543. Based on a system of mutual trust, this system has been acclaimed by some, even if Francis, reacting only to the immediate needs of war, allowed the practice to drop.

Such ingenuity did not solve Francis' problem and in 1523 he was once again without resources to pay for his campaigns. Now he began to suspect his officials of embezzlement and so in January 1523 he set up the *Commission de la Tour Carrée*, another expedient to look into fiscal administration.

For some reason, possibly jealousy, Semblançay, the King's loyal finance minister, was the principal target. However, the final verdict of the commissioners was that the King owed his minister 1 190 374 livres! In 1527, Semblançay was arrested and thrown into the Bastille. His trial was a farce, for his judges were handpicked by the King, rather than by the Parlement. He was hanged at Montfaucon in August and aroused the sympathy of the Parisiens due to his dignified manner and age (he was 80!). Apart from the fact that Francis wanted to be rid of this older and wiser minister, it is difficult to find evidence against him. Since his capture by the Spaniards in 1525 he had attempted to recover his debts, and it was a time of national crisis, but this hardly justifies judicial murder. This affair shows Francis at his most ruthless.

For a short time after the Peace of Cambrai in 1529, France was at peace with her neighbour and Francis seized the opportunity to refill his coffers. As a result of the Ordinance of Rouen in 1532, revenue was to remain at the Louvre rather than with the mobile court, and ensure a reserve of ready cash. Yet substantial sums levied by the *Trésorier de l'Epargne* never passed through his Treasury and went straight to pay for the everyday living costs of the King. By 1536 the 1.5 million livres saved by Francis had been absorbed in the war against the Emperor which cost over three million livres, and the same was true in 1542. Again, Francis used every expedient to raise cash including extending the *gabelle*, the salt tax.

Francis was fortunate that he endured relatively few instances of resistance to royal taxation compared with his contemporaries or his successors in seventeenth century France. He only levied one new tax and even this was not entirely new. This was the *solde des 50 000 hommes* levied on all towns. What was new in 1543 was that from then on it was to be levied annually, even in peacetime. Although the paying of the tax created problems, as for example in Lyon where they had to borrow from Italian bankers to do so, there was no unified resistance to it.

There were only a few instances of popular rebellion against taxation, despite the financial strain on the French people. In 1542, in western France people took up arms against Francis' attempts to reform the salt tax in the Edict of Châtellerault of 1541. This introduced a single salt tax to be levied at the salt marsh. Severe penalties also aimed to eradicate fraud and smuggling and, by a further edict in April 1542, the King tried to increase the yield of the *gabelle* by simplifying the levy. To the government this might have been reasonable and fair but to those affected it seemed to threaten their whole way of life. Ten thousand men, aware that the king was occupied with war against the Emperor, took up arms and forced the royal commissioners to retire.

The measure of Francis' concern is shown by the fact that, despite being at war, he himself came to La Rochelle to pass the final judgement. The rebels expressed their remorse and Francis reminded them of the seriousness of their crime, particularly at a time when he was defending the kingdom. But he concluded that he could not refuse them a pardon if they truly repented and he did not wish to be seen to treat his subjects in a similar vein to Charles V and the people of Ghent *(see page 191)*.

Francis' treatment appears very magnanimous compared with Charles and Henry's policies towards their rebels but it has to be remembered that he could be little else when this part of the country was particularly vulnerable to English attack and although the ordinance of 1542 was revoked, a similar policy was put into practice in 1544. This was not characteristic of his policy towards rebels. In November 1544, following a rebellion at Lagny-sur-Marne over the *gabelle*, he ordered the Seigneur de Lorges to sack the town and forbade the inhabitants from prosecuting de Lorges or his troops.

Francis has enjoyed the reputation of being a shrewd business man because he left several million livres in his treasury despite his many years at war. However, this is misleading because when he died Francis owed the Lyons bankers 6 860 844 livres (his income in 1547 was 7 183 271 livres). Francis had in reality left a huge debt that his successor had to pay off. Despite his various fiscal experiments Francis had failed to improve the financial situation of the Crown, not through lack of ability but because both his time and money were absorbed by foreign affairs.

(d) Faction
Even though the unification of the kingdom was well advanced by the reign of Francis, there was still opportunity for the powerful families who continued to control various parts of France to challenge the authority of the Crown. This could and did occur in different ways but it needed a strong and effective king to suppress it.

The defection of Charles of Bourbon is one example. The Bourbon feudal demesne consisted of an unusually consolidated block of territories in central France and, like other such landowners, within his demesne his word was law. Francis honoured him with the office of Constable of France in 1515 and this gave him control of the army in peacetime as well. Although Francis could be criticised for entrusting him with too much power, this was not unusual for the time. It made for effective government—until a problem arose.

In 1521 a crisis did occur on the death of Bourbon's wife, the Duchess Suzanne who had inherited the Bourbon lands in her own right but had been challenged for them by the man who later became her husband. The Duchess had made a will leaving her lands to her husband but it was challenged by Francis' mother, Louise of Savoy, on the grounds that she was the nearest blood relative. Francis naturally sided with his mother, particularly as the lands had officially been absorbed into the kingdom. Although the whole question was submitted to Parlement, Francis disposed of some of the lands before their verdict was issued. This led to Bourbon's treacherous decision in 1523 to throw in his lot with Charles V and Henry VIII and lead a rebellion in France whilst the King was away in Italy.

Was this just because of the loss of his lands or was Bourbon power-hungry and looking for an excuse to rebel? Whatever the answer, the King showed who was ultimately in control. The plot was discovered and, although Bourbon escaped, his property was ceded to the Crown. However, this was not before Francis had been forced to forbid the publication of the Parlement's decisions as it had virtually acquitted Bourbon and his accomplices. When Bourbon was killed at the sack of Rome in 1527 the Bourbon lands reverted to Francis and his mother, and when she died in 1531 the Crown acquired them all.

A second example of faction came from within the King's family and intensified in the last years of Francis' life, particularly as his health deteriorated. There was rivalry between his two surviving sons, the Dauphin Henry and Charles, Duke of Orleans. After the death of the Dauphin Francis in 1536, Charles became Francis' favourite son and the rift between the two brothers widened in 1541 when Montmorency, the chief royal minister, fell from favour. Henry remained loyal to him throughout but Charles fell under the influence of the king's chief mistress Madame d'Etampes, Montmorency's greatest enemy. The war of 1542 made the situation even worse; whereas Charles conquered Luxembourg, Henry had to retreat from Perpignan. Had the Treaty of Crèpy in 1544 been implemented, Charles might have become Duke of Milan, married the Emperor's daughter and gained four French duchies from his father. This was very insulting to the prestige of the Dauphin but, fortunately for him, Charles died in 1545.

Francis and Henry did grow closer but on his accession to the throne, one of Henry's first moves was to restore Montmorency. Francis had found that power struggles could occur even within his own family and again the importance of the personality of the king is emphasised. Francis had contained the problem; a weaker monarch might not have done. This was an omen for the future.

Faction abounded in the last five years of Francis' life probably because, although still in control, he was a sick man as an ultimately fatal illness took its toll. It showed that the fragile position of even an authoritative king such as Francis could be challenged and how he always had to be vigilant even amongst his most trusted advisers and friends.

3. Religious Policy

(a) The Concordat of Bologna
As Francis was king of France during one of the most turbulent periods in the history of the Roman Catholic Church, religion was bound to be an important issue. When Francis came to the throne the French Church enjoyed the unusual privilege of relative independence from Rome. The question was whether he would be able to maintain this and cope with the challenge of Protestantism.

The Concordat of Bologna was an agreement made by Francis with Pope Leo X in 1516, by which the King permitted papal taxation in France in return for the right to nominate bishops. Its diplomatic context was the Italian Wars. It has been said that it gave the King control over the French Church, so much so that there was never any inducement for him to ally with the Protestant reformers against the authority of the Pope. However, Knecht has shown that the relationship of Church and state in France was already one of close mutual dependence, whatever the relationship between King and Pope. After the passing of the Pragmatic Sanction in 1438 which increased the development of Gallicanism (the independence of the French Church from Rome), Louis XI by 1471 was freely controlling clerical appointments and by 1515 this royal control was an accepted fact. However, Francis had made financial concessions to the Pope which aroused some of the most concerted opposition he had to face.

The Paris Parlement was a staunch defender of Gallican privileges and delayed registration of the Concordat. In January 1518 the King received a memorandum from two representatives of the Parlement which repeated the objections to the Concordat: fear that all benefices would become liable to papal taxation, and of large-scale papal interference in the French Church. Francis was thrown into a fit of rage. He roared that there would only be one king in France and no senate as in Venice, and threatened to turn the Parlement into a nomadic institution, making it 'trot after him like those of the Grand Conseil'. The two *Parlementaires* were ordered to leave but when they pleaded for respite, they were told that if they were not gone by six the following morning they would be thrown into a pit by twelve archers and left there to rot for six months! Rumours then spread that Francis planned to establish a new Parlement at Orleans. Royal intimidation finally triumphed; on 22 March 1518 the Concordat was registered, though under protest.

The Parlement had capitulated but Francis still had to face the opposition of the Sorbonne, then the Faculty of Theology of the University of Paris, that bastion of Gallicanism, which had a vested interest in a system which reserved a third of vacant benefices for graduates. The Sorbonne was important—it was the leading theological school in Europe and its support was vital in influencing public opinion. But under threat of banishment it too capitulated.

Did the Concordat do nothing, then, to increase the Crown's control of the Church? Although recognising the King's right to appoint to major benefices, it did not give him unlimited power:

> Henceforward, in the case of vacancies now and in the future in cathedral and metropolitan churches of the said kingdom (of France) whoever is king of France shall within six months counting from the day on which the vacancy occurred present and nominate to us and to our successors, as bishops of Rome or to the Apostolic See to be invested by us, a sober or knowledgeable master or graduate in theology, or a doctor or graduate in all or in one of the laws taught and rigorously examined at a famous university, who must be at least twenty-seven years old and otherwise suitable . . .
>
> . . . and should the king not nominate a person with such qualifications, neither we, nor our successors nor the Holy See shall have to invest such a person . . . If, within the stipulated six months, the king should present to us, our successors or the Holy See a secular priest or a regular priest of another order or a minor under twenty-three years or someone unsuitable in another way, such a person will be rejected by us and will not be invested with the office.

1   Why did age limits have to be stipulated?
2   How far could these clauses of the Concordat really limit the royal power?

If the limitation embodied in the Concordat had been adhered to, the Crown would not have gained as much control over the Church as it did. But the Pope did not qibble over details of application because the authority of the Holy See, undermined by the Pragmatic Sanction, was now much restored, 'the thorn removed from the eye of the Church' as it was put at the time. Even if Francis did not gain all he had hoped for from the Pope in a political sense, he was never inclined to repudiate the

Concordat, because to do so would have meant humiliation before the Gallican opposition and loss of domestic advantages gained from the agreement.

The Concordat of Bologna was not simply a triumph for Francis I. It was part of the traditional policy of kings of France to put pressure on the Papacy to further their Italian ambitions. In this it ultimately failed *(see page 232)*. Nor in France did the Concordat produce the revolutionary changes ascribed to it. The independence of the French church from the Crown was already in decay; the Concordat merely endorsed this.

(b) Reform and Reformation within France

In the early sixteenth century, as in other parts of western Christendom, there existed the paradox of a lowering of standards within the French Church, combined with the flourishing of humanist ideas at the highest academic levels. Jacques Lefèvre d'Etaples was the first French academic to break away from a scholastic approach towards spiritual matters. Deeply concerned about the state of religion, he deliberately chose to become a teacher and keep in touch with events rather than retreating to a monastery. In 1512 he published an edition of St Paul's Epistles. Lefèvre was important because he was the first French Christian Humanist (classical scholarship aimed at instilling new life into the Christian religion by going back to the original scriptural text). He was following the example of Erasmus, who had visited France in the 1490s. Lefèvre's influence was tremendous, particularly after he joined the household of the Bishop of Meaux.

If French humanism was to revive the French Church properly, it needed support from the top. The higher clergy were not particularly inspiring but there were exceptions, for example Guillaume Briçonnet, Bishop of Meaux. Appalled at the state of his diocese when he visited in 1518, he immediately set about remedying the situation and was soon joined by Lefèvre and a group of evangelical preachers who became known as the Circle of Meaux. Briçonnet, inspired by Bishop Giberti of Verona *(see page 306)*, imported a printing press and divided up his diocese into 26 zones, allocating preachers to each of them for Lent and Advent, while he himself preached every Sunday in his cathedral. Unfortunately this annoyed the local Franciscans, who were dependent for their survival on payment for their services as preachers. In the long term it had far greater significance: they accused the Bishop and his evangelical circle of heresy and put their claim before the Sorbonne and the Parlement of Paris. Their fate rested on the definition of heresy.

France could not for long escape the infiltration of Luther's works. Although the Sorbonne sympathised with his attack on indulgences, they could not tolerate his later ideas. Finally on 15 April 1521 the University issued its *Determinatio* condemning Luther's ideas as heresy, but it was too late to retrieve the seeds that had already been sown.

But what precisely did the critics mean by heresy? Was it just Lutheranism or did it include evangelical humanism practised in France before 1519? The dividing line between evangelical humanism and Lutheranism is difficult to pinpoint in the 1520s. Both emphasised the importance of the writings of St Paul and an improved understanding of Scripture. There were points where they differed; for example, Lefèvre could not accept Luther's reduction in the number of sacraments but other members of the Circle of Meaux, notably Guillaume Farel, soon became totally convinced by Lutheranism. The scholar and preacher Louis de Berquin was a disciple of both Erasmus and Luther. To the Sorbonne, there was no question about it; both were detestable. So the infiltration of Luther's ideas into France in the early 1520s put a slur on the more orthodox reformers at Meaux.

(c) Francis I and the question of heresy

As the 'Most Christian King' Francis could not tolerate heresy, it would have completely contradicted his aim for national unity. However, Francis' interpretation of heresy did not coincide with that of the Sorbonne and this was to be the cause of future problems. Francis liked to portray himself as the ideal Renaissance monarch and from the beginning of his reign, although himself no classical scholar, he had been an enthusiastic patron of humanism. He enjoyed the company of well-educated men and his household included several humanists: his secretary Guillaume Budé, his doctor Guillaume Cop and his old tutor Francois de Rochefort.

Francis invited Erasmus to France in 1517 to take charge of a college devoted to the study of classical languages. Erasmus declined and the idea waned, but in 1530 the King established what would become the Collège de France, a society of professors paid by him to give lectures on Greek, Hebrew, mathematics and Latin. By actions such as these, Francis was stressing the importance of the study of the classics in reaching a correct understanding of Scripture: but to the Sorbonne only the Latin Vulgate was respectable. There were also close links between the court and the Circle of Meaux due to the influence of the King's beloved sister, Marguerite, who in 1527 became Queen of Navarre. She sought Briçonnet's spiritual guidance and corresponded with him from about 1521, becoming acquainted with the ideas of Lefèvre. Her influence on the King must not be underestimated.

Francis was none the less hostile to the German heresies spread by Luther. In June 1521, Francis instructed the Parlement to examine all printers and booksellers and check that nothing was published without the University's approval. When this proved difficult to impose, Francis followed it up by a proclamation issued on 3 August 1521. This stated that anyone owning Luther's works had one week in which to hand them over to the Parlement or face a fine and imprisonment. This proved to be little more effective than the first measure.

One reason for this was the difference of opinion between the King and the Sorbonne and Parlement in their interpretation of heresy. The best example of this is the treatment of a young scholar, Louis de Berquin, who was found in possession of Luther's books in 1523. Berquin's own works were examined by the Sorbonne and proclaimed heretical: he was reported to the Parlement and arrested on a charge of heresy. In the meantime, the University had seized the opportunity to examine works by Lefèvre and Erasmus. Whereas Francis did not wish to be seen protecting heretics, this he refused to tolerate. So he referred the case to his Grand Conseil and Berquin was released. Francis had over-ridden the Sorbonne's traditional right to judge doctrine.

The University took up the challenge and accused two members of the Circle of Meaux, Caroli and Mazurier, of heresy. It also condemned all editions of Scripture in Greek, Hebrew and French. Francis again had the last word; he simply forbade all discussion of Lefèvre's work and referred to him as an internationally acclaimed scholar.

It has been said that Francis failed to crush heresy at this stage because of the inconsistency of his policy. But, as we have seen, heresy in the early 1520s in France was not clearly defined. Francis' policy was consistent in that he was constantly ordering the authorities to stamp out heresy: the problem was that their interpretation differed from his, and Francis' patronage of evangelical humanism provided a breeding ground for the infiltration of more Protestant ideas.

The Parlement had an equally rigid view of heresy. In 1525, it seized its opportunity to become involved in the persecution of heretics during Francis' captivity in Spain after the Battle of Pavia. Although Parlement met at the invitation of the regent, Francis' mother Louise of Savoy, it took advantage of her vulnerable position and criticised a number of royal policies that had been pursued since the beginning of the reign. Although no direct accusation was made it implied that Francis was guilty of protecting heretics and demanded that Louise pursue a tougher policy of persecution. Only in religion did she go some way to satisfying their demands: having applied to the Pope, Clement VII, she set up the *juges délégués* which formed a commission made up of two Sorbonnistes and two *Parlementaires* with powers to deal with all heresy cases without consulting the ecclesiastical courts. So heresy jurisdiction was now directly under the control of the orthodox extremists.

The new machinery was immediately put into action against the Circle of Meaux which resulted in the King making one of his few interventions from captivity in the domestic affairs of the realm. No doubt Francis had been warned of what was happening by his sister who had recently visited him in Spain. He ordered proceedings against Lefèvre and other defendants to be suspended until his return but the Parlement ignored this and the *juges délégués* were ordered to continue with their work. Berquin was also harassed in the King's absence: he was arrested for a second time in January 1526 and accused of heresy but sentence was not passed as it became known that the King had been released.

On his return, Francis expressed his disapproval of the persecution by appointing Lefèvre librarian at his new chateau of Blois, allowing Caroli to resume preaching in Paris and demanding Berquin's release. The following year, 1527, he abolished the *juges délégués*, which led people to believe that he was moving closer to Luther, particularly as the Emperor now had control of the Pope. This was not the case; all that Francis was doing was once again showing the Sorbonne and parlement who was ultimately in control of the kingdom.

Early in 1528 Duprat, Archbishop of Sens, put forward a list of harsh penalties for heresy and in July a horrific device known as *l'estrapade* was first used for putting heretics to death at Meaux. Instead of being burned at the stake, the victim was suspended by means of iron chains over the flames, into which he was alternately lowered and raised so as to prolong the agony. This was obviously meant as a deterrent to heretics and it was in fact quite successful.

1528 also heralded the first of a series of iconoclastic attacks in Paris when a statue of the Virgin and Child was deliberately damaged. Francis offered a large reward for information about the culprits, showing the extent of his concern. This event is significant because it was just the first of many such acts and reveals that the more fundamental ideas of the radicals were already being absorbed by the lower classes. Even amongst the reformers in France there was a split of opinion, as Farel, one of the original members of the Circle of Meaux, rejected Lefèvre in favour of Karlstadt and the Swiss reformer, Zwingli *(see Chapter XI)*, thereby showing his essentially Protestant beliefs.

(d) Heresy and politics 1530–47

This growth of radicalism concerned not only the University and the Parlement but also the King. In December 1530 the Chancellor was instructed to appoint judges to supervise any heresy cases throughout the kingdom. This did not mean that relations between Francis and the Sorbonne became any more harmonious: if anything they grew worse as the Faculty increased its efforts to control the King's patronage of Christian Humanists. It believed that heresy would never be eradicated from the whole of France, whatever legislative action the King might take, as long as it was allowed to flourish at court. There followed a series of contests between King on the one hand and Parlement and the Sorbonne on the other.

It was this situation which led to the final downfall of Berquin in April 1528. Parlement took advantage of the King's absence from Paris and Berquin was burned on the Place de Grève.

Another target for the Catholic extremists was Gérald Roussel, a member of the Queen of Navarre's household. In 1533 he was accused by the Sorbonne, for the second time, of preaching heresy before her in the Louvre. This was particularly embarrassing for Francis as he was about to meet the Pope at Marseilles. To show who was in control, the King left Roussel to Marguerite's congenial care, ordered his critics more than 20 leagues from the capital and postponed any decision on the charge of heresy. University circles were livid but when they blacklisted a poem of

Marguerite's, it resulted in the University having to make an abject apology to the King.

These frequent contests between the King and the Catholic extremists did not mean that Francis tolerated heresy. The spread of heretical ideas would not only threaten the unity of the kingdom but also jeopardise his delicate diplomatic negotiations. It was at the King's own request that, on 30 August when Francis and Pope Clement VII met at Marseilles, a Bull was drawn up to quicken the procedure in heresy trials, and a later one made special provision for the punishment of ecclesiastics. These were meant only to be used in emergencies, but this very soon occurred.

After Nicolas Cop, the rector of the University of Paris, had delivered his traditional sermon on All Saints' Day, 1533, in the Church of the Mathurins, the Sorbonne complained to the Parlement because he had referred to the ideas of Lefèvre. Fearing the worst, Cop vanished taking with him the University's seal; he was followed by his young friend John Calvin. Three months later he turned up in Basle. In the aftermath of this incident there broke out a wave of persecution.

Having made around 50 arrests, Parlement informed the King of the terrifying growth of heresy in the capital. With due concern, Francis ordered the publication of the two recent Bulls against heresy and that a commission of *Parlementaires* should be set up to try heretics already detained. It has been suggested that Francis was obeying the dictates of his foreign policy in reacting so quickly to this appeal from the Sorbonne and Parlement, particularly as Cop had recently defended his sister and considering that the content of his sermon was no more radical than many people's ideas at court. It is more likely that Francis was merely responding to a situation that he had only heard of: he was not in Paris to judge the situation for himself. The Sorbonne and Parlement exaggerated the dangers of the situation to force the King into action. Once the King had returned he was able to assess the situation for himself —persecution soon ended. Only at this point was Roussel finally cleared of heresy.

Tranquillity remained till the Affair of the Placards broke out in the autumn of 1534. On the Sunday morning of 18 October, Parisians on their way to Mass were aghast to find that Protestant placards attacking the doctrine of the Mass had been put up during the night in various public places. The Parisians' hysteria grew when it was reported that identical broadsheets had been found in the Chateau of Amboise where the King was in residence and in five provincial towns, Orleans, Blois, Amboise, Tours and Rouen. To make matters worse, the placards did not flaunt Luther's more moderate view but Zwingli's extreme position on the Mass which denied the physical presence of Christ in the sacrament altogether. (The followers of Zwingli in France were known as sacramentarians.)

The Affair of the Placards was a significant event in itself for two reasons: firstly in showing that the Eucharist had ceased to be merely an academic debate, and secondly in the reaction of the people to the placards, it can be seen that the Reformation in France was becoming more popular and more easily defined. In short, it polarised people's opinions.

Almost immediately there followed a swift campaign of persecution on a scale as yet unknown to French reformers. A special commission of twelve *Parlementaires* was set up to judge heresy cases (along with a subcommission to deal with suspects within the Parlement's own ranks). By the end of November six 'Lutherans'/dissenters had been burned in Paris. Francis was actually complimented by the Sorbonne for his zeal in dealing with this bout of heresy! Then on 13 January, just after Francis had returned to the capital, some copies of the *Petite Traité*, a sacramentarian tract, were discovered in the streets. Although seemingly of less significance than the first episode, this incident was more provocative considering the measures being taken to stifle heresy. It was probably this flouting of his authority that made Francis on the same day ban all printing till further notice and to order a procession for 21 January.

This must have been one of the most dramatic demonstrations of orthodoxy that the capital had ever witnessed as shrines and relics were carried through the streets. The relics included the Crown of Thorns and, in pride of place, the Blessed Sacrament, which the placards had insulted, reverently borne under a canopy by the King's three sons. Immediately behind walked Francis, his dismay at recent events openly expressed by his black attire, bare head and the lighted torch in his hand symbolising his own orthodox Catholic view of the Eucharist. After a service at Notre-Dame, he urged his subjects to denounce all heretics, and ended the day by burning six heretics. Further legislation was passed against those who harboured and concealed heretics.

The traditional explanation of Francis' harsh reaction was the appearance of a placard on his own bedchamber door. Although contemporary accounts differ over detail, it is almost certain that at least one such placard was found in the King's apartments at Amboise. Was this a crime grave enough to provoke such a violent campaign of repression in a town as far away as Paris? Also, unauthorised persons drifted in and out of his apartments with ease. Nothing in his behaviour suggests an outburst. He did not rush back to the capital but travelled at his usual leisurely pace.

Was Francis then responding to the international situation? This is unlikely as he was sounding out the German Lutheran princes at the time and the persecution could hardly have been more embarrassing, and this incident ruined his anti-Habsburg coalition.

It was the Parlement of Paris who acted first over the Affair of the Placards and who quite legally ordered the search for the culprits in the King's name. Previously, as for instance over Cop's sermon, the King had called a halt to persecution ordered in his name. This time he did not, and the reason must be that he felt Parlement had correctly assessed this Protestant challenge. The Placards were a violent attack on a fundamental belief of the Catholic faith and were on display to all the

King's subjects. Their language was abusive even for the sixteenth century and it quite clearly showed the radical path the French Reformation had been taking since the mid-1520s. For once the Parlement and the Sorbonne got their way, but as the Most Christian King, Francis could hardly dispute the seriousness of the offence or the popular hysteria it had provoked. Francis acted astutely in giving his blessing to the persecution.

It has been traditional to see the Affair of the Placards as marking a radical change in the King's attitude to heresy, from one of toleration to one of persecution. But Francis had never tolerated what he considered to be heresy; he had just disputed the definition of heresy with the Catholic extremists. Francis did not immediately break off negotiations with the German princes or stop patronising humanists, but from 1534 onwards the King worked with the Parlement, rather than against it, to eradicate what both recognised as a more aggressive and dangerous type of Protestantism at large in France.

(e) The growth of persecution

Francis was now much more aware of heresy and far less tolerant of it. However, this did not prevent him from allying with Protestants abroad, in spite of Imperial agents making propaganda out of the situation by contrasting the King's treatment of his Protestant subjects with the hospitality given to Turkish envoys. To foreign ambassadors, Francis claimed that persecution in France was political and not religious: he had gone no further than any other ruler in stamping out sedition. None the less he did suspend persecution while he needed the alliance of the German Protestant princes. Then, after the Truce of Nice in 1538, he was freed from the constraints of foreign policy and turned his full attention to the problem of heresy.

The parlements needed more power if heresy was to be eradicated. So on 1 June 1540 the Edict of Fontainebleau gave the parlements what they had long wanted, control of heresy cases. This proved insufficient and finally in July 1543 Francis decided that the power of search and arrest would now be shared by the secular and ecclesiastical authorities, and further decrees continued to be issued till the end of the reign, with one aim—to hunt down heretics. The numerous draconian measures taken suggests that it was becoming increasingly difficult to stifle the growing Protestant challenge.

As in the rest of Europe, French Catholics were bewildered and confused by the contradictory doctrines put forward by the different reformers. The Sorbonne, frightened by the threat of Protestantism despite the King's policy of persecution, attempted to define the doctrine of the Catholic Church in a series of 25 articles which were published in July 1543. These were an orthodox statement of traditional Catholic practice with regard to dogma, worship and organisation. This Confession of Faith gave the campaign against heresy a clearer sense of direction. The dangers of the printing press as a means of spreading subversive ideas had long been recognised. In 1543 the Sorbonne drew up the first Index of Forbidden Books, consisting of 65 titles amongst which were Luther, Melanchthon and Calvin's works.

Persecution intensified during the last years of the reign and the number of prosecutions for heresy by the Parlement of Paris increased. Heretical ideas spread deeper into the kingdom and penetrated a wider spectrum of the population in the late 1530s and throughout the 1540s. In particular, the lower classes and the burghers and artisans of the towns were 'contaminated'. In 1545, five commissioners were assigned to particular areas with full powers of search and punishment. Heretics were hunted down all over France but none more viciously than the inhabitants of the Provençal villages of Merindol and Cabrières who were massacred in 1544.

As we have seen, it is too much of a simplification to say that until 1534 Francis was well-disposed towards reformers, protecting them from persecution by the Sorbonne and the Parlement and that after the Affair of the Placards, he suddenly rounded on them and unleashed a savage campaign of repression which continued intermittently till the end of the reign. The constant U-turns in foreign policy had their effect on religious policy as did the influence of his sister, Marguerite, who sympathised with the reform movement. In fact Francis was not as inconsistent as commonly supposed. Although the importance of the Placards in the French Reformation cannot be overlooked, it did not cause a fundamental change in Francis' attitude to heresy. Francis had always been hostile to what he considered to be heresy. The aura of sanctity that surrounded the monarch and enhanced his authority bore with it the obligation to attend to his people's religious welfare; an obligation that was all the more important since the negotiations of the Concordat of Bologna. It was just that until 1534, Francis' interpretation of heresy did not coincide with that of the Sorbonne and Parlement. Once it became apparent that the French Reformation had taken a more radical turn and was infiltrating all sectors of society, Francis' attitude hardened. Although there were instances when he seemed to ease the pressure of persecution to meet the demands of an international situation, it was no more than Charles V or the Pope did; one must remember Francis was a politician as well as the Most Christian King.

4. Foreign Policy

Much of the detail of Francis' foreign policy has been dealt with in relation to the Italian Wars and Charles V *(see pages 72 and 191)*. Here we shall review some of the main features, assessing Francis' goals and achievements.

(a) The issue of Milan
For most of his reign, the key issue for Francis was Milan. He felt he had a

hereditary right to the duchy and it was of great strategic importance, dominating the Alpine passes into Italy. Also he had to avenge the defeat of his predecessor, Louis XII, by the Swiss.

Francis' invasion of Italy on becoming King in 1515 was an unqualified triumph. As the Swiss blocked the obvious routes across the Alps, Francis chose a pass used only by local peasants and their herds, so that he was able to take the Milanese by surprise at Villafranca. A Venetian eyewitness commented that the Alps had seen nothing comparable since Hannibal's famous crossing! His defeat of the seemingly invincible Swiss at Marignano covered him with glory.

However, Francis' pre-eminence was short-lived. Charles of Burgundy became King of Spain in 1516 and put himself forward to succeed his grandfather as Holy Roman Emperor in 1519. Francis put himself forward as a rival candidate. He spent 400 000 crowns in bribery of the Electors but to no avail. It seemed as though he suffered from too great a sense of his own grandeur. But he had more practical motives. He wrote that he wished to gain the Empire 'to prevent the said Catholic king from doing so. If he were to succeed, seeing the extent of his kingdoms and lordships, this would do me immeasurable harm; he would . . . doubtless throw me out of Italy'. Even in the case of the Imperial election the issue was Milan, although now part of the larger issue of Habsburg encirclement of France.

Francis was right. By 1522 Milan was in Habsburg hands—after Francis had tried to take advantage of Charles by attacking Spain during the Revolt of the *Comuneros*. Still, the French successfully resisted an Imperial invasion in the region of Marseilles and Francis managed to re-take Milan in 1524. However, there was not to be another Marignano —in 1525 Francis was defeated and captured at the Battle of Pavia. He had shown great personal bravery during the battle but the consequence for him was imprisonment in Madrid.

(b) The consequences of defeat

By the Treaty of Madrid in 1526, Francis was forced to concede Milan to Charles and he promised to return the Burgundian territories taken by Louis XI. He was then freed, leaving behind him his two young sons as hostages. Charles thought he had won hands down but Francis was not to give in so easily.

In May 1526 the Viceroy of Naples visited Francis, having heard that he intended to disregard the Treaty of Madrid and hoping to persuade him otherwise. This was his official answer:

> It has been resolved that the Viceroy will be called to the Council tomorrow, and after his demands have been heard, they will be answered. First, should he speak of the king's promises, oath and obligation, he will be told that the King is under no obligation whatever and that he is not bound to keep his
> 5   promises, since they (the Imperialists) did not trust his word, but kept him under guard, setting him free only after they had received hostages. Nor is he obliged to keep promises which may be attributed to him, since they were

extorted from him under the fear of life imprisonment and of death
10 consequent on the grave illness caused by melancholy into which he had
fallen.

He feared also that his mother would not be able to carry the regency for
long, given the onerous nature of the task and her sorrow over the King's
capture. He was afraid, too, that the kingdom would fall into ruin and civil
15 strife and that his children, who are young, would be cheated of their
inheritance.

1   What does this extract tell us about Francis' attitude towards his children (line
    15)?
2   How real was the threat of 'ruin and strife' (line 14)?
3   What does this show us about sixteenth century diplomacy?

Taking as an excuse Charles' capture of the Pope after the Sack of
Rome, Francis declared war again in 1528. However, the defection of the
Genoese admiral to Charles and defeat at Landriano in 1529 brought
about the Peace of Cambrai in the same year. This left Milan firmly in
Charles' hands but it was not a complete defeat for Francis. His right to
the Burgundian territories in France was recognised and his sons were
returned to him.

(c) The last conflict in Italy

After six years of careful diplomacy, negotiating with such diverse
potential allies as the Pope and the Ottoman Emperor, Francis again
attempted to take Milan in 1536. This was extremely rash as there were
already promising negotiations with Charles in progress, with the
possibility of one of Francis' sons becoming Duke of Milan after the
death of the last of the Sforzas in 1535.

Francis did capture some Italian territory and he won glory in
repelling an Imperial attack on Provence. However, in financial terms it
was disastrous; within a year Francis had spent all he had saved since
1532. Charles had certainly been defeated and Francis now had a
foothold in Italy but most of Provence was laid waste and the succession
of Milan, over which the war had been fought, remained as doubtful as
ever.

The influence of the King's favourite, Anne de Montmorency, on
foreign policy cannot be overestimated at this time. He changed Francis'
strategy in the Habsburg-Valois conflict from aggression to defence and
he now went even further by attempting a reconciliation between his
master and the Emperor. The main objective of French foreign policy,
the recovery of Milan, remained the same, only the method was now
different.

The consequence was the Truce of Nice in 1538 arranged by Montmorency and the Pope. Francis and Charles refused to meet each other
initially at Nice, even in front of their spiritual father. Perhaps it was
fortuitous, for when Francis' wife, Queen Eleanor, went alone to meet
her brother Charles, a wooden pier, specially constructed between the

boats, collapsed and the Queen, the Emperor and many of their retinues were flung into the sea.

Francis retained Savoy and Piedmont but the peace achieved little else. While Montmorency remained in power, the spirit of friendship was maintained and in 1539, when Charles was faced with a revolt in Ghent, Francis invited him to take a short cut through France and entertained him royally.

(d) Conflict in northern Europe
In October 1540 when Charles formally invested his son, Philip, with the Duchy of Milan, Montmorency's policy appeared to have failed and he was sent from court in disgrace. Without him at the helm, Francis reverted to his old ways and war broke out once again.

This time Francis faced a two-pronged attack by Charles V and Henry VIII on northern France. The Imperial army came within leagues of Paris before retiring owing to exhaustion. Francis was criticised at the time for not doing anything to halt the Imperial advance but it could also be argued that he showed sound judgement in reserving his army for the defence of Paris, given that the war was on two fronts.

The Peace of Crèpy in 1544 restored the status quo but a significant change had come about in the shape of the Habsburg–Valois conflict. The main arena was now to be northern Europe. Francis I died in 1547 but his son, Henry II, was to take the German cities of Metz, Toul and Verdun in 1552. His gains in the north were ratified by the Peace of Câteau–Cambrésis in 1559—and also ratified was the surrender of French ambitions in Italy.

(e) Success or failure?
Despite the gains in the north, the Peace of Câteau–Cambrésis heralded the beginning of Spain's hegemony in Europe which lasted till the early seventeenth century. Was this outcome inevitable and had Francis been foolish to challenge Habsburg power on the Italian peninsula? Certainly this Italian dream seems to have been almost an obsession and driven him on, as at Pavia when it would have been more sensible to retreat. It was, of course, a matter of prestige and, although Francis possibly put his priorities in the wrong order, he was right to recognise the importance of military glory in the eyes of his subjects and the rest of Europe. But Francis could still have offered a challenge to Charles' authority, considering the Emperor's other distractions, by pursuing a more defensive policy. This was apparent during the ascendancy of Montmorency but the balance swayed once more in Charles' favour when Francis took over again and reverted to the offensive. Although Francis showed that he could be tactical, as in his defence of Paris in 1544, he could not afford, in terms of manpower and money, to wage war abroad for such a continuous length of time and the kingdom paid the penalty in terms of financial weakness in the future.

He did allow foreign policy to dominate his religious and domestic policies which prevented consistency at home. It is debatable whether Francis' foreign policy brought any advantages to France. In the short term there was the prestige and satisfaction of thwarting the Emperor on occasion but in the long run Francis gained little in terms of territory and prosperity to balance the losses sustained.

5. Bibliography

R J Knecht *Francis I* (CUP, 1982); *French Renaissance Monarchy: Francis I and Henry II* (Seminar Studies, Longman, 1984). D Parker *The Making of French Absolutism* (Edward Arnold, 1983). G Mattingly *Renaissance Diplomacy* (Penguin, 1973).

6. Discussion Points and Exercises

A *This section consists of questions or points that might be used for discussion (or written answers) as a way of expanding on the chapter and testing understanding of it:*

1 In what ways, if any, were central and provincial administration improved by Francis?

2 Did Francis' financial reforms merely complicate the system?

3 How damaging were Francis' financial expedients?

4 What was the King's attitude towards rebellion?

5 What effect did faction have on government?

6 Why did Francis fail to crush heresy in the 1520s?

7 Why did Francis need to struggle with the Parlement and the Sorbonne over religion?

8 Why did persecution of heresy increase after 1534?

9 Was Francis consistent in his religious policy?

10 How far did foreign policy determine Francis' religious and domestic policies?

11 What errors did Francis make in his foreign policy before his capture at Pavia, and were they avoidable?

12 Was Francis wise to renew the war in Italy after 1526?

13 'Francis' foreign policy was most successful while Montmorency was directing it.'

14 Did France gain at all from Francis' foreign policy?

B *Essay questions*

1 'The monarchy of Francis I had less solid foundations than its magnificent façade suggested.' Discuss.

2 In what sense can Francis I be regarded as a product of his age?

3 How far was Francis I able to utilise the power of the monarchy?

4 'He personified all the virtues and weaknesses of the typical Renaissance prince.' How far is this a fair judgement of Francis I?

5 'He subordinated religion and national interests to the pursuit of personal glory.' Is this a valid comment on the foreign policy of Francis I?

6 'A failure, but a glorious failure.' Do you agree with this assessment of the reign of Francis I?

7. Documentary Exercise—Francis I, An Absolute Monarch?

Was Francis I an absolute monarch, i.e. a monarch recognising no legitimate restraint on his authority?

This question has long fascinated historians. Absolutism is usually applied to seventeenth century France and particularly the reign of Louis XIV. Can it, however, apply to Renaissance France? Certainly the doctrine of royal absolutism was to be found in the early sixteenth century in the work of contemporary writers.

Two of these, Claude de Seyssel, an important churchman, and Guillaume Budé, a leading humanist scholar, illustrate the two schools of thought at the time. Seyssel, in his *La Monarchie de France*, admired the moderation of the French monarchy because it was checked from exceeding its powers by the aristocracy which he identified with the sovereign courts. Budé's *L'Institution du Prince* saw the role of the aristocracy differently. To him they were privileged but should not share power with the king. Budé realised the importance to the king of wise advice but stated that he was free to reject this as long as he was not overriding the precedents set by his predecessors.

A. From Claude de Seyssel's La Monarchie de France*:*

The authority of the king in France is regulated and restrained by three checks . . . the first is Religion, the second, Justice and the third, Police . . .

With regard to the first, it is an indisputable fact that the French have always been, and still are . . . pious and God-fearing . . . For that reason it is both proper and necessary that whoever is king should make it known to the people by example and by visible and outward signs that he is a zealot, an observer of the Faith and of the Christian religion, and that he is resolved to use his power to strengthen and sustain it . . . So long as the king respects . . . the Christian religion he cannot act as a tyrant. If he is guilty of such an act, it is permissible for a prelate or any other devout man who respects the people, to remonstrate with and to upbraid him.

1 How far could the French Church, according to Seyssel, act as a check on the authority of the king?
2 In what way was this merely a theoretical check?

Justice, which is the second check . . . indubitably carries more weight in France than in any other country in the world, especially because of the institution of the Parlements, whose principal role is to bridle the absolute power which the kings might seek to use.

3   *Using examples from the chapter, how would you describe Francis' relationship with the Parlement?*

4   *Did the Parlement act as a check on the King, as Seyssel argues?*

> The third check is that of the Police, by which is intended those many laws that have been passed, and subsequently confirmed and approved from time to time, which help to preserve the kingdom as a whole and the rights of the individuals who compose it.

5   *What does Seyssel mean by the 'Police'?*

6   *Were there any other checks on the authority of the king in practice?*

B.   Contemporary historians also debate as to how absolute, if at all, the French monarchy was under Francis I. J Russell-Major has described early sixteenth century France as 'popular and consultative', but Knecht argues that, although absolutism in the seventeenth century use of the word was not achieved, 'the king's actions and informal pronouncements certainly pointed that way.'

Russell-Major's argument rests on the following:

(a)   'The French Renaissance monarchs ruled according to the law, not in defiance of it.' He argues that their claim to the Crown 'was based on law, not force' and they in turn respected the rights of their subjects.

(b)   '. . . they (French kings) accepted the decentralisation of the state, and made little effort to centralise it.' For example, newly acquired lands kept their own institutions and laws, provincial governors attempted to usurp royal power, and there was the establishment of local parlements and the continuation of provincial estates.

(c)   '. . . they were inherently weak, not strong.' France had neither an adequate army nor bureaucracy.

(d)   '. . . that the dynamic elements in society were the nobility and the bureaucracy, not the bourgeoisie.' The Renaissance monarchs did suppress rebellious nobles but not indiscriminately. In fact the nobility were the natural advisers and companions of the king and, therefore, their economic status improved accordingly.

(e)   '. . . that the basis of a king's power lay in the support he could win from the people, not in a standing army or a bureaucracy.' Kings restored order after a period of civil unrest through the use of assemblies and there was no other 'safe, logical alternative to their rule.'

List these 5 arguments and apply them to the reign of Francis I, finding examples for and against each one.

Knecht bases his argument on the 'abeyance of the Estates General' in the early sixteenth century and the position of the Parlement which was the only body left to check the power of the king. He refers to Francis' 'authoritarian disposition' and the way in which he departed from tradition and the existing methods of government.

1 Can you think of occasions when Francis displayed this characteristic?

Knecht disagrees with Russell-Major over the lack of centralisation in France. He refers to the 'radical' changes made in the financial administration, the extended control in local government and increased linguistic unity within the kingdom.

Also he points out that 'Francis I's fiscal expedients won him the international reputation of being a tyrant . . . The king's religious policy also derived from his authoritarianism . . .'

2 Using examples from the chapter, how far is it true that Francis treated his subjects 'tyrannically' over fiscal demands?

3 In the same way, could Francis be termed 'authoritarian' in his religious policy?

Knecht does qualify his argument:

> If we take the line that absolutism precludes any form of consultation, any ceiling to the amount of taxation which can be realistically exacted, and any dependence on the support of a powerful social group, then clearly Francis I was not absolute . . . Absolutism in practice has always fallen short of its theoretical completeness but Francis would appear to have been as absolute as any European monarch of his day could hope to be.

4 Was Francis as 'absolute as any European monarch of his day could hope to be'?

X The Ottoman Empire

1. Introduction

At about half past one in the morning of Tuesday, May 29, 1453, Sultan Mohammed II gave the order for the final assault on Constantinople. The first attack by his irregular troops, the Bashi-Bazouks, was beaten off after two hours. A second assault by trained regiments of Turkish troops also failed. Finally, a way in was discovered through a small gate and Mohammed's élite troops, the Janissaries, fought their way into the city. The last emperor of Constantinople, Constantine XI, threw himself into the battle and was never seen again.

Constantinople had been one of the great cities of Europe for over a thousand years, since the Roman Emperor Constantine had made it his capital. Although its importance had declined, it remained a great centre of Christian culture and of trade. Its capture by an Islamic ruler horrified and terrified Europe.

For the next one hundred and fifty years the Ottoman Empire can fairly be described as more successful and powerful than any other state in Europe. Under Suleiman the Magnificent (1520–66), the state dominated the Balkans, the Middle East and much of north Africa. The Ottoman navy controlled the eastern Mediterranean and the Black Sea and its armies were considered invincible.

It seems surprising, therefore, that so few historians have written at length on the Ottoman Empire. In part, this reflects a traditional European stereotype of the 'cruel Turk' and a lack of understanding of Islamic culture and society. Modern historians, such as the French historian of the Mediterranean, Fernand Braudel, and the Turkish historian, Halil Inalcik, have justly drawn attention to the remarkable impact of the Ottoman Empire. The American historian, Stanford Shaw, is equally convinced of the strength and importance of the Empire, but points out its rapid decline after the death of Suleiman the Magnificent. In particular, he stresses the geographical problems which limited further expansion, the cultural and intellectual divisions which made the Empire suspicious of innovation, and the rise of factional divisions in its government. But even today, serious historical research is discouraged by the inaccessibility of the major archives and the skill in languages that is required before they can be used.

Despite these problems, it is now accepted that the major events of the sixteenth century, such as the Habsburg–Valois rivalry and the Reformation, were, directly or indirectly, deeply affected by the Ottoman threat. Not only this, the Ottoman system of government was so different and arguably so much more effective than that of, for example, Charles V, that a study of the Ottoman Empire provides an invaluable point of comparison and contrast to the rest of Europe.

2. The Rise of the Ottoman Empire to 1453

Throughout European history, nomadic tribes have drifted from Central Asia towards Europe and Asia Minor. These tribes have often posed a serious military threat, especially because of their skills as horsemen. Tribes of Turkic race began to colonise Anatolia (modern Turkey) from the end of the eleventh century. Anatolia was the frontier zone between the Christian and Islamic worlds and great opportunities were available to successful fighting tribes. There was a chance of plunder and a relative freedom from government. The frontier therefore attracted the most aggressive and militaristic elements amongst the Turkic tribes and successful leaders gained great prestige. The violent nature of this frontier society was augmented by the justification granted by Islamic Law (the Shari'a) to those who fought people who did not share their faith. The central idea was that of the *Jihad* or Holy War. Like Crusaders, it was the duty of the *Ghazis* (Holy Warriors) to fight against the non-Muslims until they submitted. One of the most successful *Ghazis*, Osman, who lived in western Anatolia, destroyed a Byzantine army in 1301 and established the Ottoman dynasty. His grandson, Suleiman, crossed into Europe and the victory of Suleiman's brother Murad over the combined armies of Serbia and Bosnia at Kossovo in 1389 confirmed the Ottoman Turks as the greatest power in the Balkans. Only the cunning diplomatic intrigues of the Byzantine emperors and the sudden danger posed by the armies of Timur (Tamberlaine) who invaded Anatolia in 1402 and destroyed a Turkish army at Ankara delayed the now inevitable fall of Constantinople for the next fifty years.

The capture of Constantinople in 1453 brought enormous prestige to Mohammed II. To the world of Islam, he was now Mohammed the 'Conqueror', one of the greatest *Ghazis* in history. The Turkish historian H Inalcik has written: 'The Islamic world came to regard Holy War as the great source of power and influence'. Mohammed also saw himself as the heir to the Roman tradition of a universal empire. In 1466, a Greek scholar George Trapezuntius wrote: 'No-one doubts that you are Emperor of the Romans. Whoever is legally master of the capital of the Empire is the Emperor and Constantinople is the capital of the Roman Empire'. Mohammed undoubtedly believed that control of Constantinople would provide a springboard for the conquest of the whole Christian world.

Not only did the city have great prestige, but its situation, where Europe meets Asia and the Black Sea joins the Mediterranean, had made Constantinople traditionally a great trading centre. Although Islam preached the duty of Holy War, its laws forbade the forced conversion of Christians and Jews. A great opportunity now existed to re-build Constantinople as the cosmopolitan trading centre of the eastern Mediterranean, which had been united in the Byzantine Empire and was now being gradually re-united under Ottoman rule. The Empire would offer Greek Orthodox Christians and Jews a more tolerant environment than was likely under the rule of Venice or the Spanish monarchy.

3. The Expansion of the Ottoman Empire 1453–1520

Mohammed II and his successors Bayezid II (1481–1512) and Selim I 'the Grim' (1512–20) continued the expansion of the Ottoman state. By 1464, Mohammed had eliminated the small states of Trebizond and the Morea (the Peloponnese), both of which were ruled by families with a claim to the Byzantine inheritance. His main threat to the west, however, was Venice. The Venetians possessed a far stronger navy than the Ottoman Empire, which had traditionally been a land power. They were also, however, reliant on the goodwill of the Turks to maintain their trade and had been granted important trading concessions in 1454. The Venetians were reluctant to commit themselves to a lengthy war against the Ottoman Empire. Over the next century and a half, there were many wars, but economic necessity invariably forced Venice to make peace and the Venetian Republic could never be relied on in any European coalition against the Turks.

Despite this, with the support of the Pope and in alliance with the Hungarians and the Albanian chieftain, Scanderbeg, the Venetians went to war in 1463. This war clearly demonstrated the superiority of the Ottoman military system. In 1468, Scanderbeg died and Albania passed under Ottoman control and in 1470, Euboea off eastern Greece was seized. The Venetians hoped to take advantage of the hostility towards the Ottoman Empire of the Islamic state of Karaman, which Mohammed wished to bring under direct control, and of Uzun Hasan, the ruler of the so-called 'White Sheep' of eastern Asia Minor. These nomadic tribesmen lived in remote and mountainous districts and were particularly formidable opponents. In 1472, the Venetians allied with Uzun Hasan and the Knights of St John, whose naval base at Rhodes constantly menaced Ottoman trade in the Aegean. The response to this challenge emphasised the formidable nature of the Ottoman army. Over 70 000 men were sent against Uzun Hasan, who was defeated at Bashkent in 1473. Ottoman power, as a result, now extended to the Euphrates.

After this overwhelming victory, the Ottoman army advanced to

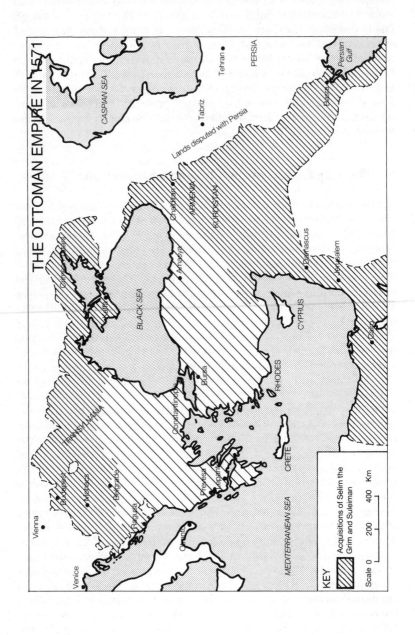

THE OTTOMAN EMPIRE IN 1571

PERSIA

Tehran •

CASPIAN SEA

• Tabriz

Lands disputed with Persia

Basra •

Persian Gulf

Chaldiran •

ARMENIA

KURDISTAN

Amasya •

Damascus •

• Jerusalem

Georgian states

BLACK SEA

CYPRUS

• Cairo

Constantinople

Bursa •

RHODES

Vienna •

TRANSYLVANIA

• Budapest

• Mohacs

• Belgrade

Ragusa

Prevesa

Lepanto

CRETE

Otranto •

Venice •

MEDITERRANEAN SEA

KEY

Acquisitions of Selim the
Grim and Suleiman

Scale 0   200   400   Km

within sight of Venice and the peace treaty of 1479 confirmed Ottoman control of the Balkans and forced the Venetians to pay an annual tribute.

Mohammed was also able to subdue the Genoese colonies in the Black Sea and the acceptance of vassal status by the Crimean Tatars in 1475 confirmed complete Ottoman control of the Black Sea.

The last years of Mohammed's life were dominated by the twin aims of subjugating Rhodes and invading Italy. On December 4 1479, the siege of Rhodes began and on August 11 1480, Otranto in southern Italy was seized and the Pope prepared to flee to France. Only the death of Mohammed in 1481 caused these campaigns to be abandoned. This may well have been fortunate for the Turks, since an attack on Italy would almost certainly have unified Christendom in the defence of the Papacy.

Even so, Mohammed's achievement was remarkable. Ottoman rule in the Balkans and Asia Minor was to last for four centuries.

The reign of Bayezid II, 1481–1512, is generally seen as one of consolidation. He succeeded to the throne only with some difficulty and relied on the support of the élite troops of the army, the Janissaries, to whom he was forced to offer bribes when he came to the throne, establishing a most unfortunate precedent. He did succeed in extending Ottoman power beyond the Black Sea and by 1503, Moldavia and Wallachia had become vassal states. Moreover, economic pressures forced the Venetians to make peace after the war of 1499–1503 and Bayezid must take credit for the effective foundation of the Ottoman navy.

Along with these advances, the growing importance of the Ottoman control of the great trade routes was becoming ever more clear and public revenues almost doubled in Bayezid's reign.

Despite this, he must be considered a failure in two areas. First of all, the war with the Mamluks (1485–91) was unsuccessful. The Mamluks were the rulers of Egypt and Syria and at no time during this conflict was any major Syrian town captured. Bayezid failed, therefore, to win the military prestige of his predecessor, which was so vital for any successful sultan. Much more critical, however, was the growing threat of heresy and war in the eastern part of the Empire. There are many deviations of religious belief within Islam, but the most fundamental is between the Sunni, the orthodox majority which included the Ottoman Sultans, and Shi'ism. In the thirteenth century the Safavid movement emerged, which became one of the most militant elements within Shi'ite Islam. The Safavids became known as Kizilbas ('red heads') because of their distinctive red headgear and won a strong following among the nomadic tribes of eastern Anatolia. Under the leadership of Ismail (1487–1524), a descendant of the founder of the Safavid movement, seven Kizilba tribes emigrated at the end of the fifteenth century and by 1500 the strong Safavid state of Persia had been founded on the eastern border of the Ottoman Empire. There were many sympathisers with these Shi'ites, particularly in Anatolia, causing constant threats of rebellion, which did in fact break out in 1511.

The Janissaries felt that Bayezid was too ineffectual to cope with this threat and he was forced to abdicate in favour of Selim I in April 1512. Selim shared Mohammed's vision of a world empire and had the forceful and martial spirit required to put these aims into practice. After seizing the throne, he ruthlessly executed all other possible claimants to the throne and paid substantial 'tips' to the Janissaries to secure their loyalty. The Janissaries were based in Constantinople and Selim did not rely on a landed aristocracy in the manner of western Europe. Selim saw his main danger as coming from Ismail and the Safavids. Kizilbas in Anatolia were massacred as his armies marched east to Tabriz, Ismail's capital. On August 13 1514, Selim won a bloody but decisive victory at Chaldiran near Lake Van in eastern Anatolia and temporarily occupied Tabriz. He did not maintain the occupation but kept control of the high plateau of eastern Anatolia which provided an excellent natural barrier against invasion. Moreover, the mountain tribesmen of Kurdistan accepted vassal status. Although the Safavid state continued to exist, it was significantly weakened and pressure on this frontier ceased to be a major problem.

This was only the start of Selim's outstanding career as an energetic conqueror. He once wrote to Tuman Bey, the Mamluk ruler of Egypt, that he intended to become the ruler of east and west like Alexander the Great and between 1515 and 1517, he launched a series of dramatically successful campaigns in Syria, Egypt and Arabia. The Mamluks had originated as a military class of slaves and had managed to impose themselves as the rulers of Egypt and Syria. By 1515, however, their fortunes were in decline. In the Red Sea, the Portuguese fleet posed a major threat and had established bases at Socotra on the Gulf of Aden and Ormuz in the Persian Gulf. The great fear of all Muslims was that they would seize the Holy Cities of Mecca and Medina. The Arab population of these cities became increasingly convinced that the Mamluks could not defend them effectively, particularly after the Portuguese defeated the Mamluk navy in 1509. Any Muslim leader who could effectively defend the Holy Cities would dramatically enhance his reputation as the champion of Islam.

In 1516, Selim marched into Syria. In the only significant battle near Aleppo on August 24, the Mamluks were routed, thanks mainly to the superiority of Turkish artillery and musket fire. On September 27, the important city of Damascus was occupied and Selim's army marched into Palestine. After a slight hesitation, the Sinai peninsula was crossed in only five days at the beginning of 1517. On January 22, the Mamluk army was defeated. 25 000 were killed and by the end of 1517 Egypt was under effective Ottoman control. The capture of Syria and Egypt brought enormous wealth to the Empire. These were areas of great economic value themselves and also controlled vital trade routes. Even more important in some ways was the establishment of control of the Holy Cities on July 3 1517. This brought the title 'Servant and Protector of the Holy Places'. The Ottoman sultans were now the protectors of

Mecca and Medina and the guardians of the pilgrimage routes, a position which brought enormous honour and prestige in the Islamic world.

However, a description of the growth of the Ottoman Empire does not in itself explain the rapid expansion of Ottoman power. In its organisation, the Ottoman state possessed qualities that were not to be found in its European rivals. An examination of the civil and military organisation of the state is essential if its growth is to be understood. By the time that Suleiman the Magnificent succeeded to the throne in 1520, most of the characteristic institutions of the Ottoman state at its peak were functioning.

4. The Civil and Military Organisation of the Ottoman Empire in the Fifteenth and Sixteenth Centuries

There is no doubt that the actual power of the sultans was far greater than that of the major European monarchs. Islamic law and tradition regarded strong royal authority as the basis of the whole social system. The main task of the monarch was to protect his subjects from exploitation by the more powerful members of the community. One of the most striking features of the Ottoman Empire was the absence of a powerful, hereditary aristocracy. Problems of particularism and a dissident aristocracy were far less than, for example, in France and the Low Countries. An Ottoman bureaucrat and historian, Tursun Bey wrote in the fifteenth century: 'Without a sovereign men cannot live in harmony and may perish altogether. God has granted this authority to one person only and that person, for the perpetuation of good order, requires absolute obedience'.

In order to rule effectively, however, any ruler needs a reliable and efficient administration. The method adopted by the Ottoman rulers was to use slaves as the vast majority of the ruling class of the Empire. Most slaves were obtained by the *Devshirme*, which was a levy of Christian children, the word having its origin in the Turkish word meaning 'to collect'. The main sources for this levy were the Christian villages of the Balkans. Urban areas were excluded and so were only sons. A levy was taken every three or four years and between 1000 and 3000 children were taken. These were converted to Islam and underwent a rigorous process of selection. Some were used for military service, as will be described later in this section. However, the best were selected as *Icoglans*—Imperial pages—and were sent into the direct service of the sultan at the Topkapi Sarayi, the sultan's palace in Istanbul.

Under the supervision of the 'white eunuchs' of the sultan's Palace, these pages received a rigorous education in the Koran, Arabic, Persian, Turkish, music, calligraphy and mathematics. They also learned horsemanship and archery and artistic skills, such as miniature painting, or bookbinding. A page once wrote that the aim of this education was to produce 'the warrior statesman and loyal Muslim, who at the same time should be a man of letters and polished speech, profound courtesy and honest morals'.

Some of these slaves stayed within the palace and served the sultan directly. Others became provincial governors, or entered the religious establishment.

The most important office of state was that of Grand Vizier. The Grand Vizier was the sultan's deputy in all matters of state. He conducted the Imperial *Divan* (Council) every day except Friday (the Muslim holy day) and its decisions were sent to the sultan for approval. The Grand Vizier was given the sultan's seal of office and the council dealt with finance, foreign policy and government appointments. Mohammed the Conqueror's last Grand Vizier, Nisanci Mohammed, was in fact a Turkish aristocrat, but after the Sultan's death he was murdered and from that time on the sultans accepted that the Grand Vizier should be a slave. In the sixteenth century slaves, such as Lufti Pasha in the reign of Suleiman the Magnificent and Mohammed Sokullu in the reign of Selim II, became Grand Viziers of enormous power and influence. Machiavelli was, therefore, entirely correct when he described the Ottoman Empire as an 'absolute monarchy dependent on slavery'.

No state in the fifteenth and sixteenth centuries had the effective power of the modern state, but the use of slaves did bring great advantages to the sultans. The slaves did identify their interests in general with those of the central government and lacked the power bases in the provinces that made many territorial aristocrats, who served other European monarchs, actively suspicious of any expansion of central authority. Quite simply, the power and influence of the slaves depended on a strong and stable government.

Slavery was not only the basis of the civil administration of the Ottoman state; the core of the army—the Janissaries—were also recruited by the *Devshirme*. The use of slaves in the standing army dates back to the capture of Adrianople in 1361, when prisoners of war became the first Janissary corps. Mohammed II increased the size of the corps to 10 000. It was to be the nucleus of his army. The sultan chose the commanders personally and the corps took its orders directly from the sultan, wherever it was serving in his Empire. The Janissaries were supposed to be on a war footing at all times. They lived in barracks, trained regularly and were not allowed to marry. Estimates of their numbers vary, but in Suleiman the Magnificent's reign there were probably 12 000. They were armed with hand guns, pikes, bows and arrows and had their own cannon corps, miners and mortar men. In battle, they held the centre of the sultan's army. Most Janissaries were infantry, but there was an élite of about 6000 cavalry, the Kapi Kulu, who acted as the sultan's personal bodyguard. Janissaries tended to be devout Muslims and Muslim preachers were attached to them to maintain their zeal as *Ghazis*. The advantages of a trained, disciplined and fanatical standing army cannot be overestimated in Early Modern Europe. Although the loyalty of the Janissaries was already being undermined by the end of the sixteenth century and the practice of bribing the corps dated back to the accession of Bayezid II in 1481, at their best they were loyal servants of the sultans and lacked the attachment to a particular locality and region that so often existed elsewhere in Europe.

Although the Janissaries provided the élite of the Ottoman army, they were in fact only a minority of its total strength. Indeed, the entire provincial administration of the Empire was designed to provide for the Empire's military needs. The typical Ottoman province was organised under the *timar* system. A *timar* was a piece of land held for life by an individual from the sultan in return for military service. The system originated in the first place in response to a shortage of currency. The soldiers would collect their income in kind from a village, which released the government from any obligation to pay them a salary. The main aim of this system was to provide a large number of *sipahi*, or light cavalry, for the army. In the sixteenth century, it is estimated that there were about 40 000 *timar*-holding sipahi.

The successful functioning of the *timar* system stemmed from the view of property ownership in the Ottoman world. Virtually all the land in the Empire was regarded as the property of the sultan; in 1528 about 80 percent of land was owned by the Crown. The *sipahi* were not given the land itself, but only the right to collect a fixed amount of revenue from it. They lived in their villages, but did not farm and could not take any land from the peasants. They could arrest a wrong-doer, but had no power to administer punishment, which was the responsibility of the local *kadi* (judge).

The power of the *sipahi* over the peasantry was therefore very limited. The peasant was protected by the state and an independent legal system. The *sipahi* provided their own horses and carried a bow, sword, shield, lance and mace. Large *timars* would be expected to provide an extra horseman and the wealthier *timar* holders wore armour. In campaigns, they served under the *bey* (local provincial governor) and formed the light cavalry on either wing of the army, whose aim was to outflank and encircle the enemy. While the Janissaries held together the centre of the sultan's armies, the *sipahi* would attack on the flanks. The Ottoman armies were particularly well placed in battle to use the speed of the *sipahi*, who were far more mobile than heavy European cavalry, to surround their enemies in a classic pincer movement. The campaigning season lasted from March to October and generally the *sipahi* were very anxious to return home at the end of the season. Their horses would be exhausted and they had received no money wages. It was at this time that the Ottoman army was traditionally at its weakest.

The *timar* system offers a further example of the powers of the central government. The government controlled the granting and revocation of *timars*. Although the son of a *timar* holder inherited his father's military status and received a *timar* similar in size to his father, *timars* could not be passed on to sons, as the land was the property of the state. Also, any *timar* holder who did not perform military service for seven years would lose his military status. In other words, a strong hereditary aristocracy, which could pass on its land and wealth, did not exist in the Ottoman Empire.

The advantages of this system were the subject of letters written by Ogier Ghiselin de Busbecq, a horticulturalist (he introduced the lilac and tulip to Europe) and Imperial ambassador in Constantinople from 1554 to 1562. He wrote to a fellow ambassador in Portugal:

> The Sultan's headquarters were crowded by numerous attendants, includ-ing many high officials. All the cavalry of the guard were there and a large number of Janissaries. In all that great assembly no single man owed his dignity to anything but his personal merits and bravery; no one is distin-guished from the rest by his birth, and honour is paid to each man according to the nature of the duty and offices which he discharges. Thus there is no struggle for precedence, every man having his place assigned to him in virtue of the functions which he performs. The Sultan himself assigns to all their duties and offices, and in doing so pays no attention to wealth or the empty claims of rank, and takes no account of any influence or popularity which a candidate may possess; he only considers merit and scrutinises the character, natural ability and disposition of each. Thus each man is rewarded according to his deserts, and offices are filled by men capable of performing them. Those who hold the highest posts under the Sultan are very often the sons of shepherds and herdsmen, and, so far from being ashamed of their birth, they make it a subject of boasting, and the less they owe to their forefathers and to the accident of birth, the greater is the pride which they feel. They do not consider that good qualities can be conferred by birth or handed down by inheritance, but regard them partly as the gift of heaven and partly as the product of good training and constant toil and zeal . . .
>
> Thus, among the Turks, dignities, offices and administrative posts are the rewards of ability and merit; those who are dishonest, lazy and slothful never attain to distinction, but remain in obscurity and contempt. This is why the Turks succeed in all they attempt and are a dominating race and daily extend the bounds of their rule. Our method is very different; there is no room for merit, but everything depends on birth, considerations of which alone open the way of high official position.

1 *How did the Ottoman system enable the sultan only to have to consider 'merit', 'character', 'natural ability' and 'disposition'?*

2 *In what ways would the system that Busbecq describes give the sultan greater power than other contemporary European rulers? Does this contrast help to explain Busbecq's intentions in writing these letters?*

3 *Why might 'sons of shepherds and herdsmen' prove to be better state adminis-trators than aristocrats?*

4 *What problems might the Ottoman system eventually produce?*

At its most effective, the *timar* system provided the sultan with both a provincial police force and a large element of his standing army. Moreover, the desire to create more *timars* provided a strong motivation for the expansion of the Ottoman Empire. By the late sixteenth century, however, weaknesses were starting to appear in the system. *Timars* were no longer exclusively granted to fighting men, but increasingly were given as favours and pensions to palace and government officials. Moreover, growing economic problems weakened the loyalty of many *timar* holders.

5. The People of the Empire 1450–1580

It was clearly understood that the stability and prosperity of the people was essential if the military and economic strength of the Empire was to be maintained. The military and administrative classes were exempt from taxation and were legally totally separate from the wealth-producing classes, who were known as the *Reaya*, literally 'flock'. The sultan was seen as the guardian, guide and protector of the *Reaya* and in return they were the financial backbone of the Empire. To move from the *Reaya* to the military classes required the permission of the sultan, which was very rarely granted. The laws of the Empire stated that, 'The *Reaya* and the land belong to the sultan'. There was, therefore, no powerful aristocracy holding great legal powers over the peasantry, such as existed in most European countries.

There is no doubt that one of the reasons for the outstanding speed of Ottoman expansion was that the peasantry in the Balkans was treated with far more justice after the Ottoman conquest than had been the case under previous Christian rulers. Before the Ottoman conquest, the peasantry had been subject to many harsh and varied burdens, imposed by local aristocrats or monasteries. The sultans abolished all of these. For example, it was no longer legal to demand forced labour from the peasantry and obligations, such as the transportation of firewood and hay, could no longer be imposed. Instead, all the peasantry paid one poll (head) tax, which replaced all their former duties to their lords. For many of the peasantry, therefore, Ottoman rule provided a stability and security that they had never known under Christian rule, when the Balkans in particular had been notoriously unstable. Only those who resisted Ottoman rule were subjected to intimidation and violence.

Moreover, although it was seen as the duty of all *Ghazis* to extend *Darulislam* (the abode of Islam) by campaigning in the non-Islamic world, which was known as *Darulharb* (the abode of war), Islamic tradition totally rejected the idea of forced religious conversion of Christians and Jews. There were occasions when Christians converted *en masse* to Islam, for example in Bosnia. But Bosnia was an area with a tradition of heresy and religious dissidence and there is no evidence of forced conversion. Moreover, many Orthodox Christians had been subjected to the rule of Latin Christians from Venice or Genoa, and found Islamic rule far more tolerant and acceptable. Indeed, the attempts made by the Emperor John VIII to save the Byzantine Empire from the Turks by reunion with Rome at the Council of Florence in 1439 had split his Church and been bitterly unpopular with the ordinary people.

In 1451, the 'Unionist' Patriarch of the Greek Orthodox Church, Gregory Mammas, fled from Constantinople and was generally held to have forfeited his throne. The most gifted and respected opponent of the Union with the Roman Church was the scholar George Scholarius Gennadius. After the fall of Constantinople, it was discovered that he had been bought as a slave by a wealthy Turk in Adrianople, but Mohammed the Conqueror insisted on his return to Constantinople and in January 1454, as Emperor, he installed Gennadius as Patriarch of the Orthodox Church. Mohammed was clearly aware that he could capitalise on the hostility of his Greek Orthodox subjects toward the Catholic Church.

Mohammed's aim was to use the Patriarch as the head of the Greek Christian community within his Empire. The Patriarch's role was not simply that of a religious leader; he was to be the political leader of the Orthodox community and would be responsible for maintaining their political loyalty.

The system, known as the *millet*, was later extended to the Armenian Christians and to the Jews. They were to be self-governing communities within the Empire under the authority of their religious leader. The Sultan would hold him responsible for their good behaviour. The leading figures within the Orthodox Church, who formed the Holy Synod, were granted freedom from taxation and deposition and freedom of movement. Ecclesiastical courts would deal with all disputes between Orthodox Christians of a religious nature, such as marriage and divorce. Only criminal cases and those involving a Muslim went to the state's courts. In return for these privileges, it was to be the duty of the Church to discipline Christians who did not pay their taxes or disobeyed the state. Christians were supposed to wear a distinctive dress and could not carry weapons.

Although the status of the non-Islamic peoples within the Empire was clearly inferior, equally they did enjoy the right to practice their religions and maintain their culture. In this, Islamic society was notably more tolerant than that of most of Europe.

The Ottoman Empire also provided a refuge for religious groups who were persecuted in the rest of Europe. Many of the Jews expelled from Spain came to the Ottoman Empire and settled in large numbers in cities such as Salonika. They were often welcomed because of their intellectual and scientific expertise and their trading links with the west. Members of the Mendes family, who were originally from Spain, came to Istanbul in 1553 in flight from religious persecution and effectively controlled the European spice trade. One of their relatives, Don Joseph Nasi, became one of the wealthiest men in the Ottoman Empire. He gained a monopoly of the wine trade and was made Duke of Naxos, which was a very important wine-producing area. Not only could the Jewish community provide much intelligence and advice about conditions in the west, they were often naturally very sympathetic towards anti-Spanish and anti-Habsburg policies.

There were of course many religious and racial tensions within the Empire. However, it is clear that racial and religious minorities and the peasantry were treated with relative justice, efficiency and tolerance in the Ottoman Empire of the fifteenth and sixteenth centuries.

The American historian Stanford Shaw has written of Mohammed II: 'To the mass of people he offered an end to the feudal oppression of their former Christian masters, security of life and property, and an opportunity to preserve their old traditions and ways as well as their religion through the *millet* system'. It can be said that at least until the 1580s, Mohammed's successors maintained the spirit of these policies with some success.

Indeed, popular disaffection was arguably more common amongst the Islamic rather than the non-Islamic elements of the Ottoman Empire. The *Devshirme* system gradually excluded the old Turkish aristocracy from any significant role in the government of the state. Sixteenth century Anatolia saw the emergence of many heretical Muslim sects, influenced by Shi'ism and often encouraged by the Safavid emperors. In 1519, there occurred the first of the so-called Celali revolts in Anatolia, which recurred spasmodically for the rest of the century. In these revolts, the discontent of the old aristocracy, the peasantry and the religious dissidents merged. While it was essential to be Muslim to be a member of the military and administrative classes, Muslims outside these classes were not notably better off than their Christian counterparts.

6. Economic Life

One of the greatest advantages that the Ottoman Empire possessed over its main rivals from 1450 to 1580 was its superior wealth. Despite the discovery of America and the opening of the route to India via the African coast by the Portuguese, major trade routes were still concentrated on the eastern Mediterranean, through which Europe had to import valuable commodities that it could not produce for itself. Constantinople itself stands at the crossroads of land routes from Asia and the sea route from the Black Sea. The acquisition of Syria and Egypt increased the wealth of the Empire partly through control of their resources and brought a virtual monopoly of all the traditional trade routes. This gave enormous advantages. The Venetian Republic, which would have been such a formidable opponent, was heavily dependent on the Ottoman Empire for the maintenance of its trade and became increasingly cautious about commitment to a long war. Moreover, the wealth of the Empire made it more capable than its European rivals of sustaining the enormous cost of sixteenth century warfare.

When Constantinople fell in 1453, it had lost most of its former population and glory. Its population had fallen to below 30–40 000, which was far smaller than could be contained within its massive fortifications. Moreover, since the city had not surrendered voluntarily, it was pillaged according to Ottoman tradition, and much property was destroyed. Mohammed was determined to restore the city as a great Imperial capital. First of all, immigration was encouraged. Christians were settled from captured cities, such as Trebizond and Kaffa. Merchants and skilled artisans came from all areas of the Empire and the leaders of the Greek Orthodox, Jewish and Armenian communities were ordered to live in the city. By the 1470s, about 60 percent of the population was Muslim, about 25 percent Greek Orthodox and about 15 percent Jewish. Each group had its own quarter within the city. Turks wore white turbans, Greeks blue turbans and Jews yellow turbans. During the next century, the population of Istanbul rose spectacularly. In 1478, it was c80 000. By 1530, it had reached c400 000 and by 1600, c700 000. This made Constantinople by far the biggest city in Europe with a population twice the size of Paris and four times that of Venice. One simple reason for the growth of Constantinople was that it was now the political and administrative centre of a great empire. The growth in population created great demand, especially for the grain of the territories which surrounded the Black Sea, which increased their dependence on the goodwill of the Ottoman Empire.

The unique situation of Constantinople, whose harbour—the Golden Horn—was the only safe anchorage between the Sea of Marmara and the Black Sea, enabled the Ottoman state to establish virtually complete control of the Black Sea trade. Italian ships were subjected to close inspection each time they passed into or out of the Black Sea and the influence of Genoa as a result declined dramatically in the sixteenth century. Certain vital and valuable commodities were traded through the markets of Constantinople. For example, the Khan of Crimea, a tributary state of the Empire, shipped 1000–1200 tons of salt every year. Even more important was the slave trade, which was the chief source of income for the Khan and his Tatar horsemen. The Tatars raided for slaves far into Russia and Poland and these were shipped through the port of Kaffa to the slave markets of Constantinople. A tax of four gold ducats on each slave raised 100 000 gold ducats each year. All major cities in the Ottoman Empire had their bedestan (covered market) where merchants could meet and store goods, and that of Constantinople was of course the largest and most famous. As well as being a focal point of the Black Sea trade, Constantinople became the centre of an extensive road system. The Turkish historian H Inalcik has written: 'Not since the fall of the Roman Empire has any state in Europe devoted such care to its system of roads'. Undoubtedly the Ottoman road system was vastly superior to that of western Europe. Between six and ten caravans arrived each year from Iran and there were also caravans from Basra, Aleppo, Ragusa and Poland. Military roads, which basically followed Roman routes, were driven through the Balkans to the important centre of Adrianople and then to Sofia and Belgrade. By wagon the journey from Belgrade to Istanbul took one month. Charitable foundations known as *Waqfs* were endowed with property to provide the income to pay for road maintenance. These built hostels and maintained roads and bridges. Money was also allocated to pay forces of soldiers whose job was to guard the roads against bandits. Perhaps the most ambitious feature of this trade network was the construction of caravanserais where caravans could be lodged. These could have as many as 200 rooms and space for 5000–6000 horses.

But although Constantinople was the most important economic centre of the Empire, other cities maintained a vital role. Persian silk remained, in the sixteenth century, one of the most desirable commodities in Europe. The major trading centre for Persian silk was Bursa in Anatolia. The market here was the greatest centre for the exchange of Persian silk for European goods, such as woollens, and despite decline in the sixteenth century, partly because of the Persian wars, Bursa remained a city of prime economic importance.

Trade with Europe had traditionally been handled mainly by the Venetian Republic and this remained largely the case, at least until 1564. But the sultans gave great privileges to the city state of Ragusa (modern Dubrovnik) which was a tributary state of the Empire and a useful counterweight to the Venetians. In October 1564 the French were granted trading rights—a typical example of the alliance of convenience between the Ottoman Empire and the French with their shared dislike of the Habsburgs—and by 1600 there were 1000 French ships in the Mediterranean.

Of course the expansion of the Ottoman Empire greatly boosted its economic resources. Of particular significance was the capture of Syria and Egypt. In 1528 they alone provided one-third of the Imperial revenue. They also enabled the Empire to acquire control of more vital trade routes. By 1517, with the capture of Aleppo, all outlets for Persian silk were in Ottoman hands.

An even more important acquisition in many ways was the port of Alexandria. In the sixteenth century spices still dominated world trade. The main source of these was the east and a major market was Europe, which did not produce pepper, ginger, cinnamon, nutmeg, cloves and frankincense, but did have an inexhaustible demand for them. It has often been suggested that the opening of trade routes around the Cape of Good Hope by the Portuguese such as Vasco da Gama in the late fifteenth century destroyed the economic importance of the Mediterranean. The reality is far more complicated. Indeed, the French historian, Fernand Braudel has written, 'The circumnavigation of the Cape of Good Hope did not strike an immediate death blow to the Mediterranean spice trade.'

251

The Portuguese did attempt to block the trade routes through the Persian Gulf and the Red Sea. In 1509 they defeated the Mamluks at Diu; their viceroy, Alfonso de Albuquerque failed to take Aden in 1513, but did seize the Red Sea island of Karaman. But Portugal was a small state and could not sustain a Red Sea fleet of more than 20 ships, which was defeated in 1517. Despite the Portuguese alliance with Ethiopia, the Safavids and the states of south India, they were never able to mount a complete blockade of the Ottoman trade routes to Alexandria, Damascus and Beirut.

It is true that, in the early sixteenth century, there were times when the Portuguese were near to success. In 1504, for example, the Venetians found no spices at Alexandria or Beirut. But by the 1540s, the Mediterranean trade route was again dominant. It was less risky than the route via the Cape of Good Hope and brought enormous profits to the people of the Empire. Between 1560 and 1564 an average of 17 000 quintals of spice (a quintal is about 100 pounds) were shipped through Alexandria, about half of which was bought by the Venetians. This quantity was as high as it had been before the voyages of Vasco da Gama. The importance of this trade was a vital factor in the Venetian reluctance to sustain a long war against the Turks and it was only in the early seventeenth century that the Dutch succeeded in taking over the bulk of this trade, ending the economic control of the Ottoman Empire.

The economic resources of the Ottoman Empire in the sixteenth century were undoubtedly far greater than any of its European rivals. The Empire controlled the most valuable trade routes in the world and retained this control, despite the competition of the other European states.

The government was concerned to protect the peasantry and, in the Balkans at least, the peasantry was far more prosperous than in previous centuries. At the same time, the relative weakness of the aristocracy ensured that income went to the government rather than being intercepted elsewhere. Above all, the Turks appreciated the vital importance of Constantinople, whose wealth, splendour and rapidly growing population provided a massive market for trade and for the agricultural region around the Black Sea. Success in war created a stable trading area on which Europe was still dependent for all kinds of goods. The wealth of the Empire was combined with an administrative and military system generally superior to that of other European states.

It is hardly surprising, therefore, that the reign of Suleiman the Magnificent (1520–66) brought the Ottoman Empire to the pinnacle of power and success.

7. The Reign of Suleiman the Magnificent 1520–66

Suleiman the Magnificent came to the throne on September 30, 1520. Known as Suleiman Kanun, 'the lawmaker', to his own people, he is remembered both for the constant expansion of Ottoman power during his reign and for the firmness and justice of his administration at home. The pattern of his life reflected these two concerns. Each summer he would lead his armies on campaigns to the distant frontiers of his Empire. The winter, in contrast, would be devoted to administrative activities and he would stay in Constantinople, rarely visiting any of his provincial capitals. During this time he was renowned as an outstanding interpreter of Islamic law who regulated the laws of property, the duties of his servants and the terms and conditions of military service.

Suleiman inherited a very advantageous position. There were no rival claimants to the throne and so he avoided a bloody struggle for power and gained the immediate loyalty of the Janissaries, who were probably at their most powerful and effective as a fighting force at this time. Selim the Grim, Suleiman's predecessor, had doubled the size of the Empire. Egypt and Syria were not simply the source of vast revenues which made Suleiman the wealthiest ruler in Europe, they also provided the money and expertise to enable Selim to develop a great shipyard in Constantinople which was to be the basis of Ottoman naval power. Moreover, none of the principal rivals of the Ottoman Empire in the eastern Mediterranean or the Middle East was in a position to challenge Suleiman effectively; both the Venetians and Safavids had been humiliatingly defeated quite recently and had no desire to fight.

If there were to be effective opposition to Suleiman, therefore, it would have to come from western Europe. There is no doubt that Suleiman gained enormous benefits from the suspicions and rivalries of the major European powers, which prevented a unified front being formed against him, despite the consistent and sometimes frantic efforts of the Papacy. In particular, Suleiman was aided by the rivalry between France and the Habsburgs which dominated Europe at this time *(see Chapters VIII and IX)*. To ally with the infidel Turks was an act which would draw the condemnation of all Christian Europe, but Francis I repeatedly, if sometimes secretly, sought Suleiman's assistance. After the Battle of Pavia in 1525, the French ambassador in Constantinople asked Suleiman to attack the Habsburgs by land and sea or face the prospect of complete Habsburg supremacy in Europe. The Venetians echoed this view. In 1532 Francis I admitted to the Venetian ambassador that the Ottoman Empire was the only power that could prevent the complete domination of Europe by Charles V.

At this time, the Ottoman and French fleets began to co-operate in the Mediterranean. On February 18 1536, a trade agreement, subsequently named the 'capitulations', was negotiated between the two powers which was followed soon after by a secret military alliance, and when the Ottoman fleet besieged Corfu in 1537 it was reinforced by the French navy. After Papal pressure, Charles and Francis did make peace in July 1538 and promised to organise a crusade, but the alliance between the French and the Ottoman Empire was a natural one against a common foe, and in 1543 formal military co-operation took place. It was relatively ineffective, but served to illustrate the continuity of the links between the two states although French policy was regarded as shocking by the rest of Europe, particularly when the Ottoman fleet wintered at Toulon.

Suleiman was also aided by the emergence of Protestantism in Europe. Indeed, it has been argued that the Protestant Reformation would have been crushed by Charles V if he had not been continually distracted by the Turkish threat. This is not to suggest that Protestant reformers had any sympathy for Islam. In typical fashion, Luther described the Turks as the 'scourge of God', Mohammed the Prophet of Islam as the 'servitor of the devil' and once claimed 'that the spirit of Antichrist is the Pope, his flesh the Turk'. Nevertheless, Luther opposed the idea of a crusade against the Turks. He regarded crusades simply as a means of furthering papal financial and military influence. Moreover, the German Lutheran princes utilised Charles' need for military support against the Turk to gain concessions from him. Inevitably, therefore, the divisions within Christendom which the Reformation brought about were capitalised upon the Turks who were well aware of the close identification of the Habsburgs with the Catholic faith. Suleiman's only consistent opponents were, therefore, the Habsburgs. Charles V, and later Philip II, contested control of the Mediterranean where their fleet was under the command of the Genoese admiral, Andrea Doria, while Ferdinand faced the army of the Ottoman Empire in Hungary. The clash between the two empires was not simply a clash between two rival dynastic states; it was also a clash between two cultures and civilisations. Suleiman was an Ottoman *Ghazi* and the leader of a state which was geared to expansionist religious wars. The Habsburgs were the chief defenders of Catholic Europe, despite the frequent suspicion of the Papacy. Suleiman was also the inheritor of the traditions of the Roman Empire as the conqueror of Constantinople which had been its capital, and certainly hoped to capture Rome itself. Charles V as Holy Roman Emperor, on the other hand, inherited another tradition of universal monarchy from Charlemagne.

There is no doubt that Suleiman possessed significant military and economic advantages over the Habsburgs, but there were certain weaknesses in his system which might be exploited. First of all, there was the constant threat from the Safavid Empire to the east which had a reservoir of potential support in the large number of Shi'ite sympathisers in eastern Anatolia. Despite the development of an Ottoman navy, the Christian powers were regarded as having superior naval resources. In particular, the island of Rhodes which was held by the Catholic Knights of St John was a nest of Christian pirates, who constantly disrupted Ottoman trade in the Aegean Sea. Finally, Suleiman set out on campaigns from Constantinople each campaigning season and the *sipahi* cavalry needed to return for the winter. This meant that much of his fighting was conducted at a great distance from his home base and campaigns often had to be broken off after only a few weeks so that the troops could be home for the winter.

Despite this, Suleiman's armies enjoyed a record of almost uninterrupted success. So great was the prestige of his armies that his enemies were always very reluctant to initiate war against him, which was one reason for his success in avoiding conflicts on different fronts at the same time. Ottoman diplomatic techniques were also perhaps more sophisticated than those of their Christian rivals. In the Crimea, Transylvania, Hungary, North Africa and Ragusa, the Ottoman Empire controlled client states on its distant frontiers. These might be ruled by Christians or by Muslims, but all were clearly dependent on Ottoman friendship. In Hungary and Transylvania the alternative to Ottoman rule was the Habsburgs, while the Crimean Tatars and Ragusa were dependent on trade with Constantinople.

Militarily and economically, the Ottoman state commanded far greater resources than its rivals. The sultan did not need to fear over-mighty subjects. Although there were religious tensions within the Ottoman Empire, they were tackled in a far more flexible fashion than was usual in western Europe. Quite simply, in the time of Suleiman there was no aspect of government in which the Empire was clearly weaker than its European rivals and in most it was far stronger.

8. The Campaigns of Suleiman the Magnificent 1520–66

(a) Belgrade and Rhodes

In order to establish himself as a worthy *Ghazi* in the Ottoman tradition, Suleiman needed swift and spectacular military success. In the Balkans, his primary military target was Hungary. The city of Belgrade provided the major barrier to rapid advance along the Danube and Mohammed the Conqueror had been checked there by the Hungarian king, John Hunyadi, in 1456. Belgrade was captured on August 8 1520, which opened the way for a future assault on the plains of Hungary itself.

Rhodes was controlled by the crusading order of the Knights of St John. They threatened the stability and prestige of the Ottoman Empire in many ways. They were notorious pirates, who fulfilled their religious vows and filled their pockets by attacks on Ottoman shipping in the Aegean Sea. In particular, they disrupted trade with Egypt, which was of such economic importance to the Empire. Moreover, they weakened the prestige of the sultan amongst devout Muslims by their success in transporting Christian pilgrims to the Holy Land. Rhodes was attacked in the summer of 1520. It possessed strong fortifications and over 60 000 defenders, many of whom were experienced soldiers. Eventually the island fell in December 1522. It seems that the slaves and servants of the Knights of St John, most of whom were of the Orthodox faith, aided the Sultan's forces and preferred Ottoman to Catholic control. The threat of the Knights of St John was not removed altogether. They were allowed to evacuate to Malta and their control of this island, in alliance with

Charles V, proved a consistent menace to the forces of the Ottoman Empire. But the eastern Mediterranean, except for some Venetian outposts, was now under undisputed Ottoman control and Christian piracy diminished in importance.

(b) The western frontier

After the defeat of Francis I by Charles V at Pavia in 1525, Suleiman considered a land and sea assault against Italy but eventually decided to attack Hungary.

This was a well-considered choice. In the fifteenth century, under John Hunyadi and Matthias Corvinus, Hungary had been considered a formidable military state and an effective opponent of the Turks. Under their successors, Ladislas (1490–1516) and Louis (1516–26), Hungarian power declined. The aristocracy strongly opposed any extension of royal power and its leader John Zapolyai was himself ambitious for the throne. In 1514, there had been a peasant rebellion which was brutally suppressed by the gentry, who followed their victory by imposing on the peasantry a particularly harsh form of serfdom. Hungary was therefore ruled by a weak king who was dominated by an irresponsible aristocracy who harshly exploited the peasantry.

In 1526 the Ottoman armies invaded Hungary. On August 29 the Hungarian army was destroyed at the Battle of Mohacs. The discipline of the Janissaries and the superiority of the Turkish cannon proved too much for the Hungarian cavalry and King Louis was killed as he fled the battlefield. John Zapolyai offered to acknowledge Ottoman overlordship and pay a tribute if he was left in control of the country and this was agreed by Suleiman. Hungary was a great distance from Constantinople and a puppet ruler suited his interests. The Turkish army withdrew and the French granted recognition to Zapolyai. The Crown was then disputed between Zapolyai and Archduke Ferdinand, Charles V's brother, who married Louis's sister. He invaded Hungary and drove Zapolyai from Buda in 1527.

The Sultan agreed to restore Zapolyai to the throne and the second Turkish campaign into Hungary was launched in 1528. Buda was recaptured on September 3 and John Zapolyai was restored to his throne, while Suleiman's interests were protected by the establishment of a garrison of Janissaries at Buda and the payment of an annual tribute.

Suleiman's armies then advanced to Vienna which was besieged from September 27 until October 15 1529, when the end of the campaigning season forced the Ottoman army to retire. Vienna itself was safe but its suburbs had been destroyed and isolated Ottoman raids penetrated as far as Regensburg in Bavaria and Brno in Bohemia, causing great panic throughout Europe. Ferdinand was also fortunate that the Peace of Cambrai with France enabled Charles V to send him reinforcements. Nonetheless it is probably true that Vienna was beyond the effective campaigning range of the Ottoman Empire. The organisation and government of the Empire required Suleiman to winter in Constantinople, from which each new campaign was begun. It was always late summer before his army arrived in Hungary and it had to return home in October, not simply because of climatic problems, but also because the *sipahi* had to return to their *timars*.

Despite these problems, a third campaign took place in 1532. This was a response to the siege of Buda by Ferdinand in December 1530. 300 000 troops advanced into central Europe in 1532 causing renewed panic.

On this occasion, however, Suleiman proved incapable of drawing the Habsburg prince into a decisive conflict. The small town of Guns resisted heroically for three weeks until August 28, by which time the campaigning season was coming to a close. Suleiman retreated and by October 12 had returned to Belgrade. The historian V J Parry summarised the problem quite well when he wrote, 'The Sultan realised that time and distance were enemies as least as formidable as the power of the Habsburgs'.

In 1533 peace was made after mediation by Poland. Archduke Ferdinand recognised Suleiman as 'father and suzerain', while the Grand Vizier was his 'brother' and equal in rank. He also abandoned all claims to Hungary except for the border area. Suleiman had made no concessions and had established a stable border and recognition of his superior status. In 1540 John Zapolyai died. The succession issue was very complicated and Hungarian opinion was divided between the supporters of Ferdinand and Zapolyai's young son, John Sigismund. Suleiman decided to settle this issue and invaded in 1541. In August he made his camp at Buda, having destroyed all opposition, and established a new Ottoman province with Buda as its capital. A stable frontier was coming into being.

After further Ottoman attacks in 1543 and 1544, Ferdinand sought and obtained a truce in 1545. In 1547 this was converted into a five year truce after discussions at Adrianople and Ferdinand agreed to pay an annual tribute of 30 000 gold pieces for those parts of northern and western Hungary which he still controlled. Meanwhile John Sigismund was to rule Transylvania which was effectively an Ottoman puppet state.

Hostilities re-opened in 1551 when Ferdinand attacked Transylvania. The Habsburg campaign was unsuccessful, Ottoman armies defeated them twice in 1552 and created the new Ottoman province of Temesvar in south west Transylvania. The war continued in an indecisive fashion. Suleiman was pre-occupied in the east and Ferdinand lacked the military strength to take advantage of this. The peace of 1562 more or less repeated the terms of 1547.

After this, the frontier stabilised. Ferdinand concentrated on the construction of a strongly fortified frontier and strengthening the defences of small towns. He avoided pitched battles and forced the Ottoman Empire into a war of long sieges. For example, when Suleiman was persuaded into one last campaign against the Habsburgs in 1566, he left Constantinople on May 1 and travelled for 97 days before meeting serious resistance. It then took 34 days to capture the small town of Sigetvar which fell on August 29. Even if the Sultan had not then died it would have been impossible to continue the campaign. It seemed as if the Ottoman Empire was incapable of further expansion in this area.

(c) The eastern frontier

The second major area of conflict for Suleiman the Magnificent was his eastern frontier. There was always the threat of social and religious unrest in Anatolia. In this part of the Empire there were many Turkish aristocrats who resented the domination of the slaves of the *Devshirme* and also many peasants who were economically insecure and sympathetic to the Shi'ite doctrines of the Safavid Shah Tahmasp. Charles V had tried to exploit these problems by sending envoys to the Safavids in 1529 and the Shah had encouraged the Celali in Anatolia. By 1533 Suleiman had decided that an eastern campaign was essential for his security. He also feared that Tahmasp would block the vital trade routes, and needed to defeat the man who was executing Sunni Moslems, of whom Suleiman was the great protector.

In 1534 Tabriz was captured although this remote and isolated city in the mountainous region of Azerbaijan was later abandoned. Later in the year Baghdad, a city of great wealth and prestige in the Muslim world, was also captured. Suleiman stayed there until the spring of 1535 and it became the centre of a new province with a garrison of 2000 Janissaries. By 1538, Basra in the Persian Gulf also accepted Ottoman authority. The important Basra-Baghdad-Aleppo trade route was now firmly under control and Syria fully protected. Suleiman had, however, failed to commit the Safavids to a decisive battle. The threat was greatly diminished but had not entirely disappeared.

There was no further serious conflict until 1548, although there was much skirmishing on the frontiers. In the summer of 1548, Suleiman marched once again on Tabriz, but found that the Shah had abandoned it rather than commit his army to battle. The fortress of Van was taken but over the next years the Shah recovered some ground. In April 1554 Suleiman again attacked and devastated much of the frontier as an alternative to the destruction of the Shah's army.

After this, peace negotiations were opened and conducted at Amasya in May 1555. Suleiman abandoned his claim to Tabriz but retained Iraq, most of Kurdistan and western Armenia. These campaigns against the Safavids were largely undertaken in remote and mountainous regions, where water and food were scarce and the winters exceptionally harsh. Although Suleiman was never able to inflict another decisive defeat, such as Selim's victory at Chaldiran, he greatly extended and strengthened the frontiers of his Empire. Considering that he was fighting, as in Hungary, at an enormous distance from his capital his success was remarkable.

(d) The Mediterranean

The third major frontier and war zone for the Ottoman Empire was the Mediterranean. Even at the time of Suleiman's accession, the key islands of Rhodes, Crete and Cyprus were not in Ottoman hands and the eastern Mediterranean could not be navigated safely. Of course, the capture of Rhodes did improve the position. Equally important was the emergence of Muslim pirates, usually known as corsairs. These saw themselves as sea *Ghazis* and the north African coast provided many potentially useful bases for them. Most important was the city of Algiers. In 1516, two Turkish corsairs established themselves in Algiers. One was killed in 1518; the other, Hayreddin Barbarossa, became the most famous and effective Muslim sea captain of the sixteenth century. Although the Barbary pirates placed themselves under Suleiman's protection, initially Barbarossa and his followers acted more or less independently. Algiers became the greatest threat to Habsburg dominance in the western Mediterranean and a haven for pirates and renegades of all races. In particular, many *Moriscos* fled to Algiers and took with them their hostility to Christian Spain. In 1529, Barbarossa seized the Peñón d'Argel, the fortified island at the entrance to the harbour of Algiers which had been a Spanish base. Despite this, the Spanish–Genoese alliance which brought Andrea Doria's fleet over to Charles V seemed to tip the naval balance against the Ottoman Empire, especially when Doria captured outposts in the Morea in 1532.

But Suleiman's response was to appoint Barbarossa Governor General of Algiers and Grand Admiral of the Ottoman fleet in December 1533 and to begin to construct a new fleet. At a stroke, he had gained an experienced and gifted naval commander and a valuable base in the western Mediterranean. In 1534, Barbarossa re-captured the outposts in the Morea seized by Doria and expelled the King of Tunis who was an ally of Spain. An invasion of Italy seemed imminent and a struggle for control of the central Mediterranean ensued.

The recapture of Tunis by Charles in 1535 was certainly a major blow, but Barbarossa's navy was not significantly weakened. In September 1538, at Prevesa near the entrance to the Adriatic Sea, Barbarossa was able to exploit the distrust within the combined Imperial and Venetian fleets and the hesitations of Doria to inflict a significant if not overwhelming defeat. This confirmed Turkish dominance of the eastern Mediterranean and in October 1540 Venice was forced to surrender her remaining possession in the Morea. On the other hand, Barbarossa's expedition to the western Mediterranean in 1543 was equally unsuccessful. Initially the French co-operated in the unsuccessful siege of Nice, but Francis I changed his policy. After Barbarossa occupied Toulon for a while he retired without significant success.

The death of Barbarossa in 1546 caused a temporary halt to naval activity but excellent sea captains such as Turgut Reis, known more familiarly as Dragut, remained. He took Tripoli in North Africa from the

Knights of St John in 1551 and established himself as its ruler. Moreover, an attempt by Philip II to remove him ended in a disastrous rout at the island of Djerba in May 1560. One of the last great campaigns of Suleiman's career was the attempt to capture Malta from the Knights of St John in 1565. The capture of Malta would have given the Turks control of the central Mediterranean and it was only with great difficulty that the Christian forces raised the siege in September.

Suleiman's reign saw the continued expansion of his Empire by land and sea. In the end it was not the military skill of his opponents that contained him, but the problems of time and distance. By land and sea the Ottoman Empire continually proved superior to its opponents, despite campaigning on very distant frontiers.

Many of the advantages that Suleiman enjoyed on land also applied at sea. His captains, such as Barbarossa, were more loyal and dependable than the Genoese Doria, who was always concerned to protect the interests of his city even when they clashed with those of his Habsburg allies. Equally, the Venetians were unreliable in their attitude and rarely opposed the Turks for long periods.

9. The Decline of the Empire

It is easy simply to say that after 1566, the great days of the Empire were ended. It is certainly true that Suleiman's successors were not as competent as his predecessors. Selim II (1566–74) was nicknamed the 'Sot' (the drunkard) and neither he nor Murad III (1574–95) provided strong leadership. Moreover, the devastating defeat of the Ottoman navy at Lepanto (October 7 1571) seems an obvious illustration of its declining power. Some historians have argued that only the defection of Venice from the Holy League in 1573 prevented the decisive defeat of the Ottoman Empire.

The historian Andrew Hess strongly and effectively disputes the view of Ottoman decline. First of all he points out that the Venetians were never able to recapture Cyprus which fell to the Empire in 1571. Moreover, the Ottoman fleet was rebuilt to its former strength with remarkable swiftness. The Grand Vizier, Mohammed Sokullu, is quoted as saying in 1572, 'The Ottoman State is so powerful, if an order was issued to cast anchors from silver, to make rigging from silk and to cut the sails from satin, it could be carried out for the entire fleet'. Indeed, the collapse of the Holy League after Lepanto when Venice deserted it and the rapid reconstruction of the Ottoman fleet illustrate that the traditional Ottoman advantages of economic superiority and a divided opposition still applied. No long-term strategic gains were attained by the Holy League. In fact Ottoman naval expansion continued along the North African coast. Tunis was recaptured in 1574 and, along with Tripoli and Algiers, guaranteed the Islamic dominance of this coast. Expansion continued towards Morocco, which greatly worried the

The Expansion of the Ottoman Empire

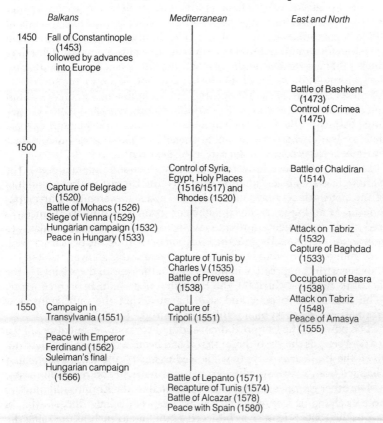

	Balkans	Mediterranean	East and North
1450	Fall of Constantinople (1453) followed by advances into Europe		
			Battle of Bashkent (1473) Control of Crimea (1475)
1500			
		Control of Syria, Egypt, Holy Places (1516/1517) and Rhodes (1520)	Battle of Chaldiran (1514)
	Capture of Belgrade (1520) Battle of Mohacs (1526) Siege of Vienna (1529) Hungarian campaign (1532) Peace in Hungary (1533)		
			Attack on Tabriz (1532) Capture of Baghdad (1533)
		Capture of Tunis by Charles V (1535) Battle of Prevesa (1538)	Occupation of Basra (1538) Attack on Tabriz (1548)
1550	Campaign in Transylvania (1551)	Capture of Tripoli (1551)	Peace of Amasya (1555)
	Peace with Emperor Ferdinand (1562) Suleiman's final Hungarian campaign (1566)		
		Battle of Lepanto (1571) Recapture of Tunis (1574) Battle of Alcazar (1578) Peace with Spain (1580)	

Portuguese. At the Battle of Alcazar, 4 August 1578, the Portuguese King, Don Sebastian, was killed and Morocco became a tributary state of the Ottoman Empire. It was not, therefore, until the truce of 1580 with Spain that the expansion of the Ottoman Empire in the Mediterranean ceased and this truce left North Africa under almost unchallenged Ottoman control, again using client rulers.

Nonetheless, weaknesses in the Ottoman system which were to become clear in the seventeenth century can in fact be seen as early as the reign of Suleiman himself.

One of the great criticisms of the Ottoman system in the next century was the growing importance of court intrigue and favouritism. In particular the Sultanate of Women, in which factions within the Emperor's harem secured advancement of their own favourites, is seen as a significant factor in the declining quality of the government of the Empire. Suleiman himself seems to illustrate the vices of favouritism. His first Grand Vizier, Ibrahim Pasha, was chosen above many long-serving and efficient ministers and then ruthlessly strangled after 13

261

years. The influence of Suleiman's favourite wife, Hurrem Sultan, more commonly known as Roxelana, is often seen as the main reason for this. Roxelana clearly put her position and that of her sons, rather than those of the Emperor's other wives, above considerations of good government. It was an Ottoman tradition that, in order to secure a peaceful accession, the brothers of the heir to the throne were strangled. Roxelana particularly abused this cruel tradition by her attempts to secure the succession for one of her own sons. She secured the strangling of Suleiman's ablest son, Mustafa, because he was the child of a different favourite. Her two sons, Selim and Bayezid, then fought a civil war in 1559 before Bayezid fled to Iran, where Suleiman arranged his execution. Such palace intrigue became commonplace over the next century.

Even more important were the growing economic problems that the Empire began to face. Inflation disrupted the Empire in the second half of the sixteenth century and weakened the *timar* system, in particular. The *sipahi* no longer received sufficient income to support themselves and *timars* were often granted to favourites and government officials as salaries or pensions. Despite the tradition of treating the peasantry well, they suffered a growing burden of taxation and this showed itself in the Balkans with the spread of banditry and in the repeated uprisings of the Celali in Anatolia. In 1590, the Spanish ambassador in Venice wrote, 'The Empire is so poor and so exhausted that the only coins now circulating are aspers made entirely from iron.'

The power of the Empire did not suddenly evaporate, but after 1580 it was not seen as the great threat that it had been in the reign of Suleiman. Even the Janissaries were now allowed to marry and learn a trade and changed from a loyal standing army to a privileged and rebellious caste.

The other European states were fascinated by the Empire and quick to note its changing features. The Empire's power declined very slowly. As late as the 1680s Vienna was besieged again, but as early as the 1590s the growing problems of the Turks were reported to the rest of Europe. The Venetian Republic maintained ambassadors at Constantinople who provided some of the most interesting first-hand accounts of the Empire's problems.

In 1592, Lorenzo Bernardo was sent as the Venetian Ambassador to Constantinople. Extracts of his report appear below, providing a representative contemporary analysis of Turkish decline.

> Three basic qualities have enabled the Turks to make such remarkable conquests and rise to such importance in a brief period: religion, frugality and obedience. In former times, all Turks held to a single religion whose major belief is that it is 'written' when and how a man will die, and that if he dies for his God and his faith he will go directly to Paradise. But now the Turks have not a single religion, but three of them. The Persians are among the Turks like the heretics among the Christians. Then there are the Arabs and Moors, who claim they alone preserve the true, uncorrupted religion, and that the 'Greek Turks' (as they call these in Constantinople) are bastard Moslems with a corrupted religion, which they blame on their being

mostly descended from Christian renegades who did not understand the Moslem religion.

As far as frugality, which I said was the second of the three sources of the Turks' great power, at one time the Turks had no interest in fine foods, in splendid decoration in their houses. But now that the Turks have conquered vast rich lands they too have fallen victim to the corruption of wealth. They are happy to follow the example provided by the Sultan, who cares nothing about winning glory on the battlefield and prefers to stay at home and enjoy the countless pleasures of the harem. Modelling themselves on him, all the splendid pashas, governors and generals, and the ordinary soldiers too, want to stay in their harems and enjoy their pleasures and keep as far as possible from the dangers and discomforts of war.

Obedience was the third source of the great power of the Turkish Empire. They are all slaves by nature, and the slaves of one single master; only from him, can they hope to win power, honours and wealth and only from him do they have to fear punishment and death.

Four years ago I found the Turks less obedient than they had earlier been. This time I learned that the situation had deteriorated still further.

The Janissaries set fire to the houses of Jews in Constantinople and burned down a quarter of the city. For all this they were never even threatened with punishment.

1 Explain the reference to the 'Persian heretics' and the 'Greek Turks'.
2 How valid is the ambassador's analysis of the traditional strengths of the Ottoman Empire?
3 What aspects of the Turkish system of government were clearly not working effectively by the 1590s?
4 What other factors in Turkish decline does the ambassador ignore? Why might this be so?

10. Bibliography

F Braudel *The Mediterranean and the Mediterranean World in the Age of Philip II* (Fontana, 1975). P Holt (ed.) *Cambridge History of Islam* (CUP, 1977). H Inalcik *The Ottoman Empire: the Classical Age 1300–1600* (Weidenfeld & Nicolson, 1973). S Runciman *The Fall of Constantinople* (CUP, 1955). S Shaw *The History of the Ottoman Empire and Modern Turkey Vol. 1* (CUP, 1976).

11. Discussion Points and Exercises

A *This section consists of questions or points that might be used for discussion (or written answers) as a way of expanding on the chapter and testing understanding of it:*

1 Why was the Ottoman Empire so important in the history of sixteenth century Europe?
2 'Dedication to *Jihad* was crucial to Ottoman success.'
3 Which were the most significant areas of Ottoman expansion up to 1520?

4   Why was the *timar* so eminent a feature of Ottoman strength?
5   How effective was the religious policy of the Ottoman Empire?
6   What were the main economic strengths of the Ottoman Empire?
7   How did Suleiman exploit the divisions amongst Europeans?
8   Why was a limit reached to Ottoman expansion in the Balkans?
9   How crucial was Barbarossa to Ottoman success in the Mediterranean?
10 What effects did court intrigue have on the Ottoman Empire in the late sixteenth century?

B *Essay questions*
1   In what ways did Ottoman power menace Europe in the sixteenth century?
2   What were the distinctive features of the Ottoman system of government in the sixteenth century?
3   Why was the expansion of Ottoman power so rapid in the sixteenth century?
4   Were the successes of Suleiman the Magnificent the result of the strengths of his Empire or the weaknesses of his opponents?

C *Exercise*
Geography is clearly a vital factor in helping to explain both the successes and the failures of the Ottoman Turks. Find a map of the Mediterranean in which the physical geography of the whole region is shown clearly. Then answer the following questions.

1   How does the map help to explain the importance of Constantinople, Belgrade, Rhodes and Malta?
2   Why did Barbarossa's control of Algiers pose such a problem to the Spanish monarchs?
3   What would you see as the key frontier zones between Christian and Muslim?
4   Is the geography of the region the most important explanation for the establishment of these frontiers?
5   How far from Constantinople were the land borders of the Ottoman Empire?
6   How large was the Ottoman Empire in comparison with that of Charles V?
7   Do you feel that any further expansion would have been possible?

XI The Swiss Reformation

1. Introduction

In 1518, a year after Luther made his protest against indulgences, Huldrych Zwingli (1484–1531) became a preacher at the Great Minster in the Swiss city of Zurich. There he gradually moved away from the Church of Rome, finally making the breach clear in 1523. He claimed to have developed his views independently of Luther and certainly his doctrine was sufficiently original to make the Swiss Reformation distinct from the Lutheran Reformation in Germany and Scandinavia.

The importance of the Swiss Reformation does not derive just from its being different. It was more its international impact which was to set it apart. Zwingli's Reformation was to spread throughout northern Switzerland and into southern Germany, although he was to be killed in battle in 1531, having failed to secure any further gains. Ironically, the first religious initiative originating in Zurich which was to spread across much of Europe in one form or another was not that of Zwingli but that of the so-called Anabaptists.

The Anabaptists' name derives from their denial of the sacrament of infant baptism in favour of the baptism of adults who could make a confession of faith. This was not just a minor doctrinal variation. It symbolised the Anabaptists setting themselves apart from normal society and the state, given that baptism introduced the individual into the community as well as into the Church. The Anabaptists were the mainstay of the Radical Reformation and as such were to be attacked by the leaders of the Magisterial Reformation, such as Luther and Zwingli.

Eclipsing both Zwinglianism and Anabaptism in long-term significance was the movement established in Geneva by John Calvin (1509–64). He was the leader of the second generation of reformers, bringing the Reformation to its high point through his intellectual and organisational energies. The success of Calvinism was international. Geneva having been secured, Calvinism was to spread first into France, Calvin's homeland, and then to the Rhineland, the Netherlands, England, Scotland and into eastern Europe as far as Transylvania. While Calvin's clarity of doctrine and the strength of his missionary organisation obviously played a role in this expansion of the Reformation, historians have now begun to question whether this is a sufficient explanation. The contributors to *International Calvinism*, edited by Menna Prestwich, have shown just how much Calvinism adapted itself to its various national settings, developing in ways which Calvin himself never envisaged.

However Calvin's role is assessed, sureness of purpose combined with adaptability ensured the triumph of the Swiss Reformation and made it international. More than that, it has been claimed to be the foundation of the modern world in unintentionally fostering democracy, revolutionary theory and capitalism. We must bear these ideas in mind but we must also remember that they were far from the minds of the Swiss reformers themselves. They had their attention focused sharply on religious issues and when they were drawn, mostly unwillingly, into affairs of politics or economics they often reflected the age they lived in rather than being set to transform it.

2. Zwingli

(a) Zwingli's early career

Huldrych Zwingli was born in 1484 at Wildhaus in Toggenburg, a region loosely attached to the Swiss Confederation. His family was not rich but, given a tradition amongst the Zwinglis of making a career in the Church, Huldrych was sent away to be educated. He was bright and he was set to climb the ecclesiastical career ladder.

Unlike Luther, he does not seem to have been obsessed by the problem of sin. Although he was quite a conscientious priest, he was not above the ordinary abuses of the Church. When he left Glarus, his first parish where he worked between 1506 and 1516, he carried on drawing his salary, paying over only some of it to the vicar who took over the work there. He was happy to accept a papal pension. He found the priest's vow of celibacy a burden so he had an affair with a barber's daughter—quite acceptable behaviour at the time although Zwingli later had to defend himself against enemies who claimed that he had seduced a virgin. Zwingli was not outraged by the corruption of the Church. He was to abandon his former ways only when he became intellectually convinced that Catholic doctrine had to be purified.

It was Christian Humanism which first changed the way Zwingli thought. From the earliest days of his education he had assimilated a humanist style and love of the classics. He studied Greek and Hebrew as well as Latin. These skills became truly important when Erasmus' edition of the New Testament in its original Greek became available in 1516. Zwingli began to read the text itself rather than accept the standard interpretations. He also met Erasmus and corresponded with him, while growing in his appreciation of Erasmus' *Philosophy of Christ*, his emphasis on the knowledge and love of Christ Himself as opposed to mechanical, outward piety. Like Erasmus, Zwingli saw the need for reform in the Church.

(b) The Reformation in Zurich

In 1518 Zwingli took up a prestigious appointment as preacher in the Great Minster of Zurich. By this stage he may have been moving further than Christian Humanism towards a break with the traditional doctrine of the Church but he did not publicise his thoughts.

In Zurich the environment was as favourable to the Reformation as it could be in any city. The magistrates were used to regulating Church activities and were open to discussion about reform. Zurich was controlled by its guilds and so had a broad electorate of about 2000 out of 6000 citizens—there was no small ruling group of conservative Catholic families, as in some other cities, to stand in the way of religious innovation. But Zwingli was still very cautious when in 1522 he criticised the Catholic practice of fasting during Lent, and followed this by an attack on celibacy, the first public signs that Zwingli was moving away from Catholic tradition.

Having tested the water over fasting and celibacy, Zwingli started to make his general position clear in an open letter, known as the *Apologeticus Archeteles*, which he wrote to the Bishop of Constance in August 1522. He set out to prove that he was not a heretic but he also attacked the authority of the Pope, the errors of General Councils and the unnecessary rituals of the Church. Zwingli was now as clearly an adherent of the Reformation as Luther. Having stated his position, he had to defend it so the Council of Zurich agreed to a public debate on January 29 1523.

In preparation for this debate, Zwingli wrote his *Sixty Seven Articles*. They detailed his beliefs and what he saw as the regrettable innovations of the medieval Church. Amongst other things he attacked the powers of the Papacy and the use of excommunication, the sale of indulgences and the idea of Purgatory, the worship of saints and going on a pilgrimage to curry favour with God. Zwingli argued all this from the same starting point as Luther—that only God, not the oppressive apparatus of the medieval Church, could justify the sinner. And he claimed the backing of an indisputable authority: 'We have the infallible and impartial judge, Holy Scripture, in Hebrew, Greek and Latin.' The Bishop of Constance refused to debate all this with Zwingli in person. Instead he sent Johannes Fabri who, although he remained a Catholic, had been an admirer of Zwingli. He urged the reformer not to set himself against the rest of the world but Zwingli was as unimpressed by that argument as Luther had been—he would not surrender the truth for anything. The people of Zurich were also unimpressed by Fabri's arguments. The doctrine of the Reformation was established in Zurich in 1523.

The Council took action but in a limited way. The monasteries were gradually taken over, the monks often accepting a pension and leaving quite willingly, the buildings being put to other uses such as a hospital for the poor and schools. All preaching was to conform to the evangelical model established by Zwingli. But the churches remained Catholic in appearance and the Mass was still celebrated in the traditional way even though Zwingli had condemned the doctrine behind it in his *Sixty Seven Articles*. In part, the Council did not want to be too hasty in alienating Catholic neighbours and there were hopes that the Pope himself could be persuaded to repay certain debts he owed to Zurich. Also Zwingli urged that reform be carried out slowly so as not to leave the weaker brethren behind. But some of the more eager brethren forced the pace.

In September 1523 a cobbler named Hans Hottinger overturned a crucifix which stood on a road outside Zurich, on the grounds that you should worship only Christ and not a material image of Him. This started a series of writings and disputations, with Zwingli continuing to have the commanding voice. He was tactful, though—he suggested that images be covered over until the Council ordered their removal. That duly occurred in June 1524. The careful, organised removal of altar-pieces, statues and crucifixes was iconoclasm of a sort but it was most unlike the frenzied iconoclastic riots which were to break out in other parts of Europe. The ultimate effect was the same—the churches were no longer Catholic to look at but were bare and simple, which the reformers hoped would concentrate hearts and minds on Christ and His Word alone.

Only one feature of Roman Catholic worship was left but it was the most significant—the Mass. Condemned by Zwingli two years previously, it was at last abolished by the Council in April 1525. This did not mean that Zwingli had dispensed with the sacraments. Like Luther he cut them down from seven to two—baptism and the Eucharist. But the Eucharist, now no longer the Catholic Mass, was a simple service commemorating the Last Supper, with only ordinary bread and wine distributed from a Communion table rather than from an altar. This showed the reformers' rejection of the Catholic doctrine of transubstantiation. For Zwingli, the Eucharist was a necessary outward sign of faith but there was to be no magic about it. All the outward signs of Reformation worship had now been established in Zurich in a way that was rather more austere but still much the same as in the Lutheran cities of Germany.

(c) Zwingli and Luther—the split in the Reformation

Despite their common Protestantism Zwingli always distanced himself from Luther. In 1523 he wrote: 'The Papists say, "You must be Lutheran, you preach just as Luther writes." I answer, "I preach just as St Paul writes, why not call me a Pauline?"'. At this stage Zwingli's aloofness was probably a matter of policy rather than doctrine. He did not want his enemies to brand him as a heretic too easily by associating him with Luther and so endanger Zurich's international position. Also Zurich could be an independent centre of reform in the Swiss Confederation being remote from the political orbit of Lutheran Saxony. But just as the abolition of the Mass was the final symbolic break with Catholicism, so the problem of the Eucharist was to divide Zwingli and Luther and split the Reformation permanently.

In the Bible story of the Last Supper, Christ indicates the bread and says 'This is my body'. As we saw in Chapter VI, Luther took this in its physical sense—he thought that, in the Eucharist, Christ's body is physically present in the bread although without it changing in substance, as heat can be said to be physically present in red-hot iron. Zwingli saw this as an unwarranted compromise with the Catholic doctrine of transubstantiation. More of a humanist than Luther, he was less prepared to interpret the Bible in so literal a way. He took the words 'This is my body' to mean 'This represents my body', the idea being put to him in a letter of 1524 written by the Dutchman Cornelis Hoen. This re-interpretation of Christ's words meant that, in the Eucharist, the bread was just symbolic of Christ and did not contain Him in any way. Historians used to think that on this issue Zwingli took up an extreme radical position, denying the presence of Christ altogether in the Eucharist. In fact, as his recent biographer G R Potter has shown, he did believe that Christ was present, if only spiritually in the heart of the believer. Still, the division of opinion between Luther and Zwingli was profound. For Luther, even an unbeliever would consume Christ physically in the Eucharist, albeit blasphemously, whereas for Zwingli, only the believer received Christ spiritually—a point of view known as receptionism. Parties unable to agree on this essential point of doctrine began to form around the two reformers.

Most of the reformed areas of northern Germany took their lead from the Wittenberg reformer but in south west Germany and Switzerland Zwingli had the greatest following, his party becoming known as the Sacramentarians. This geographical division was not just a matter of which reform centre was closest. Thomas Brady has argued in his book *Turning Swiss* that the south west German cities gravitated towards the Swiss Reformation as they tended to identify themselves constitutionally and socially with the Swiss cities. However, uppermost in the minds of the people at the time was the war of words between the two reformers. In a series of publications Zwingli stated his position in a cool and reasonable tone. He even praised Luther as the David who had slain the Papist Goliath. But he also schooled his followers well in the *Prophezei*, a theological college opened in 1525 and designed to turn out a superior brand of Sacramentarian preacher. Finding that Zwingli was consolidating his position, Luther put heat into the debate. He wrote in 1527 that Zwingli 'neither holds nor teaches any part of the Christian faith rightly and he is seven times more dangerous than when he was a Papist'. Such hostility within the ranks of the reformers was dangerous at a time when the Catholics were organising their forces for a counter-attack.

As early as 1526, the tireless von Eck had won a victory at a religious conference in the Swiss city of Baden. He had even had the support of some Lutherans against the Zwinglians present. (Zwingli had decided it was too dangerous to attend in person.) The result was that nine of the Swiss cantons declared their support for Catholicism. After the 1529 Diet of Speyer it looked as though the whole of Protestantism, as it then became known, was in danger from the Emperor and the Catholic princes. The most dynamic Protestant leader, Philip of Hesse, saw that safety lay in unity so he summoned a conference of all the leading reformers to try and hammer out a compromise between the Lutherans and the Zwinglians. The Colloquy of Marburg, as it was called, opened in October 1529.

Here is some of the dialogue spoken at Marburg:

> Luther (in response to the argument that Christ's physical body cannot be in more than one place at a time): 'I repeat again that I do not accept mathematical dimensions as applicable to Holy Scripture, because God is greater than all the mathematicians.'

> Oecolampadius (the reformer of Basle and a supporter of Zwingli): 'Where, doctor, does it say in the Bible that we should close our eyes to its meaning?'
> Luther: 'If we debated for a century it would make no difference. Show me the text and I will be satisfied. We must not interpret in our own way the words of our Lord.'

> Zwingli (on a verse from the Bible which supported his case): 'This passage breaks your neck.'
> Luther: 'Don't be too sure. Necks are not so easily broken. You are in Hesse here not in Switzerland.'

1 *What obstacles to compromise do the above illustrate?*
2 *What is the significance of Luther's last comment?*

The Colloquy of Marburg was not a complete disaster. The reformers came away with greater respect for one another, and of fifteen articles under discussion they had been able to agree on fourteen of them but not, of course, on the article concerning the Eucharist. This being the critical issue, the Swiss Reformation was to remain permanently distinct from Lutheranism and the two parties of reformers had to fight their battles against Catholic reaction separately.

(d) The Reformation in Berne

Far more critical than the attitude of Lutherans for the survival of the Swiss Reformation was the attitude of the rulers of Berne. It was the most important canton both in terms of size and military resources and it carried much weight within the Swiss Confederation. Zurich was one of Switzerland's leading cities but, with five mountain cantons to the south remaining fiercely Catholic (in receipt of papal pensions and without major cities to spearhead the Reformation) and with the power of the Habsburgs not far away, Berne's support was vital.

At first it looked as though that support would not be forthcoming because of a clash of interests between the two cities. Zurich in north eastern Switzerland looked to Germany; Berne to the west looked towards France. Zwingli had campaigned successfully in Zurich against the hiring out of mercenaries to France and this ran clean against Berne's policy. But there were also forces in Berne working in Zwingli's favour.

The Bernese had resented the leading Swiss Catholic, Cardinal Schinner, and his recruitment of mercenaries to serve the Pope. And, perhaps more importantly, there were effective preachers in the mid 1520s converting the people of Berne to Zwingli's way of thinking.

The Council of Berne tried to avoid disturbance by maintaining Catholic worship while encouraging evangelical preaching. This simply allowed the Zwinglians to gather enough support to dominate the Council after the 1527 elections. In January 1528 a formal disputation between Catholics and reformers was held in Berne. Zwingli was present with distinguished supporters from northern Switzerland and southern Germany. It was more a triumphal declaration of opinions by the reformers than a disputation. The Council declared that Berne was now reformed. Soon the Mass was abolished and images of saints were removed from the churches. The reform was not carried through without cost—Berne had to put down a rising in the surrounding countryside —but it was established firmly. Given Berne's dominant position in Switzerland there was no power which could reverse the reform. That was the best guarantee for the Swiss Reformation—not just for Zwinglianism but for the Calvinism of Geneva in the next generation.

(e) Zwingli and politics

Zwingli saw the need to be active in politics in order to further the Reformation. He sometimes attended Council meetings and he influenced voters to ensure that the necessary legislation was passed to abolish the Mass and remove the trappings of Roman Catholicism from the churches. He also made his views known on non-religious issues; even before he became a reformer he had campaigned against the Swiss selling their services as mercenaries. This involvement in politics has sometimes been seen as a move to create a theocracy, a state controlled by priests or, more specifically, by Zwingli himself. Zwingli would have indignantly denied this.

In 1523 in his commentary on the *Sixty Seven Articles*, Zwingli made it clear that Church and state were to be separate. The popes had failed to maintain that distinction, he thought, and so had become politicians rather than spiritual leaders. Zwingli stated a view similar to Luther's that the secular authorities should be obeyed by everyone; he did not claim any special authority for priests.

There were instances, however, where spiritual and secular affairs overlapped, one such being marriage. When a couple wanted to separate they were both abandoning a union made before God and breaking a civil contract. So to decide divorce cases it was necessary for clergy and magistrates to join together. But this is far from an indication of theocracy—in the marital court there were four magistrates and only two ministers.

Public morality was also of concern to both the clergy and the magistrates. In March 1530 a code of conduct was issued which affirmed that church-going was compulsory, restricted the sale of alcohol and forbade certain games which might lead to disorder. (Surprisingly, chess was thought to be one such game.) This could be interpreted as Zwingli taking control of the lives of Zurich's citizens, even as something approaching totalitarianism. However, such legislation was not new; many medieval cities had passed laws governing public morality. And the councillors of Zurich had issued the code of conduct quite willingly —it had not been imposed by Zwingli.

(f) Zwingli and war

One final area where Zwingli was politically active was with regard to neighbouring cantons. He supported the foundation in 1527 of a defensive league of seven reformed Swiss cities called the Christian Civic Union. He was keen to spread the Reformation and he pressed Zurich's Council to be expansionist in its policies. Zurich was one of the four protectors of the Abbey of St Gall, which controlled a territory to the north. When there was an election to the post of abbot which could be disputed, Zurich moved in on that territory. Other areas particularly under issue were the subject territories in north eastern Switzerland jointly administered by Zurich and other cantons. In these territories, Zurich claimed that the local people had the right to reform their parishes; the five Catholic cantons of central Switzerland asserted that only a majority vote amongst the 13 cantons could make such innovations in religion and in 1529 they formed the 'Christian Alliance' with Ferdinand of Austria to protect their position. The scene was set for conflict.

The specific cause of war was the right of Unterwalden, one of the Catholic cantons, to appoint in 1529 the new governor of the Freie Aemter, one of the jointly administered territories, of strategic importance to both Protestants and Catholics. Zwingli was determined to stop the Catholics gaining this advantage so he threatened to leave Zurich unless the Council agreed to a declaration of war. The councillors, keen enough on expansion and confident of Zurich's superior military strength, did not need too much persuading and in June war was declared on the Catholic cantons. The problem was that Zwingli's influence did not extend to Berne which doubted that faith could be brought 'by means of spears and halberds' and which did not want to disrupt the Swiss Confederation with civil war. Berne forced a compromise on the combatants. The Catholic cantons did agree to give up their 'Christian Alliance' and that local majorities in jointly administered territories could decide on reform. But this first Peace of Kappel of 1529 had frustrated Zwingli's hopes that war would lead to a united Protestant Switzerland.

Zwingli did not give up. He continued to work towards the political downfall of the Catholic cantons. He was encouraged by Philip of Hesse's aggressive stance towards the Catholics in Germany after the Diet of Augsburg in 1530 had failed to solve the religious problem there. He had hopes that Francis I would see the light and join the evangelical cause. He was well pleased by the economic blockade which the Protestant cantons imposed on the Catholics in 1530. The trouble this time was that it provoked the five Catholic cantons of central Switzerland to declare war before Zurich was ready to resist them. Zwingli was politically active but that does not mean he was altogether politically realistic.

Earlier in his career Zwingli had been an army chaplain and had come to despise war fought for human profit. But this war was fought for God and Zwingli went with the army, such as it was, to join in the fighting. The Battle of Kappel in October 1531 was a disaster for the forces of Zurich and Zwingli himself was killed. His enemies quartered his body, burnt it and mixed the ashes with dung. Zwingli had been one of the early victims of those religious wars which were to plague Europe for generations. As an active citizen as well as a reformer he had tried to transform Zurich, with a view to transforming all Switzerland, and had entered politics as necessary. The result was that the Swiss Reformation had both furthered the civic aspect of the Reformation but also helped to embroil it in political conflict.

After the second Peace of Kappel in November 1531 Zurich gave up its expansionist policies in north eastern Switzerland and allowed its contacts with German Protestant forces to lapse. Zwingli was succeeded by Henry Bullinger, a dedicated, effective reformer like his predecessor but more prepared to keep out of politics. With Berne maintaining a low profile, the Reformation in Switzerland was only to develop political and international aspects again when John Calvin began work in Geneva. In the meantime, the Radical Reformation which had begun in Zurich in the mid 1520s was to have both a political and an international impact.

3. The Radical Reformation

(a) The origins of Anabaptism

Zwingli insisted that reform must be introduced gradually so as not to leave behind those of a naturally conservative temperament. He recognised the need for order and so worked in co-operation with the magistrates. Not all of Zwingli's followers in the years after 1523 saw it his way. Some followed instead his emphasis on the Bible as the sole authority and took it to what they saw as its logical conclusion. Not finding any clear instance of infant baptism in the Scriptures they insisted that it should be abandoned and replaced by the baptism of adults. On this issue they refused to tarry for those more conservative or for the decision of the magistrates. These were the people who were first labelled as Anabaptists.

The simple ceremony in Zurich in 1525 when Conrad Grebel re-baptised George Blaurock, who then re-baptised others present, would seem to most of us to be entirely inoffensive. To Zwingli and most of his contemporaries, it threatened anarchy. Infant baptism meant that everyone in a community became a member of the Church; adult baptism meant that every individual could choose for himself whether to join—or not to join—the Church and that might lead to competing religious sects with a divided community as a result. Zwingli, like Luther, felt the need to argue from circumstantial evidence in the Bible that infant baptism must be the rule and he condemned his former followers who had become Anabaptists.

Baptism was not the only issue. The Anabaptists wanted to separate themselves off from the official Church in other ways. They tried to stop paying tithes, the dues paid to support the officially appointed ministers. They wanted to elect their own ministers rather than have them vetted by the authorities. They exploited the tensions between the city and the surrounding countryside it ruled, persuading some of the rural parishes around Zurich, starting in Zollikon, to make changes in religion without reference to the city magistrates. As K Deppermann put it, 'The tension which had existed since the later Middle Ages between the city and its rural communities was one of the principal causes of the origin and spread of Anabaptism'. In being a threat to the existence of an official Church, the Anabaptists were necessarily a political threat as well. Anabaptist involvement in the Peasants' War of 1525 served to confirm this.

The political threat was made even clearer by the Schleitheim Confession of 1527. The Anabaptists, once persecution had begun, could not form a single coherent movement but this was the nearest they came to a manifesto of their views. In some ways it was a moderate document. Rebellion was rejected as a means to religious reform. The basic Protestant belief in the authority of the Bible was upheld against the spiritualists, those who relied on individual inspiration alone. But there was also the extreme view that once an adult was baptised and began to live the life of a perfect Christian, disciplined only by his religious brethren, the state would become irrelevant. The Anabaptist was not to serve the state in any office, he was not to bear arms in support of the state and he was not to swear oaths of loyalty. For sixteenth century rulers this was unacceptable. It threatened their power at its roots.

Zwingli continued his attack on the Anabaptists in words, justifying the existence of the state as the only way of keeping order in a corrupt world. He condemned the notion that a perfect Christian life was possible given that all men are necessarily sinners. He denied the existence of free will which the Anabaptists claimed they were exercising when they chose the path of righteousness. The authorities were to go further than words in Zurich and elsewhere as Anabaptism spread, in seeking to persecute the recalcitrant Anabaptists out of existence.

(b) The persecution of Anabaptists

In 1526 the Council in Zurich passed a law prescribing the death penalty for unrepentant Anabaptists. The following year a leading Anabaptist, Felix Mantz, was drowned in Lake Zurich, a punishment thought appropriate for one who insisted on adult baptism. As a result the Anabaptists left Zurich, dispersing to remote Alpine communities or other parts of central Europe and along the Rhine. But few parts of Europe were safe for them as other authorities followed Zurich's lead and legislated against them. In 1528 an Imperial edict imposed the death penalty on them and one of the few things agreed by Lutherans and Catholics at the Diet of Speyer the following year was that this should be followed up as a matter of urgency.

In only a few areas were the Anabaptists tolerated. Bucer persuaded the authorities in Strasbourg that they should remain unmolested; he regarded the Swiss Brethren, as they were known, as sheep who had gone astray and should be coaxed back into the fold. Up to 2000 of them found refuge in Strasbourg, although only until 1534 when the Lutheran line, which excluded such radicals absolutely, was accepted by the city. Another area where Anabaptists found toleration was the lands of Philip of Hesse. As he showed at the Colloquy of Marburg in 1529, he was interested only in uniting Protestants in order to stand up to the threat posed by the Catholics. His lack of dogmatism regarding the variations of Protestantism seems to have been shared by some of the noblemen of Moravia where, there being no strong central authority to interfere, sympathetic lords could provide a haven even for those radicals who practised a primitive communism.

Even though these areas of toleration existed, the Anabaptists were dispersed. They lost what coherence they had had in Zurich as a small movement. They were no longer the champions of rural communities with regard to free elections, tithes and village autonomy so they lost their mass support. Persecuted and generally scattered in small groups, they became more socially as well as religiously sectarian, cut off from larger communities. And the more persecuted and scattered they were, the more their faith was confirmed. They were sustained by *nachfolge* —their sufferings were the sufferings of Christ and were to be welcomed rather than feared. In Augsburg in 1527 the so-called Martyr's Synod was held in which missionary work was called for as a matter of urgency; they believed that the world was about to end and the faithful must be gathered in before the Day of Doom arrived. They also anticipated martyrdom as the Bible prophesied that the Antichrist would strike before Jesus came again to judge the world. And they were right about the martyrdom. The more martyrs there were the more convinced were the survivors of the righteousness of their cause.

As Anabaptism became more fragmented, greater scope developed for a black legend to develop about them. Horror stories relating to one group or a few individuals could be taken as isolated examples; where stories were simply fabricated there was no way of giving them the lie. One Hans Hergot, for instance, preached that the rule of the Holy Spirit was about to be established and that would eliminate the nobility and bring in the age of the common man. He was beheaded in Leipzig in 1526 but fear of his like, especially in the aftermath of the Peasants' War, lived on. There was a story about some Anabaptists who made love on an altar to prove their purity. The truth of such a story was taken for granted; it fitted in well enough with the generally assumed deviancy of Anabaptists. Balthasar Hübmaier worked through landed nobility in Moravia and upheld the authority of the state. But he was not remembered for his relative moderation; he was burnt at the stake in 1528 and his wife was drowned. Much more notable news from Moravia was the establishment of the *Bruderhof* by Jacob Hutter. He judged that property was selfish and all should be abandoned to God. A system of communal farming was established without any private property. Hutter even managed to win the support of some lords who exempted the Anabaptists from taxes and services. But, however peaceful and voluntary and unusual this communal experiment was, it caused an early version of a 'red scare'. Philip Melanchthon, Luther's close supporter, was loud in his condemnation of all aspects of Anabaptism and, in particular, their supposedly widespread communism.

The Anabaptists were few in number, under one percent of the population and often in groups of five and six. They were drawn from different classes but there were few powerful men amongst them. Artisans and yeoman farmers predominated in most areas with a few aristocrats in Moravia and more peasants in Württemberg and other areas nearer to Switzerland. Their aim in general was to separate themselves off from the larger, sinful society rather than to subvert it. Still, they were regarded as a profound threat to true religion and the social order. The fear they inspired seems out of all proportion to their capacity to do harm. But a liberal society was inconceivable to most in Early Modern Europe and any threats to authority had to be dealt with severely before the radicalism spread like an epidemic. Also, if one was disputing the issue of the danger of Anabaptism with the like of Philip Melanchthon, he might well have strengthened his argument by referring to the Peasants' War and later to the blood-letting at Münster in 1535.

(c) Apocalypse at Münster

There was a strong pacifist strain in Anabaptism. Ironically, that was regarded as a threat by rulers who needed to command troops made up of their subjects. However, as Anabaptism fragmented, its characteristics could vary enormously. Melchior Hoffmann represented a more militant strain, looking to the violent transformation of the world rather than withdrawal from it. He wandered in the Rhineland and as far as Sweden prophesying a violent apocalypse, the triumph of the 144 000 virgins at the end of time, and all this to take place in 1533. He identified himself with the Anabaptists from 1529 although, like those called Spiritualists, he relied much on an 'inner light' for religious guidance rather than the Bible. He announced that he was the second Elijah preparing for the day of wrath when all the unrighteous would be cut down. Shortly after the end of time was due in 1533, he found himself in prison where he was to die in 1543, but his followers, the Melchiorites, most of them in the Netherlands, awaited that day of wrath.

Their opportunity to prepare the way for it came in 1534 in the German city of Münster just over the border from the Netherlands. The year before, after a struggle to free itself from the power of its Bishop, the Reformation had triumphed in Münster. The city's mayor, Bernt Knipperdolling, had met Melchior Hoffmann in Sweden and approved of the radicals. From the beginning of 1534 Melchiorites poured into the city. Jan Matthys, a baker from Haarlem, and Jan Beukels, formerly a Leiden tailor, took charge, forcibly rebaptising the population, Matthys declared the abolition of private property. Resistance to these measures was overcome by a mob which supported the Melchiorites, having been stirred up into apocalyptic belief by the earlier struggles to introduce the Reformation and by the threat of the Bishop of Münster who was gathering his forces to besiege the city.

Under siege conditions, an ever greater hysteria seized Münster. Matthys believed God had commanded him to face the Bishop in battle and had granted him invulnerability for the purpose. He was killed by the Bishop's troops. Jan Beukels then became the dictator of the city. He made sins punishable by death, including scandal-mongering or complaining. Polygamy was introduced and Jan himself married 16 wives, although he reduced their number when he had one beheaded for impertinence. He declared himself to be King Jan and reigned over his holy city-kingdom in the grip of terror and famine as the siege continued into 1535.

Finally the besieging forces, the Catholic Bishop now aided even by the Lutheran Philip of Hesse, found weak spots in the walls and took the city by storm in June 1535. After a slow, painful death, the corpses of King Jan and Knipperdolling were suspended in a cage from a church steeple as a sign that there had been a day of wrath but not the one the Melchiorites had anticipated. It was a symbolic day of wrath for all Anabaptists. Whatever their various, often pacifist, views they were identified with the dangerous and lunatic regime at Münster.

(d) The survival and diversity of the Radical Reformation

After Münster, the persecution of Anabaptists intensified. Some 2000–3000 lost their lives in the Netherlands within forty years. This did not exterminate them, however. They lived quietly, seeking to avoid the gaze of the authorities rather than preaching their beliefs too enthusiastically. Numbers were kept up and some unity was attained through the missionary work of Menno Simons between 1536 and his death in 1561. His *Foundation of Christian Doctrine* made clear the ways of saintliness expected of believers and maintained the separatism of Anabaptists from official Churches with their demand for infant baptism, and from the state with its demand for the swearing of oaths which Anabaptists said Christ had forbidden. Menno journeyed for most of his 25 missionary years through the Netherlands and northern Germany as far as Danzig, showing how the faith could be preserved under severe persecution. In 1572, just over a decade after his death, his followers, the Mennonites, were granted toleration in Holland and later in parts of Germany.

The various Anabaptist sects—the Mennonites, the Swiss Brethren, the Moravian Brethren and other subdivisions—were not the only radicals to emerge in the aftermath of the Reformation. There were other yet more exclusive groups, sometimes more extreme, sometimes more intellectual. There were the Spiritualists who rejected even the Bible, that 'paper pope' as they called it, in favour of inner spiritual revelation. There were the Evangelical Rationalists, an offshoot of Italian humanism, who rejected the Trinity and were the first Unitarians.

Some historians now dispute the significance of the Radical Reformation. Even the term itself, given currency by G H Williams' exhaustive study *The Radical Reformation* published in 1962, has come into question. Interest in the radicals had grown in the 1960s amidst an atmosphere of anti-authoritarianism and the dissenters of four centuries earlier acquired a new academic importance. This merged with a particular interest in America, given that some of the sects, such as the Mennonites and the Schwenkfeldians, had migrated there to escape persecution in Europe and still exist. Now that the atmosphere has changed since the 1960s, more emphasis has been placed on how marginal the radicals were to the larger society of Early Modern Europe, how little institutional and political impact they really made.

The radicals, however, cannot be written off by historians any more than Luther or Zwingli could ignore them. They had deep roots in the heretical sects of the Middle Ages, as C-P Clasen has shown, and they have persisted through to the modern day when they are allowed to practise their brand of religion unmolested. In the sixteenth century, they demonstrated what Christian freedom could mean in a way that the 'magisterial' reformers had just not anticipated. And they did much, however unintentionally, to fashion the Reformation when they forced the realisation that organisation and discipline were vital if the reformed Church were not to splinter into innumerable small sects. More than any other reformer, it was John Calvin who provided that organisation and discipline.

4. Calvin and Calvinism

(a) John Calvin
The Calvin family of Noyon in northern France were, in today's terms, upwardly mobile. John, born in 1509, was all set for a lucrative career in the Church or the law. However, in the course of his studies, John came under the influence first of Christian Humanists and then of those who believed in Reformation, not just reform. It is not certain when he was converted but he was implicated with Protestants in 1533 and had to flee France. He wandered for two years visiting Swiss reformers and the

Duchess Renée of Ferrara, a French princess who created a small refuge for Protestant thinkers in her husband's Italian duchy. By 1536 he was also ready to publish the *Institutes of the Christian Religion* which was to be the religious handbook of all Calvinists.

(b) *The Institutes of the Christian Religion*

The *Institutes* was the single most important book written by any of the Protestant reformers. Luther's thought had emerged through innumerable pamphlets and, although his helper Philip Melanchthon had tried to impose some order on Lutheran ideas in his *Loci Communes*, it was Calvin's *Institutes* which provided a truly systematic statement of Protestant thinking. He announced it as 'the Basic Teaching of the Christian Religion comprising almost the whole sum of godliness and whatever it is necessary to know on the doctrine of salvation.'

Calvin had the advantage of being a second generation reformer, summarising a Protestant position after nearly twenty years of debate with Catholics. And he had the intellectual power to know the Bible and the writings of early Church Fathers so well and to clarify his ideas so effectively that he could never be forced to back down on a theological point or express uncertainty. The *Institutes* was to expand through several editions from the six chapters of 1536 to a completely re-organised 80 chapters in 1559 but in order to explain in greater detail or deal with objections rather than make any change to the underlying principles. This publication makes the other aspects of Calvin's biography seem almost inconsequential. As E W Monter has put it: 'Calvin was not so much a personality as a mind . . . In most cases (his) influence was based upon the fact that he knew more about something than anybody else, expressed himself about it more readily, and seldom changed his mind.'

Much of the *Institutes* was in line with Lutheran and Zwinglian teaching. *Sola fide* was taken as the guiding principle, only faith being able to make up for mankind's entire feebleness with regard to obeying the laws of God. The priesthood of all believers was accepted as a logical consequence of that and *sola scriptura*, the Bible alone being the source of authority for Christians rather than the traditions of the Church or the statements of a pope.

On the subject of the sacraments Calvin agreed with the other reformers (once Luther had dropped penance) that there were only two, baptism and the Eucharist. However, Calvin was distinctive in his doctrine of the Eucharist. He rejected the early Zwinglian teaching which seemed to reduce the Eucharist to nothing more than a commemoration of the Last Supper. He denied that it was 'a vain and empty symbol' and asserted that the believer is 'fed with the substance of Christ'. On the other hand, he could not accept that the believer was fed with the *physical* substance of Christ, as Luther maintained. For Calvin, Christ could not be contained within corruptible material things so it was as a real but spiritual substance that He fed the believer at the

Eucharist. Calvin also felt that the whole debate got off the point of the Eucharist's importance as a seal of God's promised grace. As he said of the working of the Eucharist: 'I rather experience than understand it.' Luther was more dogmatic about his understanding and fell out with Calvin on this issue. There were other points of difference but it was the debate over the Eucharist which again stopped reformers from joining forces and led to the setting up of separate Protestant Churches. For a time the Eucharist was one of the critical issues which kept Zwinglians and Calvinists apart as well, although a compromise was to be reached by 1549.

In the *Institutes* Calvin developed the traditional doctrine of predestination. St Augustine had written that God has predestined those who are to go to Heaven (the elect) while leaving the rest to a fate determined by their sin, and Luther had followed him in this view. Calvin's doctrine, though, earned the name of *double* predestination, given that God made a definite decision as to who to consign to Hell (the reprobate) as well as who to select for Heaven. For Calvin, this was arguing a basic principle, the overwhelming majesty of God, through to its logical conclusion. For his opponents it turned God into a harsh and even capricious figure who was prepared to create men just to cast them into everlasting flames.

The controversy it provoked made double predestination a far more significant issue than Calvin had ever intended. He did not claim that it had any practical effects in that no man could tell who was elect and who not. He said that, as long as someone claimed to be a Christian, acted like a Christian and participated in the sacraments, he or she must be assumed to be elect. And in the case of those who failed such tests, it might just mean that they had not yet been brought to Christ. As for the individual's own salvation, the simple existence of faith was assurance of being elect. But moderate statements like this did not lessen the argument over the doctrine. Calvin found himself giving it more and more space in later editions of the *Institutes* as he justified himself against his critics. It was to become one of the distinguishing features of Calvinism even though much of that was due to the crude emphasis on it given by Beza, Calvin's successor. Calvin had aimed for balance in his theological scheme, as T H L Parker has stressed, but that was difficult to maintain amidst the religious turmoil of the sixteenth century.

(c) Geneva in the sixteenth century

Geneva was a frontier city of some 10 000 people between France and Switzerland. It was part of the Duchy of Savoy and technically under the direct control of its Bishop, but by the 1520s it was seeking to free itself and enter into a pact with one or other of the Swiss cities.

The city's Bishop in the 1520s was Pierre de la Baume. His tactic was 'divide and rule', backing first one faction and then another until no-one trusted him. In 1526 some Genevans were at Berne negotiating an alliance with that powerful Swiss city. De la Baume sent two messengers, one supporting the negotiations and one opposing them. Rather than 'divide and rule', the Bishop's inconsistency allowed his opponents to take advantage of him. He was forced to leave the city and thereafter he tried bullying Geneva, placing it under an Interdict in 1528 (in effect a strike by the Church), varying that with offers of concessions. His habitually inconsistent policies got him nowhere. Geneva was quite secure given the protection of Berne although some rural nobility, rejoicing in the name of the Fraternity of the Spoon, did engage in guerrilla action on behalf of Savoy and had to be fought off.

Geneva was independent but not stable in the 1530s. Its three councils and its four chief magistrates, the Syndics, governed the city but they were still split into factions. And the future of the Church in Geneva was not clear. The Genevans themselves did little in the way of reform beyond overthrowing the power of the clergy. Berne, however, intervened and sent the reformer Guillaume Farel under a safe-conduct to Geneva. Exploiting fears of the Bishop's return and the popular unrest which had led to iconoclasm in the churches, Farel persuaded the authorities to suspend the Mass in 1535 and the Reformation in Geneva had begun. Savoy soon threatened further attacks in 1535 and 1536 but Berne's commitment proved firm enough to fend that off. As in the case of Zurich five years earlier, the power of Berne proved crucial in defending the independence of reformed cities in the region of Switzerland.

Farel, however, had not triumphed completely. There was a faction opposed to him known as the Articulants who rejected any religious regulation by Protestant clergy just as much as they had rejected that by Catholics. Farel felt he needed support and so he was delighted when John Calvin, diverted by troop movements from his original route to Strasbourg, passed through Geneva. Calvin at first would not agree to stay in that troubled city but Farel accused him of refusing the task God had decreed for him. So Calvin stayed although he was never to feel much affection for Geneva. On his deathbed he was to recall how, on his arrival in the city, '. . . there was no reformation. Everything was in disorder'. His opinion was to improve little: 'I have lived here amid continual bickerings . . . For you are a perverse and unhappy nation, and though there are good men in it the nation is perverse and wicked . . .'. But once Calvin had accepted that God's task for him was to serve in the 'perverse and unhappy nation' of Geneva he applied himself with a will.

In 1537 Farel and Calvin put forward their blueprint for the reform of the Church, the 21 *Articles on the Organisation of the Church and its Worship at Geneva*. The councils accepted the *Articles* although with some modifications to reduce clerical control. Participation in Communion (the Eucharist) was to be compulsory, not once a week as the reformers wanted but once every three months. The reformers had provided for the excommunication of any whose views were heretical or behaviour outrageous—that was accepted by the all-important Small Council but the Councillors insisted that they should have a role in deciding when such a penalty should be imposed. The reformers had largely got their way but they failed to recognise the strength of feeling with regard to the renewal of clerical control in a city which had so recently staged a revolution against the clergy which had governed it. A Confession of Faith was put to the people with demands that every individual sign it. There was much reluctance to accept such orders from foreign reformers. There were refusals to sign and rumours spread through the city that Farel and Calvin were agents of the French seeking some political advantage.

The reformers became impatient and in 1538 tried to deny Communion to those who refused to sign the Confession of Faith. The Council, increasingly dominated by the hostile Articulants, then stepped in to restrain the reformers from exercising an independent power. They were not permitted to deny Communion on their own decision to anyone and, as an indication of who was in charge, the Council decreed that the Church of Geneva should adopt certain of the services of the Church of Berne. Farel and Calvin responded by refusing to celebrate the Eucharist on Easter Day. The situation was not eased by a blind friend of Farel's referring to the magistrates as a bunch of drunks. Relations between the reformers and the secular authorities had broken down and the only solution was for Farel and Calvin to leave Geneva.

Calvin had displayed a clear vision of doctrine and the requirements of a strong, disciplined Church but he had shown little political sensitivity. Geneva needed direction after its revolutionary years in the early sixteenth century but would not submit quickly to a new clerical yoke. In 1538 therefore Calvin continued his journey to Strasbourg which he had broken off two years earlier, but he went there as an exile from Geneva.

(d) Calvin in Strasbourg

In Strasbourg the Reformation was well established and the city's leading reformer, Martin Bucer, welcomed Calvin who became pastor there to the Protestant exiles from France. As well as a new job, he acquired a wife after his friends had persuaded him to marry so that his domestic life could be better organised and his irritability softened. He did not allow marriage to distract him from his studies, however. In 1539 he published a new edition of the *Institutes* three times the length of the original. As a result of this work Calvin's reputation as a leading Protestant thinker was spreading and becoming international.

As his failure in Geneva had shown, however, Calvin had much to learn about the setting up of a reformed Church. It was from Bucer that he learned how to reconcile the authority of the Church with that of the magistrates and councillors through the close involvement of the latter in Church government. *(See 'Ecclesiastical Ordinances' on p. 284.)* And Calvin saw how important education could be in informing both mind and character when he taught in Jakob Sturm's Academy in Strasbourg. Sturm's Academy was to be the model for Geneva's own twenty years later. Calvin, already the master of doctrine, was now learning more about institutions.

While Calvin was in Strasbourg Geneva was once again suffering from lack of direction. The two leading ministers who had replaced Farel and Calvin proved to be inferior as preachers and organisers. An attempt was made by Archbishop Sadoleto to bring the Genevans back within the Catholic fold. In 1539 he wrote a letter to the city regretting past abuses and suggesting that all could be rectified once the Genevans had returned to the faith of their fathers. It seemed only Calvin could offer a satisfactory reply to this. From his exile he strengthened the Protestant case in Geneva by writing to Sadoleto pointing out the doctrine rather than just the abuses which, he said, lay at the root of the Catholic Church's corruption.

It was not just the religious situation which opened a way back to Geneva for Calvin; political circumstances were also very different. Two of the four Syndics (chief magistrates), who belonged to the Articulants faction and had opposed Calvin, were disgraced after they bungled some negotiations with Berne. In 1540 the remaining two Syndics of the Articulants faction got themselves involved in a brawl in which a man was murdered. One Syndic was executed and the other, trying to escape through a window, slipped and was killed. The supporters of Calvin now had the upper hand politically and, given that the two ministers who had taken over in Geneva had given up and left, arrangements were made to invite Calvin to return.

Calvin wrote to Farel: 'Whenever I call to mind the wretchedness of my life there, how can it not be but that my very soul must shudder at any proposal for my return?' But he did go back to Geneva in 1541 and now he had more constructive ideas on how to manage the affairs of the Church there.

(e) The Calvinist Church

As soon as he returned to Geneva in 1541, Calvin picked up where he had left off to the extent of preaching on the verse of the Bible where he had ended his last sermon in the city 3 years previously. Immediately, Calvin presented to the Council his plan for a re-organised Church. This was the *Ecclesiastical Ordinances* of 1541.

Learning from Bucer, Calvin proposed four types of officers in the Church. These were:

1   *Pastors*. Their duties were to preach, to teach, to administer the sacraments and to guide the people in a Christian way of life. They were to be chosen by those who were already pastors and their appointment was to be confirmed by the Council. The Council added the words 'as it thinks fit' to the sentence about its confirmation of appointments. It was clearly not going to be regarded as a rubber stamp, and Calvin, with his newly learned tact and diplomacy, accepted that.

2   *Doctors*. Their task was to instruct the people in true doctrine, so taking some of the load off the shoulders of the pastors.

3   *Deacons*. Looking after the sick and the needy was their role. In line with humanist reforms in other cities, both Catholic and Protestant, an aim was to keep beggars off the streets through poor relief, an early

version of the welfare state. This was especially necessary given the ending in Geneva of support for the poor through Catholic alms-giving.

4 *Lay Elders.* These were to be twelve worthy citizens whose duty was to supervise every person's conduct, issue warnings and, where necessary, report those who were not up to the mark to the Company of Pastors. They were to come from every part of the city so that they could keep an eye on all of it. They were chosen by the Small Council from amongst their fellow Councillors in Geneva. Calvin was not setting up a Church in rivalry to the authorities of the state, he was incorporating those authorities into the Church.

These lay elders were not Calvin's invention; the reformer of Basle, Oecolampadius, and Bucer in Strasbourg had both used them. However, they gave Calvinism its characteristic of strong social control, given that the lay elders joined with the pastors in the consistory, a court to supervise beliefs and morals, which the *Ecclesiastical Ordinances* established as follows:

> A day should be fixed for the consistory. The elders should meet once a week with the ministers on a Thursday to ensure that there is no disorder in the Church and to discuss together any necessary action to put things right . . .
>
> If any one fails to come to Church to such a degree that there is real dislike for the community of believers manifested, or if any one shows that he cares nothing for the ecclesiastical order, let him be reprimanded, and if he is reasonable let him be sent back in a friendly way. If however he goes from bad to worse, after having been warned three times, let him be cut off from the Church and be denounced to the magistrate . . .
>
> All this must be done in such a way that the ministers have no civil jurisdiction nor use anything but the spiritual sword of the Word of God as St Paul commands them; nor is the authority of the consistory to diminish in any way that of the magistrate or ordinary justice . . . In cases where, in future, there may be a need to impose punishments . . . the council . . . will judge and sentence according to the needs of the case.

1 *What were the organisational strengths of the consistory?*
2 *How was pressure gradually built up on the wayward or rebellious in order to make them conform?*
3 *Of the above three paragraphs which one was added to Calvin's original proposals by the Council and why?*

Menna Prestwich has argued that 'Calvin's revolutionary innovation was to require his churches to be established on the basis of a consistory'. There was already a consistory in Zurich, it must be said, but it had not been able to impose the same social and moral control as Calvin's consistory did in Geneva. In 1546, for instance, Amblard Corne, a leading citizen of Geneva, a Syndic and President of the consistory itself, was reprimanded for dancing at a wedding. (Dancing was thought to be dangerous to sexual morality.) Corne submitted. And it was the consistory which was to be the key element in Calvinist Churches all over Europe. Involving as far as possible the leaders of a community ('the aristocratic principle of the consistory', as Beza called it), it was able to impose religious order on the rest of that community.

If one of the pastors was wayward he could be summoned before the consistory but more than this threat was needed to maintain the standard of spiritual leadership. Calvin had a low opinion of his fellow pastors. He wrote in a letter in 1542: 'Our other colleagues are rather a hindrance than a help to us: they are rude and self-conceited, have no zeal and less learning'. Calvin could dominate the Company of Pastors in Geneva through force of intellect and character but he saw the need to create a strong corporate identity. The Company of Pastors therefore met once a week to study Scripture and once every three months for what was known as the *grabeau*. The *grabeau* was a session of mutual criticism. In the words of T H L Parker it 'was a little day of judgment when, flattery and convention laid aside, each man saw himself through the eyes of his fellows, and, if he were wise, harboured no resentment but knew the uniquely joyful release of voluntary humiliation.' This is an idealistic view of a most effective psychological technique. With the prospect of the *grabeau* each pastor would be more thoughtful in his approach to his work and his life in general. Each time a pastor admitted a weakness the Calvinist values of the Company as a whole could be reinforced. The *grabeau* caused the individual to merge much more into the group.

The consistory and the *grabeau* gave Calvinism an institutional strength which Lutheranism lacked. Lutheran pastors had no similarly effective way of disciplining their congregations and they themselves were only irregularly supervised by superintendents and visitation committees. But important as the consistory and the *grabeau* were as institutions, it was Calvin who animated them and the Calvinist Church in general.

Calvin trained Genevan congregations in the certainties of his religion. After the turmoil of the years before he arrived in Geneva, most citizens were prepared to conform and listen to their irritable but still inspiring preacher. General respect for Calvin guaranteed the maintenance of his Church in Geneva as he had established it through the *Ecclesiastical Ordinances* and developed it through his writings and sermons. This did not mean, however, that Geneva ceased completely to be 'a perverse and unhappy nation'. After Calvin's return to Geneva in 1541 there were still opponents who helped to fashion the Calvinist Church through their challenges.

(f) Calvin and his opponents

Calvin faced three types of opposition within Geneva. There were pastors who would not or could not submit to the discipline of the *grabeau* and the consistory. There were theological opponents who protested that Calvin's pronouncements on some issues were too extreme. Finally, there were the political opponents who would not submit to Calvin's moral authority and who wanted to limit his power as much as possible.

In line with Calvin's earlier experience it was the political contest which was most difficult to win.

The pastors fell into line fairly rapidly. By 1546 all was well in Geneva itself, and the surrounding rural parishes, where the most stubbornly individualistic ministers were to be found, had largely been purged of the incompetent and the wayward. It did, however, take three years to dismiss one unsuitable minister, Philippe de Ecclesia, because of political opposition to Calvin on the Council.

There had also been opposition from theologians, more serious in that they gained publicity outside Geneva. Sebastian Castellio had been appointed as principal of the college in Geneva with Calvin's approval. But they soon fell out over interpretation of the Bible and, in particular, the Song of Songs which Castellio described as 'a lascivious and obscene poem'. By 1544 Castellio's attacks on Calvin and the Company of Pastors had become so general that he was forced to leave. Nonetheless Calvin was not vindictive, as he had tried to secure a teaching job for Castellio at Lausanne.

A former monk called Jerome Bolsec met Calvin in a face-to-face debate in 1551 which did more to threaten the latter's theological supremacy. Bolsec argued that 'Scripture does not say we are saved because God has elected us, but because we have believed in Jesus Christ'. This was a direct attack on the doctrine of predestination. Calvin's response was to overwhelm Bolsec with his superior knowledge of the Bible and St Augustine. The minutes of their debate record that 'M Jerome did not know what to say'. In 1551 Bolsec was exiled from Geneva so that 'the sacrament might not be polluted by him'.

It was the Council which exiled Bolsec. They still wanted to limit Calvin's authority but not at the expense of allowing views to spread that might be heretical. This was as much for the sake of social unity as religious unity—the experience of many other cities and countries demonstrated how religious differences could lead to violence.

The most outrageous opponent of such unity was Michael Servetus. He was a disbeliever in the Trinity, like some of the other radicals discussed earlier. He wandered from country to country taking on an assumed name once his writings had made him notorious. He learned medicine and even became physician to the Archbishop of Vienne but his urge to enter theological debate was irrepressible. He recognised Calvin as one of his most serious opponents and exchanged letters with him until Calvin decided he was irreformable. When Servetus had been recognised in France in 1553 he was forced to go on his travels again and he decided to go to Geneva to hear Calvin preach. He was recognised there and brought to trial for heresy. Calvin's condemnation of him was backed up formally by the various reformed Churches which were consulted, and Catholics and Lutherans alike were united in approval of the execution of this arch-heretic. (He was burnt even though Calvin argued for more merciful beheading.) Calvin's international reputation was much enhanced by the Servetus case.

Calvin could rely on the Council to crush heretical opposition but the Council was the source of much political opposition for a decade and more after his return to Geneva. From 1545 a faction emerged known as the Libertines because they would not submit to Calvin's moral authority. One of the most awkward of the Libertines was Philibert Berthelier. He and his friends would interrupt Calvin's sermons with coughing. When Calvin complained, Berthelier threatened to burp and fart instead. This was an irritant but the powerful Favre family was even more difficult to control. Members of the family were accused of a variety of sins from sexual immorality to playing darts instead of attending Easter Communion. The Favres were continually called before the consistory where their 'astounding insolence' was recorded in the minutes along with their extensive use of obscene gestures. A particularly dedicated opponent to Calvin was M. Favre's son-in-law, Ami Perrin, who was the Captain-General.

Perrin had been a supporter of Calvin when he had returned to Geneva in 1541 but he became one of the leading Libertines. This was not just due to a moral unruliness or his family connection with the Favre clan. Perrin was ambitious and came to see Calvin as a rival for political influence. Perrin's political career had its ups and downs—he was in prison for a time and was charged with treason in 1547 after some negotiations with the French—but by 1553 his fortunes reached a high point when he became first Syndic as well as Captain-General and the Libertine faction took control of the Council. The issue on which they chose to challenge Calvin was that of excommunication. Calvin viewed the exclusion of someone from the most important service of Communion as a spiritual matter but, given that membership of the Church and citizenship were then so closely interlinked, it was a sensitive political issue as well.

Berthelier and two others had insulted one of the pastors and had been excommunicated in 1552 without any objection from the Council. This willingness to accept the consistory's decision over excommunications was in line with Council policy since 1541. However, Perrin and his supporters asserted themselves in 1553 insisting that, after due apologies, Berthelier be allowed to take Communion. The controversy over this dragged on for 18 months. Calvin offered his resignation but Perrin and the others would not accept it. They had no fundamental religious opposition to the reformer but they did want to see him thoroughly tamed. The weakness of Perrin and his supporters, however, was that they could find no legal basis for denying the consistory the right to decide on excommunication. And then in February 1555 Perrin and his supporters lost the elections.

The Perrin faction had been too disruptive and too greedy, monopolising government posts for its own supporters. Finally, there was a brawl in May 1555 during which Perrin seized the black baton, the symbol of authority, of the new First Syndic—an act of treason. He fled the city and was condemned to death in his absence. The religious issue had clearly not been the only one but the overthrow of the Perrin faction meant an end to Libertine opposition. From 1555 until his death in 1564, Calvin dominated the Church in Geneva and his supporters controlled the Councils. This was so owing to Perrin's errors but also to the fact that Calvin had by now become indispensable and a new generation of Genevans had grown up who were much more willing to conform than the revolutionary generation of the 1520s and 1530s.

Calvin was triumphant and it seemed to some that Geneva was a new theocracy, a state ruled by its priests. This is an exaggeration. It was not Calvin himself or the Company of Pastors which passed judgement but the consistory, which included the lay elders nominated by the Council. Most cases anyway ended not in punishment imposed by the consistory but in reconciliation. Calvin had fought over the issue of excommunication because he thought it vital to the spiritual purity of the Church. He recognised that purely secular issues were no concern of the clergy and, unlike Zwingli, he did not attend all Council meetings. When he did attend he did not necessarily get his own way, as on the occasion when he demanded the arrest of the ambassador from Savoy on a charge of seduction. That would have been diplomatically unwise and the Council politely rejected his advice. Insofar as Calvin did play a dominant role in Geneva after 1555, it was because the rulers of the city respected his religious leadership rather than because they were blindly obedient or forced to obey.

It is true that the religious sphere was broad in the sixteenth century and that can make Calvin seem more interfering. There was a brief attempt to replace taverns with religious eating houses where grace would be said and there would be no idle gossip or swearing. There were many cases of the control of an individual's morals such as when Bonivard, the official historiographer, was forced to marry his house-keeper who had seemed too much like a concubine. Bonivard was in fact impotent and his wife and her lover, a servant, were executed for adultery in 1565. Such cases seem to us to bear the mark of a repressive regime. However, it was not all Calvin's doing: the magistrates had taken most of the initiative in the Bonivard case, for instance. And it was normal for city authorities to control closely the morality of citizens. As Gillian Lewis has stressed, the regulation of morals was 'designed not so much to transform the community so that it became more godly as to protect traditional decencies and preserve the status quo'. Calvin did not impose himself on Geneva: for all the opponents he had to face and the riots which Genevans were prone to stage, the city in general was prepared to accept his guidance.

(g) The expansion of Calvinism
By the 1550s Calvin had fallen out with Luther over the Eucharist but had come to an agreement with the Zwinglians in the *Consensus Tigurinus* of 1549. He kept up a constant correspondence with his fellow reformers, encouraging them and firmly letting them know his views. The Swiss

agreement was to be extended in 1566 with the Second Helvetic Confession. Calvinism had become dominant in the Swiss Reformation but its mission extended to the whole of Europe and in particular to France.

Geneva became home to large numbers of exiles, Calvin amongst them. In the 1550s alone there were 5000 immigrants to the city which itself only had a population of 10 000. Some of those immigrants had come to Geneva to be trained as missionaries for service in their own countries. There were to be 120 missions, peaking in 1559, with 32 to France alone.

Calvinism spread through these missions but Calvin was aware that the training was inadequate given that the Company of Pastors, only numbering 18 in Geneva and its rural parishes, was hard pressed to attend to its normal duties let alone prepare missionaries. Finally one of his long-term aims was realised when the money was raised for an Academy which opened in 1559. It incorporated the old school of Geneva and also offered courses at a higher level, principally in theology which the missionaries needed to offer the certainty to their congregations which Calvin offered to his.

As well as the Academy, Geneva's printing presses were crucial to the spread of Calvinism. Not just Calvin's works were published but also those of the exiles writing for their home markets. The psalms for French Protestants printed in 1561 and 1562 made up one of the biggest printing ventures in the sixteenth century. There was economic incentive here as well, with printing becoming the growth industry in Geneva.

The missionaries and Calvinist books were by no means guaranteed a friendly reception in the countries where they went. In France, for instance, persecution had steadily become more consistent and more severe since the 1520s. Calvin let his followers know what he expected of them in his *Letter to the Nicodemites* in 1544. Nicodemus had come to Jesus in secret and Calvin urged those who had embraced the reformed faith not to hide the fact behind a pretence of Catholicism. The only choice was to face up to persecution or to flee. Either way, it was a hard path to take but it may have been made easier by the Calvinist theories of Providence and predestination. There was the conviction that Calvinism would necessarily triumph over what were seen as the Catholic forces of darkness. Divine Providence was recognised when the Protestant military leader Coligny found a vital ford across the Loire: it was hailed, without irony, as being like Moses' crossing of the Red Sea. And if the individual had to face martyrdom for his faith, he went to his death in the belief that he was one of 'the elect', chosen of God. In his letters Calvin kept stressing how martyrdom was a sign of God's favour which should be greeted warmly.

Calvin's teaching was to suffer persecution rather than offer resistance to it but he has a reputation for having established a revolutionary ideology *(see p. 296 for a documentary exercise on his political thought)*. It is true that Calvinists were involved in armed resistance to sovereigns in France and the Netherlands but, as can be seen in Chapters XIV and

XV, this was due to local political circumstances rather than Calvin's political thought. Out of these conflicts there did arise some revolutionary theory but the authors of it, such as Beza, were writing after Calvin's death. In any case, more important for the survival of Calvinism in a hostile environment was its organisation.

When a few Calvinists, perhaps ten or twelve, had been converted in any one place, they gathered together in a conventicle for Bible reading and worship. Once there were enough to form a congregation a pastor was requested, possibly to be sent from Geneva, and a full parish organisation was set up including a consistory. Calvinist leaders in a locality would gather together in a colloquy to discuss common problems and policy. Beyond that, when there were enough churches in a province to warrant it, an assembly called a provincial synod could be held and ultimately a national synod.

Such a structure brought with it both flexibility and strength. The conventicles could spread in an almost cellular way, members of one moving off and setting up another. And if one conventicle was destroyed through persecution there were many others which could continue to grow and develop. But Calvinism was not just a religion of flexibly organised local groups; its organisation at regional and national level gave it great political strength.

The classic example of such a structure developing was France where Calvinists were known as Huguenots, a name deriving from the pro-Swiss faction in Geneva. Conventicles were set up with support from both inside and outside France. The government tried to close the frontier but booksellers and missionaries got through, often displaying ingenuity and heroism. Farel escaped from Metz on one occasion disguised in a cart full of lepers.

In the first place Calvinism was an urban movement. Artisans, such as cobblers with time to think and talk as they worked or printers with their high degree of literacy, made up the majority of Huguenots. Also being converted were urban élites—the lawyers, the merchants, the government officers—who were to dominate the consistories when they were set up from 1555. Calvin had delayed the setting up of consistories. He was cautious and had hopes of converting the rulers of France first in order to prevent any backlash. However, the growth of the Calvinist Church was running beyond Calvin's control, particularly in Paris.

The Paris Church was founded in 1555 and three years later there were demonstrations of 3000–4000 Huguenots singing psalms on the left bank of the Seine. This was provocative enough and some Calvinists were even more militant, anticipating civil war. It was also in Paris that the structure of the Calvinist Church was completed with the meeting in 1559 of a national synod. Calvin, still cautious, had opposed this meeting and, although he sent it advice, the synod reached its own decisions with regard to discipline and a Confession of Faith.

It was stated by Coligny that, by 1562, there were over 2150 Calvinist churches in France. This was an optimistic Huguenot estimate but the true number was probably not far short of 2000. Calvin and Geneva were regarded as sources of inspiration by these churches but they were too many to be controlled by them. Similarly, some 50 percent of the French nobility, bringing their supporters and dependent peasantry with them, had converted to Calvinism, but they very much followed their own policies. They provided the Calvinist churches with a parallel military organisation and, caught up in faction fighting with Catholic militants and with a crisis of Crown authority as well as religious conflict, they led the Huguenots of France into thirty years of civil war *(see Chapter XV for an account of this)*. Whatever Calvin's hopes for orderly conversion, Calvinism had become a revolutionary force.

The same was to occur in the Netherlands, ruled by Philip II of Spain. The contacts with Geneva were limited. In the 1560s there were no missionaries sent to the Netherlands although some preachers from there had visited Geneva. Most of those urging reform in the Netherlands were the so-called 'hedge-preachers' who would attract large numbers of people to leave the more closely regulated towns in order to attend a *prêche* in the countryside where they could hear 'the Word of God'. Calvin would probably have approved of the evangelical *prêche* but, as Phyllis Mack Crew has made clear, 'these early hedge-preachers were certainly Reformers in spirit, but they were not formal Calvinists'.

In 1567 the Duke of Alva had arrived in the Netherlands to punish the iconoclastic rioters and others who had rebelled in 1566 *(see Chapter XIV)*. His persecution of those of the reformed faith (irrespective of whether they had been responsible for the riots or not) encouraged the imitation of Calvinist organisation in France which had successfully stood up to Catholic attempts at repression, although a fully Calvinist organisation did not emerge in the Netherlands until the Synod of Emden in 1571.

The roots of the Reformation in the Netherlands had not been specifically Calvinist but it was Calvinism which provided a structure strong enough to withstand persecution. And stories of Calvinist martyrs made the Dutch and the Flemish more willing to die for their faith as one of 'the elect'. This did not mean that the Calvinists took over the Netherlands. They remained a minority of well under ten percent and they were divided by religious controversies which culminated in the ferocious disputes at the Synod of Dort in 1618. However, Calvinist zeal and organisation were key elements in the resistance to Philip II during the Dutch Revolt to come. Even magistrates in the north of the Netherlands who remained Catholic but were anti-Spanish accepted that Calvinism should be the official religion of their newly independent United Provinces.

Scotland's Reformation was more Calvinist in origin owing to the mediation of its leading reformer, John Knox. In the mid-1550s, after a spell as a French galley-slave, Knox was in Geneva where he learned about the Calvinist faith and organisation. He was to call the Academy 'the most perfect school of Christ'. He held the author of the *Institutes* in high regard and when he returned to Scotland he argued for a Reformation on Calvinist lines, a goal which was achieved in 1560 when the Protestant Lords of the Congregation had driven out the French forces of the regent, Mary of Guise, and passed the Reformation through the Scottish Parliament. Knox was largely responsible for the *Scots Confession*, which made clear the reformed faith, and the *First Book of Discipline* which established the organisation of the Kirk, the Scots Church. However, in establishing the Reformation in Scotland Knox did not consult Calvin in Geneva. And the Scottish reformer was much less cautious than Calvin would have liked. In 1557 Knox had published in Geneva his *First Blast of the Trumpet against the Monstrous Regiment of Women*, an uninhibited attack on female Catholic rulers. Calvin was much embarrassed by this undiplomatic piece of propaganda. Also Knox went much further in urging resistance to Catholic rulers than Calvin would allow. Knox and the Scottish Reformation were Calvinist but Calvin had no control over either.

In England Queen Elizabeth had no liking for the uncompromising nature of Calvinism and she particularly disliked Knox for his authorship of the *Monstrous Regiment*. Also many exiles who had left during Queen Mary's reign had returned to England from Zurich or German cities, bringing reformed but not directly Calvinist ideas with them. Still, several of the Bishops of the Church of England were influenced by Calvin's views and that influence, if anything, was to grow during the religious disputes of the next century.

Germany was more resistant to Calvinist inroads than other areas of northern Europe, as Lutheranism was well established in north Germany and the Counter-Reformation was at last becoming organised in parts of south Germany such as Bavaria. However, a vital conversion was made in the person of Frederick III (1559–76), the Elector Palatine, a leading prince of the Empire controlling extensive territories along the Rhine. The effective discipline of Calvinism appealed to him as visitations (official inspections) had shown how insecure the Reformation was in the Palatinate, how much social as well as religious division there was between Lutherans and those still Catholic on the one hand and Anabaptists on the other. He made his capital city, Heidelberg, almost as important a refuge for exiles as Geneva and the Heidelberg Catechism of 1563 became the most important statement of the reformed faith for the Empire and later the Netherlands and also eastern Europe.

Again, however, Calvinism was adapted rather than simply adopted. The Heidelberg Catechism was largely Calvinist but it also displayed the influence of Zwinglians and some followers of Melanchthon. And although consistories were introduced they never had the importance in the Palatinate that they had in Geneva or elsewhere. Power was concentrated in a state controlled Ecclesiastical Council which had influence at every level of Church organisation and so penetrated society more thoroughly than any other political institution. And the Elector's physician, Thomas Erastus, provided a political theory which asserted the supremacy of the state. The Calvinist Church in Geneva had never become a theocracy or defied the state but Calvin had won for it some independent control over excommunication. Erastianism in the Palatinate ensured that the Church bowed to the state in everything including excommunication.

By the first decades of the seventeenth century, Calvinism had become the religion of 28 German states, albeit generally small ones. It spread eastwards into Poland where ten percent of the nobility became Calvinist although that did not last owing to weak organisation. In Bohemia Calvinism influenced the home-grown Bohemian Brethren. In Hungary the anti-Habsburg Magyars embraced Calvinism largely in its Heidelberg form although with much local variation. In Transylvania Prince Bethlen Gabor (1613–29) established Calvinism as the state religion and played his part in the attempt to fend off the power of the Catholic Habsburgs in the Thirty Years' War. Calvinism even had an effect as far east as Constantinople where one of the Patriarchs of the Orthodox Church, Cyril Lucaris, sympathised with its teaching.

Only in the most firmly Catholic and the most firmly Lutheran countries in Europe was Calvinism limited. Wherever there was religious confusion, the certainty of the Calvinist faith and the strength of its organisation enabled it to take root.

(h) The historical impact of Calvinism

Calvinism dominated the second, expansionist stage of the Reformation. Lutheranism was largely confined to Germany and Scandinavia whereas Calvinism spread, as we have seen, across much of Europe. Certainty of faith, a belief in Divine Providence and strength of organisation were crucial to this but there were other ways in which Calvinism was distinctive.

Luther, especially in his clinging to the doctrine of a physical presence in the Eucharist, seemed to be still in the grip of scholastic thinking and therefore intellectually more conservative than Calvin, perhaps even making a false start to the Reformation. However, Steven Ozment has posed the question whether Calvinists were really Protestants at all. Calvin asserted the centrality of 'justification by faith' but Calvinist discipline laid so much emphasis on a Christian morality that it seemed as though 'works' were once again a way to Heaven. The logical problem in this was dealt with by Calvin who said that we 'should rely wholly on the free promise of righteousness (i.e. justification by faith alone). We do not, however, forbid the Christian from under-girding and strengthening his faith by signs of the divine benevolence towards him'. Luther, in his overwhelming emphasis on faith, had cut away the Catholic sanctification of the works of everyday life; Calvin's revolution away from Catholicism seemed to have come full circle in restoring the sacred importance of actions in everyday life. Ozment calls this 'the "re-Catholicizing" of Protestant theology at its most sensitive point'.

It may be that Calvin filled a gap in Christian life left by the destruction of medieval Catholicism. On the other hand, there are those who feel that his emphasis on *beruf*, as German scholars were to call it, a divine calling or sense of purpose in everyday activity, was vital to the creation of the modern world. Calvin described this calling in the *Institutes*:

> The Lord bids each one of us in all life's actions to look to his calling. For He knows by what restlessness human nature is inflamed, what waywardness carries it here and there, how its ambition longs to embrace various things at once. Therefore, lest through our own stupidity and rashness, everything is turned topsy-turvy, He has appointed duties for every man in his particular way of life . . . It is enough if we know that the Lord's calling is in everything the beginning and foundation of well-doing.

1 *Why does Calvin judge a 'calling' to be necessary?*
2 *How might this sense of a 'calling' affect a Calvinist's attitude towards his everyday work?*

For Max Weber, a sociologist writing at the beginning of this century, the 'calling' became the Calvinist work ethic and worldly success was thought by some to be evidence of being one of 'the elect'. That in turn operated as the 'spirit of capitalism' and so Calvinism was crucial to the development of the modern capitalist world.

The problem with the Weber thesis is the lack of supporting evidence. Calvin himself urged the faithful to share what they had rather than to pursue profit for themselves and later Calvinist literature as well was critical of unrestrained capitalism. Studies of capitalists in the Early Modern period show characteristics other than a strict Calvinist morality—some examples, Catholic as well as Protestant, have flight from religious persecution as the common denominator. Amongst the commercially enterprising Dutch, although Calvinism was the official religion, only a small minority were committed Calvinists and they were not identified with the mercantile interests.

While the economic impact of Calvinism on the modern world is doubtful, its political impact on Early Modern Europe is more certain. Calvin, for all his caution, had set in motion an international conflict. It was not just that his creed became revolutionary within other countries in the hands of his successor Beza and others. Calvinists across Europe looked to each other for support in their various battles, given that they feared an international Catholic conspiracy against them. Catholic princes in turn, such as Philip II of Spain, saw an international Protestant conspiracy threatening them. Even when it was political ambition rather than religious zeal which motivated the conflicts and even when the battle-lines between Catholics and Protestants became confused, the religious wars of the century after Calvin lasted longer and bred more bitterness because of the determination and the ability of Calvinists to stand up to the Counter-Reformation.

Calvin died in 1564, urging his fellow pastors that they should change nothing. That was not possible given changing historical circumstances as well as the liking of his successor, Beza, for crude propaganda which over-emphasised predestination and encouraged armed resistance to a Catholic government, if only by lesser magistrates. And by 1600 Geneva itself had declined as a 'holy citadel'. Morale was low in the Company of Pastors and Perrot commented: 'The School has gone cold'. However, Geneva had by then done its work. Europe, from Scotland to Transylvania, was the home of an aggressive Calvinism.

5. Bibliography

G R Potter *Zwingli* (CUP, 1976). T H L Parker *John Calvin* (Dent, 1975). F Wendel *Calvin* (Fontana, 1965). G R Potter and M Greengrass *John Calvin* (Edward Arnold, 1980). M Prestwich (ed) *International Calvinism 1541–1715* (OUP, 1985).

6. Discussion Points and Exercises

A   *This section consists of questions or points that might be used for discussion (or written answers) as a way of expanding on the chapter and testing understanding of it:*

1   What made the Swiss Reformation so important?
2   What were the most significant early influences on Zwingli?
3   Why did it take several years to establish the Reformation in Zurich?
4   What made Zwingli's view of the Eucharist so controversial?
5   Why and with what success did Zwingli involve himself in politics both within Zurich and in Switzerland as a whole?
6   Why were Anabaptists almost universally condemned?
7   How did persecution affect the radicals?
8   Was the Radical Reformation in the end of any importance?
9   What made the *Institutes of the Christian Religion* distinctive?
10   Why did the authorities in Geneva find it so difficult either to accept Calvin or to dismiss him altogether?
11   What were the features of the Calvinist Church which enabled it to penetrate society so thoroughly?
12   Why did Calvin face opposition in Geneva and how did he overcome it?
13   What made Calvinism capable of such extensive expansion?
14   How far did Calvinism come to differ from the views of Calvin during that expansion?

B   *Essay questions*
1   Assess the significance of Zwingli's contribution to the Reformation.
2   Compare Luther and Zwingli *or* Luther and Calvin as Protestant reformers.

3   Why were the Anabaptists subject to so rigorous a persecution and
    what were its effects?
4   What made Calvin so distinctive as a reformer?
5   'A Protestant Rome'. How accurate is this as a description of
    Calvin's Geneva?
6   'The Calvinist faith and discipline could not be persecuted out of
    existence.' Account for the international spread and survival of
    Calvinism.

7. Documentary Exercise—Calvin's Political Thought

Read these extracts and then answer the following questions.

A   *From the* Institutes *(1543 edition) on the office of magistrate, a term applying
to rulers in general:*
    The Lord has not only testified that the office of magistrate is approved by
    and acceptable to him, but he also sets out its dignity with the most
    honourable titles and marvellously commends it to us . . . (Magistrates)
    have a mandate from God, . . . Accordingly there should be no doubt that
    civil authority is a calling, not only holy and lawful before God, but also the
    most sacred and by far the most honourable of all callings in the whole life of
    mortal men . . .

B   *From the* Institutes *(1543 edition) on obedience to magistrates:*
    We are not only subject to the authority of princes who perform their tasks
    towards us uprightly and faithfully as they ought, but also to the authority of
    all those who, by whatever means have control of affairs, even though they
    perform only a minimum of the prince's office . . . (God) says that those who
    rule for the public benefit are true patterns and evidence of His benevolence;
    and those who rule unjustly and incompetently have been raised up by Him
    to punish the wickedness of the people; that all equally have been endowed
    with that holy majesty with which He has invested lawful authority.

C   *From the* Institutes *(1543 edition) on the best form of government:*
    If the three forms of government which the philosophers discuss (monarchy,
    aristocracy and democracy) are considered in isolation, I will not deny that
    aristocracy, or a system compounded of aristocracy and democracy, far
    excels all the others: not indeed in itself, but because it is very rare for kings
    to control their will that it never is at variance with what is just and right; or
    for them to have been endowed with sufficient prudence and shrewdness to
    know how much is enough. Therefore man's weakness causes it to be safer
    for a number of men to exercise government so that each one can help, teach
    and admonish the other. If one of them asserts himself unfairly, there are a
    number of censors and masters to restrain him.

D   *From the* Institutes *(1543 edition) on resistance to kings:*
    For if the correction of unbridled despotism is the Lord's to avenge, let us
    not at once think that He has entrusted it to us, to whom no command has
    been given except to obey and to suffer.

I am speaking here of private individuals. If there are any magistrates appointed by the people to moderate the power of kings—as in ancient times the ephors were set against the Spartan kings, or the tribunes of the people against the Roman consuls, or the demarchs against the senate of the Athenians; and perhaps, as things now are, such power as the three estates exercise in every realm where they hold their chief assemblies—I am so far from forbidding them to withstand, in accordance with their duty, the violence and cruelty of kings, that, if they connive with kings in their oppression of their people, then I declare that they are guilty of the most wicked betrayal of trust . . .

E *From a letter dated 16th April, 1561, from Calvin to Admiral Coligny, one of the leading Huguenot nobles in France. Calvin was writing with reference to the Tumult of Amboise, a plot the previous year involving some Huguenots who aimed to seize the young king, Francis II. There was a question as to whether Calvin had supported the plot:*

Seven or eight months before the event, a certain person (La Renaudie, the organiser of the plot) . . . consulted me, whether it was not lawful to resist the tyranny by which the children of God were then oppressed . . . I strove to demonstrate to him that he had no warrant for such conduct according to God; and that even in worldly terms such measures were ill-organised, presumptuous and could have no successful outcome . . .

. . . if a single drop of blood were spilled, floods of it would deluge Europe; it were better we should perish a hundred times, than expose Christianity and the gospel to such shame. I admitted, it is true, that if the Princes of the Blood (i.e. royal princes) demanded to be maintained in their rights for the common good, and if the Parlement (a supreme court) joined them in their quarrel, that it would then be lawful for all good subjects to lend them armed assistance. The man afterwards asked me, if one of the Princes of the Blood, though not the first in rank (referring to the prince of Condé), had decided upon taking such a step, we were not then warranted to support him. I answered in the negative. In a word I adopted so decided a tone in condemning all his proposals that I was convinced that he had completely abandoned them . . .

If I should be asked why I did not more formally oppose the proceedings, I answer, that first of all I thought there was no great necessity for doing so, because I despised the enterprise as a childish affair . . . yet it is an undoubted fact that at that time people heard me preach several sermons in which I combated their cause with as much vehemence as I was master of. This can easily be verified, inasmuch as these sermons were copied word for word as I delivered them with the date of the month and the day, whence, it is evident, that I did not play a double part, nor avail myself of silence to spring a mine under ground.

1   *What was Calvin's attitude in general towards rulers or 'magistrates' and what reasoning lay behind that attitude (Extracts A and B)?*

2   *What were Calvin's reasons for preferring a government made up of aristocracy, or aristocracy and democracy? Might his political experience in France and Geneva have influenced his opinion (Extract C)?*

3   *On what grounds and by whom could a king be resisted, according to Calvin (Extracts D and E)?*

4   How definite is Calvin on whether that resistance should be passive or active (Extracts D and E)?
5   What do you think was Calvin's purpose in writing to Coligny (Extract E)?
6   How far would you judge from the above evidence that Calvin himself was the author of a Calvinist revolutionary theory?

XII The Counter-Reformation

1. Introduction

In the immediate aftermath of Luther's protest it looked as though the Church of Rome might be ruined. Protestantism seemed to be unstoppable in Germany and it was threatening to spread through all Europe. However, after decades of ruinous delay, the Catholic Church began to take corporate action. A General Council met at Trent in northern Italy in three sessions between 1545 and 1563. Its decrees gave Catholic militants a cause to be sure of, a new morale and a new discipline. Given its renewed vigour, the Roman Catholic Church could not only survive but fight back. With the help of crusading Catholic princes and new religious orders, especially the Jesuits, it could reclaim souls and territories previously lost to the Protestants. The term which best suited this renewal and attack seemed to be 'the Counter-Reformation'.

The term 'Counter-Reformation', however, is regarded by many as being inadequate, even misleading. It was coined by those accustomed to thinking about strategies and counter-offensives, about matters military. This cannot do justice to a positive, and not merely reactionary, spiritual movement which had its origins long before Luther made his protest and which, diverse enough in Europe, spread with Catholics around the world far from the battle against Protestants. The Council of Trent itself seems to shrink in its relative importance amidst the other events and variations of what is now sometimes renamed the Catholic Reformation, as in the title of Pierre Janelle's book on the topic.

As you read this chapter think carefully about the terms used, and be critical of them, but not just that. Try to sense the living faith of the time and how it could be manipulated. Also consider whether the roles of the traditional heroes of the Counter-Reformation—the Councillors of Trent, the popes, Philip II of Spain—are still to be seen as crucial for the people of Catholic Europe or whether it was the case that Catholicism was developing slowly and diversely, only occasionally reaching up to more visible expression in the attitude of a pope or a decree at Trent. It is certainly necessary to look for the origins of Catholic renewal before the Council of Trent and before Luther even thought of making his protest.

2. The Reformers

Long before 1517 there had been those seeking to revitalise the Church. There were groups of pious laymen, referred to in general as 'the devout', such as the Brethren of the Common Life *(see page 138)*, and there were individual Catholic reformers such as Erasmus *(see page 119)*. Because Luther's protest was more radical and more noisy, it tended to obscure the quiet work of reform going on within the Church.

When Luther visited Rome in 1510, he discovered that the heart of the corruption of the Church was to be found in Italy, where the popes played out their power politics and where, for many, the Church was nothing more than a financial racket. While true, this is not the whole truth. Already reformers were at work. New brotherhoods had been founded at Vicenza in 1492 and 1493 and at Genoa in 1497. These were men gathering together to pray and to fast, and by their example to make an impact on the society around them. In a hierarchical society, the scale of that impact depended in part on the rank of the reformers. That is why the foundation in about 1514 of the Oratory of Divine Love, a sort of reform club, was so important.

The list of those associated with this Oratory reads like a roll-call of the leaders of the Catholic Reformation. Giberti, Sadoleto, Thiene —these would all reform dioceses, or advise the popes on reform or create new monastic orders. One, Reginald Pole, was even a connection of the English royal family.

Another member of the Oratory was Gasparo Contarini. He had no intention of becoming a priest at all. He was a Venetian aristocrat and statesman, and stayed so until the mid-1530s. But, inspired by a friend who became a hermit, he tried to measure and direct his active public life by his interior faith. He became a cardinal in the end (1535) and led a Catholic delegation in one of the last attempts at compromise with the Lutherans (the Colloquy of Regensburg, 1541), where he hoped in vain that a negotiated settlement might be reached. Contarini and Pole as well, while working within the Catholic fold to restore the Church, had some sympathy with the basic Protestant belief in justification by faith alone. In this they drew, as Luther had, on the ideas of St Augustine. They, and other Catholic reformers who thought like them, became known as the *spirituali*.

The most austere member of the Oratory, with no sympathy whatever for Protestant views, was Gian Pietro Carafa. He had shown his dedication to the Church at the age of 14, when he attempted to run away from home in Naples to become a monk. This adolescent commitment was to remain with him as he aided in the foundation of the Theatine Order, and later on as he worked out new ways of isolating the contagion of heresy: a reorganised Papal Inquisition (1542) and an Index of Prohibited Books (1559). He was the leader of the *zelanti*, those bitterly opposed to any compromise, dedicated to the crushing of Lutheranism. In 1555 Carafa became Pope Paul IV.

Clearly, the men of the Oratory were to be of great significance in the attempt to strengthen the Church in the face of Protestant attack. But their reform club was founded before they had ever heard of Martin Luther. And within the Oratory there were very different attitudes towards Luther's ideas when they had heard of him. The split between the *spirituali* and the *zelanti* was to become apparent during the crisis of the early 1540s *(see page 307)*. Before then 'the devout' continued their attempt to regenerate the Church, and not just by example. They aided the setting up of new orders of reforming monks and priests and made their protest to the pope about the state of the Church.

3. The New Orders

The development of new orders at the beginning of the sixteenth century took place largely in Italy, remote from the centre of Lutheran controversy in Germany. Many of 'the devout' favoured this development as they were particularly dissatisfied with the old orders where monks and nuns had grown complacent, performing rituals mechanically, enjoying good collective incomes and failing to set an inspiring example to the people. One group of 'the devout' was the Camaldolesi, an eleventh century order revitalised by Venetian noblemen who became hermits in 1510 to escape the corruption they saw all around them. More positive were the Theatines (founded 1524), a group of ordinary priests receiving training as reformers, and the Somaschi (1528) who dedicated themselves to caring for the sick, for orphans and for those prostitutes who would turn to God. Such social concern was one way of bringing religion to the people. Dramatic preaching was another way, a speciality of the Barnabites (1530). A new order of nuns called the Ursulines (1535) stayed firmly in the community, continuing to live with their families and devoting themselves to girls' education.

The simple fact of these new foundations and their activities shows that there was a reforming spirit alive in the Catholic Church. But few could be compared for their impact with the Capuchins and the Jesuits.

The Capuchins (1529) were not strictly a new order at all, but an offshoot of the Franciscans. In the twelfth century, St Francis had set a standard of humility and skill in preaching which was thought to be unsurpassable. He and his followers had been instrumental in saving the newly growing towns of Europe from drifting away from the Church, Matteo da Bascio wanted to follow his example in bringing the Christian message to the people, and symbolised this by wearing a pointed hood or *capuccio* supposedly like St Francis'. His followers, the Capuchins as they became known, did the same. Their zeal disturbed many of their self-satisfied fellow Observants, a branch of the Franciscans, who tried to crush the new offshoot, but unsuccessfully. The Capuchins were lucky to have powerful patrons, such as the Duchess of Camerino, whose uncle conveniently enough was Pope Clement VII. Surviving the factional politics of the Church, the friars with their pointed hoods became familiar and welcome figures throughout Catholic Europe. They were skilled in preaching and in the use of down-to-earth language. But they were most renowned for their fearlessness in combating deprivation and disease. Right from the start in Camerino, the Capuchins had nursed those afflicted by the plague despite the risk of infection to themselves. This selflessness was to be the mark of these friars; they brought their living faith and their Church to the people in the most practical way possible.

The Jesuits (1540) were the most outward-going of all the new orders, following the example of their first 'General', reared in the tradition of the Spanish Reconquista, Ignatius Loyola. A unique blend of commitment to obedience to the pope with the freedom to go anywhere and to adapt to local circumstances (unlike ordinary monks confined to one place and with a set routine), they have been seen as the most dynamic element of the Counter-Reformation. They consolidated the Church in the Catholic south and reclaimed lost souls in parts of the Protestant north; their first aim, however, had been to combat the Infidel Turk and they became the leading missionaries to the newly explored lands of South America and the Far East. They shared with the other new orders the spirituality of the early Catholic Reformation and they are too often seen exclusively as part of militant reform from the 1540s onwards. Their methods and successes will be dealt with in looking at how the Catholic Reformation reached the people and, in detail, as part of a documentary exercise at the end of the chapter.

Whether in caring for the sick or the destitute, in preaching or in teaching, the new orders had started to reinforce not just the spirituality of clerics, but also the involvement of laymen. Left as mere spectators of church rituals the ordinary church-goer in Italy, not just in the north, might have found the Protestant declaration of the 'priesthood of all believers' very enticing. This is not to suggest that the new orders or any of 'the devout' intended in the early days specifically to pre-empt Protestantism. In fact they were reacting to the same problem as Luther—how to channel the growing piety of the age. But it cannot be denied that, in keeping that channel Catholic, 'the devout' helped to save the Church of Rome from collapsing in the face of the challenge from Germany.

Before such collapse could definitely be averted, though, 'the devout' had to find ways of increasing their power. Otherwise their work might have been local to Italy, sporadic and ultimately of limited effect. Only power could spread and consolidate reform. For power it was necessary to look to the princes of Europe and to the popes.

4. Power and Reform before Trent—The Princes

Princes frequently professed themselves to be good servants of the Church. But they usually preferred to be its masters. There has been much mythology in talk of 'new monarchies' in the early sixteenth century, but it is true that princes were slowly if unsteadily increasing their powers at the expense of privileged groups such as the Church. Hand in hand with this mastery went the possibility of bringing power into the service of reform.

A traditional example of power supporting reform is the work of Cardinal Cisneros de Ximénez, the Archbishop of Toledo. He was a committed crusader confessing that for him, 'the smell of gunpowder was sweeter than the perfumes of Arabia'. However, he was also dedicated to reforming the Church as well as adding new territories to it. He drew on the support of the Catholic kings, Ferdinand of Aragon and his wife the devout Isabella of Castile, in order to reform monastic orders in Spain, establish a new university at Alcalà and encourage the biblical scholarship of Christian Humanists *(see page 119)*. His attempts at reform were, however, of limited importance in the end. They were local to Spain, the land of the Reconquista, where racial and religious purity were seen as one in the fight against the Moors, and where the Spanish Inquisition had been safeguarding that purity since 1478. Nonetheless, Cisneros' work does reveal some willingness by princes to back reform.

Such commitment to reform was present but even rarer in other parts of Europe. In England some Franciscan friars were reformed, but for Henry VII churchmen were largely seen as useful Crown servants. For Henry VIII, this was even more marked in his patronage of Cardinal Wolsey, the personification of such abuses as absenteeism and pluralism, although Henry did also cultivate the friendship at least of reformist figures such as Erasmus and Sir Thomas More and could be a pious man on occasion. Just how secular Henry was in his public interests, however, is shown in his execution of More when this old friend of his refused to acknowledge the King's supremacy over the Church.

Across the Channel Louis XII of France and his successor Francis I found war and its attendant chivalry to be far more suited to their ideals than reform of the Church. But Francis did take an interest in the Church in 1516. His agreement with Pope Leo X in the Concordat of Bologna *(see page 220)* guaranteed him much control over the personnel and revenues of the Church in France. It was secular interest rather than spiritual renewal which lay behind this. In contrast, Francis' sister Marguerite was a patroness of the reformist circle of the Diocese of Meaux but this was local and élitist. The key figure in the Church in France in the early years of the sixteenth century was Cardinal Georges d'Amboise. He had been made a papal legate in 1501 with the supposed purpose of reforming the 'Conventuals'. However, as the Italian Wars continued to absorb attention and cash, it became clear that the suppression of a monastery was as useful for the confiscation of its wealth as for any improvement of religion.

It was difficult to reform a monastery in Germany. At Deddingen the monks broke a reformer's carriage to pieces. At St Ulric's, Augsburg, a would-be reformer found himself jailed for a fortnight. In the Tyrol the great fifteenth century churchman, Nicholas of Cusa, the Bishop of Brixen, was continually obstructed by the local duke who rather liked the unreformed habits of a convent and its nuns. The developing piety of many Germans was flouted and frustrated. This paved the way for Luther's protest and in turn for the conviction of the Emperor, Charles V, that reform was vital for the maintenance of the Church and the Holy Roman Empire. The problem for Charles was that he was too late. For the first 20 years of his reign he had been preoccupied with the wars against the French and against the Turks. In these same years up until 1542, the reforming instinct in Germany had quickly found its main expression in Luther's new doctrine and the adherence to it of many free cities and some powerful princes. Charles V's belated attempts to reform were futile. He sent Matthew Held to the German princes and cities in 1536 to offer reform; Held was soon reduced to plotting war against the Protestants. Charles backed compromise with the Protestants at the Colloquy of Regensburg in 1541. The attempt failed and with drastic consequences, as we shall see. Charles had to press even harder then for what he had long expected was the only solution: the Pope had to reform his own administration and summon a General Council to spread that reform throughout the whole Church.

Charles was right. Princely authority was insufficient to organise reform. Some princes were just not interested. Others, as Charles had been, were preoccupied with what seemed to be more urgent secular matters. To reform the 'members', the body of the church, so much depended upon the 'Head', the Pope. The problem that remained was that popes often acted more as Italian princes than as vicars of Christ.

5. Power and Reform before Trent—The Popes

Renaissance popes have often been portrayed as sensual, power-thirsty betrayers of the Church. This portrayal made a good argument for the Protestants and it still makes a good story, but it is not the whole truth. Princes and bishops had taken advantage of the Great Schism *(see page 5)* to whittle down the powers of the Papacy through the movement known as Conciliarism which held that General Councils, not popes, governed the Church. The Councils of Constance (1414–17) and Basle (1431–49) nearly succeeded in making the popes puppet rulers of the Church. But at Basle the Conciliarists quarrelled amongst themselves and Conciliarism faded. Authority once again passed to one pope resident in Rome.

In the aftermath of Conciliarism the popes had one principal aim— security against attack. In pursuit of that, they self-consciously acquired not spiritual virtues but the refinement of the worldly arts of the Renaissance which raised the status of churchmen, as they had done that of merchants and princes. Also, as in the case of Cisneros, gunpowder smelt sweet in the nostrils of some popes as they fought to control their own anarchic territories in central Italy, the Papal States. And they saw a need to concentrate not on the religious life but on the new game of international diplomacy to guarantee their position threatened by the onset of the Italian Wars. It is this quest for security which helps us understand why the popes dealt with the question of reform so gingerly for so long; and, given the threats to their authority at Constance and Basle, it shows us why the popes were so reluctant to summon a General Council of the Church.

The attitude of the Renaissance popes to reform can be seen in the fate of Savonarola, a new style reformer in Florence who wished to turn his native city into a City of God, with Renaissance vanities—books, priceless paintings—being cast into the fire. In 1498 Pope Alexander VI (1492–1503) applauded when the reforming Savonarola was cast into the fire instead. But Alexander was not just acting with the immorality typical of his family, the Borgias. Savonarola was an ally of the Pope's enemy France during this dangerous period of the Italian Wars. It was politics not religion which called the tune.

This was true for Pope Julius II (1503–13). He was more comfortable in armour than in priestly robes as he sought to drive the French out of Italy and to crush the petty tyrants who had carved up much of the Papal States between them.

The French threatened Julius with deposition and summoned a 'reforming' Council at Pisa. The Pope responded in 1512 by calling the Fifth Lateran Council (in effect an advisory committee) to attract genuine reformers to his side. Much was decided about the need to improve Church law and to co-ordinate the work of Bishops and of monks but little was done. The new Pope, Leo X (1513–21) was not inclined much to reform. ('Now God has given us the Papacy', he is reputed to have said, 'let us enjoy it.') And he was preoccupied with politics and with the shortage of money which decreed the further sale of indulgences.

Cuts could be attempted to solve the financial problem. That was tried by the reformist Pope Adrian VI (1522–23), formerly Charles V's austere tutor. There were howls of protest from citizens of Rome now unemployed; and vested interests in the Curia (the Papal civil service) resisted the Pope's every move. The epitaph on Adrian's tomb reads 'Woe! How even a most righteous man's power to act depends upon the times in which he happens to live.' But times were about to change.

Pope Clement VII (1523–34) was a surprisingly virtuous pope, for a Medici, but one still obsessed with politics. His hopelessly bad diplomacy prepared the way for the Sack of Rome in 1527 *(see page 194)*. For weeks a motley band of Spaniards, Italians and German Lutherans murdered, stole and raped their way quite methodically across Rome. The Pope was a helpless prisoner inside his fortress of the Castel Sant'Angelo. Gone were those Renaissance visions of the glory of Man. Even when Rome had recovered physically from the Sack, the atmosphere had changed drastically. The disaster was seen as a visitation of

God upon the sins of Rome. Gian Matteo Giberti, already a member of the Oratory of Divine Love, exemplifies this new spirit. In 1528 he gave up his lucrative post as Datary, in effect a broker for the sale of dispensations (permits for otherwise forbidden practices). He then remedied his years of absenteeism by moving to his bishopric of Verona where he became the first 'model Bishop' of the Catholic Reformation, raising the standards of the clergy and giving more direction to the spiritual lives of the laity. Pope Clement himself did not respond fully to this new spirit. He played politics to the end of his reign, shadow boxing with the Emperor, Charles V. But it was clear to Clement's successor that political security would avail the Papacy nothing. The only way forward was to raise its moral status.

While not being a model of pure living himself, Pope Paul III (1534–49) was shrewd enough to pay attention to the reform of the Church in order to avert its ruin. It was he who first tried to assemble a General Council in 1536, but was forestalled by war between Francis I and Charles V. It was he who was to perceive the unique potential of the Jesuits, establishing them as a religious order in 1540.

Paul had already seen the possibility of renewal through the work of the Oratory of Divine Love, raising five of its members to the Cardinalate in the two years after becoming Pope. He then asked four of these Cardinals, along with five others, to take part in a reform Commission, rendering advice on the improvement of the Church—the *Consilium de Emendanda Ecclesia*.

Here is an abstract from the Report presented to the Pope:

> Most blessed father, we are very far from able to express in words what thanks Christendom ought to give to Almighty God for making you pope at this time and shepherd of His flock, and has given you the mind you have . . . For the Spirit of God, by which the heavens are held up (as says the prophet), has decreed that Christ's Church, falling and indeed almost collapsed, should be restored by you and that your hand should save it from ruin; and that you should re-erect it in its earlier glory and return it to its pristine splendour . . . And Your Holiness . . . knows well that the origin of all these evils arose from the fact that several popes, your predecessors, . . . collected expert (opinions) according to their desires, not in order to learn from them what they should do, but to find by their zeal and craft a reason to justify their wills. . . .
>
> Concerning the institution of ministers by means of whom, as by instruments, the worship of God is to be well administered and Christ's people are to be well instructed and guided in the Christian life, the first abuse here is the ordination of the clergy, and especially of priests, in which no care is taken or diligence displayed. Whoever they might be—totally unlearned, of the vilest origins and appalling morals, or under age—they are regularly admitted to holy orders, and particularly to the priesthood, that condition which most notably expresses Christ . . .
>
> Concerning the Bishop of Rome. This city and church of Rome are the mother and teacher of other churches. Therefore the worship of God and honesty of manners should flourish here above all . . .

1 *What evidence is there here of a new sense of urgency in the higher councils of the Church?*

2 *Why, in the opinion of the Commission, had earlier popes sought reformist advice?*

3 *What seemed to be the first obstacle in the way of impressing the people with the true Faith?*

4 *The authors of this report, all resident in Italy, were particularly concerned with Rome. Bearing in mind where the greatest threats to the Church were at this time, what weakness in the Catholic reform movement might this indicate?*

5 *Doctrine was not dealt with by the Consilium. Given that, how would convinced Lutherans react to these proposals? Why might some of the Cardinals on the Commission have been reluctant to broach matters of doctrine?*

The *Consilium* was indicative of a new attitude in the Church and a reform 'congregation' (committee) did follow it up with reforms in the Curia reducing the favours and dispensations from Church law which could be bought for cash. Nonetheless its effect was very limited.

Paul III was sympathetic to the Commission's report but he was not the man to overcome the deadweight of the Curia. He had what he saw as the greater matter of Catholic peace to establish—he was in Nice in 1538 arranging a truce between Charles V and Francis I. It soon became clear that the *Consilium* had only just touched on what threatened the ruin of the Church.

6. The Crisis of the Catholic Reformation 1541–42

Charles V had been distracted by wars against the Turks and the French for most of his reign. By the late 1530s he urgently required a negotiated settlement with the Protestants before the structure of the Catholic Church in Germany collapsed completely. A conference of Protestant and Catholic representatives, planned in 1539, finally took place in 1541 in the form of the Colloquy of Regensburg. The leader of the Catholics at the conference was Cardinal Contarini, prominent among the *spirituali*, those churchmen with leanings towards Lutheranism *(see page 300)*. At the head of the Protestants was Philip Melanchthon, a close colleague of Luther but placing a much higher value than he did on Church unity.

Within a few weeks the two delegations had managed to agree on the first five articles of the draft agreement, *The Book of Regensburg*. The atmosphere of optimism was tremendous. It seemed as though the end of the schism was at hand. Thorny questions about the nature of original sin had been sorted out. The even thornier question of justification by faith alone or by faith and works was resolved in the doctrine of 'double justification'. It was agreed that faith was fundamental to salvation and that while the value of good works depended entirely on the faith underlying them (that satisfied the moderate Protestants), they were vital (sufficiently traditional for the moderate Catholics). The problem was that, while the moderates were at Regensburg, the dogmatists at Wittenberg and Rome were to have the final say.

Luther and the Pope were swift to condemn 'double justification'. For them such a compromise would be a betrayal of the cause. It would also have been very difficult to persuade their embattled followers to accept the subtle theological formulae involved. The collapse of negotiation, however, was not due just to the dogmatism of Luther and the Pope but also to the impossibility of finding a compromise to cover every doctrinal issue.

Five articles of *The Book of Regensburg* had been agreed upon by the moderates, but there were eighteen other articles under consideration. Of these, the issue of transubstantiation, the starkest symbol of the difference between Catholics and Protestants, seemed to defy all attempts at compromise. While it may be wrong to say that the failure of conciliation was inevitable, the day of the moderate was certainly passing.

The failure of the Colloquy of Regensburg convinced many Catholics that a definitive, uncompromising statement of Catholic doctrine was long overdue. Machinery was immediately set in motion to preserve the purity of the Faith even before such a statement could be issued. In July 1542 the Papal Inquisition was reorganised after years of ineffectiveness. Cardinal Carafa, that leading representative of the *zelanti*, obsessed with the need to stamp out heresy, was put in charge of it. No doubt the model for it was in part the successful Spanish Inquisition. But Carafa was not concerned mainly with those who lent towards Judaism or Islam, as in Spain. He was obsessed with the Lutheran heresy spreading like a disease in Italy. The Papal Inquisition had been revived as a direct response to the fear that two Italian cities, Modena and Lucca, were about to turn Protestant. Those cities actually remained Catholic but there was evidence enough that the crisis of the Catholic Church was not confined to northern Europe but was spreading to the heart of the Church in Italy itself. In August 1542 Bernardino Ochino, General of the Capuchins and a renowned preacher, fled, just after another great preacher Peter Martyr Vermigli, across the Alps into Protestant Switzerland.

They had fled, at the height of their preaching careers, because they felt that the logic of their *spirituali* ideas, drawn like Luther's to a great extent from St Augustine, led inescapably towards Protestantism. Their decision, though, had more than personal consequences. The responsibility for stemming heresy in Italian cities had lain largely with *spirituali* bishops—at least, that was so until the flight of the two preachers who had been so eagerly employed by the same bishops to keep the Italian people within the embrace of the Catholic Church. In the same month as the flight to Switzerland, Contarini died. It was symbolic of a change in the direction of reform. With the reformers in disarray and the *spirituali* suspected of heresy, the resolution of the crisis was found in a new emphasis on defence against Protestantism. Carafa, the *zelanti*, set the tone. And amidst fears of an independent national settlement in Germany, as well as fear of heresy at home in Italy, a General Council was at last summoned to Trent to put the Church to rights.

7. The Council of Trent—The Meetings

Paul III summoned a General Council to meet in 1542. Yet again, that was forestalled by war when Francis I in that year invaded Charles V's territory in the Netherlands. In 1544 the Peace of Crèpy established the peace Paul III had been waiting for. The Council opened on the 13th December 1545 in the small town of Trent, a compromise location in that it was on the Italian side of the Alps which pleased the Pope, while it was a free city of the Empire which pleased Charles V. There were to be three meetings of the Council: 1545–47, 1551–52, and 1562–63.

The remote, cramped town with its poor climate did not seem to please many Bishops. Only 31 turned up for the opening session. The numbers, however, did grow and in later sessions there were 237 voting members of the Council. But even that number does not indicate a truly 'General' Council. The Protestants were not included, despite a brief and redundant appearance by their representatives at the second meeting of Trent in 1551. And there were only very few Catholic bishops from north of the Alps. On July 15th 1563 during the third meeting a complete list of those present was taken. Out of 235 there were 135 Italians. This did not guarantee papal control, however, as has sometimes been suggested. Of the 135 Italians, 89 were from Spanish-controlled or independent territories.

While the debates were quite free and wide-ranging this does not imply a democratic approach. Whereas at the Council of Basle (1431–49) the joke had been that anyone turning up could vote, only the Fathers at Trent bishops and monastic leaders) took part in the final decisions. They in turn were not merely subject to the Papal Legates, but were under pressure all the time from secular princes.

Ambassadors were present at all the meetings at Trent and played a relentless diplomatic game on behalf of their princely masters, often diverting the Council from its decision-making. Considering the political turmoil of the time it is more surprising that the Council ever completed its business at all than that it took so long.

The first meeting at Trent (1545–47) ended when an epidemic of plague broke out. But it would have ended anyway given that Charles V was seeking to impose an independent settlement on the German Protestants by use of force, beating the Schmalkaldic League at the Battle of Mühlberg in 1547. The Emperor had planned force for some time, but he was also disappointed that the Council had concentrated so much on the reform of doctrine, a papal priority given the threat of heresy in Italy. Charles wanted the reform of abuses first which he felt held the key to recovering Germany.

Pope Julius III (1550–55) recalled the Council to Trent for its second meeting in 1551–52. It made little headway given the presence of hostile Protestants and was again overtaken by war. In 1552 Charles V's policy of force and reform of abuses was in ruins. The Peace of Augsburg in 1555, engineered by his brother Ferdinand, acknowledged the permanent religious division of Germany.

The Peace of Augsburg might have been the immediate cause of a third meeting of Trent to try and pick up the pieces. However, there was a new Pope in Rome—Carafa had become Paul IV (1555–59). Obsessed not just with the purity of doctrine but also with the undivided authority of the Papacy, he decided that he would direct reform on his own. His action was fast and furious. He attacked the extravagance of Church leaders, he suppressed simony (the sale of Church offices) and in 1559 established the Index of Prohibited Books, banning any publication that was remotely deviant from loyalty to Rome and its orthodoxy.

The immediate problem was that even a vigorous pope like Paul could be no substitute for a General Council. His authority, in reality, extended little beyond the Papal States. Frustrated by this, and even driven near to madness, Paul declared war on Philip II, that most zealous of Catholic princes. He then went on to accuse Cardinal Pole of heresy at the very time when Pole had abandoned his earlier suspect views, those of the *spirituali*, and was faithfully seeking under Mary Tudor to reclaim England to the Catholic fold. It was clear to the cardinals after Pole's death that this divisive approach had to be terminated, especially after the Counter-Reformation had come to an abrupt halt in England upon the death of Mary Tudor. (This aborted Pole's reform decrees of 1556 which were almost a model of what the Fathers of Trent were trying to achieve.)

On his election, Pius IV (1559–65) was made to promise that the Council would be recalled to continue the spiritual regeneration of Christendom. Pius, much influenced by his holy nephew Archbishop Carlo Borromeo of Milan, kept his word, but it was due more to his diplomatic skill than to his spiritual dedication that the Council actually met. The Emperor, now Ferdinand I, wanted no continuation of dogmatic Trent, as he feared to provoke the Protestants in recently settled Germany. The Cardinal of Lorraine, the dominant ecclesiastic in France at this time, wanted conciliation with the French Protestants, the Huguenots. And so he sided with Emperor Ferdinand. Philip II of Spain, a more dogmatic Catholic, wanted to continue Trent if anything, but preferred to delay as he made his bid to woo the new Queen of England, Elizabeth.

These political obstacles were finally overcome with some papal sleight of hand. The Cardinal of Lorraine conveniently panicked Ferdinand and Philip on to the Pope's side by arranging for a separate national Council in France. The Pope then followed this up by fooling the Cardinal of Lorraine into thinking that the new meeting at Trent would start afresh and not be a continuation of the previous two meetings. With these clear indications that reform depended on political manoeuvre as well as on spiritual renewal, the third meeting (1562–63) of the General Council opened at Trent.

This time the meeting was to end not because of the outbreak of war, but because the work of the Council was complete. However, this was not achieved easily.

The Papal Legate Cardinal Morone had had to fight off an attack on papal authority led by the Spanish Archbishop of Granada, Guerrero. The independent-minded Spaniard had used the issue of Bishops being made to reside in their sees in order to raise the further issue of whether Bishops received their authority direct from God by divine right or from the Pope. Morone undermined Guerrero's position, promising papal favours to Ferdinand, the Cardinal of Lorraine and, most importantly, Guerrero's own prince, Philip II. And he finally clinched agreement with a compromise formula. That formula guaranteed the dignity of Bishops with a promise that papal interference would be restricted, but it firmly established the principle of the papal monarchy over the Church.

The decrees of the Council could now be formally 'promulgated' (issued). There were still obstacles in the way of reform but, as we shall see in the next section, at last the Church had a clear statement of what ought to be believed by all Catholics, and of how the Church hierarchy, from Pope to parish priest, should organise and behave itself. The Council had also empowered the Pope to continue reform, to encourage the greater growth of Catholic renewal and to prevent any further inroads of Protestantism into Catholic territory.

8. The Council of Trent—The Decrees

The Decrees of the Council of Trent (the 'Tridentine' Decrees) fall into two categories: doctrine and discipline. Doctrine was decided upon first, largely during the first two meetings of the Council. The Pope and the Fathers of the Council, unlike Charles V, recognised that the strength of the Lutheran offensive was in its doctrinal certainty and that many more Catholics, unless guided by clear authoritative beliefs, would follow Ochino and become apostates, religious 'deserters'.

The Council affirmed the basis of all its doctrine. That was to be Scripture but tradition as well, not 'Scripture alone'. And where direction was sought from Scripture, the Vulgate, the official text of the Church, was to be used. This was not to be publicly vetted, as Erasmus had done, but issued in an amended version by the Pope.

These are some extracts from the major doctrinal decrees:

(a) If anyone says that nothing is commanded in the Gospel apart from faith, that everything else, whether commandment or prohibition, is indifferent and up to the individual, and that the ten commandments have nothing to do with Christianity, let him be anathema (excommunicated).

(b) If anyone says that the grace of justification is granted only to those predestined to life, and not to the others who are definitely called but do not receive grace, because they are predestined to evil by God's power, let him be anathema.

(c) If anyone says that the sacraments of the new law were not all established by Jesus Christ, Our Lord; or that they are more or less than seven, that is, baptism, confirmation, the Eucharist, penance, extreme unction, orders and matrimony; or even that any one of these seven is not truly and properly a sacrament; let him be anathema.

(d) If anyone says that in the most holy sacrament of the Eucharist there remains the substance of the bread and wine together with the Body and Blood of our Lord Jesus Christ, and denies that marvellous total conversion of the substance of the bread into the Body and of the wine into the Blood, even though the appearance of the bread and wine remain, which the Catholic Church most appropriately calls transubstantiation, let him be anathema.

(f) If anyone says that in the Catholic Church there is not a hierarchy established by divine ordination, consisting of bishops, priests and ministers; let him be anathema.

1 *Draw up two lists side by side from the decrees. One should be the name of the Catholic doctrine being re-asserted; the other should be the implied Protestant doctrine which is being condemned.*

2 *How might such statements of doctrine help the Catholic Church?*

In their urgent attention to doctrine the Fathers of the Council did not want to neglect discipline, even if the main bulk of that legislation had to wait for the third meeting (1562–63). They recognised that it was the essential counterpart to a clearer doctrine. It was not just that abuses were morally objectionable in themselves, it was that they weakened the central activities of the Church. A seven-year-old archbishop could scarcely oversee his province effectively, a bishop who never visited his diocese could hardly check up on his clergy and an ignorant priest could not set the Mass in its proper context or preach correct doctrine to the people. The following are some of the major disciplinary reforms.

With regard to bishops:

(a) Preaching was established as a bishop's chief duty. Severe penalties were threatened for neglect of this duty to instruct the faithful.

(b) Pluralism was condemned.

(c) Absenteeism was condemned. Absence without permission was to last no more than three months unless on state service, which was not unusual. If the bishop failed in his attendance, his revenue was to be used to repair churches or given to the poor rather than to him.

(d) A bishop had to attend a provincial synod (Church conference) every three years and hold one in his own diocese every year.

(e) Visitation was to occur regularly, meaning that the bishop had to go on tours of inspection in his own diocese.

(f) The authority of the bishop to do all this was reinforced as he was to be the delegate of the 'Apostolic See', i.e. of the pope himself, empowered to over-rule other clerics in his diocese. So the pope's reinforced authority actually enhanced rather than competed with that of the Bishop, in the work of Catholic renewal.

With regard to parish priests:

(a)　Preaching was, of course, as much the duty of the parish priest as of the bishop. And it was to be 'in conformity with the capabilities of its hearers'. For too long, Protestants, with their emphasis on preaching and aptitude for it, had had the ear of the people.

(b)　In dress and in speech, priests were to show themselves to be a distinct and worthy group of men. Concubinage would result in dismissal. House-keepers were to be respectable older women.

(c)　Wandering priests and relic pedlars were to be banned, as were the quaestors—indulgence sellers—just 46 years too late!

(d)　Admission to the priesthood was to depend upon a knowledge of Latin and the Bible as well as an upright life. Candidates for ordination had to be at least 23 years old.

All the above would, however, just be airy idealism unless action was taken to produce men of the right quality for the priesthood. The Council's action was to decree that a seminary, i.e. a training college should be set up in every diocese where there was no university. Boys were taken in at secondary school age and then given a decade or so of training, concentrating heavily on theology, before they became priests. Despite all the educational difficulties of this project, and despite it taking more than a century before the Council's decree was effective throughout Catholic territories, the seminaries more than anything else guaranteed that priests remained a distinct caste, doing their jobs properly and maintaining their status in whichever society they found themselves.

This does not exhaust the list of disciplinary decrees. Amongst other things the Council continued the reform of monastic orders which had long been such a notable feature of the Catholic Reformation. But however much reforming zeal the Council Fathers had shown and whatever their joy when the work of the Council seemed complete in 1563, the fate of the Tridentine Decrees was still uncertain.

Now, the application of the decrees of the Council depended on the popes and on princes as well as on the bishops and priests.

9.　Power and Reform after Trent—The Popes

The Popes of the later sixteenth century did not fail the Council of Trent. Pius IV's successors, Pius V (1566–72), Gregory XIII (1572–85) and Sixtus V (1585–90), were all dedicated to building on the work of the Council and could rely on reformist Bishops, led by Carlo Borromeo, Archbishop of Milan, to help them.

The most immediate task for these Popes was the restoration of the liturgy, that is, the form of Church services which had to express the doctrines newly clarified at Trent. In 1568 the Pope issued a Breviary, the order of service to be recited by a priest each day. In 1570 this was followed up by the Missal, specifying the procedures followed during

Mass. These, with the authorisation of a new Catechism, an instruction manual for the faithful, gave a new direction to what went on inside Catholic churches day by day.

The Popes did not just address themselves to the work left over by Trent. There were plenty of longstanding problems in Rome itself. The Curia, although not purged completely of its abuses, was at last cut down to size. Pius IV dismissed 400 excess officials, while Pius V, when dismissing more, reassured them with the words: 'Better starve yourselves than lose your souls'. The Curia was, anyway, being starved of corrupt business. With the only recently halted shrinkage of the Church in Europe and with the disciplinary legislation at Trent, there was simply not so much trade in dispensations from Church laws or the sale of Church offices. Also, the money that was coming into the Curia came from the better administration of more legitimate revenue such as taxation of the Papal States and the papal monopoly of alum, a valuable chemical.

Curial administration of the Church as a whole was improved. The twenty new cardinals created by Pius V included not just pious men but efficient ones as well. More and more administration was entrusted to specialist committees. These were known as 'congregations'. In 1588 Sixtus V confirmed fifteen permanent congregations, able to overcome the uncertainty in earlier, more chaotic, papal decision-making. Eventually a congregation was set up in 1622 to take charge of spreading the Faith—*Congregatio de Propaganda Fide*. The new dynamism and efficiency of the Counter-Reformation had given a name to 'propaganda'.

The whole tone of life in Rome changed after the Sack of Rome and more so after Trent. There was a new austerity. Moral fashion as much as papal decrees had changed. The glorious nudes of Renaissance art were suddenly seen as little more than pornography. Many courtesans, high-class prostitutes, had been reformed or had left the city. Church leaders could work without the secular distractions of an earlier generation. What was suitable for the Papacy in its earlier quest for security had given way to the new power of morality and efficiency that was fitting to a much more genuinely self-confident and renewed Papacy.

The cardinals of the *Consilium* would have been pleased to see this. But that serves to remind us that any reform of Rome would be insignificant if it were to stop there. After Trent, the Popes and the reformed Bishops could attend to renewal in Italy but, for the rest of Europe, so much depended on the princes and their reaction to the Tridentine Decrees.

10. Power and Reform after Trent—The Princes

In January 1564 the Pope issued a Bull declaring the decrees of Trent obligatory in all Catholic lands. That in itself was one cause of Catholic princes being reluctant to accept the decrees. While they might be genuinely enthusiastic for the reform decrees themselves, they were deeply suspicious of the assertion of papal authority they involved. The zealous Philip II was to complain that he had sent Bishops to Trent and they had come back parish priests.

Philip II nevertheless agreed to the publication of the decrees in Spain in 1564, although he inserted a 'catch all' clause that his royal rights were not thereby to be infringed. Too much has been made of that clause. It did lead to some jurisdictional wrangles—as to whether the Pope or the royally controlled Spanish Inquisition should try a Bishop for heresy, for instance *(see page 344)*—but this did not prevent the implementation of the important reforming decrees.

Those decrees were to have greater consequence in the Netherlands, where they were also published, than they had in Philip II's Spanish dominions where the Reconquista tradition made them easy to adopt without much change or turmoil. In the Netherlands Philip was carrying out a policy of religious and political centralisation in which the Tridentine Decrees had a major role. The problem was that this policy offended noble and urban liberties to the extent that it stimulated what was to become the Dutch Revolt *(see Chapter XIV)*. This had two effects on the Counter-Reformation. In one way it was a disaster in that the largely moderate Catholic population of the northern Netherlands were to come under the sway of a minority of Calvinists in the new United Provinces. It was a success, though, in that from 1590 onwards the southern Netherlands were thoroughly reclaimed for Catholicism. Calvinists fled north or submitted to the combined efforts of papal ambassadors called *nuncios*, Bishops conscientious in their visitations and 3000 Jesuits and Capuchins. By the time of the long postponed peace settlement between the Spanish and the Dutch in 1648, once great centres of Protestantism like Antwerp and Brussels in the Spanish Netherlands again looked to Rome for guidance. The foundations of a Catholic Belgium had been laid.

It was also by 1648 that the religious lines of Germany were more clearly drawn than they had been at the Peace of Augsburg in 1555. Many supposedly Catholic territories in the mid-sixteenth century, such as the Habsburg lands themselves, were riddled with Protestantism. In 1556 the Catholic princes accepted the Tridentine Decrees, with just a few modifications. The dukes of Bavaria were among the first to back the setting up of that most effective of Jesuit seminaries at Ingolstadt in 1556, co-operating with Peter Canisius, the Jesuit who masterminded the Counter-Reformation in southern Germany. The dukes had already done much towards undermining those protectors of Protestantism, the local Estates, and when they accepted the Tridentine Decrees the grateful Pope made over ten percent of clergy income in Bavaria for princely use. It is clear that princes could expect to make nearly as much out of the Counter-Reformation as the princely followers of Luther had made out of Protestantism.

Of all the Catholic princes, the Emperor Ferdinand seemed the most reluctant actively to support the Tridentine Decrees. He was fearful of strife with the Protestants and even touchier than his nephew Philip about his prerogatives with regard to the Church. It was not until his Jesuit-trained great-grandson Ferdinand became the Emperor Ferdinand II in 1619 that there was a concerted effort to purge the Habsburg lands of Protestantism. This effort merged into the Thirty Years' War (1618–48) during which the Emperor in the Edict of Restitution (1629) tried to take back all Church lands which had been illegally secularised by Protestants. This would have been the high point of the Counter-Reformation—if it had worked! However, the Habsburg failure on a European scale in that conflict should not obscure the fact that, at home in the Bohemian and Austrian lands, Protestants had finally lost their liberties and Jesuit education had provided the basis for a triumphant Catholicism.

The character of southern Germany was changed by the Counter-Reformation but even more affected was the character of Poland. With much power in the hands of noblemen, the elected kings of Poland could only exert their authority if they were men of a remarkable personality. While the Papal Nuncio persuaded the King of Poland to accept the Tridentine Decrees almost immediately in 1564, it was not until the reigns of the vigorous Stephen Bathory (1576–86) and then Sigismund III (1587–1632) that energetic reform began. There was little concerted opposition to the Catholics as Poland was as anarchic religiously as it was politically with at least six different religious affiliations vying with each other. The kings enjoyed the legacy of reform in Poland conducted by Cardinal Hosius (d1579) and the continuing support of Jesuits teaching in colleges and preaching on missions. This activity gave Poland a Catholic identity which has been a mainstay of its national tradition down to the present day.

While Poland was the scene of an undoubted triumph of the Counter-Reformation, France in the later part of the sixteenth century looked as though it would be the scene of its most signal failure. No Tridentine Decrees were accepted there in the 1560s. Instead the country was plunged into the Wars of Religion which were to last over 35 years *(see Chapter XIV)*.

In 1598 peace was made when Henry IV, having converted to Catholicism five years earlier as a political expedient, came to a compromise settlement with his former supporters the Huguenots (French Protestants) in the Edict of Nantes *(see page 422)*. This looked like a major Catholic defeat in that it guaranteed the security and near independence of large Protestant areas in the south and west of France. In fact, it effectively quarantined Protestantism in those areas and paved the way for a triumphant Catholic renewal in the seventeenth century. The early seventeenth century in France saw a whole gallery of saints, St Vincent de Paul, St Jean Eudes, St Francis de Sales and many others, who were to revitalise the Catholic priesthood and Catholic devotion in France, with the aid of aristocratic patronage. The kings of seventeenth century France gave their tacit approval even though they continued to foster some abuses such as pluralism. (Henry IV even gave two abbeys to the Protestant Duc de Sully.) While the Tridentine Decrees were never officially registered in France, an Assembly of the Clergy in 1615 did acknowledge their acceptance of them, without opposition from the King. Men of power might be diverted from spiritual matters—the reformist Bishop of Luçon became that scheming politician Cardinal Richelieu—but their whole way of thinking was coloured by Catholic reform.

By the end of the seventeenth century reformist vitality had ebbed although the Counter-Reformation reached its climax in a dubious way in the reign of Louis XIV. Where saints had failed Louis seemed to think troops would succeed; he tried to convert the Huguenots by force, finally revoking the Edict of Nantes in 1685, which merely deprived Protestants of their civil liberties rather than enhancing Catholic renewal. And there had emerged in France a brand of reform Catholics called the Jansenists whose views on predestination made them, for Louis and the Jesuits, dangerously like the Calvinists. The King's unsuccessful attempt to rout the Jansenists by destroying their convents and by calling on the Pope for help shows us how sterile the Counter-Reformation could become. It showed also how resilient diverse brands of Catholic reform could be, with the Jansenists maintaining their influence on into the eighteenth century.

Catholic reformers were confined to certain areas—England after 1558, northern Germany and Scandinavia were to be closed to them—but it is clear that we cannot confine Catholic reform or Counter-Reformation to the sixteenth century. Varieties of political circumstances determined where and when the reformers could do their work, spreading it out over at least one and a half centuries. However, historians writing recently have begun to realise that the exact nature of its impact upon the people must also be taken into account, and that makes us take up an even broader perspective.

11. The New Catholicism—Reaching the People

The people of Europe had undoubtedly witnessed the preaching friars, the pious Brethren of the towns, the reformist writers, the 'devout' of the later Middle Ages. However, the impression made could be superficial, particularly as the 'devout' tended not to venture into what could be a semi-pagan countryside, and even in the towns there were numerous parishes not remotely touched by this sporadic movement of piety. The Fathers at Trent thought they had answers. The people could be reached through an invigoration of the hierarchy: Pope—Bishops—parish priests, with the last being newly capable of answering the religious needs of the people.

The Council Fathers were not wholly unrealistic. Albeit slowly the

Tridentine Decrees did change the parish priest as visitation records, for instance for France in the seventeenth century, clearly show. The priest knew his Latin and the liturgy, he preached effectively and he set a moral example to his parishioners. The problem with these improvements was that they were variable even within dioceses and they took time just when the Counter-Reformation was demanding speedy results. The new priest needed new auxiliaries to reach the people.

(a) Saints

Sociologists have noted that the starting point of popular movements is often an individual possessing 'charisma', that capacity to express in personality, action and words the profound aspirations of a whole group of followers. (One historian has more prosaically described it as star quality.) In the late sixteenth and early seventeenth century there were large numbers of men and women with marked charisma. The Church recognised their value. Nearly all have since been made saints. Some of these saints found their strength in preaching. St Philip Neri in Rome, for instance, provides a most extraordinary example. He would make his mark by joking and dancing even during Church services and his preaching became enormously popular. St Philip did not just reach the people direct. He passed on his skills by gathering together his followers in a new Oratory, the Roman Oratory. This in turn inspired Pierre Bérulle to found a French Oratory in 1611. Preaching was to be conducted not just by old-style friars or workaday priests, but by newly-trained professionals.

St Philip was not just a preacher; he was also something of a mystic—someone blessed with ecstatic visions of the workings of God. The classic mystic of the later sixteenth century was St Teresa of Avila. In her autobiography she told of her ecstasy when a most beautiful angel thrust his great arrow into her three times, consuming her soul with the love of God. But Teresa was not by any means obsessed by visions; her success also lies in the fact that she was an intensely practical person. In her opinion true religion found its origin in common sense, and common sense told her to reform her own order of nuns, the Carmelites. She did that with great success. Many in Castile were suspicious of that success. Mysticism smacked of bypassing the Church on the route to Paradise and there were interests vested in the old ways of the Carmelites. But Teresa was unstoppable. She was too valuable in bringing Catholicism to the people.

Similarly suspect earlier in Rome had been St Ignatius Loyola, founder of the Jesuits. He too was a mystic and yet an intensely practical man. His 6000 letters show how well he kept his finger on the pulse of reform all round the world. His 'charisma' was to find its way into his *Spiritual Exercises*, methodical prayers to enhance spiritual fitness, and into the *Constitutions*, the rules of the Jesuit Order. We shall be looking at those at the end of the chapter.

While St Ignatius attended to missionary work in Europe as a whole and far round the globe, St Carlo Borromeo worked on a smaller scale and with a minute attention to the detail of the Christian life. Active as Archbishop of Milan between 1566 and 1584, he copied and expanded upon Giberti's work in Verona as a model Bishop. His was to be the model execution of the Tridentine Decrees. He held frequent synods and set up six seminaries in his archdiocese. To ensure his detailed reforms were carried out, he founded the Oblates of St Ambrose, a local version of the Jesuits, their oaths of loyalty being to the Archbishop. Borromeo saw the need to control the laity as well as the priests. He used police to arrest those who obstructed his policies, as well as employing sophisticated techniques of social control *(see page 323)*.

This sounds like the sort of repression which might stimulate reaction rather than reform, but Borromeo's charisma carried it through. The people saw the Archbishop threaten to excommunicate the hated Spanish governor, who quailed at his moral authority. The people saw him give away all his possessions and set an example of self-denial hitherto unknown in Milan. In 1576 the people saw their saintly Archbishop follow the example of the lowly Capuchins, tending plague victims in person. It was moral authority which gave Borromeo his hold over people. And this hold was not confined to northern Italy. In 1582 the *Acts of the Church of Milan* were published and became the textbook for every would-be reforming Bishop in Europe. Again 'charisma' had carried reform to the people and had not perished with the person of the saint.

(b) Teachers
It was realised by the saints described above, as by other reformers, that efficient preaching, organisation and charity were not enough by themselves. The new Catholicism required a full understanding as well as outward compliance. That could only be achieved through education.

This had been perceived, of course, in the early days of the Catholic Reformation. Erasmus saw the need for efficient education. In France, Jean Standonck had made Montaigu College an exemplary academy of learning from 1499 onwards and Loyola was one of its former pupils —but so was Calvin. Clearly a more systematic 'Counter-Reformation' approach was needed. In the realm of secondary schooling, as in missionary training, this was largely at the initiative of the Jesuits. At first Loyola had thought of training only his own Jesuit priests. But, flexibility being the mark of his character and his order, he saw the education of ordinary children as the invaluable tool it was. In 1552 the first Jesuit non-clerical school was opened at Billom in France. Thereafter the number of Jesuit colleges, combining Jesuit training with secondary schooling for ordinary children, grew to around 200 by 1650.

To ensure that their educational investment was earning a maximum return, the Jesuits were highly selective as to ability in their admissions policy. As with so much effective education, the Jesuits indoctrinated their pupils with basic principles but also gave them the capacity to

319

apply them independently. This may be contrasted with the failures of Lutheran schooling where indoctrination pure and simple was tried and largely failed *(see page 156)*. Parents, even if lukewarm in religious terms, sent their children to the Jesuits for the best education available. Good Catholics were produced, often more pious than their parents, and with a sense of mission.

Not all pupils were as high-born as Ferdinand of Styria, later to be Emperor Ferdinand II, but most were aristocratic and many were destined to be men of influence. They remained loyal to their schools, organised in later life into 'sodalities' (old boys' associations, in effect). In 1640 there were 11 300 members of Jesuit sodalities in the Franco-Belgian province alone.

Coupled with their activities as confessors to kings and the high-born, the Jesuits' role as teachers more than anything else consolidated the Catholic renewal among the upper classes of Catholic Europe. But they, along with other reforming orders, were not content with that. There was a missionary impetus to take a re-invigorated Catholicism beyond the bounds of the élite of Catholic Europe.

(c) Missioners

The Jesuits provide the most dramatic examples of missionary work across the globe. They were received by suspicious Samurai in Japan, executed by Protestants in England and eaten by Huron Indians in North America. At the Jesuits' English college founded in 1568 at Douai in Flanders, Fathers Campion and Parsons were trained for what proved to be their fatal mission to England in 1580. Their execution has been made much of in English history but despite the hue and cry surrounding their capture, their work did not go beyond succouring a few of the faithful and must, quantitatively, be put into perspective beside the immense task of bringing Christianity to the pagans of Asia and America *(see page 324)* and the semi-pagans of rural Europe. It is the latter whom we shall look at next.

'Missions being necessary everywhere, we shall preach everywhere, but with preference in the country.' (St Jean Eudes, one of the leading French missioners of the seventeenth century). The Jesuits had seen the need to make religion a country matter but all manner of men and orders were also employed to do so. Many who answered St Vincent de Paul's call to preach to the 'poor people of the fields' came from that saint's establishment at St Lazare founded in 1632. It offered priests fortnight 'refresher courses' as well as basic training for missioners.

As might be expected from newly efficient Catholics, the rural missions were characteristically methodical. Preaching took place when it would interfere least with agricultural work. The people were for a start taught simple basic prayers and learned to sing hymns set to popular tunes. Success was judged to be when all the parishioners had recognised their sins. As St Vincent de Paul put it in 1639: 'Our maxim is not to leave a village until everybody has made his general confession; and there aren't many in the places we visit who don't.' Of course, it could not simply end with that. Missioners had to leave behind them the signs of greater devotion in attention to the sacraments and feast days and the machinery of instruction in the form of catechism classes, where the essentials of the faith would be recited, and primary schools. The missioner also had to return every few years to check up on it all.

This sounds quite straightforward. The Tridentine priest, supplemented by saints and missioners, would bring the Catholic renewal to rural Europe. But perhaps 'renewal' is an important word. While one must be wary of exaggerating the point, Jean Delumeau has shown, in *Catholicism between Luther and Voltaire*, that there were many ways in which people of the Middle Ages had scarcely ever been Christianised at all. With regard to them it was not so much renewal, as starting from scratch.

12. Popular Culture and 'Christianisation'

'The Age of the Cathedral Builders'. That cliché is too often used to imply that the Middle Ages was an era of simple, constructive faith in comparison to our own secular age. In fact, recent historians, acquainted with the methods of anthropology, have revealed a faith that is far from simple. A primitive rural society grapples with forces—storm, flood, disease—which are not naturally controllable and which require a religion to provide remedies in this world as much as redemption in the next. Delumeau claims that animism—the belief that spirits inhabit all material objects—was prevalent in Europe at least until the Industrial Revolution. Festivals, processions, relics all helped to ward off those evil spirits *(see page 22)*. Protestants and, up until recently, historians, wrote this off as superstition. It now seems necessary to take it more seriously.

Quite consciously, the Church itself had taken these superstitions seriously in its early missionary days. In 601 AD Pope Gregory the Great had recommended that churches be erected on the sites of ancient temples. There is debate about how far the Church went in compromising itself in order to Christianise pagans, but there is firm evidence that the Church was alarmed about the capacity of the people to turn the tables and paganise the Christian religion. Even as late as 1674, the peasants at Autun in France sacrificed a heifer to the Virgin Mary to win protection for cattle against the plague. But the Church was fearful of worse paganism than this—witchcraft.

Although the witch hunts started before this period, it is no coincidence that they intensified during this time of Protestant and Catholic reform, although there were other factors involved *(see Chapter VI)*. Delumeau's argument is that both Protestantism and Catholic reform, for all their differences, were part of a more general movement of 'Christianisation'. There was a demand for a distinctively Christian commitment and no tolerance for folk magic. There was to be no tolerance for the sort of custom in Brittany where women threw dust from the floor of their chapel into the air in order to charm a good wind for their menfolk at sea. There was to be no tolerance for the healing at St Die where the cure for a peasant's dislocated hip was to hang up his breeches, full of ritually gathered horse dung, in the church.

Not just magic charms and folk healing were to be censured by the reforming Church; communal rituals and celebrations were to be condemned where they were too much akin to paganism. May Day fertility rites were banned by Borromeo. He also condemned Carnival as a period of gross self-indulgence. In doing so he was reiterating the opinion of so many Catholic reformers starting with Savonarola and Erasmus, and duplicating the attitude to be found amongst the Calvinists of Geneva or the Puritans of seventeenth century England.

However, while it is true that Protestants and Catholics shared a common aim in Christianisation involving an onslaught on witchcraft and the lesser evils of popular custom, it was the Catholics who were more willing to accommodate the old ways. Semi-pagan customs might be transformed. The Fires of St John, with accompanying rituals the night before the Feast of St John the Baptist, could be made acceptable. In Catholic Germany the main ritual was the burning on the bonfire of an image of Luther.

Alternatively the Church might find substitutes for popular customs. Veneration of saints was encouraged. There was no need for a traveller to appeal to a pagan god for protection when St Christopher could do the job. Saints could be popularised by being portrayed in art. St Joseph, often a figure of fun in the Middle Ages, had his reputation enhanced by many a pious painting of the Holy Family.

The great age of baroque art thus derived in part from the need to give the Catholic Church visual appeal and to provide a 'book for the unlearned'. Great artists like van Dyck and Rubens belonged to Jesuit sodalities, and owed much to the Counter-Reformation in the form of patronage and subject matter. Baroque art resided in ornate baroque churches, dramatic buildings designed to impress the people. The Jesuits amongst others were great builders in this style.

Where passive contemplation of art was insufficient, the people could be organised in processions winding their way around the new churches. A wake, a boisterous celebration in the church the night before a Saint's feast day, could be replaced by a vigil, a night spent in religious contemplation under the guidance of a priest. It was seen that popular activity was useful to the Church if only it could be channelled properly.

The guidance of a priest, that was what was necessary to combat paganism and to reform popular culture. The renewal of Catholicism in the sixteenth century and beyond ensured that guidance was available. However, simple guidance alone did not guarantee success.

13. Social Control and the New Catholicism

In a sense the Church was fighting on two fronts—to stop the people from becoming Protestant and to prevent them clinging to a virtually pagan tradition. To pre-empt both of these, priests did not just have to guide people or, as a last resort, to burn them when they proved stubborn. Priests had to learn subtle methods of social control.

Some of these methods have already been touched on. Education was of great importance. Primary education was virtually invented in the Early Modern period to catch the individual young and bring him up with a basic knowledge of Church doctrine and of course the authority of the Church.

That authority was reinforced when the priest sat in one side of the Confessional box, brought into use by Carlo Borromeo, while the individual sinner, alone and in the dark, sat in the other side. At a psychological advantage, the priest could then try to ensure inner repentance rather than just a ritual show of 'satisfaction' for sins committed. The Church, through the Confessional, learned how to manipulate guilt in an individual rather than relying on society in general to inspire shame in him for his sins.

The Church relied on society in general as little as possible. Parish registers were introduced to ensure that the major events of life were recorded and controlled. After the Council of Trent, marriage, for instance, was no longer regarded as purely a matter of family alliances; it had no validity unless carried out in the proper sacramental manner before a priest with the free consent of bride and groom. Ordinary people were no longer allowed to organise themselves into free religious associations. These confraternities either died out or were taken over by the Church and placed under the Bishops' control, following the example of Borromeo in Milan. Ironically, the Brethren of the Common Life, a confraternity and a fount of Catholic renewal, could not have flourished under this new regime.

In a *Past and Present* article (No. 37, 1970), John Bossy emphasises how this destructive side of the Church's social control could be self-defeating. Social structure in the Middle Ages depended very much on kinship—real as in marriage alliance, or artificial as in a confraternity. The Church's new controls hit that structure hard. However, the basic social unit remained the family and the Church failed to use that to further its cause. Protestants used it successfully in family prayer and domestic Bible reading. Bossy suggests it was for that very reason, the Protestant example, that the Counter-Reformation Church was afraid of working through the family, domestic religion being seen as 'a seedbed of subversion'. Owing to the Church's reluctance to use the family, 'its educative programme misfired' and its whole impact was brought into question.

Much more research needs to be done before the success of the Church's control of the people in the Early Modern age can be assessed.

There was much regional variation and that has yet to be mapped. But the story of one extraordinary character, a miller called Menocchio from Friuli in Italy, pinpoints something of the success and the failure of the Church.

Menocchio drew on wide reading, much conversation and some original thinking to come to the conclusion that the universe had existed before God and it could best be compared to cheese. The cheese had putrefied and out of it had emerged worms which were God and His angels. The Inquisition could not tolerate these views, especially as Menocchio would preach them to anyone who would listen, and forced him to recant in 1584. The miller, however, was irrepressible. He appeared before the Inquisition again in 1599 and this time he was handed over to the secular authorities to be burned.

In one sense the case of Menocchio shows the Church's failure. He could not be psychologically controlled. Also, Carlo Ginzburg, who has written his life story entitled *The Cheese and the Worms*, suspects that in Menocchio's talk 'we see emerging, as if out of a crevice in the earth, a deep-rooted cultural stratum'. There were certainly others like him —another miller called Pighino living near Modena, for instance. There may have been many more still who were afraid to talk. The Church could force a show of devotion, boosting the numbers taking Holy Communion at Easter for instance, but it could never be quite certain that those communicants were really devout.

In another sense, though, the Church could face up to Menocchio and his kind as a success. It had kept him under physical control for a time and then kept track of him when his behaviour lapsed. There was an efficiency in that, albeit a cruel one. And Menocchio was at least out of date when he claimed that 'the law and commandments of the Church' were 'all a business'. Even if it was not entirely successful, even if it had to resort to terror tactics sometimes, the Church was more than a business. It had a renewed spiritual mission by the end of the sixteenth century. This meant that the Catholic Church did advance into enemy territory on both fronts, against Protestantism and against independent popular traditions, even if the forces of Catholicism did not entirely win the war.

14. The Missions Overseas

The clearest indication that the Catholic Church of the sixteenth century was not merely responding to the Protestant threat is the extraordinary dynamism with which it undertook missions to the newly discovered lands around the globe. By 1500 Franciscan and Dominican friars had started to cross the Atlantic to use their skills in popular preaching to convert the pagans. Before Ignatius Loyola thought of combating Protestantism, he was all set to convert the Infidel. Jesuits went on to show as much dedication in China or South America as they did in Europe. Some contemporaries saw this activity abroad as compensation for the souls lost to Protestantism at home. But this compensation may be more of an effect than a cause. A vision of Christendom embracing a whole New World certainly pre-dated Luther's protest.

There was as complex a relationship between power and conversion across the world as between power and reform at home. This was especially true in central and southern America where the Spanish Conquistadores brought Christianity as part of their imperial baggage. For these crusaders the notion of a just war involved the *requerimento*: a notice could be read to the Indians instructing them to convert. If they ignored it, not surprisingly, that was the justification for the glorious slaughter to begin. The Conquistadores, however, did not get it all their own way. Bartolomé de las Casas was just one of the leading missionaries to contest this soulless approach. The Pope was persuaded to issue the Bull *Sublimis Deus* (1537) which stressed the humanity of Indians and even their willingness to be converted if only a chance was given.

The rate of conversion was enormous. For instance, moving on from South America, the Spaniards had started to colonise the Philippines in the middle of the sixteenth century. By 1620 there were two million converts to Christianity there. Supposedly the natives, impressed more by rituals than words, were much taken with the feasts and processions of the renewed Catholicism. They submitted readily to the mass baptisms which could admit thousands each day to the Catholic faith. But that raises the question of just how far these converts were actually Christianised.

It is likely that many went through the motions of Christianity because they were scared, at least where the missionaries came with conquistadores. Prestige was also a great incentive for conversion. Lower caste Hindus were tempted by the offer of joining that superior caste, the Portuguese. In some cases the simple novelty of a strangely dressed missionary appearing from nowhere would convince natives that here was a visitation from a superior god. There is no certain method of assessing or counting faith or its superficiality across the sixteenth century world. There is one acid test though—martyrdom.

In 1549–51 there took place the first Jesuit mission to Japan. St Francis Xavier was the missionary. He had already helped to confirm Goa, a Portuguese settlement on the west coast of India, as a 'little Rome'. During his lifetime he was responsible for about 30 000 baptisms. He was clearly a saint of the charismatic type and Loyola did right to entrust him with the mission to the East. Xavier was to leave a solid base of about 1000 Christians in Japan. By the 1590s there were 300 000 responding strongly to the Christian message during a period of religious and political decadence in their own land. But a national reaction led to the persecution of Christians in 1613 in which many thousands of Japanese Christians died. Their martyrdom suggests a deeper faith than fear of Europeans, power, prestige or novelty value would explain.

Even with martyrdom as a test, the nature of the faith could be disputed. The problem of the Church accommodating itself to a pagan culture was raised in the global mission as much as it was in Europe. A fierce debate known as the Rites Controversy beset Matteo Ricci, a missionary in China from 1582 to 1610. His Chinese philosophical writings were thought by some to be adulterating rather than transmitting the Christian message. There was the fear that anything deviating from the culture of the Christian élite was a threat to Christianity; and that was a feature of the Catholic renewal in Europe as it was in the missions abroad.

The unique capacity of the Jesuits to operate successfully in the political sphere showed itself in the overseas missions as in Europe. The Jesuits in China, the Peking Fathers, kept the favour of changing emperors by acting as advisers, even showing their intellectual breadth in running the royal observatory. At the other end of the social scale, the Jesuits of South America organised the territories of the Guaraní along the Paraná and neighbouring rivers. The territory was granted to them by Philip III of Spain in 1608 and it accommodated about 100 000 Indians in what evolved into an almost classic Utopia. A peaceful population lived in well-planned towns, serving the community and holding goods in common. The Jesuits were in fact creating a secular version of themselves, the Indians being living elements of a monastic life while outside the usual monastic discipline. These 'Reductions', as the Guaraní autonomous territories were known, lasted until the aggression of slave traders, and the waning of Jesuit fortunes, spelt their end in the eighteenth century.

The example of the Guaraní shows how the Catholic renewal of the sixteenth century could find the fullest expression beyond the confines of Europe. In that remote part of South America, there had been no political obstacles, the deadweight of tradition in that sense being absent. And there were no Protestants to combat—this was something more than just Counter-Reformation.

15. Bibliography

M Mullett *The Counter Reformation* (Lancaster Pamphlets, 1984). N S Davidson *The Counter Reformation* (Historical Association, 1987). (Both of these are readable and concise pamphlets.) M R O'Connell *The Counter Reformation* (Harper Torchbooks, 1973). A G Dickens *The Counter Reformation* (Thames & Hudson, 1968). B Bradshaw 'The Reformation and the Counter Reformation'—a review of the recent historiography in *History Today*, November 1983.

16. Discussion Points and Exercises

A   *This section consists of questions or points that might be used for discussion (or written answers) as a way of expanding on the chapter and testing understanding of it:*

326

1 How have historians changed in their approach to the history of Catholic renewal in the sixteenth century?

2 Was Catholic reform having any impact before the need to react to Luther?

3 In what ways did the New Orders help to restore the Church?

4 Why did Catholic princes before Trent fail to make Church reform a priority?

5 Why were the Popes also so reluctant to embark on reform?

6 What eventually caused the Council of Trent to be summoned?

7 'The political obstacles at Trent almost prevented the Council achieving anything.'

8 What was the main aim behind the Council's doctrinal decrees?

9 What were the disciplinary decrees designed to achieve?

10 How did the Popes after Trent further the work of the Council?

11 'Even after Trent the backing of princes counted for little in the Counter-Reformation.'

12 Why were saints, teachers and missioners important to the cause of reform?

13 How did the Catholic reformers react to popular beliefs and culture?

14 What techniques did the Church use to improve its social control over its congregations? How far were they successful?

15 What were the achievements of Catholic missionaries beyond Europe?

B *Essay questions*

1 How adequately does the term 'Counter-Reformation' describe the Catholic renewal of the Early Modern period?

2 What was the role of the Popes in the Counter-Reformation?

3 'It was the work of the New Orders rather than the Council of Trent which was most important to the Catholic renewal of the sixteenth century.' Discuss.

4 Assess the significance of the Jesuits in the Counter-Reformation.

5 'The Catholic princes of Europe did more to hold back than to advance the cause of Catholic renewal in the sixteenth century.' Do you agree?

6 What impact did the Counter-Reformation have on the people of Early Modern Europe?

17. Documentary Exercise—The Jesuits

The purpose of this exercise is to establish what made the Jesuits unique and what made them successful.

1 The Jesuits have been mentioned in this chapter in relation to various aspects of the renewal of Catholicism *(see pages 302 and 319)*. Gather the relevant information together in note form as the starting point

of your investigation. As you do so, give emphasis to what made the Jesuits most important to the Church.

2   Ignatius Loyola (1491–1556) was the founder of the Jesuits. His life story was important as his *Autobiography* was to be an inspiration to his followers. Consider the following information and extracts drawn from the *Autobiography*.

> (a)   Loyola was a professional soldier until injured at Pamplona in 1521. While convalescing he read religious works including Lives of the Saints who became his heroes. Thereafter he decided to dedicate his life to the service of God.
>
> (b)   In 1522–23 he lived the life of a holy beggar at Manresa near Barcelona. There in his own words 'often and for a long time while at prayer, I saw with interior eyes the humanity of Christ. The form that appeared to me was like a white body, neither very large nor very small . . . I have also seen our Lady in a similar form . . . if there were no Scriptures to teach us these matters of the faith, I would be resolved to die for them, only because of what I had seen.'
>
> (c)   In 1527 Loyola's unusual appearance and preaching landed him in prison in Salamanca where he was investigated by the Inquisition, albeit only for a short time. To a lady who sympathised with him he replied: 'Does imprisonment seem to be such a great evil to you? Well, I will tell you that there are not so many grills and chains in Salamanca that I would not wish for more for the love of God.'
>
> (d)   Loyola moved to Paris where he furthered his education from 1528 to 1535. There with eight friends he took the three monastic vows and a special one of obedience to the Pope.
>
> (e)   At first the aim was to serve as missionaries in Palestine but war made this impossible. By 1537 Loyola and his followers, now going by the name of the Society of Jesus, were in Rome. But being Spaniards and without a clearly defined role, they were not well received by all whom they encountered there. Some accusers said of Loyola and his companions that they 'were fugitives from Spain, from Paris, from Venice . . . The legate ordered silence to be imposed on the whole affair, but I did not accept that, saying that I wanted a definite sentence . . . I went to speak to the Pope at Frascati . . . he ordered sentence to be given and it was in my favour . . .'

1   *In what ways might these examples drawn from Loyola's life have strengthened his followers' resolve?*

2   *What difficulties does the historian face in using the* Autobiography *as evidence of Loyola's life?*

3   While at Manresa in 1522–23 Loyola was developing his 'Spiritual Exercises'. They were to be a distinguishing feature of Jesuit practice, but the exercises were often used by non-Jesuits, even including that leader of the *spirituali*, Cardinal Contarini. Here are some extracts from the day-to-day programme of meditation intended to last about a month under the guidance of a spiritual director.

> (a)   'First preliminary. The picture. In this case it is a vivid portrayal in the imagination of the length, breadth and depth of hell.' 'Second preliminary.

Asking for what I want. Here it will be to obtain a deepfelt consciousness of the sufferings of those who are damned, so that, should my faults cause me
5 to forget my love for the eternal Lord, at least the fear of these sufferings will help to keep me out of sin.'

'First Heading. To see in imagination those enormous fires, and the souls as it were with bodies of fire.'

'To hear in imagination the shrieks and groans . . .'
10 'To smell in imagination the fumes of sulphur . . .'

'To taste in imagination all the bitterness of tears . . .'

'To feel in imagination the heat of the flames . . .'

(b) 'I will try to be ashamed of all my sins, using illustrations; for example, I may think of a knight, standing before his king and the whole court, utterly
15 ashamed at having greatly offended one from whom he had received many gifts and acts of kindness.'

(c) 'Another picture. A great plain, comprising the entire Jerusalem district, where is the supreme commander-in-chief of the forces of good, Christ our Lord: another plain near Babylon, where Lucifer is, at the head
20 of the enemy.'

(d) 'To arrive at complete certainty, this is the attitude of mind we should maintain: I will believe that the white object I see is black if that should be the decision of the hierarchical Church, for I believe that linking Christ our Lord the Bridegroom and his Church, there is one and the same Spirit,
25 ruling and guiding us for our souls' good.'

(e) 'Whilst it is absolutely true that no man can be saved without being predestined and without faith and grace, great care is called for in the way in which we talk and argue about all these matters'.

1 *What technique did Loyola use to increase the impact of a religious idea (lines 1–12)?*

2 *Why does Loyola refer to a knight (line 14) and to armies (lines 17–20)? What response was he trying to stimulate?*

3 *Why was it necessary to give entire obedience to the 'hierarchical Church' (line 23)? Is there a connection with Loyola's caution over discussing predestination (lines 26–28)?*

4 In 1539 Loyola put forward a draft charter for the Society of Jesus. It was difficult to get it accepted as there was much suspicion of these monks who did not spend most of their time in prayer and monastic rituals but were free to do other work and to travel wherever they were needed.

Here is an extract:

All members shall be aware . . . that this entire Society and its members serve as soldiers in faithful obedience to the most holy lord Paul III and his successors. . . . We are bound to carry out instantly, as far as in us lies, without any evasion or excuse his orders: whether he sends us to the Turks, or into the New World, or to the Lutherans, or into any other realms of infidels or believers . . .

The Pope accepted the charter in 1540. In 1547–50 Loyola perfected the organisation of the Society in his *Constitutions* which included:

One who is sent to an extensive region such as the Indies or other provinces and for whom no particular district is marked out, may remain in one place for a longer or shorter period. Or, after considering the reasons on one side or the other, while praying and keeping his will indifferent, he may travel about wherever he judges this to be more expedient for the glory of God our Lord.

And as to qualifications the *Constitutions* laid down:

The profession (to join the Society) should be made only by persons who are selected for their spirit and learning, thoroughly and lengthily tested, and known with edification and satisfaction to all after various proofs of virtue and self-denial.

1 *Why did Loyola place such emphasis on the so-called 'fourth vow' of obedience to the Pope?*
2 *What prevented the Jesuits from being mere automatons in the service of the Pope?*

5 Clear evidence of the Society of Jesus in action comes from letters written to and by Jesuits.

Margaret of Parma, later Regent of the Netherlands (1559–67), wrote the following to Father Polanco, a leading Jesuit, in 1556:

... I can only tell you, therefore, that you can depend upon my assistance in everything as far as lies in my power, and that you will always find me ready to further your interests and do whatever I can for you in all things.

Accordingly I beg you not to hesitate to address yourself to me on any question which may arise and to remember me in your holy prayers. This will always give me the greatest satisfaction and this we ask in the conviction that it will also be acceptable to God our Father.

A keen follower of Loyola in 1554 was Joanna of Austria, sister of Philip II and shortly Regent of Spain (1555–59). She applied to become a Jesuit, but the Society of Jesus was an all-male order, and it was also necessary that Joanna should remain available for a marriage arranged to suit Habsburg diplomacy.

Much correspondence passed between Castile and Rome, Joanna being referred to by the pseudonym 'Matteo Sanchez' in order to keep the delicate matter secret. It was decided to admit Joanna, ignoring her sex. She was also allowed to take her vows in the knowledge that although she could not break them, the General of the Order could release her from them as was the case with any novice. On this basis Joanna became the only Jesuitess in history. In connection with this, Loyola wrote in 1554 to the leading Jesuit in Spain, Father Borgia (the Duke of Gandia):

... As to the rest, this person shall not have to change their dress, or residence, nor to give any demonstration whatever of what it is sufficient should be kept between themselves and God our Lord. The Society, or someone from it, shall have the obligation of the care of this person's soul, in so far as it is demanded by God's service and the comfort of that soul, to the glory of God our Lord.

1 *What do these letters tell us about how the Jesuits worked?*
2 *The Jesuits have been accused of casuistry—tortuous moral argument or the assumption that the ends justify the means. How far does the case of Joanna of Austria support that accusation?*

6 To summarise: make a list of the important ways in which the Jesuits were distinctive, identifying their special strengths.

XIII Philip II: The Mediterranean

1. Introduction

Philip II inherited a collection of states that formed a Mediterranean empire comprising Spain, Milan, Naples and Sicily and some outposts in North Africa. Then there were his Atlantic possessions consisting of the Netherlands and the New World. To this was added, in 1580, Portugal and its immense empire. The Atlantic states had the potential to become a powerful empire to match that of the Mediterranean but Philip failed to forge any links between them, preferring to treat them as distinct entities connected only through Madrid. However, like his father Charles V, Philip was continually beset by problems spread across Europe, making conflicting demands on his resources.

The reign of Philip II saw a decisive shift in Spanish orientation. For the first 20 years, Philip pursued a defensive policy seeking to minimise conflict. Spain was a Mediterranean power, concerned above all with the menace of Islam and the Ottoman Turks. The conquest and annexation of Portugal brought a dramatic change. The focus of attention swung away from the Mediterranean to the Atlantic and Philip became much more aggressive in his foreign policy, waging war not only in the Netherlands but also against England and France.

2. The New King and His Empire

Philip II was born in 1527, the much-loved son of Charles V whose influence had a profound and lasting effect on his son. Philip was the effective ruler of Spain from 1543 when he became Regent at the age of sixteen. His father took the opportunity to give him detailed advice which Philip followed for the rest of his life. In it, Charles exhorted Philip not to trust anyone and to take advice from as many as possible. He was to rely on God, conceal his feelings and be just to all men. These became the hallmarks of Philip's rule. His piety was unquestioned, he attended Mass daily and religion pervaded all aspects of his life. He kept his emotions under strict control, greeting both the triumph of Lepanto and the disaster of the Armada with the same lack of emotion. He endeavoured always to be just in his dealings although at times he justified involvement in assassination, as we shall see.

Most of the above characteristics could be seen as strengths but the same is not true of Philip's obsessive lack of trust which poisoned the atmosphere at court and bred uncertainty and faction. It also made him reluctant to delegate responsibility and this slowed the workings of his empire to the speed at which he alone could transact business. Although Philip was extremely hard-working, spending some eight or nine hours a day at his desk, he could not hope to deal with all the business of empire unaided and have an efficient administration. The problem was compounded by Philip's inability to distinguish the important from the trivial. When the Armada was in preparation, he was engaged in correspondence with Rome about clerical vestments.

Philip was aware of the delays in sending and receiving instructions and it made him determined to make the right decision first time. Unfortunately this slowed the process still further as he sought to consult as widely as possible before making up his mind. His own lack of incisive thought can be seen in this margin note on a suggestion by the Duke of Alva that councillors be given correspondence early enough to make an informed judgement about it: 'Of the zeal of the Duke I am very sure; about the rest, although he is often right about many things, still in some instances perhaps not, and therefore I do not expect to look into all (he says) in order to arrange matters suitably, unless there is more time for it, but for now I will go on thinking about it. In order to take care of this it is necessary to look into other matters, but as I said, all will be studied in order to do what I believe is suitable.'

While Philip deliberated, his empire suffered. Pius V wrote sternly, 'Your Majesty spends so long considering your undertakings that, when the time to perform comes, the occasion has passed'. Philip was not entirely to blame for the slowness of communication but he exacerbated the problem by his hesitant indecision and his refusal to delegate responsibility so that everything had to go through the centre.

Philip II's empire spread across Europe and over into the New World. Its king, however, was Spanish and determined to remain so. Although Philip was in the Netherlands when he became King of Spain and did not return for another three years, in 1559, he never left the peninsula again. Unlike his father he did not regard it as important to see, and be seen in, his different dominions. He told his son, 'Travelling about one's kingdoms is neither useful nor decent'. Philip established a permanent capital at Madrid, in the centre of Spain conveniently close to the great palace of the Escorial. Philip also relied almost exclusively on Castilian advisers. Only one non-Iberian, Cardinal Granvelle, reached high office in his reign, and he had also served Charles V. This all sent clear messages to the rest of Philip's territories about the nature of his empire.

Philip II's empire, like that of Charles V, was an empire of inheritance except in America, conquered by the conquistadores. In other respects Philip's empire was very different from that of his father. He did not inherit the Imperial title nor the world vision that had inspired Charles to seek to be leader of Christendom. However, his inheritance of the Netherlands was to entangle him in the affairs of northern Europe.

Philip did not regard his dominions as having any unity beyond himself and he did not try to foster a wider sense of commitment between the constituent parts. Thus, he rejected Granvelle's suggestion that members of the high nobility in the Netherlands should be given influential positions in Italy, in order to give them a sense of belonging to the empire. Instead, Philip increasingly came to appear as a Spanish, and specifically Castilian, king, who regarded all his other territories as subordinate, whatever he might profess to the contrary. This inevitably increased dissatisfaction in the outlying states and the distinction between the good prince and his evil advisers which usually characterises rebellion became blurred. So, in the Netherlands, Philip himself came to be the focus of opposition. The issue for the whole empire was whether it would become a Castilian dependency or whether an honourable partnership could be maintained between the centre and the outer members. For the relatively free Netherlands, the possibility of being reduced to the condition of Castile with its compliant Cortes and all-powerful Inquisition was highly alarming. If he had been willing to visit his dominions Philip would have been able to reassure his subjects and convince them that he still regarded them as important.

Philip's dependence on Castile is hardly surprising since it was not only his home but also the major supplier of revenue and soldiers for the empire. In theory each part of the empire was self-supporting but in many instances Spain had to subsidise the rest. Italy made a valuable contribution to the war against the Turks, and America produced ever-increasing quantities of bullion (12 500 000 ducats in the first half of the reign, 52 000 000 ducats in the second) but all other non-Castilian territories were a burden on the central treasury. It is a particular irony that it was the attempt to make the Netherlands financially independent through the imposition of the Tenth Penny that sparked off revolt and placed an intolerable burden on government finance. As Kamen has pointed out: 'The limited role of Spain under Charles V was in sharp contrast to its new role under Philip II. By imposing on Spain the Burgundian territories (the Netherlands) and other obligations, Charles forced it to take on the leadership of an empire which neither its military nor its economic capacity had earned.' The burden of empire simultaneously made Spain a great power and promoted a 'golden age' of cultural achievement, while sowing the seeds of decline as the economy struggled to meet the enormous demands placed upon it. The price of pre-eminence was to be very high.

Creating a sense of unity in the empire would always have been very difficult. As Braudel wrote, it 'depended on what was for the period an unprecedented combination of land and sea transport. . . . The Spanish Empire, which was poorly situated from the point of view of its European and world possessions, expended the better part of its energy in struggles against distance.' Communications in the sixteenth century were always uncertain, subject to the activities of pirates and the attitude of one's neighbours as well as the vagaries of the weather. For Spain, the presence of France dominating her lines of communication was always disturbing, even though for most of the reign of Philip II, the French were too occupied with their civil wars to disrupt Spanish traffic.

3. The Administration

Philip ruled his empire through a series of councils which had responsibility either for territory, such as the Council of Italy and the Council of the Indies, or for some aspect of government, for example the Council of War. These councils would receive reports which they would consider and then send with their recommendations to the King. He would annotate these and send them back for further consideration by the council, which would comment before the King made a final decision. (This process was capable of being repeated.) It was painstaking and extremely cumbersome. Philip disliked transacting business directly and therefore everything had to be written down. Not surprisingly, the King often complained that the volume of work was becoming excessive: 'We will see to all this tomorrow, for now I have neither the time nor the head for it'.

The Council of State was nominally the most important council but its function was purely advisory and Philip frequently ignored its suggestions. In practice, all the councils reported directly to the King and functioned independently of one another. I A A Thompson has detailed the way in which the authority and function of councils clashed, even allowing petitioners to play off one council against another. This led to conflicting orders and disagreements over each council's legitimate sphere of activity. In 1581, for instance, the Council of War protested against the issue of exemptions from billeting obligations by the Council of Castile and the Council of the Indies. Such conflicts were bound to limit the effectiveness of conciliar government, especially as Philip himself often reversed council decisions without bothering to inform them. In these circumstances it is hardly surprising that the councils failed to develop policies of their own. The Spanish empire was unrivalled in the sixteenth century for its depth of knowledge about its territories and the attention that was given to detail, but since the entire system rested on the speed at which Philip could work, the almost daily flow of information from the provinces was not utilised effectively and the councils were unable to develop their potential administrative efficiency.

It became apparent that some changes would have to be made because the whole system was liable to break down in a crisis, and the last years of the reign were a time of greater stress as the King's capacity to deal with it was declining. Thus, in the 1570s as the financial crisis worsened, Philip turned to the Council of Finance and an assortment of other advisers for a solution. By 1574 a course of action had been agreed upon but nothing was done and a decree of bankruptcy was forced on the King the following year. Ten years later it became physically impossible to transact all business with the old informality, and with Spain taking the offensive in the north a change in the structure of government became essential.

From 1586 the Grand Junta acquired an important role in government. This was an informal committee of Philip's chief ministers and it supervised the overall direction of policy. Philip often disregarded its advice at first, but increasingly he came to rely on its recommendations. The Grand Junta had a number of sub-committees which dealt with specific problems and were convened for as long as was necessary. The real power in the Grand Junta was exercised by an inner ring, known as the Junta of the Night. As Philip's reign drew to a close, this inner ring was formulating overall strategy and taking decisions that were referred to the King for his approval. This relieved much of the burden on Philip and enabled Spain to prosecute her wars against the Atlantic powers.

A key figure in the conciliar system was the secretary of state who acted as an intermediary with the King and had an important role in directing the business of the councils. Philip's secretary from 1543 to 1566 was Gonzalo Pérez who enjoyed enormous influence. On his death the secretaryship of state was divided into two, one dealing with northern Europe and the other with the Mediterranean. This division may have been because of the volume of work but it is equally likely to have been dictated by Philip's excessively suspicious nature—he disliked anyone but himself having a total knowledge of events. Gabriel de Zayas became secretary of the north and Gonzalo's illegitimate son, Antonio Pérez, became secretary of the south and came to wield great influence over the King.

The secretaries all came from the class of university-educated lawyers. This was the group that Philip preferred to employ because, unlike the *grandees*, they owed their position entirely to him. Diego de Espinosa (1502–72) was typical. He was a priest who had trained in law and he became president of the Council of the Inquisition in 1564 and additionally president of the Council of Castile in 1565. He was described a year later as 'the one man in all Spain in whom the King places most confidence and with whom he discusses most business'. No-one else was allowed to approach the position of trust which Espinosa had enjoyed.

Philip could not, however, ignore the *grandees* and they were given the most important and lucrative posts but Philip did not allow them much influence. Koenisberger has pointed out that Philip, like Charles V, tried to rule his empire through his personal control of patronage and all official appointments. Unfortunately, as Philip did not follow his father's practice of constant travelling, the non-Castilian parts of the empire felt excluded from the King's favour. It also made Philip more reliant on his secretaries since he needed advice, and the nature of his government excluded a free flow of information. This gave the secretaries enormous power because all petitioners had to work through them and it is hardly surprising that the system was open to abuse. Philip wished to choose only good ministers but because he insisted on rigid personal control, he actually promoted corruption and secrecy.

4. Faction and the Pérez Affair

'Transact business with many and do not bind yourself to or become dependent upon any individual.' Philip took these words of his father's to heart and encouraged subordinates to spy on their masters and report back to him. He also encouraged quarrels between ministers and institutions in the vain hope that he would have a clearer idea of what each was doing and be in a position to control them more easily. In fact, the results were wholly negative. Mediocrity and conservatism were encouraged as no-one wished to draw unfavourable attention to himself. At times there was an almost complete breakdown in government as different factions struggled against each other, which could even produce the conditions for revolt as in Andalucia before the revolt of the *Moriscos* in 1568.

Rivalries that might have been held in check at court in fact spread all across Spain through family networks and paralysed administration as each side tried to block the proposals of the other. Philip II bears a heavy responsibility for the atmosphere at court which encouraged such unhealthy struggles to develop.

There were two main factions, one led by the Duke of Alva and the other by Ruy Gómez de Silva, Prince of Eboli, who had married into the powerful Mendoza family. Gabriel de Zayas was linked to Alva's faction and Antonio Pérez to Eboli's, and on the latter's death in 1573, Pérez became leader of his faction. These factions opposed each other at all levels but their conflict was most clearly demonstrated in the debate on what to do about the outbreak of revolt in the Netherlands *(see page 368)*. In the event, Alva's policy of ruthless repression carried the day, but throughout his governorship there were contrary voices at court warning Philip against him and it is hardly surprising that Alva became the first of many governors to be recalled in disfavour owing to court intrigue, allowing an alternative strategy to be pursued.

By the time Alva was disgraced in 1573, the leadership of the Eboli faction had passed to Antonio Pérez. Philip already relied heavily on him and Pérez exploited this dependence. In the Netherlands, Don John of Austria, the King's half-brother, was made governor in 1576. Don John was ambitious and sought a kingdom for himself. He had hoped to carve one out in North Africa and only tolerated being sent to the Netherlands because of the possibility of invading England and marrying Mary Queen of Scots. Don John's secretary, Juan de Escobedo, had been a protégé of Pérez who expected to be kept informed of Don John's plans.

Conflict between these and the wishes of Philip, who suspected the ambitions of his brother, was to lead to trouble.

Escobedo was sent to Madrid in 1577 to try and obtain more money. To further his cause Escobedo apparently threatened to reveal to Philip that Pérez had been selling state secrets and that he was involved in a liaison with the Princess of Eboli, which might have involved negotiations with the Dutch rebels. Pérez decided Escobedo must be eliminated and he persuaded Philip that Escobedo was a danger to the state. Three assassins murdered Escobedo in March 1578. Popular rumour immediately blamed Pérez and Escobedo's family demanded vengeance which Philip was not prepared to take since he was implicated himself. His suspicions about Pérez were, however, aroused and these deepened during the negotiations about the Portuguese succession in 1578. Pérez was working with the Princess of Eboli to secure the throne (which Philip wanted himself) for the Duchess of Braganza, in the hopes that a marriage could be arranged between Eboli's daughter and Braganza's son.

These suspicions were confirmed when Don John's private correspondence arrived in Madrid in 1579 and showed that Pérez had been lying when he persuaded Philip that Escobedo was a danger to the state. All that Philip needed before he could take action was an alternative adviser. The Duke of Alva had been banished to his estates for allowing his son to make an unauthorised marriage, so with both factions discredited, Philip turned to Cardinal Granvelle who had been in Italy since 1564. The night he arrived in Madrid Pérez was arrested and the two factions disappeared from court. No real action was taken against Pérez until 1589, in the soul searching which followed the defeat of the Armada. He was tortured, made to confess to murder and sentenced to death, whereupon he escaped and fled to Aragon where he was instrumental in provoking revolt in 1590 (see page 353). The factions might have been overthrown by 1580 but their effects were to dog Philip into the last decade of his reign.

5. The Army

Philip's attempts to exert a centralised control over every aspect of government were seen in the army. Under Charles V, much of the permanent military establishment had been farmed out to contractors, so the North African fortresses, for instance, were virtually hereditary possessions of the great noble families. Philip reasserted royal control; for example, in 1556 the Duke of Medina Sidonia handed back the fortresses of Melilla which his family had held since 1497. By 1580 the entire military establishment had been restored to the Crown and was run by royal ministers. The demands of war placed great strains on the administration, especially after 1580 when Spain took on a more aggressive role and had to create a high seas fleet. The Council of War was in control of military organisation but it did not function entirely satisfactorily; in February 1586 there were only three members left in the Council and the secretaryship was vacant, yet this was the moment when it was decided to send an Armada against England. This caused a breakdown in the system of centralisation and private contractors and the localities gradually assumed responsibility for military matters again.

The Spanish *tercios* who fought in northern Europe were justly feared but they were the élite of Spain's fighting forces, seasoned in Italy before being exposed to the stresses of warfare. The soldiers who were responsible for the defence of their native land were much less impressive. They were always first to go short when money was lacking and mutiny was not a practicable option. Consequently morale, discipline and standards were all low and the military machine was permanently undermanned. In 1579 the three corps of Navarre were at half strength and this was not untypical. The great failing was that there was no firm financial settlement for either the regular or extraordinary expenses of war. Payments were made when they were unavoidable, from whatever sources were available. The revolt of the *Moriscos* broke out partly because they knew there was no militia, the guards were undermanned, the towns had no military supplies and the coasts were incapable of resisting enemy attack. It was fortunate for Philip that the Turks were more interested in seizing Cyprus than in exploiting his weakness.

6. Checks to Royal Authority

It was once fashionable to assert that Philip II was an 'absolute' king, in other words he had no effective checks to his power. This is a misleading view. Philip may have appeared to be free from constraints but there were many features of his rule that prevented it being absolute. These checks included physical factors such as distance and the lack of sufficient royal officials to keep a firm hand on administration. It has already been noted that the military establishment was insufficient to meet the threat of rebellion from an alien minority, let alone impose the royal will on a hostile population. Taxes were farmed out with a corresponding lack of control. Inefficiency was rife at all levels, from the King down, and it was only in co-operation with local oligarchies of nobility or clergy that the Crown could enforce its wishes. There were 66 *corregidores* in Castile who acted as the King's representatives but they were powerless on their own and could only hope to be effective working with local élites. The Cortes of Castile, although reduced to little more than a tax-voting machine, did retain some hold on the King because it voiced popular feeling about government policy and, if the Cortes became too insistent, the King was unwise to ignore it. Thus, in the 1590s the Cortes refused to grant more money for nearly four years because of the exhaustion of the country.

Outside Castile, Philip respected the traditional liberties which put considerable restraints on royal power, especially in Aragon. But the biggest restriction to his power was the large part of the country which was outside his jurisdiction. For example, as Kamen shows, in the province of Salamanca 63 percent of the territory was under noble jurisdiction and six percent under Church control. Some of the nobles ran their holdings as virtually independent states and this gave the *grandees* great power. The Duke of Medina Sidonia was able to raise 10 000 militia from his estates; like many nobles he increased the size of his holdings under Philip II because the King sold the lands of the three military orders. Eighty towns were transferred from royal to seigneurial jurisdiction between 1516 and 1575. The motive behind this diminution of royal authority was finance. Lack of sufficient resources was the biggest constraint on Philip as absolute ruler.

Michele Suriano, a Venetian ambassador, commented on the limits to Philip's authority in 1559:

> The Aragonese claim to be independent and to govern themselves as a republic of which the king is head. He may not succeed to the government unless they have elected him. They are so zealous to preserve their independence that they contest every little thing to prevent the king from having greater authority over them. They make difficulties even where they have no right, so that Queen Isabella used to say that her husband, King Ferdinand, would have been pleased if the Crown of Aragon had actually rebelled, since he would then have been able to reconquer it and impose his own laws. The kingdom of Castile, on the other hand, is governed by councillors and ministers whom the king appoints, because he is the supreme arbiter of laws, finances, grants, justice and matters of life and death. All the nobles, however, are so privileged that they have no other obligation than to serve the king in time of war, at his expense and then only for the protection of Spain. When Charles wished to abolish their privileges, he was opposed by all the grandees . . . So the Aragonese maintain their liberty, and the nobles of Castile their privileges, openly challenging their kings if they try to abolish or modify their privileges and jurisdictions.

1   *What problems did the King face in governing Aragon?*
2   *Summarise in your own words the King's position in Castile.*

7. Royal Finance and the Castilian Economy

Like most monarchs, but more acutely than many, Philip was always short of money. He was in a state of perpetual financial crisis that was temporarily alleviated by bullion shipments from the New World but not solved because the underlying problems were not tackled. Spain's problem above all was that her resources were insufficient to meet the demands of empire that were placed on them. The Castilian economy simply could not cope with the constant warfare which resulted from her imperial commitments and therefore short-term expedients were employed in order to maintain the next season's campaigns, which resulted in mortgaging the future to pay for the present. Thus the burden of debt and consequent repayments became increasingly heavy as the reign progressed and made the financial problems of the latter part much more severe.

Finance in Castile

	Estimated Income	National Debt (in millions of ducats)	Debt Interest
1560	3.1	25.5	1.6
1575	5.5	40.0	2.7
1598	9.7	85.5	4.6

(from *Philip II* by G Parker, 1979)

The figures speak for themselves. Although Philip more than trebled his income, the debt rose even faster and with it the burden of interest. What made matters worse was that Crown expenditure was much heavier at the end of the reign, largely because of the enormous increase in the cost of war. The Lepanto campaign of 1571 cost 1 100 000 ducats, of which 400 000 came from the Italian kingdoms. Seventeen years later the Armada cost about 10 000 000 ducats, of which Castile contributed around 70 percent. These appalling costs destroyed the financial viability of the state. Philip had inherited financial difficulties from his father. The first state bankruptcy of 1557 was a legacy of Charles V's wars. The only way for Philip to resolve his financial problems and establish a firm foundation for future expenditure was to have a prolonged period of peace during which the Exchequer could be reformed and the country's economy built up. He never achieved this and so his financial plight worsened, not helped by such projects as the building of the Escorial.

The King relied principally on two sources of revenue—the Indies and Castile. His other dominions were in theory self-supporting and in the case of Italy this was largely true. Although Castile bore the bulk of the cost of campaigns against the Turks, the Italian kingdoms contributed according to their means. They were not prepared to be as generous for hostilities in the Atlantic. The Netherlands, which had made an important contribution to Charles V's imperialism, became the most serious drain on the Treasury. Between 1567 and 1600 about 80 000 000 ducats was sent to the Netherlands. The eastern kingdoms of Spain were too poor to yield much and too hedged about by liberties to make it worth pressing them. Only Castile and the Indies were left.

The amounts received from the New World showed a steady increase throughout the reign, from about 500 000 ducats a year to 2 000 000 ducats in the 1590s. Even in the best years it never amounted to more than one-fifth of government revenue but its great value lay in the fact that it was hard currency, it could be relied upon and financiers were willing to make loans on the basis of repayment from the treasure fleets. It thus enabled Philip to continue with his grandiose projects for longer than would otherwise have been possible.

Castile provided almost all of the rest of Philip's income and there were three different sources. There was the King's own revenue, Church dues and votes by the Cortes. The King's own revenue included Crown lands, feudal dues, salt taxes and mineral rights and the lands of the Castilian military orders. Together, all these brought in about 600 000 ducats a year but this tended to diminish over time as the King sold land for immediate profit.

The Church revenues were much more significant. They included the 'Royal Third' which was a third of all tithes. This yielded 400 000 ducats a year rising to 800 000 ducats by the end of the reign. There were also the 'Three Graces', Church taxes which included the *cruzada* and *excusado* dependent on periodic renewal by the Pope, an important political issue. All three brought in 1 400 000 ducats by the 1590s when the Church was providing more than one-fifth of government income. It seems likely that a bishop who complained in 1574 that the Crown was taking more than half of the wealth of the Church was speaking the truth.

The final and most important source of all was taxation voted by the Cortes. Existing taxes were tripled between 1559 and 1577 (compared with overall inflation at 25 percent). This was a turning point: many towns were unable to pay and the *alcabala*, the main sales tax, had to be reduced by 1 000 000 ducats to 1 900 000 ducats a year. The limit had been reached in Castile's taxable potential but even so, faced with the financial crisis caused by the Armada, the Cortes reluctantly agreed to a new subsidy, the *millones* of 8 000 000 ducats to be collected over 6 years. The municipalities raised this money by excise taxes on basic foodstuffs, meat, wine, oil and vinegar, so that the poor were hardest hit. In 1592–93 Philip got nearly 10 000 000 ducats from Castile but this was the peak; the Castilian economy could no longer tolerate such heavy exactions and its decline was hastened.

Even these levels of support were insufficient for Philip's needs and he resorted to the sale of lands, titles and offices with a corresponding diminution in his future revenues and an additional burden of salaries, as well as the inevitable increase in corruption and inefficiency of inferior officials. The worst expedient in terms of its long term effect was the sale of *juros* or state bonds which brought in immediate cash at the price of mortgaging future income. By 1600 interest payments to *juro* holders took 40 percent of total income. With all his efforts, Philip was unable to prevent himself going bankrupt three times—in 1557, 1575 and 1596—and the reign ended as it had begun, in financial chaos.

Philip II's warfare did not bring the benefits to the Spanish economy that might have been expected. Spanish industry was unable to provide the necessary munitions so that four-fifths of the firearms used to suppress the revolt of the *Moriscos* were imported. Much of the bullion was immediately re-exported to foreign financiers in payment of debts and most of the soldiers were overseas and those countries received the benefit of their wages. Thus there was a lack of capital investment in Spanish industry which was coupled with crippling taxation to create industrial stagnation. Spain became vulnerable to imports of manufactured goods, especially as she was unable to supply the expanding American market and this further depressed local industrial initiative. Seville boomed because of the activities of foreign merchants but it was a false prosperity relying on external investment. It created a temporary illusion of economic activity but there was no solid base for long-term growth. A series of epidemics made matters worse with a dramatic effect on the population—some areas, for example Segovia, a city of 28 000, lost 12 000 in the plague of 1598–99. Deserted villages and the decay of agriculture became increasingly common phenomena from 1570 onwards. The imperialism of Philip II brought little benefit to his native land.

8. The Church—Relations with the Papacy

'The King of Spain, as a temporal sovereign, is anxious above all to safeguard and to increase his dominions . . . The preservation of the Catholic religion which is the principal aim of the Pope is only a pretext for His Majesty whose principal aim is the security and aggrandisement of his dominions.' Thus wrote Pope Sixtus V in 1589, illustrating that, far from the Pope and Philip II working in harmony as the two halves of the Counter-Reformation, there was considerable friction between them. Philip's relations with Sixtus were particularly bad but there were conflicts with virtually every pope on two main issues: foreign policy and ecclesiastical jurisdiction.

Men said there was no pope in Spain and Lynch has stated that the Crown's domination of the Church was 'probably more complete in Spain than in any other part of Europe including Protestant countries'. The King made all the major ecclesiastical appointments, he controlled the Council of the Inquisition and he enjoyed the revenues of vacant sees. In 1572, appeals by Spaniards to Rome were forbidden and the King insisted on his right to scrutinise papal bulls and, if necessary, forbid their publication in his dominions.

In foreign policy, religious considerations were secondary to political and economic ones. Philip would not be rushed into war against England, nor was he prepared to follow up the Battle of Lepanto in the eastern Mediterranean. It was the question of France after the accession of the Protestant Henry of Navarre as Henry IV which caused most friction.

Philip wrote stiffly to Sixtus V:

> Nothing has surprised me more than to see Your Holiness, after an act inspired by God (the Bull against Henry IV) leaving time to the heretics to take root in France, without even ordering that the Catholic partisans of 'the

Béarnais' (Henry) should separate from his cause. The Church is on the eve of losing one of its members; Christendom is on the point of being set on fire by the united heretics; Italy runs the greatest danger, and in the presence of the enemy we look on and we delay! And the blame is put upon me because, looking at those interests as if they were mine, I hasten to Your Holiness as to a father whom I love and respect, and as a good son remind him of the duties of the Holy See! . . . God and the whole world know my love for the Holy See, and nothing will ever make me deviate from it, not even Your Holiness by the great injustice you do me. . . . But the greater my devotions the less I shall consent to your failing in your duty towards God and towards the Church, who have given you the means of acting; and, at risk of pressing Your Holiness and displeasing you, I shall insist on your setting to the task.

1 How would you characterise the tone of this letter?
2 What effect would such a letter be likely to have upon the Pope's relations with France?
3 'Looking at those interests as if they were mine.' Why would Philip and the Pope have divergent views on what were properly Philip's interests?

Philip was greatly relieved when Sixtus died in 1590 and made great efforts to secure Spanish nominees for the next two popes, but both died within months and eventually the cardinals rebelled and chose Clement VIII who was reluctant to serve Spanish policy and recognised Henry IV as King of France.

Although relations with the Papacy were often strained, neither side wished to push them to breaking point. This had been illustrated at the beginning of the reign by the case of Carranza, Archbishop of Toledo, who was arrested in 1559 on a charge of heresy, although it was more a matter of his having clashed with the Inquisitor-General. The Pope claimed the right to try so important an Archbishop, rather than the Inquisition, but Philip was determined to keep the case within Spanish jurisdiction. As a result, the unfortunate Carranza was kept in jail without trial for 17 years. He was moved to Rome in 1566 because Philip needed his ecclesiastical revenues and the *cruzada* and *excusado* relied on periodic renewal by the Pope. He was then detained in Rome until 1576, being released just before he died. The Pope had not released him earlier because he, for his part, needed Philip to lead the struggle against the Turks and to promote the Counter-Reformation which both sides valued. Carranza had been the victim of jurisdictional conflict in which neither side would give up nor push the other too far.

9. The Church—Counter-Reformation and Orthodoxy

The Spanish Church of the mid-sixteenth century was badly in need of reform in spite of Cisneros' work under Ferdinand and Isabella. Pluralism was widespread—in the diocese of Barcelona in 1549 only six out of

67 parish priests were resident—the clergy were uneducated and ignorant and there were extremes of wealth and poverty. Philip was anxious to reform the Church. The Jesuits were welcomed by him and they undertook important missionary work. Six new bishoprics were created in Aragon and religious houses were revitalised by the suppression of some and the merging of others. The decrees of the Council of Trent were promoted to improve the standard of the clergy and to impose uniform services. The effects must not be exaggerated, but gradually a new spirit of religious fervour became apparent. All theatres were closed in 1597, church buildings became completely dedicated to sacred use and parish priests were instructed to record the attendance of their parishioners.

This new spirit was encouraged by the activities of the Inquisition which concentrated less on the discovery of heretics, since there were very few, and more on the moral education of the people. Nearly two-thirds of those arrested in this period were ordinary Catholics unconnected with heresy, and the emphasis was on re-education rather than mere punishment. However, there was much fear of Protestant heresy in Spain, even though there was so little of it.

Throughout Europe, the middle years of the century saw an end to reconciliation and the growth of militant theology of which both the Jesuits and the Calvinists were examples. Spain was already sensitive to the presence of large numbers of barely assimilated *Moriscos* who might at any time link up with the Turks, and of *conversos* (converted Jews) whose allegiance to Christianity could justifiably be doubted. The discovery in 1557–58 of a number of supposed Protestants in Valladolid and Seville was sufficient to unleash repression against anyone who seemed to deviate in any way from the established orthodoxy. In fact the 'heretics' were not all Protestants—some were mystics who sought direct communion of the soul with God, continuing a tradition begun decades before. It was a sign of the new nervousness that such a harmless deviation should lead not only to severe measures against those involved, but also to a ban on the import of foreign books and to the licensing of all books by the Council of Castile.

From mid-century onwards, the Inquisition, firmly backed by Philip, gradually cut Spain off from external ideas. In 1559 all study in foreign universities was forbidden. The index of censorship was extended until it included over 2500 books, many of them by Spaniards of unquestionable orthodoxy. Spain, which had been culturally one of the most open of societies, became virtually isolated.

Philip was determined to eliminate all traces of heresy. He also saw that the Inquisition was a useful instrument to do this and that it simultaneously increased his control. King and *La Suprema*, the Council of the Inquisition, were in complete harmony.

10. The Succession

Philip II was married four times and all of his wives and most of his children predeceased him. To die without a male heir would have been to risk anarchy in Spain but this was the position in which Philip found himself in 1568. The only surviving son of his first three marriages was Don Carlos, born in 1545, the son of Philip's first wife Maria. His parents were closely related, both grandchildren of Joanna the Mad, and Don Carlos revealed an unstable character from an early age. He could be unpleasantly violent and sadistic. In 1562, Philip made him president of the Council of State hoping this would produce a sense of responsibility but in fact Don Carlos became more erratic and began to criticise his father openly. In the mid-1560s he began plotting to escape to the Netherlands and he was in contact with the rebels. Philip decided something must be done and in January 1568 Don Carlos was arrested. In July he died in prison. Men blamed Philip for his death and there was considerable speculation that Philip had ordered his murder. In fact this is highly unlikely; Don Carlos indulged in a hunger strike and then excessive eating and it is far more likely that his constitution could not take the strain. It was also perfectly reasonable that Philip should imprison his son who was obviously a menace to society and no fit ruler.

Don Carlos' death left Philip with a problem over the succession which was increased when his much-loved third wife, Elizabeth of Valois, died later in 1568 leaving two daughters. As his fourth wife Philip chose his own niece, Anna of Austria, whom he married in 1570. She bore him a succession of sons but only one, the future Philip III, survived beyond infancy. The succession was safe-guarded but only by a hair's breadth.

11. The Revolt of the *Moriscos*

1568 was a black year for Philip; not only did he have the personal tragedy of the deaths of his wife and son but there were also major political upheavals including strained relations with both England and France. The worst of these was a major rebellion by the *Moriscos* of Granada which broke out on Christmas Eve 1568, and which took two years to suppress, laying the heart of Spain open to an attack by the Turks.

The causes of *Morisco* dissatisfaction were deep-rooted. They were brought to breaking point by the ill-considered policies of the government and the insidious effects of faction. The *Moriscos* were dangerously concentrated in a few areas of Spain; in Granada they comprised over 50 percent of the population. Here they formed a race apart with their own language, customs and lifestyle. These had been prohibited under

Charles V but the edicts had not been strictly enforced and the Captain-General of Granada, the Marquis of Mondejar, acted as their protector, keeping in check the hostility of the Christian population.

At the time of Philip II's accession, a number of factors combined to bring about a drastic decline in *Morisco* fortunes which were not entirely planned. The *Moriscos* derived much of their income from silk cultivation and weaving; this industry suffered when export restrictions were imposed in the 1550s and the tax on silk was more than doubled between 1560 and 1565. A further threat to *Morisco* livelihood came after 1559 when agents of the Crown checked all title deeds in order to reclaim Crown lands. Those who had no legal evidence of ownership were fined or lost their land. Those who suffered were almost all *Moriscos*: 100 000 hectares was transferred to Christian hands in the period 1559–68 alone.

These difficulties for the *Moriscos* coincided with a weakening of the position of Mondejar, exposing them to further attacks. Mondejar was in dispute with the Church, the *audiencia* (the supreme court in the south of Spain), the municipal council and the Inquisition. These feuds brought local administration in Granada to a virtual standstill. The enemies of the Captain-General found a spokesman at court in the Marquis de Los Vélez, so the protests and warnings of Mondejar about new measures against the *Moriscos* went unheeded. After the siege of Malta in 1565, there was much greater fear about the existence of the Moorish community and in 1567 new restrictions were issued prohibiting the use of Arabic, native costumes, Moorish surnames, customs and ceremonies. Philip showed no awareness of the likely backlash to such cultural oppression.

Petitions by the *Moriscos* and Mondejar for the suspension of the edicts were ignored. There was a complete harvest failure in the south in 1567 and this, together with the failure of the *audiencia* to protect the *Morisco* farmers from bandits, led to a breakdown in public order and the plotting of rebellion which erupted at the end of 1568.

The rebellion involved about 30 000 *Moriscos* at its height. The two years before it was suppressed were the most dangerous of the reign for Philip. Spain had been stripped of troops to send with Alva to the Netherlands and the internal defences were pitiful. Philip was saved because the Turks and the Algerians contented themselves with sending messages of support while seizing the opportunity to take Cyprus and Tunis. Eventually, Don John re-established royal control at the end of 1570 after a campaign marked by atrocities on both sides.

It was decided to settle the *Morisco* problem by breaking up their communities and relocating them throughout the peninsula. Long processions of chained and fettered *Moriscos* were led away, at least 20 percent dying on the way. Granada lost about 120 000 people and the Christians sent to replace them lacked their skill in agriculture. This did not solve the *Morisco* problem but merely extended it. They remained an unassimilated minority and a final solution was adopted in 1609 when the *Moriscos* were expelled.

12. The Turks and the Struggle for the Mediterranean

The *Moriscos* represented one part of the struggle against Islam. The greater part of Spanish effort was directed to the continuing war in the Mediterranean against the Ottoman Turks and their North African clients *(see Chapter X)*. Spain was open to attacks by corsairs and Barbary pirates but it was Italy which was in real danger from the Ottoman offensive. With some exceptions, the major sea battles concentrated on the narrows between Sicily and Tunis. This was to prove the decisive line between east and west, Turk and Christian.

Philip did not entertain the grandiose dreams of Charles V; he had no desire to lead a crusade to Constantinople. After a brief and disastrous expedition to Djerba in 1560, his policy was strictly defensive, with the aim of containing the Ottoman advance as much as possible. In this he was relatively successful. The 1550s were a bad decade for the Christians; the Knights of St John were expelled from Tripoli, the Spanish fortress of Bougie was lost, a Turkish force penetrated to Minorca and Corsairs severely disrupted trade from Spain to Italy. It is no wonder that the defence of the Mediterranean was considered to be of first importance by Castilians, and it was in this area that the resources of the monarchy were concentrated until 1567, when the Netherlands came to the fore.

It was the Peace of Câteau-Cambrésis which freed Philip from his northern commitments and enabled him to plan an offensive campaign in the Mediterranean. The King's aim was to recapture Tripoli, lost in 1551, and so restore the barrier across the central Mediterranean, leaving Algiers isolated. The original idea of a swift raid was abandoned, against Philip's better judgement, for a more ambitious project which took six months to prepare. The element of surprise was lost and the island of Djerba was taken as an advanced base in 1560. This was an exposed position and the Turks attacked. Twenty-eight galleys were lost and 10 000 troops were stranded and forced to surrender. This was a great blow to Spanish power and prestige and the loss of 25 more galleys with 4000 crew in a freak storm in 1562 meant that the fleet was almost halved in size. Spanish resources had to be diverted to a costly programme of reconstruction and all operations in the future were designed to safeguard the fleet. In the meantime, Italy and Spain had to endure attacks by squadrons of Barbary corsairs which they were powerless to prevent. So, in 1561, Naples was blockaded by 35 vessels and there was a raid into the interior of Granada which carried off 4000 prisoners. Every summer the Christian powers braced themselves for the next attack and it was not until the end of September that the tension relaxed as the campaigning season drew to its close.

By 1564 Spain had nearly 100 galleys, which were soon to be needed as in May 1565 the Turks attacked Malta. Twenty-five thousand troops confined the Knights of St John to a few forts but they continued to resist stoutly until September when a relief force eventually arrived. Philip has

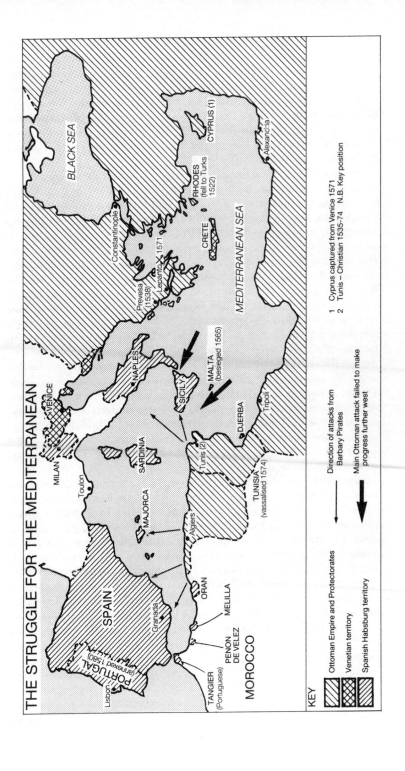

THE STRUGGLE FOR THE MEDITERRANEAN

BLACK SEA

MEDITERRANEAN SEA

Constantinople

Prevesa (1538)

Lepanto X 1571

CRETE

RHODES (fell to Turks 1522)

CYPRUS (1)

Alexandria

VENICE

MILAN

Toulon

NAPLES

SARDINIA

MAJORCA

SICILY

MALTA (besieged 1565)

Tunis (2)

DJERBA

Tripoli

TUNISIA (vassalised 1574)

Algiers

Granada

ORAN

MELILLA

PENON DE VELEZ

TANGIER (Portuguese)

Lisbon

PORTUGAL (annexed 1580)

SPAIN

MOROCCO

KEY

Ottoman Empire and Protectorates	
Venetian territory	
Spanish Habsburg territory	

Direction of attacks from Barbary Pirates

Main Ottoman attack failed to make progress further west

1   Cyprus captured from Venice 1571
2   Tunis – Christian 1535-74   N.B. Key position

been criticised for the time taken to relieve the island but he did not want to risk losing an inferior force. The successful relief of Malta raised Christian morale and they were given a respite over the next four years as Suleiman I died in September 1566 and it took some time for Selim II to establish himself as Sultan. Philip was thus enabled to send Alva to the Netherlands with the best troops from Italy and he also turned his attention to the revolt of the *Moriscos*. These problems meant that Spain was less prepared than she might have been for the new Turkish offensive when it came in 1570.

The Turks returned in force and seized Tunis and then invaded the valuable Venetian possession of Cyprus. This new threat caused the Christians to overlook their differences and to form a Holy League of Spain, Venice and the Papal States in 1571. In return for appointing the commander, Spain contributed half of the money and forces, but in practice it was an Italian campaign with major contributions from Naples and Sicily. The Pope also granted a special tax, a *subsidio*, for the maintenance of 60 galleys. The commander-in-chief was Don John. On 7th October 1571 he led his forces in the last great galley battle off the coast of Greece at Lepanto. The Christians' victory was absolute. Only 35 out of 230 Turkish galleys escaped, 30 000 were killed or wounded while the allies lost 12 galleys. The whole of Christendom rejoiced at the humiliation of their apparently invincible foe.

In fact the victory solved nothing. It gave a boost to morale but did not change the unfavourable military situation. The Turks completed their conquest of Cyprus thus driving the Christians out of the east Mediterranean. A massive rebuilding programme was undertaken so that the Turkish fleet in 1574 was larger than it had been in 1571. However, it was a severe blow to the prestige of a Muslim leader who depended for support on his success in the Holy War and it paved the way to eventual disengagement by both sides.

In the short term, there was no follow-up to the victory because Philip was not prepared to risk his fleet in the eastern Mediterranean, especially when there was the possibility of an attack by France. He also told his ambassador in Rome in June 1572 that he wanted 'to gain some benefit for my own subjects and states from this league and all its expenses, rather than employ them in so risky an undertaking as a distant expedition in the Levant'. This illustrates that the differences between the allies were surfacing once more. Don John remained in Sicily, firmly in the western half, while the interests of Venice lay in the eastern Mediterranean. It was only the persuasiveness of the Pope, Pius V, which had brought them together and it came as no surprise to Philip when Venice abandoned the League and made a separate peace with the Sultan in March 1573. Reverting to a Spanish policy, Don John took Tunis in 1573, providing an obvious target for the rebuilt Turkish fleet in 1574. The Sultan tried to link up with the rebels in the Netherlands and the *Moriscos* in Spain but the effort of co-ordinating attacks over such great distances proved too difficult. However, Philip was aware of the diplomatic activity and, as he was also on the verge of his 1575 bankruptcy, Tunis was abandoned to the Turks once more in 1574.

In 1576, Morocco was captured by a Turkish vassal and turned into an Ottoman protectorate, completing Turkish control of North Africa. Then the Persian Shah died, which opened possibilities to the east while those in the Mediterranean were becoming increasingly difficult to exploit as the frontier of Ottoman power grew further from Constantinople. For his part, Philip was very anxious to have a respite in the Mediterranean because of the collapse of royal authority in the Netherlands. He held secret talks about peace which led to a truce in 1578 and that became a formal armistice in 1580. Two generations of conflict ended favourably for the Turks who had greatly extended their territory and power. The Mediterranean became a historical backwater as the centre of conflict shifted to the Atlantic. Philip's policy had not defeated the Ottoman menace but it had been contained and peace was eventually secured.

13. The Annexation of Portugal

While Philip was recognising the futility of further conflict against the Turks, his nephew King Sebastian of Portugal was planning a crusade against the new puppet ruler of Morocco. In 1578, Sebastian and the greater part of the Portuguese nobility were killed at the Battle of Alcazar. The childless king was succeeded by his elderly uncle, Cardinal Henry. Philip immediately saw his chance as the next legitimate heir, especially as the destruction of the army had left the country undefended.

Philip adopted a two-pronged policy with considerable skill. He sent one of his chief ministers to Portugal to build up a party in his favour and ransomed the Portuguese nobles captured by the Moroccans. The towns and lower clergy remained violently anti-Castilian but the nobility and rich merchants backed Philip's claim against his two main rivals, the Duchess of Braganza and Dom Antonio, prior of Crato, who was illegitimate. Philip also assembled a large army, ready to press home his claim as soon as the moment came. It was at this time that Philip began to suspect the ambitions of Antonio Pérez and removed him in favour of Cardinal Granvelle who in effect became chief minister until about a year before his death in 1586. Granvelle favoured a more active, imperialist policy and fully supported the King's actions in Portugal. He persuaded Philip to restore the disgraced Alva to favour and to appoint him commander of the army.

Cardinal Henry died in January 1580 having failed to designate his successor. The supporters of Dom Antonio seized Lisbon, the royal arsenals and the Crown treasury, and the commons proclaimed him king. On the expiry of an ultimatum, Philip ordered his troops across the border in June. They encountered little determined resistance. Dom

Antonio fled abroad after the fall of Lisbon and by September the conquest was complete and Portugal was absorbed into the Spanish monarchy. Over the next few years Dom Antonio made a number of attempts to win back the country, helped by England and France, but none of these posed a real threat.

Philip made a triumphal entry into Lisbon in December 1580. He then had to decide what policy to adopt for his new country. Granvelle favoured major changes of law and government which would closely identify Portugal with Castile but Philip ignored these suggestions and instead left Portuguese traditions and institutions virtually intact. In part this may have been out of a desire to minimise opposition but it also reflected his conviction that preserving local government was the best way to rule his kingdoms. Thus, he announced that the Portuguese alone would administer their country and its overseas possessions and their commercial and colonising monopolies would be respected. In effect, Portugal remained an autonomous country under a foreign king.

The annexation of Portugal coincided with other events to bring about a decisive shift in Spanish orientation and policy. It had already become clear that the Atlantic was becoming the battleground of the future, leaving the Mediterranean in comparative obscurity, and the acquisition of Portugal with its huge empire, its large fleet and its long Atlantic seaboard completed the change in orientation. Together Spain and Portugal had a combined fleet of 250–300 000 tons (compared with 232 000 tons in the Netherlands and only 42 000 tons in England). Their empires complemented each other. Portuguese possessions stretched from Africa to Brazil, India and the Moluccas, and the empire was essentially commercial. The Spanish empire was concentrated largely in the New World and provided the bullion necessary for trade with the Far East for pepper, spices and silks. Already Lisbon had been dependent on Seville for the gold and silver only the Spanish American mines could produce.

The 1580s saw dramatic increases in the amount of bullion arriving from America because of the introduction of amalgam of mercury into the refining of silver. Two to three million ducats began to arrive annually on the treasure fleets and this gave Philip a freedom of manoeuvre he had not enjoyed before. His foreign policy, which had been defensive for the first two decades of the reign, changed to aggressive imperialism. England and France were alarmed at the increase in Spanish power and the stage was set for a major confrontation. Granvelle advised moving the capital to Lisbon which was well-placed for the new battlefield but Philip preferred to return to Madrid in 1583. It was to be a symbolic withdrawal into the heart of Castile. Before the end of the reign it had become apparent that the battle for the Atlantic had been lost; Portugal was not effectively absorbed into the empire and Castile was to remain the centre and chief support of an increasingly unwieldy monarchy.

14. The Crisis of the 1590s—The Revolt of Aragon

1580 was the high point of Philip's reign. Spain dominated Europe and the last outposts of resistance in the Netherlands did not appear to have much chance against the brilliant tactics of Alexander Farnese. Ten years later, the position was very different. Spain was at war with England and had failed in the most costly military endeavour of the reign, there was a real possibility that a heretic would be accepted as king of France and Spanish intervention there allowed the Dutch rebels to counter-attack. These additional commitments involved heavy extra expenditure and therefore demands for tax increased. Discontent within Spain was widespread. The Cortes complained vociferously against new taxes and said that if the rebels in Flanders and France 'wanted to earn damnation, let them'. Inflation was high in the 1590s: the price of grain increased by more than 50 percent in Castile between 1595 and 1599. By the end of the reign, Philip's popularity had been considerably diminished and the high cost of his imperialist policies was openly questioned. The 1590s also saw the most serious constitutional crisis of the reign which broke out not in over-taxed Castile but in the neglected eastern kingdom of Aragon.

Philip had paid little attention to Aragon because of its poverty and its concern with its liberties, the *fueros*, which made extracting either money or troops extremely difficult. He visited his eastern kingdoms in 1563 and then not again until 1588. These long absences were resented. There was more concern over Catalonia, given its proximity to France and the danger of Huguenot infiltration, but this concern took the form of harsher censorship and the arrest of some nobles. Aragon itself became an increasing worry for the government as the reign progressed because the growth of lawlessness made it virtually ungovernable and Philip could not ignore his duty to protect his weaker subjects. The nobility in Aragon enjoyed absolute rights over their vassals but when they began to shelter bandits, a large proportion of whom were *Moriscos*, Philip could no longer ignore the threat to security.

The violence and disorder which was endemic in Aragon surfaced when Philip tried to take a firmer grip on the country. In 1588 a Castilian, the Count of Almenara, was appointed viceroy. The Aragonese protested that this was infringing their liberties but Philip insisted that the choice was his and the Justicia, who was the guardian of Aragon's *fueros*, accepted his argument.

There was thus already a tense atmosphere when Antonio Pérez escaped from prison in 1590 and fled to Aragon, claiming the privilege, as an Aragonese, of being tried in the open court of the Justicia rather than a closed court in Castile. He thereby effectively removed himself from royal justice and began making sensational allegations, using secret state papers, implicating Philip in the murder of Escobedo and claiming that the appointment of Almenara was the start of a campaign to undermine the *fueros*.

353

The only way for Philip to silence Pérez was to accuse him of heresy, because the Inquisition was not subject to the Justicia's court. (Here we see the importance to the Crown of the Inquisition, the only institution to operate throughout Spain.) But as an attempt was made to move Pérez to the Inquisition's prison in May 1591, riots broke out and Almenara was fatally wounded. A second attempt in September also ended in failure and a group of young nobles seized Zaragoza's armouries. Philip was uncertain what to do. He was heavily committed against England, France and the Dutch and there were fears for Portugal. On the other hand: 'If there is no action at once, with a strong hand and a rapid punishment, Aragon will be like the Netherlands'. Such arguments won the day and in October an army of 14 000 was sent into Aragon while Philip announced that only the leaders of the troubles would be punished and 'my wish has always been that the *fueros* be maintained'. There was no resistance and the rebellion was over in four days. Most of Pérez's supporters had come from the minor nobility who were fighting to preserve their feudal rights. The mass of the people stood to gain nothing from the revolt or from defence of the *fueros* and trouble was confined to Zaragoza. The new young Justicia who had supported the revolt was executed; otherwise there was a general pardon. Pérez fled to France where he spent the rest of his life writing a vicious attack on Philip.

With Aragon at his mercy, the King could have destroyed the *fueros* if he had so wished. In fact, his policy mirrored that in Portugal eleven years previously. With minor amendments, he scrupulously observed the traditional liberties and, learning from his experience in the Netherlands, he went in person to ensure that order was restored. In 1592 he presided over the Cortes which approved the changes that were made. The Justicia was to serve at the King's pleasure; majority votes, not unanimity, would suffice in the Cortes; nobles younger than 22 were not to sit in the Cortes; and the King had the right to choose non-Aragonese as viceroys.

15. Philip II's Legacy to Spain

Philip successfully surmounted the problem of Aragon and annexed Portugal with great skill. When he died in 1598 he left a united peninsula with Castile at the head of the first empire on which the sun never set. However, there would be trouble in the future: the burden on Castile was enormous and the Dutch Revolt, as we shall see, was not yet over. The *Moriscos* were still a problem, there was no effective machinery of government to take over if the king was deficient, the financial predicament of the monarchy was well nigh insoluble, and the empire had no coherence to make it a manageable unit. Nonetheless Philip had inherited many of these problems himself and by unstinting application and a heavy sense of responsibility he had maintained a functioning empire that struck fear into the rest of Europe. His failure to resolve the

Philip II

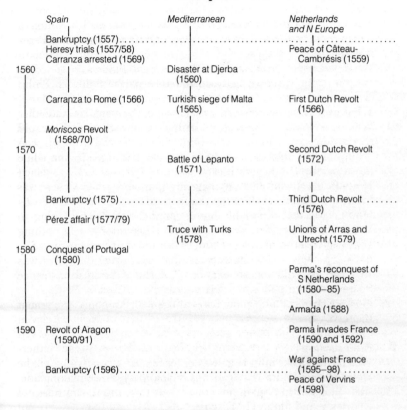

Spain	Mediterranean	Netherlands and N Europe
Bankruptcy (1557)		Peace of Câteau-Cambrésis (1559)
Heresy trials (1557/58)		
Carranza arrested (1569)		
1560	Disaster at Djerba (1560)	
Carranza to Rome (1566)	Turkish siege of Malta (1565)	First Dutch Revolt (1566)
Moriscos Revolt (1568/70)		
1570		Second Dutch Revolt (1572)
	Battle of Lepanto (1571)	
Bankruptcy (1575)		Third Dutch Revolt (1576)
Pérez affair (1577/79)	Truce with Turks (1578)	Unions of Arras and Utrecht (1579)
1580 Conquest of Portugal (1580)		Parma's reconquest of S Netherlands (1580–85)
		Armada (1588)
1590 Revolt of Aragon (1590/91)		Parma invades France (1590 and 1592)
Bankruptcy (1596)		War against France (1595–98)
		Peace of Vervins (1598)

contradictions and weaknesses within his empire was not entirely his fault owing to the burdens of office which allowed no respite for the resolution of problems. This failure is comprehensible but meant that his less capable successors faced an impossible task which increasingly they proved themselves unable to manage.

16. Bibliography

P Pierson *Philip II of Spain* (Thames & Hudson, 1975). G Parker *Philip II* (Hutchinson, 1979). J Lynch *Spain Under the Habsburgs Vol. I* (2nd edition Blackwell, 1981). H Kamen *Spain 1469–1714: A Society of Conflict* (Longman, 1983). J H Elliott *Imperial Spain 1469–1716* (Edward Arnold, 1963). H G Koenisberger *New Cambridge Modern History, Vol. 3, Chapter IX.* F Braudel *The Mediterranean and the Mediterranean World in the Age of Philip II* (2nd edition Fontana, 1975).

17. Discussion Points and Exercises

A *This section consists of questions or points that might be used for discussion (or written answers) as a way of expanding on the chapter and testing understanding of it:*

1 What was the place of Castile in the empire of Philip II?
2 Why was the distance between different parts of the empire so crucial?
3 What were the strengths and weaknesses of the conciliar system?
4 Why did Philip's method of ruling give rise to faction and corruption?
5 'Philip II had absolute jurisdiction over national affairs but could intervene little in the localities.'
6 How effectively did Philip manage his finances?
7 What was the main role of the Inquisition?
8 How far was it Philip's fault that the *Moriscos* rebelled?
9 What was the significance of the Battle of Lepanto?
10 Why was it in the interests of both Philip and the Ottoman Sultan to have a truce in the Mediterranean after 1577?
11 In what way did the annexation of Portugal bring a change in Spanish foreign policy or government?
12 How wisely did Philip act in his dealings with Aragon at the time of the revolt there?

B *Essay questions*

1 Was the reign of Philip II a disaster for Spain?
2 How far were Philip II's problems in Spain of his own making?
3 'Rebellions within Spain posed a serious threat to the authority of Charles V and Philip II.' Discuss.
4 How successful was Philip II as a Mediterranean monarch?
5 Does Philip II deserve to be known as the 'Prudent King'?
6 Compare Charles V and Philip II as rulers of Spain.

18. Essay Writing—Comparison

It is always a good idea to compare rulers or countries in order to sharpen up your arguments but some essay questions require you to do so systematically. Consider question 6 above: 'Compare Charles V and Philip II as rulers of Spain.'

One approach would be to write one half of the essay on Charles and the other half on Philip. However, even if it was a good assessment of the ways they governed Spain, such an essay would really be two short essays rather than one comparison.

The best approach would be to compare the two monarchs issue by issue.

(a) Make a list of the main issues concerning Spain and its government in the sixteenth century. This would certainly include:

Administration	The Nobility
Patronage	Rebellion
Finance	The *Fueros* of Aragon
The Economy	The Church

(b) Then under each of the above headings summarise in a couple of sentences the main relevant policy of each of the monarchs with a comment on the degree of their success.

(c) Next, review what you have written and decide where the two monarchs' policies were alike and where they differed. This should help you to structure your essay—you could start with the similar policies and then move on to the differing ones.

(d) Finally frame your overall argument. In your Introduction you could comment on how far Philip did follow his father's example as he intended to. In your Conclusion you could compare their respective legacies to Spain.

19. Documentary Exercise—The Character of Philip II

Philip II has aroused extraordinary passions among historians. He has been vilified and praised in ways that are almost impossible to reconcile. Many historians have not displayed objective judgement in the case of Philip and have allowed their own strong prejudices to colour their accounts. For this reason it is important to identify the preconceptions of a historian before one can fully assess the accuracy of his or her portrayal.

Unfavourable views of Philip II and the Spanish, 'heretics, schismatics, accursed of God, the offspring of Jews and Marranos, the very scum of the earth' (Pope Paul IV), originated in Italy. This so called 'Black Legend' was given greater strength by Dutch propaganda during the Revolt of the Netherlands. In order to further their own cause, it was in the interests of the Dutch to blacken the name of Philip II as much as possible. Their pamphleteers therefore exaggerated the actions of the Spanish and even resorted to outright forgery which was to be a fruitful source for later Protestant historians.

The most notorious forgery of the Dutch which was not exposed until early this century was 'The Advice of the Inquisition'. This was supposedly a sentence passed in February 1568 and confirmed by royal decree by which the entire population of the Netherlands, with very few exceptions, was declared guilty of high treason and therefore lost any right to either life or property.

The 'Black Legend' was given a particular boost by the 'Apology' of Philip's arch-opponent, William of Orange.

A. Having just claimed that Philip murdered his own wife Elizabeth in order to form an incestuous union with his niece, Anna of Austria, Orange went on to write:

It was not a single murder that was perpetrated for the sake of this extraordinary marriage. His son too, his only son, was sacrificed, in order to furnish the Pope with a pretext for so unusual a dispensation; which was granted, in order to prevent the Spanish monarchy from being left without a male heir. This was the true cause of the death of Don Carlos, against whom some misdemeanours were alleged; but not a single crime sufficient to justify his condemnation, much less to vindicate a father for imbruing his hands in the blood of his son . . .

In response to Philip's orders to have Orange assassinated, the latter continued:

For there is not, I am persuaded, a nation or prince in Europe, by whom it will not be thought dishonourable and barbarous, thus publicly to authorise and encourage murder; except the Spaniards, and their King, who have been long estranged from every sentiment of honour and humanity. In having recourse to private assassinations against a declared and open enemy, does not this mighty monarch confess his despair of being able to subdue me by force of arms?

B. A later historian, Robert Watson, commented on Philip as follows in 1794:

Philip II possessed, in an eminent degree, penetration, vigilance, and a capacity for government. His eyes were continually open upon every part of his extensive dominions. He entered into every branch of administration; watched over the conduct of his ministers with unwearied attention; and in his choice both of them and of his generals, discovered a considerable share of wisdom. He had at all times a composed and settled countenance, and never appeared to be either elated or depressed. His temper was the most imperious, and his looks and demeanour were haughty and severe; yet among his Spanish subjects, he was of easy access; listened patiently to their representations and complaints; and where his ambition and bigotry did not interfere, was generally willing to redress their grievances. When we have said this much in his praise, we have said all that justice requires, or truth permits. It is indeed impossible to suppose that he was insincere in his zeal for religion. But as his religion was of the most corrupt kind, it served to increase the natural depravity of his disposition; and not only allowed but even prompted him to commit the most odious and shocking crimes. Although a prince in the bigoted age of Philip might be persuaded that the interest of religion would be advanced by falsehood and persecution; yet it might be expected, that, in a virtuous prince, the sentiments of honour and humanity would on some occasions, triumph over the dictates of superstition: but of this triumph there occurs not one single instance in the reign of Philip; who, without hesitation, violated his most sacred obligations as often as religion afforded him a pretense; and under that pretense exercised for many years the most unrelenting cruelty, without reluctance or remorse. His ambition, which was exorbitant; his resentment, which was implacable; his arbitrary temper, which would submit to no control; concurred with his bigoted zeal for the Catholic religion, and carried the sanguinary spirit, which that religion was calculated to inspire to a greater height in Philip, than it ever attained in any other prince of that, or of any former or succeeding age.

C. J L Motley, the great nineteenth century historian of the Revolt of the Netherlands, portrayed Philip thus:

His power was absolute. With this single phrase one might as well dismiss any attempt at specification. He made war or peace at will with foreign nations. He had power of life and death over all his subjects. He had unlimited control of their worldly goods. And he claimed supreme jurisdiction over their religious opinions . . . The whole machinery of society, political, ecclesiastical, military, was in his single hand . . . If Philip possessed a single virtue, it has eluded the conscientious research of the writer of these pages. If there are vices—as possibly there are—from which he was exempt, it is because it is not permitted to human nature to attain perfection even in evil. The only plausible explanation . . . of his infamous career is that the man really believed himself, not a king, but a god . . .

Homicide such as was hardly ever compassed before by one human being was committed by Philip when in the famous edict of 1568 he sentenced every man, woman and child in the Netherlands to death. That the whole of this population, three millions or more, were not positively destroyed was because no human energy could suffice to execute the diabolical decree. But Alva, toiling hard, accomplished much of this murderous work. By the aid of the 'Council of Blood', and of the sheriffs and executioners of the Holy Inquisition, he was able sometimes to put eight hundred human beings to death in a single week for the crimes of Protestantism or of opulence, and at the end of half a dozen years he could boast of having strangled, drowned, burned, or beheaded somewhat more than eighteen thousand of his fellow creatures.

D. A more recent historian, R Trevor Davies, wrote of Philip in 1937:

He was an exceptionally dutiful son, a devoted husband, and a singularly understanding and affectionate father. His letters written to his daughters Isabella and Catherine during his journey in Portugal (1581–83), show a mixture of kindly interest in their childish doings together with a homely humour that is altogether charming. His love for his children is important in view of the accusations brought against him in connection with the death of Don Carlos . . . Duplicity and even crime are possibly, though by no means certainly, to be found as incidents in his diplomatic and political life; but such things were no part of his normal behaviour. Philip set out in life to train himself for the duties of a king. He gradually acquired an iron self-control expressed in immobile features that would register no sign of emotion . . . Every decision, great or small, rested with the king. This was the strength and the weakness of the system. Its strength, in that no favouritism and no undermining of royal power was possible . . . the weakness of the system was the inevitable and intolerable delay that resulted from it. . . . This failure to distinguish between the great and the small was the most glaring fault of his system. . . . The papers fought an inevitably winning battle against the king. As time went on, the piles of them awaiting attention grew ever larger, and the king, though working almost all the hours of the day and much of the night, was falling ever more and more behind with his decisions, so that the Spanish Government achieved world-wide notoriety for its delays. 'If death came from Spain', said Philip's Viceroy of Naples, 'we should live to a very great age.'

1   a) *Why does William of Orange (Extract A) allege that Philip murdered his
        wife and son?*
    b) *Does this seem credible?*
    c) *What justification can you offer for William making such outrageous
        accusations?*
2   *Robert Watson (Extract B) uses a familiar technique to make one believe he is
    being impartial. What is it?*
3   *Re-read Extract B and identify where it has drawn on Extract A.*
4   *Extract C contains major errors of fact (as opposed to interpretation). What are
    they?*
5   *Is Extract D more believable than the others and, if so, why?*
6   *Read through the extracts again and note down what you think are the prejudices
    of each writer.*
7   *In your own words write a summary of the character of Philip II, giving specific
    examples where possible to support your case.*

XIV Philip II: Northern Europe—The Revolt of the Netherlands

1. Introduction

The Revolt of the Netherlands was in fact not one revolt but several, motivated by different causes and involving different groups of people: It has suited Dutch historians to imply that all the revolts were part of a larger movement which led to the creation of a new nation—the modern Netherlands, often incorrectly called Holland. It must be remembered, however, that the aims of those involved in the revolts were much more modest than the end result might suggest. Certainly, they did not set out with the intention of creating a republic; this was forced upon them by circumstance. The pressures leading to rebellion were political, religious, economic and local and each was present to a different degree in all the revolts. The multiplicity of the revolt cannot be overstressed. While it is not unreasonable to regard William the Silent, the main opponent of Philip II between 1567 and 1584, as the father of the Dutch nation, it is important to recognise how accidental was the final shape of the country and that, if William had had his way, there would have been no division between north and south nor would religion have driven men apart.

The northern Netherlands were not to be finally recognised as an independent state by Spain until 1648, after 80 years of nearly continuous warfare. However, effective independence was conceded in 1609 when a twelve year truce was agreed by each side. It seems incredible that so small a territory should have been able to withstand the might of the most powerful state in Europe. The answer lies in Spanish commitments elsewhere. As the rebels themselves realised, events in the Mediterranean were crucial to their progress. Up to 1578, events in southern Europe took precedence over the north. Also to be considered were Dutch control of the sea, the boost that Dutch trade gave to the rebel war effort, the distance from Spain to the Netherlands and the consequent difficulty of transporting men and money along the 'Spanish Road' between them, and the intervention of foreign powers, especially

France and England, which at some points gave a vital boost to rebel morale.

Thus the revolt cannot be viewed in isolation from the Spanish government's other concerns. The most important modern work on the revolt has been done by Pieter Geyl and Geoffrey Parker, but it is the latter who has studied both Dutch and Spanish sources and who has therefore been able to take the necessary broader perspective.

2. The Netherlands in 1555

The Netherlands were in no sense a 'nation' in the mid-sixteenth century, although there was the beginning of a sense of the country or *patrie*. The 17 provinces were geographically compact, but they enjoyed a common link only through the person of their ruler and, except in the north eastern provinces, through the States General. The titles which Philip II held indicate that his position in each province was subtly different. For example he was Duke of Brabant, Count of Flanders and Lord of Friesland; in each province he had to swear to uphold their liberties at the same time as he was recognised as ruler. These entrenched local privileges were a source of annoyance to the government since they made any centralisation extremely difficult and the simple voting of taxes was a cumbersome affair. It was the duty of the provincial States to resist any breach of their privileges, and they carried out their role with energy so that government edicts would only be published after they had been examined and found to comply with local privileges. If there was any conflict, the edict would be modified accordingly. Inevitably this particularism was a source of tension with the government.

Equally frustrating were the activities of the States General which was nothing more than a meeting of representatives of the provinces who were not given any delegated authority. All requests and decisions had to be relayed back to the provincial States for agreement, a process which could be repeated two or three times, making rapid progress impossible. This was annoying for the government but less dangerous than a more powerful and organised States General might have been, so no drastic reforms were undertaken. In 1559, after the States had drawn up a list of political grievances, Philip went so far as to tell his half-sister Margaret, the Regent, not to convoke them again, since the States General were not responsible for voting new taxes.

It will already be clear that particularism was a powerful force and over-rode any feeling for a wider community. It was a problem that was seriously to hinder William the Silent's later efforts for a united opposition. There were enormous differences between the provinces. The south was French-speaking with a powerful landed nobility. The north was Dutch-speaking and had very few noble families; the rich merchants of the towns were more influential. In the centre was Antwerp, a town of 80 000, the greatest commercial centre in Europe. These all sought to promote their own interests, if necessary at the expense of others.

While there was not much fellow feeling between the provinces, there was a definite identification of the Low Countries as a unit distinct from foreigners. This sense of identity was reinforced by the accession of a foreign Spanish king in the form of Philip II who had little understanding of the traditions of his new possession. Under Charles V, the Netherlands had enjoyed the reflected glory of his Imperial title. In the reign of Philip II they were relegated to be the northern outpost of a Spanish empire. No longer would the high nobility cluster around the King as trusted advisers and the prestigious Order of the Golden Fleece was allowed to decline in status. Even before Philip left the Netherlands for Spain in 1559, never to return, there were fears amongst the nobility about their position.

3. Prelude to Revolt 1559–65

These fears were soon to be justified. Outwardly Philip acted correctly and made the great nobles members of the Council of State and stadholders of the provinces and appointed his half-sister, Margaret of Parma, as Regent. However, he left secret instructions that she was to consult only with an inner ring of three ministers, known as the *consulta*, of whom the most important was Cardinal Granvelle, who had served Charles V. It was rapidly apparent to the native nobility that they were excluded from all real power, a position in which Margaret of Parma also found herself since Philip insisted on retaining all executive power himself and ordered that no decision was to be made without first consulting him. This would have been an unwieldy process at the best of times but when uncertain communications were added to Philip's notorious inability to make up his mind, the prospect of anarchy in government became a real possibility.

The alienation of the high nobility from the government unleashed forces neither it nor they were able to control. The nobility were in no sense revolutionary; they merely wanted to improve their own position. They were suffering from a fall in their effective income because of inflation and with the French wars at an end, no longer was military service and plunder a way to a quick fortune. This left them dependent on government posts to increase their income and they disliked the influence of the Spanish. The French ambassador wrote that Margaret was 'surrounded by Spanish minds which are hated here to the death . . . nothing here is well said, well done or well considered unless it comes in Spanish and from a Spaniard'. In order to put pressure on the government to wring concessions from it, the nobility therefore resisted attempts to put down the growing Protestant movement because this was the issue which would most gravely embarrass the King. In doing so

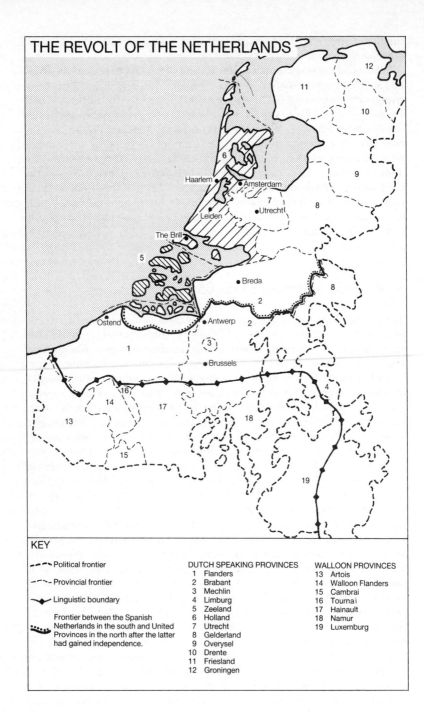

THE REVOLT OF THE NETHERLANDS

KEY

- – – Political frontier

- – – Provincial frontier

- Linguistic boundary

Frontier between the Spanish
Netherlands in the south and United
Provinces in the north after the latter
had gained independence.

DUTCH SPEAKING PROVINCES
1 Flanders
2 Brabant
3 Mechlin
4 Limburg
5 Zeeland
6 Holland
7 Utrecht
8 Gelderland
9 Overysel
10 Drente
11 Friesland
12 Groningen

WALLOON PROVINCES
13 Artois
14 Walloon Flanders
15 Cambrai
16 Tournai
17 Hainault
18 Namur
19 Luxemburg

Haarlem
Amsterdam
Leiden
Utrecht
The Brill
Breda
Ostend
Antwerp
Brussels

they encouraged the spread of a revolutionary movement which soon developed a momentum of its own.

There had been severe persecution of heresy under Charles V but this had evoked little sympathy because most of the victims were Anabaptists. In 1559 a new element was added by the opening of the border with France. This enabled increasing numbers of Protestant preachers to penetrate the Netherlands. (These Protestants were not yet fully organised as Calvinists but they held very similar views.) The Netherlands was a tolerant country placed as it was at the centre of European trade. This meant that the courts charged with enforcing the severe anti-heresy laws were reluctant to do so. Unusually, in the Netherlands the vast majority of alleged heretics were tried by civil courts because the ecclesiastical courts might seek to persuade the accused to renounce his beliefs, which delayed the process. While Philip was pressing for harsher measures against heretics, Protestants were taking over England, Scotland and, to some extent, France. Margaret of Parma complained that the strict orthodoxy which might be suitable for Spain 'closed by sea and by mountains' was impracticable for a trading country ringed by heretical neighbours. The fear that anti-heresy legislation was infringing local liberties (particularism was very marked in the Netherlands) joined with dislike of Spanish garrisons and deep suspicion about planned reform of bishoprics to produce pressures for change which the Regent was unable to resist.

Philip had left behind 3000 Spanish troops to guard the French frontiers. This was resented by the States General which felt their status was being undermined and they refused to release any money until the garrisons left. Reluctantly the King was forced to give way in 1561, to the jubilation of the Netherlanders. As Granvelle forecast: 'There will be trouble here sooner or later on some other pretext.'

This pretext was the 'new bishoprics' scheme. This appeared to be an admirable and long overdue reform of the structure of the Church. There were only four bishoprics in the Netherlands with its population of 3 000 000 and Philip proposed to create 14 new bishoprics under the new Archbishopric of Mechlin (Malines in French). Ten of the new bishoprics were to unite with wealthy abbeys and receive the abbot's revenue. When the reorganisation became known in 1562 there was immediate and widespread opposition. Antwerp, one of the proposed new sees, protested so strongly against the arrival of a bishop, fearing for its trade with heretic states, that Philip agreed to suspend the appointment of a bishop. The scheme was (wrongly) seen as the first step towards the introduction of the Spanish Inquisition; there were fears about the growing power of the Crown because the new bishops would sit in the States. The Archbishop of Mechlin would have the first voice in the States of Brabant and the new Archbishop was the hated Granvelle. William of Orange, one of the greatest noblemen of the Netherlands and nicknamed 'the Silent' because of his alleged deviousness, saw that the plan would dangerously strengthen royal power. It

365

would not only increase religious persecution but also render unnecessary the co-operation of nobles and towns.

For the first time, there was a point of focus for different groups of opposition. Over the next 40 years religion was often to be the unifying feature of the revolt, not provoking rebellion on its own but acting as a powerful secondary motive to compel people to action. Philip was heavily committed in the Mediterranean and could give little attention to the Netherlands, whose government rapidly lost authority. There was a continuing financial crisis caused by the debts from the French wars and Margaret had to appeal to the States for financial help. Granvelle was seen as the source of the trouble and every occasion was taken to attack him and the government's religious policy. When Orange and Counts Egmont and Hoorn withdrew from the Council of State and the States of Brabant withheld their taxes, Philip bowed before the storm and in 1564, Granvelle was transferred to Italy.

The high nobility on the Council of State began to assume a more active role in government, working closely with Margaret of Parma. The greatest problem facing them was a marked spread of Protestantism. Many exiles had returned when Granvelle left and in several provinces persecution had virtually ended. In Holland, no-one had been executed for his beliefs since 1553. The Brussels government therefore moderated the anti-heresy laws to make them more acceptable and sent Count Egmont to Madrid in 1565 to explain their actions and seek approval of the new position of the Council of State in government. Egmont arrived at a bad time for Philip, as he had just heard that the Ottomans were planning a great expedition in the Mediterranean. It may be that the King was accordingly very conciliatory in attitude and Egmont returned to the Netherlands convinced that Philip approved of all they were doing, although there is a suspicion that Egmont deliberately misunderstood in order to take advantage of the government in Brussels.

In any case, it came as a tremendous blow to the Netherlands nobility when Philip was finally able to state his case clearly and unambiguously after the relief of Malta in September in the notorious 'letters from the Segovia Woods' which he wrote to Margaret of Parma, the Regent, on 17th October 1565:

> Madame, my dear sister . . . You say that I did not make it clear in the afore-mentioned instruction that it was not my intention to ask you or the seigneurs of the State Council in the Netherlands for more advice in this matter but in fact you were made to understand my definitive intention. As to whether I would wish to ask the advice of the private and great councils and of the governors and provincial councils, this would be a considerable waste of time since my mind is made up . . .
>
> As to the resentment you have noticed at some of the things which the Prince of Gavre (Count Egmont) says I told him and which don't seem to correspond with my letters from Valladolid and with the negotiations in progress over the matter of religion, I don't see or understand that I wrote anything different in these letters from what was entrusted to the Prince of

Gavre. For as to the Inquisition, my intention is that it should be carried out by the inquisitors, as they have done up till now . . .

If one fears disturbances there is no reason to think that they are more imminent and will be greater when one does allow the inquisitors to perform their proper duties and when one does assist them. You know the importance of this and I command you urgently to do in this matter all that is so necessary and not to agree to any different policy. You know how much I have these things at heart and what pleasure and satisfaction this will give me . . .

1 *What was Philip's response to the idea that the Council of State should have a greater say in government?*
2 *What religious policy did Philip instruct his sister to pursue?*
3 *What does the extract reveal about Philip's understanding of the situation in the Netherlands?*

4. The First Revolt and the Sending of Alva

The nobility were appalled at the complete disregard of their views. About 400 of the lesser nobles drew up a 'Compromise' in December 1565 which opposed the Inquisition and forced Margaret to suspend the anti-heresy laws. The high nobility held aloof from the 'Beggars', as those who signed the Compromise became known, but they sympathised with its aims. This challenge to the government coincided with a period of great hardship in the Netherlands, caused by harvest failure in 1565 linked with the closure of the Baltic which drove prices to famine levels. In addition, England had placed an embargo on the cloth trade with the Netherlands which had caused widespread unemployment. All the ingredients of an explosive situation merely needed a spark to set them off.

It is now disputed as to whether the spark was provided by Protestant 'hedge-preachers' who, throughout the summer of 1566, had been addressing crowds of thousands in fields outside the towns. However in August, after a rise in prices, mob violence broke out that became directed against churches and images (i.e. religious paintings and statues) in an orgy of destruction known as the iconoclastic fury. The nobility were appalled and, with the exception of Orange who seemed uncertain in his allegiance, allied themselves with the government. Slowly, order was restored but not before Margaret had written to Philip in the most lurid terms about the desperate plight she was in. There was little opposition to the activities of the iconoclasts which pointed to a strong anti-clericalism and a corresponding readiness to listen to the message of the Protestants, even if the 'hedge-preachers' were not responsible for the riots. The revolt was over and open Protestant worship at an end by May 1567 but by then Philip had decided there was only one course of action—force.

In July 1566, Philip had been preparing to make some concessions but the outbreak of the iconoclastic fury hardened his attitude. His decision to use force in the Netherlands changed the history of his reign and has been hotly disputed. Philip has been blamed for sending the Duke of Alva with a large army to crush a revolt that was already over, although he was merely following the conventional wisdom of the day which said that rebellions must be crushed in their infancy. The Spanish Council of State unanimously supported this view: 'If the Netherlands situation is not remedied, it will bring about the loss of Spain and all the rest'.

What was not agreed upon was the degree of force necessary. This division reflected, and was a part of, faction struggles within the Spanish court, with each side vying for the King's confidence—a situation Philip encouraged. The Prince of Eboli favoured limited use of force and a personal visit by the King to settle matters. The Duke of Alva argued that firm measures taken immediately would end the problem and the King, profoundly shocked at the presence of open Protestantism in his dominions, supported his view. Conditions were favourable. The Ottoman Emperor, Suleiman I, had just died so a Turkish attack was unlikely in the near future. France and England were preoccupied with internal divisions and, for once, financial constraints were less pressing because a treasure fleet had just arrived.

However good the omens seemed in 1566 for Spanish policy, in retrospect it can be seen as a grave mistake, probably the worst of Philip's reign. The conflict in the Netherlands was to become a terrible burden which crippled Philip's other enterprises. As Arias Montano wrote in 1573: 'I see clearly an unending problem, unbearable expense and the loss of innumerable lives, both theirs and ours.' A more conciliatory policy which sought to win back the favour of the nobility might well have produced a quick resolution to the problem, especially as the general population returned to political apathy once the economic crisis of 1565–66 had passed. There would have remained only the Protestants. It is impossible to guess whether they would have been easy to deal with. Certainly Philip would have been most unlikely to tolerate the pragmatic co-existence that the Crown was trying to achieve in France. In 1566 he wrote to the Pope: 'Before suffering the slightest damage to religion and the service of God, I would lose all my estates, and a hundred lives if I had them, because I do not propose, nor do I desire, to be the ruler of heretics.'

5. Alva's Rule 1567–72

The despatch of the Duke of Alva with 10 000 Spanish and Italian troops not only transformed the situation in the Netherlands but also caused grave concern to England and, above all, France, along whose borders the troops marched. Philip assured the French government of his peaceful intentions, but not until Alva had safely arrived in the Netherlands in August 1567 were the French towns on the borders able to relax.

Alva had not been the King's first choice of commander, but those preferred had excused themselves. His instructions went only so far as the restoration of royal authority. He was to work with the Regent, Margaret of Parma, and prepare the way for a visit by Philip either at the end of 1567 or in 1568. Unfortunately for Spain and the Netherlands, events made these orders meaningless. Margaret found the Duke difficult to work with and resented her loss of power. She therefore resigned within a few weeks of Alva's arrival. In the absence of any other candidate, Alva himself took over her position by becoming the Governor-General. Then Philip found it impossible to come to the Netherlands, first because Alva informed him that it would be dangerous to do so, and then because of the disasters of 1568 beginning with the arrest and subsequent death of Don Carlos and ending with the revolt of the *Moriscos*. A visit to the Netherlands in such troubled times had to be postponed indefinitely. In the event it was never to occur, a serious deficiency in this age when kings were respected in person so much more than their deputies.

Alva was left in control of the Netherlands even though he was ill-fitted and unprepared for such a role. It is typical of Philip's haphazard way of providing for his northern provinces that he was happy to let such a state of affairs continue, even though he was aware of the unpopularity of the Duke's rule. In 1572, he went so far as to send the Duke of Medina Celi to spy on Alva's activities—at least, the Duke was encouraged to send secret reports back. Philip wrote to his secretary Vázquez: 'I have seen the letters of the Duke of Medina Celi and I approve of your telling him that he can continue our arrangements. . . . I want no-one to learn of this.'

It is not difficult to understand why Alva's rule was unpopular. The Duke had come to crush any sign of rebellion and he was determined to show no mercy. A 'Council of Troubles' was set up which soon became known as the 'Council of Blood'. It tried over 12 000 people, of whom between 1000 and 2000 were executed and about 9000 lost all or part of their lands. Counts Egmont and Hoorn were arrested and executed in 1568, a fate that would certainly have been shared by Orange if he had not prudently remained in Germany. In Spain, Baron Montigny, who was putting the nobles' case to Philip, was secretly garrotted in prison. These punishments had the desired effect and when William the Silent mounted an invasion in 1568 not a single town rose in his support. It seemed as if the policy of force was vindicated.

As a military commander, Alva had shown his effectiveness; as Governor-General, he proved unable to contain the discontent his policies aroused. Philip was anxious to make the Netherlands easier to govern and administer. He instructed Alva 'to make all the states into one kingdom with Brussels its capital.' This would involve attacking local liberties and Alva's attempts to do so met with immediate hostility even from staunch Catholics. In beheading Egmont and Hoorn, he had executed two members of the Order of the Golden Fleece, the great chivalric order of knights, and that was an attack on all noble privilege. He surrounded himself with Spanish and Italian advisers and left posts vacant rather than fill them with Netherlanders. Thus, the class upon which the administration of the country had always depended became alienated from government.

This alienation was turned into outright opposition by Alva's response to Philip's insistence that the Netherlands must become financially self-sufficient. Alva decided to impose new taxes known as the Hundredth and Tenth Pennies. The former, to which the States General agreed in 1569, was a one-off tax of one percent on all capital; the latter, which provoked an outcry, was to be a permanent sales tax of ten percent. If it came into effect, the Tenth Penny would remove the need to call the States again since it would apply to everyone, and it would hit the wealthiest most—usually they passed the burden of taxes on to the lower classes. A temporary grant by the States postponed the conflict but in 1571 Alva proposed to collect the Tenth Penny by force, although he was not in a position to do so. Philip was totally occupied by a new offensive against the Turks and could spare neither money nor attention for the Netherlands. With discontent mounting rapidly, William of Orange saw his chance and the second revolt of the Netherlands began.

6. The Second Revolt 1572–76

Initially, everything went wrong. A four-pronged simultaneous invasion had been planned for 1572 by sea, from France, and two invasions from Germany. In the event, the Sea Beggars, refugees from Alva's rule in the Netherlands who had been operating as pirates from English ports, were expelled by Elizabeth I and this led them to capture the little port of Brill in Holland in April 1572. William's brother, Louis of Nassau, led a Huguenot (French Protestant) invasion which took Mons in May, but the main invasion force under Orange himself was not ready until August and the massacre of St Bartholomew's Day in that month *(see page 411)* put an end to French help. Alva was able to recapture Mons and then turn against the heart of the revolt in Holland and Zeeland. The loss of French help was a severe blow to Orange. When Philip heard the news of the massacre he laughed out loud and danced around the room. It seemed that it would only be a matter of time before the revolt was utterly crushed.

Alva marched north and sacked Mechlin, whereupon the rest of Brabant surrendered. Orange retreated in despair to Holland. In November 1572, Zutphen was sacked and the rest of the north east returned to obedience; only Holland and Zeeland were left in defiance. Alva moved in to complete his work and found he had gone too far. After a seven month siege, Haarlem surrendered in July 1572 on condition that no-one in the town would be harmed. In fact, the garrison of 2000 was massacred. This seemed to be a warning to other towns and all preferred to fight on to the death since they could not trust any surrender proposals. The loss of Haarlem cut the rebel provinces in two but, more important, it gave them the will to resist, turning the revolt into a nightmare for Philip.

The survival of the second revolt was due to the reaction to Alva's repressive regime but also to the ceaseless efforts of William of Orange to regain his place in the Netherlands. He was a sovereign prince in his own right (along with his great estates in the Netherlands, he had inherited Orange, a tiny independent principality in the south of France) and he used his status to cultivate international contacts. He had spent his years in exile negotiating with the German princes, Elizabeth I and the Huguenots. He had most success with the latter: in 1568 they signed a treaty promising mutual assistance, and he and Louis of Nassau had served with the Huguenots later that year. This campaigning only bore limited fruit in 1572 but was to be of much greater significance later.

The opposition to the Tenth Penny and the widespread hardship that had resulted from efforts to avoid it, which had created unemployment, provided fertile ground for the spread of the revolt but the importance of religion cannot be ignored. The Sea Beggars were Calvinists and anxious to spread their creed. William of Orange had become a Protestant in exile and in 1573 was to become a Calvinist to harness the support of this determined group. There could be compromise over taxes but Philip II would never consent to toleration on religious matters and this kept the revolt alive.

The Sea Beggars followed a clear strategy in their seizure of towns. The town councils were overwhelmingly loyal Catholics but they hated Alva and his centralisation and taxation and were therefore unwilling to accept Spanish garrisons. In each town, the Sea Beggars could usually rely on a small number of fanatical Calvinists who would open the gates to them. In most cases the town militias, the *schutters*, thoroughly alienated from Alva's regime, were quite prepared to let this happen. Once the Sea Beggars were inside, they ignored any agreements that might have been made with the authorities; churches and monasteries were plundered and priests murdered. Open Protestant worship was permitted and those magistrates thought to favour Catholicism were replaced by supporters of the Sea Beggars. The behaviour of the Sea Beggars was so extreme that Orange was forced to dismiss their leader in order to retain the support of the magistrates for the revolt.

The geography and traditions of Holland and Zeeland were in large part responsible for the survival of the revolt in its crucial years when only a small area maintained its resistance (a mere 30 towns by December 1572). The terrain was extremely inhospitable to an invading army, composed as it was of a network of rivers, dykes and islands which made the movement of large numbers of men and their supplies difficult. In addition, much of the country was below sea-level so that the dykes could be broken to flood the fields around towns and prevent their capture, as happened at Alkmaar in 1573 and Leiden in 1574. The advantages of Holland as a centre for revolt had been recognised in 1571 by one of William's advisers: 'Once you have got a foothold in the maritime provinces, it will be easy to resist all attempts at expulsion. Next time, therefore, Holland should be the objective. There is to be found the converging point of trade routes which he who obtains a firm footing there will be able to command. It will be unnecessary to occupy more than a few towns . . . that will at once give to our privateers a safe retreat and a market. The enemy, hampered by the rivers and lakes, will not easily surprise us there.'

Geyl has stressed the importance of the great river barriers in obstructing the Spaniards, along with the fortresses built by Charles V which the rebels now took over. In Geyl's view, it was strategic and geographic factors, rather than any pre-determined linguistic or cultural boundaries, which were ultimately to settle the boundary between an independent north and a Spanish south. And the religious division between a Protestant north and a Catholic south was to follow the revolt rather than precede it.

Before these geographic factors could come into play, the one precondition for possession of Holland and Zeeland was control of the sea. This was obtained by the Sea Beggars in 1572 and the war fleet of the Brussels government was destroyed by them between 1572 and 1574 and never allowed to regain its strength.

If the physical conditions were favourable to the revolt, so too were the political traditions which enabled the rebel provinces to set up a government to challenge that of Brussels. Without such a government the revolt could not have succeeded in establishing a new nation because there would have been no alternative to Philip II's rule, except annexation by a foreign power. The support of the urban ruling class (known as the 'regents') for the revolt and their consequent retention of power was another important reason for the successful avoidance of anarchy and chaos. There was no social revolution and therefore no chance for extremist elements to take over. William of Orange recognised how vital the support of the regents was for the success of the revolt and he took few decisions without assuring himself of their consent first.

The long tradition of particularism meant that the institutions of administration were already there. In 1572 the States of Holland agreed to recognise Orange as (technically) the King's Stadholder (governor) for Holland, Zeeland and Utrecht and to fight against Alva to recover their lost rights and liberties. In effect they merely transferred allegiance from Brussels to the Prince of Orange. They also agreed to pay for the army and navy fighting for the province and to grant freedom of worship for all. This latter did not last long. In 1573 Catholic worship was forbidden in Holland in the interests of public order. From very small beginnings (in Delft, a town of 14 000, there were 200 communicant Calvinists and three pastors), Calvinism became the official religion. The active Calvinists remained in a small minority but they were the most dedicated, organised and powerful religious group.

To assist Orange in governing the country, a number of committees were set up, the most important of which was the Standing Committee of the States. Much power was retained at local level by the town councils and it was a constant complaint of Orange that he was hampered in the war effort by the unwillingness of each locality to consider the needs of the whole. Where Alva had used repression, Orange was to use all his gifts of diplomacy to overcome such particularism.

If Orange faced difficulties in governing, these were insignificant compared to those of Philip II for whom the revolt could not have come at a worse time. The victory of Lepanto in 1571 had been a splendid triumph, but the King knew that the Turks would be back and he must maintain his Mediterranean fleet. Ironically, the second revolt had been precipitated by Philip's needs for money in the form of the Tenth Penny. Now his needs were greater than ever before. The early 1570s were a financial nightmare—Philip was spending almost twice as much of his revenue and it was essential for him to find relief from somewhere. In these circumstances it is hardly surprising that he decided the Duke of Alva must be replaced. The Duke was slowly overcoming the rebels but Philip could not afford a siege of several months at every town. Realising that Alva's harsh measures had provoked the revolt, Philip decided on a change of policy and appointed, in December 1573, the moderate Don Luis de Requeséns, then in Milan, as the new Governor-General.

The new governor faced an unenviable task. The Spanish troops had mutinied in July 1573 over their lack of pay and had refused to attack Alkmaar in the autumn. No money was likely to be forthcoming in the near future and Requeséns' own position was unclear. He was still officially governor of Milan and his status in the Netherlands was not settled until Alva seized the opportunity to return to Spain as soon as Requeséns arrived. The greatest difficulty, however, lay in the lack of instructions from Madrid, coupled with a refusal to delegate any power.

A few quotations from Philip's letters will illustrate the problem. Requeséns was 'to effect the said pacification and settlement in accordance with my future commands'. 'As I do not know the truth of the matter I cannot suggest a remedy. The safest thing is to distrust both sides equally. . . . You should try to adopt a middle course using the maximum circumspection.' 'I want you in all things to appear as if you place great confidence in the local officials and that you are gaining their strong support. At the same time you must not allow anything detrimental to our interests.'

Requeséns was unhappy about his appointment but he made determined efforts to be successful. In March and November the army mutinied, allowing the Orangists to consolidate their hold on the north west. Philip doubled his remittances to the Netherlands but it was still not enough. The cost of the army was estimated at 1.2 million florins a month (2 florins = 1 ducat) which was more than Philip's combined revenue from Castile and the Indies. At the same time, the war in the Mediterranean was going badly with the loss of Tunis. Philip was in despair. He wrote in June 1574: 'I believe that everything is a waste of time, judging by what is happening in the Low Countries, and if they are lost the rest (of the monarchy) will not last long, even if we have enough money.'

Requeséns decided that direct peace talks with the rebels was the only answer. These were held at Breda in 1575 but the governor was pessimistic from the start because of differences over religion. He complained bitterly to his brother about the government's silence during the talks: 'They have not made a single remark with reference to my suggestions about the talks and negotiations which have been held with the rebels.' 'They do not reply to my requests because they wish to make me responsible for what is done or not done at the peace talks.'

When, predictably, the talks failed, Requeséns launched a successful attack to divide the rebel provinces. However, Philip's decree of bankruptcy in September 1575 spelt ruin for his efforts, as he realised: 'I know full well that those who arranged and advised the Decree have lost these states for the Catholic Church.' Requeséns died in March 1576 and before his successor could be appointed, the situation was transformed by a mutiny of the army in July. It turned into the 'Spanish Fury' when the mutineers invaded Brabant in search of plunder.

7. The Third Revolt 1576–81

The death of the Governor-General left the Council of State, composed largely of southern Catholic nobility, in control of the government. The Council proved unable to cope with the menace of the mutineers and so it was replaced by the States General which began negotiations with William of Orange to end the war and expel the Spanish. Agreement was reached five days before the Spanish mutineers attacked Antwerp on November 4th and in the 'Spanish Fury', an orgy of looting and destruction, laid waste to the greatest city in northern Europe. Eight thousand people died in one of the worst outrages of the century. The entire Netherlands, horrified and revolted by the actions of the troops, united to expel the hated foreigner. All internal differences were temporarily forgotten and it would not be an exaggeration to say that the mutineers had lost the revolt for Philip. On November 8th the Pacification of Ghent proclaimed the existence of a united Netherlands led by the States General.

The Pacification of Ghent ended what had been a state of civil war between the loyal provinces and the rebels of Holland and Zeeland. Now it was agreed jointly to drive out the Spaniards and then submit all differences to the States General. Religion was a worrying issue for the future but the heresy edicts were suspended on condition that 'those of Holland, Zeeland or others shall not be allowed to disturb the common peace and quiet outside the provinces of Holland, Zeeland and associated places, or in particular to attack the Roman Catholic religion.'

Orange was recognised as Stadholder of Holland and Zeeland although his authority was restricted to those territories he already had under his command.

1576 represented the high point of the revolt. Philip was faced with the reconquest of the entire Netherlands and the new Governor-General, Don John, appointed because he would have greater authority as the son of Charles V, was forced into humiliating concessions. Philip recognised that compromise was necessary to allow Don John to establish his position but he included the important proviso: 'Safeguarding religion and my authority as much as may be'. In other words, there would be no movement on the real issues in dispute.

The government of the Low Countries was now in the hands of the States General. This was an unwieldy body as all agreements had to be referred back to the provincial States and achieving agreement, except on the expulsion of foreign troops, was difficult. William of Orange persuaded them to sign the Union of Brussels in January 1577 which restated the Pacification of Ghent but he was unable to prevent the Perpetual Edict being agreed between the States and Don John in February. In return for the maintenance of Catholicism in all areas and their recognition of Don John as Governor-General, all Spanish troops were removed. Holland and Zeeland, firmly opposed to the religious clauses, withdrew their delegates from the States General. The first signs of division had already appeared, but they were temporarily covered again when Don John, fretting at his lack of real power, unexpectedly seized Namur. Orange was invited back to Brussels where he made a triumphal entry in September 1577 at the same time that Don John was forced to accept an ultimatum from the States to surrender all loyal towns, retire from Luxemburg and ask the King to recall him.

Meanwhile the States themselves appointed a new Governor-General —the Archduke Matthias, the nephew of Philip II. This was designed to restrict Orange's power and the conditions imposed on Matthias made him totally dependent on the States. In fact, Orange became Matthias' deputy and the latter had little real power during his three years in the Netherlands.

By the end of 1577, Spanish power in the Netherlands had again almost collapsed. However, a dramatic change was already under way. In March a truce had been arranged with the Turks, freeing Philip from war in the Mediterranean. In August a shipment of 2 000 000 ducats arrived from the Indies, the largest yet received. Philip was able to reschedule his debts and the Spanish army of Flanders was ordered to return. On their arrival in January 1578, they inflicted a crushing defeat on the army of the States at Gembloux. The reconquest of the Low Countries had begun.

The progress of the royal troops was made more rapid by the internal disagreements of their opponents. It was soon apparent that the aims of the Catholic Walloon (southern) nobility were almost irreconcilable

375

with those of the Calvinists. This became obvious as Calvinists began to take control of towns in the south (where their numerical strength lay at this stage) and to impose their will by force, contravening the Pacification. A notable example of this was Ghent where the Calvinists took power and in 1577 went so far as to arrest the Duke of Aerschot, a leading Walloon nobleman and committed opponent of Orange. Unlike the north, the Calvinists of the south, as in Ghent, were often artisans and social revolution was threatened by their ousting of the Catholic magistrates. In these circumstances, continued allegiance to the revolt began to appear more dangerous to the nobility than loyalty to the King and this combined with the traditional particularism of the provinces to produce serious rifts in the States General.

The States were already experiencing problems in financing the war and maintaining an army of 50 000. In 1578, Don John died. His successor, Alexander Farnese, later Duke of Parma, proved himself a master of diplomacy, well able to exploit the divisions in his opponents' ranks. He was also an excellent soldier and tactician and under his leadership the Spanish cause prospered as never before. In January 1579 the three southern provinces of Hainault, Artois and Walloon Flanders formed the Union of Arras to preserve the Catholic religion. In May the Union signed a treaty with Parma in which he agreed to the removal of foreign troops from its provinces and the restoration of all old provincial and aristocratic privileges in return for renewed allegiance to the King. Parma now had a strong territorial base from which to attack the north.

The reconciliation of the Walloon provinces prompted those in the north into their own Union, signed at Utrecht in January 1579. This Union was opposed for some months by William of Orange because he realised that it formalised the separation between north and south which had already begun. It would be much harder to unite the two sides after the Unions had been signed.

The Union of Utrecht was formed by Holland, Zeeland, Utrecht, Friesland, Gelderland and the Ommelanden of Groningen. It was a formal alliance of provinces that acted as if they were independent states. They agreed to act as a single province in matters of peace and war; otherwise each province would retain its independence, including the question of religion.

The Netherlands was now divided into three. In the south, the rule of the King had been restored and with it Catholic worship. In the centre, the States General were increasingly unable to cope with the strains of war and unresolved religious differences. In the north, the Union of Utrecht had effectively thrown off all allegiance to the King and Calvinist worship was imposed. The States General had little option but to seek negotiations with Spain and they were ready to attend a peace conference at Cologne.

At the same time Parma continued his steady progress north, following the strategy of isolating each centre of resistance and then starving it out. In June 1579 he captured Maastricht and Mechlin surrendered soon after. Parma's generous terms to the defeated towns encouraged others to return to the royalist fold, for example Groningen in March 1580.

As the area covered by the revolt slowly diminished it became clear that the peace negotiations would not bring a settlement. Complete surrender or outright rejection of the King were the only options. In July 1581 Philip was deposed as head of state in the northern provinces by the Act of Abjuration. This made explicit a situation that had long existed, but it did nothing to solve the problem of whom to put in Philip's place. The search for foreign allies, which had been conducted ever since the revolt began, took on a new urgency.

8. The International Context of the Dutch Revolt

The Revolt of the Netherlands was more than an internal Spanish matter from the start. Because of its position in northern Europe neither England nor France could ignore events there. If the Spanish army was victorious, where would it turn next? To the English, especially after Elizabeth's excommunication in 1570, the answer seemed obvious. Consequently Elizabeth was ready to listen to the rebels' pleas for aid, although she rarely assisted them until after 1585. In fact Philip was so concerned at the prospect of French control of England through Mary, Queen of Scots, that he was prepared to overlook a number of English provocations including the seizure of a treasure fleet that was blown into English ports in 1568. And he actually opposed the excommunication of the English Queen in 1570.

Relations with the French were complicated by the position of the Huguenots to whom many of the Netherlands nobility were related; for example, the leading Huguenot nobleman, Admiral Coligny, was a relative of the brothers Hoorn and Montigny. Philip was a supporter of the Guise faction which meant that their enemies tended to support the Netherlands rebels. Thus there was the curious spectacle of the French King's brother, the Catholic Duke of Anjou, in alliance with Calvinist opponents of the King of Spain. Initial assistance was given to the rebels by Anjou in 1578 when he assembled an army, but more importantly in 1581 he agreed to become the new sovereign of the Netherlands. William of Orange was behind this move in order to harness permanent French support for the rebel cause.

This alliance across the religious divide indicates French dislike of Spanish power which reached new heights after the annexation of Portugal and her empire in 1580. Neither France nor England could tolerate the increased power this gave to Spain, and the Netherlands became the focal point of resistance. There had been a 'cold war' operating for decades in the Channel, partly in response to the Spanish monopoly in the New World, but in the 1580s this broadened into open intervention in the Netherlands themselves. The tireless efforts of

William of Orange to procure foreign involvement in the revolt led to him being branded as an outlaw by Philip II in 1580, with a price on his head. William was seen as the main obstacle to the suppression of the revolt which was a necessary precondition for the subjection of England. Assistance for the Netherlands rebels was therefore a matter of state security for England. Ironically it was not to be forthcoming until after the assassination of Orange in 1584.

9. The Spanish Reconquest 1581–85

The States General had not sought a revolution and did not want supreme power themselves, but merely a different sovereign. They proved incapable of holding the provinces together given the strength of local particularism. The Duke of Anjou was accepted as the new head of state with reluctance—and by Holland and Zeeland not at all—and severe restrictions were placed on the Duke's authority. He found this galling and made an abortive attempt in January 1583 to seize the principal towns of Flanders, including Antwerp. The United Provinces turned against Anjou after this 'French Fury' and he left for good in June 1583 but there now seemed no alternative to submitting to Spain. Anarchy was rapidly developing and only Holland and Zeeland provided determined resistance to Spain under the leadership of William of Orange. It seemed that the revolt must inevitably fail when Orange was killed in July 1584 by an assassin paid by the Spanish. He had seemed the only man capable of holding the revolt together.

The tensions in the north had been made more acute by the steady success of Parma. His strategy was to capture the coastline and block the River Scheldt above Antwerp because this would fatally weaken all the great towns of Flanders and Brabant which were heavily dependent on water transport. In 1583 he captured the major Flemish ports, except Ostend, and the towns along the Scheldt estuary. In 1584 Parma continued his attack on towns on the Scheldt, capturing Aalst, Bruges and Ghent amongst others. In March 1585, Brussels was taken and then Antwerp was cut off from the sea by the construction of a bridge across the Scheldt. In August the great city fell without a shot being fired. In three years Parma had doubled the area under royal control.

The apparently unstoppable progress of the Spanish army finally decided Elizabeth I that open intervention could no longer be delayed and in August 1585 she signed the Treaty of Nonsuch with the rebels. Elizabeth agreed to send a force of 4400 (later increased to 8000) and pay the States 600 000 florins. The Earl of Leicester was to become the Lieutenant-General, advised by a Council of State. In return the Dutch were to surrender to the English Flushing, Rammekens and Brill until all the Queen's expenses were repaid after the war.

English intervention was the major turning point in the revolt because it finally pushed Philip into the decision that England must be defeated before the Netherlands could be dealt with. For a few years the Netherlands had been Philip's major concern. At the end of the reign they were pushed into second place again, not by the Mediterranean conflict this time but by war first against England and then also against France.

Parma had less money than his predecessors but at least remittances were regular and this enabled him to make plans and to avoid the mutinies which crippled the Spanish war effort on many occasions. The table illustrates how great was his achievement given the inadequacy of his means.

Money received from Spain by the Military Treasury of the Netherlands
(in millions of florins)

1572–77	22.4	(Alva, Requesens)
1580–85	14.95	(Parma's Reconquest)
1585–90	44.7	(the Armada)
1590–95	37.8	(French aid)
1595–99	52.9	(French aid)

(From *The Army of Flanders and the Spanish Road* by G Parker, 1972)

The enormous sums after 1585 were mainly spent on foreign enterprises. For example, between August 1590 and May 1591 nearly four million was received by the Treasury. Three million was spent on the war with France which left less than one million for the Netherlands. This explains why, despite the enormous sums received, there were few real gains after 1585 and mutinies again began to paralyse the army.

There were five mutinies between 1572 and 1576 and 37 between 1589 and 1607. The major ones involved up to 4000 men and could take a year to settle. The mutineers were highly disciplined and made reasonable demands—their arrears of pay often ran into years—but they presented a grave problem to the government who could not continue the war effectively until the mutiny was settled. Consequently they nearly always ended successfully with each mutineer paid in full and in cash. Despite this, mutinies destroyed the offensives of 1589, 1593 and 1600 and led to the loss of Groningen in 1594. Philip's inability to pay his troops promptly is one of the main reasons for Dutch success in the campaigns of the 1590s under Maurice of Nassau.

Parker stresses that the major reasons why the Dutch were able to maintain their independence and so keep the Netherlands divided were the distraction of the Spanish almost continually to wars elsewhere in Europe, their financial difficulties and the consequent mutinies. He has also highlighted the logistical (transport and supply) difficulties of the 'Spanish Road' which had to be used because the English and the Dutch had closed the sea route. Sending armies and supplying them along this lengthy land route around the borders of France was bound to be slow and uncertain. The rebels of the north were that much safer because the power centre of their opponents was not in the southern provinces but hundreds of miles away in Spain.

10. Relations between the Dutch and the English

The alliance between the Dutch and the English was riven by tensions but Parma was unable to exploit these fully because he was ordered to be ready for an invasion of England in 1587 which was then delayed until 1588. The tensions arose because of the different viewpoints of the Queen and the Dutch. Elizabeth rejected their offer of sovereignty because she wanted a return to the position of the 1560s with the Netherlands under weak Spanish control. This was totally unacceptable to the States who resented the pressure put upon them to reach a negotiated settlement with Parma. They had long ceased to regard such a settlement as feasible.

The activities of Leicester also created ill-feeling. In January 1586 he accepted the post of Governor-General offered to him by the States General which wanted to tie the English closer to their cause. Elizabeth was furious and then Leicester tried to break down local independence, especially with the introduction of new taxes that were not under the control of the States. This created opposition and, when two of Leicester's commanders betrayed Deventer and a fort near Zutphen to the Spanish in February 1587, he was discredited. Mistrust between the English and the Dutch was completed when Elizabeth ordered the English troops in Holland to return in May 1588 to defend the English coast. Dutch morale had been lifted at a critical time by English intervention but if it had not been for Philip's decision to turn against England instead of pressing north, it is unlikely that their gratitude would have lasted long.

11. The Enterprise of England

For both Spain and England, the traditional enemy was France and the two countries had pursued a fairly consistent policy of friendship since the end of the fifteenth century. Philip had begun his reign as husband to Mary Tudor and he even offered to marry Elizabeth after her accession. England had been an important ally. It therefore took a considerable time before Philip would seriously consider attacking England even though their differences and rivalries might have made such an attack seem highly justified and even prudent. Religion was not the main factor in Philip's decision, although it was obviously a secondary consideration and the one that Philip chose to emphasise. More important were political and economic factors.

For many years, English privateers had been preying on Spanish shipping, especially in the New World. France and England disputed Spain's exclusive claim but attempts to break the monopoly led to violent clashes—for example, the three Hawkins expeditions ended in pitched battles in the 1560s and two colonies of French Protestants in Florida were massacred by Spanish forces in 1566. The activities of Drake, which culminated most spectacularly in his circumnavigation of the world in 1577–80 and his capture of Spanish treasure in the Pacific, were a serious irritant to the Spanish although his practical effect was small. English piracy was in fact a tribute to the superior power of Spain, as was the assistance given to Dom Antonio of Portugal and even to the Dutch. This did not make them more acceptable to the Spanish and from about 1585 onwards Philip became convinced that he would have no success until England had been taught a lesson. When Drake raided Vigo on the Spanish mainland in 1585 this confirmed Philip's intentions and plans were made for an invasion of England in 1587.

It would have been impossible to mount a full-scale invasion from Spain; therefore it was decided to send a strong fleet which would join up with Parma's army and escort it across the Channel. This plan ignored the vital point, repeatedly made by Parma, that there was no deep-water port in Spanish hands where such a junction could occur. Nevertheless the plans went ahead, to be delayed for a year by a daring raid by Drake on Cadiz which sank a number of ships and, importantly, destroyed the barrels in which stores were to be carried—a deficiency that was never remedied so much food and water was spoiled before it was used. The death of the Armada's commander, the Marquis of Santa Cruz, in February 1588 was another set-back which was not allowed to halt proceedings. His replacement, the Duke of Medina Sidonia, was not a sailor but he was a powerful *grandee* who could exercise authority over the captains of the fleet. By May the fleet was as ready as it ever would be and it set out on its fateful mission.

We can follow Spanish perceptions of the progress of the Armada through the despatches of Girolamo Lippomano, Venetian Ambassador in Spain:

30 April 1588
Here in all churches they make constant prayers; and the King himself is on his knees two or three hours every day before the sacrament. Everyone hopes that the greater the difficulties, humanly speaking, the greater will be the favour of God.

12 July 1588
The wiser wonder what can induce the King to insist quite against his natural temper, that the Armada shall give battle to the English, who are known to be awaiting the attack with eager courage, and so they surmise that, over and above the belief that God will be on his side, two motives urge the King to this course; first, that he has secret understandings which will fail if there is any delay; secondly, that these expenses of a million of gold a month cannot be supported for long, and so he has resolved to try his fortune, believing that if the enemy win a battle it will have been so bloody that they will immediately be compelled to make peace, whereas if they lose a battle they lose all at one blow.

20 August 1588

Don Bernardino de Mendoza announced from France, in letters of the second of August, that the Armada has given battle to the English, sunk some of their ships, won a victory, and passed on to join the Duke of Parma; but the report is so confused, and that ambassador is so accustomed to deceive himself, that they are waiting confirmation of the news.

6 September 1588

The bad news received in dispatches from the Duke of Parma, and dated the tenth of August, though kept strictly secret, yet pain the King and the court all the more that they were unexpected, and moreover quite contrary to the news sent by Don Bernardino de Mendoza, the ambassador in France, who by three different couriers confirmed the statement that the Duke of Medina Sidonia had sunk many of the enemy, and was on the point of effecting a junction with the Duke of Parma. The dispatches from the Duke of Parma detail the misfortune which befell the Armada on the eighth of August, and how it has been driven toward Scotland and Norway.

17 September 1588

... so the reports from Rouen and Don Bernardino de Mendoza, the Spanish ambassador in France, have done much to console His Majesty, for they announce that the English fleet, in its endeavour to prevent the Armada from entering a certain port in Scotland, has been severely damaged, with the loss or capture of many ships ... The ambassador affirms that the Queen and the whole country are in a panic, for only thirty ships have come home, and those very roughly handled; also that in various parts of the English army mutinies have broken out ...

1 *There was obviously widespread agreement that the Armada would face enormous difficulties. What reasons are given for it continuing?*
2 *This is Philip's answer to Medina Sidonia after he asked for the expedition to be abandoned: 'If the fleet remains in Corunna ... it would be likely to encourage the enemy to more hostilities, thinking we are weak. ... Even if our purpose were solely to make peace, this could not be done on honourable terms without the fleet proceeding.' What is Philip's reasoning here?*
3 *What do the extracts tell you about the nature of sixteenth century communications?*

The real story of the Armada is quickly told. Scattered in a storm on leaving port, it was forced to regroup at Corunna and take on fresh supplies. It appeared in the Channel at the end of July 1588 and there was a week of dog-fights with the English, who tried unsuccessfully to break the Spanish crescent formation. The decisive moment came when the Spanish anchored off Calais, unable to effect a junction with Parma and his troops. The English sent in fireships which caused the Armada to break up. Strong winds then drove it nearly onto the Dutch sandbanks but at the last moment the wind changed and the fleet was blown up the North Sea. Some ships were destroyed or captured by the English, who had the enormous advantage of being able to replenish their ammunition, but most were wrecked in storms around the Scottish and Irish coasts as the fleet straggled home. Of the 130 ships which set out, about a third failed to return.

The failure of the Armada dealt a fatal blow to Philip's prestige in both France and the Netherlands, but as far as England was concerned, it was not the end of the war but only the beginning. Fears of Spanish invasion continued throughout the 1590s and there were two more armadas in 1596 and 1597, both scattered by gales, and a further fleet in 1599 was diverted to the defence of the Canaries and the Azores. The Armada was the start of an Atlantic fleet for Spain; priority was given to making good the losses suffered. The English found that their spectacular raids on shipping were harder in the 1590s than before. More bullion reached Spain between 1588 and 1603 than in any other 15-year period. However, the costs of defence were very heavy. The Earl of Essex led a dramatic raid on Cadiz in 1595 but otherwise the English had little success and the war became a costly stalemate. Philip became increasingly anxious for peace as the financial burdens mounted, especially as from 1589 he had started to intervene in France.

12. Intervention in France

For the first 30 years of the reign, Philip's policy in France had been to aid the enemies of the Huguenots, usually by verbal encouragement but occasionally by financial assistance. This position was changed by the death of the Duke of Anjou in 1584; the new heir was the Huguenot Henry of Navarre. Philip was faced with the prospect of his greatest national enemy and near neighbour becoming Protestant. To avert such a catastrophe he signed the secret Treaty of Joinville in December 1584 with the Guises, the leaders of the Catholic League in France (see page 418). Philip agreed to pay a monthly subsidy of 50 000 crowns to defend Catholicism, suppress heresy and keep Henry of Navarre from the throne. In return, the League promised to help Philip to take French Navarre and Cambrai and to keep France neutral in the event of war with England. The League used its formidable strength to force Henry III to recognise the Cardinal of Bourbon as his heir and to outlaw Protestantism, which led to a re-opening of the French Wars of Religion (see page 419). However, Henry finally asserted himself and ordered the assassination of the Duke of Guise and his brother, the Cardinal of Lorraine, in 1588 and recognised Henry of Navarre as his heir. A year later he paid the price for his stand when a friar stabbed him to death in August 1589. Philip's fear of a Huguenot succession had been realised. He decided he must intervene in the French wars himself.

'The affairs of France are at this moment the principal thing.' Thus Philip wrote to Parma in 1589 and this remained his view until 1598. It was a disastrous decision for the reconquest of the Netherlands. Under their new leader, Maurice of Nassau (William the Silent's son), the United Provinces were able to win back some of the territory conquered by Parma and so consolidate their position. The Dutch were also well served by their chief diplomat, Johannes Oldenbarnevelt, who did much to maintain the international alliance against Spain. Spanish victory became impossible, especially as intervention in France meant that Philip was fighting three opponents.

The early 1590s was the first and last time that the lines of political and religious division were exactly the same. It seemed that at last a decisive clash between the two faiths was to take place which would settle the religious question. Of course, it was not that simple: relations between the Dutch and the English were bad and the Pope was furious at Philip's claims to be the protector of the Catholics in France.

It was necessary to have an alternative monarch to Henry IV. Philip put forward the claim of his daughter Isabella, the granddaughter of Henry II of France, although the Estates General rejected it. The prospect of Habsburgs in control of almost the whole of western Europe was not an appealing one to any but the most fanatical of Catholics, and was always unlikely to succeed. Ignoring this, Philip turned away from his legitimate interests in the Netherlands, where the war became purely defensive, and used it merely as a base for the operations against France. As money was diverted away from the Netherlands, the mutinies which destroyed the Spanish war effort began. Parma suggested a peace plan which would grant private Calvinist worship in specific towns but Philip was only interested in victory, not compromise, ignoring the fact that he was denying Parma the means to make victory possible.

Henry of Navarre besieged Paris in 1590. Parma was ordered to raise the siege, which he did successfully, but meanwhile the States General won their first military success for twelve years, capturing Breda. The Dutch then mounted a major campaign in 1591 in which they captured Zutphen, Deventer and Nijmegen. Disobeying Philip's order, Parma marched north to meet the new threat and it was five months before he obeyed the King's express instruction to return to France and relieve the siege of Catholic Rouen. Parma was disillusioned by his new role and its inevitable failures and he had already begun to lose Philip's confidence, typically but quite unjustifiably. This act of insubordination led Philip to decide on his dismissal but before his replacement arrived, Parma died in December 1592 and so Philip lost his best general.

In the confusion which followed Parma's death, Maurice of Nassau was able to capture all the Spanish outposts north of the Maas. Two men claimed to succeed Parma—the Count of Fuentes who was sent from Spain as Commander-in-Chief, and Count Mansfelt who had been Parma's deputy in Brussels. Neither would recognise the other and two parallel governments were set up with a combined result of anarchy. Spanish authority ebbed dangerously and there were riots when new taxes to pay for the French war were announced. In July 1593 the Brussels government was forced to conclude a truce with Henry of Navarre. In 1593 he became a Catholic and captured Paris in 1594. Gradually the whole of France rallied to his cause. Further fighting was profitless to Philip but nevertheless the war continued. In January 1595 Henry IV formally declared war and in 1596 formed the Triple Alliance with England and the Dutch. The United Provinces were now recognised as a sovereign state by two of the major powers of Europe.

Philip was in a desperate position. The Spanish war effort continued and Calais was captured in April 1596 but the cost was immense. Eighty eight million florins was sent to the Netherlands in the 1590s and by 1598 Spanish government debts were estimated at 100 000 000 ducats, while interest payments amounted to two-thirds of revenue. The strain on the Treasury could not be continued and in 1596 Philip had gone bankrupt for the third time. It was essential to make peace.

Elizabeth I was not interested in negotiations and war continued until after her death, the Treaty of London (1604) being one of the first acts of James I. Philip was not prepared to relinquish the northern Netherlands so the conflict dragged on there until 1609. With France he was more successful, and the Treaty of Vervins was signed in May 1598. Spain gave up Calais and other conquests and in other respects the Treaty of Câteau-Cambrésis was reaffirmed.

The war had gained little for Spain. Although Henry IV had become a Catholic he was still Spain's committed enemy. The legacy of this war, and that against the English, would be felt in Spain for decades to come in a crippled economy and a Treasury that staggered from one crisis to another.

13. The Revolt of the Netherlands—The Final Phase 1598–1609

The independence of the United Provinces was not officially recognised by Spain until 1648 but in practice the conclusion of a twelve year truce in 1609 marked the end of the revolt and the emergence of a new nation. The death of Philip II in 1598 made no difference to Spanish determination to continue the war but it was recognised that some new system of running the country was necessary. In 1596 Philip's nephew, the Archduke Albert, was made Governor-General. Two years later he married the Infanta Isabella and, known as the Archdukes, they became joint sovereigns of a partially independent Netherlands. Spain still provided the army and decided foreign policy and so retained overall control but other matters were left to the discretion of the Archdukes who therefore had more freedom than their predecessors. With some restoration of order and prosperity, they soon became popular in the south but the north was not impressed by the apparent new independence.

In 1599 Albert opened peace negotiations but advances were rejected by the northerners who instead launched an attack on Flanders in 1600. Maurice defeated a Spanish army but the towns of Flanders failed to rise in his support and the campaign ended in failure. It became clear that the south was not prepared to endure further protracted warfare against

Spain in order to be reunited with the northern provinces. It was also apparent that Spanish capture of Ostend, which the Dutch still retained, must be a priority to prevent further, damaging attacks. The siege of Ostend lasted three years and 77 days because the Dutch were able to reinforce it from the sea. During the siege, Henry IV invaded Savoy and blocked the 'Spanish Road' and Maurice captured some towns south of the Scheldt. The position appeared desperate for Spain. Eventually Ostend fell in 1604, thanks to the leadership of Ambrogio di Spinola of Genoa who became Commander-in-Chief in 1605.

Spinola's great gift was that he was an excellent soldier who was also able to raise money. His arrival coincided with peace being made between England and Spain, leaving the Dutch with no allies. In 1606 Spinola launched an offensive which won back the recent gains made by Maurice of Nassau. The war had become a stalemate. 'The net result of nine summer campaigns (1598–1606) was a few towns gained and a few towns lost' (P Geyl). Both sides became anxious for peace. The war had cost the United Provinces 10 000 000 florins a year in 1604–06 and Spain needed a respite from the continuous warfare she had endured.

A ceasefire was agreed in 1607 but it proved too difficult to negotiate a permanent peace. Instead a twelve year truce was concluded in 1609 which was a great victory for the seven northern provinces. Their independence was implied, if not openly stated, trade with the Indies and the position of Catholics in the north were not mentioned, and the Scheldt remained closed so that Antwerp would not revive as a trading competitor to the booming Dutch city of Amsterdam. All that the south obtained was 12 years' rest. The tiny United Provinces of the northern Netherlands had defeated the greatest power in Europe.

14. The Division of the Netherlands

Particularism had always been a potent force in the Netherlands but there had also been a strong sense of common ties. By the time hostilities ceased, however, clear differences were beginning to emerge between the two new countries. In the north, Catholics were probably still in the majority, partly because the lack of ministers meant that priests who agreed to accept the reformed religion remained in their posts. Open Catholic worship was, however, forbidden and Calvinism made rapid progress so that outwardly the United Provinces was a completely Protestant country.

Equally significantly, the north had prospered while the south stagnated. Holland and Zeeland were no longer a battlefield after 1576 and a burgomaster of Amsterdam was able to write: 'It is known to all the world that whereas it is generally the nature of war to ruin land and people, these countries on the contrary have been noticeably improved thereby.' The merchants of Holland had grown rich supplying the war needs of their enemies which the Spanish lacked the capacity to obtain for themselves. In 1590 the first Dutch ships entered the Mediterranean and this led to an enormous expansion in their overseas trade. They also exploited the routes to the Indies—both East and West—much to the annoyance of Spain. In 1596 the States of Holland acknowledged: 'In the command of the sea and in the conduct of the war on the water resides the entire prosperity of the country.'

Not only trade flourished in the United Provinces. Industry too experienced a great expansion, helped mainly by the 100 000 refugees from the south. Many were Calvinists seeking sanctuary in the north. Others came because of the disruption from endless fighting; thus linen production at Oudenarde and textile production at Hondschoote were severely damaged by army activity in the 1580s and profitable industries were set up in the United Provinces.

As time passed, the difference became increasingly marked between the States General of the north, which wielded sovereign power, and their sister body in the south, which lost even the power to refuse new taxes. The United Provinces only wanted re-unification on the basis of complete surrender by the south. Although there was a war party, led by Maurice of Nassau, which was willing to attempt that, the 'regents', the Dutch merchants who ran the towns and held the purse strings, wanted neither the expense nor the disruption to their trade.

The conquest of the south was in any case impractical. Not only were the Spanish capable of defending the south, if not re-taking the north, but the population of the south would give no support to Dutch invaders, as had been shown in 1590. They saw the Dutch not as liberators but as a threat. The Spanish Netherlands had emerged as a distinct entity.

Under the ordered rule of the Archdukes, the population began to increase and a reorganised local economy developed. The fruits of that can be seen in the fine houses built for merchants in Antwerp in the early seventeenth century, in spite of the closure of the Scheldt and the loss of artisans to the north.

Many of those artisans had been Calvinists and their departure helped to settle the religious problems of the south, which became firmly Catholic. This renewal of Catholicism was not just a matter of inquisitions and heresy trials—there were 3000 Jesuits and Capuchins at work in the south to restore the faith of the people.

By the time that war was renewed in 1621, the division of the Netherlands had become a firm reality. Philip II's provocative policies had ultimately led to this. In spite of immense Spanish efforts, Spain did not in the end have the resources or organisation sufficient to dominate north western Europe.

15. Bibliography

G Parker *The Dutch Revolt* (Allen Lane, 1977). G Parker *Spain and the Netherlands 1599–1659* (Collins, 1977). P. Geyl *The Revolt of the Netherlands*

(2nd edition, Ernest Benn, 1958). K W Swart *William the Silent and the Revolt of the Netherlands* (Historical Association Pamphlet, 1978). G Mattingly *The Defeat of the Spanish Armada* (2nd edition Jonathan Cape, 1983).

16. Discussion Points and Exercises

A *This section consists of questions or points that might be used for discussion (or written answers) as a way of expanding on the chapter and testing understanding of it:*

1 What legacy did Philip II inherit in the Netherlands?

2 Why did the high nobility feel dissatisfied with Philip's rule up to 1566?

3 What was the role of religion in the outbreak of the first revolt?

4 What do the 'letters from the Segovia Woods' show about Philip's government of the Netherlands?

5 How successful was the Duke of Alva as Governor-General, 1567–73?

6 Explain the physical and political conditions in Holland and Zeeland which favoured successful defiance of the Crown.

7 What problems did successive governors face in their relations with the King?

8 What effect did the 'Spanish Fury' of 1576 have?

9 Why were the 17 provinces unable to maintain for long their united opposition to the King?

10 Explain the international significance of events in the Netherlands.

11 Why was Parma so successful up to 1585?

12 What is the importance of the Treaty of Nonsuch in the Revolt?

13 What was the effect for the Netherlands of Spanish intervention in France in the 1590s?

14 Why was there increasingly a stalemate in the Dutch Revolt from the 1590s onwards?

B *Essay questions*

1 What was the role of religion in the revolts in the Netherlands up to 1609?

2 What was the contribution of William the Silent to the outbreak and success of the Revolt of the Netherlands?

3 How did the United Provinces succeed in their struggle for independence against the might of the Spanish Empire?

4 Why did only seven provinces in the Netherlands succeed in breaking away from Spanish rule?

5 'Spanish commitments elsewhere'. How far do these explain the failure to crush the Revolt of the Netherlands?

6 When and why did resistance to Spanish rule in the Netherlands become a movement for independence?

17. The Role of Religion in the Revolt of the Netherlands

The Revolt of the Netherlands used to be classed as one of the religious wars of the later sixteenth century. But did religion provide a fundamental cause of the Revolt? Read the three extracts from recent historians writing on this issue and then answer the questions which follow.

A.   From K W Swart   The Black Legend during the Eighty Years War in Britain and the Netherlands, Vol. 5, eds J S Bromley and E H Kossmann, 1975:

> The Revolt of the Netherlands broke out for a multiplicity of reasons and was not exclusively, nor even primarily, caused by strong opposition to ruthless persecution of heresy. Yet in the early manifestoes of the Revolt discontent with the government's religious policy was almost invariably cited as the only serious grievance of the population. By restricting their programme to a demand for greater religious freedom and by not professing their other further-reaching, utterly different political and religious objectives—which divided the opposition to the government—the early leaders of the Revolt hoped to establish a united front, concentrating their attacks on the weakest link of the establishment: the Catholic clergy of the Netherlands in general and the Inquisition in particular.

B.   From H G Koenigsberger   Estates and Revolutions, 1971:

> At first it seemed as if the situation of the Netherlands was that of an outlying dominion in which the power of the crown was sufficiently secure to allow the estates the luxury of overthrowing an unpopular minister, Cardinal Granvelle. But religious divisions made the opposing parties virtually irreconcilable and the Netherlands were much too important for the king to allow his authority to be seriously challenged. Philip II sent the Duke of Alva with his best army to the Netherlands, and the Duke abolished the former balance between crown and estates, in favour of the absolute supremacy of the crown.

C.   From G Parker   The Dutch Revolt, 1977:

> The defence of local privilege against the encroachments of the new central power proved to be the mainspring of the early opposition to Philip II. The various provinces, and the different social groups within them, were drawn together by the threat to their corporate 'liberties' posed by the 'novelties' introduced by Philip II and his ministers: the Spanish garrisons, the control of policy by Cardinal Granvelle, the 'new bishoprics' scheme and the rigorous persecution of heretics by a special Inquisition. Religion played its part in all this, but support for the Protestants came principally from those who were not themselves prepared to join the Reformed church. Calvinism was exploited by politicians for their own ends and the small band of devoted Protestant ministers who made many converts in 1566, while they

enjoyed the support of the political leaders, were to see most of their flocks executed or exiled when their political support evaporated in 1567.

1   *What is the different role ascribed to religion in the initial outbreak of revolt by the authors of Extracts A, B and C?*
2   *Why does Swart (Extract A) suggest that religion achieved such prominence?*
3   *What do the authors of Extracts B and C believe to be the main cause of the first revolt, if it is not religion?*
4   *Which interpretation do you find most convincing and why?*

18. William of Orange—A Biographical Study

At the age of thirty-four, William of Nassau, Prince of Orange (1533–1584), better known as William the Silent, became the leader of the people of the Dutch Netherlands in their revolt against Philip II. William has been called by some 'the wisest, gentlest, and bravest man who ever led a nation,' and by others a 'deceitful, self-seeking politician, and traitor.' The Dutch referred to him as 'the Father of his people,' but to the Spanish he incarnated the evils of the Reformation, the cunning of the Flemings and the ingratitude of an upstart. William's character represents a blending of both virtues and vices, making him, like Philip II, the subject of heated discussion to this day.

(J C Rule and J J Te Paska (eds)
The Character of Philip II, 1963)

Read the following account of William's career and the primary (headed in bold italics) and secondary sources interspersed in it. Then answer the questions at the end in order to assess William's character and his importance in the Revolt of the Netherlands.

William of Orange was the eldest son of a minor German count. At the age of eleven, his cousin left him vast estates in the Netherlands and France including the tiny but sovereign principality of Orange. William had to leave his Lutheran home and be brought up as a Catholic at the court of Charles V, who took a special interest in his welfare and arranged his first marriage to a rich heiress, Anne of Buren (d.1558).

By the age of 23, William was a member of the Council of State, held a major army command and had been admitted to the Order of the Golden Fleece. Three years later he became Stadholder of Holland, Zeeland and Utrecht. William was now the most important member of the nobility and thus was all the more dangerous when he began to oppose the King. This move began in 1561 when Orange made two important decisions. The first was to marry Anne of Saxony, the niece of the Protestant Elector of Saxony. Secondly, Orange began a campaign against Granvelle, annoyed at his own exclusion from real power. At this stage Orange was motivated entirely by the desire to further his own ambitions. It was not until later that 'he increasingly felt called upon to perform an historic mission, the success of which became more important to him than the promotion of his family interests' (Swart).

An open break with the King came closer when Orange told a shocked Council of State in December 1564: 'The King errs if he thinks that the Netherlands, surrounded as they are by countries where religious freedom is permitted, can indefinitely support these bloody Edicts [against heresy]. However strongly I am attached to the Catholic religion, I cannot approve of princes attempting to rule the consciences of their subjects and wanting to rob them of the liberty of faith.'

Inevitably, Philip began to suspect William's loyalty. Religious toleration was to become the issue that drove William from a discontented but obedient servant into an outright rebel. William clung firmly to no creed. He was happy to accommodate all churches and religious fanaticism was entirely foreign to him. He became a Calvinist for reasons of state because Protestants provided the basis of his power, but he always sought religious peace.

Orange played an ambivalent role in the revolt of 1566–67. He wanted a united national opposition to confront Philip II but he refused a position of leadership when the Calvinists and radicals decided on open rebellion. He also refused to take a new oath of unqualified obedience to the King and, rightly suspecting the Duke of Alva's intentions, he withdrew into exile in Germany. At this time, William showed few of the qualities that were to make him respected and loved as father of a nation.

A.   *From K W Swart*   William the Silent and the Revolt of the Netherlands *(Historical Association, 1978):*
Convinced that necessity breaks any law, Orange was not too particular either in the choice of his new allies or in that of his methods of warfare. It is very likely that Orange was a party to plans to assassinate the Duke of Alva, and during his abortive invasion of the Netherlands in 1568 his mercenary troops surpassed the Spanish army in maltreating the civilian population. At the same time, the numerous pamphlets issued under Orange's authorisation not only exaggerated the atrocities committed by the enemy out of all proportion to their actual misdeeds but also accused the Spaniards of many devious designs of which they were entirely innocent. In the time-honoured art of vilifying the enemy, the advantage clearly rested with Orange.

B.   **William of Orange to the States and people 1572:**
Attack that monster, (Alva) hated by Spaniards, Italians and Germans alike, see that this rogue of rogues . . . does not escape you, this prototype of utter cruelty, who littered the gates, harbours, and streets of your fine towns with the corpses of your citizens, who spared neither sex, age nor rank, who slaughtered free-born men like cattle, who made children into orphans and accused innocent men, who plunged all your homes into mourning, who either laid out the slaughtered bodies on the wheel or would not allow them to be fetched for burial or at least made it impossible for you to give them a decent funeral; I, on my part, will never desert you.

It was not until after the 1572 invasion, when the restoration of Spanish power seemed only a matter of time, that William revealed his true greatness. He took refuge in Holland and Zeeland with little hope for the future: 'I am bent on going to Holland and Zeeland to maintain the cause there as far as that may be possible, having decided to make my grave there.' In fact he was to establish himself as a statesman of international importance and a serious obstacle to Philip II.

C. *From N M Sutherland* Princes, Politics and Religion 1547–89 *(1984):*

> Historians tend to confine William narrowly within the affairs of the Netherlands. While it is not to be contested that the Low Countries were, and remained, his principal concern, it is because they became the political hub of western Europe that William's life and role should be placed in a broader European context . . . Besides his involvement in the variegated elements of the Netherlands—of close concern to all their neighbours —William steadfastly opposed the international Catholic movement whose guiding purpose was, necessarily, the extermination of Protestantism everywhere . . . William was publicly proscribed by King Philip . . . as the supreme enemy of Spain. As such, William obstructed the subjection of the Netherlands, whose resistance depended, if not uniquely, upon Calvinist fervour. He also obstructed an enterprise of England for her restoration to Rome, without which it was alleged, and Philip fitfully believed, there could be no settlement of the Netherlands. This supreme enemy of Spain was also the supreme enemy of the Roman Catholic crusade . . . the Papacy, the Queen of Scots, English exiles and Catholics everywhere all cast him in that role and periodically induced him to assume it.

It was largely because of William's skill in handling the States that the opposition to Philip in Holland and Zeeland did not seriously waver. Nor did he allow the radicals to take control, which meant that he retained the vital support of the 'regents', the merchants who controlled the towns, and prevented the growth of anarchy which developed in the south after the Pacification of Ghent. On the other hand he retained a broad vision for a united, liberated Netherlands which made him attack the deeply entrenched particularism by which he was confronted. William's grasp of the wider realities made him push the States into offering the sovereignty of the Netherlands to a foreign power because he knew they could not continue the revolt indefinitely without assistance.

D.   *From H G Koenigsberger* Estates and Revolutions *(1971):*

> In the Articles of Union which Holland, Zeeland and West Friesland concluded in 1575 . . . the provinces agreed that resolution taken by the estates in common should have binding force, and that if any one of the allies refused to be bound by them, he should be compelled to do so by the others. Even so, the insistence of the towns on withholding from their deputies full powers in financial matters still led to much friction with the prince. In practice, it was the prince's skill in handling the estates which overcame the inherent difficulties of the system. Thomas Wilkes, Leicester's representative in The Hague in 1587, has left us an account of William's methods:

'He always entertained some five or six of the most credit; the needy ones with pensions, the rest with presents, and all with calling them to his table and society. Through these he wrought upon the rest, and there was nothing handled in their assemblies but he knew of it beforehand.' When he had anything to propose, he always consulted with these persons 'whether the matter would pass or be impugned (discredited).' He knew the arguments that would be brought against his proposition and came 'armed with all the answers and counter-reasons to the wonderful admiration of all, and so prevailed.'

E. William of Orange to the Deputies of the Union, September 1579:

His Excellency answers that unless peace is offered by the deputies of the king on terms favourable to the fatherland as well as to religion, and assurances are given that there shall not be the slightest reason for suspicion that on the pretext of peace the King and his servants should want to tyrannise once more over the country and exterminate religion, the provinces may want to choose a prince as their protector. All things considered His Excellency thinks that in that case no lord or prince could be found whose authority and means are of greater importance and consequence than those of the kingdom of England or the Duke of Anjou . . . But if the provinces think it more advisable not to elect a prince as their protector, His Excellency will comply with their discretion and counsel. In that case too he promises to serve and assist them as much as he can in all matters that they may consider advisable for the benefit and prosperity of these countries.

F. William of Orange to the States General, January 1580:

Your first and foremost mistake is that as yet neither you nor your masters, the provincial States, have established any assembly or council on behalf of the States which has the power to take decisions beneficial to the whole of the country. Everyone in his own province or town acts as he thinks is beneficial to himself and his particular affairs without realising that when some town or province is under attack, it may be useful not to help it for the time being so that in the end the whole country, including these towns and provinces, may be saved.

That is why we are forced to fight not in areas chosen by ourselves and indicated by the interest of the country but in areas determined by the enemy who attacks one part of the country this time, and another part the next time, so that we must follow him as if he alone has the power to decide both on the time and the place to give battle. As a result we are always compelled to stay on the defensive without daring to attack because each time it is difficult for us to use more than the army of a single province. This of course is not sufficient to resist the forces which the enemy can easily concentrate while our army is scattered . . .

We meet often enough and deliberate long enough, but are as negligent in implementing our decisions as we are diligent in deliberating at length.

William liked to put forward the idea that he was the father of his people who had sacrificed his own interests and those of his family in order to liberate the Netherlands from Spain.

G. William of Orange 'Apology' presented to the States General, December 1580:

It is this head they have destined for death, putting upon it so high a price (25 000 crowns) . . . and saying that as long as I remain among you this war will not come to an end. I wish it were God's will, gentlemen, that either my eternal exile or even my death could indeed deliver you from all the evil and misery the Spaniards have in store for you . . . how delightful a death for such purpose! For why did I leave all my goods at the mercy of the enemy? Was it to get rich? Why did I lose my own brothers, who were dearer to me than life? Was it to find others? Why have I left my son so long under arrest, my son whom, did I correctly call myself a father, I should long for? Does it lie within your power to give me another or to give him back to me? Why have I risked my life often? What price or reward could I expect for my long trouble and toil in your service, in which I have grown old and lost all my goods, other than to win and buy your freedom even; if necessary, with my blood? If, gentlemen, you therefore believe that my absence or even death may be of use to you, I am willing to obey. Bid me go to the end of the world, and·I shall willingly do so. Here is my head over which no prince or potentate but you alone have power.

1   Using this section and the previous chapter, make a time-line of William's life under the following headings:
      Early Career (1533–60)
      Move into Opposition (1561–72)
      Alone against Spain (1572–76)
      The Years of Triumph (1576–78)
      Division and Resistance (1579–84)
2   In your own words, sum up William's attitude to the following and then find a quotation from him to support your view:
      a) religion
      b) the States
      c) particularism
      d) foreign assistance
      e) the intentions of the Spanish
      f) his own role in the revolt.
3   How did William manage the States (See Extracts D, E, F and G)?
4   In what ways could William be seen as an idealist? (Take care not to accept his words at their face value.)
5   Could the Revolt of the Netherlands have succeeded without William of Orange?

XV The French Wars of Religion

1. Introduction

The celebrations marking the Treaty of Câteau-Cambrésis in 1559 ended in tragedy when Henry II was mortally wounded by a lance piercing his eye whilst jousting. His unexpected death opened the floodgates to discontent which had been gathering over the years but had been kept in check by the strength of the monarchy under Francis I and Henry II. The problems under Henry had been similar to those faced by his father, namely the resolution of the old Habsburg–Valois conflict, inadequate revenue and the increase in the spread of Protestant ideas. The new King, Francis II, was only 15 years old and incapable of exerting the personal authority that was needed to defeat the opposition.

That opposition was to plunge France into over 30 years of civil wars. Those wars are usually referred to as the 'French Wars of Religion' and certainly the growth of a militant Calvinism and the Catholic reaction to it made the nation much less stable. However, religion was by no means the only cause of war. The nation was to be torn apart by the faction fighting of the great aristocratic families and their clients. And the wars were not fought out just at a national level. As royal authority broke down local feuds had free play and foreign powers began to interfere in the internal affairs of France. The situation could only be saved by the Crown, the unifying force in France, but the problems of royal authority seemed too severe and the inadequacies of those who wore the crown in this period too marked.

2. Problems of Royal Authority

In an age of personal monarchy, as has been seen in the reign of Francis I, the success of a king in France depended to a large extent on the strength of his character; he had to be able to dominate and weld together the large and unruly noble class and control the diverse institutions on which France's past greatness had developed. Unfortunately, the children of Henry II and Catherine de Medici lacked their parents' strength, in both personality and health. Of those who inherited the throne, Francis II (1559–60) was a weak, sickly and easily influenced youth; Charles IX (1560–74), a minor on his succession, never rose above the factions which surrounded him; and Henry III (1574–89), although the most capable of the trio, was governed by his emotions rather than his mind. And the problems which these feeble monarchs had to face were enormous.

Despite possessing the power to tax at will and the introduction of fiscal reform under Francis I, money was a major problem for the French monarchy by the mid-sixteenth century. The reasons for this were twofold: firstly, the burden of the Habsburg–Valois wars and secondly, the inflation which had accelerated in the last phases of the war between France and Spain. In order to cope with the huge sums of money involved in war on this scale, which went far beyond their respective existing revenues, both sides developed the use of credit. Francis I and Henry II had resorted to permanent state loans in an attempt to remedy the situation. These *rentes* had been taken up by the lower orders of urban society as the interest formed annuities for those investing in them. Another expedient was to borrow on the new money markets of Lyons and Antwerp, but that was not an inexhaustible source. In 1557 Henry II had to follow the example of his rival, Philip II, and admit that France was bankrupt. Without supplies, both kings had to make peace.

Financial stability is essential for the well-being of any state and France was now about to be overtaken by one of the most turbulent periods of its history with its credit in ruins. The debt at the death of Henry II has been estimated at about 40 000 000 livres whilst royal income then averaged about 12 000 000 per year and a great part of this never reached the Treasury.

In its desperate need for money the Crown, as we have seen under Francis I, resorted to the sale of offices. The king's ultimate control was sacrificed by this procedure, for a bureaucracy cannot be disciplined without the right of dismissal. The Crown also created new posts and increased the existing ones. In the early sixteenth century it was not absurd to think that France did need more royal judges and administrators, but it was exploited out of all proportion by both Francis I and Henry II to fulfil a primarily financial need. The policy was extremely shortsighted; the salaries of royal officials only added to the royal debt and to the crippling demands for taxation.

Appointment to office, however, was also a means by which royal power could penetrate to every part of the kingdom through the distribution of patronage. One of the best positions from which to exercise this degree of control was through the provincial governorships *(see page 215)*. Governors were able to promote people to offices in their own vast households and to use their authority to appoint to offices within their jurisdiction. The system could work in the opposite direction too. Provincial Estates and towns began to shower pensions and gifts on their governors in the hope of protection, which was usually met. So the need to control patronage became ever greater in order to maintain royal authority over the diverse and sometimes wayward provinces of France.

We have spoken about the growing centralisation of French government under Francis I, but this must be put into perspective. Compared to medieval government, France now had something that could be called a bureaucracy, but compared to what was to come it was still in its embryonic state. There were still no uniform laws or taxes; the provincial Parlements and Estates ensured this. Here lies the paradox: kings of France had recognised the difficulties of moulding the different provinces into one state and had developed local institutions to aid this process, upheld by powerful noblemen and their intricate network of officials. The Renaissance monarchs had extended their own power and the instruments of central government but simultaneously had institutionalised the authority of their provincial deputies, who could get out of control. More than ever before, an effective king was required.

3. The Aristocracy and Faction

The relationship between king and aristocracy depended on mutual respect and recognition of landed interests and honour. Just how disastrous this could be when it turned sour can be seen in the treason of Charles, Duke of Bourbon *(see page 219)*. Most nobles never went this far, but they did retain an attachment to fighting, fostered by the continuing Habsburg–Valois conflict and roaming bands of mercenary soldiers, which was not always in the Crown's interest. Although it was made treasonable for anyone to raise their own army without royal permission, the repetition of such legislation is indicative of the difficulties of implementing it. To maintain the political loyalty of the nobility, kings of France in times of weakness had been required to make concessions. The most important of these was the principle of tax exemption begun in 1404 which, of course, proved to be a permanent deficiency in the Crown's access to the realm's wealth. The great princes received *appanages* (semi-independent territories) with substantial judicial and economic powers; others were satisfied with royal pensions and gifts. By 1523 the cost of pensions was 800 000 livres, almost equivalent to the proceeds from the *aides*, the main sales tax.

By the mid-sixteenth century the aristocracy were becoming aware of the discrepancy between their local influence and their declining role in central government at a time when central administration was rapidly expanding. Increasingly, legal, financial and administrative experts were used to cope with the ever-growing government business, and the royal council was developing a more complex and professional make-up. In addition to political exclusion from central government, the aristocracy suffered economically from the chronic inflation enveloping France. This resulted in a steady drop in the value of fixed rents which were the nobles' chief sources of income, whilst the cost of living continued to rise. As their economic status gradually declined, the nobles clung desperately to their rank by increasingly luxurious dress, display and disorder. Some of them turned to brigandage and piracy for a livelihood, others sought the patronage of wealthier lords.

The lesser nobility were also resentful; primogeniture, the inheritance of the whole estate by the eldest son, was not rigorously applied and estates were broken up in such a way that the wealth of the main line of a noble house was diminished. They had been compelled to contribute to forced loans and had been lured into lending the Crown money at enticing but unpaid rates of interest. To make matters worse, a ban was placed on the entry of French noblemen and their children into trade. Unlike their English counterparts, younger sons found themselves bearing an empty dignity of nobility with war their only permissible occupation and, in 1559, even that was snatched away from them. It was hardly surprising that some nobility were drawn to Huguenotism, not merely as a spiritual comfort, but in an attempt to maintain their prestige and as a way of attacking the government.

In this highly inflammatory atmosphere there hovered three most important families, all wishing to assume control of the young Francis II. The leading protagonists were the Guise family who had profited enormously from the favour of Francis I and Henry II at a time when it was royal policy to favour noble families rather than princes of the blood. So the Guises as royal favourites and provincial governors had acquired vast territory in the northern and eastern regions of France; they had also built up diverse ecclesiastical holdings and international influence. In return they had served their kings well, particularly in Italy in the Habsburg–Valois conflict. Head of the family was Francis, Duke of Guise, defender of Metz and winner of Calais in 1558. His brother, Charles, Primate of France, Cardinal of Lorraine and Archbishop of Rheims, was an experienced diplomat and played an influential role at the Council of Trent. Staunchly Roman Catholic, their great advantage in 1559 was that Francis II was married to their niece, Mary Stuart, which automatically gave them a head start in the fight for control over the young King.

The family most closely related to the Valois (and thus Princes of the Blood), and great rivals of the Guises, were the Bourbons. They were also kings of Navarre through the marriage of the head of the family, Antoine, to Jeanne d'Albret, Queen of Navarre. Antoine, an occasional Huguenot, was rather spineless and not quite as independent in attitude as was usual in the Bourbon family; he was preoccupied with the Spanish threat to Navarre and with keeping safe his estates in south west France and Picardy. His brother Louis, Prince of Condé, was a Huguenot, but though brave, lacked the qualities of reliability and leadership. In many ways the strongest character in the family was Antoine's wife, Jeanne, a devout Huguenot.

The Montmorencys were the oldest noble family in France with a tremendous record of loyalty to the Crown. Their head was Anne de Montmorency, Constable of France, the most important military officer in the realm. He had been raised to high favour by Francis I up to 1540 and returned to prominence under Henry II as his chief minister. The Guise family had rivalled Montmorency's influence, as reflected in the last phase of the Italian Wars. This had been a triumph for Guise war policy over the Constable's desire for peace, and whilst the Duke of Guise was hailed saviour of the country, Montmorency was defeated and captured at the disastrous battle of Saint Quentin in 1557. Montmorency was unswervingly Catholic, but his nephews were Huguenots and his sons at any rate sympathetic to Protestantism. The nephews from the Châtillon branch were led by Gaspard de Coligny, Admiral of France, who combined all the finer qualities of the family. The Montmorency lands were in the Midi and the Île de France.

The regional power bases of these three great families were important but to divide control of France in 1559 geographically into three portions, Bourbons in the south west, Montmorencys in the centre and Guises in the east, is to simplify what was in fact a complex situation. Many noble families did not belong to the clientage system of these three and, even in their own territories, they still faced opponents. This made them all the more determined to gain control of the royal council. However, they all faced a fourth rival, a personality much closer to the young King than anyone else, his mother Catherine de Medici.

The widowed Queen Mother represented the one consistent element in French government during the religious wars and her life spanned those of three of her sons. In 1559 she was pitied as the neglected wife of Henry II, driven into the wings by his powerful and beautiful mistress, Diane de Poitiers. Catherine was also scorned for the commercial associations of her family and viewed with suspicion because of her foreign background, although on her father's side she was descended from a Florentine family of popes and on her mother's she was related to the highest French nobility. Without any deep religious conviction. Catherine's main aim was to preserve the French monarchy intact for her sons (see biographical exercise, page 424).

4. Religion

Francis I had flirted with reformist ideas (see page 223) but drew a sharp distinction between Christian Humanists and Lutherans whom he treated as heretics. Suppression of heretics was even more vigorous under his son, Henry II. The Edict of Châteaubriant of 1551 drew together various enactments against heresy and later in 1557 the Edict of Compiègne added that there was only one penalty for heresy: death. This proved successful against Lutheranism, but was not so effective against Calvinism.

In France the Protestant faith was slow to establish itself, but by the 1540s the pace of conversions was increasing. This owed much to Calvin's influence from Geneva once he had re-established himself there in 1541. This base gave him the opportunity to train ministers who could then easily carry their good news across the border into France. The French Catholic Church was in no state to resist, wracked as it was with abuses. From a diplomatic point of view it might have been advantageous for the French monarchy to embrace the new faith, but the Concordat of Bologna (1516) ensured that there was no constitutional incentive to breaking with Rome. So persecution continued but the anti-Protestant campaign of the government only succeeded in promoting Calvin's cause as his doctrine and organisational skills were those best suited to a situation of extreme danger to the Protestants *(see Chapter XI)*.

J Garrisson-Estèbe estimates that around 1560 there were 2 000 000 Calvinists in France, or ten percent of the population. The amazing growth of Calvinism at this time can be mainly attributed to the missionary zeal of John Calvin and his Geneva Company of Pastors. From 1555 these missionaries, carefully vetted and trained, were sent into France in utmost secrecy to previously planned locations. The provinces of south and south western France, particularly the cities, soon numbered many Huguenots among their inhabitants, as did Normandy and much of central France. In the north and east the missionaries were ultimately less successful, as they were in Paris and several other big cities such as Toulouse and Bordeaux. The reaction of particular areas to Calvinism had much to do with social and economic factors. For example, the missionaries did well in Normandy where the burden of fiscal demands was heavy; in Lyons, a great commercial centre and open to influence from Switzerland, one of the earliest Huguenot churches was founded in 1546.

Their greatest success in converting was amongst the urban classes, the artisans and small tradesmen, but this soon spread to those of higher status such as doctors, lawyers and local officials. The turning point for the Huguenots was winning the support of the lower nobility and later the great magnates and Princes of the Blood. By the outbreak of war in 1562, it is estimated that one half of the French nobility was on the side of the Huguenots. This eventually had its effect on the peasants, as the nobility were the holders of political power in the countryside, but of even greater significance was the dominance they brought to the movement through military leadership and political influence. The nobility imposed a military type of organisation on the church by acting as 'protectors'. During 1560 and 1561 most of the Huguenot churches placed themselves under the guard of a 'protector', either a great magnate or a simple country gentleman. The consistories and synods encouraged this and soon there was no Huguenot community, however small, which was not defended in some way or another. They were well placed to threaten not only the Roman Catholic Church in France, but also the Roman Catholic monarchy.

The motivation behind these aristocratic converts has caused much debate amongst historians. Lucien Romier has spoken convincingly of 'a dissident nobility under the cloak of religion'. Others distinguish between 'religious Huguenots' striving to convert all France to their beliefs, and 'political Huguenots' whose energies were directed principally against the Crown. Look at the leaders of the Huguenot movement as you come across them, examine their motives for yourself, bearing in mind their economic and political position at the time. Contrast Louis, Prince of Condé, whose conversion Calvin himself always suspected, with the devotion and sincerity of Gaspard de Coligny who, having long agonised over whether or not to embrace the Huguenot cause, became a source of inspiration to all his followers. Bear in mind the cynical remark of the then Chancellor, L'Hôpital: 'Several take shelter beneath the cloak of religion even though they have no God, and are more atheist than religious; among them there are lost souls who have consumed and wasted their all, and can only survive in the troubles of the realm and the possessions of other men.'

Blaise de Monluc was one individual who reacted strongly to the religious changes. In his memoirs he tells us of the situation he discovered when he returned home to Gascony as the wars were about to begin:

> Some months after my return home, I had news brought me from all sides of the strange language and most audacious speeches the ministers of the new faith impudently uttered, even against the royal authority. I was moreover told that they imposed taxes upon the people, made captains and listed soldiers, keeping their assemblies in the houses of several lords of the country who were of this new religion . . . I saw the evil daily to increase but saw no-one who appeared on the King's behalf to oppose it. I heard also that the greatest part of the officers of the treasury were of this religion (the nature of man being greedy of novelty) and the worst of all and from whence proceeded all the mischief, was that those of the long robe, the men of justice in the parlements and seneschalseys, and other judges, abandoned the ancient religion and that of the king to embrace the new one.

When Monluc went to Guienne as royal lieutenant in 1562 he found this situation:

> The ministers publicly preached that if they would come over to their religion, they should neither pay duty to the gentry nor taxes to the king, but what should be appointed by them. Others preached that kings could have no power but what stood with the liking and consent of the people.

Monluc supervised the first execution of Huguenots at St Mézard in Guienne, February 1562:

> The other two I caused to be hanged upon an elm that was close by, and being the deacon was but eighteen years old I would not put him to death, as also that he might carry the news to his brethren; but caused him nevertheless to be so well whipped by the hangman that, as I was told, he died within ten or twelve days after. This was the first execution I did at my coming from my own house without sentence or writing; for in such matters, I have heard, men must begin with execution, and if everyone that had the charge of provinces had done the same, they had put out the fire that has since consumed all.

1   *Why was Monluc so outraged by judges adopting Calvinism?*
2   *What other reasons had he for fearing the spread of the new religion?*
3   *What was his remedy for the dangerous religious situation? Why might that
    remedy be counterproductive?*

5. Prelude to the Wars of Religion—The Reign of
Francis II

There was no-one to offer an effective challenge to the Duke of Guise and
the Cardinal of Lorraine when they assumed dominance of the council
for Francis II, the husband of their niece Mary, Queen of Scots. Antoine
de Bourbon, although he was the first Prince of the Blood, was handi-
capped by his Protestantism and was not the man to make so decisive a
move; Catherine de Medici was too stunned by the sudden and
unexpected death of her husband.

Two problems confronted the Guises: a debt of over 40 000 000 livres,
the legacy of Francis I and Henry II's wars, and the growing strength of
the Huguenots. In an effort to deal with the former, the Guises sensibly,
but rather too energetically, cut back on pensions which particularly hit
the nobles returning from the Italian wars, which created an incentive
for them to join the anti-Guise faction. As regards the Huguenots, the
Guises began a fresh wave of persecutions. The most notable victim was
Anne du Bourg, councillor of the Paris Parlement, who was executed for
heresy in December 1559. This inflamed violent passions and the
Huguenots quickly retaliated by openly defying the government; open
air services were held outside many towns including Paris, and in May
the first national synod (a Huguenot parliament) met.

It was during the 17 months of Francis II's reign, or rather the Guises'
supremacy, that the real coalition between many of the nobility and the
Huguenots occurred. Each needed the other; the Church found a
protector against persecution in the nobility and the aristocracy were
attracted by the Church's men and money. So by the spring of 1560,
what had been a rather passive evangelical movement was transformed
into an active party of resistance both at court and in the provinces. This
was first apparent in the attack on the Guises known as the Tumult of
Amboise.

This conspiracy was the work of a number of Huguenot nobles, mainly
La Renaudie and Condé, who plotted to seize the young King, assassinate Guise and the Cardinal of Lorraine and elevate Antoine of Navarre
as chief adviser to the Crown. Its aim was purely political; to remove the
Guises from power and replace them with the Princes of the Blood,
the Bourbons. In the event it failed, and La Renaudie was killed in the
skirmish. Once the existence of armed insurrection against the King had
been established, the government retaliated severely. Fifty seven leading
Huguenots were found guilty, although Condé escaped blame. On
Catherine's orders the executions were staged for public display and

windows for viewing procured at the exorbitant price of ten livres! The royal family and court watched as the victims mounted the scaffold in the square beneath the walls of the Château of Amboise.

However, the significance of the event goes much deeper, for it drew together diverse elements of the Huguenot movement and gave it a common purpose. Religion now became entwined with high politics. For the first time, the passive resistance advocated by Calvin was thrown aside and the Huguenots began to project an organised political front. When consulted, Calvin hesitated, but offered no compromise, so the Protestant movement passed from the hands of the disciplined evangelists into those of politicians and extremists.

Although the Tumult of Amboise had demonstrated the potential threat of the Huguenots, their leaders had shown that they were not yet ready for open opposition. The attack on Guise rule gave Catherine de Medici the excuse she needed to intervene. Her desire for appeasement was shared by the new Chancellor, Michel de L'Hôpital, a lawyer and Christian Humanist. Together, they persuaded the Guises to permit the calling of a great council composed of the leading men in the kingdom in the hope of gaining some toleration for Huguenots. The assembly met at Fontainebleau in August 1560 with Gaspard de Coligny representing the Huguenots. It was agreed that, due to the unprecedented financial crisis, the Estates General should be summoned plus an assembly of prelates to review the religious situation.

The Bourbons boycotted the meeting and the Guises now determined to bring matters to a head. Antoine of Navarre, always the more pliable, eventually persuaded his brother that they should attend the meeting of the Estates General at Meaux and agreed to Guise's summons. Meanwhile the Guises changed the location of the meeting to Orleans and by the time the two Bourbons reached the city on October 31, it was teeming with soldiers loyal to the Guises. Navarre was put under constant surveillance but Condé was sentenced to death. His life was saved only by the death of Francis II on 5 December 1560 and the ensuing political re-alignment.

6. Catherine and Conciliation

Francis II's sudden, though not altogether unexpected, demise from an ear infection spelt the end of Guise supremacy, at least temporarily. Their final desperate attempt to oust the Bourbons was outmanoeuvred by the machinations of the Queen Mother, who this time was determined to win control of the regency for the new King, her ten year old son, Charles IX. Catherine's political deviousness is well illustrated in her treatment of her closest rival, Antoine de Bourbon. Three nights before her son's death she summoned him to her apartments and, playing on his cowardice, pressurised him to renounce his possible rights as regent, in return for the title of 'lieutenant-general', a title carrying exceptional powers and bestowed on a great personage only in a time of emergency.

In private she was capable of breaking down in tears, and wrote to her daughter, Elizabeth, Queen of Spain: 'God . . . has deprived me of your brother, leaving me with three small children and a kingdom divided among itself, in which there is not a single person whom I can trust, as each has some compelling interest.' In public she presented a commanding and capable presence. Determined to keep the Crown intact for her son, she skilfully negotiated with the various factions by short-term diplomacy, retaining the dubious allegiance of Navarre, whilst persuading the Guises not to undertake acts of repression.

At the meeting of the Estates General in Orleans in December 1560, Catherine hoped to win support for a period of compromise in which to re-unite Christians. She also wanted assistance in solving the Crown's financial problems. The Estates General ignored Catherine's requests and simply demanded immediate reforms in Church and state. A problem throughout for Catherine was that when the Crown's authority was at its weakest there was no other institution in France which could or would give it support.

Despite this, Catherine went ahead and put her moderate principles into practice in the Edict of Amnesty in early 1561, which released religious prisoners in the hope that they would return to Catholicism. This was not meant as a general edict of toleration, but as a way of prolonging the uneasy peace. In reality it was to have the reverse effect. Until this point the Huguenots had been prepared to meet in secret; now they began to come out into the open, and dispute possession of churches with the Catholics. If reformers won, then the buildings were desecrated, statues and paintings destroyed.

Catherine began to lose her grip on the situation, as she wrote in December 1560: 'This farce has so many different actors that one of them is bound to spoil things'. She was right; the following spring three of the leading Catholics, Montmorency, Guise and the Marshal de Saint-André, worried about the apparent favour shown to the Huguenots, put aside their personal rivalries and formed the Triumvirate. Catherine had been foolish to concentrate on keeping Guise and Bourbon satisfied and neglecting the middle party on whose independence the monarchy ought to have been based in a crisis. It was important in the history of the wars of religion in France for, as Sir John Neale says, 'a party existed, menacing in its power, whose object was to defend the Catholic faith, apart from the king and if need be against him'. This became more dangerous when an international flavour was added with the Pope, Philip of Spain and the Duke of Savoy all offering help to the Guises. The royal edict of July 1561 condemning Protestant assemblies came too late to have any effect.

In a desperate attempt to reach some settlement in the religious controversy, Catherine daringly called an assembly of the French clergy to meet with Huguenot leaders in September 1561 at Poissy, as mooted at Fontainebleau. Toleration had been Catherine's temporary policy; now she wished to reach a permanent solution. She hoped that the Colloquy would act as a national council of the French Church, working out a much-needed programme of reform that would also reconcile Protestants and Catholics. Notorious Protestants, such as Theodore Beza from Geneva and Peter Martyr of Zurich, were received at court and faced the leading Catholics across the assembly hall.

Despite this auspicious beginning, the Colloquy was a catastrophe and no agreement was reached. Catherine deserves praise for her idealism in trying to reconcile the religious parties for the sake of France but she failed to understand that this was not just a political debate but a fundamental disagreement over religious doctrine. Whereas both sides could agree about the necessity of reform of abuses, unity over the Eucharist was an impossible dream. If anything, it imbued Huguenot ranks with increased daring and the seizing of churches spread, whilst on the other side it enraged the Catholics to such an extent that they vented their frustrations on the Huguenots.

The failure of the Colloquy plus the alliance of Guise and Montmorency meant that there now existed a party determined to defend the Catholic faith, if necessary apart from the Crown. 1561 was a turning point because it heralded the beginning of the wars of religion proper. Until this point the struggle had been primarily political, a fight for power at the top. After 1561 two organised parties, Catholic and Huguenot, existed, both intent on self-preservation and the extinction of the opposition. Providing the moderate force between them was the Crown under Catherine de Medici.

7. Aristocratic Rivalry and the First Decade of War 1562–72

Beza and Coligny remained at court in the hope that their presence would help restrain the excesses of Huguenot revolt. The final expression of Catherine's moderate policy before the outbreak of war was the so-called January Edict of 1562. This gave legal status to the Protestant religion in France, granted the Huguenots places of worship in the city suburbs, authorised their assemblies of synods and consistories and forbade the involuntary imposition of additional taxes upon them. The significance of the Edict was that the Huguenots had at last achieved legal recognition; they would not win as favourable a settlement till the Peace of Monsieur in 1576. The edict was extremely unpopular and the Queen Mother had difficulty in persuading the Parlement of Paris to register it.

Its immediate results were to increase religious tensions: Catholics feared that Catherine de Medici was aiming to Protestantise France. The Triumvirate were in touch with the Papacy and Spain. The final blow for Catherine was the defection of Navarre in December, lured by

The French Wars of Religion

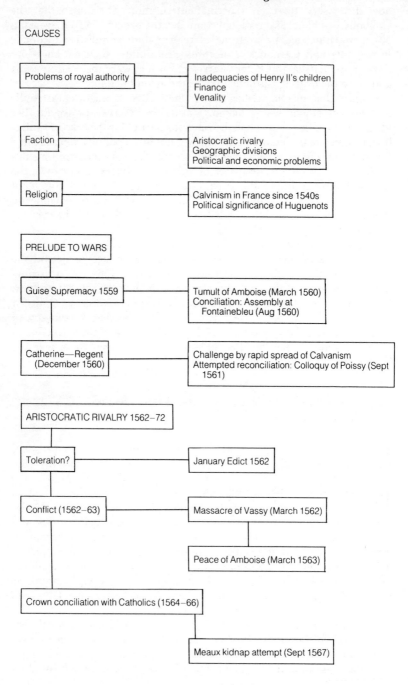

CAUSES

Problems of royal authority — Inadequacies of Henry II's children
Finance
Venality

Faction — Aristocratic rivalry
Geographic divisions
Political and economic problems

Religion — Calvinism in France since 1540s
Political significance of Huguenots

PRELUDE TO WARS

Guise Supremacy 1559 — Tumult of Amboise (March 1560)
Conciliation: Assembly at
Fontainebleu (Aug 1560)

Catherine—Regent
(December 1560) — Challenge by rapid spread of Calvanism
Attempted reconciliation: Colloquy of Poissy (Sept 1561)

ARISTOCRATIC RIVALRY 1562–72

Toleration? — January Edict 1562

Conflict (1562–63) — Massacre of Vassy (March 1562)

Peace of Amboise (March 1563)

Crown conciliation with Catholics (1564–66)

Meaux kidnap attempt (Sept 1567)

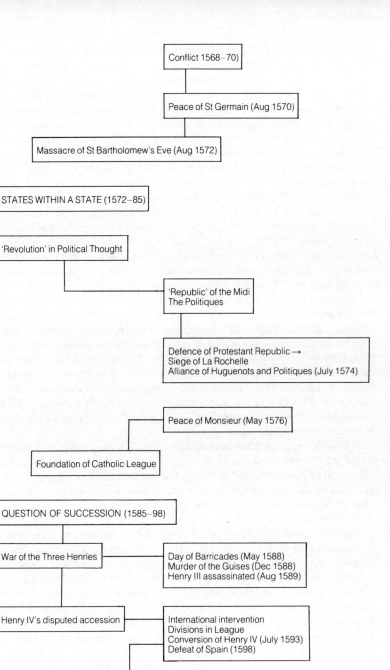

Conflict 1568–70)

Peace of St Germain (Aug 1570)

Massacre of St Bartholomew's Eve (Aug 1572)

STATES WITHIN A STATE (1572–85)

'Revolution' in Political Thought

'Republic' of the Midi
The Politiques

Defence of Protestant Republic →
Siege of La Rochelle
Alliance of Huguenots and Politiques (July 1574)

Peace of Monsieur (May 1576)

Foundation of Catholic League

QUESTION OF SUCCESSION (1585–98)

War of the Three Henries

Day of Barricades (May 1588)
Murder of the Guises (Dec 1588)
Henry III assassinated (Aug 1589)

Henry IV's disputed accession

International intervention
Divisions in League
Conversion of Henry IV (July 1593)
Defeat of Spain (1598)

Edict of Nantes (April 1598)

the Guise faction with the promise of the regency after the Queen Mother had been deposed. It was the prospect of a Catholic rising supported from abroad that made Catherine appeal to the Huguenots for armed support. Coligny replied that there were 2150 churches at her disposal. But Catherine had unleashed an as yet unknown force. Her action provided the Huguenots with the invaluable argument that they were really fighting for their King and so direction of their policy passed more forcibly from the more cautious leaders to those girding themselves for war. Both sides were ready for war and any spark would be enough to cause an explosion.

This came in the Massacre of Vassy. On 1 March 1562 the Duke of Guise, returning to Paris from his seat at Joinville, came across a Huguenot assembly worshipping in the town of Vassy, contrary to the January Edict. In the ensuing slaughter his men killed about 30 of the congregation and wounded another 120. Guise had not planned the incident; in fact earlier he had avoided Vitry where he knew that there were Huguenots breaking the law, and he was at the time involved in negotiations with the German Protestants. However, as it had occurred, he took advantage of the situation and, determined to break Catherine's alliance with the Huguenots, marched to Paris to seize the royal family. The Huguenots immediately looked to Condé for leadership, but seeing that they were greatly outnumbered, he fled to the Midi. This left the royal family defenceless and left Paris, which at times had seemed ready to embrace Protestantism, now permanently in the hands of the Catholics. The monarchy was stranded; Catherine's policies were in shreds and she had no choice but to join with the Catholic forces. After Vassy, war was inevitable.

Both sides appealed for outside help, the Catholics and Catherine to Spain and Savoy, and the Huguenots to the German Protestants and Elizabeth of England. The latter offered her support in exchange for Le Havre and at the end of the war she would exchange it for Calais; Condé's promises to Elizabeth revealed the desperate situation in which he found himself.

Fighting centred on the Loire Valley and, compared to later bouts, consisted more of a series of skirmishes than battles. Condé advanced from Orleans, Guise and Montmorency from Paris. The war went well for Catherine de Medici and the Catholics won the only pitched battle of the war at Dreux in December 1562. Condé and Montmorency were both captured here though. Navarre had been killed at Rouen and Guise was murdered in February 1563. (The Huguenot assassin of Guise, Poltrot, revealed under torture that Coligny had authorised the murder. Revenge for this act was to influence events leading to the Massacre of Saint Bartholomew nearly ten years later.) The two rival armies disintegrated and Catherine de Medici was able to negotiate a peace, exchange captives and unite them to drive the English out of Le Havre.

This ensuing Peace of Amboise in March 1563 allowed the Huguenots freedom of belief, but their freedom of worship was severely restricted.

Huguenot worship could continue in the homes of the nobility in places where it was already established and in the suburbs of one town in each administrative district, but none was to be permitted in Paris. When Calvin heard the terms he accused Condé of having 'betrayed God by his vanity in his desire for a settlement and freedom'. Certainly one result of the peace was that Protestantism began to lose its mass appeal and became more of a religion for the nobility. The peace had brought the fighting to an end, but only temporarily. Old feuds were as intense as ever and the murder of the Duke of Guise was not forgotten by his family. Coligny, alone of the Huguenot leaders, opposed the settlement, but he was voicing the opinion of the Calvinist pastors who thought it a betrayal and prepared for further conflict. The Catholics were dissatisfied that any concessions at all had been made to the Huguenots but they had no need for resentment. Catherine de Medici now realised that she had overestimated Huguenot support in the past and insisted that the Peace of Amboise be strictly enforced. This, plus the fact that the results of the Catholic revival had begun to take effect in France and the refusal of the Parlement of Paris to register the peace, meant that the Huguenots grew restless.

Having expelled the English from Le Havre by the Treaty of Troyes (1564), Catherine tried to restore unity and rally public opinion behind the Crown. Throughout 1564 and 1565 she and the King, Charles IX, progressed around France. In each of the great towns they were solemnly received and lavishly entertained. Catherine's energy was inexhaustible. In the course of this, Catherine had arranged to meet her daughter, the Queen of Spain, in Bayonne in 1565 and to have an interview with the Duke of Alva in the hope of arranging several marriage alliances for her offspring and reducing the tension between France and Spain. This destroyed the positive effects gained by the royal progress, as Alva had been ordered to demand that the Queen Mother take the threat of heresy seriously. But the importance of this meeting lay not so much in what was said, but in what the French Huguenots thought was said. They believed the interview was to seek Spanish help against them and they appeared to have judged the situation correctly when Alva led his army from Milan along the eastern frontier of France to the Netherlands in 1567.

Alarmed by Alva's march, the Huguenots attempted to seize the King who, with his court, was at Meaux, a town to the north east of Paris. Their failure was the signal for a fresh outburst of civil war. The second round of fighting achieved nothing and was over by March 1568: in the only battle, fought at Saint Denis, the 75 year old Montmorency was fatally wounded. The Treaty of Longjumeau that followed merely confirmed the Edict of Amboise.

But this was a truce more than a peace, and meant little to the leaders of the individual parties. The central regions of the country remained in turmoil, whilst the Catholics began to organise themselves into groups known as 'holy leagues', which foreshadowed the Catholic League of the latter stages of the conflict. Catherine de Medici, enraged by the surprise attack at Meaux, now had little sympathy for the Huguenots; she became convinced that her earlier policies had been misguided and that the Huguenots planned a political revolution. The moderate L'Hôpital was dismissed and edicts were issued withdrawing previous grants of freedom of worship to the Huguenots and ordering Protestant ministers to leave the country. Fearing the Queen Mother, Condé and Coligny fled from Burgundy to La Rochelle; their retreat symbolised the end of any hope of Huguenot victory in France. The Huguenot headquarters was no longer Orleans, in the centre of France, but on the western coast, around which future conflict would be based.

On the death of Montmorency at Saint Denis, control of the Catholic forces passed to Henry, Duke of Anjou, Lieutenant-General of France and the third son of Catherine de Medici. Eager to flaunt his ability as a soldier, he pursued the Huguenot leaders to La Rochelle where he defeated Condé at the Battle of Jarnac (March 1569) and afterwards shot him in cold blood. In October, Anjou followed this up by defeating Coligny and his Franco-Germanic Protestant army at Moncontour. The Huguenots lost Poitiers, but Coligny and another Huguenot noble, Francis la Noue, escaped into the Midi.

The war had restored the Guises to power but the Cardinal of Lorraine's overbearing nature had turned the Queen Mother against him. Short of money too, she opened negotiations with the Huguenots. The Peace of Saint Germain, agreed in August 1570, was yet another version of the Edict of Amboise. This time Huguenots were granted freedom of worship in two towns in each administrative district, plus the assurance of civil and judicial equality. As a guarantee of Catherine's good faith, the Huguenots were also given the right to hold four towns, La Rochelle, La Charité, Montauban and Cognac, for two years. The Pope called this 'the most deadly blow the faith has received since the beginning of the religious troubles.' His reason was that the Huguenots now had political security as well as religious toleration. For her part, Catherine, seeing complete defeat of the Huguenots to be impossible, was returning to her former policy of moderation.

Since 1559 the Crown had faced one of the most traumatic periods in its history. The policies of Catherine de Medici are often criticised, but she had at least brought the monarchy through intact. Diverse religious opinions still existed but the experience of civil war had evoked moderate responses on both sides. Royal officials made every effort to carry out the latest peace settlement advocating toleration and the Huguenot leaders even returned to court. It was at this point in 1571 that the King took over the reins of government for himself. Conflict intensified and continued over the next 20 years, mainly because of the lack of ability of Charles IX and his two younger brothers. Ineffective and incompetent, their rivalries helped deepen the divisions in the realm and without firm direction from the centre, the factions took power into their own hands.

8. The Massacre of St Bartholomew 1572

The events that led to the Massacre of St Bartholomew were directly connected with French foreign policy. Having abandoned the ultra-Catholic side, the King and his mother were now influenced by the Huguenot leaders and Charles began to consider intervention in the Netherlands on behalf of the Dutch rebels. The traditional view, that the King favoured this policy owing to the insistence of Coligny who had become one of his closest advisers, has been disproved. In fact it seems to have been the younger Huguenot nobles who wished to involve themselves in the Netherlands and forced Coligny to join them.

There were positive reasons for intervention in the Netherlands—the traditional anti-Spanish foreign policy, particularly with Spain's dominant position in Europe since her victory in Italy, and the new threat to France in the north with Alva's occupation of the Netherlands. Also Charles was following the long-standing idea of uniting his subjects by directing their attention to foreign war.

If French intervention in the Netherlands was to succeed, English co-operation had to be agreed. It was to this end that a marriage between Elizabeth I and the Duke of Anjou, the King's younger brother, was proposed. Although major religious differences ensured that nothing came of this, a defensive treaty between England and France was signed at Blois in April 1570. The French did manage semi-official raids into the southern Netherlands during the early summer of 1572 and this successfully diverted Alva's attention from the Sea Beggars' invasion of Holland, thereby ensuring their success. However, the Queen Mother, although initially agreeing to this policy, became fearful that it would provoke all-out war with Spain, as well as antagonising the Catholics at home. Charles dithered but allowed plans for a full-scale invasion of the Netherlands to go ahead.

So tensions were already rife when, on 18 August 1572, both Huguenots and Catholics were in Paris for the marriage of Charles' sister, Marguerite, to the young Huguenot King Henry of Navarre, outside Notre Dame since Henry could not attend Mass inside. This was yet another part of Catherine's earlier policy of compromise, but the situation was far from conciliatory. The Guises obviously found it intolerable that Coligny, the presumed murderer of Francis of Guise, should have so much influence over royal policy and Catherine de Medici had her own reasons for destroying Coligny: not only had he alienated the affections of her son, but he was connected with what now seemed to her as disastrous policy abroad.

On 22 August a Catholic assassin shot and wounded Coligny, it is thought on the orders of the Guise family, although whether the Queen Mother was implicated as well is difficult to ascertain. The Huguenots rashly threatened to attack the royal family and this was more ominous with the closeness of Huguenot forces to Paris, preparing to march to the Netherlands.

It is impossible to establish exactly how the decision to authorise the massacre was taken on 23 August. One can only assume that, in the ensuing panic, Catherine persuaded the King that they must strike first. But their intention seems to have been confined to a small group of Huguenot leaders, primarily Coligny, and sparing Princes of the Blood.

The murder of the Admiral on the streets of Paris in the early hours of 24 August set off an orgy of killing as the Paris mob ran wild, hunting down and killing between 2000 and 3000 Huguenots in the next few days. Noblemen were slaughtered in their beds and their bodies dragged through the streets before being cast into the Seine. What had been intended as a purge of the Huguenot leadership erupted into a bloodbath in which all manner of Protestants, and some who were not, were victims. Every feud was now resolved by murder; plunder was the prime motive of the mob but others, like the goldsmith who boasted that he had cut the throats of four hundred men that morning, were carried away by the hysteria in the city. Students did not even spare a pregnant woman on their rampage. The Queen Mother's adviser, Tavennes, wrote, 'there was no alley in Paris, however small, in which they did not assassinate someone.' The streets of the capital ran with 'torrents of blood as if it had rained heavily.'

News of the massacre inspired similar carnage in a number of other towns, Rouen, Orleans, Toulouse, Lyon and more, where it is estimated that 10–15 000 Protestants died, despite royal protests to prevent this.

The Crown could do little else but accept responsibility for the massacre and justify it as an act of self-defence. Earlier generations of historians have seen the chief instigator of the massacre as Catherine (see biographical exercise page 424). This view has now been overturned, and Salmon attributes most blame to the King himself, seeing one of the few occasions when Charles took control of foreign policy as prompting the domestic crisis. We can only make calculated guesses but whoever was the culprit, the Crown had to pay the price of its mistake for the next 30 years. Catholic Europe reacted with jubilation; Protestant countries, horrified, saw it as a pre-meditated plan revealing the duplicity of Catherine and her son. The immediate consequences of the massacre were to end any danger of a war with Spain and to force the Crown into an alliance with the Guises.

The carnage of Saint Bartholomew soon turned into a legend that has only intensified down the centuries. As Natalie Zemon Davis argues, this massacre was not an unusual occurrence. It was on a larger scale than local insurrections but that was because it had been authorised from the top. Religious violence, on both sides, was a fact of life at this time; society itself was more accustomed to bloodshed, e.g. public executions, and the most unusual feature of 1572 was that the Huguenots did not immediately retaliate. It is important, therefore, to put the Massacre of Saint Bartholomew in perspective.

9. States within a State—The Republic of the Midi

To the Huguenot movement it must have seemed to be the greatest crisis they had ever faced, but in fact this ruthless act pulled the Huguenots even closer together. Previously divided amongst themselves over politics, war and religion, these differences mattered little now and their bitterness became centred on the monarchy. The numbers of Huguenot converts did not increase after 1572, and they concentrated on defending their provincial strongholds in the towns. This exclusiveness was to their advantage and they abandoned all hopes of national toleration. Initially the Huguenots had not set out to be rebels. They acted as faithful followers of Calvin who deplored resistance to the lawful ruler. As Coligny said, 'They claimed to be fighting not against the King, but against those who have tyrannically forced those of the reformed religion to take up arms in order to defend their lives.'

In the 1560s their aims and arguments were conservative, wanting freedom of worship for their sect with political safeguards guaranteed by the Crown. In the post-massacre period, Huguenot propaganda began for the first time to defend the right of rebellion by subjects and the idea of kingship itself was critically questioned. *(The nature of kingship at the beginning of the century has been discussed in an earlier chapter, see page 234).* This new attitude of resistance is apparent in the work of Francis Hotman, a Huguenot lawyer who appealed for a limited monarchy controlled by the Estates General and aristocratic magistrates. In 1574 Beza opened a new phase of controversial religious literature against the government in his *The Right of Magistrates over Subjects* which emphasised that a king's power rested on the fulfilment of his religious and political duties. But Huguenot ideology did retain a conservative core. Beza had stressed that resistance could only be through 'lesser magistrates'. Likewise Philippe du Plessis-Mornay's *Vindiciae Contra Tyrannos* did not allow ordinary people to initiate resistance. They could only act through their superiors. Therefore, to the Huguenots, popular sovereignty was the privilege of the people to follow their aristocratic or ecclesiastical leaders in opposition to a government that those leaders have pronounced to be in violation of divine law. (This change in Huguenot theory only survived until the Protestant Henry of Navarre became heir to the throne in 1584, whereupon Huguenot political thinkers became royalist once more.) The importance of the printing press in spreading these ideas, and so hardening the lines of conflict, cannot be overestimated. As Zagorin says, 'The press became for the first time an important means of combat and propaganda by both rebels and their opponents.'

On the first anniversary of the massacre, the Huguenot churches in Languedoc formed a militant organisation that would develop for a time into a republic independent of the Crown in military and civil affairs. Languedoc was divided into two administrative districts with Montauban and Nîmes as their capitals. Each was put under the charge of an appointed general, the Viscounts Paulin and Saint-Romain, who had to work with an elected council. Taxation, justice and administration of each Protestant city lay in the hands of a council of 100 members, chosen indiscriminately from amongst its inhabitants. The ideals of government—no pluralism or venality of office, officials elected on the basis of merit rather than rank—were indeed worthy but within a year many of these had to be compromised when the Huguenots allied with the Politiques.

10. The *Politiques* and the Defence of the Protestant Republic

Moderate Catholics disliked the fact that the Crown was now linked with the extremists. A party known as the 'Politiques' emerged; to them the unity of the state was the most important problem which they felt could best be remedied by the restoration of strong monarchical power. Religious uniformity was of secondary importance, but they considered it not worth the price of political upheaval and war which would weaken the state. Desire for peace and national unity compelled the Politiques to advocate religious tolerance. They included leading members of the court, Francis, Duke of Alençon, Catherine's unscrupulous youngest son, and Montmorency's younger son, Damville, governor of the important province of Languedoc. Many lawyers and administrative officials were drawn to the Politiques because of their desire for return to strong government, and merchants and financiers because their businesses had suffered from civil war. The varied composition of the party is shown by the identification of some pacifist Huguenots with the Politiques.

Jean Bodin in his *Six Books of the Republic* (1576) states the theoretical position of the Politiques. His theory, that ideal order was the result of men obeying a prince who governed according to the laws of God, was something to which all parties could subscribe. But as for the rights claimed by the Huguenots to revolt against an unjust ruler, Bodin concluded that 'a subject is never justified under any circumstances in attempting to do anything against his sovereign prince, however evil and tyrannical he may be'. This was the theory but it was not always to be the practice of the Politiques—they recognised that the Protestants might need to be supported and the policies of the King resisted in order to save the Crown as an institution from further decline.

The Protestant cause was saved at this vital stage by the unstifled enthusiasm of its urban followers, led by their preachers. The war which followed the Massacre of St Bartholomew was due entirely to their fervour. This took the form of a struggle for La Rochelle. The city refused to admit a new governor, Armand de Gontaut, Baron de Biron, sent from the court, and held out for seven months under the leadership of the Huguenot, Francis la Noue. But the besiegers were divided amongst themselves. In particular, the two younger brothers of the King, the Dukes of Anjou and Alençon, showed their antagonism towards each other. In June 1573 the Rochelais were saved by the departure of Anjou to take up his new position as the elected King of Poland.

The Crown then offered compromise in the Peace of La Rochelle which followed in July. This granted freedom of worship all over France for noble households and also in the towns of La Rochelle, Montauban and Nîmes, where similar waves of unrest had occurred. These terms, less favourable than before, showed that the massacre had failed to destroy the Huguenot movement but had altered its character by killing so many of its leaders and frightening away noble support. The Huguenot numbers were reduced, the movement was now confined mainly to the south of France and its survival depended less on its own strength than on the weakness of the Crown.

On 30 May 1574 Charles IX died, aged 24, from tuberculosis. Catherine de Medici became Regent once more whilst Henry III made his way back from Poland. The new King was a strange personality. Highly intelligent and an able soldier on the one hand, but weak, effeminate and unpredictable on the other, he was to face a situation at which even a strong prince would have baulked. His tendency to favour a small clique of his personal followers only increased tensions at court and the dissolute activities of Henry and his male favourites known as the *mignons*, chosen for their beauty and courage, became the talk of Paris. His biographer, Martha Freer, sums him up thus: 'Never did any prince seem more worthy to ascend a throne . . . and never did a monarch more thoroughly disappoint such expectations . . . France imagined her king to be a hero, and found him imbecile.'

One who was disappointed was the Politique, Damville, one of the Montmorency family and governor of Languedoc. He had been loath to bring the rebellious Huguenots there to heel. With the accession of Henry III, he entered a military alliance with the Huguenots in July 1574 for the common defence and, they said, for the good of the realm, in what was an extension to the Huguenot state within a state. The southern provinces of Languedoc, Provence, Dauphiné and Guienne levied their own taxes and customs duties and Damville negotiated as an equal with the royal council. The realm of France seemed to be disintegrating and such separatism would prolong the wars.

The following year Damville gained the support of Condé (son of the one killed in 1569) and Francis, formerly Duke of Alençon and now Duke of Anjou. The rivalry and antagonism between the ambitious and unprincipled Anjou and his elder brother intensified after Henry became King, despite Catherine's attempts to reconcile them. In 1576, having escaped from court where he had been held captive since the Massacre of St Bartholomew, Henry of Navarre, the head of the Bourbon family, joined Damville and Anjou and, as king of an independent sovereignty, declared himself Protector of this 'state'. So, in spite of the Politique claims of loyalty to the Crown, Damville and his associates pursued a very independent course for many years. Policy was dictated by expediency, so sometimes they allied with the Huguenots and at other times with the government or the Catholics. The wars for them were not solely Wars of Religion.

11. States within a State—The Catholic League

Terrified by the advance on Paris of Henry of Navarre, Damville and Anjou, the King sued for peace in 1576. The resulting treaty, signed at the Château de Beaulieu and known as the Peace of Monsieur (in honour of Monsieur, le duc d'Anjou), was the most favourable settlement the Huguenots were ever to obtain. In short, the Huguenots were granted full religious liberty, except in Paris, and eight fortified towns as security. The weakness of the King's position was shown in another clause which made Henry of Navarre Governor of Guienne, Condé Governor of Picardy and left Damville supreme in the Midi.

In the long run, the treaty was worthless, as it proved as impossible to enforce as its predecessors. It was soon clear that Protestants would never be able to convert the whole of France; that opportunity had been missed before 1572. The issue at stake now was how much toleration the minority would receive. Catholic zealots were horrified by the Peace of Monsieur and this led to the formation of the Catholic League. At this stage its character was predominantly aristocratic. Its chief was Henry, Duke of Guise and its centre, Paris. By demanding blind obedience to its head, negotiating independently with Philip of Spain and in its administrative and financial organisation, it was emulating the Huguenot stance and Damville's success. It presented just as much of a threat to the Crown's sovereign authority as the Huguenots. The League in its manifesto promised obedience to the King's authority but in reality here was another state within a state.

Henry III was forced to recognise the power of the League and he decided to deal with it by declaring himself its head. The League promptly dissolved itself, albeit only temporarily. There had also been a division between the Huguenots and the Politiques at the time of a new outbreak of war in 1577. Anjou deserted the Huguenots and Damville was reconciled with the King. The Huguenots therefore had to accept the loss of some privileges granted in the Peace of Monsieur when the Peace of Bergerac was signed in 1577. This was a return to the old terms of Amboise, plus the dissolution of all religious leagues.

An eight year truce followed, with only a brief assertion of strength by Henry of Navarre. The King and the now ageing Catherine de Medici used the interval to strengthen royal government. The Ordonnance of Blois, issued in 1579, recommended various reforms in almost every branch of general administration. Life at court became much more regulated, emulating the formal court of Philip II and with every aspect of the King's life becoming part of an elaborate ceremony to enhance his prestige and to dispel any easy familiarity with the royal person. But Henry's extravagance and debauched life style, combined with religious

416

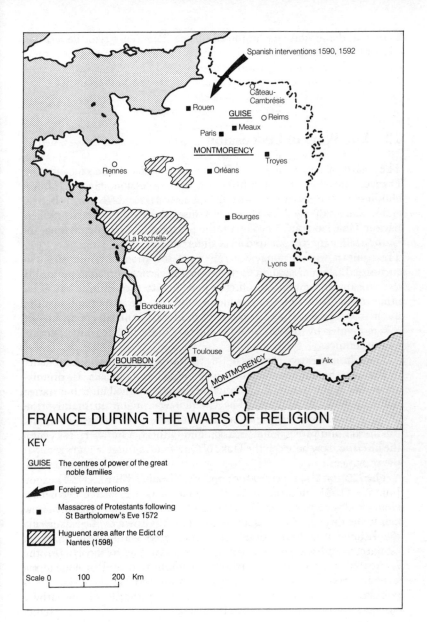

Spanish interventions 1590, 1592

Câteau-
Cambrésis

■ Rouen

GUISE

○ Reims

Paris ■ ■ Meaux

MONTMORENCY

○ Rennes

■ Orléans

■ Troyes

■ Bourges

La Rochelle

Lyons ■

Bordeaux ■

BOURBON

Toulouse ■

MONTMORENCY

Aix ■

FRANCE DURING THE WARS OF RELIGION

KEY

GUISE   The centres of power of the great
         noble families

Foreign interventions

■   Massacres of Protestants following
     St Bartholomew's Eve 1572

Huguenot area after the Edict of
Nantes (1598)

Scale 0   100   200   Km

bigotry and the honours bestowed on his favoured circle the *mignons*, offset any ideas of reform, and divisions in the country rendered them unenforcible. His only attempt to exploit Spain's weakness was to send Anjou on an unsuccessful private expedition to the Netherlands.

12. The Wars of Succession

The death of Anjou in June 1584 led to the last phase of conflict in France, and this time it centred on the succession. Henry III was childless so the heir to the throne was now Henry of Navarre but his claim was challenged by Henry of Guise who could trace his descent back to Charlemagne. Faced with the prospect of a Huguenot king, the Catholic League reappeared in a different but more dangerous form. This time it was no longer merely an association of noblemen. The revitalised League began in Paris among the clerics, spread to the guilds, the artisans and municipal officials and then to the lower orders of the other towns. Although some noblemen did join the movement, inspired by their aggression as well as religious motives, the urban classes flocked to it motivated by the additional problem of material hardship increased by the conflict.

The administrative nucleus of this revitalised League was established in Paris on the initiative of a group of lawyers and officials. Its organisation was in the hands of a Council of Sixteen, named after the sixteen political divisions of Paris. The Council was made up mainly from lawyers with some clergy and only two from the artisan class, 'Poccart, a tin-worker and professional assassin and Gilbert, a butcher'. It became the intermediary between the Duke of Guise and similar leagues set up in the provinces.

The League also received the support of Spain by the secret Treaty of Joinville (1584) negotiated by the Duke of Guise, which recognised Henry of Navarre's aged Catholic uncle, the Cardinal of Bourbon, as heir to the throne. The danger presented to the Crown by the existence of the League was tremendous for it separated Catholicism from the monarchy and was as threatening to the King as to the Huguenots. It created a third party which only complicated and prolonged the struggle. Soon the League's advocates were writing their theories of popular sovereignty and limitations to the authority of the Crown, similar to those put forward by Huguenots.

In 1585 at Péronne, the League published a manifesto which laid down their ideas for restoring peace and religious unity in the name of the Cardinal of Bourbon. This was followed by the League seizing control of most of the towns of the northern and central provinces. Henry III had little choice but to submit to the League, and in July he made the Treaty of Nemours with the Duke of Guise. This withdrew all religious concessions, condemned heresy and offered the choice of conversion or exile. Henry of Navarre claimed that half his moustache turned white on hearing these terms!

After further successes in war by 1587, in contrast with the failures of the King's *mignons*, a wave of popularity for Guise swept the north-east of France. Since 1574, when Damville had made the south more or less independent, the entire burden of taxation had fallen on the northern provinces. Henry III and the Politiques were therefore unpopular in the north. Henry III, in 1588, then alienated the Catholic Parisians even further by doing what he could to help Elizabeth of England who was faced by the Spanish Armada.

Invited to Paris by the radical Catholics of the Council of Sixteen, on May 9 1588 the Duke of Guise defied a royal command and entered the capital. The King attempted a counter-attack but on May 12, the famous Day of the Barricades, the Parisians drove out his Swiss Guards, and he fled west. Analogies are often made with the revolution of 1789, but on that occasion the Paris mob drove the King, Louis XVI, into his capital and captivity. Guise and his associates never intended to get rid of the King, merely to force him to recognise the League's claims. This Henry was obliged to do by the Edict of Union, whereby he agreed to eradicate heresy and recognise the Cardinal of Bourbon as Lieutenant-General of France. This was negotiated by Catherine and Guise. In what was to be her final intervention in affairs of state, the Queen Mother had restored Henry to his place as King of France even if it involved compromising his views. Henry also summoned an Estates General which met at Blois in the autumn of 1588. Dominated by Leaguers because the south sent no representatives, their proposals would only have weakened the power of the Crown.

The King not unnaturally identified Guise influence behind these proposals. Spurred on by the setback to Guise's ally, Philip II, with the defeat of the Spanish Armada, Henry decided on the elimination of his rivals once and for all. On December 23, the Duke of Guise was summoned from the council chamber to a meeting with the King but in a preconceived plan he was murdered in the royal ante-chamber by the King's guard. The Duke's brother, the Cardinal of Guise, suffered the same fate the next day. The King might have rejoiced at the removal of his main enemies at one stroke but his mother warned him to beware of the towns. It was her last piece of advice for she too died on January 5 1589, worn out by the continuing conflict she had striven to end. Catherine de Medici was proved right for, when news of the Guises' murders spread, the alliance between the League and the towns tightened. Paris erupted and, unlike the Day of the Barricades, this rebellion radiated out to the provinces. The King had rid himself of the leaders of the extremists but their followers remained. The youngest Guise brother, Charles, Duke of Mayenne, assumed control of a League region stretching from Burgundy across northern France to Brittany. There was less support south of the Loire but the League did control Marseilles and Toulouse. Of the most important towns, only Blois,

Tours, Saumur and Bordeaux remained loyal to the King. As in 1563, assassination had not resolved matters, only intensified conflict.

With Paris in uproar, the Council of Sixteen began a formal trial of the King in his absence. The Sorbonne proclaimed that the King's subjects were released from any allegiance to him and Catholic publicists declared Frenchmen were free to defend themselves against a tyrant, as the Huguenots had earlier advocated. In this political climate Henry had little choice but to seek reconciliation with Navarre. Negotiation proved difficult but eventually the two kings mustered their armies to march on Paris and began the siege of the capital. Just before the final assault was accomplished, on 1 July 1589 Jacques Clément, a fanatical young friar, assassinated the King at Saint-Cloud.

The death of Henry III saw the extinction of the House of Valois, for Henry of Navarre was a Bourbon. It also meant that the three-cornered struggle in France was now over. The divisions that remained were simply between the new Henry IV and those who refused to accept him as King. Initially it resulted in Henry abandoning the siege of Paris for, as a Protestant, he could not command the allegiance of those Catholics who had remained loyal to Henry III. However, he regrouped his forces and by the end of 1589 the path to Paris lay open.

13. The Triumph of Henry IV

As in 1561–62, 1572 and 1585, the role of other European countries had a significant part to play in the outcome and the prolonged nature of events. Elizabeth I rallied to the cause of Henry on his accession, sending him generous supplies of money and munitions that played an important role in his early victories. The Dutch and German princes also contributed to what they saw as the fight against the forces of international Catholicism.

Philip II, concerned about Henry's growing support, ordered the reluctant Duke of Parma to abandon his campaign against the Dutch rebels and take support to Mayenne. Henry now found himself facing part of the supreme army in Europe.

Parma relieved the King's sieges of Paris in 1590 and Rouen in 1592, but he was unable to inflict a resounding defeat on the royal forces. This was partly due to the King's nerve and partly due to his tactics. Prior to the siege of Rouen Henry, with 7000 cavalry, had attacked Parma and his Spanish army of 23 000 at Aumâle as they marched into France from the north-east border. This was a reckless move but fortunately Parma fell into Henry's trap; believing that no-one would be foolish enough to attack with so inferior a force unless it was backed by a powerful reserve, he ordered his men to withdraw. Otherwise, Henry avoided a head-on battle and the result was deadlock, but it was a tremendous psychological advantage for the King and his followers to have kept Parma at bay.

Meanwhile divisions amongst different sections of the League were becoming more marked, in particular those between the aristocratic and popular elements. The Council of Sixteen still governed Paris and faced hostility from the higher ranks of urban society. Matters reached a climax in November 1591 when these popular, radical leaders vented their hatred on the conservative Parlement of Paris by executing the president and two councillors for alleged treason. Even Leaguers were stunned and the Duke of Mayenne was forced to intervene and put to death four of the instigators. This left Paris in turmoil. The radicals of the Council of Sixteen had been enraged but not defeated. So the Parlement and the upper ranks of urban society were still prey to the radicals and they felt betrayed rather than protected by Mayenne.

Disillusionment with the Leaguers was not unique to the capital. After the initial enthusiasm of a League victory had waned, towns found themselves governed by political careerists or religious fanatics who did little to halt the misery of war. The presence of Spanish troops on French soil, war exhaustion, rampaging soldiers, a series of poor harvests and consequent rise in prices, all led to a desire for peace, a return to strong government and a move away from extremism.

In 1590 Cardinal Bourbon, the League's claimant to the throne, had died. This put the League in a dilemma for there was no other obvious Catholic candidate. Philip II proposed his daughter, fortuitously the grand-daughter of Henry II. Apart from being contrary to Salic law, which barred women from succession to the throne, the thought of a Spanish queen created a deeper rift within the League and alienated yet more of their supporters. This revival of national feeling was only enhanced by Parma's arrival in France.

In 1593 Mayenne summoned an Estates General to resolve the question of the succession and to find an alternative to the Spanish suggestion. To this end Mayenne invited some of the Catholic royalists hoping to lure them over to his side by the election of a Catholic prince.

At this point, in July 1593, Henry IV conveniently chose to announce his return to the Catholic Church. He had calculated that the gain in Catholic support would more than compensate for any loss of Huguenot loyalty. And he is reputed to have remarked genially: 'Paris is well worth a Mass'. He knew that only as a Catholic could he take control of this most important city.

The League preachers protested that the King's conversion was insincere but their influence was diminishing. Henry was crowned at Chartres in February 1594 and in March entered the gates of his capital, Paris. The newly acclaimed King showed his diplomacy by allowing the small Spanish garrison to depart in peace and granting a pardon to his opponents and generous bribes to their leaders. The League collapsed as its members took advantage of the clemency of the King. By the summer of 1594 most areas around Paris were royalist; resistance centred on the borders of the kingdom, around Champagne under the Guises, Brittany under Mercoeur and Languedoc under Joyeuse, but their surrender began in November 1594 with that of Guise.

14. War with Spain and the Edict of Nantes

What finally brought about the unity of France was war with Spain in 1595; many rallied to their King to drive out the Spanish. At Fontaine-Francaise in Burgundy, Henry encountered a small force of Spanish cavalry which he promptly attacked. Unfortunately, the King had failed to realise how close the major part of their army was and he soon faced the entire Spanish force. The obvious solution was retreat, but although outnumbered two to one, Henry stayed put. Aumâle was repeated; the Spanish commander, Velasco, believed the French must be supported by a more powerful force and withdrew. This victory made superb propaganda for Henry and his valour won over Mayenne and Burgundy in October 1595.

Throughout 1596, the Spanish clung on to key towns on the north-east border but were eventually driven from Amiens in September 1597. By 1598, Philip was close to death and suffering the effects of bankruptcy. He sued for peace, formalised by the Treaty of Vervins. Similar in terms to the earlier Treaty of Câteau-Cambrésis, Spain agreed to relinquish Brittany and Calais, together with her conquests on the Netherlands frontier. France had thrown off the last fetter of foreign involvement. This phase of the old Franco-Spanish rivalry, which had been rekindled by France's internal conflict but also prolonged her agony, now ended and this time it ushered in domestic peace. Without Spanish support the last area of resistance, Brittany, could no longer hold out and Mercoeur surrendered.

On 30 April 1598, two days before the conclusion of the treaty with Spain, Henry IV signed the Edict of Nantes for the 'union, concord and tranquillity' of both his Huguenot and Catholic subjects.

This was really a repetition of previous edicts of pacification in its granting of freedom of worship in a number of designated areas except Paris. It was slightly extended in that two further towns in every *bailliage* (district) were added to those specified in 1577. The Huguenots were guaranteed full civil rights protected by special chambers in the parlements and some 100 small towns as security, garrisoned at royal expense.

Much has been written about the Edict of Nantes, but in fact there was nothing radically new to it except the King's determination that this time it would last, despite the opposition from the Parlement of Paris and initial dissatisfaction in Catholic and Huguenot ranks with the terms. It was really just another in a long line of religious truces and the King had little choice as the Huguenots were preparing for another war. This time, however, given that it preceded a restoration of royal authority, the religious truce was to last. It has been suggested that Henry sacrificed some of the Crown's authority by sanctioning a 'state within a state' with the Edict of Nantes. In practice, however, the Huguenots, now shrinking in numbers and influence, knew that their best hope of defence for their freedoms was the Crown—and in any case, it was the King who was the paymaster of their garrisons.

Peace with Spain and the end of the religious wars meant that Henry IV was now able to begin the restoration of France in the consolidation of the administration at home and in her role on the European stage. His record so far boded well for a new era of French politics as the first Bourbon king led France into the seventeenth century.

15. Bibliography

R Briggs *Early Modern France 1560–1715* (OUP, 1977). D Parker *The Making of French Absolutism* (Edward Arnold, 1983). P Zagorin *Rebels and Rulers Vol. 2* (CUP, 1982). N M Sutherland *Princes, Politics and Religion 1547–89* (Hambledon, 1984). J H M Salmon *Society in Crisis: France in the Sixteenth Century* (Ernest Benn, 1975). H R Williamson *Catherine de Medici* (Michael Joseph, 1973). N M Sutherland *Catherine de Medici and the Ancien Regime* (Historical Association Pamphlet, 1966).

16. Discussion Points and Exercises

A   *This section consists of questions or points that might be used for discussion (or written answers) as a way of expanding on the chapter and testing understanding of it:*

1   What were the main problems that faced France in 1559? Which were the most important?

2   Why was Calvinism particularly able to gain support in France?

3   In what ways could rivalries among aristocratic families be dangerous?

4   How did Catherine try to provide France with good government and why did it prove disastrous?

5   What was the significance of the Massacre of Vassy?

6   How did Catherine try to conciliate the Catholics in 1564–6?

7   Why did conflict continue after 1570?

8   Do you consider the Massacre of Saint Bartholomew to have been a pre-meditated action or an impulsive one?

9   What were the long term results of the massacre?

10   Under what circumstances did the Politiques now emerge?

11   What was the character of the Huguenot movement after 1572?

12   Did the personality of Henry III prolong the conflict?

13   What was the significance of the alliance between the Huguenots and the Politiques?

14   Why did the Catholic League form in 1576?
   How did the character of the League change and with what success?

15 What was the significance of international intervention throughout the French Wars?

16 How did Henry IV become the undisputed king of France?

B *Essay questions*

1 What problems faced the French monarchy on the death of Henry II?

2 Who or what was responsible for the weakening of the French Crown from 1547 to 1589, during the reigns of Henry II and his sons?

3 'To dismiss Catherine de Medici as a failure is to misunderstand her aims and to underestimate her achievements.' Discuss this comment.

4 Why did the French Wars of Religion last so long?

5 Discuss the view that the French Wars of Religion were fought over issues that were only indirectly religious.

6 Why did the Edict of Nantes succeed in terminating the French Wars of Religion when earlier attempts had failed?

17. Catherine de Medici: A Biographical Study

Few historical figures have received so bad a press as Catherine de Medici. The legend of the 'wicked Italian Queen' began at the hands of extreme Protestant pamphleteers and reached its climax in the nineteenth century. This stigma is only just being lifted. It is, however, interesting to discover that during her lifetime Catherine attracted not only hostility but also admiration, from Catholic and Protestant alike.

Catherine's influence was felt as much in Europe as in France. She is important as one of several women active in top-level sixteenth century politics. Her career, which spanned nearly half a century, revealed at its height a subtle diplomat capable of restoring peace to Catholic Europe and, at its depth, tearing France into two warring factions.

In order to assess Catherine, first summarise what you have read about her. A convenient way to do that would be a date chart set out as follows:

Date   Event   Aim of Catherine   Extent of her influence   Result

Now consider Catherine's personality and try to work out the reasons that lay behind her actions. You will need to expand on the information you have gathered from the chapter and do some personal research. Consult the bibliography at the end of the chapter. Then read the extracts below and answer the questions which follow them.

A. *From Sir John Neale*   The Failure of Catherine de Medici *1943:*
She was undoubtedly a woman of great qualities, if not a great woman. Her vitality was boundless: she was always ready, with tireless energy, to tackle

every difficulty that arose. But she lacked any grasp of principles and was apt to see political problems in terms of a Palace intrigue which could be solved by getting folk together and making them shake hands. She was, in fact, a very able politician, not a statesman; and her charm coupled with her vitality made her most successful at the game.

Modern psychologists would shake their heads over her possessive maternalism. She loved her children and dominated them with her affection and personality that was ruinous to them . . .

Catherine's solution for the religious problem (in 1560), while bound to command respect in the more tolerant atmosphere of later centuries, was no more statesmanlike in its own milieu than her handling of the political problem. She contemplated a temporary policy leading to a permanent solution . . .

The practical consequence, of course, was to encourage the growth of the Huguenot movement, increase the bitterness of religious feeling every-where, and make the religious problem graver than ever.

B. *From J Heritier* Catherine de Medici *1963:*
On August 24, 1572, Paris proved to Catherine that she had made a mistake . . . The battle on which Catherine had insisted had ended in disaster. Indomitable fighter that she was, she first of all covered her retreat. She had gambled and lost; now she paid up, without arguing. She went over to the victors. Machiavellism had failed her because she was a woman and a mother before she was a politician. Faced with the domestic tragedy of her sons' mutual hatred and the submission of the elder to Coligny, the Queen had given way to the woman. Yet Machiavellism was an instrument that should not be discarded. Since violence adopted for the reasons of State had only made the situation worse it was better to resort to perfidy (treachery). Catherine pulled herself together with her usual willpower. She would lie to everyone and she would not be believed—that she knew. Nevertheless, behind this smoke-screen of lies that she would spread over the battlefield on which she had been beaten, the Florentine Queen would be able to retreat in order to prepare her rehabilitation . . . Her genius for dissimulation and deceit was now to be given full rein.

C. *From R Briggs* Early Modern France 1560–1715 *1977:*
The Queen Mother and Charles's Catholic councillors, over-impressed by Spanish power . . . became determined to withdraw from the dangers of involvement in the Netherlands, the King wavered, and French policy collapsed in an undignified mess. Charles IX pressed on with the plan for a marriage of reconciliation between his sister Margaret and Henry of Navarre . . . Coligny was preparing to leave court and lead an army into the Netherlands, but on 22 August he was wounded in an attempt on his life, probably instigated by one or another of the pro-Spanish Catholic leaders. With extraordinary imprudence the Huguenot nobles threatened the King and the royal family with revenge; the threats were given substance by the presence of Huguenot forces near Paris, preparing to march to the Nether-lands. In what seems to have been a panic reaction, the Queen Mother and her associates, persuaded the King that the Protestants were planning a coup, and that he must strike first; the result was the massacre . . . Making the best of a bad job, the court claimed that the massacre had been a

deliberate act, fully justified by the conduct of the Huguenot leaders over the previous decade.

D. *From N M Sutherland* Princes, Politics and Religion 1547–89 *1984:*
Charles had not governed for himself . . . but it is clear . . . that Catherine expected Henry to do so. Far from resenting any consequent change in her own position, she had always wanted France to possess an effective king. No other authority could ever restore the realms of Francis I and Henry II . . . Her attitude is clearly illustrated in a long letter of advice to the king; it also disposes of the traditional allegation that her judgement was impaired by her maternal affections.

This long and remarkable memoir, dated 8 August 1574, began with an expression of her love for Henry and her hopes for his future greatness . . . She exhorted him to take magisterial possession of his kingdom, and to restore order with firmness and benevolence . . . The memoir urged him to stand alone, as master in his realm, and to avoid provoking opposition by the entertainment of favourites. To obtain the support of the provinces . . . Similarly, Henry was to maintain a well-ordered court, himself providing the example . . . (he) must personally assume all control and direction . . . thus all policy and advancement would proceed from him, and all allegiance and gratitude return to him . . .

She affirmed her belief in his opportunity and her fear of his insufficiency . . . Catherine's fears were indeed, well-founded, and nothing reveals more clearly the extent of her moral courage than her love for Henry and her considered opinion of the king.

E. *From H R Williamson* Catherine de Medici *1973:*
The following year (1577) Catherine set out on her last great undertaking —a journey of pacification in the south, which lasted for sixteen months, though she had hoped to accomplish it in three. She visited Guienne and Languedoc, Provence and Dauphiny, even Navarre itself. Frequently she found the towns and chateaux of the lesser nobility had shut their gates against her but she pitched her camp wherever she could find a suitable site, set up a portrait of the king, summoned the important men of the district and addressed and argued with them. Hostility and suspicion, bad roads and brigandage, plague, her gout and her age—nothing deterred her. The Huguenots who came at her summons were impressed in spite of themselves. Nowhere was she attacked or insulted.

1 *How far was Catherine working, in the short term, for the survival of her sons or, in the long term, for the interests of France?*
2 *How religious was Catherine, if at all? How far did religious considerations affect her policies?*
3 *Do you notice any shift in the direction of her policy at any time? If so, why?*
4 *How would you describe the 'style' of the Queen Mother's involvement in government? How Machiavellian? How moderate?*
5 *How successful were her policies?*

XVI Ivan the Terrible

1. Introduction

'I surpassed in iniquities all of the transgressors from Adam to this day . . . I have desecrated my very head with unseemly desires and thought; my mouth with murderous and lustful words; my tongue with obscenity and profanity, with uttering words of anger and wrath; my hands for reaching for what I should not, with insatiable robbery.'

This extract from the will of Ivan IV of Russia, which he wrote in 1572 and which is translated in George Vernadsky's history of Russia, provides a justification for the traditional view of Ivan the Terrible. His lengthy reign was an odd combination at home of sensible reform in the 1550s followed by the horror and barbarism of the 1560s and 1570s. In foreign policy, a neat parallel can be seen; there were early triumphs against Tatars in the 1550s which were followed by the costly and ultimately fruitless Livonian War.

Interest in Ivan lies both in an examination of his own personality and motivation and of his role in Russian history. He can be seen as a clear example of the typical Russian autocrat, who strangely combined sensible and progressive ideas with outbursts of irrational and sadistic brutality. He can also be seen as ruling the country at a vital time in its history, when it began to emerge as a major power and also to develop internally in a curious and unique fashion.

2. Background: Russia before the Accession of Ivan

All states are deeply influenced by their geography and the emergence of Muscovy, which was the core of the Russian state, clearly illustrates this. In his book, *Russia under the Old Regime* the historian Richard Pipes wrote: 'In the case of Russia the geographic element is particularly important because the country is inherently so poor that it affords at best a precarious existence.'

In the north lies the tundra, which can only support very limited plant life and is incapable of supporting organised human life. The tundra merges into the forest zone, which lies approximately between 45 and 50 degrees latitude. South of this is found the steppe which is an enormous grassy plain of great fertility. These features combine with a harsh climate of long, cold winters and short, hot summers, which leads to a short growing season and a constant degree of crop failure. Equally important is the lack of easily defensible natural frontiers. Most of Russia consists of a flat plain. Indeed, no point in European Russia is more than 1400 feet above sea level and even the Urals, which are usually taken as the boundary between Europe and Asia, present no great geographical obstacle. Although the forest regions presented a formidable barrier to movement before the modern age, there is a unique network of navigable rivers, which mostly flow from north to south. These have made transportation significantly easier than might be expected. The result of all this was to create an environment where the struggle for survival was especially harsh and the fear of invasion and conquest ever present.

The history of Kiev, which was the earlier Russian state, illustrates many of these problems. Kiev was probably founded by Vikings, who used the Russian rivers to trade with Constantinople. In the thirteenth century Mongol invaders from the east destroyed the Kievan state and drove the Russians from the steppe lands to isolated settlements in the north east, such as Moscow, where the forest afforded some protection from the invincible Tatar (the Russian word for Mongol) cavalry of the Golden Horde.

Historians are in complete agreement as to the importance of the Tatar influence on Russian history, but there is great debate as to the nature of that influence. There is no dispute that, for 200 years, there was no strong Russian state. The small principalities, such as Moscow, which emerged in north eastern Russia were cut off by the Tatars from any significant contact with western Europe. Kiev and the western Ukraine were, on the other hand, eventually absorbed into the Polish-Lithuanian state.

Many historians of Russia are concerned to play down the Asiatic element in Russian history. Riasanovsky argues that the nomadic and unstable Tatar state barely influenced Russian history and government, which was far more affected by the traditions of the Byzantine Empire, from which the Russians derived their orthodox religion. George Vernadsky, on the other hand, belongs to the Eurasian school of historians, who argue that the Tatars deprived the Russians of the best land and also cut them off from any contact with the Renaissance and Reformation in western Europe.

Richard Pipes further developed Vernadsky's arguments. He is anxious to explain the emergence of Moscow as the centre of the Russian state, when it was initially a minor principality overshadowed by the wealthier and more powerful city-states, such as Novgorod and Vladimir. Pipes argues that the early princes of Muscovy were notorious for their subservience to the Tatars. Ivan I, who was the first prominent Muscovite prince, made his name by crushing a revolt against the Tatars in the city of Tver in 1327. In gratitude, the Tatars appointed him to collect tribute. Karl Marx described him as 'possessing the characters of the Tatars' hangman, sycophant and slave in chief'. Pipes suggests that the tradition of Russian autocracy derived from the regular contact with the Golden Horde, whose capital Sarai on the lower Volga was regularly visited by Ivan I and his successors, where they were treated in a humiliating fashion by the Khans. Constantinople, on the other hand, was distant and inaccessible. He notes that key words of government in Russia, such as 'Kazna' which means treasury, are of Mongol origin, and argues that the princes of Moscow learned from the Tatars a view of politics in which the ruler was responsible for the collection of tribute, the maintenance of order and the preservation of security, but not for the well-being of the public. What is clear is that between the fourteenth and sixteenth centuries, a strong principality was established in Muscovy, in which the absolute power of the ruler gradually increased to a level only matched by the Turkish Sultan.

However, it was not simply subservience to the Golden Horde which caused the rise of Muscovy to its dominant position within Russia. The princes of Muscovy were shrewd and surprisingly healthy and long-lived, which gave a stability to the state. Great prestige came to the principality at the beginning of the fourteenth century, when the See (Head) of the Russian Orthodox Church was moved to Moscow. After 1439, the Greek Orthodox Patriarch at Constantinople lost all control over the Russian Church and the princes of Muscovy emerged as the protectors of orthodoxy.

By tradition the Orthodox Churches subordinated themselves to the rule of the state. After 1448 the Church in Moscow had its own Metropolitan (next in rank to a Patriarch) who was seen as the equal of all others in the Orthodox Churches but these men were appointed by the ruler of the state and rarely challenged his authority.

3. The Reigns of Ivan III 1462–1505, and Basil III 1505–33

Ivan III was the shrewdest and most successful of the early Russian princes and Ivan IV based much of what he did on the achievements of Ivan III's reign. It was during his reign that the 'gathering of the Russian land'—the conquest of Russia by Moscow—accelerated. Ivan III annexed various smaller principalities, such as Tver, but most important was his conquest of Novgorod which was the most prosperous trading city of north western Russia. He followed this by the suppression of the traditional liberties of the city and the annexation of its land after a campaign in 1478. Ivan III's reign coincided with the disintegration of the Golden Horde into the Khanates of Crimea, Kazan and Astrakhan. Probably, effective Tatar influence over Moscow had ended by 1452, but in 1480 Ivan III formally renounced Tatar control and kept for himself the tribute that had previously been sent to the Golden Horde.

Gulf of Finland

LIVONIA

Narva

Novgorod

Pskov

Archangel

Tver

Moscow

TATARS OF KAZAN

Kazan

Kiev

Volga

Don

ASTRAKHAN

COSSACKS

NOGAY TATARS

KHANATE OF CRIMEA

Azov

COSSACKS

Astrakhan

CASPIAN SEA

BLACK SEA

RUSSIA IN THE AGE OF IVAN THE TERRIBLE

KEY

Russia in 1533

Acquisitions of Ivan the Terrible

Northern limit of steppe (grassland)

Scale 0   200   400 Km

Ivan III's reign also saw a growing ideological justification of the power of Moscow and its princes. In 1472, he married Zoe Paleologos, the niece of the last Byzantine Emperor. The marriage was the idea of the Pope in an unsuccessful attempt to create an anti-Turkish coalition, but through it the Muscovites began to develop a view of themselves as the heirs to the traditions of Constantinople and Rome. Ivan III added the Byzantine doubled-headed eagle to his standards and over the next century elaborate genealogies were developed, which were supposed to prove the descent of the princes of Moscow from the Emperor Augustus.

At the same time the doctrine of the 'Third Rome' emerged. This was developed after 1500 by Filofei of the Eleazer Monastery in Pskov. He argued that, when Rome broke with the doctrines of the Orthodox Church in the Middle Ages, Constantinople became the 'second' Rome. However, the Greeks had lost their position as the 'second' Rome when they betrayed the tradition of Orthodoxy in their attempted re-unification with the Church of Rome at Florence in 1439. Their punishment had been the fall of Constantinople to the Turk in 1453. Now, only Moscow preserved the true traditions of the Orthodox Church. In 1512, Filofei wrote: 'Two Romes fell down, the third is standing, and there will be no fourth.' He also argued that it was the ruler's task to protect and encourage Orthodoxy, since Russia was the only truly Orthodox state. He advocated a close unity, a 'symphony' of Church and state. In practice, these ideas greatly increased the prestige of the rulers of Moscow. Ivan III and Basil III started occasionally to use the title Tsar (Caesar) with its imperial connotations.

Basil III, in particular, built monasteries and churches, while at the same time strictly subordinating the Church to his power. He continued the expansion of Muscovy with the annexation of Pskov in 1511 and Riazan in 1517. Three campaigns were fought against Lithuania, which was the other major state with a significant Russian population. As a result of these, Smolensk was captured in 1514 and its acquisition was confirmed by treaty in 1522.

By 1533, Moscow had established itself as the strongest Russian state. Various factors had contributed to this. The location was favourable; Moscow lay at the crossing of three roads, one of which was the major route from Kiev to the north east, and close to four major rivers, the Oka, the Volga, the Don and the Dnieper. There were no geographical barriers to expansion and the forest brought relative freedom from invasion. Moscow's rulers were shrewd in their policy towards the Golden Horde; they were healthy and produced male children to maintain the family line, while the establishment of the Metropolitan See had brought power and prestige to the state and favoured the development of strong monarchy. But inevitably a reaction was always likely against the system of government that had emerged in Muscovy.

By tradition, Russian princes had divided their realms equally between their sons. This was one reason for the emergence of so many small principalities in Russia, which were constantly subdivided between sons. These so-called *appanage* princes might only rule relatively small estates, but within these they levied taxes and administered justice. The system of *Votchina* or hereditary landholding involved no loyalty to any great prince, or obligation to provide military service. It was common, before the sixteenth century, for the *appanage* princes and the *boyars*, the great aristocrats, to choose the great prince whom they would serve. The right of 'free departure' might even involve going to serve the ruler of another country.

The princes of Moscow had gradually abandoned the principle of equal subdivision of the realm between sons. The eldest son gained more and more land until he automatically inherited about three-quarters of his father's land. It also became the practice for the *appanages* of the younger brothers to revert to the prince on their death. By these methods, the principality was held together and conquered *appanages* were added to it.

Ivan III used the land that had been seized after the conquest of Novgorod to foster the development of a different system of landholding by the nobility, known as *Pomestia*. *Pomestia* land was given to his servants in return for their military or administrative service. It could not be sold, or divided among their heirs. By this method, a service aristocracy began to emerge in the sixteenth century which was far more dependent on the ruler than were the *appanage* princes.

Basil III continued to encourage the system of *Pomestia* and by 1533, it was only in central Muscovy that *Votchina* landholding predominated. However, the *Votchina* aristocrats obviously resented their decline in status. Many were of royal blood and regarded themselves as equal to any ruling prince. They would have favoured the development of a state in which the aristocracy held the real power, such as did in fact emerge in the neighbouring state of Poland-Lithuania. Naturally the aristocracy would attempt to take advantage of any weakness in royal authority. The early death of Basil III brought such an opportunity. Although the nominal power of the ruler was very great, like all European rulers he depended on the aristocracy to enforce his authority and lacked the military force and bureaucracy of the modern state.

Sigmund von Herberstein travelled to Muscovy in 1517–18 and again in 1526–27 as an ambassador of the Holy Roman Empire. He produced the first substantial first-hand account of life in Muscovy in the time of Basil III and commented interestingly on the way in which the Russians viewed their rulers:

> All in the land call themselves Kholopi, or sold slaves.
>
> The Grand Duke exercises his power over both clergy and laymen, both property and life. None of his councillors has ever dared to gainsay his Lord's opinion. One and all agree that their Lord's will is the will of God, hence what the prince does is divinely inspired. Thus they call their prince God's Klyuchnik or key bearer, in the sense of chamberlain, and only regard him as the fulfiller of God's purpose. So when someone pleads for a prisoner he will say 'What God orders will take place without your plea'. And when

one asks about something to which there is no proper answer they say: 'God
10 knows and the Grand Duke'. It is debatable whether such a people must
have such oppressive rulers or whether the oppressive rulers have made the
people so stupid.

Albeit he (Basil III) has been unfortunate in war, yet his people call him
successful. And when there remained not half of his troops they dared to say
15 they had not lost a man. He surpasses all other kings and princes in the
power that he has and uses over his own people; what his father began he
completed. That is, he turned out the princes and others from all the
fortresses neither leaving nor entrusting any fortress to his brothers. He
holds one and all in the same subjection.

1 Why is it significant that the people called themselves 'sold slaves' (line
   1–12)?
2 Why do you think that Basil entrusted no fortress to his brothers (line 18)?
3 In the light of this passage, what was the difference between the power of Basil
   III and that of Charles V?
4 What are the advantages and disadvantages in relying on the evidence of a foreign
   ambassador?

4. Ivan IV's Early Years 1530–47

Ivan IV was born in August 1530 and was the first son of Basil III and
his second wife, Elena Glinskaya, a member of the Glinsky family who
were great landowners on the Lithuanian border and had recently
transferred their allegiance to Basil III.

In any European state at this time, the accession of a child brought
fear of social and political discontent. In December 1533, Basil III died
and in accordance with Muscovite law and custom, Ivan's mother Elena
became Regent during his minority. Elena was not popular with the
boyars; she was seen as heavily influenced by her Lithuanian connections
and western ideas. After two strong rulers, who had consciously sought
to advance their power at the expense of the great aristocrats, it was
inevitable that there should be an attempt to reverse the growth in royal
power.

In fact, Ivan's childhood was a time of almost continuous violence and
civil strife, the effects of which were never to leave him. Until her death in
April 1538, Elena maintained some semblance of royal authority.
Princes Ivan and Andrei Shuisky, who had been imprisoned by Basil III
and belonged to one of the great princely families, were released from
prison and began a conspiracy with Yuri, Ivan's uncle, to seize power.
Other conspirators included Mikhail Glinsky, Elena's uncle, on whom
she had relied for advice and guidance, Ivan's other uncle, Prince Andrei
Staritsky, and Simeon Belsky, whose family was very powerful.

Naturally, neighbouring states attempted to capitalise on these problems. The aristocratic conspirators turned to Sigismund I of Lithuania
and to the Crimean Tatars, whose close links with Suleiman the

Magnificent made them especially dangerous enemies. Elena maintained some control but after her death, possibly from poisoning, royal authority virtually collapsed.

From 1538 to 1543, the great aristocratic families ruthlessly struggled for power. The struggle centred around the rival Belsky and Shuisky clans. Ivan suffered various traumas and humiliations such as the dismissal of his nurse, Agrafena, to a nunnery and these experiences helped to foster the violent and autocratic streak in his character. Suddenly on 29 December 1543, Ivan ordered the arrest of Andrei Shuisky and had him thrown to a pack of hounds, who tore him to pieces. This decisive and ruthless action broke the hold of the *boyars* on the government of the country and gave a clear indication of Ivan's temperament and approach. For the rest of his life, he often showed himself to be capricious and violent. He never lost his suspicion of the *boyars* and consistently sought to advance his power at their expense.

The next four years showed no clear direction in policy. Generally, Ivan left direction of the affairs of state to his unpopular Glinsky relatives.

5. Ivan's Coronation 1547

On January 16 1547, Ivan was crowned Tsar of all Russia. Although Ivan III and Basil III had used this title on occasions, Ivan IV was the first Muscovite ruler actually to be crowned Tsar. His title was approved by the Patriarchs of the Greek Orthodox Church and he now used the title regularly at home and in his dealings with foreign countries. In the coronation ceremonies, which were conducted by the Metropolitan Makary, a cross and regalia were used which it was claimed had been sent by the Byzantine Emperor Constantine to Prince Vladimir of Kiev in the early twelfth century. This claim was false, but it illustrates the lofty view that Ivan held of his role. He intended to be a great Tsar and to continue the expansion of the Muscovite state which had grown dramatically over the previous century and which was to double in size during Ivan's reign.

Ivan saw his task as being the completion of the 'gathering of the Russian land' and bringing together under his rule all those of the Russian Orthodox faith. Obvious targets for expansion were Lithuania whose population was predominantly Orthodox and Russian, the Tatar states of Kazan and Astrakhan which blocked access to the fertile steppe of the south and east, and Livonia, possession of which would bring access to the Baltic Sea and western Europe.

Ivan's coronation was followed by his marriage to Anastasia, a member of the Zakharin family, who were Muscovite *boyars*, but not of princely blood. He did not, however, yet seem to have shown the qualities required in a Tsar of such lofty ambition. But in April 1547 there was a serious fire in Moscow, which was a city mainly built of wood. This was followed by an uprising in Moscow in the summer, during which the Tsar's uncle, Yuri Glinsky, was murdered.

These events seem to have shocked Ivan, who was prone to sudden personal and spiritual crises and constantly tormented by a not unjustified view of himself as a sinner. He became far more responsible as a ruler and the next twelve years were the most successful of his reign. At home, a policy of reform was followed with many positive results; in foreign policy, Ivan continued the expansion of Muscovy with great success. After 1560, however, inconsistent and brutal policies were introduced within Muscovy and an inconclusive and ultimately unsuccessful war gradually drained the resources of the state. Undoubtedly Ivan instigated and directed most of the dramatic changes in direction. Some historians, such as Ian Grey, while not defending his violent excesses, argue nonetheless that many of his policies were justified and in the interests of the Russian state and people, who clearly preferred his rule to that of the *boyars*. Certainly expansionism and autocracy, which are two major themes in Russian history, were Ivan's central preoccupations. At the same time, like any sixteenth century European monarch, practical obstacles and the need to keep the support of the ruling classes greatly restricted Ivan's autocratic ambitions. When he did try to challenge his opponents in Muscovy, the result was to be the greatest crisis of his reign.

6. The Foreign Policy of Muscovy 1547–83

(a) The conquest of Kazan
Although the Golden Horde had broken up and the Khanates of Kazan, Astrakhan and Crimea could not match its strength, they still provided formidable obstacles to the expansion of Muscovy. The strength of these nomadic tribesmen of Turkic race and Islamic faith lay in their skill as horsemen. They excelled at mobile warfare, to which the steppe was particularly suited. Muscovites had suffered at the hands of the Tatars for centuries and there was undoubtedly a widespread sense of military inferiority. Tatar raids from Kazan constantly devastated the villages to the south and east of Moscow. The villagers were killed or taken as slaves. In 1551 alone, it is estimated that 100 000 prisoners were taken. If Muscovy was to expand to the east and south, the conquest of Kazan was essential. The defeat of Kazan would open up the fertile steppe to Muscovite farmers, to whose way of life the nomadic Tatars were particularly hostile. It would ease the problem of defending Muscovy's enormous land frontier, along which there were few natural barriers to Tatar raids except the forest. Finally, the conquest of Kazan could be presented as a crusade against the Infidel, which could bring Ivan much credit in the Christian world and unite his people behind him.

As early as 1545, Ivan launched an unsuccessful campaign against Kazan. A winter campaign in January 1548 failed when the frost and snow, which often made movement in winter easier than at any other time by hardening the ground, did not materialise. But in March 1549 Safa Girey, the Khan of Kazan, died. His successor Utemish was a child of two, which encouraged further invasion plans.

In 1550, after another unsuccessful campaign, Ivan began to re-organise his forces. A particular problem was that military appointments were based not on merit, but on birth. The system of *Mestnichestvo*, or 'place order', meant that no-one would take an army position if it entailed his subordination to a person of equal or inferior descent. The fundamental principle of the system guaranteed that no-one need serve under another, if he could show that one of his ancestors had held a higher position than the ancestors of his proposed superior. Although this system clearly showed how highly regarded service to the Tsar was among the aristocrats, it prevented Ivan from selecting by merit alone. The system was too deeply entrenched to be abolished, but a decree of 1550 modified it by strengthening the power of the commanding officer over the *boyars* who served him. In the same year, the Streltsi were created; these were a force of about 3000 arquebusiers, who were to be the nucleus of the regular army.

In the spring of 1551, the campaign was launched. The fortress of Sviyazhsk was built as a stronghold near Kazan and many of the nomadic Tatar tribesmen gave their allegiance to Ivan. In August, the siege of Kazan began. Ivan had 150 000 troops against 30 000 defenders and in October the city fell. Despite opposition by some Tatars supported by the Crimeans, further expeditions in 1552 and 1556 consolidated Russian control.

The conquest of Kazan was followed by a successful expedition to Astrakhan in 1554, which was followed by its annexation in 1556. The only Tatar Khanate not in Muscovite hands now was the Crimea. The Crimean Khan, Devlet Girey, presented a constant threat and could rely on the backing of the Turkish Sultan. He supported Kazan and Astrakhan and raided Muscovy. In response, in the summer of 1556, an expedition reached as far as Ochakov, which was over 700 miles from Moscow and in 1554, the Crimea itself was raided.

The impact of the conquest of Kazan and Astrakhan was enormous. Ivan was given the title 'Grozny' which is commonly translated into English as 'Terrible', but should more accurately be rendered as 'Awe-inspiring'. It was a great victory for Christendom and to mark this, St Basil's Cathedral was built in Moscow. For the Russian people, great opportunities now appeared. Much of the black earth belt, which was land of outstanding fertility, was now available for settlement. The peasants saw this opportunity and mass settlement of these regions, which had formerly been too dangerous, began. Russian agriculture was no longer restricted to the relatively unproductive forest region. More-over, the Nogay Tatars east of the Volga now recognised Ivan as overlord and the whole of the Volga was now in Russian hands. This secure eastern frontier gave Muscovy access to the Caspian Sea and the trade routes to central Asia, Persia and the Caucasus, which had previously been in enemy hands. Moreover, there was now no obstacle to expansion into Siberia, into which Russian settlers advanced with astonishing rapidity over the next century.

(b) The Livonian War 1558–83—the debate over foreign policy
After the great triumphs against the Tatars, there was no doubt that the expansion of the Muscovite state should continue, but much disagreement as to the direction. Three possible courses were open to Ivan: he could attack the Crimean Tatars; he could attack the parts of Poland-Lithuania largely inhabited by Orthodox Russians; or he could expand towards Livonia and the Baltic Sea.

Many of Ivan's advisers strongly favoured a campaign against the Crimean Tatars. It was argued that they had actively opposed Ivan in Kazan and Astrakhan and that their constant raiding for slaves posed a threat to the security of the state. It was also true that this campaign could be presented as a crusade. Ivan rejected this idea. He believed that it would be impossible to cross 700 miles of steppe with 100 000 men and feared the possibility of a war with the Ottoman Turks. Despite the successful raids against the Crimea, in 1560 Ivan adopted a defensive policy on his southern frontier. Defences, which mainly consisted of trenches and ramparts and fortified stockades, were constructed along the southern frontier and eventually a frontier guard was established.

A campaign against the Polish-Lithuanian state was considered. At this time Poland and Lithuania were two separate states which shared the same ruler. Lithuania contained the heartland of the state of Kiev, to which the Muscovites had a rather spurious claim. But Poland-Lithuania was a strong state, in which there was a growing mood of unity. This was to lead to the Union of Lublin in 1569, which established a proper constitutional union. Moreover, in case of war, it would not be difficult for Poland-Lithuania to make a tactical alliance with the Crimean Tatars and the Turks.

Livonia was certainly the weakest of Muscovy's neighbours. Originally Livonia had formed part of the territories of the Order of Teutonic Knights, which had been formed initially to convert the Lithuanians to Christianity. These German knights had established themselves along the Baltic coast, but by 1550 their military power was in decline. Most had become Lutheran and they were divided into pro-Polish and pro-Russian factions.

There is no doubt that the capture of Livonia and access to the Baltic Sea would have given Muscovy what Vernadsky describes as a 'corridor to Europe'. Ivan's western neighbours constantly blocked contact with the west and the Baltic states allowed trade with Muscovy only in goods that were of no military or industrial value. In 1547, Ivan had sent a German named Schlitte to the Baltic States to recruit skilled men to serve Muscovy. One hundred and twenty three men assembled at Lubeck, but the Livonians protested to Charles V and the men were

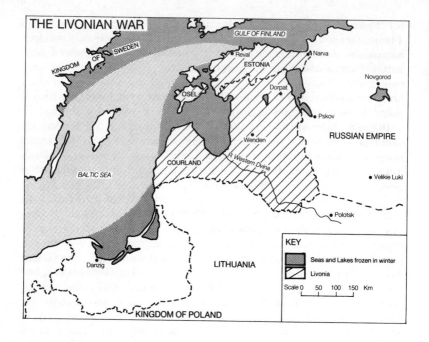

THE LIVONIAN WAR

GULF OF FINLAND

KINGDOM OF SWEDEN

Reval
ESTONIA
Narva
Novgorod

OSEL
Dorpat

Pskov
Wenden
RUSSIAN EMPIRE

BALTIC SEA
COURLAND
R. Western Dvina

Velikie Luki

Polotsk

Danzig
LITHUANIA

KEY

Seas and Lakes frozen in winter

Livonia

Scale 0   50   100   150   Km

KINGDOM OF POLAND

prevented from sailing. One of the Germans, who tried to make his own way to Moscow, was executed on the border by the Livonians. There was similar opposition to the English expeditions of Chancellor and Jenkinson, who travelled to Muscovy in the 1550s via the White Sea and Archangel and made contacts which continued for the remainder of Ivan's reign. Poland-Lithuania, Sweden, Denmark and the Holy Roman Emperor all protested against the alleged English sale of arms to Muscovy.

Ivan's decision to invade Livonia was to be unsuccessful and to have terrible consequences for the Russian people. Historians are divided as to the wisdom of his move. George Vernadsky argues that the war was not necessary. He feels that the true enemies of the Russians were the Crimean Tatars, who constantly menaced the Russian peasantry, and that Ivan imposed upon himself a war on two fronts, since in only three of the 24 years of the Livonian War was there no Tatar raid. For Vernadsky, the war was a disastrous mistake. Ian Grey and J L A Fennell, on the other hand, stress the enormous advantages that the capture of Livonia would have brought. The economic and strategic benefits of an outlet to the Baltic would be vast; not only would trade benefit, but Poland-Lithuania would have been threatened from the north and the east and Muscovy would never again have been blockaded. They also point out the practical difficulties and dangers of a campaign in the Crimea. Ivan's policy—and the Livonian War was certainly his decision—must be regarded as controversial, but not as irrational or foolish.

(c) The outbreak of the Livonian War

The war itself was a lengthy struggle of great diplomatic and military complexity. Apart from the Livonians, Sweden, Denmark and Poland-Lithuania were all deeply concerned in its action and outcome. Ivan also constantly suffered from the lack of a fleet, which made it very difficult to hold any bases on the coastline. A lengthy and complex war was, therefore, to be expected.

Initially, the war brought great success. A huge invading army captured Dorpat and Narva in 1558. Control of Narva gave Ivan an invaluable port on the left bank of the River Narova, which was only ten miles from the Gulf of Finland. In 1559, there was a further Muscovite invasion; an army of 130 000 men conquered the northern territories of the Livonian Order.

The inevitable result of this was to frighten all the other powers, especially after a further Russian campaign in 1560 led to the virtual collapse of the Livonian Order. In a treaty of 28 November 1561 all the possessions of the Order were ceded to Poland-Lithuania. The Grand Master, Kettler, who had replaced the pro-Russian Furstenberg, became Duke of Courland and a vassal of the Polish king. The Swedes occupied northern Estonia and the important port of Reval while the Danes occupied the island of Osel. Livonia had effectively ceased to exist and was now a battleground for the major powers of the region.

It was important for Ivan not to fight all his opponents at the same time. Eric XIV of Sweden was at war with Denmark (1563–70), and was strongly anti-Polish, so Ivan chose to maintain good relations with Sweden and concentrate his efforts against Poland-Lithuania. The 1560s were a time of domestic upheaval and diplomatic confusion. The major success for Ivan was the seizure of Polotsk in 1563. This gave him control of the western Dvina which was the major waterway to the Baltic. This war was followed by a lengthy period of diplomatic bargaining, which brought little change to the situation.

(d) The strengthening of the opposition to Muscovy

In the late 1560s, the international position of Muscovy began to deteriorate rapidly. In Sweden the mad, pro-Russian Eric XIV was overthrown by John III, who was the brother-in-law of Sigismund Augustus of Poland-Lithuania and followed a pro-Polish policy. In June 1569, the Poles and Lithuanians concluded the Union of Lublin. The aristocracy of these states would now elect a king jointly. Each country was to remain independent internally, but in foreign affairs and war the two countries now formed a single state, which was a formidable threat to Muscovy. Nor could the threat of the Ottoman Empire be ignored. Sultan Selim II wished to control Astrakhan.

In 1569, a campaign was launched by the Turks to build a canal from the Don to the Volga and then seize Astrakhan. This over-ambitious scheme was a complete failure, but the Turks did not abandon their claims and began to seek an alliance with Poland-Lithuania against

Ivan. Ivan's only allies were the Danes. He appointed Magnus, the brother of King Frederick II, 'king' of Livonia, but when Magnus unsuccessfully besieged the Swedes in Reval in 1570–71, Frederick II failed to come to his assistance.

Within Muscovy, many *boyars* still argued that the greater threat came from the Crimean Tatars. This opposition increased the violence and brutality of Ivan's policies. In 1571, Devlet Girey, the Crimean leader, invaded Muscovy and on May 23 Moscow was set on fire. The city recovered with remarkable speed, but the increasing burden that was being placed on the people of Muscovy is clear. Except for the palace of the Kremlin, the whole city with its wooden buildings was destroyed and 150 000 Russians were captured. Although a further Tatar invasion was defeated in 1572, these problems prevented Ivan taking any initiatives in the west.

This was unfortunate, because Polish-Lithuanian affairs were in some confusion at this time. After the death of Sigismund in 1572, Ivan advanced himself as a candidate for the throne in this elective monarchy. Some Orthodox Lithuanians did favour Ivan, but his chances of election were never serious. It is clear that after the short and disastrous interlude of Henry of Anjou, who fled back to France in 1574, Ivan's main aim was to advance the claims of the Habsburg Archduke Ernest over those of Stephen Bathory, Prince of Transylvania. The election of Bathory would be a disaster for Ivan. He was a close ally to the Sultan, whose vassal he was. He clearly intended to maintain good relations with the Ottoman Empire and the Crimean Tatars and fight Muscovy. In addition, he was an energetic leader and a capable soldier.

Bathory's successful election and assumption of the throne in early 1576 demonstrated the failure of Ivan's diplomacy. In late 1576, Ivan attempted to take advantage of a rebellion against Bathory in Danzig and launched one final attempt to conquer Livonia. He met with initial success but the siege of Reval, which was still held by the Swedes, was unsuccessful and abandoned in March 1577. Ivan was now without allies and faced the forces of Poland and Sweden, combined with a constant threat of Tatar raids on his southern frontier. In 1578, the counter-attack began and the Swedes defeated a Russian army at Wenden. In the following year Bathory, with the help of the Danish prince Magnus, attacked and seized Polotsk, which gave him control of a vital river route. His capture of Velikie Luki in the following year cut off Ivan's troops in Livonia and provided a base for a possible invasion of Muscovy. Bathory's further plans were limited by the lack of enthusiasm of the Polish Diet and his own financial problems which, along with stubborn resistance, prevented the capture of Pskov in 1581. Nonetheless, Ivan's armies had now been driven from Livonia and the war had devastated his country. It was essential that he should make peace.

(e) The Treaty of Yam Zapolsky

Papal mediation led to the Treaty of Yam Zapolsky with Poland-

Lithuania in January 1582. Ivan renounced all claims to Livonia and the districts of Polotsk and Velizh; the only concession was the return of Velikie Luki. In the following year the whole of Estonia, including Narva which the Swedes had captured in 1581, as well as the districts of Ivangorod and Yam were ceded to Sweden. Only the extreme eastern end of the Gulf of Finland around the mouth of the River Neva was left to Muscovy. Russia was left with even less of the Baltic seaboard than before the war. It is worth noting that one reason for the weakening Russian resistance in the last years of the war was the raids by the Nogay Tatars on the Lower Volga, further emphasising the problem of fighting a war on two fronts.

(f) England and Siberia
It is not strictly true that the capture of Kazan and Astrakhan were the only gains of Ivan's foreign policy. Although the discovery by the English of the White Sea route to Russia was quite accidental, this opened up an important trade route to England and the Low Countries, which came into regular use. Ivan genuinely, if somewhat inconsistently, encouraged and saw the importance of this. Ivan's interest in close contact with England never waned. At the very end of his reign, it was revived in his rather eccentric proposal of marriage to Elizabeth I's cousin, Lady Mary Hastings.

Even more significant were the Russian advances into Siberia. As early as the fifteenth century, the powerful Stroganov family had begun to develop the east and they always took great care to maintain good relations with Muscovy. The capture of Kazan and Astrakhan opened the way to the colonisation of Siberia. The peoples of Siberia, many of whom were Tatars, were few in number and constantly feuding with each other. The extensive river systems made communications far easier than might initially be imagined. In 1558, the Stroganovs were given a charter for 20 years to develop territories to the east of Kazan. In 1573, settlers crossed the Urals into Siberia and were authorised by Ivan to pursue aggressive tactics against the Siberian Khan. The Stroganovs raised a private army of Cossacks, renegades from a variety of backgrounds who lived in the steppe. Tribesmen raided the Russian settlements in 1581 and in September, the Cossack leader Ermak mounted a retaliatory attack. His tiny force defeated the Siberian Khan in October 1581. Ivan received representatives from the Cossacks and was officially proclaimed Tsar of Siberia. Although Siberia was thinly populated, its resources, especially furs, were invaluable. Ivan's appreciation of the value of his acquisition, in which he was keenly interested, serves to emphasise the breadth of his vision.

(g) The outcome of Ivan's foreign policy
The Livonian War was an unmitigated disaster for Muscovy. Ivan lacked reliable allies and found himself constantly threatened to the south as well as to the west. It is certainly true that a Crimean expedition

The Campaigns of Ivan the Terrible

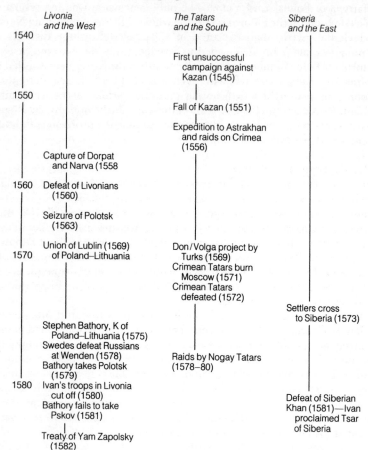

	Livonia and the West	The Tatars and the South	Siberia and the East
1540			
		First unsuccessful campaign against Kazan (1545)	
1550			
		Fall of Kazan (1551)	
		Expedition to Astrakhan and raids on Crimea (1556)	
	Capture of Dorpat and Narva (1558		
1560	Defeat of Livonians (1560)		
	Seizure of Polotsk (1563)		
1570	Union of Lublin (1569) of Poland–Lithuania	Don/Volga project by Turks (1569) Crimean Tatars burn Moscow (1571) Crimean Tatars defeated (1572)	
			Settlers cross to Siberia (1573)
	Stephen Bathory, K of Poland–Lithuania (1575) Swedes defeat Russians at Wenden (1578) Bathory takes Polotsk (1579)	Raids by Nogay Tatars (1578–80)	
1580	Ivan's troops in Livonia cut off (1580) Bathory fails to take Pskov (1581)		Defeat of Siberian Khan (1581)—Ivan proclaimed Tsar of Siberia
	Treaty of Yam Zapolsky (1582)		

would have posed enormous difficulties and that Ivan was almost certainly right to reject that policy. The choice of Livonia was based on sound reasoning and its capture would have brought enormous economic and strategic benefits. It is not without significance that a century later Peter the Great chose to concentrate his own efforts there, while the Crimea was not acquired for nearly two centuries. Despite this, the actual result of the Livonian War was economic devastation and it also had a direct bearing on the political upheavals of the second part of Ivan's reign.

7. Ivan's Domestic Reforms 1547–60

(a) The 'Chosen' Council

There is a close parallel between domestic and foreign affairs in Ivan's reign. In both cases, the early years saw a rational and coherent policy, which was quite successfully sustained. This was followed in domestic affairs by a growth in violent and autocratic behaviour, much of which casts doubt on Ivan's mental state.

It does seem that the great fire in Moscow in 1547 was seen by Ivan as a punishment for his sins and encouraged him to pursue a policy of reform. He was strongly influenced by a group of advisers, who have commonly been described as the 'Chosen' Council. The 'Chosen' Council should not be seen as a formal political institution, but simply as an influential group. These saw the *boyars*, who were strongly represented on the State Council, as obstructive to a policy of reform. There were three men who seem to have had most influence on Ivan. Sylvester was a scholarly and devout priest, who had been the young Ivan's personal confessor. He hoped to reform Ivan's character and to reform the administration of the country. The Metropolitan Makary also encouraged Ivan to reform. Makary favoured an autocratic Tsar, who would enhance the position and prestige of the Orthodox Church. But Sylvester's closest ally was Alexei Adashev. Adashev's origins lay in the minor gentry. He became a court official and by June 1547 had become keeper of the Tsar's bedchamber, which gave him daily contact with Ivan and the management of his personal treasury. Adashev was an attractive and popular character who was regarded as possessing almost saintly qualities.

It is not realistic to ascribe an absolutely rigid political outlook to the 'Chosen' Council. But it does seem that these men feared a return to the princely strife and feuding of earlier years and particularly sought to diminish the power of the *appanage* princes. They believed that Muscovy had to be a strong centralised state with an autocratic Tsar, or there would be constant danger of civil strife. If a general theme can be discerned in the reign of Ivan, it is the weakening of the power of the great aristocracy and the strengthening of that of the service gentry, who were granted land in return for service to the state.

(b) The Zemsky Sobor 1549

In 1549, the Zemsky Sobor (Assembly of Land) was summoned. This contained representatives of the clergy, the aristocracy and the service gentry. There were no representatives of the towns or the peasantry and its members were probably appointed rather than elected. There is no doubt that the administration of the state needed to be overhauled to cope with the phenomenal growth of Muscovy over the previous centuries. Typical proposals came from a man called Peresvetov, who had served in various countries before settling in Muscovy. In a petition, he urged the need for strong autocratic rule, the centralisation of finance and justice, and the creation of a standing army. He urged the Tsar to consider the example of the Turkish Sultan, who ruled without fear of his great aristocrats. These general principles were attractive to many Muscovites and Ivan's reforms of the 1550s made some attempt to satisfy them.

443

In February 1549, the service gentry were granted almost complete freedom from the legal control of the provincial governors, who were widely regarded as corrupt and incompetent. They were paid for their services usually by taking goods from the people in their province. The arrangement was known appropriately as *kormlenie*, which means 'feeding', and was an obvious cause of corruption and exploitation. The more important an aristocrat was, the larger his *kormlenie* would be. They held these appointments for a short time and were expected to accumulate enough to provide for themselves when they were out of office.

(c) The Sudebnik of 1550

A further attempt to control the provincial governors was made in the Sudebnik of June 1550, which provided the country with a new legal code. This was an impressive and wide-ranging reform of the legal system, which did not simply revise the earlier law code of 1497 but contained 99 articles, of which 37 were new and many others completely re-written. If there was a general aim of the Sudebnik, it was to protect the people from aristocratic abuses. The presence of locally elected representatives of the people at the courts of the provincial governors was made compulsory. Special clerks were appointed to advise the people on the amount of taxation that could legally be levied by the provincial governor. Finally, in 1555, each district was now permitted by law to replace their governors by elected authorities which would be responsible for local administration, justice and the collection of taxation. Taxes were now to be paid to the Treasury and not to the governor. This measure increased the control of the state and weakened the system of *kormlenie*; it was not compulsory, but offered the population of the provinces the opportunity to free themselves from the arbitrary control of their governors.

(d) The aristocracy

A clear trend in the history of Muscovy at this time was the growing control of the Tsar over the *boyars* and the attempt to create a ruling class which acted as the Tsar's servants. The development of the service estate (the *Pomestia*) has already been mentioned *(see page 432)* and Ivan's dislike of the hereditary *appanage* princes who owed him no service was clear. Equally, it was never easy for any sixteenth century monarch to rule without the co-operation of the great aristocrats and many of Ivan's reforms were undoubtedly more impressive in theory than in practice, since they relied on the co-operation of the nobility for their enactment. Land was, however, needed for the service gentry. In 1550, Ivan granted estates close to Moscow to many members of the service gentry. This was to provide land for about half the members of the court and central government close to the capital and increase the speed and efficiency of mobilisation in war. It was also intended to be a massive extension of the system of *Pomestia*, although there was clearly the practical problem of insufficient land being available for this policy to work.

The connection between serving the state and ownership of land was further stressed by the statute on military service of 1556. Each owner of land was now required by law to serve the Tsar personally. He was also, according to the size of his land, expected to provide armed men and supplies, or make a financial payment. In return it was permitted for sons to inherit their father's land, provided that they continued to provide service to the Tsar. Again, a policy of this nature would have been very difficult to enforce.

(e) The peasantry

The growing demands that were placed on the nobility were bound to lead to growing demands on the peasantry by the nobility. One of the odder developments of Russian history is that serfdom developed in the sixteenth and seventeenth centuries at a time when it was in decline in western Europe. A key element of serfdom is that the peasant may not freely leave the estate on which he works. The Sudebnik (Law Code) of 1497 had restricted the date when a peasant could leave his master to the period around November 26, which was St George's Day. St George was considered by Orthodox Russia to be in charge of the whole growing season, which came between his two holidays, April 23 and November 26. The time chosen for movement was, therefore, the end of the agricultural season. The Sudebnik of 1550 confirmed the peasant's right to move freely at this time and this quite clearly shows that the Russian peasants were by no means completely enserfed in the reign of Ivan. These years were a time of growing population and relative prosperity and there was little need to control the peasants.

But the conquest of Kazan and Astrakhan opened up the fertile black earth lands of the central and lower Volga to the Russian peasantry and a great shift of population to the south east began, in particular during the chaos of the second half of Ivan's reign. In late 1580 or early 1581, the government did begin to restrict the right of the peasants to move on St George's Day, probably on an annual basis initially. Ivan's reign therefore saw the beginning of a process of enserfment, which was to last into the nineteenth century and distinguish developments in Russian society so dramatically from those in western Europe.

(f) The Church

The spiritual, political and economic power of the Russian Church was as great as anywhere else in sixteenth century Europe. In a country with no universities, education was effectively a monopoly of the Church and monasteries were great landowners in their own right. It was therefore inevitable that the summoning of the Zemsky Sobor should be followed by that of a Stoglav Sobor (Council of the Church) in 1551.

First of all, Ivan submitted to this Council the Sudebnik and the local government reforms, which were approved. But the Church itself contained divisions and factions which needed to be reconciled. The two major factions were the Josephans and the Trans Volga Hermits. The

445

Josephans, who were named after the Abbot of Volokolamsk, maintained that the Church must retain all its wealth and land and the protection of the state if it was to fulfil its religious tasks effectively. The Trans Volga Hermits followed the teachings of Nils Sorski and argued that the Church must reject luxury and the ownership of land and dedicate itself purely to prayer and spiritual activity. At the beginning of the century, the Josephans had emerged as the stronger faction, but clearly some of the ideas of the Trans Volga Hermits appealed to a Tsar who constantly needed land to provide *Pomestias* for his serving gentry. In particular, it seems probable that the plan to settle many serving gentry on estates near Moscow, which was advanced in 1550, never came into effect because of a shortage of land. Acquisition of Church lands would solve many of Ivan's problems.

Of Ivan's close advisers, Sylvester and Adashev were both attracted to the ideas of the Trans Volga Hermits and favoured the secularisation of Church lands. The Metropolitan Makary and most of his bishops were Josephans but were anxious to reform the Church, in part to protect its land from critics. Two major proposals were submitted to the Stoglav Sobor: first of all that the clergy should no longer be exempt from the Tsar's laws, and second that the Church should not obtain land as a result of special privileges. But although it was agreed that the laws of the Church should be more strictly enforced, the Stoglav Sobor rejected the trial of priests and monks in the Tsar's courts and was totally opposed to the loss of any Church lands. Ivan was not prepared to confiscate Church lands and risk a dangerous conflict. But the position of the Trans Volga Hermits was strengthened and in May 1551 the Church's purchase of further lands without the Tsar's permission was forbidden. Despite this, it appears that the Josephans remained dominant and were able in 1553 to press successful charges of heresy against leading supporters of the ideas of the Trans Volga Hermits.

(g) The fall of the 'Chosen' Council

There may be reservations about the overall success of the work of the 'Chosen' Council. Despite the curbing of *kormlenie*, it is likely that corruption continued in the countryside. The Sudebnik did provide the basis for a just legal system, but a just legal system needs just administration, and many judges were probably corrupt and came from those very aristocratic classes whose powers Ivan was anxious to curb. Nonetheless, as J L A Fennell has written, the reforms of the 'Chosen' Council were 'far sighted and shrewdly conceived'. The major aims were increased centralisation and administrative efficiency. This was necessary in a state whose frontiers had rapidly expanded. Moreover, the constant strengthening of the *Pomestia* as opposed to the *Votchina boyars* was a natural and legitimate reaction to the anarchy of Ivan's childhood. It is not at all clear how far Ivan instigated, or approved of, all these policies. What is clear, however, is that he gradually became disillusioned with this group of advisers and, having cast them aside, adopted dramatically different policies after 1560.

As early as 1553, there were signs of tension. In March 1553, Ivan fell ill and there were inevitable fears of another succession crisis. Ivan wanted his leading *boyars* and advisers to swear loyalty to his son, Dmitri. Leading members of the 'Chosen' Council showed great reluctance to do this and supported Ivan's cousin, Vladimir, as heir to the throne. Their main reason was distrust of the family of Ivan's wife, Anastasia. It was feared that they would be the true rulers of the state if Ivan were to die. Despite the fact that there was clearly no military conspiracy, Ivan's paranoia, which was never far below the surface, was aroused. He was always intensely suspicious of any hint of a conspiracy and a return to the aristocratic feuds of his childhood.

On August 7 1560, Anastasia died. It was a sign of Ivan's growing instability that he held his opponents on the 'Chosen' Council responsible. But Ivan's mental instability is by no means the only explanation of his change of policy. Indeed, although his behaviour could be exceedingly brutal and acutely suspicious, there was usually an underlying rational purpose. On this occasion it is clear that most of the members of the 'Chosen' Council, especially Adashev, opposed the Livonian War and strongly favoured a campaign against the Crimea, which Adashev had raided so daringly and successfully. It was above all differences of policy and questions of loyalty which destroyed the 'Chosen' Council and ended the period of reform.

Ivan's treatment of Adashev and Sylvester illustrated his growing violence and disregard of the law. They were tried in absentia, which was against the principles of Russian law. In 1560, Adashev was imprisoned and died, possibly after poisoning. Sylvester was exiled to a monastery near the White Sea, where he also soon died. This was followed by a series of executions of aristocrats, especially after the loss of the restraining influence of the Metropolitan Makary who died in 1563.

Sigismund Augustus took advantage of the fears of the *boyars* and received many exiles, the most notable of whom was Prince Andrei Kurbsky in 1564. Those who remained loyal to Ivan joined with the new Metropolitan, Afanasi, in urging him to stop the executions and concentrate on the Crimea. To do this would have been to admit that Adashev had been right and Ivan wrong. As Vernadsky has written: 'The alternative facing him was either to resign or to enforce his dictatorship by extraordinary measures.'

8. The Oprichnina

Fear of conspiracy by the *boyars* and the difficulties resulting from the Livonian War brought about the most infamous and controversial events of Ivan's reign. In December 1564, Ivan suddenly deserted Moscow for the village of Alexandrovsk, which was about 60 miles away.

About a month later, the Metropolitan Afanasi received two letters from Ivan. The first letter contained a denunciation of the *boyars* and the clergy. He accused them of treachery and wrote: 'Consequently, not wishing to endure your treachery, we, with great pity in our heart, have quitted the Tsardom and have gone where God may lead us'.

He commanded that the second letter be read to the people. In this he stated that he was not angry with them and assured them of his goodwill. The letters caused panic, especially among the ordinary people, for whom the Tsar was the pivot of society and their protector against the *boyars*. After a deputation had visited him, Ivan agreed to return, but only after certain conditions had been met.

When his conditions had been met, Ivan returned to Moscow, having aged almost beyond recognition. He had clearly suffered a mental and physical breakdown. The conditions of his return suggested that he was now determined to suppress all opposition to his will. First of all, he was given full power to punish and execute traitors and confiscate their possessions, where he saw fit. The second and extraordinary demand was that Muscovy be divided in two and that a subdivision, called the 'Oprichnina' be created. Here Ivan would rule entirely as he wished.

Oprichnina derives from the word 'Oprich' which means apart, and it was to be entirely separate from the rest of the nation, the Zemshchina, where traditional methods of government would be maintained. A force, initially of about 1000 men, was recruited to serve as the Oprichniki, who would be Ivan's personal servants. They came from a variety of backgrounds. Many were from the minor gentry, but there were some great *boyars* and a few foreigners. Their numbers eventually rose to about 6000, all of whom had sworn personal loyalty to the Tsar. They wore a black uniform and rode black horses, which carried a dog's head and a broom on the saddle to symbolise the idea of sweeping traitors from the country. Alexandrovsk was used by Ivan as his chief base. It was strongly fortified and Ivan's life there represented a conscious parody of that of a monastic order, in which bouts of riotous self-indulgence were followed by guilt and self-denial.

Many areas were put under the direct control of the Oprichnina, although Alexandrovsk remained the great stronghold. A part of Moscow was included and other groups, such as the English Muscovy Company and the Stroganov family in the east, with their great commercial and industrial interests, petitioned to be included. In this way, they hoped to be protected and not subjected to harassment from the Oprichniki. In central Muscovy, the estates of many *boyars* were confiscated and they were settled in the middle Volga around Kazan.

The establishment of the Oprichnina and the debate as to its nature and purpose bring into focus all the major arguments about Ivan's character and motivation. There is a case for arguing, as do historians like Platonov, that the 'Chosen' Council had seized power from the Tsar and that it was the tool of the *boyars*. In creating the Oprichnina, therefore, Ivan was making his own significant contribution to the establishment of the strong and autocratic monarchy so necessary in Russia and which, in the seventeenth century, proved so much stronger than Poland-Lithuania, where the aristocracy retained great power.

There is no doubt that one of the main reasons for the creation of the Oprichnina was the opposition to the Livonian War. Equally, it is quite possible that this opposition came mainly from the *boyar* class and that the people as a whole generally supported Ivan. In 1566, Ivan summoned a Zemsky Sobor (National Assembly). This mainly included representatives of the gentry class, but about one-fifth of those present were merchants and it supported Ivan's opposition to concessions in the Livonian War. It is, of course, futile to speculate on the opinions of the ordinary people, but the reaction of the people of Muscovy to Ivan's departure to Alexandrovsk in 1564 does suggest that he did retain much popular support and that Tsarist rule was preferred to that of the aristocracy.

Moreover, those people who see a rational purpose in the creation of the Oprichnina point out that most of the land that was seized and taken into the Oprichnina was in central Muscovy and of great economic importance. It also included the vital trade route from Archangel to central Muscovy. Many *appanage* princes were driven from their hereditary estates where they had great prestige and authority over the peasantry and had kept the rights to act as judges and collect taxes. In their new estates, their power and prestige were dramatically reduced and they were replaced by reliable new men, who saw themselves as servants of the Tsar. In this way, Ivan was able to ignore the system of *Mestnichestvo* and create a nobility whose prestige was based on service to him rather than hereditary succession. This service nobility was to be the cornerstone of Tsarist authority in the next centuries.

This view of Ivan IV as a far-sighted and rational ruler does merit serious consideration. It is equally possible, however, to see in the creation of the Oprichnina the fantasies of a paranoid and unpredictable ruler, who saw conspiracy all around him. The Oprichniki themselves may have been intended to be unselfish servants of the Tsar, committed to the purification of the administration of the state, but they usually behaved as a bunch of sadistic thugs who encouraged Ivan's propensity for violence.

It is certainly hard to see any constructive success resulting from the creation of the Oprichnina. It may have weakened the control of many *appanage* princes by driving them from their estates, but these estates were then often ruined economically by exploitation and mismanagement, so that for many years central Muscovy suffered from dreadful economic difficulties and many peasants fled to the south and east.

The local *boyars* had been responsible for military mobilisation within their regions and this system was severely disrupted, which may help to explain the dramatic success of the Tatar raid which led to the burning of Muscovy in 1571 and the capture of 150 000 Russian slaves. It is surely significant that the defeat of the Tatar invasion of 1572, which brought such relief to the Tsar, was the work of *boyars* under the leadership of Prince Mikhail Vorotynsky who was a member of the Zemshchina and not the Oprichnina.

Executions had always been common in Muscovy, where the loyalty of the aristocracy could not be guaranteed any more than elsewhere in Europe, but the Oprichniki undoubtedly employed cruel and sadistic methods which suggested that, for many of them, violence was an end in itself.

The Metropolitan Philip, who had succeeded Afanasi in 1566, was a pious and worthy man. His criticism of random executions and terror led to his deposition in 1568, after which he was tried and sentenced to life imprisonment. In December 1569 Malyuta Shuratov, one of Ivan's favourites, strangled him in his cell.

The greatest atrocity of this period was that inflicted on the city of Novgorod. Novgorod had a long tradition of independence and trading contacts with the west. In 1569, documents were produced which suggested that Novgorod was about to defect to Sigismund Augustus of Poland-Lithuania. It seems likely that these documents were forgeries. A Pskovian chronicle states: 'Wicked men slanderously informed Tsar Ivan that both Novgorod the Great and Pskov wanted to go over to the Lithuanian side.' These rumours coincided with the death of Ivan's unpopular second wife, Maria, on September 6; her brother, Mikhail Cherkassy, was a leading figure in the Oprichnina. Ivan assumed that she had been poisoned and blamed his own cousin Prince Vladimir Staritsky, who had been advanced as a possible successor to Ivan in 1553. Vladimir's lands had been confiscated already and exchanged for new land where he had no traditional authority, but Ivan believed that he had supporters in Novgorod. In October, Vladimir was forced to take poison and in December Ivan set out for Novgorod.

Ivan's force consisted almost entirely of Oprichniki. There were atrocities in Tver, where about 9000 were killed, but Ivan's attention was mainly concentrated on Novgorod. His forces arrived there in early January under his personal command. Estimates vary as to how many were killed in the five weeks of unrestrained violence that followed, but it may have been as many as 60 000. Archbishop Pimen of Novgorod was taken to Moscow, put on trial and sent to a monastery. His escape from execution suggests the flimsy nature of the evidence against him. But in the trials for conspiracy, leading Oprichniki were also implicated. About 200 were executed in all and this included close advisers of the Tsar, such as Alexei Basmanov and his son Feodor who had been trusted members of the Oprichnina.

9. The Abolition of the Oprichnina

It does seem that the discovery of treachery in these men contributed to Ivan's decision to abolish the Oprichnina in 1572, although the divisions in the state persisted until 1575. A further factor was the failure of the Oprichniki to organise effective defence against the Tatars in 1571, for which Mikhail Cherkassy was executed.

The next decade did see a decline in violence, but Ivan's behaviour continued to show irrational and unpredictable elements. For example, in 1575–76 a converted Tatar prince was given the name Simeon and the title Grand Prince of All Russia, while Ivan used the lesser title of Prince of Muscovy. Ivan's motives in taking this action remain obscure. It may have been superstition, since he had been told to beware of this year, or to make his position less exposed. Suddenly, on August 31 1576, he resumed the title of Tsar and re-asserted his supreme power. Against the laws of the Church, Ivan took six further wives, although none played a significant role in the government of the state. Perhaps, however, the most significant evidence of the uncontrolled violence of one part of Ivan's character is to be found in the accidental killing of his son in a fit of anger in 1581, an act which further increased Ivan's sense of guilt.

10. The Kurbsky Letters

One of the oddest features of Ivan's reign is that he did try to justify his actions in correspondence with Prince Andrei Kurbsky. Andrei Kurbsky was a member of an ancient princely family and had been a prominent adviser of Ivan. After the fall of the 'Chosen' Council, he became disillusioned and crossed to Lithuania in 1564. His wife, son and mother were put to death by Ivan. Kurbsky became a leading critic of Ivan and entered into a lengthy correspondence with him, in which the major issues of dispute in Ivan's reign are discussed. Although Professor Keenan has suggested that these letters are forgeries, their authenticity seems almost certain and they provide a fascinating insight into the political dispute about the 'Chosen' Council and the Oprichnina. Here are some selected extracts from the correspondence:

Ivan:
And so the priest Sylvester joined Alexei too in friendship and they began to hold counsel in secret and without our knowledge, believing us to be incapable of judgement; and they began to give worldly counsel in the place of spiritual and little by little to lead all the boyars into resistance to authority taking the splendour of our power from us and leading you into opposition . . .

. . . And so neither in external affairs nor in internal affairs, nor in the small and pettiest things (and I refer to such things as footwear and sleeping) was anything according to my will; but everything was done according to their desire, while we remained, as it were a child . . .

Is it then light or sweetness for servants to rule? And is it darkness or bitterness for a divinely ordained sovereign to rule? . . .

Yet concerning the German towns how can I but recall the opposition of the priest Sylvester and Alexei and all of you (who said) on every occasion that we should not wage war.

You might also have remembered how, thanks to the Grace of God, in the time of your days of piety, things prospered for you according to your will, owing to the prayers of the saints and the Chosen Council of your eminent advisers; and how, afterwards, when the most wicked and cunning flatterers seduced you, the destroyers of you and of their fatherland, events turned out and what plagues were sent by God; hunger, I say, and the arrows of pestilence, and afterwards the sword of the barbarian, the avenger of the law of God, and the sudden burning of the most renowned city of Moscow, and the laying waste of all the land of Russia.

1   Explain the references to 'German towns', 'wicked and cunning flatterers, and 'sudden burning of the most renowned city of Moscow'.
2   What justification does Ivan advance for his behaviour? How does this illustrate the view that he took of the role of the Tsar.
3   How effectively do these extracts summarise the conflicts of Ivan's reign?

11. Conclusion

Despite his outbursts of violence and lapses into insanity, Ivan's overall aims seem quite clear. He wished to expand the frontiers of the state and to increase his power within the state. The conquest of Kazan and expansion into the steppe country were great triumphs, as was the move into Siberia. But his most ambitious project, the Livonian War, although a reasonable and imaginative idea, proved a complete disaster.

At home, Ivan feared and wished to control the aristocracy and create a strong autocratic monarchy. But the most successful period of his reign, the time of the 'Chosen' Council in the 1550s, came when he co-operated closely with at least a section of the aristocracy. Ivan did prevent the development of an aristocratic state, such as Poland-Lithuania, in Russia, but the failure of the Oprichnina demonstrates that he could not rule without the co-operation of at least a large portion of his most powerful subjects.

It is surely not insignificant that Ivan's death was followed by a lengthy period of turmoil and crisis, the so-called 'Time of Troubles'. The death of his son Feodor in 1598 was followed by an immensely complex period of civil war, during which Poland-Lithuania and Sweden almost brought about the collapse of the Russian state. But Tsarism did survive under the Romanov dynasty and the policies of powerful successors, such as Peter the Great in the late seventeenth century, echo those of Ivan.

Peter the Great acknowledged the influence of Ivan and Ivan has remained a potent and controversial figure in Russian life ever since. It is surely no coincidence that, in the time of another great autocrat, J V Stalin, the famous Russian film maker Sergei Eisenstein produced an unforgettable portrait of Ivan the Terrible which caused enormous controversy within the Societ Union. Ivan the Terrible left a permanent imprint on the Russian state.

12. Bibliography

J Blum *Lord and Peasant in Russia from the Ninth to the Nineteenth Century* (Princeton, 1961). J L Fennell *Ivan the Great of Moscow* (Macmillan, 1961). R Pipes *Russia under the Old Regime* (Penguin, 1977). N V Riasonovsky *History of Russia* (2nd edition, OUP, 1969). G Vernadsky *The Mongols and Russia* (Yale, 1953). G Vernadsky *Russia at the Dawn of the Modern Age* (Yale, 1959).

13. Discussion Points and Exercises

A *This section consists of questions or points that might be used for discussion (or written answers) as a way of expanding on the chapter and testing understanding of it:*

1 How far did geography shape the history of Russia in this period?
2 What was the significance of Muscovy's subservient relationship with the Golden Horde?
3 'It was Ivan III who laid the firm foundations for later Russian power.'
4 What were the main dangers to the authority of the Crown revealed in Ivan's childhood?
5 Assess Ivan's goals and character at the beginning of his reign.
6 Why was Ivan's conquest of Kazan such a success?
7 Was there any wisdom in Ivan's decision to embark on the Livonian War?
8 What was the balance between Ivan's success and failure in foreign policy?
9 What was the significance of the 'Chosen' Council?
10 What were the advantages and disadvantages of the legal and social policies carried out under the 'Chosen' Council?
11 How far was Ivan in control of the Church?
12 Why did Ivan destroy the 'Chosen' Council?
13 'The Oprichnina was just the product of an unbalanced mind.'
14 How did Ivan justify the violent actions he had taken in the latter years of his reign?
15 What was Ivan's legacy to Russia?

B *Essay questions*
1 What did Ivan IV contribute to the development of Russia?
2 How important was the domestic opposition to Ivan IV and his policies?
3 To what extent can the 'Oprichnina' of Ivan IV be regarded as a rational policy?
4 Can Ivan IV fairly be considered an 'oriental despot'?
5 Do you agree with the view that the Livonian War was the greatest error of Ivan IV?

C *Exercise—Comparison between East and West*

It is clear that the history of Russia differs from that of western Europe but how much and in what ways?

1 Compare the powers of Ivan, Charles V and Francis I. Write a paragraph on each of the following issues, drawing attention to what was most alike and what differed most in the experience of the three rulers:
   (a) The relationship of the aristocracy with the Crown.
   (b) Faction.
   (c) Religious conflict.
   (d) Representative assemblies—the Zemsky Sobor, the Diet, the Estates.
   (e) Trade.
   (f) Absolutism.

2 Compare the Russian Orthodox Church, the Lutheran Church and the Roman Catholic Church.
   (a) Which was most powerful and why?
   (b) How did the structure and attitudes of those Churches affect the development of the state?

3 Compare the status of the peasantry in Russia with that of western Europe *(see pages 12 and 145)*.
   (a) In which part did the peasantry have greater freedom?
   (b) How, if at all, was the relative status of the peasantry changing in the sixteenth century?

Index

r. = dates of reign
? = date of birth uncertain